The Modern Language Association of America

Reviews of Research

The English Romantic Poets: A Review of Research and Criticism. Third revised edition. Edited by Frank Jordan. 1972.

Victorian Prose: A Guide to Research. Edited by David J. DeLaura. 1973.

Anglo-Irish Literature: A Review of Research. Edited by Richard J. Finneran. 1976.

Victorian Fiction: A Second Guide to Research. Edited by George H. Ford. 1978.

Victorian Periodicals: A Guide to Research. Edited by J. Don Vann and Rosemary T. VanArsdel. 1978.

Victorian Fiction: A Guide to Research. Reprint of 1964 edition. Edited by Lionel Stevenson. 1980.

Recent Research on Anglo-Irish Writers: A Supplement to Anglo-Irish Literature: A Review of Research. Edited by Richard J. Finneran. 1983.

RECENT RESEARCH ON ANGLO-IRISH WRITERS

A Supplement to
Anglo-Irish Literature: A Review of Research

Edited by
Richard J. Finneran

The Modern Language Association of America
NEW YORK
1983

Library of Congress Cataloging in Publication Data

Main entry under title:

Recent research on Anglo-Irish writers.

Supplement to: Anglo-Irish literature.
Includes index.
1. English literature—Irish authors—History
and criticism. 2. English literature—Irish authors
—Bibliography. I. Finneran, Richard J. II. Title:
Anglo-Irish literature.
PR8712.R4   1983   820'.9'9415   82-12575
ISBN 0-87352-259-1

Published by The Modern Language Association of America
62 Fifth Avenue, New York, New York 10011

CONTENTS

PREFACE

This volume has two purposes: to provide supplements to the chapters in *Anglo-Irish Literature: A Review of Research* (1976) and to provide new chapters on modern fiction and modern poetry. With the exception of the chapter on George Moore, coverage of important work is complete through 1980, and we have added as many 1981 items as possible. It should be noted, however, that each chapter is to some degree selective; thus readers in search of a comprehensive listing must still consult the standard bibliographical sources.

The editor and contributors note with regret the death of Helmut E. Gerber on 29 April 1981. His chapter is complete therefore only through 1979.

Each chapter has been read by another contributor and by at least one outside reader. We are grateful to the following for their assistance: Ron Ayling; Bernard Benstock; Zack Bowen; Robert Boyle, S.J.; Terence Brown; Alan M. Cohn; Janet Dunleavy; Michael Durkan; Richard Ellmann; John Wilson Foster; Edwin Gilcher; George Mills Harper; Robert G. Lowery; Dan H. Laurence; Ann Saddlemyer; and Jack W. Weaver. We are also indebted to the staff of the Modern Language Association, particularly Walter S. Achtert and Claire Cook.

Since *Anglo-Irish Literature: A Review of Research* is planned as a continuing project, with periodic revisions and supplements, we remain interested in receiving offprints, review copies, and news of forthcoming publications. In the next edition, the chapter on George Moore will be provided by Jack W. Weaver. That edition will also include a new chapter on Samuel Beckett by Peter J. Murphy.

R. J. F.

ABBREVIATIONS

ABC   American Book Collector
AI   American Imago: A Psychoanalytic Journal of Culture, Science, and the Arts
AIS   Anglo-Irish Studies (Cambridge, Eng.)
AJES   Aligarh Journal of English Studies
AL   American Literature
ALM   Archives des Lettres Modernes
ALT   African Literature Today
AN&Q   American Notes and Queries
Anglia: Zeitschrift für Englische Philologie
AntigR Antigonish Review
AQ   American Quarterly
AR   Antioch Review
Archiv   Archiv für das Studium der Neueren Sprachen und Literaturen
ArielE   Ariel: A Reivew of International English Literature
ArQ   Arizona Quarterly
ASch   American Scholar
ASNSP Annali della Scuola Normale Superiore di Pisa: Classe di Lettere e Filosofia
AWR   Anglo-Welsh Review (Pembroke Dock, Wales)
BB   Bulletin of Bibliography
BC   Book Collector
BDEC   Bulletin of the Department of English, University of Calcutta
BJA   British Journal of Aesthetics (London)
BMQ   British Museum Quarterly
BNYPL Bulletin of the New York Public Library
Boundary Boundary 2: A Journal of Postmodern Literature
BRH   Bulletin of Research in the Humanities
BuR   Bucknell Review
BUSE   Boston University Studies in English
C&L   Christianity and Literature
Caliban (Toulouse, France)
CanL   Canadian Literature
CathW   Catholic World [now *New Catholic World*]
CCEI   Cahiers du Centre d'Etudes Irlandaises

CD	Child Development
CE	College English
CEA	CEA Critic
CentR	Centennial Review (Michigan State Univ.)
Centrum	Working Papers of the Minnesota Center for Advanced Studies in Language, Style, and Literary Theory
ChiR	Chicago Review
Cithara: Essays in the Judaeo-Christian Tradition	
CJIS	Canadian Journal of Irish Studies
CL	Comparative Literature
CLAJ	College Language Association Journal (Morgan State Coll., Baltimore)
CLC	Columbia Library Columns
ClioI	CLIO: An Interdisciplinary Journal of Literature, History, and the Philosophy of History
CLQ	Colby Library Quarterly
CLS	Comparative Literature Studies (Univ. of Illinois)
CollL	College Literature
CompD	Comparative Drama
ComQ	Commonwealth Quarterly
ConP	Contemporary Poetry: A Journal of Criticism
ContempR	Contemporary Review (London)
CP	Concerning Poetry (Bellingham, Wash.)
CQ	Cambridge Quarterly
Crane Bag	(Dublin)
CRCL	Canadian Review of Comparative Literature/Revue Canadienne de Littérature Comparée
CRev	Chesterton Review: The Journal of the Chesterton Society
CritI	Critical Inquiry
Criticism: A Quarterly for Literature and the Arts (Detroit, Mich.)	
CritQ	Critical Quarterly
CRUX: A Journal on the Teaching of English	
CS	Critical Survey (Manchester, Eng.)
CSLBull	Bulletin of the New York C. S. Lewis Society
CVE	Cahiers Victoriens et Edouardiens: Revue du Centre d'Etudes et de Recherches Victoriennes et Edouardiennes de l'Université Paul Valéry, Montpellier
DilR	Diliman Review (Quezon City, Philippines)
DM	Dublin Magazine [as *The Dubliner*, 1961–64]
DNB	Dictionary of National Biography
DQR	Dutch Quarterly Review of Anglo-American Letters
DR	Dalhousie Review
DramaS	Drama Survey
DUJ	Durham University Journal
EA	Etudes Anglaises
E&S	Essays and Studies by Members of the English Association
EB	Eastern Buddhist
EFT	English Fiction in Transition

EI	Etudes Irlandaises (Villeneuve d'Ascq, France)
EIC	Essays in Criticism (Oxford, Eng.)
Éire	Éire-Ireland: A Journal of Irish Studies (St. Paul, Minn.)
EJ	English Journal
ELH	Journal of English Literary History
ELLS	English Literature and Language (Tokyo, Japan)
ELN	English Language Notes (Univ. of Colorado)
ELT	English Literature in Transition (1880–1920)
ELWIU	Essays in Literature (Macomb, Ill.)
EM	English Miscellany
English	(London, Eng.)
EngS	Englische Studien
Era	(The Curragh, County Kildare, Ireland)
ES	English Studies
ESA	English Studies in Africa (Johannesburg)
ESC	English Studies in Canada
ETJ	Educational Theatre Journal
EUQ	Emory University Quarterly
Expl	Explicator
Explor	Exploration: Journal of the MLA Special Session on the Literature of Exploration and Travel
FDP	Four Decades of Poetry 1890–1930
FortR	Fortnightly Review
FR	French Review
FS	French Studies
Gambit: An International Drama Quarterly (London)	
GaR	Georgia Review
GL&L	German Life and Letters
HAR	Humanities Association Review
HC	Hollins Critic
Hermathena: A Dublin University Review	
HLQ	Huntington Library Quarterly
HQ	Hopkins Quarterly
HS	Humanities in the South
HSL	University of Hartford Studies in Literature: A Journal of Interdisciplinary Criticism
HSt	Hamlet Studies: An International Journal of Research on *The Tragedie of Hamlet, Prince of Denmarke* (Delhi, India)
HudR	Hudson Review
IB	Irish Book
IBl	Irish Booklore
ICarbS	(Carbondale, Ill.)
IFR	International Fiction Review
IM	Irish Monthly
IndL	Indian Literature
IRA	Irish Renaissance Annual
IrishR	Irish Review

IrishS	Irish Studies (Cambridge, Eng.)
IUR	Irish University Review
IW	Irish Writing
JAAC	Journal of Aesthetics and Art Criticism
JAF	Journal of American Folklore
JAPS	Journal of the American Portuguese Society
JBeS	Journal of Beckett Studies
JEGP	Journal of English and Germanic Philology
JEn	Journal of English (San'ā Univ.)
JENS	Journal of the Eighteen Nineties Society
JFI	Journal of the Folklore Institute (Bloomington, Ind.)
JGE	Journal of General Education
JIL	Journal of Irish Literature
JJCL	Jadavpur Journal of Comparative Literature
JJQ	James Joyce Quarterly (Univ. of Tulsa)
JJR	James Joyce Review
JML	Journal of Modern Literature
JNT	Journal of Narrative Technique
JRUL	Journal of the Rutgers University Libraries
JSL	Journal of the School of Languages
KanQ	Kansas Quarterly
KM	Kilkenny Magazine
KQ	Koreana Quarterly
KR	Kenyon Review
L&P	Literature and Psychology (Teaneck, N.J.)
Lang&S	Language and Style: An International Journal
LangQ	USF Language Quarterly (Tampa, Fla.)
LBR	Luso-Brazilian Review
LCrit	Literary Criterion (Mysore, India)
LCUT	Library Chronicle of the University of Texas
LHR	Lock Haven Review (Lock Haven, Pa.)
LHY	Literary Half-Yearly
Lit	Littérature (Paris)
Literatūra:	Lietuvos TSR Aukštųjų Mokyklų Mokslo Darbai (Vilnius, Lithuania)
LitR	Literary Review: An International Journal of Contemporary Writing (Madison, N.J.)
LonM	London Magazine
LWU	Literatur in Wissenschaft und Unterricht (Kiel, W. Germany)
MBL	Modern British Literature
McNR	McNeese Review
MD	Modern Drama
MFS	Modern Fiction Studies
MHRev	Malahat Review
MissQ	Mississippi Quarterly
MLN	Modern Language Notes
MLQ	Modern Language Quarterly

MLR Modern Language Review
Mosaic: A Journal for the Comparative Study of Literature and Ideas
MP Modern Philology
MR Massachusetts Review (Univ. of Massachusetts)
MSLC Modernist Studies: Literature and Culture 1920–1940
MSpr Moderna Språk (Stockholm)
MTJ Mark Twain Journal
MuK Maske und Kothurn: Internationale Beiträge zur Theater-
wissenschaft
N&Q Notes and Queries
NBR New Boston Review
NCBEL New Cambridge Bibliography of English Literature
NCF Nineteenth-Century Fiction
NCFS Nineteenth-Century French Studies
NConL Notes on Contemporary Literature
NEQ New England Quarterly
NewS New Statesman
NL Nouvelles Littéraires
NLH New Literary History (Univ. of Virginia)
NM Neuphilologische Mitteilungen
NRF Nouvelle Revue Française
NVT Nieuw Vlaams Tijdschrift
NY New Yorker
NYFQ New York Folklore Quarterly
NYLF New York Literary Forum
NYRB New York Review of Books
NYTBR New York Times Book Review
OCR Oxford and Cambridge Review
OJES Osmania Journal of English Studies
OL Orbis Litterarum
Parnassus: Poetry in Review
PAus Poetry Australia
PBA Proceedings of the British Academy
PBSA Papers of the Bibliographical Society of America
PCP Pacific Coast Philology
PEGS Publications of the English Goethe Society
PLL Papers on Language and Literature
PMLA: Publications of the Modern Language Association of America
PoetryR Poetry Review (London)
PoT Poetics Today: Theory and Analysis of Literature and
Communication (Tel Aviv, Israel)
PP Philologica Pragensia
PQ Philological Quarterly (Iowa City)
PR Partisan Review
PRR Pre-Raphaelite Review
PrS Prairie Schooner
PsyR Psychoanalytic Review
PTL: A Journal for Descriptive Poetics and Theory

PTRSC	Proceedings & Transactions, Royal Society of Canada
PULC	Princeton University Library Chronicle
QJS	Quarterly Journal of Speech
QQ	Queen's Quarterly
RAA	Revue Anglo-Américaine
RDM	Revue des Deux Mondes [now *Nouvelle Revue des Deux Mondes*]
REL	Review of English Literature
Renascence: Essays on Value in Literature	
RES	Review of English Studies
RLC	Revue de Littérature Comparée
RLM	Revue des Lettres Modernes
RLR	Revue des Langues Romanes (Montpellier, France)
RLSt	Rackham Literary Studies (Ann Arbor, Mich.)
RLV	Revue des Langues Vivantes (Bruxelles)
RMS	Renaissance & Modern Studies
RR	Romanic Review
RS	Research Studies (Pullman, Wash.)
RUS	Rice University Studies
RUSEng	Rajasthan University Studies in English
SAB	South Atlantic Bulletin
SAQ	South Atlantic Quarterly
SARev	South Asian Review
SatR	Saturday Review
SB	Studies in Bibliography: Papers of the Bibliographical Society of the University of Virginia
SBHC	Studies in Browning and His Circle: A Journal of Criticism, History, and Bibliography
SEL	Studies in English Literature, 1500–1900
SELit	Studies in English Literature (Tokyo)
SELL	Studies in English Language and Literature (Fukuoka, Japan)
SF	Sinn Féin
SFQ	Southern Folklore Quarterly
SH	Studia Hibernica (Dublin)
Shaw: The Annual of Bernard Shaw Studies	
ShawR	Shaw Review
SHR	Southern Humanities Review
SIR	Studies in Romanticism (Boston, Mass.)
SJW	Shakespeare-Jahrbuch (Weimar)
SLitI	Studies in the Literary Imagination (Georgia State Coll.)
SMLit	Studies in Mystical Literature (Taiwan, Republic of China)
SNNTS	Studies in the Novel (North Texas State Univ.)
SoQ	Southern Quarterly (Univ. of Southern Mississippi)
SoR	Southern Review (Louisiana State Univ.)
SoRA	Southern Review: An Australian Journal of Literary Studies (Univ. of Adelaide)
SORev	Sean O'Casey Review (Holbrook, N.Y.)

Southerly: A Review of Australian Literature (Sydney)
SP   Studies in Philology
Spirit: A Magazine of Poetry
SQ   Shakespeare Quarterly
SR   Sewanee Review
SSF   Studies in Short Fiction (Newberry Coll., Newberry, S.C.)
StHum   Studies in the Humanities (Indiana, Pa.)
Studies   (Dublin)
Style   (Fayetteville, Ark.)
SWR   Southwest Review
TA   Theatre Annual
TC   Twentieth Century
TCL   Twentieth-Century Literature
TDR   Drama Review [formerly *Tulane Drama Review*]
TFSB   Tennessee Folklore Society Bulletin
Thoth: Syracuse University Graduate Studies in English
Thought: A Review of Culture and Idea
ThR   Theatre Research International
ThS   Theatre Survey: The American Journal of Theatre History
TJ   Theatre Journal [formerly *Educational Theatre Journal*]
TJQ   Thoreau Journal Quarterly
TLS   [London] Times Literary Supplement
TN   Theatre Notebook: A Journal of the History and Tech-
                 nique of the British Theatre
Topic: A Journal of the Liberal Arts (Washington, Pa.)
TQ   Texas Quarterly (Univ. of Texas)
TriQ   Tri-Quarterly
TSE   Tulane Studies in English
TSL   Tennessee Studies in Literature
TSLL   Texas Studies in Literature and Language
UES   Unisa English Studies: Journal of the Department of
                 English
UI   United Irishman
UKCR   University of Kansas City Review
UNCSCL   University of North Carolina Studies in Comparative
                 Literature
Unitas: A Quarterly for the Arts and Sciences (Manila, Phillipines)
UnivR   University Review (Dublin)
UTQ   University of Toronto Quarterly
UWR   University of Windsor Review (Windsor, Ont.)
VC   Virginia Cavalcade
VIJ   Victorians Institute Journal
VN   Victorian Newsletter
VP   Victorian Poetry (Morgantown, W.V.)
VQ   Visvabharati Quarterly
VQR   Virginia Quarterly Review
VS   Victorian Studies (Indiana Univ.)
WascanaR   Wascana Review

WHR	Western Humanities Review
WN	A Wake Newslitter: Studies in James Joyce's *Finnegans Wake*
WWR	Walt Whitman Review
WSCL	Wisconsin Studies in Contemporary Literature
WSJour	Wallace Stevens Journal: A Publication of the Wallace Stevens Society
XUS	Xavier University Studies
YCGL	Yearbook of Comparative and General Literature
YeatsS	Yeats Studies
YER	Yeats Eliot Review
YES	Yearbook of English Studies
YR	Yale Review
YULG	Yale University Library Gazette

GENERAL WORKS

Maurice Harmon

1. Bibliographies

GENERAL BIBLIOGRAPHIES

The new material in the area of general bibliography includes, first of all, additions to existing bibliographies. Richard J. Hayes's *Manuscript Sources for the History of Irish Civilisation* (1965) now has a three-volume *First Supplement 1965–1975* (1979); and Alan R. Eager's *A Guide to Irish Bibliographical Material* (1964) has a much expanded second edition (1980), which covers "catalogues; bibliographies completely devoted to Irish material; bibliographies appended to books and articles; general bibliographies which include Irish material; bibliographies printed in Ireland, but which are not Irish in character; periodicals and indexes; unpublished material and work in progress; and other primary sources." Frank L. Kersnowski et al., *Bibliography of Modern Irish and Anglo-Irish Literature* (1976), noted in the postscript to Richard M. Kain's chapter in the first review of research, proved seriously unreliable.

Two new general bibliographies have appeared: Maurice Harmon, *Select Bibliography for the Study of Anglo-Irish Literature and Its Backgrounds: An Irish Studies Handbook* (1976), and Brian McKenna, *Irish Literature, 1800–1875: A Guide to Information Sources* (1978).

Harmon's handbook is divided into four parts: Background: General Reference; Background: Ireland; Anglo-Irish Literature; and Chronology. The first lists major reference works dealing with libraries, bibliographies of bibliography, biographies, dissertations, books (catalogs, indexes, and serial bibliographies), and periodicals and newspapers (catalogs, indexes, and guides). The second emphasizes the interdisciplinary nature of Anglo-Irish literary studies by providing selective, annotated bibliographies under the headings of history, archaeology, biography, topography, folk culture and anthropology, the arts, language (both Anglo-Irish and Irish), Gaelic literature (including mythology), and newspapers and periodicals. In Anglo-Irish Literature the emphasis is on literary history, reference material, and bibliography. The section begins with general works and moves on to poetry, fiction, and drama; it concludes with bibliographies of individual authors and with a descriptive list of literary periodicals. The fourth part, Chronology, runs from the middle of the eighteenth century to the present. The *Handbook* is a practical work of reference and a guide for students and researchers.

McKenna's *Guide*, volume 13 in the Gale Information Guide Library, will be followed by *Irish Literature, 1876–1950*. The present volume seeks to reflect the development and the variety of Anglo-Irish literature in the nineteenth century "by listing works by and about the more prominent and representative authors and, in listing anthologies, periodicals, and general bibliographical, biographical, and critical works, to place these authors in their proper perspective and to give a sense of their literary world." The book is divided into two parts. The first, which is by far the shorter of the two, lists relevant anthologies of fiction and poetry, periodicals, bibliographies, biographies, and criticism. The first section of part 1 describes the "world" of Anglo-Irish literature, its associations and research bodies, its periodicals, and its sources of information, and it concludes with a list of works about Irish music and song. The book's major emphasis, in part 2, is on about 120 individual authors. Chosen are "those who have exercised an influence over the course of Irish writing, who have attracted critical attention, or who, although not influential, represent important elements in the total picture." For each the critical list is selective, but the list of primary books and books of criticism tries to be complete and includes biography and bibliography.

McKenna's *Guide* presents the materials for research; it is not explicitly evaluative, although the selectivity of its critical lists involves judgment. The scope is broad; it points to writers and works that give a sense of their period, instead of confining itself to those of proved literary merit.

Richard Kain's lament at the lack of a dictionary of Irish biography comparable to the DNB is still valid. But three works have now been published in this area: Henry Boylan, *A Dictionary of Irish Biography* (1978); D. J. Hickey and J. E. Doherty, *A Dictionary of Irish History since 1800* (1980); and Robert Hogan, *Dictionary of Irish Literature* (1979). While Boylan's book is not the answer to every scholar's prayer and contains occasional factual errors, it is useful. Published a hundred years after Webb's *Compendium of Irish Biography* and fifty years after Crone's *Concise Dictionary of Irish Biography*, it attempts to be up-to-date. No living people are included. Birth in Ireland has been taken as a requirement for inclusion, but this rule is wisely modified to admit those who worked in Ireland or made a considerable contribution to Irish affairs. The book has over a thousand entries, ranging from the fifth century to the present and excluding the merely legendary or mythical.

Hickey and Doherty's more concentrated *Dictionary*, because of its range, is particularly useful to the literary scholar. While political and military concerns are central, it includes many entries on social affairs, literature and the arts, folk customs, religious developments, economics, and population.

The bulk of Hogan's *Dictionary* "is made up of biographical and critical essays on approximately five hundred Irish authors who wrote mainly in the English language." A handful of general topics such as folklore are also included, together with many entries on major historians, political writers, editors, orators, and journalists. There are entries for important literary organizations and publications, such as the Abbey Theatre, the Cuala Press, and the *Nation*. In his introduction Hogan, the general editor, discusses the qualities that have formed Irish writers—geography and climate, the memory of the dead, the land, religion, drink, sex, violence, "the judgment of saints and the language of scholars." There are also a historical survey of Gaelic literature by Seamus O Neill and a survey of Irish writing in English. The *Dictionary* fills a need, despite the occasional factual errors and the uneven quality of its critical comments. It could be argued that by trying to be both a factual dictionary and a kind of potential literary history the book falls between two stools. Nevertheless, on balance, it is an indispensable work of reference. Each entry is followed by a bibliography of primary work, criticism, and reference material.

Mention should be made here of C. J. Woods's useful "A Guide to Irish Biographical Dictionaries" (*Maynooth Rev.*, May 1980).

To the list of regional bibliographies one should add Helen Maher's *Roscommon Authors: A Biographical and Bibliographical Contribution towards an Index of Roscommon Authors* (1978). Ann Saddlemyer's contribution to *English Drama (excluding Shakespeare): Select Bibliographical Guides* (ed. Stanley Wells, 1975), entitled "The Irish School," should also be noted. Finally, Liam Miller's *Dolmen XXV: An Illustrated Bibliography of the Dolmen Press* (1976), beautifully designed and illustrated, is a fitting tribute to a publishing house that has been central to Irish writing for a quarter of a century.

2. Journals

To the list of periodicals having wide interest for literary historians one should add *Studia Hibernica* (1960–   ), published annually and dealing with general literary, historical, and cultural matters. Several periodicals had special issues on Irish literature. Three should be mentioned here: *The Literary Review* (Winter 1979)—*Irish Poetry after Yeats; Mosaic* (Spring 1979)—*The Irish Tradition in Literature;* and *Genre* (Winter 1979)—*The Genres of the Irish Literary Revival.*

3. General Studies

SURVEYS: ANGLO-IRISH LITERATURE

There has also been a quickening of interest in literary history and general studies. A small number have already appeared and several have been announced. Recent studies may be divided into three kinds: literary surveys; studies of a particular geographical region, a particular theme, or a particular period; and collections of essays. The surveys include Roger McHugh and Maurice Harmon, *A Short History of Anglo-Irish Literature from Its Origins to the Present Day* (1982); Alan Warner, *A Guide to Anglo-Irish Literature* (1981); Augustine Martin, *Anglo-Irish Literature* (1980); Richard Fallis, *The Irish Renaissance* (1977); Robert Welch, *Irish Poetry from Moore to Yeats* (1980); Micheál Ó hAodha, *Theatre in Ireland* (1974); Hugh Hunt, *The Abbey: Ireland's National Theatre, 1904–1978* (1979); and Robert Hogan and James E. Kilroy, *Modern Irish Drama: A Documentary History* (1975–   ).

The McHugh-Harmon history is an authoritative, chronological study of the growth and development of an indigenous Irish literature from the old Irish period to the present. It shows how the literature borrows, adapts, and renews itself from native sources and at the same time places it within the broad contexts of English and European literature; it has a valuable bibliography. Warner's "personal and selective guide" is a general introductory account of nineteenth- and twentieth-century literature. Martin's book is a short illustrated account of Anglo-Irish literature from 1690 to the present.

The first four chapters of Fallis' *Irish Renaissance*, which is intended as a basic history of modern Irish writing, describe the gradual development of Irish literature in the 1880s and 1890s; the next two briefly describe the literature and the history that preceded Yeats and his contemporaries. Part 2, which covers the period from 1900 to the end of the civil war, is divided into chapters on the emergent nationalism of the first two decades of this century, the Abbey Theatre, and poetry. The final section of the book deals with postrevolutionary writing up to World War II, with chapters on the social and political background, drama, the emergence of prose fiction, poetry, and writing since 1940. Fallis' claim that he wanted to write a basic history is not seriously invalidated by his occasional inaccuracies or lapses in judgment. The book is a good introductory account of the literature and of its social, political, and cultural contexts.

After the abundance of McKenna's bibliography we have in Welch's *Irish Poetry from Moore to Yeats* a study of seven poets, chosen because they are "probably the best the century had to offer" and because "they illustrate the central concerns of Irish poetry of the period." The poets are Thomas Moore, J. J. Callanan, James Clarence Mangan, Sir Samuel Ferguson, Aubrey de Vere, William Allingham, and W. B. Yeats. Welch sees the rhetorical simplicity into which the poets fell but notes their "moments of poignant intensity, of clarity and energy, especially when in touch with the native tradition." Nineteenth-century Irish culture, he says, should not be hastily dismissed, because from "its passion and complexity, its misguided and often dangerous intensities, came many of the preoccupations of twentieth-century Irish consciousness." His book complements Thomas Flanagan's on the novelists in its discussion of poets and poetry in the complex world of Irish society, politics, and culture. Welch's sense of history and his knowledge of English and Gaelic literature enable him to write with understanding and insight about each poet. His book is the best account we have of nineteenth-century Irish poetry.

John Cronin's *The Anglo-Irish Novel: Volume One, The Nineteenth Century* (1980) is a short study of the fiction as represented by seven novels: Maria Edgeworth, *Castle Rackrent*; John Banim, *The Nowlans*; Gerald Griffin, *The Collegians*; William Carleton, *The Black Prophet*; Charles Kickham, *Knocknagow*; George Moore, *A Drama in Muslin*; and Somerville and Ross, *The Real Charlotte*. The study is guided by Yeats's identification of two accents in Irish literature, that of the gentry and that of the peasantry. In effect, Cronin examines seven novels that "deserve such analysis in their own right and for the light they throw on the period." The book is a collection of separate essays rather than a coherent study.

Of the books on Irish drama, two were discussed in the first edition of this book, although not in Kain's chapter. The Ó hAodha study is a compact, straightforward account of theater in Ireland, elementary but useful. The Hogan and Kilroy project continues; six volumes are contemplated. The series provides interesting background material in selections from contemporary documents, periodicals, letters, and so on. Hunt's *The Abbey* and Katharine Worth's *The Irish Drama of Europe from Yeats to Beckett* (1980) represent significant new material.

As an authorized history of the Abbey Theatre, Hunt's book is disappointing. The first half deals with the period up to 1922, when Yeats gave up the struggle for a poetic theater; the second half deals with the somewhat dreary years since 1922, when the theater had a state subsidy but lacked a Yeats or a Synge. The main reasons for the book's failure are the almost total lack of dramatic criticism and the lack of authorial judgment. Too much reliance on obscure journalistic pieces as comments on plays and players undermines one's confidence. At best the book is a history of the externals of theater—its business, management, and people—not of its intellectual and imaginative life. The book provides a list of productions up to 1978.

Philip Edwards, *Threshold of a Nation: A Study in English and Irish Drama* (1979), deals with Irish drama in part 2, in just over fifty pages, but the theme of the interaction between drama and nationalism in Shakespeare's England and Yeats's Ireland—the one at the beginning of a single historical cycle, the other at the end—is of considerable interest. "Each of them draws artistic strength from the idea of a new nation which in truth he helps to bring into existence, and each of them recoils from everything which, in practical terms, the creation of the new nation involved. For each of them, the past of the nation is of intense importance. . . ." Edwards' book is intellectually stimulating much of the time, especially when he deals with Yeats, although the discussion of O'Casey and Behan, for example, seems to go over familiar ground.

Edwards' emphasis on the close connection between drama and nationalism, which comes up again in books about Irish literature in general, contrasts strongly with that of Katharine Worth's *The Irish Drama of Europe from Yeats to Beckett*. This innovative and challenging study discards the nationalist dimension for a European perspective, "bringing Yeats, Synge and Beckett, Wilde and O'Casey under the same light with Maeterlinck and, above all, showing how Yeats's evolution of a modern technique of total theatre and his use of it to construct a 'drama of the interior' makes him one of the great masters of twentieth century theatre." Through an examination of Maeterlinck, Worth argues persuasively for placing Irish dramatists within a symbolist tradition; she sees their characteristics as the search for a new language and a new theatrical syntax. Yeats is the central example, because of his use of music and dance and because of his influence on the development of modern drama. Beckett comes as the latest example, successor to Yeats, Synge, and O'Casey, who belong to what Worth calls "the main line of modern drama."

Her dismissal of the nationalist dimension, shown to be central by Philip Edwards and many other critics, is regrettable, but the demonstration of the European connections is of great importance. Worth knows that her perspectives also exclude the eighteenth-century rational, rhetorical mode one sees in Shaw and detects in Lady Gregory. She is right to emphasize Yeats's sensitive feeling for the visual side of the theater. He came to see that all the resources of the theater—scene, color, music, dance, and movement—had to be used; "only a synthesis of the arts, supporting and highlighting the words, drawing attention to their value by allowing spaces between them, stretches of silence, unanswered questions, could hope to render anything like the complexity of the mind's processes, its intuitions of fine shades of feeling, the whole undertow of the stream of consciousness." This is a wide-ranging, scholarly, and authoritative work, a challenging alternative to the standard accounts of Irish drama by Una Ellis-Fermor and A. E. Malone.

Four other general studies on Irish drama may be mentioned: Annelise Truninger, *Paddy and the Paycock: A Study of the Stage Irishman from Shakespeare to O'Casey* (1976); Elizabeth Hale Winkler, *The Clown in Modern Anglo-Irish Drama* (1977); Hans-Georg Stalder, *Anglo-Irish Peasant Drama: The Motifs of Land and Emigration* (1978); and Brenna Katz Clarke and Harold Ferrar, *The Dublin Drama League 1918-1941* (1979).

There are two studies of the literature of a particular region—Terence Brown, *Northern Voices: Poets from Ulster* (1975), and John Wilson Foster, *Forces and Themes in Ulster Fiction* (1974)—and two on particular themes—Peter Costello, *The Heart Grown Brutal: The Irish Revolution in Literature, from Parnell to the Death of Yeats, 1891-1939* (1977), and G. J. Watson, *Irish Identity and the Literary Revival: Synge, Yeats, Joyce and O'Casey* (1979).

Brown's book is a chronological study of the poetry of Northern Ireland from colonial times to the present. It combines a critical reading of individual poets, including Samuel Ferguson, William Allingham, John Hewitt, Louis MacNeice, W. R. Rodgers, and John Montague, with a historical and contextual awareness. It dispels the notion that the poetry may be seen in simplistic or narrow terms by presenting the Northern province in its "cultural, social and emotional complexity." A similar effect is found in Foster's study of the fiction, despite its tendency to link its "topographical scenario" with mythic interpretations à la Mircea Eliade. The emphasis, however, is on individual works, and the discussions of William Carleton, Benedict Kiely, Brian Moore, and Forrest Reid are particularly useful. In more general terms the book's interest in regions within the province, in specific settings, and in recurrent themes gives a lively sense of Ulster's social, religious, and cultural complexity.

Peter Costello's study of violence and culture explores changing attitudes and responses throughout its chosen period, as though trying to slow down the tempo of history in order to focus on the complexity of contemporary moments. At times it is a lively and illuminating work, if not original in most of its observations—as, for example, in its presentation of reactions before, during, and after the civil war, when writers like O'Faolain and O'Connor seemed to reek of literature as they went gadding about like gunmen. Costello believes that a revolution in thought or feeling is the prerequisite for any revolution. "I hope to show that the Literary Revival in Ireland created the possibility of the political revolution; that the writings of the revival record the true reality of the war; and that the literary movement emerges from the disillusioning events of the Civil War with its integrity intact, which is more than can be said for the politics of Irish nationalism." The thesis is pursued much too earnestly at times and Costello overgeneralizes. But he brings Gerald O'Donovan into focus and treats Somerville and Ross in an original manner. At his best he illuminates "the flux of emotions, loyalties and ideas" that prevailed at specific periods.

G. J. Watson's unifying theme is "each writer's attempt to grapple with, or define, the nature and meaning of Irish identity, and the resultant effects on the content and form of their art." One might be tempted to ignore this book on the assumption that the subject is already well known. Watson, however, writes clearly and compactly and gives perceptive and intelligent readings of many, even the well-known, individual works. The book is perhaps more suited to the general reader and the undergraduate than to the advanced scholar; it is a useful, sensible study of the four writers mentioned in its title.

Two studies of particular periods are Wayne E. Hall's *Shadowy Heroes: Irish Literature in the 1890s* (1981) and Terence Brown's *Ireland: A Social and Cultural History 1922-79* (1981). Hall studies the work of Somerville and Ross, George Moore, Edward Martyn, George Russell, and W. B. Yeats within an economic and political context, especially the relationship of literature to the issues of land reform and the decline of the Protestant Ascendancy. Brown's three-part work, which focuses on intellectual, cultural, and social history, is particularly useful in showing the rapid social and cultural changes of the last twenty years.

Several recent collections of essays, though inevitably somewhat uneven in quality, represent current research. Many indicate critical trends and literary developments in various countries and within the organizations formed to promote interest and research in Anglo-Irish literature. Among these are the following: *Two Decades of Irish Writing: A Critical Survey* (ed. Douglas Dunn, 1975); *The Irish Novel in Our Time* (ed. Patrick Rafroidi and Maurice Harmon, 1976); *Literature and Folk Culture: Ireland and Newfoundland* (ed. Alison Feder and Bernice Schrank, 1977); *Myth and Reality in Irish Literature* (ed. Joseph Ronsley, 1977); *Place, Personality and the Irish Writer* (ed. Andrew Carpenter, 1977); *Pleasures of Irish Literature* (ed. John Jordan, 1977); *Views of the Irish Peasantry, 1800–1916* (ed. Daniel J. Casey and Robert E. Rhodes, 1977); *Image and Illusion: Anglo-Irish Literature and Its Contexts* (ed. Maurice Harmon, 1979); *Genres of the Irish Revival* (ed. Ronald Schleifer, 1980); *The Irish Short Story* (ed. Patrick Rafroidi and Terence Brown, 1980); *Yeats, Sligo and Ireland: Essays to Mark the 21st Yeats International Summer School* (ed. A. Norman Jeffares, 1980); *Literature and the Changing Ireland* (ed. Peter Connolly, 1982); and *The Way Back: George Moore's* The Untilled Field *and* The Lake (ed. Robert Welch, 1982).

SURVEYS: ENGLISH LITERATURE

To the surveys already listed by Kain one should add Albert C. Baugh et al., *A Literary History of England* (2nd ed., 1967). This edition, which has extensive bibliographical supplements, is particularly good on Irish writers. James M. Ethridge, *Contemporary Authors: A Bio-bibliographical Guide to Current Authors and Their Works* (1962–   ), includes Irish writers. James Vinson, *Contemporary Writers of the English Language* (1970–73), revised every three years, is also good on Irish writers. G. S. Fraser, *The Modern Writer and His World* (rev. ed., 1975), places Irish writers in a survey of twentieth-century literature. M. L. Rosenthal, *New Poets: American and British Poetry since World War II* (1967), devotes one long chapter to contemporary Irish poetry.

REMINISCENCES

John Ryan's *Remembering How We Stood: Bohemian Dublin at the Mid-Century* (1975) and Anthony Cronin's *Dead as Doornails: A Chronicle of Life* (1976) provide considerable insight into a state of literary life in Dublin in the 1940s and 1950s. Hugh Leonard's *Home before Night* (1980) is a witty account of a Dublin childhood and goes over some of the material that appears in the plays *Da* and *A Life*.

ANTHOLOGIES

Almost all the recent anthologies are primarily concerned with the current state of Irish writing—an interest that indicates how the literary scene has changed in the past twenty years.

In April 1968 the *Irish Press* began a weekly page devoted to Irish writing, mainly short stories and poems. Since then the literary editor, David Marcus, has edited a number of anthologies based on this material: *New Irish Writing 1* (1970), *Best Irish Short Stories* (1976), *New Irish Writing* (1976), and *Best Irish Short Stories 2* (1977). A similar emphasis is found in William Vorm's *Paddy No More* (1977), which presents the work of the younger writers, such as Michael Foley, Desmond Hogan, Neil Jordan, and Lucile Redmond. These anthologies are discussed by Maurice Harmon in Patrick Rafroidi and Terence Brown's *The Irish Short Story* (1979). Anthony Bradley's *Contemporary Irish Poets* (1980) deals with the whole twentieth century. Similarly, *The Bodley Head Book of Irish Short Stories* (ed. David Marcus, 1980) consists mainly of work from the twentieth century.

Three anthologies concentrate on Northern Ireland. Padraic Fiacc's *The Wearing of the Black* (1974) is somewhat unusual in that it includes only poetry that reflects the violence of the North. As a result, the book may seem gross at times. Still, it contains work by most of the major poets who have dealt with the tragedy and by many of the younger poets as well. Frank Ormsby's *Poets from the North of Ireland* (1979) is a serious attempt to define a tradition within the poetry written by poets from Northern Ireland. The idea was implicit in Terence Brown's *Northern Voices* (1975), and the work it contains, from twenty poets born since 1900, supports the argument for a separate tradition. John Hewitt's collection *Rhyming Weavers and Other Poets of Antrim and Down* (1974) discusses their work and "throws light upon rural life in the eastern part of Ulster in the period 1800–1900." There is, as Hewitt observes, no Robert Burns or John Clare, but "the reader will encounter several companionable men and a number of memorable lines of verse."

Grattan Freyer's *Modern Irish Writing: A Prose and Verse Anthology* (1979) also reflects contemporary developments, although it is somewhat uneven in its selections and omissions. Peter Fallon and Sean Golden's *Soft Day: A Miscellany of Contemporary Irish Writing* (1980) is refreshingly unacademic in tone and approach. Presenting the work of twenty-six living writers of prose, poetry, drama, and translation, with an emphasis on new work and on poetry, it is perhaps the best introduction to the whole range of contemporary Irish writing. Maurice Harmon's *Irish Poetry after Yeats: Seven Poets* (1979) has a long introductory essay on the developments in Irish poetry during this century and a bibliography of the work of all the poets. The seven poets included are Austin Clarke, Patrick Kavanagh, Denis Devlin, Richard Murphy, Thomas Kinsella, John Montague, and Seamus Heaney. The selections for each are generous. James Simmons' *Ten Irish Poets* (1974) is a slim volume that includes George Buchanan, John Hewitt, Padraic Fiacc, Pearse Hutchinson, James Simmons, Michael Hartnett, Eiléan Ní Chuilleanáin, Michael Foley, Frank Ormsby, and Tom Mathews.

These four anthologies indicate that there is no diminishment in output. Unlike the early fifties, when it seemed that Irish writing had faltered and might even die, the seventies appear vital and growing.

4. General Topics

Sooner or later every student of Anglo-Irish literature has to recognize that English as spoken in Ireland is not standard English. Until recently one had almost no help in trying to understand the nature, origins, and development of this language or to learn whether it was uniform throughout Ireland or fragmented by regional variations (see Maurice Harmon, *Select Bibliography for the Study of Anglo-Irish Literature and Its Backgrounds*, pp. 81–84). Alan Bliss, *Spoken English in Ireland 1600–1740: Twenty-Seven Representative Texts Assembled and Analysed* (1979), is a major contribution in this field. It begins with a general account of the fortunes of the English language in Ireland from medieval times down to 1740, when Cromwellian English displaced the earlier forms. The massive shift of people to the west helped greatly to establish English in the Big House and on the large estates. The language has two basic peculiarities: lack of change and considerable influence from Irish. Bliss's treatment of the Irish influence on phonology, vocabulary, morphology, and syntax is particularly useful. The author gives ample evidence for all his observations and provides many references for every form in the glossarial index. The book is both a reference work and a guide for those who want to study Hiberno-English for themselves.

Diarmuid O Muirithe's *The English Language in Ireland* (1977) is a collection of nine papers on various aspects of the subject, such as the emergence of modern English dialects in Ireland, the Irish background, the Anglo-Norman dialect of Wexford, the Ulster dialects, the dominance of English in the nineteenth century, and dialect and literature. It may also be noted that P. W. Joyce's *English As We Speak It in Ireland* has been reprinted (1980).

In the recent upsurge of publishing in Ireland and in England, the coffee-table kind of book has proliferated. Brian de Breffny, *The Irish World: The History and Cultural Achievements of the Irish People* (1977), has beautiful illustrations and a reputable list of contributors. Nevertheless, some of the essays contain factual errors, some have a seriously restricted scope, and some tend to see Irish life through the windows of the Big House. The *Treasures of Early Irish Art 1500 B.C. to 1500 A.D.* (1977) is the superbly illustrated catalog of the exhibition that toured America and Europe in recent years with works drawn from the collections of the National Museum of Ireland, the Royal Irish Academy, and Trinity College, Dublin.

NINETEENTH-CENTURY WRITERS

James F. Kilroy

Interest in nineteenth-century Irish literature continues to intensify, and the published research tends to improve in quality. The most valuable contributions of the past five years have been the publication of a useful research guide and the reprinting of a series of novels of the period. Brian McKenna's *Irish Literature, 1800–1875* (1978) serves particular needs of historians and literary scholars, for reliable bibliographical information on the many minor writers of the period has been difficult to obtain. McKenna provides brief listings of editions and published criticism on over one hundred authors, as well as a useful list of the periodicals of the period. Although many recent editions and some important criticism are omitted, the guide will serve as a starting place and should prompt further inquiries into nineteenth-century Irish writing. Robert Lee Wolff has selected seventy-seven works, mostly novels and story collections of the period, for reprinting in the Garland series, Ireland: From the Act of Union, 1800, to the Death of Parnell, 1891 (1979); here, finally, are reliable texts and excellent informative introductions to the works. Wolff brings a historian's skills to the task, arguing that the novelists best describe this period of great suffering and bold aspirations. But he is also a careful literary critic, sensitive to fictional techniques and responsive to language. Included in the series in addition to Irish novels of the century are five novels by Trollope and one by Harriet Martineau, English writers on Irish subjects, and Allingham's narrative poem, *Laurence Bloomfield*.

The essays in Daniel J. Casey and Robert E. Rhodes's *Views of the Irish Peasantry: 1800–1916* (1977) provide historical information; of special interest in that collection is James MacKillop's essay on Finn MacCool, which traces the change in treatment of that mythological hero and concludes that by the end of the century he was both the superhuman hero and the comic trickster.

In *The Anglo-Irish Novel: Volume One, The Nineteenth Century* (1980), John Cronin proposes two dominant themes of the Irish fiction of this century: a protest against colonial misrule, pronounced in *Castle Rackrent* and *Knocknagow*, and the decline of the Big House, as seen in works of various novelists from Edgeworth to Somerville and Ross. Brief biographical essays precede temperate, generally favorable essays on seven novels.

In the title essay of *The Irish Short Story* (ed. Terence Brown and Patrick Rafroidi, Lille, 1979), Rafroidi differentiates that literary form from the folktale; he even claims that the subjects, language, and techniques of the Irish story distinguish it from English and continental versions. In treating the fantastic, for instance, Irish writers resemble the continental Romantics but concentrate on a guilt that has national implications for Ascendancy writers. In a brief survey he gives special credit to William Carleton for helping to formulate the Irish short story and to Somerville and Ross for perfecting its structure. David Norris' essay in the same collection praises Somerville and Ross's R. M. stories, works in which Norris sees a rational world overcome by the imaginative anarchy of the Gaelic mind.

Robert Welch's *Irish Poetry from Moore to Yeats* (1980) claims neither a single tradition for Irish poetry of this period nor, as the title could suggest, a clear line of development. Rather, he discusses seven poets' treatments of what Welch considers the inevitable theme for contemporaries of the English Romantics and Victorians: the poet's exploration of self and the artistic uses the poet makes of the past. In this regard J. J. Callanan, Samuel Ferguson, and William Allingham receive perceptive analysis and praise for their skill in transcending self and presenting vivid pictures of Irish life and history; Thomas Moore, James Clarence Mangan, and Aubrey de Vere fare less well. Welch's focus is narrow, but his assessments are fair. The book will prove useful to scholars and should prompt reconsiderations of the poets of the past century.

A fruitful subject for continued research is uncovered by Jacques Chuto in "Militant Nationalist Verse from 1798 to 1848" (*EI*, 1979); he examines verse in *Paddy's Resource* (1798), poems by James Clarence Mangan, and verse in *The Spirit of the Nation* (1845) to show how the last volume's romantic nationalism replaces the first volume's internationalist tone and concern for human rights. The development of propagandist verse deserves further treatment.

There follow brief summaries of research of the past five years on the individual authors discussed in the 1976 review. Authors are listed in alphabetical order, with O'Grady omitted, since further significant research on him has not appeared. Of authors not included in this survey, the O'Hara brothers, John and Michael Banim, receive appropriate critical attention in Mark D. Hawthorne's monograph (Salzburg, 1975), which sensibly concentrates on their historical importance to the formulation of a national literature, rather than on their creative power.

William Allingham

Recent critics grant William Allingham credit as an accurate recorder of Irish life, if not acclaim as a creative artist. In "William Allingham and Folk Song" (*Hermathena*, 1974), Hugh Shields notes how Allingham's poems reveal folk traditions and resemble accounts in the contemporary popular press of County Donegal. Alison M. Feder's "Irish History in Heroic Couplets" in *A Festschrift for Edgar Ronald Seary* (ed. A. A. Macdonald et al., 1975) adds to this some general praise for *Laurence Bloomfield* as a narrative and a satire and for its experiments in reproducing Irish idiom. Terence Brown's comments in *Northern Voices: Poets from Ulster* (1975) are not so generous; while admitting the accuracy of Allingham's descriptions of country life, he concludes that in *Laurence Bloomfield* the poet attempted to promote peaceful reform instead of revolution but succeeded in making only vague, utopian, and confused proposals.

Dion Boucicault

A complete biography and a note on theater history add only slightly to our knowledge of Dion Boucicault. The latter, Christopher Calthrop's "Dion Boucicault and Benjamin Webster" (*TN*, 1978), provides information on an unusual partnership between playwright and manager. Richard Fawke bases his biography (1979) on manuscripts discovered in 1962 and thus supplements Robert Hogan's earlier study. But the book is directed at the general reader and does not present detailed criticism of the plays.

William Carleton

Most of the criticism on William Carleton centers on the mimetic aspect of his work. Maurice Harmon's essay in *Views of the Irish Peasantry: 1800–1916* (ed. Casey and Rhodes, 1977) praises Carleton for the accurate depiction of peasant life, and Colin Meir (*EI*, 1979) regards the two-volume *Traits and Stories of the Irish Peasantry* as superior to the later works, in which Carleton turned to explicit moralizing. While noting the unevenness and verbal excesses of *The Black Prophet*, John Cronin in *The Anglo-Irish Novel* (vol. 1, 1980) praises the novel for its powerful depiction of famine-racked Ireland in 1817 and 1822. Although Margaret Chesnutt, in both an essay on Carleton (*MSpr*, 1977) and a monograph on his short fiction (Göteborg, 1976), sets out to examine social and religious themes and literary techniques, she treats them only superficially and concludes by echoing the familiar praise of this writer as a folk historian. Eileen Sullivan goes further (*Éire*, 1977); she argues that Carleton's reality includes not only rural Ireland but the ancient world reflected in folklore and myth and that he revolted against both. Her interpretation is not complete—it is unclear why or how he rejected the ancient tradition—but this article is more precise and balanced than much earlier criticism.

Carleton receives closer critical study in Robert Lee Wolff's volume in the Garland series, *William Carleton, Irish Peasant Novelist* (1980). Wolff reexamines biographical data and published criticism and compares multiple publications of the works to determine the author's intentions and to assess the historical accuracy of the accounts. For instance, responding to Yeats's claim that Carleton's "heart always remained Catholic," Wolff, building on earlier research by André Boué, argues that Carleton had turned openly anti-Catholic even before his encounter with Caesar Otway. Supporting this thesis, he reprints Carleton's works in their earliest versions as printed books, showing how virulent the attacks on the church were. Then, by examining the published prospectus for the unpublished, incomplete novel *The Chronicles of Ballymacruiskeen*, he shows how Carleton gradually mellowed in those sentiments. He thus establishes that the changes in Carleton's religious, and political, allegiances were not abrupt or unprovoked. Wolff does not deny the literary shortcomings of Carleton's writings: the inability to convey upper-class dialect, the sentimentality, and the lapses of style; but he praises the historical accuracy and the consistency of Carleton's personal vision, so that the artistry of the novels and stories is proved. By informing the reader of Carleton's volatile but determined character and by providing a fuller picture of the historical events that prompted the writings, Wolff uncovers important aspects of Carleton's art. André Boué takes another promising critical approach in "William Carleton as a Short Story Writer" in *The Irish Short Story* (ed. Rafroidi and Brown, 1979). Boué views Carleton's contribution to the genre as the introduction of the peasant as a subject and praises the writer primarily as a historian of the Irish peasantry. While the best of his stories, "Wildwood Lodge," has exceptional economy and force, Carleton's imagination was "more reproductive than creative."

Thomas Davis

Eileen Sullivan's *Thomas Davis* (1978), in the Bucknell series, is not likely to replace Joseph Hone's 1934 study, but it does present a fair-minded if somewhat unduly enthusiastic introduction to the poet. In contrast, Alf MacLochlainn, in "The Racism of Thomas Davis: Root and Branch" (*JIL*, 1976), argues that Davis preached a theory of the purity of the Celtic race and the inevitable opposition of the Celt to the Sassenach.

Maria Edgeworth

The publication of two new collections prompts new interest in Maria Edgeworth as a vivacious, intelligent letter writer. Christina Colvin's edition, *Maria Edgeworth in France and Switzerland* (1979), supplements her earlier edition of letters from England; it consists of selections from family letters from 1802–03 and 1820, many of them previously unpublished. Edgeworth's correspondence with Rachel Mordecai Lazarus, *The Education of the Heart*, has been edited by Edgar E. MacDonald (1977); the North Carolina lady was Edgeworth's ideal correspondent, evoking comments on a wide range of political and literary subjects and revealing the most humane aspects of the Irish writer.

Two essays return to the familiar subject of literary influences and similarities. David Jackel's *"Leonora* and *Lady Susan"* (*ESC*, 1977) notes similar themes and epistolary techniques in these works by Edgeworth and Austen; the Irish novelist comes off as a moralist and caricaturist, while the younger writer is excused as an apprentice. Joseph F. Connelly's essay on *Castle Rackrent* and Thackeray's *The Memoirs of Barry Lyndon* (*Éire*, 1979) is more convincing, since it bases the comparison on specific similarities in narrative method.

While Edgeworth's historical importance has been repeatedly recognized, little close criticism of her works has yet appeared. One exceptionally informative analysis is Mark D. Hawthorne's "Maria Edgeworth's Unpleasant Lesson: The Shaping of Character" (*Studies*, 1975), which examines revisions of *Belinda* done eight years after the novel's completion, showing how the author attempted to deemphasize the moral lesson and strengthen development of the characters. Such a change in emphasis has been observed before but seldom established by exact references to texts. In the introduction Robert Lee Wolff provides to the five novels of Edgeworth he reprints, he is characteristically perceptive and useful in relating Edgeworth's family background and educational theories to her works. Finally, John Cronin, in *The Anglo-Irish Novel* (vol. 1, 1980), regards *Castle Rackrent* as the "most powerful condemnation in existence of the forces of misrule" and sees Thady Quirk as a victim of colonialism, "a magnificently realized slave."

SAMUEL FERGUSON

A Unionist who promoted Irish nationalism, Samuel Ferguson is given credit by Terence Brown, in *Northern Voices: Poets from Ulster* (1975), for being an important influence on later writers. His sympathy for pagan Celtic culture led writers and scholars back to their heritage, and in *Congal* he almost unwittingly wrote a work that would inspire the most dedicated Fenians. Robert O'Driscoll's *An Ascendancy of the Heart* (1976) goes even further, praising his translations from the Irish as closer to the originals than were various contemporary versions. That he was even partially effective in uniting Catholic and Protestant and that he was instrumental in shaping modern Irish literature are claims that O'Driscoll does not conclusively prove in this brief book; nevertheless, he recognizes Ferguson's achievements as a scholar and a dedicated writer and reasserts his influence and importance.

GERALD GRIFFIN

Finally a reliable biography of Gerald Griffin has appeared. Based on extensive use of manuscripts previously undiscovered, John Cronin's *Gerald Griffin* (1978) is thorough, and his critical assessments of the novels and of the play *Gisippus* are sensible. Even if the claims made of similarities to Joyce and other later writers are strained, the book is informative and reliable in its details. Robert Lee Wolff includes seven of Griffin's works in the Garland series, as well as the contemporary biography by Griffin's brother, an indication of the historical importance accorded to Griffin. Wolff suggests that Griffin's love for Lydia Foster may have inspired *The Rivals* and gives special praise to *Tracy's Ambitions* as second only to *The Collegians* in quality. Grace Eckley's "The Fiction of Gerald Griffin" (*JIL*, 1978) is a general introduction to and appreciation of the novels; she notes the recurrence of duels and the importance of family relationships in Griffin's works.

JOSEPH SHERIDAN LEFANU

The reissue of the collected works by Arno Press in fifty-two volumes and the inclusion of *The Purcell Papers, The Cock and Anchor*, and *The House by the Church-Yard* in Wolff's Garland series, with the editor's thorough introduction, should prompt reconsideration of this complex writer. Wolff corrects Michael Sadleir's bibliography, *Nineteenth Century Fiction* (1951), in denying major differences between the 1863 and 1866 editions of *The House by the Church-Yard*. Even more likely to promote further study is W. J. McCormack's *Sheridan LeFanu and Victorian Ireland* (1980); not only does this model literary study present more complete biographical information than has been available, but it carefully and clearly establishes LeFanu's relationships with his society. McCormack untangles LeFanu's shifting political allegiances, shows how they affected his writings, and establishes what earlier critics had only claimed: that LeFanu cannot be dismissed as merely a writer of escape fiction. The critical checklist that concludes the volume will prove particularly useful to future scholars.

Wendell V. Harris' *British Short Fiction in the Nineteenth Century* (1979) contains brief but accurate comments on LeFanu, as well as on Carleton, Edgeworth, and others; but it is essentially a historical summary of the development of the genre rather than a critical analysis of individual writers. A fuller thesis is set forth by Jack Sullivan in *Elegant Nightmares* (1978); in a chapter on LeFanu he argues that the writer's ghost stories do not derive from a reaction to religious orthodoxy or to materialist philosophy; rather they embody the author's vision of the world as hostile and horrible. "Green Tea" is analyzed in a full chapter as an archetype of the ghost story.

CHARLES LEVER

Although no entire reassessment of Charles Lever's works has yet appeared, three essays on individual novels suggest that he cannot be dismissed as a light humorist or a popular writer for the English market. While noting the structural weaknesses of *Charles O'Malley*, N. M. B. Christie (*EI*, 1979) praises it for a humor that may be termed grotesque. The later novels are cited for special praise by Robert L. Meredith in his essay on *St. Patrick's Eve* (*Éire-19*, 1977) and by A. Norman Jeffares in his essay on *Lord Kilgobbin* (*E&S*, 1975). Meredith welcomes the force and accuracy of the novel's treatment of contemporary problems and detects a weakening of Lever's earlier Tory orientation, particularly in the novel's sympathetic portrayal of the tenants; Jeffares goes so far as to claim that Lever's last novel shows a commitment to the Irish cause. Lever is much more than a local colorist, Jeffares concludes; he is a novelist in the mode of Balzac.

FRANCIS MAHONY

Only one slight reference to the mysterious Francis Mahony (Father Prout) appeared in the period; Julia Markus (*VS*, 1978) claims that he is the model for Gigadibs in Robert Browning's "Bishop Blougram's Apology." As background proof she provides accurate but brief biographical information on Mahony, including a discussion of his activities as editor of the *Globe*.

JAMES CLARENCE MANGAN

The historical importance of Mangan has long been established, and most recent commentaries merely repeat familiar praise for his ingenuity and for the force of certain poems. Henry J. Donaghy's book in the Twayne series (1974) offers general appreciative statements and undocumented claims for Mangan's artistry rather than a new understanding or a careful analysis of his peculiar techniques and dominant themes. Furthermore, Donaghy tends toward overstatement and cliché: the poet's "incredible gift of rhyme" is praised, and a poem is said to evoke a "truly moving experience." Robert Welch, examining Mangan's translations from the Irish (*Éire*, 1976), is more analytical and careful. He concludes that the translations served a personal need for the poet, providing a mask through which Mangan could express his own thoughts; thus their variances from the originals were tonic in freeing the old verses to new uses. But in "James Clarence Mangan, the Irish Language and the Strange Case of *The Tribes of Ireland*" (*IUR*, 1978), Peter MacMahon, responding to an earlier article by Jacques Chuto on Mangan's association with the scholars of the Ordnance Survey (*IUR*, 1976), concludes that Mangan knew little Irish and did not translate directly from the originals. Mangan's rendering of the text by Aenghus O'Dalaigh mentioned in the title, for example, was based on a prose version hurriedly and carelessly prepared by John O'Daly, not by John O'Donovan.

An original thematic anlysis is offered in Jacques Chuto's "James Clarence Mangan: In Exile aι Home" (*EI*, 1976); commenting on the exotic imaginary settings of Mangan's poems, he concludes that the subject of most of the poetry is Mangan's own self and that the landscapes are interior visions. An equally promising critical approach is employed by Diane E. Bessai in " 'Dark Rosaleen' as Image of Ireland" (*Éire*, 1975); tracing the symbol of the rose in Irish poetry, she finds that its identification with Ireland is not common in early poetry and that Mangan is the poet most responsible for developing the national allegory of the rose. Once established, however, the symbol acquired extraordinary force and appeared in the works of numerous poets of the nineteenth and twentieth centuries. Bessai skillfully analyzes the symbol in Mangan's most famous poem to reveal its complex, rich meanings.

C. R. MATURIN

Claude Fierobe's *Charles Robert Maturin (1780-1824): L'Homme et l'oeuvre* (Lille, 1974) will not replace Niilo Idman's 1923 biography, but it does supplement it. The biographical section, the first third of this long book, cites early printed sources, especially articles published a few years after Maturin's death, to present a coherent account of a strange personality. Critical discussions of each of the works and two essays on recurrent themes and literary style follow, leading to the carefully documented, closely argued conclusion that Maturin is a major Romantic novelist: philosophical, bold, and artful.

Of Maturin's works, *Melmoth the Wanderer* continues to evoke the most commentary. David Eggenschwiler (*Genre*, 1975) argues that the novel exploits the reader's fascination with Gothic experience and in doing so explores fiction's potentials to the extent that the genre itself becomes the novel's subject. Jack Null (*PLL*, 1977) claims Maturin's major work is much more than a Gothic novel; its intricate structure reflects a mad world, where people search, unsuccessfully, for sanity and salvation. Null claims that in the novel Maturin pleads for religious tolerance and warns against routine, meaningless existence. A narrower aspect is explored in Syndy M. Conger's *Matthew G. Lewis, Charles Robert Maturin and the Germans* (Salzburg, 1977), where the author cites Goethe's *Faust*, Mme de Staël's *Germany*, and Bürger's *Lenore* as influences on Maturin's novel.

Robert Lee Wolff's introduction to Maturin's three Irish novels—*The Wild Irish Boy, The Milesian Chief*, and *Women*—stresses Maturin's concern for his native country, which he associated with Wordsworthian Romanticism in conflict with the classicism identified with England. He has special praise for *Women*, both for the accuracy of its depiction of Irish life and for its attempt at conveying female psychology. The introductions in the Arno reprintings of *The Wild Irish Boy* (1977), *The Albigenses* (1974), and *The Fatal Revenge* (1974) are shorter and less striking, although Maurice Levy's introduction to *The Fatal Revenge* is useful in pointing out the influences of Ann Radcliffe and the German novelists of horror.

LADY MORGAN (SYDNEY OWENSON)

Criticism on Lady Morgan tends to repeat the familiar. James Newcomer, in "Lady Morgan: Generalization and Error" (*EI*, 1978), complains about the critical neglect of this writer, arguing that her knowledge of Irish life and custom make her worthy of consideration; accordingly, in his article on *Manor Sackville* (*Éire*, 1975), he points out how the drama reveals her concern for her country in 1833. A more original essay, Colin B. Atkinson and Jo Atkinson's "Sydney Owenson, Woman Writer" (*Éire*, 1980), gives special praise to *Woman and Her Master*, which, while flawed stylistically and technically, is cited as an important and early example of feminist literature. Robert Lee Wolff, in his introduction in the Garland series, calls *The O'Briens and the O'Flahertys* her best book; it is less uncritical in its liberalism and fuller in its presentation of social and political themes.

THOMAS MOORE

Of the poets in this group, Thomas Moore has received the greatest amount of critical attention: two new biographies as well as several essays on his poetic technique and subjects. The two biographies represent the poles of current methodologies. Hoover H. Jordan's two-volume *Bolt Upright* (Salzburg, 1975) cites original records and texts, providing full citations to earlier work and concluding with a sensible, scholarly, certainly not revisionist interpretation of the poet and his work. In contrast, Terence de Vere White, writing for a more general audience in *Tom Moore* (1977), concentrates on the personality: the charmer of upper-class society, the faithful friend of Byron, the loving husband of Bessy. His is not a critical biography, although his obvious appreciation of the Irish Burns makes his account enjoyable. Neither book replaces Howard Mumford Jones's interpretative biography, which provides both a scholarly approach to the works and a strong portrayal of the man. For an even fuller account of the man, we await the publication of Moore's journals, described by their editor, Wilfred Dowden, in " 'Let Ireland Remember': A Reexamination of the Journals of Thomas Moore" (*RUS*, 1975).

Moore's poetry deserves further analysis than it has received. Thérèse Tessier's *La Poésie lyrique de Thomas Moore* (Paris, 1976) provides a start, and her chapter on *Lalla Rookh* contains some careful analysis; but the overall critical examination is not thorough, so that no new understanding of the poetry is conveyed. Smaller studies continue to appear: H. J. Jackson's "Thomas Moore and Robert Burton" (*ELN*, 1975) finds the source of Moore's "The Ring" (1801) to be Burton's

Anatomy of Melancholy, and Mark D. Hawthorne in "Thomas Moore's *The Epicurean*: The Anacreonic Poet in Search of Eternity" (*SIR*, 1975) compares the poem "Alciphron" with the novel *The Epicurean* to show how uneasy Moore was both in dealing with eroticism and in addressing social questions.

SOMERVILLE AND ROSS

Hilary Robinson's *Somerville and Ross* (1980) makes use of manuscript materials, commonplace books, diaries, and letters to present a biography and a detailed account of these two writers' collaboration, including the ways they used recorded anecdotes and colorful dialogue in their novels; because they had more intimate knowledge of the rural Irish than did the leading writers of the Irish revival, their presentations of Irish characters and speech are more accurate and more sympathetic. The critical estimates, including special praise for *The Real Charlotte* and *The Big House at Inver*, are sound, and Robinson gives their comic writings due compliments. Guy Fehlmann's "The Composition of Somerville and Ross's Irish R. M.," in *The Irish Short Story* (ed. Rafroidi and Brown, 1979), also argues, on the evidence of manuscripts, that the R. M. stories were elaborately planned to achieve continuity. Wayne E. Hall, in *Shadowy Heroes: Irish Literature of the 1890's* (1980), holds that their novels present a comprehensive account of the demise of the Protestant Ascendancy, a class that was decaying from within, alienated and powerless in the face of an emerging new Ireland. In his essay on *The Real Charlotte*, included in *The Anglo-Irish Novel* (vol. 1, 1980), John Cronin presents a briefer but similarly favorable account of their skill in describing the stratified society of their time.

OSCAR WILDE

Ian Fletcher and John Stokes

Our 1976 essay began with grumbles: at the absence of an authoritative collected edition, an exhaustive bibliography, a definitive life, and a full iconography. In 1981 it might seem that we have less cause for complaint. Two major critical books have appeared, innovatory in both content and approach, together with two competent if comparatively pedestrian full-length studies and various shorter or more specialized offerings, most of them containing at least a new idea or so. Editions too have been prepared, in book or dissertation form—excellent in the case of three plays and the poems, adequate certainly in that of the shorter fiction.

One reason for this renewed activity is the rise of gay studies. There has also been increased interest in the ideological complications of Wilde's period, in Aestheticism, and in the evolutionist thought to which Wilde contributed as both commentator and example.

Yet still we await the standard life, bibliography, edition, and iconography; until these appear Wilde studies will continue to present the shadow without the substance. Happily, Richard Ellmann's biography may now be described as "imminent"; but there are no signs of a revised primary bibliography, and Oxford University Press has recently made it known that it has set aside Owen Dudley Edwards' edition for the Oxford English Texts with no present plans for reviving the proposal. N. A. Salerno's *Oscar Wilde: An Annotated Bibliography of Writings about Him* has also been withdrawn.

Grateful for what there is, we have already expressed the opinion, in our portmanteau reviews (*VS,* 1979; *YES,* 1980), that Rodney Shewan's *Oscar Wilde: Art and Egotism* (1977) is the most important academic study of Wilde yet written. This work epitomizes the best trends in recent Wilde scholarship. Shewan makes considerable use of manuscript material, he has ransacked the Clark Library, he refers whenever possible to Wilde's contemporaries, and he pays due attention to Wilde's extraliterary interests, particularly in the philosophy of science.

In the last few years E. H. Mikhail has emerged as editor and bibliographer extraordinary. Faced by the enormity of Mikhail's efforts we are humble. Should the Recording Angel still be pursuing Wilde with inquiries, we can assume that he will now reply, "Oh, don't ask me. Why don't you look it up in Mikhail?" Mikhail's *Oscar Wilde: An Annotated Bibliography of Criticism* (1978), published after our first essay, includes a great many items we ignored or were unaware of. In this essay we have, with few exceptions, listed only those items that have appeared after our 1976 essay or that, if earlier, seem to be of some interest, though previously overlooked both by Mikhail and by us. We suggest that researchers use our two essays in conjunction with Mikhail's book.

Two items in our 1976 essay were unfortunately misplaced. *Libre Parole* (24 June 1909) and *L'Action d'Art* (1 Apr. 1913) on page 80 refer to the controversy over Epstein's sculpture and should not appear among the memoirs. Since that essay was compiled, we have visited the Clark Library, where we examined Millard's own copy of his bibliography, heavily annotated and interleaved with additional secondary items, including poems and books dedicated to Wilde. Among the Clark's many other treasures are Millard's unpublished iconography and many volumes of press cuttings pertaining to Wilde. Jeffrey Weeks's splendidly radical *Coming Out* (1977) sent us to the Humanities Research Center at Austin, Texas, which now has the voluminous, though for the Wildean ultimately frustrating, diaries of George Ives. At the Bibliothèque de l'Arsenal we came across a useful collection of French press cuttings (at Re 10.968).

A peculiarly satisfying discovery was the authentic double life of Felix Paul Greve, the early German critic celebrated in our first essay. Greve, it turns out, resurfaced in later life as the honored Canadian novelist Frederick Philip Grove. (See D. O. Spettigue, *F. P. G.: The European Years*, 1973; and *The Letters of Frederick Philip Grove*, ed. Desmond Pacey, 1976.)

Our earlier feeling that the persecution of Wilde left a lasting mark on English culture has been confirmed by Martin Green in *Children of the Sun* (1977). How many adolescents learned the facts of "the life we do not lead" from *Dorian Gray*? Two at least—Cyril Connolly and George Orwell.

The ghosts of "decadence" haunt us still. Richard Gilman's *Decadence: The History of an Epithet* (1979) applies the workaday thesis that the word is but a word—a handy catchall for cultural pundits. The contributors to *Decadence and the 1890s* (ed. Ian Fletcher, Stratford-upon-Avon Studies 17, 1979), most of whom mention Wilde, would probably disagree, convinced that a fashionable epithet and a distinct historical episode should not be confused. In a comparative study of Huysmans, D'Annunzio, and Wilde (*CentR*, 1978) Lawrence M. Porter claims that "the greatest 'decadent' literature is not a weird paracriminal aberration by the counterculture of the Victorian age, but rather, a respectable tributary of modern psychoanalytical thought." Yet decadence need not be solemn, or solemnly treated. As Richard Ellmann has written recently, "Wilde was partly amused by the idea of decadence and parodied it when he lamented the decadence of lying and the loss of earnestness" (*TLS,* 15 Feb. 1980).

The wheel has turned and the eschatology of fin de siècle/fin de globe is back in vogue—as publishers and critics well know. For the Wilde devotee each new arrival suggests new leads. From *The Letters of Roger Fry* (ed. Denys Sutton, 1972) we learn that in May 1891 Fry immediately recognized Lord Ronald Gower as the original of Lord Henry Wotton. Does that morsel confirm a long-established hypothesis? Even fresh manuscript sources continue to emerge. In 1979 a bookseller's catalogue offered J. A. Symonds' copy of *The Correspondence of Sir Philip Sidney and Hubert Languet* with an autograph draft of a letter from Symonds to Wilde written on the publication of *Poems* (1881); these legendary uranians had apparently corresponded much earlier than is usually assumed. The significance of this and other discoveries someone, somewhere, will try to establish, confident, no doubt, that the last mask has been peeled away.

1. Bibliographies

E. H. Mikhail's *Oscar Wilde: An Annotated Bibliography of Criticism* (1978) contains more than its title suggests. The book lists bibliographies wholly and partially devoted to Wilde; published books by Wilde and their reviews; reviews of play productions, including dramatizations and films based on Wilde's life or works; dissertations wholly and partially devoted to Wilde; discography; and satires on Wilde in *Punch.*

Mikhail's labors are sometimes scarcely credible; their result is an essential tool, though one not always easy to use. In a work of this kind, indications of the content of particular items are necessarily scanty, and the effort of tracking down a tantalizing title may go unrewarded. Students interested in Wilde's reputation, theater historians in particular, will find the lists of contemporary reviews extremely helpful, and we are curious to see what effect Mikhail's work will have on future scholarship. We should add that we have found some errors of dating and description.

Establishing the contents of distant libraries is often a problem. William E. Conway's brief description of the Clark Library (*Book Club of California Quarterly Newsletter,* 1947) is now out of date. E. D. H. Johnson describes, in hushed tones, the collection of Robert Taylor housed at Princeton (*PULC,* 1977), which includes many presentation copies of first editions, *A Woman of No Importance* with a letter to Wilde from Beerbohm Tree giving terms of production, unpublished scenarios of *The Cardinal of Avignon* and *The Duchess of Florence* (which became *The Duchess of Padua*), and much Wilde correspondence, including twenty letters to Leonard Smithers.

Items 12995–13001 in *Dulau and Co. Catalogue 165 (1929): Books from the Library of John Lane* relate to Wilde. The advertisement at the end of a copy of *De Profundis* (1905) is dated one month earlier than the date given in Stuart Mason's bibliography (1914). The Dulau catalog is fascinating, most of all for its Beardsley and Lionel Johnson entries.

Gary H. Paterson's annotated bibliography of writings about Lord Alfred Douglas (*ELT*, 1980) inevitably includes many treatments of Wilde. The summaries are full, but the list is by no means up-to-date and could easily be increased.

Mikhail's long section "Bibliographies Partially Devoted to Wilde" can be supplemented by L. W. Conolly and J. P. Wearing's *English Drama and Theatre 1800–1900* (1978) and Linda Dowling's excellent *Aestheticism and Decadence: A Selective Annotated Bibliography* (1977), mandatory for all students of the period. Myrna J. Lundquist's dissertation (Univ. of Puget Sound 1974) gives a basic list of Wilde manuscripts and their locations.

Wilde's hitherto unknown review of *Crime and Punishment* has been identified (*N&Q*, 1980). The works of Shewan, Chamberlin, and Stokes discussed in our section on major critical studies all contain bibliographical information, the most significant being contextual.

2. Editions

The Illustrated Oscar Wilde (ed. Roy Gasson, 1977) is pleasantly produced and contains a biographical introduction by Gasson, filmography (including tv productions), a short list of productions, photos of stage productions, stills from old films, Crane and Ricketts' designs from original editions, a generous selection from the published works, and a brief but efficient bibliography. *The Portable Oscar Wilde* is now available in a Penguin edition (1977).

Isobel Murray has edited the *Complete Shorter Fiction* (1979). In her introduction Murray stresses the pervasive influence of Meinhold's *Sidonia the Sorceress*. There are useful notes. The shorter version of *The Portrait of Mr. W. H.* is given, on the grounds that it more coherently presents Wilde's central notion that when one converts another to a belief one loses that belief oneself. Murray has also written a constructive introduction to her revised edition of the Everyman volume *Plays, Prose Writings and Poems* (1975). Peter Faulkner's introduction to the Everyman *Picture of Dorian Gray* (1976) is merely predictable.

Photographic reprints of *The Happy Prince and Other Tales* (1888) and *A House of Pomegranates* (1891) appeared as a single volume in 1977; in the preface John Espey gives some bibliographical information.

Ian Small's comprehensive edition of *Lady Windermere's Fan* (1980) provides the text published in 1893 but gives cross-references to the six surviving drafts and the one unauthorized edition of the play—that is, the manuscript draft in the British Library, the typescript under the title of *A Good Woman* in the Clark Library, two early acting versions at the Clark (one in manuscript, one in typescript), the undated Samuel French edition, the revised acting typescript at the University of Texas, and the licensing copy at the British Library. Small discusses the order of revisions and, in an appendix, gives the entry of Mrs. Erlynne and the end of act 2 as they appear in versions other than the one published in 1893.

Russell Jackson's *The Importance of Being Earnest* (1980) is the most authoritative text of the play and the most widely available. Jackson has adopted the 1899 three-act edition as the copy text, but appendixes contain the Gribsby episode from the manuscript draft; the dictation episode, act 2, in the licensing copy; and the conclusion of act 2 in the licensing copy. Jackson has looked at the manuscript draft of the four-act version; the typescripts of acts 3 and 4 now in the Arents Tobacco Collection, New York Public Library; the typescript of the four-act version dated October 1894 in the same library (MS. Add. 53567); the typescript revised by Wilde to provide copy for the 1899 edition in the Arents Collection; the page proofs of that edition with Wilde's autograph alterations in the University of Texas; and the French edition of 1903.

In 1981 the Curwen Press, London, announced a two-volume edition of *The Sphinx* with decorations by Charles Ricketts, consisting of a facsimile of the original work (1894) and a companion volume containing an essay by Stephen Calloway and further illustrations by Ricketts. *Serenade* (illus. Rigby Graham, 1962) reprints a poem, probably written about Lily Langtry, from *Poems* (1881). *Mervyn Peake/Oscar Wilde* (1980) presents ink drawings made by Peake in 1946 to accompany extracts from Wilde's poems. The Tragara Press has produced a limited edition of *Hellenism* (1979), a previously unpublished article whose manuscript is divided between the Clark and Hyde collections.

The 1890s Society has brought out a facsimile of the *Chameleon* (1978), the magazine used to such damaging effect at the first trial. This beautifully made edition has an introduction by H. Montgomery Hyde and a brief essay, identifying various contributors, by Timothy d'Arch Smith. The publicity sheet produced by the society contains a fragment or two of information about Wilde's involvement with the magazine that is not to be found elsewhere.

Our previous essay omitted at least two selections of Wilde's aphorisms—*Epigrams*, "illustrated by Fritz Kredel, Mount Vernon, New York" (n.d.), and *Pensées*, with an introduction by Georges-Bazile (Paris, n.d.)—and one other printing of *De Profundis*, "translated from the German by Lord Ramsgate," in *Two Worlds* (1926).

In 1979 two satires on Wilde, *The Poet and the Puppets* and *Aristophanes at Oxford* (rpt. as a single vol.), and Guillot de Saix's *Le Chant du Cygne* were published in the series The Decadent Consciousness (ed. Ian Fletcher and John Stokes). A German version of de Saix's collocation, *Herberge der Träume*, with an introduction by Wolfhart Klee, had appeared in 1955. We continue to discover examples of de Saix's rummaging: for instance, *L'Européen* (8 May 1929—interviews with some who apparently knew Wilde, e.g., Claire de Pratz, André Sinet, Tranchant de Lunel, Max de Morès); *Les Arts et Les Lettres* (12 July 1946—Wilde and Mallarmé); *Arcadie* (June 1959—the quite insupportable suggestion that Arthur Cravan wrote *Teleny*).

3. Letters

While we naturally welcome the publication of *Selected Letters of Oscar Wilde*, edited by Rupert Hart-Davis (1979), we lament that the magnificent collected letters of 1962 should now be out of print. The new selection gives an improved text in a few instances but includes no fresh letters. That they exist we do not doubt.

Hart-Davis' own letters to George Lyttelton, which take up three volumes (1978, 1979, 1981), afford some glimpses into the rewards and tribulations of the scholar and give a rare vignette of the eccentric French Wildean Guillot de Saix.

Wilde's *Letters to Graham Hill* (privately printed, 1978)—Hill was presumably a schoolboy of the Louis Wilkinson type—are too slight even to be embarrassing.

4. Manuscripts

Our 1976 essay was in error when it stated that the New York Public Library contains an early draft of *The Sphinx* and "The Harlot's House." The entry for the library's manuscript holdings should now be canceled and the following substituted: ALS to C. Kains Jackson, 10 November 1893, inserted in *Salome*; five ALS to J. Stanley Little; "Ye shall be gods," holograph poem, six pages; *Vera*, corrections and additions to the play made for performance in New York, 1883; *The Picture of Dorian Gray*, chapter 4, sixty-five pages; *Salome*, manuscript signed by Wilde but thought to be a forgery by Fabian Lloyd; "Pan," holograph poem, two pages; "On the Decay of Lying," incomplete, twenty pages; "Notes of Travel in Greece," holograph, two pages; "Lotus Land," holograph; "Notes and Fragments on Greek Poets"; "Notes and Epigrams," holograph; "Le Jardin des Tuileries," holograph corrections to proof; "Impressions de voyage," holograph; "Impression Japonaise," holograph poem published as "Le Panneau"; "Dole of the King's Daughter," holograph of earlier verse; *The Land of Heart's Desire*, with inscribed note on Wilde by W. B. Yeats; *Dorian Gray*, presentation copy to Arthur Brett; *Dorian Gray*, privately printed, 1890; Althea Gyles's illustrated "The Harlot's House"; Frank Harris, notes in a copy of *An Ideal Husband* (1891), "Notes of a Talk after Dinner in Café Durand, 1899." The library has a typescript of the production of *A Woman of No Importance* at H. Miner's Theatre, 1894 and typescripts of the promptbook and the production of *An Ideal Husband* at the Lyceum, New York, 1895. The *Bulletin of the New York Public Library* (1971) includes an article by Avi Wortis describing the remarkable R. H. Burnside collection and explaining how, in 1968, an early variant version of *Lady Lancing* (*The Importance of Being Earnest*), presumably originating from Charles Frohman, was found among Burnside's papers.

The Pierpont Morgan Library has acquired a letter from Wilde to W. S. Blunt, c. 1883, which has already been printed in Hart-Davis, and a letter to Alfred Sternes, c. 1891, which Hart-Davis does not include.

Reading University Library now has an unpublished typescript, Daniel J. Rider, *Adventures with Frank Harris*, which contains some information about Rider's relations with Wilde, Harris, and Smithers.

The Society of Authors papers housed in the British Library Department of Manuscripts include correspondence carried out by the society on behalf of the Wilde estate. This might be useful for tracking down elusive editions, translations, and productions.

The Clark Library has obtained a set of proofs of the French text of *Salome* corrected in various hands, and John Espey (*Oscar Wilde: Two Approaches*, by Richard Ellmann and Espey, 1977) is right to remind us that the Clark has a hoard of Wildeana, some of it still unexamined. Espey notes that the Clark has the corrected and expanded typescript of *Dorian Gray* that was submitted to Stoddart, editor of *Lippincott's*; a typescript of *A Woman of No Importance*; versions of *The Sphinx* and "The Harlot's House"; and an early draft of *Vera*. He also expertly describes some of the Clark's rare editions.

Christie's in New York issued an important catalog of the Prescott Collection, for the auction held 6 February 1981. It lists many significant Wilde items, including a presentation copy to John Addington Symonds of *Poems* (1881); an edition of *Vera* dated 1882; a notebook dating from Wilde's time at Oxford; Mason's annotated copy of the Tite Street sale; a manuscript of an essay and review of Symonds' *Studies of the Greek Poets*; manuscripts of several poems; a manuscript of what became "The Rise of Historical Criticism"; Wilde's annotated copy of Aristotle's *Ethica Nichomachea*; a manuscript probably relating to *The Duchess of Padua*; a manuscript of "L'Envoi" to *Rose Leaf and Apple Leaf*; a manuscript of "Lecture to Art Students"; manuscript notes of "Personal Impressions of America"; a manuscript of what became the preface to *Dorian Gray*; a manuscript of act 3 of *Lady Windermere*; working notes for *A Woman of No Importance*; a manuscript of act 4 and a typescript of act 3 of *An Ideal Husband*; a typescript of the four-act *Importance of Being Earnest* dated 8–25 October 1894; letters from Wilde to D'Oyly Carte, John Lane, Frances Forbes-Robertson, Ada Leverson, and others; material relating to the American tour; a manuscript of Douglas' *The Wilde Myth*; and letters to Wilde from Swinburne and others.

5. Biography

The potboilers continue unabashed. Louis Kronenberger's 1976 life has no apparent errors but no originality either. Kronenberger goes to some lengths to avoid making literary judgments, and his book has a rather unconvinced introduction by the historian J. H. Plumb. Our dislike of Sheridan Morley's vulgar and inaccurate picture book (1976) has been recorded elsewhere (*VS*, 1979, *YES*, 1980). Martin Nicols' *The Importance of Being Oscar* (1981) concocts a biographical narrative out of an unusually wide range of Wildean witticisms. H. Montgomery Hyde's biography (1976)—which for the time being at any rate has assumed the status of a standard life, although it is in many ways a synthesis of his earlier works—has been widely reviewed. The novelist Anthony Powell remarked upon it in the *Daily Telegraph* (27 May 1976), and we have made our own separate comments in *JENS* (1977) and *JBeS* (1978). Also see *SR* (1976).

The second half of Brian Roberts' *The Mad Bad Line: The Family of Lord Alfred Douglas* (1981) is almost entirely given over to Bosie. Roberts provides a strong narrative line but makes no obvious use of important new material. Rumours of a hidden cache of letters sent by Wilde to Douglas in 1895, which were widely reported in the London press in the summer of 1981, appear to have been ill-founded. Douglas has also recently been recalled by two who knew him in his latter days—Stanley Allcorn in the *Standard* (London, 24 August 1981) and Donald Sinden in *A Touch of the Memoirs* (1982)—and caricatured with Wilde by Walter Dorin and George Melly in *Great Lovers* (1981).

Small additions have been made to the record of almost every phase of Wilde's career. Tim Hilton in *Studio International* (1974) gives an intelligent and detailed account of Ruskin's experiment in road building at Hinksey. A disparaging reference to Wilde's influence on Whistler is to be found in a fascinating guidebook, *Society in London* (1885), by "A Foreign Resident" (Thomas Hay Sweet Escott). Mark Girouard's *Sweetness and Light* (1977) has information on the building of the Tite Street house. The conversations with Martin Secker that are recorded in *TLS* (10 December 1976; see also 7 January 1977) tell us something about Douglas' later conduct and correct the spelling of Lord Shoreham's name in *The Importance*.

Encountering the relevant portions of Peter Conrad's *Imagining America* (1980), the Wildean finds no more and no less than meets the eye: shimmering surmise (Wilde "reduced the American language to a function of geography"), flashing inversion (Wilde's wit "disrupts morality by being so nonsensically moralistic"), and blinding comparisons—with Kipling, Brooke, and Wells. Confrontations with miners and matrons, precise belittling epigrams, even that photogenic fur coat—all are claimed as aspects of Wilde's rewarding mission to subvert American innocence. Using the present tense to affect an intimacy with his subject, ridding himself of the ballast of footnotes and bibliography, Conrad floats free, carried on, like Wilde, by his own undeniable talent for rearrangement. Earthbound scholars may wish to add to our previous list the following solid sources for the American visits: a long transcription of Wilde's lecture on the United States in the *Era* (14 July 1883); Phil Robinson, *Sinners and Saints: A Tour across the States and round Them* (1883); *The America of Jose Marti: Selected Writings of Jose Marti* (1953), a vivid account, frequently overlooked, of Wilde's appearance at Chickering Hall; Laura E. Richards and Maud Howe Elliott, *Julia Ward Howe 1819-1910* (1925); Maud Howe Elliott, *Uncle Sam Ward and His Circle* (1938); Ophia D. Smith, *Fair Oxford* (1947), a description of Wilde in Cincinnati and his influence on American Aestheticism; Forbes Parkhill, *The Wildest of the West* (1951), an account of Wilde in Denver; William Habich, "Oscar Wilde in Louisville" (*Louisvillian*, Oct. 1957); John Spalding Gatton, "The Sunflower Saint: Oscar Wilde in Louisville" (*Filson Club History Quarterly*, 1978); John

Davenport Neville, "Oscar Wilde: An Apostle of Aestheticism in the Old Dominion" (*VC*, 1978); Peat Louisa O'Neill, "When Canada Went Wilde" (*Canadian Theatre Rev.*, 1978); Annette B. Feldmann, "The Selling of Oscar Wilde" (*Phantasm*, 1979); and Barry Carman, "Oscar Wilde in America" (*Listener*, 7 Jan. 1982).

Interest in the Wilde family, that severely fractured unit, appears to be growing. James Edward Holroyd's essay on Willie (*Blackwood's*, 1979) provides a starting point for the study of an unlucky sibling. Willie's marital adventures are also referred to in Madeleine B. Stern, *Purple Passage: The Life of Mrs. Frank Leslie* (1953). Victoria Glendinning writes on Speranza with sensitivity but offers little new research (*TLS*, 23 May 1980; also printed in *Genius in the Drawing Room*, ed. Peter Quennell, 1980). A report in *TLS* (21 Nov. 1980; see also 26 Dec. 1980) tells of recently discovered family letters concerning the marriage to William Wilde.

Inevitably it is the Wilde family as a whole that draws the attention of psychoanalysts when they write on Oscar. An extended debate about the role of Lady Wilde, the importance of Isola's death, and the psychoanalytic significance of works such as "Charmides" and *Dorian Gray* can be traced through articles by Alexander Grinstein in the *Annual of Psychoanalysis* (1973) and in *American Imago* (1980), and by Jerome Kavka in the *Annual of Psychoanalysis* (1975).

The extent of Wilde's contacts, legitimate or otherwise, is revealed in several recent publications. Of these by far the most important is Richard Ellmann's study of the love affair with Douglas (*NYRB*, 4 Aug. 1977; also printed in *Oscar Wilde: Two Approaches*, 1977), in which attention is drawn to the Scarlet Marquess' eugenic poem *The Spirit of the Matterhorn*. Bringing all his skill to bear on an old story, Ellmann compels us to see it in a new way. Rivaling him in insight, Jerusha McCormack (*JENS*, 1976) shows how nature imitated art when John Gray modeled himself on Dorian: "Neither the fictive nor the actual Dorian Gray regarded this courtship of sin as subversive of their attraction to Catholicism: if anything, it was part of a logical sequence, a kind of apostasy *à rebours*. Theirs was the necessary, the therapeutic sin." Thomas Mallon has compiled a miniature biography of Edward Shelley (*Biography*, 1978). André Guillaume's *William Ernest Henley et son groupe* (Paris, 1973) documents the souring of the relationship between Wilde and Henley. Estelle Jussim's *Slave to Beauty: The Eccentric Life and Controversial Career of F. Holland Day, Photographer, Publisher, Aesthete* (1981) notes Day's contacts with Wilde and Beardsley; Nicholas Mosley's *Julian Grenfell* (1976) describes Wilde's visits to Taplow in the summer of 1891 and prints a new letter; Miriam J. Benkowitz's life of Beardsley (1981) retells the story of his relationship with Wilde; Elizabeth Longford's life of Wilfrid Scawen Blunt (1976) includes a tantalizing reconstruction of Wilde's encounters with Curzon and the Grabbet Club; Robert Secor has discovered and reprinted the novelist Violet Hunt's memoir, "My Oscar" (*TSLL*, 1979). (The character of Philip Wynyard in Hunt's *Their Lives* was based on Wilde.) Karl Beckson has provided some new documentation for the crisis at the *Yellow Book* (*N&Q*, 1979). George Hendrick's study *H. S. Salt* (1977) has a reference

to Wilde in prison, and two books deal with a significant forerunner to
the events of 1895: H. Montgomery Hyde, *The Cleveland Street Scandal*
(1976), and Colin Simpson et al., *The Cleveland Street Affair* (1978).

H. P. Clive's outline of the quarrel between Wilde and Louÿs in
Pierre Louÿs 1870–1925 (1978) may be supplemented by Guillot de
Saix's essay in *Vendémiaire* (18 Aug. 1937) and Peter Vernon's essay
"John Gray's Letters to Pierre Louÿs" (*RLC*, 1979).

The 1890s Society, which is, or at least should be, renowned for its
selfless devotion to the period, in 1979 excelled itself with Theodore
Wratislaw, *Oscar Wilde: A Memoir*, foreword by John Betjeman and
introduction and notes by Karl Beckson. Although *TLS* (11 April 1980)
remained unmoved, true devotees will be glad to have Wratislaw's
evocation of a golden weekend spent with Wilde at Goring in the summer
of 1893.

Our 1976 essay unfortunately missed Robert Pearsall's book on
Frank Harris (1970), with its spirited defense of Harris' life of Wilde,
and Charles Burkhart's sympathetic book on Ada Leverson (1973). We
should also have noted that Thomas H. Bell's *Oscar Wilde without
Whitewash* (the Clark has the English manuscript) was published in 1946
in Buenos Aires as *Oscar Wilde: Sus amicos, sus adversarios, sus ideas*.

Our tentative bibliography of the Pemberton Billing row over
Salome in 1918 has now been eclipsed by a complete book, *Salome's Last
Veil: The Libel Case of the Century* (1977), by Michael Kettle, which
quotes extensively from the trial and gives details of the lives of the prin-
cipal characters, but fails to note Edith Nesbit's early novel about Maud
Allan, *Salome and the Head* (1909).

E. H. Mikhail's lavish and expensive two volumes, *Oscar Wilde:
Interviews and Recollections* (1979), expose a current dilemma. While we
have always insisted that Wilde's life deserves the fullest documentation,
it has been with the silent proviso that sources are handled with tact,
originality, and proportion. Mikhail has scoured the memoirs and come
up with anecdotes that now occupy some five hundred pages. Apparently
intending to revive Wilde the conversationalist, he set himself a problem.
The charm of a live performance is easily lost in the retelling, and too
many of these memories have grown dull, evasive, and unamusing. Yet
the material concerning Wilde's visits abroad is well presented, the contemporary interviews are splendid, and Mikhail's editorial notes are
scrupulous, packed with further biographical and bibliographical information. Appendixes contain the dates and details of the American lecture tour and an "additional bibliography."

Having expressed our reservations about anecdotal material, we will
now list yet more memoirs, nearly all of them previously unrecorded, in
the hope that they may be of some use to discriminating scholars: James
Adderley, *In Slums and Society* (1916); Eliza Aria, *My Sentimental Self*
(1922); Sydney Blow, *Through Stage Doors* (1958); Frank A. Boyd, *A
Pelican's Tale* (1919); Oscar Browning, *Memories of Sixty Years* (1910);
G. B. Burgin, *Memories of a Clubman* (1921); Emma Calvé, *My Life*
(1922); John Coleman, *Charles Reade As I Knew Him* (1903); Stephen
Coleridge, *Memories* (1913); Ramsey Colles, *In Castle and Court House*
(1911); William Thomas Ewens, *Thirty Years at Bow-Street Police Court*

(1924); Lewis R. Farnell, *An Oxonian Looks Back* (1934); H. Felber-mann, *Memoirs of a Cosmopolitan* (1936); Moreton Frewen, *Melton Mowbray and Other Memories* (1924); Francis Gribble, *Seen in Passing* (1929); Cosmo Hamilton, *People Worth Talking About* (1933); G. P. Jacomb-Hood, *With Brush and Pencil* (1925); Henry Lucy, *Sixty Years in the Wilderness: Nearing Jordan* (1916); J. Lewis May, *Thorn and Flower* (1935); H. W. Nevinson, *Changes and Chances* (1923); Mrs. Clement Scott, *Old Days in Bohemian London* (1919); Ernest Smith, *Fields of Adventure* (1923); Cécile Sorel, *Cécile Sorel: An Autobiography* (English trans. 1953); Philip Treherne, *A Plaintiff in Person* (1923); Valentine Williams, *The World in Action* (1938); Harry de Windt, *My Notebook at Home and Abroad* (1923) and *My Restless Life* (1909); "X," *Myself not Least* (1925).

6. Major Critical Studies

The informing argument of Rodney Shewan's *Oscar Wilde: Art and Egotism* (1977) is that "Wilde remained a Romantic, according to his own definition, throughout his life." He "created himself out of his imagination," he habitually pursued the "Romantic absolute," and his works are "mythopoeic structures." Shewan's targets are the traditional accusations of insincerity and vacillation, although he subtly allows that "nothing looks more like continuity than self-borrowing." No Wildean can afford to ignore *Art and Egotism*, not the least for the new material it contains. About Wilde's sources Shewan is, for the most part, admirably precise: W. K. Clifford supplied ideas and phrases; Spencerian sociobiology and Hegelian metaphysics provided background and quotations. And even when he is more speculative, Shewan always sounds right: the importance to Wilde of d'Aurevilly's study of Beau Brummell was that it placed dandyism on a more intellectual footing; like Meredith, Wilde saw that the middle classes provided the best audience, but, unlike Meredith, he doubted that they offered the best values; Whistler supplied not only the décor for poems but the subject for "The Remarkable Rocket"—and so on, right through the complete works.

The major flaw in *Art and Egotism* lies embedded in its title. Shewan founds his argument on two possible meanings of "egotism" in the *OED*—self-absorption and self-awareness—and claims that Wilde balanced the two. But "egotism" underwent continual redefinition in the nineteenth century, and the word was adopted for many purposes. John Goode's essay on Meredith (in *Meredith Now*, ed. Ian Fletcher, 1971) might have prompted Shewan here and also, misleading though it may be, George Steiner's note on the word (*EIC*, 1952). Whether Shewan's simplification of a complex term seriously weakens his readings must remain, in this survey, an otiose question. Certainly we are reassured that there are further ways of grasping Wilde, that egotist-individualist who announced that "Under Individualism people will be quite natural and absolutely unselfish, and will know the meanings of the words, and will realize them in their free, beautiful lives. Nor will men be as egotistic as they are now." Such teasing discriminations, of words even now commonly taken to be synonymous, must surely attract more attention—"deconstruction" even.

J. E. Chamberlin's introduction to *Ripe Was the Drowsy Hour: The Age of Oscar Wilde* (1977) asks us to accept that "however arbitrary our sense of the age of Wilde, the coherence that we invent or discover in the period is not accidental, but derives quite directly from the ideas that inform the beliefs and the believers that we wonder at." Or, as one reviewer put it (*VP*, 1979), "Chamberlin's study does not entirely avoid sharing many of the mannerisms of the period he studies—its love of display, obsession with surfaces, insincerity, and its flashes of brilliance." In a weary word this book is, if nothing else, "stimulating." Chancing his luck on the board of ideas, Chamberlin plays for connections. Point sparks to point and the rewards are high: Hofmannsthal, William Carlos Williams, Wallace Stevens, Simmel, Sartre, and Picasso are just some of the markers. So too, more expectedly, are Baudelaire, Gautier, Pater, Symons, and Nietzsche. The least successful bids are the first chapter—a historical and biographical résumé—and the last, which takes a familiar circuit around the mythic figures of Marsyas, Demeter, Dionysus, Persephone, Salome, and Pierrot. Between them lie more profitable forays into the rationales for aesthetics and into the aesthetics of perception. Wildeans who study Chamberlin's footnotes will learn many things to their advantage, particularly to do with anthropology, Darwinism, and the new science of pathology. They will certainly appreciate Chamberlin's facility with the handy definition—of "egotism" and "idealism," for example, and, more questionably, of "impressionism." But Chamberlin's selection of significant events falls short; Irish politics, theater history, and the more practical achievements of Aestheticism are nowhere to be found.

The most feeble moments in Philip K. Cohen's *The Moral Vision of Oscar Wilde* (1978) are precisely those when its author claims most originality: constant reminders of the deep significance for Wilde of the death of his sister Isola (uneasily connected with his homosexuality); repeated assertions that Wilde felt himself to have been led astray by Pater, a critic sometimes crudely presented as the spokesman for naked hedonism. But elsewhere Cohen can be perceptive and useful, and he provides an extended analysis of *The Duchess of Padua* that relates the play to *The Cenci*, a bibliography for "Hylo-Idealism" as it appears in "The Canterville Ghost," background material for the fairy tales, and parallels between Plutarch and *Salome*. The chapters on the plays (which include discussions of *Love Is Law* and *The Cardinal of Avignon*) are the best argued, although their underlying direction does not become wholly apparent until the treatment of *De Profundis*, which indicates (and presumably endorses) a full-fledged Christian typology. Cohen's Wilde, then, is thoroughly earnest, by turns proselyte and apostate, striving either to disburden himself of the world or to conceive of a theology that will encompass it. The fleshly Wilde, *boulevardier*, decadent, or socialist even, is never shown.

Donald H. Eriksen's *Oscar Wilde* (1977), an oddly belated addition to the Twayne series, opens with a capsule biography and historical generalizations based, honestly enough, on Jerome H. Buckley, but otherwise the book's divisions are according to genre. Both the poems and the stories are described rather than analyzed, and Eriksen prefers not to pursue his evident perception that Wilde's critical theory evades or disguises the problems it discloses. It is not until the chapter on *Dorian Gray* that the book becomes provocative. Rebutting previous critics, Eriksen argues that the events of the novel do not in fact contradict the high Aestheticism of its preface, since "Dorian's portrait serves as a scapegoat for a life of art that succumbs increasingly to vulgar self-gratification. Only Lord Henry escapes the pitfalls of the New Hedonism." The difficulty with this reading is that it ignores the sad and uncreative spectacle that Lord Henry presents at the close, and it underestimates the urgency of Dorian's dilemma. Merely conventional in comparison, Eriksen's chapter on the drama concentrates on the shifting role of the dandy and on the final achievement, in *The Importance*, of perfect symmetry. We find it significant that the demands of a primer should so easily accommodate academic formalism.

The Germans have kept up the pace with several new books. Norbert Kohl's *Oscar Wilde: Leben und Werk in Daten und Bilder* (Frankfurt, 1976) has a remarkable range of illustrations, a bibliography of German contributions, a selection of statements about Wilde made by his contemporaries and by later critics, and a summarizing essay by the compiler himself. Ria Omasreiter's *Oscar Wilde* (Heidelberg, 1978) is arranged around topics such as the dandy, art and nature, individualism and socialism, and discusses most of the major works. Norbert Kohl's massive *Oscar Wilde: Das literarische Werk zwischen Provokation und Anpassung* (Heidelberg, 1980) has unfortunately arrived too late for us to do it justice or to estimate its originality. Five hundred pages of text survey the complete oeuvre, citing an extraordinary range of critical opinion. This is followed by a bibliographical juggernaut that includes many German editions. Anita Roitinger's *Oscar Wilde's Life as Reflected in His Correspondence and His Autobiography* (Salzburger Studien zur Anglistik und Amerikanistik, vol. 12, 1980) rests entirely on standard sources.

An essay by John Stokes (1978) has replaced James Laver's contribution to the Writers and Their Work series. Late reviews of Nassaar's *Into the Demon Universe* (1974) have appeared (*SR*, 1976; *ELT*, 1976).

7. Shorter Critical Studies

The short but stylish evaluation of Wilde's life and work has become almost a genre of its own. An early, febrile try by the anarchist poet John Barlas has been reprinted by Tragara (1978). L. H. Hugo (*UES*, 1977) gives a brisk, unfeeling summary of the life, and in a posthumously published *God's Fifth Column: A Biography of the Age, 1890–1940* (1981), William Gerhardie makes a strained comparison between Wilde and Lenin. A more recent, more stringent attempt to capture Wilde's essence has been made by Jerusha McCormack (*ELT*, 1979). In a reengagement with the terms that still seem to dog Wilde—"sincerity," "evil," "egoism,"—McCormack regrets Wilde's "inability to create a style that is more than an acquired and systematized version of that of his audience." Consequently Wilde "lost the opportunity to become something more than that creature of his age, an egoist without an ego."

Roger B. Henkle in *Comedy and Culture* (1980) puts it differently. Wilde's "elaborative" wit "illustrates what may be the particular nature of the comic impulse—the tendency to rework the existent rather than to enfigure the transcendent." Comic "transvaluation" is the keynote, though it turns out to imply a familiar version of the paradox. No mean expert with that figure himself, Henkle claims that *Dorian Gray*, which he counterposes with *De Profundis*, "evolves—intentionally—into bad art." The several biographical overstatements (e.g., Wilde "never took the slightest interest in politics," was "by no means a crusader for homosexual rights") are presumably signs of Henkle's eagerness to make Wilde an example of Renato Poggioli's theory of the avant-garde artist.

We are far less impressed by two essays in Canadian journals: James Mark Purcell's comments (*AntigR*, 1975) are unhelpful; Joseph Stein's "The New Woman and the Decadent Dandy" (*DR*, 1975) relies on Holbrook Jackson and Ellen Moers and seems more concerned with Beerbohm than with Wilde.

In John Reed's *Victorian Conventions* (1975) the content is less original than the taxonomy. The book claims that Wilde contributed to most of the "conventions" (in particular with *Salome* and *Dorian Gray*) but, typically, proved his representative nature by satirizing them.

Much of the remainder of this section is given over to listing early items discovered since 1976 and not included in Mikhail. Several minor items from the early response to Wilde have now come to light. Paul Jordan-Smith, *On Strange Altars* (1923), is an interesting specimen, though the prose is purple. There are chapters on Joyce, Hardy, Pater, and Machen as well as Wilde. Thomas F. Plowman, *In the Days of Victoria* (1918), has a long section on Wilde with illustrations. Three sympathetic essays, all written at roughly the same time, are worth mentioning: A. R. Orage (*New Age*, 4 Mar. 1909), who hails Wilde as "our English Nietzsche"; W. T. Titterton (*Vanity Fair*, 26 Oct. 1910); and J. E. Barton (*SatR*, 20 April 1912). An extreme example of the unsympathetic approach is E. Wake Cook (*ContempR*, 1910), who condemns Wilde, along with Nietzsche and Whistler, as a revolutionary enemy of natural evolution. Wake Cook was, incidentally, to take equal offense at Roger Fry's Post-Impressionist Exhibition.

The German obsession is further recorded in an article by Martin Birnbaum in the *Bookman* (New York, Jan. 1910) and in I. A. R. Wylie, *Eight Years in Germany* (1914). Hermann Bahr's important essay on decadence, which did much to establish Wilde's image, was reprinted in *Zur Überwindung des Naturalismus* (Stuttgart, 1968).

Over the years at least two French periodicals have devoted special issues to Wilde, both previously unnoticed. *Le Figaro* (Supplément littéraire, 5 Dec. 1925) has articles on *Salome*, on Wilde and Catholicism, and on Wilde and traditions of morality. *Arcadie* (Oct. 1954), a French version of the Wilde issue of *Adam* (1954), emphasizes homosexual matters. French newspaper articles that have recently come to our notice include Julien Despretz in *Gil Blas* (15 and 25 April 1925)—on the trials;

Alexandre Hepp in *Le Journal* (20 May 1897)—on Wilde's release; Paul d'Armon in *Le Signal* (21 Oct. 1904)—on the Ruskinian example; Augustin Filon in *Débats* (21 June 1905)—on *De Profundis*; G. Meesemaecker in *Mercure de France* (16 March 1917)—on the Symbolist tradition; Yvanhoe Rambosson in *Comoedia* (7 Aug. 1923)—on Wilde and Verlaine in Paris; Frédéric Boutet in *Candide* (3 Dec. 1925)—on the final phase; and two minor pieces by Cecil Georges-Bazile: in *Paris-Soir* (28 Oct. 1925)—on Wilde's last days, and in *La Volonté* (30 Nov. 1925)—on *De Profundis*. Wilde's influence in France we know to have been considerable. Jean Pierrot in *L'Imaginaire décadent, 1880-1900* (Paris, 1977) hails him as the major theoretician of the Decadence and provides an elaborate bibliography. For mention of Wilde's stays in Paris and the comments made about him by French writers, see Emilien Carassus, *Le Snobisme et les lettres françaises de Paul Bourget à Marcel Proust, 1884-1914* (Paris, 1966).

A further item in Portuguese has turned up: Eduoardo Tourinho, *Os Ultimos Dias de Oscar Wilde e outros estudos* (Bahia, 1938).

Those interested in the slightly covert American idolization of Wilde and of Aestheticism in general should hunt through the little magazines. In 1926 *Two Worlds* printed Harris' new preface to *The Life and Confessions,* Douglas' preface to the same book, and Beerbohm's "A Peep into the Past." The *Rose-Jar* reprinted "Mis-statements about Oscar Wilde's Last Days Corrected" in 1905 and, in its issue for 1904-05, an essay by Percival Pollard, characterized by his usual provincial aesthetic phrase making. Thomas Beer's *The Mauve Decade* (1926) is also of some use.

We can expect many new treatments of Wilde as gay studies burgeon. Robert K. Martin alludes to Wilde in *The Homosexual Tradition in American Poetry* (1979). Fraser Harrison's essay on Wilde's sexual development (*JENS,* 1980) takes its theory from Freud and Lenin, its facts from Rupert Croft-Cooke. Eric Bentley's polemic (*Canadian Theatre Rev.,* 1976) insists that the condemnation of Wilde was entirely motivated by a repressive sexual ideology: "He did indeed propose the most subversive of all subversions: to make love with a smile and no end in view." We have been unable to find a copy of a 1940 publication by the Friends of Oscar Wilde Society, but we suspect that it contains the two essays on homosexuality by G. V. Hamilton and G. Legman that were later published in New York in 1950; these essays are in the British Library. The Clark Library has *The Writing on the Ground* (probably 1913, "published for the author at 12 Chelsea Court, S.W., price one penny"), by "E. G. O." (possibly Gwen Otter, later a friend of Evelyn Waugh's)—an attack on Douglas and T. W. Crosland that tries to prove Douglas' uranian past. The report of Noel Annan's address to a conference on the Victorian counterculture (*VS* 1974) suggests that Annan too has done some plain speaking on the subject "The Rise of the Cult of Homosexuality in the English Upper Classes."

8. Plays

Surprisingly, Alan Bird's *The Plays of Oscar Wilde* (1977) is what it claims to be: the first book entirely devoted to Wilde's drama. It is also sensible, thorough, and a trifle dull. Bird relates *Vera* to the assassination of Tsar Alexander II and nihilist activity. *The Duchess of Padua* is analyzed in the context of Wilde's long and important letter to Mary Anderson of March 1883, and *Lady Windermere* is discussed in the light of Wilde's revisions and Alexander's policy at the St. James's. *A Woman of No Importance* is shown to be saved from outright sentimentality by its realistic attitude toward Mrs. Arbuthnot and *An Ideal Husband* successfully to reflect the contemporary intrusion of financial corruption into politics. Bird is weaker on *The Importance*, which he places under Auden's heading of "verbal opera," though as usual, he handles contextual material deftly. He is weakest of all on *Salome*, partly because he relies on secondary sources to account for the play's origin, partly because he appears to have a limited knowledge of symbolist aesthetics. *La Sainte Courtisane, A Florentine Tragedy,* and *Mr. and Mrs. Daventry* he accords more attention than is usual. *The Plays of Oscar Wilde* is not to be ignored, though readers must search for its moments of real originality.

More commonsense remarks on the drama as a whole can be found in Kate Matlock's essay (*JIL,* 1975)—though decadent, Wilde is infused with a spirit of optimism—and in David L. Hirst's *Comedy of Manners* (1979). Angela Locatelli in *Cenobio* (1977) has some structuralist comments on the relation of Wilde's theatrical language to the language of London society, and in a long, attentive piece Hélène Catsiapis (*Thalia,* 1978) explains how the plays demystify class, religion, women, and marriage by aggressive yet therapeutic use of the paradox—evidence of Wilde's ultimately Pascalian view of life.

Frances Reed's "Oscar Wilde's *Vera; or, The Nihilist:* A Critical Edition" (Diss. Univ. of California 1980) provides a welcome basis for work on that early and much-maligned play.

Salome continues to fascinate critics and producers alike. The title of Katharine Worth's book, *The Irish Drama of Europe from Yeats to Beckett* (1978), implies the interesting thesis (summarized in *MuK,* 1979) that the Irish playwrights responded to, and in some cases anticipated, continental innovations. This view finds an important place for *Salome* in theatrical history, though it does not produce a startlingly original reading of the play itself. Allowing for the proximity of absurdity and intensity in *Salome*, Worth claims that the final kiss precipitates not only "horrific ecstasy" but also "poignancy" and "an authentic sense of tragic waste." Finally she outlines Yeats's ambivalence toward Wilde's play in an analysis of *A Full Moon in March*. Wildeans will particularly value this book for its glimpses of symbolist theater history and its descriptions of individual productions, notably Lindsay Kemp's sensational staging at the Roundhouse, London, in February 1977.

The poet Richard Howard has retranslated Wilde's French text in a fine chaste version (*Shenandoah,* 1978)—a *Salome* for our times—and one or two of the poems in Howard's *Misgivings* (1979) have asides about Wilde in general. The revived interest in femmes fatales has resulted in some new comparisons between Salome and her sisters: Bettina L. Knapp, "The Hetaira Type on Stage: Thaïs and Salome" (*LangQ*, 1976)—Wilde compared with Anatole France and Massenet; Hanna B. Lewis, "Salome and Elektra: Sisters or Strangers" (*OL*, 1976)—Wilde compared with Hofmannsthal; Horst Fritz, "Die Dämonisierung des Erotischen in der Literatur des Fin de Siècle" (in *Fin de Siècle: Zu Literature und Kunst der Jahrhundertwende*, ed. Roger Bauer et al., Frankfurt, 1977)—Wilde compared with Wedekind; Margaret E. Gillies (Diss. Univ. of Alberta 1973)—Wilde compared with Flaubert and Mallarmé. We have also discovered another early examination of treatments of Salome: R. Cansinos-Assens, *Salome en la literature* (Madrid, 1919), has a translation of Wilde's play and an introduction that relates it to versions by Flaubert, Mallarmé, Eugenio de Castro, and Apollinaire. D. Radha Krishnayya, "Wilde's *Salome: Deviations from the Biblical Episode" (ComQ*, 1978), is short and ill-informed. Two articles by Robert McGinnis (*L&P*, 1968; *Komos*, 1969) argue persuasively for the influence of Swinburne on *Salome* and on other works by Wilde. Lisa E. Davis discusses the translation of *Salome* made by Guerra Mondragón in *Sin Nombre* (1980; there are also articles on Wilde's influence in the Hispanic world in *Sin Nombre*, 1975, 1977).

Gary Schmidgall proves himself an expert practitioner of the interdisciplinary approach. In "Sources of Decadence: A Genealogy" (*Literature and Opera*, 1977) he concludes that "Wilde's play is essentially of the nineteenth century. Strauss's opera decidedly belongs to the twentieth." Marilyn Gaddis Rose's "The Synchronic *Salome"* (in *The Language of Theatre*, ed. Ortrun Zuber, 1980) is markedly less tolerant. Rose considers *Salome*, as Wilde wrote it, "embarrassing" and finds "Decadent diction" in general ill suited to performance. Hence her enthusiasm for Lachmann's translation and the use to which Strauss put it. Rose's ideal is "total theatre," though she might have noted that Wilde's play has not always had to be turned into a libretto for that to be achieved.

Christopher Nassaar's "Vision of Evil: The Influence of Wilde's *Salome* on *Heart of Darkness* and *A Full Moon in March" (VN*, 1978) is disappointing, a falling-off from his earlier work. Nassaar abstracts simple moral patterns from the texts to achieve generalized parallels between Wilde and Conrad, and he sometimes confuses sophisticated Wildean decadence with the primitivism that interested Conrad. Nor does he seem aware that connections between Wilde and Yeats, in particular their use of the Salome myth, have been frequently discussed.

In *Le Dandyisme de Baudelaire à Mallarmé* (1978), Michel Lemaire sees *Salome* as a complex treatment of the Narcissus myth. Morse Peckham makes characteristically provocative remarks on *Salome* in "Victorian Counterculture" (*VS*, 1975). According to Peckham, an insistence on the supreme importance of sexual activity implies a deep conservatism. He asks, "What does Salome do that is so terrible?" and decides that Wilde "at once attacks aristocracy but at the same time confirms social structure."

Our knowledge of the actual composition of *Salome* is of course in-

complete and confused, though Rodney Shewan's examination of all
known manuscript sources should clarify matters when it is completed.
Robert Ross, we note, sent his account to the *Morning Post* (8 Dec.
1910), and the sale of Pierre Louÿs' manuscript was recorded in the London *Times* (15 April 1926) and described by J. Joseph-Renaud in *Comoedia* (10 June 1926).

The best news for enthusiasts of Wilde's drama is that carefully
prepared editions of two of his plays have been put out in the New Mer-
maids series. Ian Small's introduction to *Lady Windermere* (1980) is
scholarly and original; he details the many changes that Wilde made to
the play before, during, and after rehearsal, and he reveals how Wilde
exploited the rules of society etiquette when he made his moral points. J.
P. Mahaffy's *Principles of the Art of Conversation* (1887) and contemporary handbooks of manners are mentioned. Small sees Lord Darlington as an embodiment of the dandy's dubious freedom—Darlington
may speak, but he may not act—and considers the female characters in
the context of recent controversy over the marriage laws. In addition,
Small acknowledges the importance of the ambiance at the St. James's
and compares *Lady Windermere* with other plays having similar themes.
His textual notes continue these emphases and give much information
about London society and the drama that both reflected and catered to
it. In collaboration with Russell Jackson, Small is now preparing a
volume that will contain *A Woman of No Importance* and *An Ideal Husband*.

Nassaar's view (in *Into the Demon Universe,* 1974) that *A Woman
of No Importance* is in effect a commentary on *The Scarlet Letter* has
been extended and modified by Elissa S. Guralnick and Paul M. Levitt
(*Éire,* 1978), who argue that "Hester Worsley and Mrs. Arbuthnot can
be seen as laughable types of Hester Prynne: the first, ridiculous in her
stultifying Puritanism; the second, melodramatic in her plaintive bearing." The authors also make some astute remarks about the play as a
whole. Harsh but revealing comments on the 1893 production are to be
found in Kate Terry Gielgud, *A Victorian Playgoer* (1980).

An Ideal Husband is shown by Ann Livermore (*RLC,* 1979) to echo
Rousseau's *Confessions* at one point, but otherwise her article, which
purports to be on Goldoni, Wilde, and Shaw, is eccentric and hard to
follow.

Russell Jackson's excellent edition of *The Importance* (1980) is a
companion volume to Small's *Lady Windermere.* In the introduction
Jackson examines the conditions of production and the relation of
Wilde's play to French and other contemporary practitioners. His insistence on the generosity of Wilde's vision is refreshing. Reactions to the
first production are also described, although from John Gielgud we learn
that, in later life, Alfred Douglas, for one, could apparently remember
nothing about it (*An Actor and His Time,* 1979).

Denis J. Spininger (*PLL,* 1976) argues that *The Importance* must be
seen as tragic because it illustrates the principle that the aesthetic order-
ing of experience ultimately negates itself. "Comic" is more the word for
Tirthankar Bose's contribution to the topic (*MD,* 1978). Bose soberly in-
tones that "Structurally, then, the play may be seen as a societal model

stimulating a courtship ritual which identifies the sexual drive of man as the controlling force in social relationships," a revelation that may or may not be news to the rest of us. More useful are William Green's investigations into two possible real-life models for the ailing Bunbury (*MD*, 1978).

Adolf Barth (*Archiv*, 1979) draws on Bentley, Empson, and Marcuse to demonstrate that the exaggerations of *The Importance* should not be deemed escapist. Linda Dowling's dense survey of the Aesthetes and the eighteenth century (*VS*, 1977) reminds us that Wilde originally set *The Importance* in that time. Parallels between the plays of Wilde and Restoration comedy must therefore stress "his fundamental sympathy with the essentially aristocratic view of society and social games implicit in the earlier comedies." *Enter Certain Players: Edwards-MacLiammóir and the Gate, 1928-1978* (ed. Peter Luke, 1978) has some information on MacLiammóir's *Importance of Being Oscar* and lists the many Wilde productions at the Gate.

Our previous essay should have mentioned that *Paris-Théâtre* (Nov. 1954) celebrated Wilde's centenary by printing an illustrated translation of *The Importance* by Guillot de Saix, together with articles on Wilde's continuing popularity in France.

9. Criticism

In 1976 we inadvertently overlooked an essay by Herbert Sussman: "Criticism as Art: Form in Oscar Wilde's Critical Writings" (*SP*, 1973). Sussman argues that "intellectual formulations are, for Wilde, not to be judged by mimetic criteria, by their correspondence to a material world, but as autonomous artefacts whose validity lies in their self-sufficient coherence." That judgment—though well put—must, in the aftermath of structuralism, strike us as conventional, especially when compared, for instance, with the remarkable pages on Wilde and the distance between conversation and print that are to be found in Edward Said's essay in *Textual Strategies* (ed. J. V. Hartari, 1979). It is the perception and assimilation of those "autonomous artefacts" that now present the problem, as Bruce Bashford has explained in two closely linked articles (*ELT*, 1977, 1978). Bashford explores Wilde's espousal of a theory that is simultaneously "subjective" and "formalist" and concludes that Wilde "provides a coherent analysis of the origin, development, and fulfilment of critical activity." A large claim indeed, but Bashford justifies his case, reasonably enough, by sharing Wilde's view of criticism as progressive and self-conscious development. Consequently, "Its practitioner discovers the new not by knowing in advance where he should go but ceaselessly rejecting where he has been."

But Wilde must surely have had grounds for believing criticism to be of such primary importance, grounds that he would have located in the intellectual currents of his time. "Anarchy and Culture: The Evolutionary Turn of Cultural Crisis," by Michael S. Helfand and Philip E. Smith (*TSLL*, 1978), goes some way toward establishing the areas of influence by comparing Wilde's use of evolutionary thought with that of

Arnold. (A complete if mundane survey of Wilde's Aestheticism by John Allen Quintus, *TSLL*, 1980, moots the same comparison but without the documentation.) A study of the Clark notebooks has enabled Helfand and Smith to cite Wilde's specific reading in evolutionary theorists and to draw parallels with Grant Allen, A. R. Wallace, Kropotkin, and so on. Their conclusion, contra Raymond Williams, is that Wilde's racial theory (here rather too easily equated with "eugenics") "resolves into a dialectical unity the apparent contradiction between socialism and individualism." Although this article makes an important contribution, its worth is somewhat vitiated by the desire to make its subject consistent at all costs. However, if Helfand and Smith are read alongside Shewan, a reasonably coherent picture of Wilde's intellectual origins begins to emerge.

Other scholars help us fill in the peripheries. The witty and learned aperçus that enliven Richard Jenkyns' *The Victorians and Ancient Greece* (1980) place Wilde's learning within the context of a Victorian preoccupation. Ian Small (*BJA*, 1977) links Wilde's "impressionism" with the "associationism" that persists in Pater and Vernon Lee; Jonas Barish draws comparisons with Santayana in *The Antitheatrical Prejudice* (1981); in a well-documented piece George Stavros (*ELT*, 1977) surveys Wilde's responses to Romantic poets and aesthetics; Gabriella Micks La Regina examines the English renaissance of art in the light of its precursors: Keats, Pater, Gautier (*Itinerari*, 1980). Isaac Elimimian (*MFS*, 1980–81), in "The Preface to *The Picture of Dorian Gray* in the Light of Wilde's Literary Criticism," decides that Wilde's aesthetics follow the Blakean concept that contraries do not imply a negation. R. B. Kershner (*TSLL*, 1978) compares Wilde's and Joyce's attitudes toward Shakespeare in order to demonstrate that both "put a premium on originality" and share a relativistic approach to criticism. Joyce's interest in Wilde is of course well known. Kevin O'Brien has written "Matthew Arnold and the Hellenists of the 1890s" (*AntigR*, 1978).

10. Fiction

Few write well on the fairy tales. John Allen Quintus (*VQR*, 1977) is fairly typical in his sentimentality: "Wilde denigrates materialism while he extols the spiritual realm of human experience and constantly reminds his audience of the importance of the soul." As David M. Monaghan has realized (*CRCL*, 1974), one needs a sound theoretical basis from which to approach these deceptively simple allegories. Monaghan cites Propp, Campbell, and others and decides that at the heart of "The Happy Prince" and "The Star-Child" lies the dilemma of the would-be hero who is tied to the limitations of the world he would serve. Robert K. Martin (*SSF*, 1979) risks the charge of polemicism when he concludes that "The Happy Prince" is "an important inner journal, an account of the way in which for Wilde the recognition and acceptance of his homosexuality coincided with the rejection of his previously held Aestheticism." Michael C. Kotzin (*SSF*, 1979) sets "The Selfish Giant" in the context of the nineteenth-century fairy tale, referring to Ruskin,

George MacDonald, and others. For a largely disapproving attitude to the style of the tales, see Mary Walker (*UES*, 1976); for a comparison with Hans Christian Andersen, see Volker Klotz in *Der zerstückte Traum: Für Eric Arendt Zum 75* (ed. Gregor Laschen and Manfred Schlösser, Berlin, 1978).

One of the continuing fascinations of *Dorian Gray* is that it belongs at once to several genres. Julia Briggs in *Night Visitors: The Rise and Fall of the English Ghost Story* (1977) relates the novel to the nineties vogue for diabolism, while Elizabeth MacAndrew in *The Gothic Tradition in Fiction* (1979) claims that it is typical of its time because it "shows a heightened degree of analytical consciousness in dealing with psychological phenomena." MacAndrew believes that Wilde "reveals the possible connection between self-hatred, suicide, and murder." In a study of the tradition of the haunted portrait, *Disenchanted Images* (1977), Theodore Ziolkowski finds an alternative psychological truth: "Dorian, in his increasing self-awareness, begins to recognize in the portrait certain traits of evil that the painter, unwittingly or presciently, has painted into it." Ziolkowski maintains that everything in the text is "amenable to rational explanations," and he suggests comparisons with Hawthorne and with Bulwer-Lytton's *A Strange Story* (1862).

It is by no means obvious that homosexual fiction composes a distinct genre, and Jeffrey Meyers, *Homosexuality and Literature, 1890–1930* (1977), gives a reading that manages to foreclose both sex and art. "The real subject of the book," pronounce Meyers, "is the impossibility of achieving homosexual pleasure without the inevitable accompaniment of fear, guilt and self-hatred."

In contrast with that leaden reduction to a single secret meaning, Kerry Powell (*DR*, 1978–79) places a welcome emphasis on the theatrical aspects of Dorian's quest for transfiguration. The attempt to become a work of art is essentially a performance, bound to fail since Dorian is "unable to integrate the explosive combination of Hallward and Wotton in a single pose." Powell has an ingenious and suggestive approach, even if the unwarranted conviction that art is directly opposed to "gross reality" allows him to come up with some doubtful generalizations. For example, "Art is a role-playing medium which enables the artist to forsake a depressing if only tenuously 'real' life in order to embrace a more attractive but objectively ever less 'real' alternative. That is why Wilde's obsession with 'masks' and 'acting' is antiromantic and escapist. . . ." In a later article (*PLL*, 1980), Powell offers an engrossing study of the Gothic origins of magic-portrait fiction and argues strongly and in detail for the influence of Hawthorne's *Prophetic Pictures* and Arlo Bates's "A Problem in Portraiture." Elsewhere Powell has put forward the far less convincing suggestion that Massinger's play *The Picture* may have been a source for Wilde (*MLN*, 1979), and Robert F. Fleissner has observed the influence of Browning (*SBHC*, 1973).

Jean Delabroy's "Platon chez les dandies: Sur le *Portrait de Dorian Gray*" (*Lit*, 1977) is a glittering "article de Paris" of the semiotic or Bartheian kind. There is much along the lines of "le portrait est l'index de quelque chose d'inindexable," and "le paradoxe est une machine à désimplification." The text of the novel is inevitably discovered to be both Platonic and anti-Platonic at the same time, a judgment that is no doubt true. John E. Hart (*RS*, 1978), after an unusually close reading, concludes that "even art imitating nature offers man no more assurances of immortality than nature imitating art" and that "the survivors are Lord Henry and the picture, the art work and the spectator, the artist-critic whose function has been to explore the relation of art to man's life." This position is not inconceivable either, although it does, once again, let Lord Henry off rather lightly.

Joyce Carol Oates (*CritI*, 1980) considers Basil Hallward "the diabolical agent," since it is the artist, in love with his own image of Dorian, "his own 'motive' in art," who creates the conditions for the young man's fall: "Dorian objectifies his own physical being, and his corruption begins at once." Oates makes connections with Hawthorne, Lawrence, Dostoevsky, and even Shaw, but her conclusion sounds reasonably familiar: "The novel's power lies in the interstices of its parable—in those passages in which the author appears to be confessing doubts of both a personal and an impersonal nature."

Donald L. Lawler is preparing a new edition of *Dorian* and, in collaboration with Charles E. Knott, has related the genesis of the novel to Wilde's experience in composing "The Fisherman and His Soul" and *The Portrait of Mr. W. H.* (*MP*, 1976). Lawler's earlier essay "The Revisions of *Dorian Gray*" (*VIJ*, 1974) was presumably prepared before Isobel Murray's edition (1974) and the subsequent controversy in *TLS*. Nor does Lawler mention Murray's 1972 essay on the topic. His best points are an exposure of the Sherard-based myth that Wilde wrote the novel hurriedly and a reminder that Pater was consulted when the text was revised. This is a sound piece, devoted to proving what may now be the general opinion: Wilde's revisions were designed "to suppress a moral that was too obvious in its application by making it subordinate to new esthetic interests." John Espey's previously mentioned contribution to *Oscar Wilde: Two Approaches* (1977) rehearses the *TLS* correspondence that Lawler does not cite and suggests reasons for Dorian's singularly pagan Christian name. Pater, Symonds, Max Müller, and Lionel Johnson are Espey's points of reference.

Linda Dowling's outstanding essay on *The Portrait of Mr. W. H.* (*VN*, 1980) proclaims the newest critical sophistication. Stimulated by Foucault, and probably guided by Derrida, Dowling demonstrates that the story contains a paradox of the Decadent consciousness, an ambivalence toward the autonomy of language. Recognizing the narrator's fascination with "presence in absence," she also notes that "He has perfected all that has seemed to him inconclusive or fragmentary or empty in Shakespeare's text by recomposing the sonnets and enfolding them in his own text. Only then does he withdraw. . . . texts without secrets are empty, texts with secrets are filled, but with another kind of emptiness, imposture."

Horst Schroeder has written on "The Canterville Ghost" (*LWU*, 1977), suggesting some sources. An anecdote concerning the Rothschild family has been proposed by Adeline R. Tinter as a source for "The Model Millionaire" (*N&Q*, 1977). This possibility seems entirely likely.

11. De Profundis

In the context of the work of Jan B. Gordon and of the treatments of *De Profundis* by Shewan and by the other authors of full-length studies, Harvey Kail's argument (*Prose Studies 1800-1900*, 1979) that Wilde's letter is a confession of sins against art (embracing the traditions of both *confessio peccati* and *confessio laudis*) might seem redundant. Although unaware of Gordon's work, Kail does have his moments. Refuting the charge of "insincerity," he maintains: "If Wilde had written *De Profundis* in the language of Bunyan such criticism might have been avoided, but that would have stamped Wilde as a sinner twice over: he would have been confessing to sins against art unartfully. *That* would have been insincerity." *Mandrake* (1980) has a short, synoptic piece by Pascal Personne on the mysterious connections among beauty, pain, and truth in Wilde, Baudelaire, and others, with *De Profundis* as the key text.

With characteristic industry Mikhail gives some fifty English reviews of the 1905 edition but necessarily omits Alfred Kerr's notice in *Der Tag* (12 March 1905) and Max Meyerfeld's late account of how the first German edition came about (*NYTBR*, 21 Dec. 1924). *De Profundis* was of course an influential document in Germany.

The manuscript room at Columbia has acquired a typescript apparently taken from the copy read out at the Ransome trial.

12. Poetry

In *ELT* (1979) Bobby Fong draws attention to manuscript poems in the Clark, Beinecke, and Berg collections. Fong edits five fugitive poems and provides a purified text of two of them. More of such work needs to be done, and this piece, along with his dissertation, "The Poetry of Oscar Wilde: A Critical Edition" (Univ. of California 1978), proves that Fong is clearly the person for the job. The dissertation takes as copy text for much of the poetry the fifth edition of *Poems* (1882), arranging them in a "speculative" chronological order. Copy text for published poetry not included in *Poems* is generally the last printed version with textual authority. Poetry not published during Wilde's lifetime has, whenever possible, been taken from manuscript. There are twenty-one poems not found in Ross's edition of 1908. Fong's scrupulously professional commentary glides easily among no less than eight manuscript versions of *The Sphinx*.

At last we have a new and sophisticated approach to *The Ballad of Reading Gaol*. In *The Modes of Modern Writing* (1977) David Lodge gives a structuralist reading that reveals the poem as a "tissue of 'pseudo-statements,'" "an appeal to transcendental and specifically Christian values . . . which, though no doubt more immediately accessible and appealing to a Christian reader, are not dependent on the reader's prior belief in or conversion to Christianity for their effectiveness." The elaborate pattern of symbolism and allusion, the "centripetal" structure, makes the work "literature" and distinguishes it from "realism." These are precisely the qualities that Averil Gardner, like so many previous critics, fails to grasp (*DR*, 1974). Gardner sees the "romantic" passages as "additions" that are necessary for the poem to attain its "literary" status. The usual sources are documented, and the background of Trooper Wooldridge's hanging is given—a story that can also be found in the London *Times* (7 July 1980) and the *Reading Chronicle* (7 Nov. 1980).

A preliminary version of A. Horodisch's bibliographical study of *The Ballad* (1954) appeared in three parts in *Folium* (Utrecht, 1952, 1953, 1954). John Adlard discusses the color symbolism much favored by nineties poets, including Wilde (*Journal of the Francis Thompson Society*, 1974), and Douglas Bush suggests some sources in *Mythology and the Romantic Tradition in English Poetry* (1937). We have not come across any previous reference to Alfred Douglas' anonymous review of Mosher's edition of the poetry (*Academy*, 23 Jan. 1909).

13. Wilde among His Contemporaries and Later Writers

Among the most culpable omissions from our 1976 essay was Angus Wilson's wise and tough-minded review essay (*LonM*, 1955). The contributions of two other distinguished novelists also went unnoticed: E. M. Forster on Harris' life in the *Spectator* (29 July 1938) and Aldous Huxley on *Dorian Gray* in the *Daily Express* (30 Sept. 1926). Huxley objected to the moral conventionality of the novel, remarking, rather perversely, that "Wilde writes like a lawyer or dogmatic theologian. He assumes, gratuitously, that one class of actions is always right, another always wrong." It is a pity that Huxley could not get together with the parents of Beverley Nichols, whose autobiography *Father-Figure* (1972) describes in still quaking prose the immense, and indeed terrifying, power that *Dorian Gray* continued to hold in bourgeois superstition.

Throughout the twenties and thirties, in certain literary circles, simply to know someone who had known Wilde was enough to confirm one's own vocation. Edmund Wilson tells how Christian Gauss gained in charisma from having met Wilde in Paris in the late nineties (*The Shores of Light*, 1952), and the two volumes of Anthony Powell's reminiscences, *To Keep the Ball Rolling* (*Infants of the Spring*, 1976; *Messengers of Day*, 1978), commemorate many with Wilde connections: Herbert Vivian, George Street, Harry Melvill, Ada Leverson, and, most interestingly, Christopher Millard. (The charm of Millard had been caught earlier by Michael Davidson in *The World, the Flesh and Myself*, 1962). Powell also mentions Dolly Wilde, a member of the Paris sapphic milieu, some of whose history is told in George Wickes, *The Amazon of Letters: The Life and Loves of Natalie Barney* (1977).

It is increasingly apparent that most homosexual writers have felt the need to make their peace with Wilde—from Edward Carpenter (see esp. *Prisons, Police and Punishment*, 1905, and *The English Review*, 1916) to Cavafy (see, e.g., Edmund Keeley, *Cavafy's Alexandria*, 1977).

André Gide is, of course, a famous example, and fourteen short letters to him from Alfred Douglas spanning the years 1895 to 1929 have been printed (*RLC*, 1975). In *A. E. Housman: The Scholar Poet* (1979) Richard Perceval Graves demonstrates the mutual admiration of Wilde and Housman and quotes from some unpublished Wilde letters (see also the London *Times*, 17 June 1968).

Evelyn Waugh's bluff, impatient essay (now collected in *A Little Order*, ed. Donald Gallagher, 1977) expresses what must have been, in 1930, a consciously "up-to-date" opinion: "He got himself into trouble, poor old thing, by the infringement of a very silly law, which was just as culpable and just as boring as an infringement of traffic or licensing regulations."

Then there are continuing discoveries of Wilde's direct literary influence. In *Pater's Art of Autobiography* (1980) Gerald Monsman suggests that *Gaston de Latour* may have been, in part, Pater's attempt to answer Wilde's misguided discipleship, and Linda Dowling (*JNT*, 1978) notes Wilde's appearance as Spiridion in Beardsley's *Venus and Tannhäuser*. We are not entirely convinced by Sara Stambaugh's claim (*NCF*, 1976) that Wilde stands behind James's Gilbert Osmond or that Lady Wilde is sketched in Osmond's mother. Verbal echoes there certainly are, but the vocabulary of Aestheticism was widespread, and, as Stambaugh herself admits, "James's cold, reserved villain is a far cry from descriptions of the flamboyant, good-humoured Wilde." Martha Fodaski finds a trace of "The Happy Prince" in *The Waste Land* (*AN&Q*, 1976), which she presents as Eliot's "intellectual" and "ironic" adaptation of Wilde's "saccharine and simplistic" parable. That Nabokov added complexity to complexity when he "plagiarized" *Dorian Gray* in the composition of his own story "The Vane Sisters" has been brilliantly argued by Isobel Murray, an expert Wildean (*DUJ*, 1977). (In his essay in *Oscar Wilde: Two Approaches*, Ellmann suggests that *Pale Fire* may owe something to Douglas.) Stoppard studies are already under way, and Margaret Gold has given a sensible account of the relation between *Travesties* and *The Importance* (*MD*, 1978).

Is it really possible that Conan Doyle drew on Wilde for no fewer than three characters in the Holmes stories: Thaddeus Sholto, Sebastian Moran, and brother Mycroft? The various claims put forward by Samuel Rosenberg in *Naked Is the Best Disguise* (1974) were immediately pounced on by rival Holmesians (see the *Baker Street Journal* passim, but esp. 1975–77. See also Randy Roberts, "Oscar Wilde and Sherlock Holmes: A Literary Mystery" in *Clues: A Journal of Detection*, 1980). Since Conan Doyle himself did not doubt that Wilde's spirit had communicated with the medium Hester Travers Smith (see Karl Beckson in *ELN*, 1979), this becomes ground upon which even we fear to tread.

Our discovery of the double life of F. P. Grove, the Corvo of the outback, was perhaps even more belated than we had supposed. According to Ann Boutelle (*DR*, 1977, with a reply in *DR*, 1978–79), McLuhan's law (surely not empirically based) that American faces do not age but remain forever young is dramatized by Canadian novelists from Grove to Mordecai Richler and Margaret Atwood. Boutelle claims that *Dorian Gray*, the "first French novel in English," has a peculiar appeal for

Canadians and that the riddles of the mask have always haunted their imaginations. But whether this fascination is stronger in Canada than elsewhere is hard to say. Kevin O'Brien's *Oscar Wilde's Tour in Canada*, which promises to set the historical record straight, has been announced for 1982. Maxim Mazumbar's play *Oscar Remembered*, which was first performed at Stratford, Ontario, in 1975, and later traveled to London and New York, was finally published in Toronto in 1977. Peter Coe's *Feasting with Panthers* was performed at Chichester, England, in 1981 and widely reviewed.

The best dramatization of recent years—because both passionately and professionally conceived—is Eric Bentley's *Lord Alfred's Lover* (1981; *Canadian Theatre Rev.*, 1978). Although it turns Bentley's previously mentioned gay liberation polemic into drama, some psychological mysteries are allowed to remain. The play makes allusions to homosexuality in high places (the old hints concerning Rosebery), introduces various contradictory aspects of gay culture, and centers on the memories of an aging, ugly, but untypically generous Bosie. The affair with Wilde was, it seems, essentially platonic—a philosophical convenience that the playwright himself makes use of—and, even at the close, a scene set at the Bar Kalisaya, Wilde has few regrets. This careful misreading of "historical" events should be approached perhaps in the spirit of Bentley's own notes to the actor: "It is not exact imitation of the historical material that is needed but adaptation, transposition. Given *my* face, the actor must say, how can I make it up to suggest something of the *character* (not the dimensions) of Oscar Wilde's?"

Canada is certainly not alone in making theatrical use of Wilde. The French, like the Germans and even the English, have on several occasions adapted either Wilde's life or one or another of his prose works for the stage. There was the 1922 Paris production of *Dorian Gray*, directed by Pitoëff (see *Comœdia*, 23 Dec. 1922), and in 1976 Paris again saw an enactment of Wilde's novel—this time written and directed by Pierre Boutron. *L'Avant Scène. Théâtre* (15 Jan. 1977) has text, notes (including an essay by Jacques de Langlade), and some compelling photographs. Cocteau's adaptation of *Dorian Gray* is evoked by Jean-Marie Maquan in *Cahiers Jean Cocteau* (1979), along with some general discussion of Wilde's influence on him.

The fairy tales have inspired ballets by Mari Bicknell (recently revived in Cambridge, Eng.; see the *Daily Telegraph*, 20 Dec. 1980) and an excellent jazz record by Barbara Thompson's Paraphernalia group on MCA Records.

As we have noticed before, Wilde appeared in works of fiction early on in his career, and his memory is invoked in innumerable imaginary portraits and composite types. To the list of these novels should be added the following, again for the most part unlisted elsewhere: Frederic Carrel's *The Adventures of John Johns* (1897), which is based on Frank Harris; various works of E. Ranger Gull, in particular *The Hypocrite* (1898) and *Miss Malevolent* (1899); "Lui," a short story by Jean Lorrain included in *Heures de Corse* (1905); John Moray Stuart-Young's *Passion's Peril* (1906), in which Wilde contributes strongly to the character of "Selwyn Waring"; the comparatively well-known *The Sphinx's*

Lawyer (1906) by "Frank Danby" (Julia Frankau); Philip Gibbs's *The Street of Adventure* (1909), whose "Codrington," a cynical though heterosexual Aesthete, echoes Wilde; Stephen McKenna's *The Reluctant Lover* (1912), an Oxford novel structured like *The Importance* and an instance of the direct line that runs exultantly through to the ordeals of Bertie Wooster; Douglas Goldring's novel of London life, *The Fortune* (1917); G. W. Mathews' *The Madonna of Montmartre: A Story Oscar Wilde Never Told* (1930); and Julian Symons' *The Blackheath Poisonings: A Victorian Murder Mystery* (1978).

Poems about Wilde, many inspired by *De Profundis*, range from the absurd to the ludicrous. We can now add these: George Ives in *Reynolds Newspaper* (30 Nov. 1900); Ambrose Bierce in *Shapes of Clay* (1903); Elsa Barker in *Smart Set* (July 1907); Stephen Coleridge in *Songs to Desidera* (1907); "The Gourmand," a parody of *The Ballad*, by Harry Graham in *Familiar Faces* (1907); Gascoigne Mackie in *Andrea and Other Poems* (1908); Stephen Phillips in *New Poems* (1908); Esmé C. Wingfield-Stratford in *The Call of Dawn* (1909); a satirical epistle to Douglas ("For what were lovelier on the lawn / Than you, pearl-naked to the dawn") by Aleister Crowley in *The Winged Beetle* (1910); another favorite, "The Waiter Who Looked like Oscar Wilde," by Joseph Bernard Rethy in *The Song of the Scarlet Host and Other Poems* (1915); a "Salome" poem by Vincent Starrett in *Estrays* (1918); Mary Salford in the *Bookman* (London; Nov. 1918); Henry de Bordet in *La Volonté* (28 Oct. 1925); Samuel Loveman in *The Hermaphrodite and Other Poems* (1936); and Michael Levey in *TLS* (11 Aug. 1978).

Finally, scholars of the nineties may be glad of a partial bibliography of the first appearances of Vincent O'Sullivan's writings on Wilde. An unsigned review of Sherard, probably by O'Sullivan, was printed in *Mercure de France* (March 1903), and we are grateful to Karl Beckson for telling us of three contributions to the *Dublin Magazine*: one in 1931, two in 1939.

GEORGE MOORE

Helmut E. Gerber

The general overview of Moore in the preceding volume of this survey requires no major alteration on the basis of pre-1975 material that has since come to light. Several thousand reviews of Moore's works and biographical commentaries gathered in the course of preparing a full-scale annotated secondary bibliography, tentatively scheduled for publication in 1983, provide supporting evidence for the 1976 survey of Moore's career. His works received both favorable and unfavorable responses throughout his career; as a person he was regarded by some as charming, interesting, and capable of warm friendliness and by others as calculating, mean, and downright nasty. No one could view him with indifference.

Despite his frequent complaints about money, an inadequate audience, and a lack of critical attention, Moore was a successful writer, if not a popular one, at nearly all stages of his career after *Esther Waters* (1894). While not best-sellers, his books sold well, and they were well distributed and widely reviewed in the United States, in England, and on the Continent.

Despite Moore's reputation during his lifetime, continued scholarly interest in his work, and increased recognition of his important role in various literary and cultural movements, Moore's works are often neglected in courses on English literature. *Esther Waters* is the only one of his works regularly kept in print in modestly priced editions that can be used for teaching. That interest in Moore exists in the academies is evidenced by the high prices commanded by his manuscripts and printed works, by his inclusion as a subject of discussion at a major MLA Division meeting in 1979, and by the continuing appearance of dissertations, scholarly articles, and books on him. On the other hand, scholars' persistent demands that he be revaluated and assigned a higher place in the hierarchy of writers show that Moore has not gained general recognition on a par with, say, that accorded Thomas Hardy.

In the words of the title Moore gave one of his stories in *The Untilled Field* (in Gaelic, 1902; in English, 1903), "So On He Fares," slowly, perhaps, but steadily.

1. Bibliographies and Manuscript Locations

Letters, manuscripts, and proof copies of Moore's books and essays continue to be offered for sale. Since the publication of Edwin Gilcher's primary bibliography (1970), which for the first time accurately identified editions likely to be rare, prices of those editions have risen, as one might expect. Although the generally inflated market for rare books and manuscripts may be partly responsible, another reason is that libraries with good holdings are vying for scarcer collectibles. The major repositories listed in the previous volume of this survey (p. 143) have acquired some of the material recently offered for sale.

A few specific acquisitions or discoveries may be singled out here. The University of California, Berkeley, has acquired by gift 132 letters from Moore to Viola Rodgers, an American journalist (see *Bancroftiana*, 1977). Although many of these letters have been printed at least in part in Joseph Hone's *Life of George Moore* (1936), they can now be studied in full and Hone's frequent elisions and inaccuracies of dating and transcription taken into account. Also of some interest are fourteen letters from Moore to Frans Netscher discovered in the Letterkundig Museum, The Hague (see section on letters).

The most significant bibliographical research is a work in progress: Edwin Gilcher and Robert Becker's supplement to Gilcher's primary bibliography. Planned for publication in *English Literature in Transition,* this supplement will considerably increase listings of Moore's contributions to periodicals. A volume begun by H. E. Gerber for the Annotated Secondary Bibliography series already contains well over three thousand entries. The five thick scrapbooks of clippings that have been added to the George Moore collection at Arizona State University include hundreds of previously unlisted articles and reviews. These scrapbooks show that Moore's work was widely reviewed even in obscure periodicals and in provincial newspapers, especially in the United States. Of lesser import are the six entries for the musical settings of works by Moore, including the score for the 1948 film of *Esther Waters*, in Bryan Gooch and David S. Thatcher's *Musical Settings of Late Victorian and Modern British Literature* (1976). Of similar minor import is J. P. Wearing's listing, in *The London Stage 1890-1899* (1976), of details of the casts and productions of *The Strike at Arlingford* (1893) and *Journeys End in Lovers Meeting* (prod. 1894; pub. 1902), a play written in collaboration with Pearl Craigie ("John Oliver Hobbes").

The English department of Arizona State University has acquired a print of the 1948 film of *Esther Waters*, in which Dirk Bogarde played William Latch. For a discussion of the film's commercial failure, see Bogarde's *Snakes & Ladders* (1979). H. E. Gerber has acquired photocopies of two shooting manuscripts of the film as well as a copy of the four-part script of the BBC-TV production of the novel, most recently shown in 1978. The script of Joan Plowright's reading on BBC Radio Four (1978) of Allan McClelland's fifteen-part abridgment has not yet become available.

Although not specifically on Moore, Linda C. Dowling's *Aestheticism and Decadence: A Selective Annotated Bibliography* (1977) provides useful background material on Moore's career.

2. Editions and Textual Studies

Textual studies continue to engage scholars and, because of Moore's obsession with revisions, will probably do so for some time to come. The past five years have also seen the appearance of an annotated edition, a number of new reprints of interest, a dramatic adaptation, and a volume of previously uncollected short stories. On the whole, the period has been a prosperous one for textual studies and editions of Moore's works.

A thoroughly annotated, and better still a variorum, edition of *Hail and Farewell* (1911, 1912, 1914)—Moore's remarkable blending of autobiography, biographical portraiture, literary history, and fiction—has been needed for a long time. Richard Cave's edition (1976) approaches the requirement without wholly satisfying it. Cave's introduction is, as Jack Wayne Weaver points out in a review (*JIL*, 1977), overly oriented to the general reader, and the textual notes are inadequately documented. One may perhaps sympathize with Cave, whose effort is, as Weaver reports, "a compromise between the aims of scholarship and the needs of commerce." And one must be grateful to publisher Colin Smythe and editor Cave for having produced the most useful edition to date.

The edition of *The Untilled Field* with an introduction by T. R. Henn (1976) does not pretend to be scholarly; it has no notes and only a brief general essay on the historical background and major themes of the stories. Because this collection contains what is probably Moore's best work in the short story, one hopes an enterpising publisher will one day produce a modestly priced reprint. Meanwhile, the present edition should help Moore's title gain entry into more libraries. Henn includes the fifteen stories of the final edition (1931) rather than the original twelve of the first edition (1903) and, in the appendixes, two stories that Moore "conflated . . . into a single one called 'Fugitives.' "

Moore's short stories appear to be receiving increased attention of curious kinds. Simone Benmussa, for example, dramatized "Albert Nobbs" for a production on 22 November 1977 at Théâtre d'Orsay (petit salle). In the same year the dramatization was published as *La Vie singulière d'Albert Nobbs*, which follows the French translation by Pierre Leyris. Leyris' *Albert Nobbs, et autres vies sans hymen* (1971) is a translation of "Priscilla and Emily Lofft," "Albert Nobbs," and "Henrietta Marr" from Moore's *Celibate Lives* (1927), but it omits "Wilfred Holmes," which Moore had collected in both the English and American editions of 1927. Benmussa's French dramatization in turn was adapted, with the collaboration of Allan McClelland, as *The Singular Life of Albert Nobbs*, produced in 1978 at the Theatre at New End, but apparently not published.

Also unusual is the reprinting of *Literature at Nurse, or Circulating Morals* (1885), edited with an introduction by Pierre Coustillas (1976). Coustillas has added the explanatory subtitle *A Polemic on Victorian Censorship,* perhaps with the modern reader in mind. More important, however, Coustillas has provided an introductory brief history of circulating libraries and their "material, intellectual and moral dictatorship on authors, publishers and readers"; a detailed analysis of the milieu that gave birth to Moore's polemic; and such supplementary materials as Moore's "A New Censorship of Literature," the ensuing correspondence, and "The Case for the Publishers," all taken from *Pall Mall Gazette* of 10 through 17 December 1884. While Moore's polemic seems a trifle in comparison with J. S. Mill's *On Liberty*, it is nevertheless a perennially relevant document and, in its time, an important one. Another nonfiction work by Moore, "Tragic Novel," first published in *Cosmopolis* (1897), has been reprinted in *A Victorian Art of Fiction: Essays on the Novel in British Periodicals 1870-1900* (ed. John Charles Olmstead, 1979).

At a time when so little of Moore's work is available in inexpensive modern reprints, it is worth reporting that *Esther Waters*, in a facsimile of the first edition and with a new introduction by Helmut Gerber, was published in 1977, and a second printing in a larger format was issued in 1979. Most currently available reprints are not of the first edition. Reprints of later editions, particularly the 1920 one, do not reflect the art of the George Moore who won the initial large readership for his novel.

The record shows that Moore collected five volumes of short stories (*Celibates*, 1895; *In Single Strictness*, 1922; *Celibate Lives*; *The Untilled Field*; and *A Story-Teller's Holiday*, 1918). Of these, the first three titles overlap in complex ways, as Gilcher's bibliography demonstrates. Actually Moore wrote far more short stories than these five titles suggest, for he included portraits, sketches, and scenes, which by some standards one might classify as short stories, in his various collections of essays and autobiographical writings. More to the point, he wrote and published a considerable number of stories he did not include in any of his collections, he had partially written a number of stories late in life of which no manuscripts survive, and he had plans to gather another volume of stories. Moore's hopes have been more than fulfilled by the publication of *"In Minor Keys": George Moore's Uncollected Short Stories*, collected with an introduction by Helmut E. Gerber and David B. Eakin (in press). The volume, whose primary title Moore had proposed as an umbrella for some three to five stories, contains seventeen stories written over a period of forty-nine years. In a long introduction the compilers detail the publication history of the stories, relate the stories to relevant periods in Moore's life, link the stories to relevant novels, and reconstruct several stories, of which no manuscripts survive, from allusions in Moore's correspondence. The stories collected in this volume shed light on Moore's imaginative processes, his use of sources, and his experiments with technique.

It has become more difficult in the past five years to distinguish between textual studies in the more technical narrow sense and discussions that use textual variants to support thematic interpretations or to trace Moore's imaginative processes over a period of years as recorded in different versions of his work. It is important, however, that critics and explicators of Moore's works are writing with more awareness of revisions.

Most specifically a textual study is W. Eugene Davis and Mark J. Lidman's " 'I am still a young man': George Moore's Last Revisions of *Confessions of a Young Man"* (*BNYPL*, 1975), only briefly footnoted in the previous review of research (p. 144, n.). Here the authors discuss

Moore's revisions of the 1926 Heinemann edition in preparation for an eighth version of his text. They conclude that, while changes are relatively casual, Moore was working toward a "more perfect, more readable" prose style and distinguishing more sharply between the persona of the careless young protagonist and that of the mature editor. Jay Jernigan, in his more interpretive essay "A Protean Self-Study of the Artist Manqué: George Moore's *Vain Fortune*" (*KQ*, 1975), compares various texts of Moore's novel to show a change of emphasis from "realistic character study" to "more subjective portraitures."

Although technically not a textual study, Eileen Sarker's " 'Wonderful Meeting': George Moore's Saint Paul and Jesus" (*Éire*, 1975) examines Moore's four attempts (*The Apostle*, 1911; *The Brook Kerith*, 1916; the revised *Apostle*, 1923; and *The Passing of the Essenes*, 1930) to deal with a post-Crucifixion meeting between Jesus and Paul and Moore's insistence on the mortality of Jesus. Sarker proposes that, although Moore's chief interest was in Paul, in *The Passing of the Essenes* the novelist raised Jesus to the level of Paul and attained the dramatic effect he had been seeking. Jean C. Noël, in "George Moore's Five Finger Exercises" (*CCEI*, 1976), also uses textual variants to study the stories published periodically before being collected in *The Untilled Field;* he concludes that Moore's revisions improved the stories. Those stories that were initially either didactic or plainly reminiscent of work by Gérard de Nerval, Dostoevsky, and Sterne, Noël holds, became richer and more original as they were "Irished" and as the language was made more sophisticated. W. Eugene Davis, in " 'The Celebrated Case of Esther Waters'; Unpublished Letters of George Moore to Barrett H. Clark" (*PLL*, 1977), using substantial citations from seven letters and material in a volume of Clark's notes in the Clark Collection of Yale's Beinecke Library, analyzes the aborted effort of Moore and Clark to collaborate during 1922 on a new dramatization of Moore's own dramatic adaptation of *Esther Waters* (prod. 1911; pub. 1913). While Davis' essay is helpful in suggesting the probable essence of the two separate texts that evolved and their difference from Moore's earlier dramatization, it would be useful to have the version of Moore's published play and all the documentary evidence related to the aborted collaboration in a short monograph.

3. Autobiographies, Letters, and Biographies

Because of Moore's obsession with recording his own development and, far more important, his interest in autobiography as an art form, all the extant autobiographical writings have probably been published.

Letters, on the other hand, may continue to come to light for some time, since many of Moore's correspondents seem to have saved every scrap he wrote. Modern scholars are thus able to make the correspondence available, although not in the "imaginative" form Moore would have preferred.

Biographical writings on Moore have become more difficult to isolate, for most books on Moore as well as an increasing number of articles show an awareness of Moore's "presence" in everything he wrote. No genre seems to have remained "pure" in his hands, and scholars have begun to recognize the risk involved in treating any one aspect of Moore's life or art as separate from another. To writings on Moore's works, one is less likely to ascribe a "biographical fallacy" than a nonbiographical fallacy.

In what follows, there is no autobiographical material to report that has not been discussed in the preceding volume of this survey. The publication of an annotated edition of *Hail and Farewell* has already been noted, and Susan Dick's carefully annotated edition (1972) of *Confessions of a Young Man* (1888) was cited in the 1976 survey. Various analyses of Moore's autobiographical works will be considered in the section on criticism. There is much to report, however, on the publication of new letters and a little on biographical scholarship.

LETTERS

A modest number of previously unpublished letters and letters published only in part in Hone's *Life of George Moore* have recently appeared. Among the more important publications of the first kind are W. Eugene Davis' article, already mentioned, containing letters to Barrett H. Clark, J. G. Riewald's piece containing letter to Frans Netscher (*ES*, 1977), and Bryan Forbes's *Dame Edith Evans: Ned's Girl* (1977). Davis prints pertinent portions of seven letters. They are all included in full, with additional letters to Clark, in Helmut E. Gerber's *George Moore on Parnassus* (in press), discussed later. Riewald prints fourteen letters, dated 1885-91, that throw light on Moore's early career. The essence of this correspondence with the Dutch defender of Zola and proponent of naturalism is touched on later in another connection. Forbes prints six letters from Moore to Dame Edith, mainly in praise of her acting, and gives an account of her much acclaimed performance as the melancholy housekeeper Martin in Moore's *Elizabeth Cooper* (1913).

Any editions of letters to or by Yeats that have been prepared by exacting scholars and that include letters by Moore must be considered, if for no other reason than that such editions fully and accurately transcribe letters carelessly transcribed or only partially printed by previous editors and biographers. Thus one must note the fourteen letters from Moore to Yeats included in Richard J. Finneran, George Mills Harper, and William Murphy's admirable two-volume *Letters to W. B. Yeats* (1977). This collection also contains many letters by others who make significant mention of Moore.

A few books print a handful of letters in part or in full that are of some importance because of the special discussions they support. Thus Margaret Campbell, in *Dolmetsch: The Man and His Work* (1975), prints parts of three letters, dated 1894, from Moore to Arnold Dolmetsch that concern *Evelyn Innes* (1898); Anthony Eden, in *Another World* (1976), prints several letters from Moore to the Edens; Robert

Hogan and James Kilroy, in *The Irish Literary Theatre 1899-1901* (1975), include three letters by Moore, a speech to the National Literary Society, and an interview first published in the *Freeman's Journal*.

The most important and most massive collections of Moore's letters to be gathered since Rupert Hart-Davis' *Letters to Lady Cunard 1895-1933* (1957) and Helmut E. Gerber's *George Moore in Transition: Letters to T. Fisher Unwin and Lena Milman, 1894-1910* (1968) are *George Moore on Parnassus: Selected Letters, 1900-1933*, edited, with notes and critical-biographical commentary, by Helmut E. Gerber (in press), and Robert Becker's "The Letters of George Moore 1863-1901" (Diss. Reading 1980).

Gerber's edition of about 1,200 letters, arranged chronologically, overlaps with his earlier *George Moore in Transition*. Each section of the collection focuses on an aspect of Moore's artistic career during the relevant years covered in the section. The twenty-four major recipients have been selected to demonstrate characteristic professional and personal relationships throughout Moore's career. This volume therefore not only presents a large body of previously unpublished letters but also provides several biographical and critical contexts that groups of letters support (see discussions in sections on biographies and criticism). Robert Becker's dissertation presents 909 letters in three volumes, with scholarly annotations and sixty-eight plates. Becker is preparing a multiple-volume collection of the letters that will cover Moore's entire lifetime.

BIOGRAPHIES

Several recent articles have added details to our biographical knowledge of Moore. Jack Wayne Weaver, in "AE, George Moore, and *Avatars*" (*ELT*, 1976), for example, explains the gentle A. E.'s negative views of Moore's character as a response to the maliciousness of the Irish portraits in *Hail and Farewell* and as an expression of A. E.'s "feeling that Moore had had base motives in staying in Ireland for ten years." Richard Cave (*RES*, 1977) provides useful information on Moore's relationship with the painters Clara Christian and Ethel Walker, who were alluded to in *Hail and Farewell* as "Stella" and "Florence." T. P. Foley and Maud Ellmann (*N&Q*, 1978) identify the Father O'Donovan, mentioned by both Yeats and Moore, as the Reverend Jeremiah O'Donovan (1873-1942), who left the priesthood and wrote six novels under the name "Gerald O'Donovan." The *Dictionary of Irish Literature* (ed. Robert Hogan, 1979) includes Helmut E. Gerber's concise, yet detailed, summary of Moore's personal life and professional career and a fuller selected bibliography than is usual in such reference works.

David Bruce Eakin's "The Man in the Paper Mask: Epistolary Autobiography in Oscar Wilde and George Moore" (Diss. Arizona State Univ. 1980), based on the published letters of Moore and Wilde, concentrates on Moore's and Wilde's exploration of epistolary autobiography as a genre, but also includes interpretive biographical material, especially insofar as it analyzes the two authors' techniques for giving complex portraits of themselves as multiple personae. In many respects this thesis complements in great detail Stanley Weintraub's 1975 article "Autobiography and Authenticity" (see p. 61), Michael M. Riley's "Persona and Theme in George Moore's *Confessions of a Young Man*" (*ELT,* 1976; see previous survey), Jean C. Noël's "George Moore's Pluridimensional Autobiography: Remarks on His *Confessions of a Young Man*" (see p. 62), and Brian Greenwood Donovan's "George Moore's Fictive Autobiography" (see p. 62). Although Eakin's thesis deals with Moore's many poses, the masks he assumed in his correspondence with diverse persons, it remains free of psychological jargon. Further, Eakin cogently relates Moore's various self-representations to the novelist's theories of biography, autobiography, and truth as distinct from fact.

In Gerber's *George Moore on Parnassus* the entire first chapter and brief comments in later prefaces to various groups of letters provide information about Moore's relationships with "Three Ladies" (Margaret Gough, Ethel Palmer, and Mona Kingdon), "A Brother" (Colonel Maurice Moore), "Two Literary Agents" (J. B. Pinker and Sons and Harry Spurr), "Some Publishers and Printers" (T. Werner Laurie, James R. Wells, Riverside Press, Dunedin Press, and Richard Clay & Sons), "A Theatre Manager" (Lionel H. Barton), "Some Collaborators" (Barrett H. Clark and John Lloyd Balerston), "A Portraitist" (John Freeman), "A Biographer-Critic" (Ernest A. Boyd), and "Some Friends and Acquaintances" (Mark Fisher, James Sullivan Starkey, Samuel Chew, A. J. A. Symons, and Philip Gosse). Various notes throughout the volume also comment on recipients and writers of relatively few letters as well as persons mentioned in letters.

Two books contain, in passing, important biographical observations on Moore. Wendy Barron's *Miss Ethel Sands and Her Circle* (1977) depicts Moore's and the painter's mutual admiration for each other's work and discusses their friendship, especially during the 1930s. The second chapter of Stanley Weintraub's *The London Yankees* (1979), while focusing on Pearl Craigie, also offers pertinent comments on Moore. Inevitably, such essentially critical books as those by Cave and Farrow, which are treated later, also reinterpret various aspects of Moore's life and occasionally fill in some of the remaining gaps. In addition, two biographical studies are reliably reported to be in progress: a full-length study by Hilaire Laurie to be issued in 1983, the fiftieth anniversary of Moore's death, and a study by art critic and editor Denys Sutton that focuses on Moore's relationship with French and English artists.

4. Criticism

Of the studies of Moore that have come out during the past five years, those that are essentially "critical" have proved difficult to categorize. Without being too rigid, one might suggest that the scholarship has concentrated on (1) sources, (2) naturalism, (3) the Irish period, or (4) other special topics and that five major works have merged biography, criticism, interpretation, source studies, and so on.

SOURCES

The identification of sources for specific works by Moore and, more important, Moore's individual way of absorbing and modifying his sources to suit his artistic purposes continue to interest scholars. Because the subject has been so well mined, most such studies add little more than interesting footnotes. Only one seems to make a major contribution to Moore scholarship.

Margaret Campbell, in her *Dolmetsch: The Man and His Work,* provides evidence of Dolmetsch's influence on *Evelyn Innes* and supplements works by H. H. Noyes (1938) and Sarah Watson (1963) cited in the 1976 survey. Moore's seemingly contradictory allegiances receive attention in John J. Conlon's "Walter Pater and Zola's Literary Reputation in England" (*ELT,* 1976); Conlon observes that Moore was in the "ambiguous position of serving two masters . . . presumably considering himself apprenticed to Zola for matter and to Pater for style." Moore may not in fact be nearly so ambiguous in striving to resolve the ancient war between matter and manner, although he may not have fully attained the perfect balance for which he strove. Christopher Heywood's *Aspects of South African Literature* (1976) interestingly suggests that Olive Schreiner's *The Story of an African Farm* (1883) prefigured a subplot of *A Mummer's Wife* (1885), provided a model for Moore's breaking away from the French school, and stimulated Moore's interest in Irish land reform. Schreiner, Heywood concludes, admired Moore's novel, though not the man, and supported him in his fight with the circulating libraries. On a more familiar note, G. A. Cevasco (*RS,* 1977) discusses once more the influence of Huysmans' *À Rebours* on Moore's early work and the probable influence of his *En Route* on such later works as *Evelyn Innes.*

The best study of Moore's use of sources is Jack Wayne Weaver's thoroughly documented "George Moore's Use of Celtic Materials: What and How?" (*ELT,* 1979), which shows that Moore's absorption of Celtic folklore, Old Irish saga literature, and Middle Irish historical figures and art objects is pervasive in works from *Evelyn Innes* to *Ulick and Soracha* (1926). Weaver concludes that Moore, relying on Yeats, A. E., Richard Best, and Kuno Meyer for his information, used these materials to enrich his character portrayals, the evocativeness of his story lines, and his prose style.

Finally, Gerber and Eakin's introduction to *"In Minor Keys"* and Gerber's *George Moore on Parnassus* call attention to various ways in which Moore converted source materials into original work, or at least work that had his individual stamp. Gerber, in fact, persistently writes of Moore's "re-creation" of biblical history (*The Brook Kerith*), biography (*Héloïse and Abélard,* 1921), myth (*Daphnis and Chloe,* 1924), and Irish history (*Ulick and Soracha*). Generally, Moore's use of sources is more appropriately discussed as "re-creation," "amalgamation," "absorption," and "modification" than as straightforward borrowing or, as was common among earlier criticism, as something uncomfortably close to plagiarism.

NATURALISM

Although little that is new has appeared on Moore's best-known novel, *Esther Waters*, the familiar debate on whether or not it is a naturalist novel owing its matter and manner chiefly to French models still goes on. One notices, however, an increasing tendency to read the novel as transitional, as moving from naturalism toward some other, often vaguely defined style. In any event, the novel has recently been more often read as Moore's modified version of a naturalist work, less indebted to the French than earlier critics had insisted.

The most clearly traditional view of *Esther Waters* as a naturalist novel informs David Williams' "A Fine Naturalism" (London *Times*, 7 May 1977). Although Williams finds that the novel lacks the "imaginative power and the inner certitude" of works by Tolstoy and Dickens, he praises the depiction of the scene in the lying-in hospital and the Derby Day scene for their Zolaesque naturalism. Given the company into which Williams casts Moore, this statement seems high praise indeed. On the other hand, while the scene in the lying-in hospital may echo something of Zola's manner or that of Dickens in *Bleak House*, the three brilliant chapters on Derby Day are the result of Moore's own experiences, memories, and vivid imagination. The cinematographic effectiveness of the Derby Day scene is brilliantly represented in the 1948 motion picture of *Esther Waters*. Also familiar is the position taken by June Oechler Underwood (Diss. State Univ. of New York, Stony Brook, 1974), who sees the heroine of *Esther Waters* as an unchanging character and compares her with figures in Trollope's *Eustace Diamonds* and Thackeray's *Vanity Fair*. Underwood comments both on the recurring patterns arranged to lead the reader toward anticlimaxes and on the elimination of multiple plots and cliff-hanging suspense—all used, Underwood contends, to suggest a combined realism and aestheticism.

Rather more pointedly, John Lucas, in "From Naturalism to Symbolism" (*RMS*, 1977; rpt. in *Decadence and the 1890s*, ed. Ian Fletcher, 1979), asserts that Moore and George Gissing are "the most important naturalist writers in England," but Lucas also notes that Moore rejected naturalism in the 1890s and, like Symons and Yeats, turned toward symbolism. In fact, Moore's shift probably took place in the previous decade. J. G. Riewald, in "From Naturalism to Lyrical Realism" (cited earlier), also seeks ways to differentiate *Esther Waters* from French naturalist models. The letters to Frans Netscher, Riewald argues, reveal Moore's "growing dissatisfaction" with naturalism and evince an "evolution from an impressionistic naturalism to a lyrical-aesthetic realism." Riewald's terminology unfortunately serves only to stir up already murky waters.

In his introduction to the 1977 reprint of the first edition of *Esther Waters*, H. E. Gerber emphasizes Moore's departure from the determinism associated with the French naturalist novel and cites in support the crucial passage in the first edition where Moore writes that in the struggle between character and circumstance "a hair would turn the scale either way" (chap. 20). Compared with the French naturalists, Moore, like Samuel Butler in *The Way of All Flesh*, generally seems to have allowed for more exercise of individual will and more play of the power of instinct to ensure individual survival and human dignity. Like Hardy's Mayor Henchard and perhaps Tess of the d'Urbervilles, Moore's Esther is finally a "person" of character, not merely a victim of circumstance.

THE IRISH PERIOD

Discussions of the work Moore produced during his ten-year stay in Ireland, of work published later but drawn from his Irish experience, of his involvement in the Irish literary revival, and of his relationship with Yeats and Joyce continue to dominate Moore scholarship. No doubt this situation results in part from the scholarly interest in W. B. Yeats, James Joyce, and the Irish drama rather than from a more specialized interest in Moore. Much of what is being written on Moore's involvement in the politics of the Irish literary revival begins to have the ring of established tradition. Critics and literary historians must be cautioned not to let Moore's admitted abrasiveness, even his dubious motives, lead them to underestimate the effectiveness of his role. The most positive view that is rapidly emerging out of the scholarship touching on Moore's Irish period is the high esteem in which *The Untilled Field* is generally held.

Pleasant Larus Reed III (Diss. Indiana Univ. 1974) examines how authors of story collections establish relationships of plot, setting, character, image, and theme among separate stories to form an integrated whole. One chapter compares Moore's *Untilled Field* with Joyce's *Dubliners*, emphasizing Moore's influence on Joyce. Wilhelm Schmid's *George Moore*, The Untilled Field: *Entstehung, Thematik, Form* (Bern, 1975) provides a detailed stylistic, autobiographical, and allegorical study to show that Moore's stories are structurally interrelated and rich in evocative content. Stan Gébler Davies, in *James Joyce: A Portrait of the Artist* (1975), iterates the now commonly accepted fact of Joyce's imitation of Moore early in his career. Linda Bennett (*Studies*, 1977) once more points out the influence of Moore on Joyce and distinguishes between Moore's strengths and weaknesses in a comparison of *Confessions of a Young Man* with Joyce's *A Portrait of the Artist as a Young Man*.

Two articles further Richard Ellmann's earlier observation (*KR*, 1958) that Joyce's "The Dead" is indebted to Moore's *Vain Fortune* (1891): Thomas J. Kennedy's "James Joyce's System of Marginal Markings in the Books of His Personal Library" (*JML*, 1977) and Anita Gandolfo's "A Portrait of the Artist as Critic: Joyce, Moore, and the Background of 'The Dead' " (*ELT*, 1979). Maurice Harmon's "Generations Apart: 1925-1975," in *The Irish Novel in Our Time* (ed. Patrick Rafroidi and Harmon, 1975), links Moore and Joyce as the progenitors of the prose fiction of modern Ireland.

Important in its perceptiveness is Ronald Schleifer's "George Moore's Turning Mind: Digression and Autobiographical Art in *Hail and Farewell*" (*Genre*, 1979; rpt. as *The Genres of the Irish Literary Revival*, ed. Schleifer, 1980). Schleifer argues that Moore, seeking "what is real about his experience and himself," uses "significant digressions" that elucidate his autobiographical project and illustrate what is essential to him. A dissertation and several articles of relatively minor import also deserve mention: Elizabeth Hall Harris' "The Irish George Moore: A Biographical and Critical Interpretation" (Diss. Stanford Univ. 1976), which goes over ground already authoritatively treated by others, especially by Jack Wayne Weaver in "*A Story-Teller's Holiday*: George Moore's Irish Renaissance, 1897-1911" (Diss. Univ. of North Carolina 1966); Terence de Vere White's "Richard Irvine Best and His Irish Contemporaries" (*IUR*, 1977), which notes that Moore treated Best more kindly in *Hail and Farewell* than Joyce did in *Ulysses*; and Kevin Sullivan's "Benedict Kiely: The Making of a Novelist," in *The Irish Novel in Our Time*, in which it is asserted that Kiely's "origins are in the untilled field of George Moore," not in works by Joyce.

Views on Moore's part in the Irish literary revival remain mixed, as they have been for many years. James W. Flannery, on the whole, surveys Moore's involvement objectively in *W. B. Yeats and the Idea of a Theatre: The Early Abbey Theatre in Theory and Practice* (1976) but, curiously, asserts that Moore was "not at all a true man of the theatre," that he "always remained a man of letters who preferred to read rather than see plays acted." Thomas Rice Henn, in a lecture for the Yeats Society (1963), published posthumously in his *Last Essays: Mainly on Anglo-Irish Literature* (1976), warmly praises Moore's literary output, notes his almost unequaled malice toward his contemporaries and theirs toward him, and concludes that what remains is "a brilliant mind, and a wasted life." The essay focuses on the well-known aspects of Moore's involvement in the Irish literary revival. The clash of egos Henn alludes to is demonstrated by Sean McMahon's "The First Irish Play: *Casadh An tSugain*" (*Éire*, 1977). According to McMahon, W. G. Fay admitted that Moore was the "official director" of Douglas Hyde's play but also contended that Moore had no experience dealing with amateur actors. Moore on his part mentions Fay only in passing, dismissing him as an "energetic young actor." Moore's egotism cannot be denied, but it must be remembered that the novelist was by far the more famous man at the time and that Yeats, Symons, and others had urged Moore to come to Ireland partly because of his reputation and experience.

Three general studies of the Irish literary revival and one major edition of letters to Yeats together suggest Moore's somewhat ambiguous position during his "mission to Ireland." Robert Hogan and James Kilroy, in *The Irish Literary Theatre 1899–1901* (1975), give a detailed account of Moore's involvement, of his association with W. B. Yeats, and especially of the production of Moore and Yeats's *Diarmuid and Grania* (prod. 1901; pub. 1951). They conclude that "The modern Irish drama would not have been significantly impoverished if George Moore had not come to Dublin, but its first years certainly would have been less gay and less lively." The key word here, perhaps, is "lively." Moore certainly did not contribute much creative work to the Irish drama, but his energy, his flair as a publicist, his practical knowledge of the theater, and, simply, his reputation did much to stimulate dramatic activity.

Philip Edwards, in *Threshold of a Nation: A Study in English and*

Irish Drama (1979), while maintaining that Moore's contribution to the Irish literary revival was not large, argues that his intervention was of "striking significance." Edwards singles out *Parnell and His Island* (1887) as a book "much underestimated," *Hail and Farewell* for its discussion of a "language suitable" for the new Irish culture that Moore felt should eventually emerge, and, in general, Moore's foresight that the "subterranean or chthonic force" for nationalism needed to acquire an articulate leader to liberate Ireland. In *The Irish Renaissance* (1977), a study not restricted to the drama, Richard Fallis justly points out that although Moore was "at least as much a nuisance as a help" in the Irish literary movement, he "laid the foundations of the two major kinds of modern Irish prose narrative, the short story [*The Untilled Field*] and the autobiography [*Hail and Farewell*]." Fallis calls the latter "a brilliant book on its own terms."

The mixed view one receives of Moore's role in the Irish literary renaissance is perhaps best documented in Moore's letters and in letters by others in which he is mentioned. Thus the letters in *Letters to W. B. Yeats* show that between 1889 and 1901 Moore and Yeats's relationship, which included the poet's suggestions for the revision of *Evelyn Innes* and the collaboration on *Diarmuid and Grania*, was amiable. The letters after 1901, however, show how the relationship deteriorated—as generally happened when someone tried to collaborate with Moore on an equal basis.

OTHER SPECIAL TOPICS

A number of articles and books touch on miscellaneous topics bearing on Moore. John J. Conlon, in "Arthur Conan Doyle and George Moore: A Note on 'The Adventure of the Empty House' " (*ELT*, 1979), simply argues that Moore and Craigie's *Journeys End in Lovers Meeting* provided a remark made by Sherlock Holmes in Conan Doyle's story; Franz Wieselhuber, in *Die Faszination des Bosen in der viktorianischen Lyrik* (Heidelberg, 1976), examines Moore's *Pagan Poems* (1881) as an example of the atomistic aesthetic immoralism that fascinated many Victorians; and, more important, Lis Christensen (*Éire*, 1977) cogently studies the "Orelay" section of *Memoirs of My Dead Life* (1906) as a foretaste of the style, narrative device, tone, and mock-heroic quest motif Moore developed in *Hail and Farewell*.

Some six titles deal variously with psychology, the seduction motif, sexuality, and female portraits in Moore's works. Raymond J. Sherer's "Psychological and Mythical Patterns in the Novels of George Moore" (Diss. State Univ. of New York, Buffalo, 1974) posits that Moore's fiction is primarily narcissistic. Among the symptoms Sherer identifies are "ignorance of and fear of inner self; perception of self as feminine; latent homosexuality; feelings of disconnectedness, emptiness, and guilt; and self-perception as non-vital." The psychological patterns of Moore's novels, Sherer finds, are related to four myths: Narcissus, Demeter, Oedipus, and Pan. Sherer concludes that Moore's failure "to provide a myth of transcendence over self" was "a corollary to the general failure of his fiction as art."

Frederick M. Seinfelt's *George Moore: Ireland's Unconventional Realist* (1975), based on the author's earlier dissertation (Pennsylvania State Univ. 1967), is superficial and inaccurate (see Eileen Kennedy's review in *ELT*, 1976). Moore's "Albert Nobbs" (in *Celibate Lives*) seems to have awakened some interest in recent years. Besides the dramatic adaptations already mentioned, some favorable comments by earlier critics, and its inclusion in Christopher Isherwood's *Great English Stories* (1957), its theme of sexual alienation has attracted attention. Ernest L. Fontana (*IFR*, 1977) calls this story as "radical a study of transformation and aloneness" as Philip Roth's novel *The Breast*. Larry Simpson Longerbeam's "Seduction as Symbolic Action: A Study of the Seduction Motif in Six Victorian Novels" (Diss. George Peabody Coll. for Teachers 1975) suggests that Hardy's *Tess of the d'Urbervilles* and Moore's *Esther Waters* turn the seduction motif against the middle class, whose interests the motif's function originally defended. Moore, Longerbeam maintains, did not integrate his theme of class antagonism with the seduction motif, for William Latch is a servant with an upper-class heritage, while Esther's conflicts are with the middle class.

Two works deal with Moore's portraits of women. Lloyd Fernando's *"New Women" in the Late Victorian Novel* (1977), based on the author's dissertation (Leeds 1964), examines the somewhat ambiguous treatment of women in Moore's fiction. Fernando concludes that Moore dealt with the social injustices of women "with a tacit sympathy that could only have been the fruit of social understanding" but that he remained convinced to the end that women would be "unsexed" by liberation. Moore's best work on the subject, Fernando suggests, is in *Esther Waters*, *A Mummer's Wife*, *A Drama in Muslin* (1886), "Mildred Lawson" (*Celibates*, 1895), and *Evelyn Innes*. While not as searching as Fernando's study, Patricia Stubbs' *Women in Fiction: Feminism in the Novel 1880-1920* (1979) also insists that Moore's work shows a concerted attempt to avoid "the sexual stereotypes of mid-Victorian culture," that Moore is more "remarkably frank" than Hardy, and that he refuses to "idealize women's lives." Citing *A Mummer's Wife*, *Esther Waters*, and especially *A Drama in Muslin* as evidence of Moore's views, Stubbs maintains that Moore's portrayals of women's sexual anxieties unfortunately often lapse into melodrama.

Two writers further explore the complex narrative devices of Moore's innovative autobiographical writings, stressing his manipulation of fact and the ambiguities of tone. Thus Stanley Weintraub's "Autobiography and Authenticity: Memoir Writing among Some Late Victorians," in *Sources for Reinterpretation: The Use of Nineteenth-Century Documents* (1975; rev. and augmented in *CVE*, 1978), points out that Moore's distortion of facts in his autobiographical writings is often a deliberate attempt to rearrange life artistically, an observation that might well be applied to much of the "new" autobiographical writing of the late nineteenth and early twentieth centuries. Jean C. Noël's "George Moore's Pluridimensional Autobiography: Remarks on

His *Confessions of a Young Man"* (*CCEI*, 1979) is an excellent close reading of Moore's "masterpiece of ambiguity," a study of the kind Charles Burkhart has called for (*ELT*, 1977). Arguing that *Confessions of a Young Man* is not "inchoate," as some critics have held, Noël discusses Moore's various literary devices and concludes that his "apparent self-derision and incipient mythical magnification" accord with his counting on the shared identity of author, narrator, and character to give coherence to his many-dimensioned autobiography. (For earlier related discussions see the previous survey of research: Noël, p. 158; Shumaker, pp. 162-63; Firth, Riley, and Scotto, p. 163.)

GENERAL STUDIES INCLUDING CRITICISM

Five major book-length works on Moore have been published. They are David Bruce Eakin's "The Man in the Paper Mask: Epistolary Autobiography in Oscar Wilde and George Moore," alluded to earlier; Brian Greenwood Donovan's "George Moore's Fictive Autobiography" (Diss. Univ. of Michigan 1974); H. E. Gerber's *George Moore on Parnassus*, already mentioned in several connections; Richard Allen Cave's *A Study of the Novels of George Moore* (1978); and Anthony Farrow's *George Moore* (1978).

Eakin and Donovan both explore Moore's innovative self-representations, but they use entirely different evidence. Of these two fine dissertations, "The Man in the Paper Mask" is probably the more original, in that Eakin also undertakes to define a subgenre of autobiography not previously approached in the same way or so massively and specifically documented.

Eakin suggests that both Wilde and Moore "questioned the notion of a sincere and coherent inner self to which they should be faithful" and that in their letters "both . . . don paper masks to suit their artistic needs." The letters of each, Eakin continues, approach "an imaginative autobiography based on the doctrine expressed by Wilde: 'Man is least himself when he talks in his own person. Give him a mask, and he will tell you the truth.' " On a similar subject, based on a close analysis of *Confessions of a Young Man*, *Memoirs of My Dead Life*, and *Hail and Farewell*, Donovan shows that Moore's primary problem was to discover how to deal with a sequence of many selves and that, unlike some writers of religion-oriented autobiographies, Moore did not view his life as having "didactic value for the reader." Moore's work in this genre is coherent not in the conventional way but in the very process of discovery, of "becoming." Moore is modern, Donovan argues, in seeking "a unified self" in an apparently "fragmented and formless existence" and "in experimenting with time and planes of consciousness." Donovan insists that Moore has had more influence on modern autobiography, particularly on Joyce, than has yet been recognized.

H. E. Gerber's *George Moore on Parnassus* has been sufficiently discussed in other connections to warrant only brief mention here. The volume not only contains a massive collection of previously unpublished letters selected to focus on different types of personal relationships and on several artistic developments in Moore's career from about 1900 to 1933 but also provides biographical matter in eight essays and comments on Moore's use of sources. More important, perhaps, the integrated essays explore, as Eakin and Donovan have done in different ways, the complex workings of Moore's imagination.

Richard Allen Cave, in *A Study of the Novels of George Moore*, has turned his earlier dissertation (Cambridge Univ. 1969) into a first-rate scholarly book. He manages to compress into 239 pages a great deal of familiar information as well as many provocative observations. Like Donovan, Cave has paid more attention than most previous scholars have to Moore's variant texts for almost all his titles. He has heeded the major bibliographies and the scholarly editions of letters. He properly approaches the French works that influenced Moore with more skepticism than some earlier scholars who seemed bent on proving imitativeness rather than on showing Moore's often innovative use of source material and his generally short-lived slavishness toward any "master." One wishes that Cave had spent less time on *Esther Waters* and more on "A Phase of Experiment" ("New Influences—New Problems," "Four Novellas," "Wagner and the Novel," "*Evelyn Innes* and *Sister Teresa*," 1901) and on his discussion of *The Lake* (1905), *The Brook Kerith*, and the late historical novels. Cave is especially insightful in his treatment of Moore's innovations and technical skills: the creation of his own kind of stream-of-consciousness technique, the use of memory to give complex portraits of his characters' mental lives, the use of the epiphany, and so on. Cave, as Charles Burkhart has maintained in a review (*NCF*, 1979), convincingly shows Moore to be a forerunner of such modernists as Joyce, Woolf, Forster, Lawrence, and Beckett. Though, as Burkhart also observes, there may be "a sort of proprietary propaganda" in Cave's work, it is nevertheless "a very good book" on Moore's novels.

Though limited in depth, like most volumes in the Twayne English Authors Series, Anthony Farrow's *George Moore* is an excellent introductory survey of Moore's life and literary output, useful particularly for its examination, first, of individual works as "self-consistent artistic units" and, second, of Moore's influence on the trend of British literature. Farrow, like others before him, insists on the still unheeded observation that Moore's "overall distinction ought to place him very high in the pantheon of a literary school marked by only a few central figures of consummate merit."

As one reviews scholarship on Moore, one notes that even unsympathetic readers seem compelled to recognize his presence as a model for some literary trends and as an influential literary man. He is generally most favorably viewed as among the best English practitioners of naturalism or "new realism," with particular reference to *A Mummer's Wife* and *Esther Waters*; as a somewhat ambiguous generator of the Irish literary revival; as the author of a distinguished collection of short stories, *The Untilled Field*; and as an innovative influence on modern autobiography.

On the other hand, many scholars not particularly knowledgeable about Moore's works continue to be hampered by deep-rooted negative attitudes toward Moore, mainly having to do with his borrowings from French models for his early fiction, his questionable motives during his self-proclaimed "mission to Ireland," and by something unsavory in his character, perhaps egoism or what is taken as maliciousness or an apparent voyeurism understood as somehow perverse and lecherous. His real accomplishments, his technical skills, and his often shrewd probing of character in individual works need to be further explored without the bias of received tradition. Ironically, some of the negative views of Moore's character have their bases in his own anecdotes and fictional self-representations. What critics often miss is Moore's undercutting of a particular image by using multiple images of himself in the same work or by constantly shifting tones. In many ways, the old fox was sometimes a little too sly and the critics sometimes not sly enough.

In view of the excellent favorable studies published in recent years on Pater's and Wilde's critical theories and practices, perhaps Moore's highly personal critical essays will also receive more serious attention than they have. At least there is some evidence that authors whose critical writings were for many years dismissed as "subjective" or "impressionistic" are being reexamined without the prejudgment dictated by pejorative labels. The last word has certainly not been said on the corpus of writings, some still uncollected, made up of reviews, prefaces, introductions, essays, and sections of various published collections in mixed genres. One hopes to see more studies of the essays collected in such volumes as *Memoirs of My Dead Life*, *Impressions and Opinions* (1891), *Avowals* (1919), and *Conversations in Ebury Street* (1924). Gilcher and Becker's supplement to Gilcher's primary bibliography should be helpful in directing the student to many uncollected and, in some instances, previously unidentified titles.

Besides *A Mummer's Wife* and *Esther Waters*, a few of Moore's later works of fiction have been receiving more attention in recent years, especially *The Untilled Field*, *The Lake*, and *The Brook Kerith*. Of the earlier works, *A Drama in Muslin*, *Evelyn Innes*, and *Sister Teresa* could profitably be reexamined for their perceptive character studies as well as for thematic reasons. Among the later works, close studies of *A Story-Teller's Holiday*, *Héloïse and Abélard* (1921), and even *Ulick and Soracha* might be rewarding. *Daphnis and Chloe* and *Aphrodite in Aulis* (1930), if studied as uniquely Moore's work, could also be fruitfully analyzed. *Daphnis and Chloe* at least is not what it was advertised as being, a work "done into English." It is certainly not a translation of Longus' fifth-century version of the story, and it is at best merely "based on" Jacques Amyot's 1559 French translation. Sources are so amalgamated and manipulated that the novel must be viewed as Moore's. As so often when Moore "borrowed," "imitated," or "recreated," he put his own individual imprint on the work. Similarly, *Aphrodite in Aulis*, despite the various sources Moore used, is very much his own work.

Now that well over two thousand letters by Moore are available, with more undoubtedly forthcoming, the scholar can cull the correspondence, as David Eakin has done, for a wide range of biographical, psychological, and critical studies. Similarly, now that we have Gilcher's primary bibliography (with a supplement forthcoming), variorum editions of several works, and some excellent textual and source studies, perhaps we can look forward to more sensible critical studies of individual titles, stylistic studies, and thematic interpretations based on a sound knowledge of Moore's texts.

The most urgent need, finally, is for reprints of reliable texts at a modest price, perhaps the kind of reprints that have been published by W. W. Norton in the Critical Editions Series or the soundly edited texts published by Academy Chicago. The demand can be legitimately created; the supply of reprints in well-edited texts can, at least in the long run, have rewarding results and bring Moore "a little nearer the summit of Parnassus," as he said a little too soon in 1912. Apart from the "proprietary propaganda" of which Moore scholars—like Hardy, Joyce, Woolf, Lawrence, and Forster scholars—may be guilty, Moore's works do address the modern reader. Insofar as he speaks for art, civilization, culture, and humanity, Moore is a man of letters in the best sense. In the narrower confines of belles letters, he is a highly talented novelist, a distinguished short story writer, and certainly a brilliant imaginative autobiographer.

BERNARD SHAW

Stanley Weintraub

The original review of research on Bernard Shaw appeared in the midst of the continual revaluation of his reputation, which had reached a trough in 1956, the centenary of his birth. Ironically, the traditional centenary opportunity for rehabilitation failed to work to Shaw's posthumous advantage, for having died only a few years earlier, in 1950, he was still undergoing the equally traditional falling-off in critical estimation that follows a writer's obituaries. We are now likely to see a spurt of Shaw publications as the copyright owners use their rights before copyrights in force at Shaw's death expire in the year 2000. Once such publications go into the public domain, a deluge of reprints is inevitable. Here it should be noted that works in manuscript at Shaw's death, and copyrighted in later years, such as play manuscripts, and unpublished essays and letters, begin their published lives with new copyrights. Under the old copyright law an unpublished work had a "common law" protection that lasted indefinitely. Under the new American copyright law the period is defined; Shaw's unpublished manuscripts are protected until at least 31 December 2002. Thereafter, the manuscripts will be in the public domain, unless they are published before that date, in which case they will be protected by copyright until 31 December 2027.

Fewer and fewer valuable Shaw materials remain in private hands, and these are gradually proceeding into public collections through donation, dispersal of estates, and sale. The most recent major example is the LaFayette Butler Collection, now part of the Bucknell University Library through bequest. That much material, particularly correspondence, is still privately owned is evidenced in sale and auction catalogs each year, themselves a resource for documentation not to be overlooked by the scholar.

1. Bibliographies

A two-volume bibliography by Dan H. Laurence is now being prepared for probable publication late in 1982. It will contain full collations and a detailed history of each publication, with notes on textual variations between editions and between printings of a single edition. Included, too, will be Shaw's rehearsal copies, contributions to books by others, and a listing of every periodical publication located, as well as letters to editors and self-drafted interviews and questionnaires. The full texts of Shaw's printed-message postcards will be included, and all identified silent editings and rewritings will be described—Fabian tracts, biographies, and other publications. Archival sources of all scarce items will be identified.

In progress, as part of the Annotated Secondary Bibliography Series, is a three-volume Shaw, the segments edited by J. P. Wearing, Elsie B. Adams, and Donald C. Haberman. "A Continuing Checklist of Shaviana"—which lists new editions of Shaw as well as secondary bibliographical items from books, periodicals, theses, dissertations, films, and recordings—continued to appear thrice yearly in the *Shaw Review*, which began its checklists in 1950. In 1981 this checklist began appearing in *Shaw: The Annual of Bernard Shaw Studies*, which continues the *Shaw Review* in augmented book format.

Jill M. Phillips' *George Bernard Shaw: A Review of the Literature* (1976) is an annotated bibliography of biographies of Shaw and personal writings by him, with some citations to related writings. Two additional volumes of secondary bibliography are promised. *Twentieth-Century Literary Criticism*, edited by Sharon K. Hall (vol. 3, 1980), lists and extracts criticism on Shaw by forty-four writers, from H. L. Mencken in 1905 to writers in the late 1970s.

2. Editions

Posthumous editions of Shaw's writings continue to enlarge the prose canon. In addition, extracts from his writings, especially letters, continue to appear in memoirs and biographies by and about people whose lives touched his. Editions of Shaw correspondences—*Bernard Shaw and Alfred Douglas: A Correspondence* and *The Playwright and the Pirate: Bernard Shaw and Frank Harris*—were published in 1982. The Dan H. Laurence *Collected Letters* continues, with volumes 3 (1910–25) and 4 (1928–50) in preparation. Some new Shaw letters appear in the *Portable Bernard Shaw* (ed. S. Weintraub, 1977) and in biographies noted in part 3 of this survey. Also, numerous stage and film biographies and autobiographies continue to include Shaw correspondence—for example, Raymond Massey's *A Hundred Different Lives* (1979) and Bryan Forbes's biography of Edith Evans, *Ned's Girl* (1977).

Shaw's shorthand diaries of 1885–97 (at the British Library of Political and Economic Science), long quoted from incomplete transliterations made by Blanche Patch and Stanley Rypins, are now being edited and annotated for publication from the unfinished Rypins version by S. Weintraub, with references coordinated with the coding in the Laurence *Bibliography*. Shaw's art criticism has been further extracted in S. Weintraub's "In the Picture Galleries" (see part 3) and his music criticism in Louis Crompton's one-volume *The Great Composers* (1978). The complete and definitive music criticism has been brought together and edited by Dan H. Laurence in *Shaw's Music* (3 vols., 1981); it includes articles from the *World* and the *Star* that Shaw omitted from his own collections; other criticism, earlier and later, including unsigned reviews in the *Hornet* (1876–77), the *Dramatic Review* (1885), and the *Pall Mall Gazette* (1885–88); and miscellaneous essays on musical subjects from publications ranging from the *Musician* to the *Farnham, Haslemere and Hindhead Herald*. The index itself is a major Shavian research tool.

In *Shaw and Ibsen* (1979) J. L. Wisenthal includes *The Quintessence of Ibsenism* in a definitive text, the third, and final, edition of 1922, to which are added the numerous alterations from the 1891 and 1913 editions and the appendix to the 1891 edition, deleted in later texts. There are also copious annotations, a historical introduction, and several shorter Shavian pieces on Ibsen written both before and after 1891, including Shaw's original Fabian lecture that was the germ of *Quintessence*. Wisenthal's introduction, though it may exaggerate Ibsen's influence on Shaw's plays, is penetrating and valuable—the best single essay on Shaw and Ibsen. In Ibsen, Wisenthal claims, "Shaw saw the possibility of a drama of . . . moral indictment" and "the possibility of combining surface realism and symbolic non-realistic methods. . . . In 1891 Shaw saw mostly the realistic surface in Ibsen's plays, and this is reflected in his own work of this period. In 1912–13 (when revising the *Quintessence*) he saw more of the non-naturalistic symbolic and poetic techniques, and this is reflected in *Heartbreak House*."

F. P. W. McDowell's "Fountainhead and Fountain: Ibsen and Shaw" (*ShawR*, 1980), which uses Wisenthal's study as a springboard, is highly perceptive on Shaw's use of Ibsen and on Shaw's concept of his own plays as tragicomedies—a reason, McDowell suggests, for Shaw's preference for the dark comedies of Shakespeare. McDowell sees "an abrasive and disconcerting quality in *Candida* and *The Devil's Disciple* . . . that dilutes the comedy present in them" and finds "this antiseptic quality present even in *Arms and the Man*; and I am sure that it was just this aspect of the play that alienated Yeats when he first saw it and it led him to characterize Shaw in the unforgettable image of a sewing machine that smiled. We are more conditioned to the sardonic and the Mephistophelean perhaps than the early Yeats or the late Victorian theatre-going public were; but if this roughness of vision is characteristic of Shaw, for better or for worse, he can hardly then be regarded as representing primarily a carefree joyousness that by definition is essentially serene." Thus to McDowell there are tensions in Shaw's plays that appear Ibsenian, "though Ibsen's vision is, of course, even more sardonic and satiric than Shaw's. With the familiarity that has overtaken Shaw's plays and with the sentimentalizing of many of them in performance, the sharp edge that is present in almost everything that he did gets blunted. It is possible, even, to think of Shaw as therefore having very little relevance for the dislocated modern age."

Two other critiques of Shaw and Ibsen are of interest. In "Bernard Shaw, Ibsen and the Ethics of English Socialism" (*VS*, 1978), I. M. Britain, like Wisenthal, attacks the misconception that Shaw treated Ibsen as a socialist or that Ibsen was indeed one. Shaw, Britain writes, recognized Ibsen's individualism and even used it to criticize socialist colleagues for their inflexibility. Alfred Turco's "Shaw's Pragmatist Ethic: A New Look at *The Quintessence of Ibsenism*" (*TSLL*, 1976) examines the treatise for the consistency and cogency of its philosophy. "Shaw intuits," Turco concludes, "that the prospect of implementing his own reformist goals will depend upon an ability to resist grand designs foredoomed to failure by the nature of the world."

A minor addition to the canon is Jerald E. Bringle's first printing, with notes, of Shaw's 1879 prose sketch "The St James's Hall Mystery" (*BRH*, 1979), a rejected musical satire involving the alleged return of Mozart's ghost. Not a Shaw work, but based on one, is Robert Hogan's dramatic adaptation of Shaw's novel *An Unsocial Socialist* (1978), which largely uses Shaw's dialogue and retains Shaw's title. (Another dramatic version of a Shaw novel was the English ITV production of *Love among the Artists*, 7 Aug. 1979.) Another curious minor addition to the canon is *So He Took His Hat Round* (1981), a pamphlet published by Washington University Libraries (St. Louis) containing a preface by Dan H. Laurence and a facsimile reproduction of a 1928 charity appeal Shaw drafted for the King Edward Memorial Hospital.

The most considerable as well as the most significant editing achievement in recent years is *Bernard Shaw. Early Texts: Play Manuscripts in Facsimile*, under the general editorship of Dan H. Laurence (12 vols., 1980–81). This work, which will very likely be known as the Garland edition, includes all the early play manuscripts in the Shaw archive in the British Library that were originally drafted in longhand, plus the recently discovered, drastically revised typescript of *Heartbreak House*, of which the shorthand draft is lost. (The typescript was purchased at the sale of the Ivo L. Currall collection.) Substantial analytical introductions by individual scholars accompany each play. *Widowers' Houses* (which includes the Berg Collection's complete holograph ms) is edited by Jerald E. Bringle; *The Philanderer* (including the deleted final act) by Julius Novick; *Mrs Warren's Profession*, heavily revised, by Margot Peters; and *Arms and the Man*, as it appeared before Shaw reordered scenes, by Norma Jenckes. *Candida* and its farcical inversion, *How He Lied to Her Husband*, are paired in J. Percy Smith's edition, and *You Never Can Tell* is edited by Daniel J. Leary. Robert F. Whitman's edition of *The Devil's Disciple* includes an early shorthand sketch touching on Shaw's ideas for the play in transition, which was first drafted without its American Revolution venue, and J. L. Wisenthal's edition combines two histories, *The Man of Destiny* and *Caesar and Cleopatra*. Rodelle Weintraub's edition of *Captain Brassbound's Conversion* shows Shaw's early concern with accents and dialects, and *Major Barbara*, in Bernard Dukore's edition, includes the original final scene as well as the greatly rewritten one. Margery Morgan's edition of *The Doctor's Dilemma* includes designs for the first production. *Heartbreak House*, coedited by S. Weintraub and Anne Wright, is a much longer text than the published play, having a new beginning, a new ending (both including shorthand revisions), and Shaw's own sketches for stage settings. The editors examine the plays from the standpoint of the manuscripts, the sources, and the intentions revealed in the working-out of the text and provide other insights that supplement references to individual plays in later pages. Some of these essays are the best individual studies yet of particular plays.

Shaw's principles, as opposed to his practice, emerge in "Bernard Shaw at Oxford: GBS's Lecture on Playwriting" (*ShawR*, 1979), which salvages the transcript of Shaw's 14 March 1914 lecture from the *Oxford Times* of 6 March. The longest reconstruction of the talk, which was delivered from a few note cards, it describes Shaw's techniques of causation and of theatricality. Later Shaw play texts appear in Bernard F. Dukore's *The Collected Screenplays of Bernard Shaw* (1980), which includes *Saint Joan* (never filmed), *Pygmalion, Major Barbara, Arms and the Man*, and *Caesar and Cleopatra*, plus a fragment of a *Devil's Disciple* screenplay and a number of discarded scenes. (The edition does not include screenplays that others wrote of Shaw's works, such as the Graham Greene film version of *Saint Joan*.) Dukore's monograph-long introduction traces the genesis of the cinematic treatments.

A late work, *The Black Girl in Search of God* (1933), appears in a definitive text (ed. Dan H. Laurence) in the Penguin 1977 edition, which is otherwise a corrected reprint of the 1934 collection (with the lesser tales), and in the *Portable Bernard Shaw* (minus preface). Not so much a text as a collection of rehearsal notes and sketches is B. F. Dukore's edition, *Bernard Shaw's* Arms and the Man: *A Composite Production Book* (1982), which illuminates the playwright's ideas for productions he personally supervised. Last, defeating categorization, is *Flyleaves* (ed. Dan H. Laurence and Daniel J. Leary, 1977), which presents the results of Shaw's change of heart when, at ninety-three, he decided to create artificial book rarities by writing long inscriptions in books he was consigning to the auction rooms. The entries are fascinating "last words"—especially on Bunyan, Shakespeare, T. E. Lawrence, Elgar, and Malory, reproduced in full—and they make up yet another artificial rarity, in that *Flyleaves* itself is a limited edition.

3. Biographies and Autobiographies

The authorized biography, by Michael Holroyd, is in preparation and is likely to appear in more than one volume. A preliminary to it is Holroyd's *The Genius of Shaw* (1979), which contains essays by other hands, a number of them biographical: "The First Twenty Years," by John O'Donovan; "In the Picture Galleries," by S. Weintraub; "The Way of No Flesh," by Brigid Brophy; "The Fabian Ethic," by Robert Skidelsky; "Women and the Body Politic," by M. Holroyd; "As Lonely as God," by Margot Peters; and "Man of Letters," by Barbara Smoker.

Almost an autobiography is *Shaw: An Exhibit* (ed. Dan H. Laurence, 1978), the catalog of the exhibition at the Humanities Research Center at the University of Texas, Austin, which through quotation, illustration, and facsimile samples Shaw documentation from the earliest years to his death, the last item being Shaw's death mask (only described in the publication). The death mask itself has been reproduced as a frontispiece (*CVE*, no. 9-10, 1979). Laurence's monograph *Shaw, Books and Libraries* (1979) is an informal account of Shaw's attitudes toward letters, manuscripts, books, and book production and his public spiritedness toward libraries and the book trade in general.

The closest to a biography in a decade is Margot Peters' *Bernard Shaw and the Actresses* (1980), which chronicles Shaw's relations with actresses and nonactresses alike, beginning with Alice Lockett and Jenny Patterson and concluding with Molly Tompkins. Much on Shaw, too, appears in Josephine Johnson's *Florence Farr: Bernard Shaw's "New Woman"* (1975), which adds documentation to Shaw's love life with the actress who was the model for his Louka and whose rivalry with Mrs. Patterson inspired a tempestuous scene in *The Philanderer*. Also taking a feminine perspective are two biographical articles by Rodelle Weintraub that focus on Charlotte Shaw: "Shaw's Celibate Marriage: Its Impact on His Plays" (*CVE*, 1979) and "The Irish Lady in Shaw's Plays" (*ShawR*, 1980).

Of genealogical and perhaps biographical use is Nathaniel Harris' *The Shaws: The Family of George Bernard Shaw* (1977), and of biographical and critical interest is Arnold Silver's *Bernard Shaw: The Dark Side* (1982), which examines Shaw and his work from a largely Freudian perspective, seeing Shaw's humanity as disabled by oedipal and related psychological disturbances. Other articles with a biographical basis include Mavor Moore's "Why 'James Mavor' Morell?" (*ShawR*, 1980), about the Scot economist James Mavor; S. Weintraub's "Bernard Shaw and the Unknown Soldier" (*TLS*, 13 Nov. 1981), about what Shaw called a scenario for an antiwar play; and Weintraub's "Shaw's Other Keegan: Sean O'Casey and G. B. S.," in *Sean O'Casey Centenary Essays* (ed. R. Lowery and D. Krause, 1980). Mary O'Connor's "Did Bernard Shaw Kill John Davidson? The 'Tragi-comedy' of a Commissioned Play" (*ShawR*, 1978) details Shaw's unsuccessful attempt to revive the Edwardian poet's literary fortunes by financing a work, *The Game of Life*, that would not be a potboiler; the result was, ironically, frustration and suicide. Dealing with the same period in Shaw's life, Annie Russell's "George Bernard Shaw at Rehearsals of *Major Barbara*" (*ShawR*, 1979) is a 1908 account by the first English Barbara, once delivered by her as a lecture; it includes letters from Shaw to her and to Louis Calvert, the play's first Undershaft. Also concerning the Edwardian Shaw is Roy T. Matthews' "Shaw and *Vanity Fair*" (*ShawR*, 1980), which relates the caricatures of Shaw in that magazine to the vicissitudes of his reputation and reproduces several of the drawings. Edwardian in period, too, although more a recapitulation than anything new, is J. C. Trewin's *The Edwardian Theatre* (1976), which devotes much of its third chapter to Shaw's seasons at the Royal Court Theatre and his relationships with Harley Granville Barker. (An edition of Barker's letters, being prepared by Eric Salmon, should shed further light on this aspect of Shaw's life.) Two early critiques of Shaw suggestive of his contemporary reputation have been uncovered: "A. R. Orage on Shaw: An Unpublished Manuscript" (*ShawR*, 1979), which resurrects an article, "The Philosopher," written in 1907 by the editor of *The New Age* and apparently intended as an appendix for Holbrook Jackson's early book on Shaw; and Temple Scott's "The Terrible Truthfulness of Mr. Shaw" (*ShawR*, 1980), which used the occasion of a photography exhibition in 1909, at which Shaw lectured on photography and truth, to upbraid Shaw. "For when Mr. Shaw is condemning a work of art he is seeing his own visions; he is knowing his own truth." According to Orage, Shaw believed not that it is the world's purpose to save and perfect mankind but that it is mankind's purpose to save and perfect the world.

Timothy Kidd's "James Elroy Flecker and Bernard Shaw" (*ShawR*, 1978) chronicles the associations and possible mutual influence that grew out of G. B. S.'s attempt to help the career of a young poet-playwright who died before his gifts were fully realized. It is possible that some lines in *Saint Joan* reflect Flecker's *Hassan* (1922). *Saint Joan* is also the point of reference in Ralph W. Condee's "The Swimmer and the Patron" (*ShawR*, 1980), which suggests sources in Shaw's reading for his refusal of the 1926 Nobel Prize in literature as "a lifebelt thrown to a swimmer who has already reached the shore in safety." In a footnote to biography, "Shaw Apologizes!" (*ShawR*, 1980), R. F. Bosworth describes Shaw's ironic response to having his books briefly banned by the Needham, Massachusetts, school board in 1924.

While most of Shaw's side of the correspondence with Dame Laurentia MacLachlan, the Nun of Stanbrook, has been published in "The Nun and the Dramatist" (*In a Great Tradition*, 1956), Warren S. Smith reveals more of the relationship by presenting Dame Laurentia's side in "The Adventures of Shaw, the Nun, and the Black Girl" (*Shaw*, 1981). Also epistolary is Fred D. Crawford's "Journals to Stella" (*ShawR*, 1975), which analyzes the striking parallels between Swift's letters to his Stella and Shaw's to Mrs. Patrick Campbell, an authentic Stella.

One of a now rare category—new first-person accounts of Shaw—is "Giants in Those Days of Shaw, De Valera and Sir William Haley" (*IUR*, 1978), by the Irish playwright Denis Johnston, who prefaces the article by calling Shaw "the personality on whose shoulders most people of my generation, assuming that they have any thought processes at all, are sitting. And this applies both as regards our successes and our mistakes." Biographically, Johnston adds to the picture of the aged Shaw by depicting him as feeling "financially ruined" by taxation on every commercial success in films and play revivals.

Recent books with major sections on Shaw also contribute to the biographical picture. Stanley Pierson's *British Socialists: The Journey from Fantasy to Politics* (1979) examines the transition in the focus of Shaw's plays, from narrow and specific to general and universal, at a time when his socialist activities still involved concern over public lavatories and the municipalization of utilities. Shaw realized that a drama controlled by socialist preoccupations was too limited, and he began, while still immersed in Fabian politics, to explore human behavior in a way that went beyond promoting a socialist reorganization of society. Shaw's futuristic plays would recognize that a better world required better human beings more than idealistic legislation.

Another aspect of Shaw appears in Benny Green's *Shaw's Champions: G. B. S. and Prizefighting, from Cashel Byron to Gene Tunney* (1978), which itself is augmented by S. Weintraub's "A Passion for Pugilism" (*TLS*, 5 May 1978), an essay itself augmented in his *The Unexpected Shaw* (see next section). Diana Farr's *Gilbert Cannan: A Georgian Prodigy* (1978), a book about the then young critic-playwright whom G. B. S. caricatured as "Gilbert Gunn" in *Fanny's First Play*, has a chapter on Shaw. Victor Bonham-Carter's *Authors by Profession* (1978) devotes chapter 9 to Shaw's relationship with the Society of Authors, his methods of publishing, and his opposition to stage censorship. Jeffrey Meyers' *Married to Genius* (1977) reviews the Shaw marriage, which Meyers considers a muffinlike marriage of convenience that left both parties discontented. George Hendrick's *Henry Salt: Humanitarian Reformer and Man of Letters* (1977) details Shaw's nonsexual involvement in the nonsexual marriage of Henry Salt and his lesbian wife, Kate. Yvonne Karp's *Eleanor Marx* (2 vols., 1976) chronicles Shaw's involvement with both Eleanor Marx and the unscrupulous Edward Aveling (one of the originals for Louis Dubedat in *The Doctor's Dilemma*) in their clearly heterosexual nonmarriage. Norman MacKenzie and Jeanne MacKenzie's *The Fabians* (1977), more accurately entitled *The First Fabians* in the London edition, provides a detailed account of the Fabian Society from 1883 to 1914 and necessarily includes much on G. B. S. the politician and amateur economist. N. Mackenzie's edition of *The Letters of Beatrice and Sidney Webb* (3 vols., 1978) includes many letters to Shaw and helps further to place him in the Fabian movement as well as in the context of his friendship with the Webbs. Shaw as publicist is the subject of Dan Laurence's "What Is Your Opinion, Mr Shaw?" (*LCUT*, 1974), which details Shaw's relationships with interviewers and would-be interviewers who besieged him for his views on practically everything.

4. General Critical Evaluations

Traditional play-by-play book-length evaluations of Shaw have been mercifully few in recent years. Inevitably there has been a *Who's Who in Shaw* (1975), in which Phyllis Hartnoll provides an annotated list of characters in the produced plays and playlets. The long-running Twayne series has belatedly spawned a *George Bernard Shaw* (1978), by Eldon C. Hill, which follows the series format with chronology, biographical-critical chapters on the plays, and selected bibliography. Less successful as an introduction to Shaw is Pat M. Carr's *Bernard Shaw* (1976), in the World Dramatists series, which is flawed by omissions and errors and is written at level suggesting a secondary school audience. Taking a philosophical slant is Robert F. Whitman's provocative *Shaw and the Play of Ideas* (1977), which analyzes Shaw's intellectual development by stressing the impact—largely indirect, through E. Belfort Bax—of Hegel on the plays. Also philosophical in approach is *Shaw's Moral Vision: The Self and Salvation* (1976), by Alfred Turco, Jr., who examines Shaw's pragmatism as it emerges from the major critical essays of the 1890s, *The Quintessence of Ibsenism* and *The Perfect Wagnerite*, and moves onstage, culminating in *Major Barbara* and *Heartbreak House*. Two books that concern Shaw's religious concepts and their backgrounds are Warren S. Smith's *The Bishop of Everywhere* (1982) and Samuel A. Yorks's *The Evolution of Bernard Shaw*. While the former is more biographical in approach and the latter more critical, both are approaches to Shaw's ideas about what he labeled Creative Evolution. A more narrowly based (and previously referred to) book-length study is psychological rather than philosophical. Arnold Silver's *Bernard Shaw: The Darker Side* (1982) takes a mordant and suspicious view of Shaw's motives and creative inspiration in lengthy analyses of the novels and plays, in particular *The Simpleton of the Unexpected Isles, Candida, Man and Superman*, and *Pygmalion*, seeing sadistic and even homicidal tendencies in Shaw emerging from unresolved oedipal dilemmas. Another 1982 book, S. Weintraub's *The Unexpected Shaw: Biographical Approaches to G. B. S. and His Work*, is more traditional in approach, examining unfamiliar backgrounds of major works and significant friendships (such as those with Sean O'Casey and Frank Harris) and looking at such less familiar aspects of the man as Shaw the actor, Shaw the boxer, Shaw the art and literary critic, and Shaw the emergent Irish patriot. Alexander Woollcott's play-by-play evaluation of Shaw's work as it reached the American stage is discussed in Morris U. Burns's *The Dramatic Criticism of Alexander Woollcott* (1980), which quotes from some of the reviews and lists them all.

A many-sided examination of Shaw's principles and practice regarding feminism and feminist issues is *Fabian Feminist: Bernard Shaw and Woman* (1977), edited by Rodelle Weintraub. Although it concludes by reprinting five little-known Shavian polemics on woman suffrage, including a sardonic condemnation of forced feeding, and a checklist of works by and about Shaw that have a feminist perspective (comp. Lucile Kelling Henderson), the core of the book, following R. Weintraub's survey of Shaw's developing sensitivity toward women's issues ("Fabian Feminist"), consists of essays grouped around the topics "Literary and Mythic Influences," "Political and Economic Influences," "Shaw's Liberated Women," and "Influence of Shaw's Feminism." (Some of these essays are identified under specific plays in part 6.) Also written from a feminist perspective is Elsie Adams' "Shaw's Ladies" (*ShawR*, 1980), on his use of "lady," not as a substitute for "woman," but as a "class marker"—as when Lina in *Misalliance* claims her independence (as a "person") and identifies herself as a "woman"—something that Hypatia understands but that the class-rigid men do not.

Appropriate to the general-survey category (to be further detailed where useful under individual plays and/or other works) is Bernard F. Dukore's *Money and Politics in Ibsen, Shaw, and Brecht* (1980). All Shaw's plays deal with money (just as all of them are explicit or implicit commentaries on religion), but Dukore emphasizes *Pygmalion, Mrs Warren's Profession, The Doctor's Dilemma, Heartbreak House, Major Barbara,* and *On the Rocks,* comparing them to roughly parallel plays by Ibsen and Brecht and concluding with a drawing together of ideas on money power. Dukore notes that Shaw seldom proposes clear-cut solutions but forcefully dramatizes the money basis of contemporary society.

Special journal issues worth mention include the *New Edinburgh Review* (1975), which devoted two monthly issues to general essays on aspects of Shaw: *The Buffon* and *The Spring-Heeled Marcher.* "Shaw and Myth" (*ShawR,* 1978), edited by Timothy Vesonder, offers both an annotated checklist of research on Shaw from that perspective and articles described below under individual plays. (Perhaps also in the category of Shaw and myth are Arthur Ganz's "The Playwright as Perfect Wagnerite: Motifs from the Music Dramas in the Theatre of Bernard Shaw," *CD,* 1979, and its sequel, Robert Coskren's "Wagner and Shaw: *Rheingold* Motifs in *Major Barbara,*" *CD,* 1980. Ganz examines how the myths in Wagner's transmutation apparently influenced *Candida, Caesar and Cleopatra, Man and Superman,* and *Major Barbara,* among others, and Coskren supplements the evidences of that impact on *Barbara,* using parts of a larger Wagner-and-Shaw project in progress.)

"Shaw around the World" (*ShawR,* 1977) furnishes performance histories of G. B. S. in Sweden, Norway, the Netherlands, France, Portugal, and Japan; Ishrat Lindblad's article on Sweden, by giving details on Shaw's vicissitudes with the Nobel Prize committee, adds to Shavian biography as well. Two other articles concerned with performances are by Barbara Small (both in *ShawR,* 1979). The performance qualities as well as the performance problems in need of solution in Shaw's work for the theater are analyzed from the standpoint of voice in her "Rhetorical Style in Shaw's Plays," which points out the need to master the rhetorical style inherent in even the early plays, despite their surface realism, and in "Shaw on Standard Stage Speech," which concerns the requirement for precise stage pronunciation despite the actor's need to be "something of a virtuoso in speech" and to have the ability "to assume dialects and drop or change them at will."

"Shaw and Religion," edited by Charles A. Berst (*Shaw,* 1981), includes an extensive annotated checklist, "Shaw and Religion/Philosophy," compiled by Charles A. Carpenter, Jr.; an early Shaw "sermon," "Some Necessary Repairs to Religion"; Berst's examination of Shaw's groping toward godhead in the nineties, "The Poetic Genesis of Shaw's God"; and pieces noted later under individual works. "Shaw's Plays in Performance" (*Shaw,* 1983), edited by Daniel Leary, examines the range of Shaw's plays and playwriting strategies from the standpoint of their performance values, with emphasis by individual critics on *Major Barbara* and *Pygmalion* and on the importance of setting and "Shavian" acting and direction. Using a different lens, Gordon N. Bergquist's *The Pen and the Sword: War and Peace in the Prose and Plays of Bernard Shaw* (Salzburg, 1977) attempts to pull together Shaw's ideas on war and peace and to arrive at Shaw's philosophical positions, which prove to be pragmatic rather than consistent. Finally, there is R. N. Roy's *George Bernard Shaw's Historical*

Plays (Delhi, 1976), which treats the sources and content of the plays with a historical basis.

General yet specific is "Shaw and Dickens," edited by Martin Quinn (*ShawR*, 1977), which begins a "Shaw/Dickens File" compiled by Edgar Rosenberg on the multifarious Shavian allusions to Dickens (completed in *Shaw*, 1982), and contains articles on individual plays. Quinn's earlier "Dickens as Metaphor" (*ShawR*, 1975), describing how "the fertile world of Dickens served Shaw as a vast garden from which to pluck the ready allusion, the illustrative witticism, the characteristic metaphor," also belongs in this category. Influence studies remain an important avenue of future Shaw research. Dickens appears to be the major writer (other than Shakespeare) thoroughly tilled, with Bunyan, Butler, and Shelley some distance behind; however, the work of Valli Rao and Daniel Leary (noted under *Mrs Warren's Profession*, *Back to Methuselah*, and *Heartbreak House* in section 6) suggests that explorations of Blake will now burgeon.

5. The Novels and Early Musical, Dramatic, and Literary Journalism

Other than the two novels that have been reprinted, *Cashel Byron's Profession* (1979) and *An Unsocial Socialist* (1980, pref. M. Holroyd), little more has surfaced on the novel-writing period that has not been referred to in earlier sections. The early journalism has also been largely ignored, aside from the collected, and definitive, musical criticism noted above and the essays on the art critic, music critic, and drama critic in the Holroyd-edited *Genius* volume (1979). The single exception is Martha Hadsel's "The Common-Uncommon Metaphor in Shaw's Dramatic Criticism" (*ShawR*, 1980), which examines how Shaw used homely images rather than "intellectual" ones to broaden the base of his readership beyond the playgoing public. (Much more remains to be done on Shaw as stylist, both in the early and late work.)

6. Criticism of Individual Plays

A survey of criticism of individual plays quickly reveals which ones are attractive from the standpoint of exegesis, a phenomenon that one relates at hazard to the stageworthiness or performance record of a play. *Widowers' Houses* and *The Philanderer*, Shaw's earliest plays, have had considerable recent stage success. There is no recorded research about or criticism of *The Philanderer* (except for references in general works), and there are only two articles about *Widowers' Houses* (both in *ShawR*, 1975)—Kinley E. Roby's "Stap Street to Robbins's Row," which discusses the relationship of the play to the Report of the Royal Commission on the Housing of the Working Classes, and Diderik Roll-Hansen's "Sartorius and the Scribes of the Bible: Satiric Method in *Widowers' Houses*," which sees the biblical association in the title as less farfetched than Shaw alleged in his promotion of the play. Even *Mrs Warren's Pro-*

fession has elicited little criticism. Germaine Greer's "A Whore in Every Home" (in *Fabian Feminist*) excoriates Shaw for calling prostitution a profession (a criticism that ignores the probable irony intended) and wonders, on the basis of the text, whether Shaw ever knew, or had even met, a prostitute. Valli Rao's "Vivie Warren in the Blakean World of Experience" (*ShawR*, 1979) links *Mrs Warren's Profession* to Blake's early ideas of innocence and experience. (Shaw in the 1890s professed great indebtedness to Blake.) In "Vivie Warren and the Tripos" (*ShawR*, 1980), William A. Dolid reconstructs what Vivie Warren's academic triumph at Newnham involved and puts the achievement in the context of woman's place at Cambridge in Vivie's supposed time. In "Shaw's Use of Vergil's *Aeneid* in *Arms and the Man*" (*ShawR*, 1976), Calvin T. Higgs, Jr., suggests not only that the paradoxical title is adapted from Vergil but that the play demonstrates an intimate knowledge of the epic and follows the structural and thematic construction of the Dido episode.

A piece of playwriting history, and a potential source for influence seekers, is Tennessee Williams' "*Candida*: A College Essay" (*ShawR*, 1977), a 1930s student essay praising Shaw but declaring that Morell and Marchbanks are "fantastic" (unreal) characters. Two other influence studies also involve *Candida*. Betsy C. Yarrison (*ShawR*, 1977) sees Baudelaire's once notorious *fleurs du mal* poem on the albatross as influential in Shaw's depiction of Marchbanks as artist—"the gawkiness of the visionary in a world of Philistines." John Lucas (*ShawR*, 1979) sees Morell's complacency as like that of David Copperfield toward Dora, while Marchbanks' learning that he must resist marital domesticity may echo Dickens' own belated wishful thinking.

Elsie Wiedner (*ShawR*, 1979) examines allegedly Ibsenist elements in the plot and character of *The Devil's Disciple*, largely from *A Doll's House* and *Ghosts*, while two other studies are new readings that lift the play from Shaw's own description of it as "threadbare melodrama." Robert F. Whitman's "The Passion of Dick Dudgeon" (*ShawR*, 1978) elucidates the work as a passion play, with Dick "acting out the central Christian myth, and suffering a kind of passion in his betrayal, trial, and near-execution." R. Weintraub's " 'Only the man . . . draws clear of it': A New Look at Anthony Anderson" (*ShawR*, 1980) perceives the prevalent misunderstanding of Shaw's remark to Ellen Terry, that in every play he had written to that point he had "Prostituted the actress more or less by making the interest in her partly a sexual interest: only the *man* in *The Devil's Disciple* draws clear of it." The man may be Anthony Anderson, Judith's husband, rather than Dick Dudgeon, with whom she is smitten, even though Dick claims no amatory interest.

You Never Can Tell, although performed more in recent years, is still seldom studied. Louis Coxe's *Enabling Acts: Selected Essays in Criticism* (1977) reprints a 1955 essay on the play (*WHR*), in which Coxe observes, "The masters of reality, the cosmic dentists, of Shaw's drama are forever begging us to have it out . . . . Valentine is the actual dentist; Bohun is the spiritual dentist." Linda Herr's "Dickens' Jaggers and Shaw's Bohun: A Study of Character-Lifting" (*ShawR*, 1977) is self-evident.

Captain Brassbound's Conversion, another play produced more in recent years, has been examined only twice in journals in this period. Mac E. Barrick (*ShawR*, 1978) looks at Lady Cicely's delightful "cognatic translation of the legal maxim *Fiat justitia ruat coelum*": "Let justice be done though the ceiling fall!" Ina Rae Hark (*ShawR*, 1981) looks at the play from a conversion perspective in "Lady Cicely, I Presume: Converting the Heathen, Shavian Style."

Caesar and Cleopatra is examined from the standpoint of religion in J. L. Wisenthal's "Shaw and Ra: Religion and Some History Plays" and in C. A. Berst's "In the Beginning: The Poetic Genesis of Shaw's God" (both in *Shaw*, 1981) and from the standpoint of myth in Timothy Vesonder's "Shaw's Caesar and the Mythic Hero" (*ShawR*, 1978), which shows how Shaw shapes Caesar to make him both archetypal and acceptably realistic and down-to-earth. Harold Brooks's "Shavian Sources in the Notes to *Queen Mab*" (*ShawR*, 1977) again demonstrates G. B. S.'s profound indebtedness to Shelley, the examples here being Caesar's allusion to Rufio's murder of Pothinus as "natural slaying" and—in *Androcles and the Lion*—Lavinia's claim that we will only know God when we are gods ourselves.

Surprisingly, *Man and Superman* has not been much examined recently, despite a burgeoning of performances of the complete play (including *Don Juan in Hell*). Sally Peters Vogt's essay, in *Fabian Feminist*, sees Ann Whitefield not only as Shaw's "prototype of predatory females" but as a mythic figure whose role of "Woman Incarnate . . . subsumes all other roles," an Everywoman in both play and frame play. Daniel J. Leary (*ShawR*, 1979) elucidates the play from a Freudian perspective but observes, too, that Shaw's emphasis on female sexuality went beyond Freud and that Freud objected to Shaw's "differing conceptions of womanhood." A much different approach to the play is taken by Albert Bermel (*ShawR*, 1975), who writes that because of the humor, in particular the "good-natured chaffing" in Shaw's play, "critics have continually failed to appreciate that his wit reaches below the lines and situations and character quirks: it saturates the play's very grain. Underlying the jesting is the super jest . . . ." A source study by David Bowman, "The Eugenicist's Handbook" (*ShawR*, 1975), examines the impact of Francis Galton and Karl Pearson on Shaw's eugenic ideas.

John Bull's Other Island, the least performed of the major plays (other than *Methuselah*), also remains the least written about, although Harold Ferrar, in "The Caterpillar and the Gracehoper: Bernard Shaw's *John Bull's Other Island*" (*Éire*, 1980), sees in the play "a complicated and passionate vision of Ireland." Correcting misconceptions about audience and critical response to *John Bull* in Ireland over the years, Nicholas Grene in "*John Bull's Other Island*: At Home and Abroad" (*ShawR*, 1980) demonstrates that the play, although originally rejected by Yeats for the Abbey Theatre, has been more popular and more often produced in Ireland than in London.

Major Barbara remains the most attractive drama to Shaw scholars and critics. Among source studies, by far the most provocative is Sidney

P. Albert's "The Lord's Prayer and *Major Barbara*" (*Shaw*, 1981), which suggests that Shaw's use of the Lord's Prayer is only one instance of his appropriating religious phraseology for his own purposes. And indeed Albert persuades us that the Lord's Prayer can be seen as an intentional and ironic gloss on the play. W. T. Jewkes (*ShawR*, 1978) examines how profoundly the Mephistophelean aspect of Andrew Undershaft is indebted to Goethe, whom Shaw admired greatly. Finally, Norma Nutter (*ShawR*, 1979) contends that in *Major Barbara* Shaw illustrates Marx's concept of "false consciousness," defined as "a belief system derived from an individual's social position rather than from social and economic reality."

The meaning of the play continues to tantalize critics, and clearly the work has many dimensions. In "Logic and Religion in *Major Barbara*" (*MD*, 1978), Stuart E. Baker attempts a synthesis of meanings, explaining that the play, rather than being "confused or contradictory as many have claimed . . . , is a marvel of logical consistency, amazingly compact in its thorough dramatic exposition of Shaw's philosophy"; it is also "a profoundly religious play, and Major Barbara is not its only saint." J. Percy Smith (*ESC*, 1978) also attempts to solve the critical difficulties of the work, concluding that *Major Barbara* approaches "Euripidean tragedy. Given the materials with which he had chosen to work and his deep perplexity over the central moral problem of the play, not even Shaw, with all his zestful creativity and rhetoric, could turn it convincingly to comedy." Bernard F. Dukore's *Money and Politics in Ibsen, Shaw and Brecht*, cited earlier, is most useful on the money basis of society in *Major Barbara*, while Ken A. Baskin's "Undershaft's Challenge and the Future of the Race" (*ShawR*, 1978) draws parallels between Shaw's eugenic ideas in the play and Robert Ardrey's theories in *African Genesis* (1961).

The prewar plays before *Pygmalion* have been examined rather lightly. In *Fabian Feminist*, Michael Weimer's "*Press Cuttings* and Women's Suffrage" puts the play into historical context. (Shaw did indeed have censorship problems because of his thinly veiled references to living politicians.) F. P. W. McDowell, in "Shaw's Abrasive View of Edwardian Civilization in *Misalliance*" (*ShawR*, 1980, rev. from *CVE*, 1979), sees a steady ironic vision informing the play and observes that it is "one of Shaw's salient qualities as a dramatist in this play to inculcate some of his values through somewhat dubious spokesmen. Each of Shaw's figures has his or her moments of insight without ceasing to be limited and amusing to the spectator." The only study worth citing of another play of the period, David Matual's "*The Shewing-Up of Blanco Posnet* and Tolstoy's *The Power of Darkness*: Dramatic Kinship and Theological Opposition" (*Shaw*, 1981), suggests that Shaw's play echoes Tolstoy's "in the details of its plot and setting," although "its theological orientation underscores the basic and irreconcilable difference between Shaw and the Russian moralist." *Androcles and the Lion*, as mentioned earlier, is referred to in Harold Brooks's essay on Shelley influences. Otherwise the only look at the play to record is Susan Stone-Blackburn's essay (*ShawR*, 1978), which examines how Shaw turned the legend as told by Aulus Gellius into philosophic farce, satirizing at the same time contemporary religious melodrama. The legend becomes the frame for a discussion play about concepts of salvation.

Influence studies continue to complicate the intellectual backgrounds of *Pygmalion*, as they have ever since one critic looked behind the titular myth to see the myth of Cinderella and another suggested an episode in Smollett's novel *Peregrine Pickle*. Michael Goldberg's "Shaw's *Pygmalion*: The Reworking of *Great Expectations*" (*ShawR*, 1979) sees a Pygmalion-Galatea parallel in the Magwitch-Pip relationship and views the ending of *Pygmalion* as "a creative criticism of the ending of *Great Expectations*." E. F. Briden's "James's Miss Churm: Another of Eliza's Prototypes?" (*ShawR*, 1976) examines a character in James's short story "The Real Thing" (1892); while Sara Moore Putzell, in "Another Source for *Pygmalion*: G. B. S. and Mrs. Braddon" (*ShawR*, 1979), points to the novel *Our Adversary* (1909, just before the play was written). There Kate Lurgan is rescued from slum life and slum dialect by the Pygmalion figure Julian Danyell; he falls in love with her but so transforms her that she marries a lord, who sees the changed Kate as no different in "outward grace" from the daughter of an earl. Timothy Vesonder in *Fabian Feminist* points out that the core of both the Pygmalion myth and the Cinderella folktale is the transformation, not the marriage, which would warp the dramatic focus and merely have Eliza "trade masters—poverty and vulgarity for Higgins." Another perspective is provided in Hugo Beardsmore's "A Sociolinguistic Interpretation of *Pygmalion*" (*ES*, 1979), which reminds Shaw's audience, "It is language which is at the very core of the action of *Pygmalion* and indeed it would be difficult to give any other credible interpretation of the theme of this play than that of the relationship between code, personality and social class." Finally, Alan Jay Lerner's memoir, *The Street Where I Live* (1978), furnishes sidelights on reinterpretations of the play that occurred during the conception and production of *My Fair Lady* (1956).

Heartbreak House is rapidly approaching *Major Barbara*'s attractiveness to exegetes. Martin Quinn's "The Dickensian Presence in *Heartbreak House*" (*ShawR*, 1977) ranges through *Bleak House, Dombey and Son, David Copperfield, Oliver Twist, Little Dorrit*, and *Hard Times* for evidence of the usefulness of Dickens to Shaw; and Joseph Frank, in "Internal vs. External Combustion: Dickens's *Bleak House* and [Shaw's] *Heartbreak House*" (*ShawR*, 1977), sees further evidence of the pervasive impact of Dickens. Sally Peters Vogt (*MD*, 1978) views *Heartbreak House* as a statement on the future of England in two metaphors—the ship of state and the ship of fools. The relationships of these tropes to each other and to the literal action of the play become keys to meaning. Rhoda Nathan (*MD*, 1978) takes the idea that an insecure man might objectify his fear in a belief in malign external forces and suggests that Shaw uses this understanding for his setting and characters, who include "demon daughters" and a captain who allegedly sold his soul to the devil and married a "witch of Zanzibar." Anne Wright, in "Shaw's Burglars: *Heartbreak House* and *Too True to Be Good*" (*ShawR*, 1980), argues that Shaw saw burglars as symbolic of those classes who live on unearned income and thus represent the worst aspects of capitalist society. Fred E. Stockholder (*ShawR*, 1976) analyzes the play's thought as deriving from the philosophical pessimism not only of Nietzsche but also of Schopenhauer, while Thomas R. Whitaker, in "Dreaming the Music," a section of his *Fields of Play in Modern Drama* (1977), elicits meaning from the work's performance qualities, seeing a paradox of "rhetorical puppets" with "a surprisingly rich vitality." Ina Rae Hark (*DR*, 1978–79) sees evidences of Shaw's continuing self-satire, more obvious in earlier plays like *Doctor's Dilemma* and *Fanny's First Play* but turned inward more mordantly in *Heartbreak House*, befitting its grim rejection of much in prewar Shavianism, particularly its quasi-utopianism.

Back to Methuselah continues to interest science fiction advocates as well as its expected audience. John R. Pfeiffer's *Back to Methuselah* entry in the encyclopedic four-volume *Survey of Science Fiction Literature* (vol. 1, 1979) emphasizes the science fiction aspects, while two other essays suggest the play's continuing science fiction impact. John Aquino's "Shaw and C. S. Lewis's Space Trilogy" (*ShawR*, 1975) maintains that Lewis, despite his dislike of Shaw, was indebted to *Methuselah*, while composer Michael Tippett's "*Back to Methuselah* and *The Ice Break*" (*ShawR*, 1978) acknowledges that *Heartbreak House* and, especially, the last play in the *Methuselah* cycle influenced his opera. Warren Smith (*ShawR*, 1975) analyzes *The Tragedy of an Elderly Gentleman*, the fourth in the cycle, and death by "discouragement" (Shaw's term), basing his perspective on Alvin Toffler's concept of "future shock," while Joseph Frank (*ShawR*, 1976) sees the bleak *Tragedy* as Sophoclean in its grandeur, Shaw's *Oedipus at Colonus*. Two literary perspectives are Fred D. Crawford's "Shaw among the Houyhnhnms" (*ShawR*, 1976), which sees the *Tragedy*—clearly of increasing interest to scholars and critics—as Shaw's equivalent to the fourth part of Swift's *Gulliver's Travels*, a commentary on the inferiority of contemporary man; and Valli Rao's "*Back to Methuselah*: A Blakean Interpretation" (*Shaw*, 1981), which continues her immense study in progress of the profound Blakean impact on Shaw's work—an influence that Shaw himself acknowledged but that has remained until recently largely unexplored. (An earlier portion of this work is cited under *Mrs Warren's Profession*; Daniel Leary, it should be noted, examined *Heartbreak House* through a Blakean lens in *MD*, 1972.) Another essay with a philosophical approach is Harry Gershenowitz's "Bernard Shaw's Life Force" (*Religious Humanism*, 1979), which suggests that Shaw "interposes the meanings of biological need with the psychological concept of *wish*. . . . The poetic license taken by the artist is too often accepted by the general audience as historic truth firmly rooted in scientific thought. At some point the poetic imagination must be measured against and distinguished from scientific theory."

Little evidence of current research on *Saint Joan* exists, perhaps because the play seems to be a straightforward chronicle. William Searle's *The Saint and the Skeptics: Joan of Arc in the Work of Mark Twain, Anatole France and Bernard Shaw* (1976) elaborates on the work of comparison that Shaw began himself in his preface. S. Weintraub's

"The Genesis of *Saint Joan*" (*LWU*, 1977), an updating and extension of his preface to the Bobbs-Merrill edition of *Joan* (1971), analyzes the creative gestation of the plav from Shaw's earliest interest in his future heroine to early intimations of her in his work. Further augmented in Weintraub's *The Unexpected Shaw*, this study has been followed by Brian Tyson's *The Story of Shaw's Saint Joan* (1982), which analyzes the play's composition from the surviving shorthand manuscripts. M. A. Cohen (*ShawR*, 1977) contends that Shaw's handling of Cauchon in the trial scene is historically false and that the character is idealized—although more a "villain" than Shaw will allow—to permit him to act tragically in the passion of his righteousness. John A. Bertolini's "Imagining *Saint Joan*" (*Shaw*, 1983) analyzes subtleties of meaning in the play's visual values.

Few later plays and playlets have been examined in depth in recent years, although evidence suggests that such a trend began in the 1960s. Myron Matlaw in *Jitta's Atonement: Shaw's Adaptation and the Translation of* [Siegfried] *Trebitsch's Original* (1979) misleads in title and subtitle, since the monograph is actually a translation of Trebitsch's original *Frau Gittas Sühne*, with a preface, and does not include Shaw's very free version. Warren S. Smith's "The Search for Good Government: *The Apple Cart, On the Rocks*, and *Geneva*" (*ShawR*, 1978) picks up a line of study that will inevitably be pursued further—that few questions were as important to Shaw as "the Platonic one of what constitutes good government. That is perhaps why until the very late years all his plays skirt the problem." Another late play is examined for Shaw's developing religious thought by Daniel Leary in "*Too True to Be Good* and Shaw's Romantic Synthesis: A Religion for Our Times" (*Shaw*, 1981). (W. S. Smith's essay on Dame Laurentia, *Shaw*, 1981, mentioned earlier, also concerns Shaw's religious attitudes at the time *Too True* was written.) Another Leary exploration of a late Shaw work is "Shaw versus Shakespeare: The Refinishing of *Cymbeline*" (*ETJ*, 1978), which uses the act of "refinishing" as "a paradigm of Shaw's love/hate struggle with Shakespeare, a struggle that profoundly influenced all Shaw's major plays." Finally, on Shaw and Shakespeare there is "Determinism and Voluntarism in Shaw and Shakespeare," by Friedhelm Denninghaus (*ShawR*, 1976), translated by John J. Weisert from Denninghaus' *Die dramatische Konzeption George Bernard Shaws* (Stuttgart, 1971). Shaw's characters, Denninghaus contends, "do not make history but are shaped by history," while Shakespeare "conceives of the social action as the direct consequence of personal actions."

7. Criticism in Languages Other than English

Since 1974, the growing number of works on Shaw in languages other than English indicates a continuing interest that reaches beyond theatrical performance. Some are general-purpose introductory studies meant to put Shaw in the perspective of the national culture, such as Anna Obratsova's *Bernard Shou i evropeiskaia-teatralnaia kultura na rubezhe deviatnadtsatogo-dvadtsatogo vekov* (Moscow, 1974), Karl-

Heinz Schoeps' *Bertolt Brecht und Bernard Shaw* (Bonn, 1974), Matahiko Ichikawa's *Warau Tetsujin Bānādo Shô* (Tokyo, 1975), and Asela Rodriguez Seda de Laguna's *Shaw en el mundo hispanico* (Puerto Rico, 1981). Others concern themselves with specific aspects of Shaw, such as the sociolinguistic study by Ernst H. Andrecht, *Sprachsoziologische Aspekte in der dramatischen Sprachgestaltung Bernard Shaws* (Frankfurt, 1976). Jean-Claude Amalric's study, with extensive bibliographical apparatus, *Bernard Shaw: Du Reformateur victorien au prophete edouardien* (Paris, 1977), reveals its perspective in its title, as does Norbert Greiner's *Idealism und Realism im Frühwerk George Bernard Shaws* (Heidelberg, 1977). The impact of Shaw on Hermann Sudermann is analyzed in Walter T. Rix's "Shaw und Sudermann: Von der Gemeinsamkeit der Dramatiker und ihrer unerquicklichen Stücke beim Eintritt ins 20. Jahrhundert," in *Hermann Sudermann: Werk und Wirkung* (ed. W. T. Rix, Würzburg, 1980).

A collection of critical essays on Shaw has also appeared in Germany, *George Bernard Shaw*, edited by Kurt Otten and Gerd Rohmann (Darmstadt, 1978). Although the collection includes reprinted extracts in German from earlier German scholars, ranging from Julius Bab (1910) and Johan Huizinga (1930) to Friedhelm Denninghaus (1971) and Hansrudolph Kamer (1973), as well as extracts from familiar English-language pieces previously cited in this review, it includes others less familiar to English-language scholars. These are "Die religiose Bedeutung des Evolutionsgedankens bei Bernard Shaw," by Alfred Dutli (1950); "Sündenfall und übermensch in G. B. Shaws *Back to Methuselah*," by Rüdiger Reitemeier (1966); and "Shaws metabiologisches Testament in *Saint Joan*," by Gerd Rohmann (1976).

8. Influence and Reputation

Although Shaw's influence on the present generation of playwrights, if one judges by their remarks or by contemporary studies of their works, is receding, the evidence in the foregoing pages shows that he maintains his status as a twentieth-century master and remains much published, much examined and reexamined, and much read. Further, biographical evidence emerging from studies of his contemporaries and immediate successors confirms that his influence among his peers was profound. The many productions of his plays in the 1970s and into the 1980s, including a television dramatization of an 1881 novel that sank almost without trace on first publication, suggest the intrinsic liveliness of his work—as he put it, the jam that made the pill go down.

The familiar Shavian paradox still inhibits understanding of his work. As Robert Whitman has put it in his *Shaw and the Play of Ideas* (1977), Shaw "embodied his ideas in such delightfully witty essays and plays that there has been a very real danger . . . that the wisdom would get lost in the fun. . . . Shaw as thinker has, for both critics and readers, had to play a somewhat sour second fiddle to Shaw the comic draftsman, Shaw the pre-absurdist, Shaw the post-Victorian, and of course Shaw the writer of musical comedy." The writings surveyed here, encompassing only a half-dozen years of research on Shaw, suggest that while Shaw the thinker is indeed being taken seriously, all the other Shaws that were facets of his life and work continue to exercise their fascination. The self-described "pantomime ostrich" discovered in life that the animal, once invented, was difficult to conceal. Its shade is almost as conspicuous.

W. B. YEATS

Richard J. Finneran

Yeats scholarship continues apace, upsetting the prophecy offered at the conclusion of the first review of research—that scholars and critics would delay publication until at least some of the major projects then (and still) in progress were published. At the same time, the late 1970s did not produce a vast amount of seminal scholarship, although there were some impressive works: to name but a few, an immensely useful bibliography of criticism, an important edition of the 1925 *A Vision*, and a brilliant study of Yeats and Jung. The 1980s seem destined to be characterized by editorial endeavors: the *Collected Letters*, a new Collected Edition of the major works, and a multivolume series of manuscript editions. The publication of the authorized biography about the middle of the decade should serve as an appropriate fulcrum for new avenues of study.

In what follows I cite numerous pre-1974 items previously overlooked (most of them brought to my attention by Jochum's *Classified Bibliography*) and most of the work published from 1975 through 1980, adding as many 1981 items as possible. Nevertheless, the listing is not intended to be complete, some quite minor contributions having been deliberately omitted and one or two having eluded my searches.

1. Bibliographies and Catalogs

PRIMARY BIBLIOGRAPHIES

The fullest supplement to the third edition of the Wade-Alspach *Bibliography of the Writings of W. B. Yeats* is section AB in Jochum's *Classified Bibliography* (cited below), which lists over 350 additions, including reprints and translations.

In "When Was Yeats First Published?" (*Éire*, 1967; *Irish Times*, 5 June 1965, with the text of one poem provided), Micheál Ó hAodha argues that eleven poems published from April 1882 to July 1883 in *Hibernia* (Dublin) under the initial "Y" were the work of Yeats. The supporting evidence is not compelling. Taketosh Furomoto (*TLS*, 4 Jan. 1974) reveals that the *Irish Monthly* for February 1888 includes a lengthy quotation from Yeats's lost review in the *Gael* of Katharine Tynan's *Shamrocks*. Richard J. Finneran (*IUR*, 1978) demonstrates that a notice about Wilfrid Scawen Blunt in the London *Times* (20 Jan. 1914), assigned to Yeats by Wade and included in *Uncollected Prose*, is probably the work of Richard Aldington.

SECONDARY BIBLIOGRAPHIES

K. P. S. Jochum's monumental *W. B. Yeats: A Classified Bibliography of Criticism Including Additions to Allan Wade's* A Bibliography of the Writings of W. B. Yeats *and a Section on the Irish Literary and Dramatic Revival* (1978) lists over six thousand items of Yeats criticism, the only exclusion being the Japanese material cited in Shotaro Oshima's *W. B. Yeats and Japan* (1965). Jochum has divided the entries into ten broad categories and forty-three sections; numerous cross-references and eight indexes are also provided. About half of the items are annotated, but there is relatively little evaluation. The compilation is complete through 1972, with numerous items added from 1973 and 1974 (not all of these are included in the indexes). Since the classification necessarily entailed some arbitrary decisions, readers should carefully study Jochum's introduction and become familiar with the *Classified Bibliography* before they attempt to use it. Given the scope of the work, the errors and omissions are negligible indeed. Nevertheless, as Jochum is continuing his project, he would be grateful to have any additions and corrections forwarded to him at the University of Bamberg. One publication overlooked by Jochum was the *Ethical Record* (New York), in which George Monteiro (*PBSA*, 1976) has discovered five relevant items.

Useful selected lists of Yeats criticism are provided by Jon Stallworthy in "A Short Guide to Yeats Studies" (*CS*, 1966) and by Ann Saddlemyer in "The Irish School," in *English Drama (Excluding Shakespeare): Select Bibliographical Guides* (ed. Stanley Wells, 1975). The sections on Yeats in Harry Krawitz, *A Post-Symbolist Bibliography* (1973), and in Frank L. Kersnowski, C. W. Spinks, and Laird Loomis, *A Bibliography of Modern Irish and Anglo-Irish Literature* (1976), are inaccurate, incomplete, and of little use. In *English Drama, 1900-1950: A Guide to Information Sources* (1977), E. H. Mikhail provides a selected list of primary and secondary bibliographies. In *A Research Guide to Modern Irish Dramatists* (1979), Mikhail offers a list of bibliographical guides and review articles. His fullest and possibly last listing is in *An Annotated Bibliography of Modern Anglo-Irish Drama* (1981). Some Yeats material is also cited by Charles A. Carpenter in *Modern British Drama* (1979) and by Alan R. Eager in *A Guide to Irish Bibliographical Material* (2nd ed., 1980).

Three of the four issues of the *Yeats Eliot Review* published to date have included selected and briefly annotated lists of Yeats criticism, one by Richard Driskill (1978) and the others by Al Kazuk (1979); the criteria for inclusion have not been explained.

The following essay reviews should be added to the list in the 1976 survey of research: Ronald Dunlop (*PAus*, 1965), Richard M. Kain (*SoR*, 1967), Peter Ure (*ES*, 1967), F. S. L. Lyons (*TLS*, 10 Oct. 1975), Geoffrey Thurley (*SoRA*, 1975), Edward Engelberg (*SR*, 1976), Donald Torchiana et al. (*JIL*, 1976), Gary T. Davenport (*SR*, 1977), Edward Engelberg (*NBR*, 1977), Richard J. Finneran (*Review*, Charlottesville, 1979), and Thomas Parkinson (*SoR*, 1979).

The publication of Brenda S. Webster's *Yeats: A Psychoanalytic Study* (1973) occasioned three essays that not only review Webster's work but also comment on the value of psychoanalytical criticism: Richard W. Noland, "Psychoanalysis and Yeats" (*HSL*, 1975); Richard P. Wheeler, "Yeats" (*AI*, 1975); and Claire Hahn, "Yeats Studies and the Parameters of Psychoanalytic Criticism" (*L&P*, 1976).

CATALOGS

The Huntington Library has a copy (HM 380599) of the mimeographed catalog of the exhibit of Yeats books held in January-February 1965 in the King's Library of the British Library. The exhibit was briefly noted in the October 1964 *News Supplement* of *BMQ* and in *TLS* ("Under Ben Bulben," 21 Jan. 1965). Of greater interest is Andrew B. Myers' "The Indomitable Irishry: A Checklist" (*Gazette of the Grolier Club*, Oct. 1966), a listing of an exhibit that included many unique Yeats items. Harvey Simmonds' *John Quinn: an Exhibition to Mark the Gift of the John Quinn Memorial Collection* (1968) includes a few Yeats items.

Michael B. Yeats's *"Something to Perfection Brought": The Cuala Press* (1976), issued in conjunction with an exhibition of the part of the James A. Healy collection acquired by Stanford University, reproduces and transcribes several interesting inscriptions by Yeats. The bulk of the Healy collection is found at Colby College and has been listed by Cheryl Abbott and J. Fraser Cocks III in *James Augustine Healy Collection of Nineteenth and Twentieth Century Irish Literature* (1978).

2. Editions

Richard J. Finneran and George Mills Harper are the general editors of a new eight-volume *Collected Edition of the Works of W. B. Yeats*, to include critical editions of the major works in the canon. The texts will be corrected by reference to manuscript materials, and all allusions and references will be annotated. Finneran's *The Poems of W. B. Yeats: A New Edition* (1983) will be the first volume.

In "Yeats in the Light of Day: The Text and Some Editions," in *Editing British and American Literature, 1880–1920* (ed. Eric W. Domville, 1976), Michael Sidnell provides a good discussion of the textual complexities in several works, emphasizing the problems encountered in *Memoirs* (ed. Denis Donoghue, 1972) and in the new edition of *The Secret Rose* (see below).

POETRY

The text of "On a Child's Death," dated 5 September 1893, was privately printed by Colin Smythe in 1978; the poem is written into Lady Gregory's copy of *Poems* (1899). The text of "The Watch-Fire," also probably written in the autumn of 1893, was published in *Poetry* (1980), with a note by Christina Hunt Mahony and Edward O'Shea; the lyric is found on what appears to be a proof sheet in the collection of Anne Yeats. In "The Composition and Final Text of W. B. Yeats's 'Crazy Jane on the King' " (*ICarbS*, 1981), Richard J. Finneran discusses the evolution of the poem and concludes that the final version is that written into Lady Gregory's copy of *Later Poems* (1922).

PROSE

The publication of *Memoirs* occasioned Jon Stallworthy's "An Irish Window: Remaking W. B. Yeats" (*Encounter*, Aug. 1974), less a review than a commentary on the unfolding design of *Autobiographies*. More strictly a review is Michael Hamburger's essay in *Art as Second Nature: Occasional Pieces 1950–74* (1975).

A supplement to *John Sherman and Dhoya* is provided by J. R. Mulryne in "Printer's Copy for Part of Volume Seven of the W. B. Yeats *Collected Works in Verse and Prose* (1908)" (*SB*, 1977), which notes that the Records Office of the Shakespeare Birthplace Trust has a set of marked pages from the second 1891 edition of *John Sherman*, used (with further revision) for the 1908 printing.

The Secret Rose, Stories by W. B. Yeats: A Variorum Edition (ed. Phillip L. Marcus, Warwick Gould, and Michael J. Sidnell, 1981) includes not only *The Secret Rose* stories proper but also "Rosa Alchemica," "The Tables of the Law," and "The Adoration of the Magi." The editors properly use the 1931–32 page proofs for the "Edition de Luxe" as their basic text; all variants are presented in notes. Useful appendixes include the text of "A Very Pretty Little Story" (a "folk" version of "The Binding of the Hair," from Lady Gregory's papers), and a listing of variants between the copy-text and *Mythologies* (1959). The allusions in the stories are not annotated. A new edition of *The Celtic Twilight* (introd. Kathleen Raine, 1981) reprints the text of *Mythologies* but also includes "The Four Winds of Desire," a story included only in the 1893 volume. Raine's introduction is only of passing interest, and no notes are provided.

In "Some Further Textual Problems in Yeats: *Ideas of Good and Evil*" (*PBSA*, 1977), Jon Lanham argues that *Essays and Introductions* provides the best copy-text for any new edition, even though such a choice would admittedly involve the retention of "all accidentals and corrections of grammar and quotations, even those demonstrably posthumous." The arguments in favor of such a hybrid edition are not persuasive.

The most important text to appear in the last few years is *A Critical Edition of Yeats's* A Vision *(1925)* (ed. George Mills Harper and Walter Kelly Hood, 1978). To a facsimile of the first edition the editors have appended over eighty pages of explanatory notes and a lengthy introduction that draws on the manuscript materials to chronicle precisely the process of composition. The edition provides significant new information on Yeats's career, such as the relationship of certain poems and plays to the Automatic Script, and goes a long way toward justifying the claim that "*A Vision* (both versions) may well be the most important work in the canon to the understanding of his art and thought if not his life." In "On Editing Yeats: The Text of *A Vision* (1937)" (*TSLL*, 1977), Richard J. Finneran outlines the textual problems in the second edition of the work and demonstrates that the claim of the 1956 American version to be "A Reissue with the Author's Final Revisions" was wishful thinking; at present the best text, though far from flawless, is the 1962 London edition.

In *Yeats on Yeats: The Last Introductions and the "Dublin" Edition* (1981), Edward Callan presents edited and annotated texts of the three 1937 introductions as well as an account of the Scribner Edition and a critical commentary on the "General Introduction for My Work." Callan does not draw on the proofs of the first printing of the essays in the Macmillan Archive in the British Library, and his editing is sometimes inconsistent. In particular, he prefers the first typescript of the "General Introduction" over the second typescript because the latter is not corrected by Yeats; however, the second typescript was apparently sent to Scribner's in 1937 as copy, and it is therefore likely that Yeats had dictated it, or read and approved it, or both.

The second edition (1977) of the new *Fairy and Folk Tales of Ireland* contains a list of sources by Mary Helen Thuente, adapted from her "Bibliography of W. B. Yeats's Sources for *Fairy and Folk Tales of the Irish Peasantry* and *Irish Fairy Tales*" (*IBl*, 1976). A new edition of *Representative Irish Tales* (1979) includes not only the 1891 collection of that title but also the introduction to *Stories from Carleton* (1889); Thuente provides a list of sources (with brief indications of Yeats's modifications) and a useful foreword discussing Yeats's aims in editing the collection.

In "A Yeats and George Moore Identification" (*N&Q*, 1978), T. P. Foley and Maud Ellmann have established that the "Father O'Donovan" cited by Yeats in his 5 March 1904 speech on Robert Emmet (included in *Uncollected Prose*) was Jeremiah O'Donovan, who published novels under the name "Gerald O'Donovan."

W. B. Yeats: Interviews and Recollections (ed. E. H. Mikhail, 1977) is a disappointing collection, another lost opportunity in Yeats studies. The editing is inadequate, with numerous allusions and references passed by in silence. Many of the standard anecdotes are told two or more times—often by the same writer—while other selections are awkwardly excerpted. The cross-referencing and indexing are faulty. It is difficult to see the logic of reprinting the sole interview found in *Uncollected Prose*

when so many others remain fugitive. One that might well remain in that
state is W. C. Barnwell, "James Dickey on Yeats: An Interview" (*SoR*,
1977).

*Nobel Lectures Including Presentation Speeches and Laureates'
Biographies: Literature, 1901–67* (ed. Horst Frenz, 1969) includes the
only printing of Yeats's "Acceptance."

3. Correspondence

The *Collected Letters of W. B. Yeats* has been reorganized: John
Kelly remains as general editor, with other scholars joining him on the individual volumes. The first installment, covering the years to 1895 and
edited by Kelly and Eric Domville, is scheduled to appear in 1983. The
project is now likely to run to twelve or thirteen volumes.

In "The Friendship of Yeats and Katharine Tynan" (*FortR*, 1953),
Pamela Hinkson includes numerous quotations from unpublished Yeats
letters and offers an account of the relationship. Four letters from Yeats
are in *Agnes Tobin: Letters, Translations, Poems* (1958), in one of which
Yeats calls Tobin "the greatest poet of America since Whitman."

Of more significance is Ezra Pound, "Letters to William Butler
Yeats" (ed. C. F. Terrell, *Antaeus*, 1976), which includes nine letters
from Pound to Yeats, one from Yeats to Pound, and four from Pound
to Mrs. Yeats. Unfortunately, the material is sketchily edited, and there
is no indication that three of the Pound letters were previously published
in *Shenandoah* (1953). In " 'Intellect and Imagination Stand Face to
Face': Yeats's Correspondence with T. Sturge Moore" (*ArQ*, 1976),
Adele M. Dalsimer provides a running commentary on the
correspondence, stressing Yeats's attempt to assert "a monistic vision of
life." The essasy seems an unnecessary exercise, especially since it
ignores previous accounts of the topic, particularly G. S. Fraser's in the
Yeats issue of *Phoenix* (1965).

Letters to W. B. Yeats (ed. Richard J. Finneran, George Mills
Harper, and William M. Murphy, 1977) includes five hundred fully annotated letters from more than 150 correspondents. There is a generous
sampling of letters from Edmund Dulac, Maud Gonne, Annie Horniman, George W. Russell, William Sharp, and John Butler Yeats, as
well as from several occult associates. The editors excluded all letters
previously published in full. *The Correspondence of Robert Bridges and
W. B. Yeats* (ed. Richard J. Finneran, 1976) presents the complete ex-
change of letters, including two from Yeats not in the Wade collection.
Appendixes provide the 1897 text of Yeats's "Mr. Robert Bridges" and a
listing of each poet's collection of the other's books. The full text of one
Bridges letter that was available to the editor only in an incomplete
transcription will be included in Donald E. Stanford's forthcoming edition of Bridges' correspondence.

4. Biographies and Related Studies

F. S. L. Lyons remains at work on the authorized biography.

A useful introductory sketch of Yeats's life is provided in Frank Tuohy's well-written and well-illustrated *Yeats* (1976). Unfortunately, the work contains a number of factual errors, and one must overlook Tuohy's several prejudices, which include an animus against politically active women. Thus he describes Maud Gonne as "a virago who sweeps into rebellion on some obscure undertow of father fixation or nursery jealousy" and argues that Con Markiewicz "was using Ireland's struggle to work out some trauma of heredity or upbringing."

The 1979 edition of Richard Ellmann's *Yeats: The Man and the Masks* includes an added preface that offers new information, particularly on Mrs. Yeats (a slightly different version of the preface was published in *NYRB*, 17 May 1979, as "At the Yeatses"). Mabel Dickinson is named as the author of the infamous pregnancy scare of 1913. Because Ellmann's book is a seminal work, it is regrettable that the new preface is not documented and that the the notes of the 1948 edition have not been brought into conformity with contemporary texts.

In *Yeats: The Poetics of the Self* (1979), David Lynch draws on the work of Heinz Kohut (*The Analysis of the Self*, 1971; *The Restoration of the Self*, 1977) to argue that in Yeats "the story of the poet" "is above all a story of the vicissitudes of self-love" and thus "aesthetic psychology is the psychology not of the oedipus complex but of narcissism." These ideas are then traced both in Yeats's life and in selected works. In the concluding "Art and Madness," Lynch tries to answer such questions as "[W]as Yeats's creativity pathological?" and "Should his creativity be regarded as symptomatic or therapeutic?" This work is arguably a more successful example of its kind than Brenda S. Webster's effort (see p. 87), but it is still highly selective in its choice of materials and rigorously reductive in its interpretation of them. The same shortcomings are found to an even greater degree in the chapter "Yeats and Synge: The Cuchulain Complex," in David Wyatt's *Prodigal Sons: A Study in Authorship and Authority* (1980). Simply ignoring the work of Webster, Wyatt finds a "family romance" in the relationship of Yeats, Lady Gregory, and Synge as father, mother, and son. Thus, in this account, Yeats attains his maturity through the defense of Synge's *Playboy* in 1907.

In "W. B. Yeats and William Sharp: The Archer Vision" (*ELN*, 1969), William F. Halloran establishes that Yeats had described his 1896 vision of an archer well before Sharp completed his story "The Archer." He argues that Yeats chose to overlook the possibility that Sharp was misleading him about the originality of the story because Yeats wanted confirmation of a supernatural vision.

The sketch of Yeats in Bernard Share's *Irish Lives: Biographies of Fifty Famous Irish Men and Women* (1971) is elementary. James G. Nelson's *The Early Nineties: A View from the Bodley Head* (1971) includes some brief comments on Yeats and the Rhymers' Club, and *The Oxford Book of Literary Anecdotes* (ed. James Sutherland, 1975) retells a few of the familiar tales. Kazumi Yano's "Miscellaneous Notes on W.

B. Yeats" (*Yeats Soc. of Japan Annual Report*, 1976) corrects some minor errors in the biographies by Hone and Jeffares. More useful is Anthony Olden's "A Storm in a Chalice" (*Library Rev.*, 1976), which comments on Yeats's involvement with the short-lived *To-morrow*.

The well-written section on Yeats in Leon Edel's "Portrait of the Artist as an Old Man" (*ASch*, 1977) covers familiar ground, and Virginia D. Pruitt's "Yeats and the Steinach Operation" (*AI*, 1977) contributes little new except for the identification of the surgeon as Norman Haire. In "Blindness in Yeats" (*YER*, 1979), Paul Cohen discusses Yeats's eye problems and briefly traces the use of blindness in his works, concluding that "his most profound consideration of blindness and its implications came in the speculative poems of his middle age." More interesting is Elizabeth Heine's "W. B. Yeats' Map in His Own Hand" (*Biography*, 1978), which analyzes in detail the natal horoscope now at the University of Texas, Austin, and concludes that Yeats "could never, in astrological terms, expect a better time for marriage than 1917" and that "if 1917 was the year for his marriage, October was the month."

Hilary Pyle's "Men of Destiny—Jack B. Yeats and W. B. Yeats: The Background and the Symbols" (*Studies*, 1977) is an effective comparative study, noting the lack of much personal contact between the two during their mature years but finding parallels in such matters as "the importance of memory images," "the love of Sligo," and "their devotion to the idea of an Ireland free from foreign domination." In contrast, James Lovic Allen's "All in the Family: Artistic Interaction between W. B. Yeats and His Siblings" (*YER*, 1978) adds little to *Prodigal Father* (cited directly below) and considers it "strange that there was not greater artistic interaction between the Yeats siblings . . . in their individually full and productive lives."

William M. Murphy's lavishly illustrated *Prodigal Father: The Life of John Butler Yeats (1839-1922)* (1978) is a work of monumental and almost impeccable scholarship. Drawing heavily on manuscript materials, Murphy is able to present in great detail not only John Butler Yeats's life but also the various contexts in which that life took place. Unfortunately, *Prodigal Father* is so biased in favor of the father that the son almost becomes one of the villains of the piece, and few opportunities to criticize either Yeats's relationship with his father or Yeats's works are passed by. *Reveries over Childhood and Youth*, for instance, is attacked for lacking "even a single expression of love or gratitude from a son on whom the father had lavished so much care and affection and energy," even though Murphy's narrative itself clearly shows why the earliest memories in *Reveries* are not of Yeats's parents but of his grandparents. Thus, although *Prodigal Father* is essential reading for any advanced student of Yeats, it must be approached with caution. James Olney's essay review "Father and Son: J. B. Yeats and W. B. Yeats" (*SAQ*, 1980) offers a useful contrast between the father's choice of perfection of the "life" and the son's of perfection of the "work." More strictly on the father himself are Robert Gordon's *John Butler Yeats and John Sloan: The Records of a Friendship* (1978), a good account of the relationship, and George Bornstein's "The Antinomial

Structure of John Butler Yeats's *Early Memories: Some Chapters of Autobiography*," in *Approaches to Victorian Autobiography* (ed. George Landow, 1979), which touches on some of the parallels between the father and the son and also suggests that "the implied hero of *Early Memories* is William Butler Yeats."

Samuel Levenson's rather tedious *Maud Gonne* (1976), subtitled in the English edition *A Biography of Yeats's Beloved*, does little more than bring together the available information. A better biography is Nancy Cardozo's *Lucky Eyes and a High Heart: The Life of Maud Gonne* (1978). Although, like all other scholars, she was denied access to the letters from Gonne to Yeats held by the MacBride family, she does draw much more extensively than Levenson does on Gonne's letters to John Quinn (in the New York Public Library) and to Ethel Mannin (in the National Library of Ireland). Cardozo argues that Gonne's separation from John MacBride was precipitated by his drunken attack (rape?) on her illegitimate half-sister, Eileen Wilson. Unfortunately, Cardozo neither carefully documents her book nor addresses herself to the discrepancies between her work and Levenson's. A necessary supplement is Conrad Balliet's useful "The Lives—and Lies—of Maud Gonne" (*Éire*, 1979), which attempts to "present new, accurate information" and to correct some errors in both Levenson and Cardozo. For example, while Maud Gonne's first child is identified by Levenson as a girl, born on 24 May 1889, and by Cardozo as a boy, born in early 1891, Balliet presents convincing evidence that, although Cardozo is correct about the sex, the child was born on 11 January 1890 (d. 31 Aug. 1891). Likewise, Balliet establishes the birth dates of Maud Gonne (21 Dec. 1866) and Iseult Gonne (6 Aug. 1894), and he argues that both the episode between MacBride and Wilson (or Iseult?) and a physical liaison between Yeats and Maud Gonne in 1909 remain unproved. Balliet's "Micheál MacLiammóir Recalls Maud Gonne MacBride" (*JIL*, 1977) includes numerous references to Yeats and Gonne. In "Maud Gonne's Favorite Poem" (*AN&Q*, 1979), Balliet establishes that it was not "The Two Trees," as sometimes thought, but "Red Hanrahan's Song about Ireland."

Ann Saddlemyer's "Augusta Gregory, Irish Nationalist: 'After all, what is wanted but a hag and a voice?' " (in *Myth and Reality in Irish Literature*, ed. Joseph Ronsley, 1979) offers some brief comments on the relationship between Yeats and Lady Gregory. Mary Lou Stevenson's "Lady Gregory and Yeats: Symbiotic Creativity" (*JRUL*, 1978) is marred by amateurish psychoanalysis; it also presents a very one-sided picture of the relationship, arguing that each was using the other to fill personal needs—Yeats, for example, provided Lady Gregory with "emotional cover"—and that the friendship "was not, in itself, a thing of beauty." *Robert Gregory, 1881–1918: A Centenary Tribute with a Foreword by His Children* (ed. Colin Smythe, 1981) reprints Yeats's four poems about Gregory as well as his *Observer* notice.

Richard J. Finneran's *The Olympian and the Leprechaun: W. B. Yeats and James Stephens* (1978) draws on unpublished materials to trace the relationship, demonstrating that it was closest during the period 1912–15. Appendixes list the books by each writer in the other's library and also provide the texts of two uncollected essays by Stephens on Yeats and of Yeats's speech presenting the Polignac Prize to Stephens in 1913 (omitted from *Uncollected Prose*).

Paul Morgan's "Arthur Henry Bullen (1857–1920) and the Shakespeare Head Press," in *Frank Sidgwick's Diary and Other Material Relating to A. H. Bullen, and the Shakespeare Head Press at Stratford-upon-Avon* (1975), includes some information on Yeats's dealings with Bullen, such as the fact that Annie Horniman's subsidy of the 1908 *Collected Works* amounted to £3,455. In *Florence Farr: Bernard Shaw's "New Woman"* (1975), Josephine Johnson comments on Farr's relationship with Yeats and includes some quotations from unpublished correspondence; Johnson is hesitant about accepting the existence of a liaison between Farr and Yeats. Colin White's *Edmund Dulac* (1976) provides a useful account of Yeats's friendship with Dulac and includes some interesting photographs. Another relationship is well covered by Joan Coldwell in "Pamela Colman Smith and the Yeats Family" (*CJIS*, 1977); readers interested in Smith's artistic achievement should consult Melinda Boyd Parsons, *To All Believers: The Art of Pamela Colman Smith* (1975).

Some information about Yeats is included in Ian Carruthers' "A Translation of Fifteen Pages of Michio Ito's autobiography *Utsukushiku Naru Kyoshitsu*" (*CJIS*, 1976). More useful is Helen Caldwell's *Michio Ito: The Dancer and His Dances* (1977), which offers a scholarly account of Ito's contacts with Yeats in connection with *At the Hawk's Well*. Caldwell refutes the widely circulated anecdote that Ito practiced the dance of the hawk in front of a cage at the London zoo.

Yeats is briefly mentioned in Sandra Jobson Darroch, *Ottoline: The Life of Lady Ottoline Morrell* (1975), and eight photographs of him are included in Ottoline Morrell, *Lady Ottoline's Album* (ed. Carolyn G. Heilbrun, 1976). A more important friendship is discussed by Constance Babington Smith in *John Masefield: A Life* (1978). Smith argues that after Masefield met Yeats in 1900, "the conviction that he [Masefield] must henceforth be the Irish poet's disciple overwhelmed him in the same way that the discovery of Chaucer had overwhelmed him four years earlier."

There is little new information on Yeats in J. B. Lyons' *Oliver St. John Gogarty, the Man of Many Talents: A Biography* (1980), though two letters from Yeats are included (the first is misdated 1932 instead of 1929). Some brief remarks on Yeats's friendship with T. Sturge Moore are in Sylvia Legge's *Affectionate Cousins: T. Sturge Moore and Marie Appia* (1980). In "William Force Stead's Friendship with Yeats and Eliot" (*MR*, 1980), George Mills Harper draws on unpublished correspondence between Yeats and Stead to trace the relationship. Harper's *W. B. Yeats and W. T. Horton: The Record of an Occult Friendship* (1980), a model of precise scholarship, chronicles the long friendship and shows the influence of Horton on Yeats's thought and on the genesis and development of *A Vision*. The full texts of all Horton's letters to Yeats are provided; Yeats's letters to Horton are either quoted or summarized. Appendixes provide biographies of Horton and of Audrey Locke.

MEMOIRS

The enlarged edition of Max Beerbohm's *Mainly on the Air* (1957) includes a 1954 broadcast, "First Meetings with W. B. Yeats"; Beerbohm notes that "I felt always rather uncomfortable, as though I had submitted myself to a mesmerist who somehow didn't mesmerise me." Ninette de Valois has offered some interesting reminiscences of Yeats in *Come Dance with Me: A Memoir 1898-1956* (1957) and *Step by Step: The Formation of an Establishment* (1977); there is some further information in G. M. Pinciss' "A Dancer for Mr. Yeats" (*ETJ*, 1969). V. C. Clinton-Baddeley recalls Yeats's BBC broadcasts in "Reading Poetry with W. B. Yeats" (*LonM*, 1957). In "Players and the Painted Stage: The Autobiography of Ria Mooney," edited by Val Mulkerns (*George Spelvin's Theatre Book*, 1978), the Abbey actress offers some memories of Yeats and also provides the text of an unpublished poem, "The Hills of Mourne," and of a letter from Yeats. *Lady Gregory's Journals, Volume One: Books One to Twenty-Nine, 10 October 1916-24 February 1925* (ed. Daniel J. Murphy, 1978) contains one letter from Yeats and excerpts from several others, as well as scattered anecdotes.

Briefer reminiscences of some interest include Alvin Langdon Coburn, *Men of Mark* (1913) and *Alvin Langdon Coburn, Photographer: An Autobiography* (ed. Helmut Gernsheim and Alison Gernsheim, 1966); Henry W. Nevinson, *Changes and Chances* (1923); John Masefield, *Recent Prose* (1930), *A Book of Prose Selections* (1950), and *So Long to Learn* (1952); Edgar Jepson, *Memories of a Victorian* (1933); Louis MacNeice, *I Crossed the Minch* (1938) and *The Strings Are False: An Unfinished Autobiography* (1966); Matheson Lang, *Mr. Wu Looks Back: Thoughts and Memories* (1940); Ernest Rhys, *Wales England Wed: An Autobiography* (1940); Richard Aldington, *Life for Life's Sake: A Book of Reminiscences* (1941); Hugh Kingsmill, *The Progress of a Biographer* (1949; rpt. *The Best of Hugh Kingsmill*, ed. Michael Holroyd, 1970); Stephen Spender, *World within World: The Autobiography* (1951); R. F. Rattray, "Yeats and Vacher Burch" (*TLS*, 23 Sept. 1955); Lennox Robinson, *I Sometimes Think* (1956); Sean O'Faolain, *Vive Moi!* (1964); Herbert Howarth, "The Week of the Banquet" (*LonM*, 1965); Eileen J. Garrett, *Many Voices: The Autobiography of a Medium* (1968); Margaret Webster, *The Same Only Different: Five Generations of a Great Theatre Family* (1969); Shirley Rose, "Dorothy Richardson Recalls Yeats" (*Éire*, 1972); Basil Bunting, "Yeats Recollected" (*Agenda*, 1974); Frank O'Connor, *A Gambler's Throw: Memories of W. B. Yeats* (1975); Eric Robertson Dodds, *Missing Persons: An Autobiography* (1977); and Ben Iden Payne, *A Life in a Wooden O: Memoirs of the Theatre* (1977).

Though he is not named, Yeats appears in Richard Le Galliene's *Young Lives* (1898) as "a young Irish poet who, in the intervals of his raising the devil, writes very beautiful lyrics that he may well have learned from the faeries. It is his method to seem mad on magic and such things."

ICONOGRAPHIES AND RELATED STUDIES

James P. McGarry's *The Castle of Heroes* (1965) provides background information on Yeats's plan to establish a mystical order on an island in Lough Key. T. A. Finnegan's *Sligo: Sinbad's Yellow Shore* (1977), a detailed account of Sligo and the surrounding area, makes frequent reference to Yeats. Further background material is in *Thoor Ballylee: Home of William Butler Yeats* (rev. ed., 1977) by Mary Hanley and Liam Miller.

Although James P. McGarry's *Place Names in the Writings of William Butler Yeats* (ed. Edward Malins, 1976) does not cover all the works in the canon, it is a useful guidebook. It would have been more helpful, however, if McGarry had discussed the sources for the legendary associations that Yeats often evokes and had provided more information on some of the important locales and less on references that appear just once. A list of corrections to George Brandon Saul's *Prolegomena* to the poems and to the plays is appended.

5. Manuscript Materials

HOLDINGS

Manuscripts recently acquired by the National Library of Ireland are listed in the *First Supplement 1965-1975* (1979) to *Manuscript Sources for the History of Irish Civilisation*. Some of the Yeats items in the Robert H. Taylor Collection (housed at Princeton) have been described by E. D. H. Johnson (*PULC*, 1977), and a few unique Yeats items are listed by Donald Gallup in "Ezra Pound (1885-1972): The Catalogue of an Exhibition in the Beinecke Library 30 October-31 December 1975 Commemorating His Ninetieth Birthday" (*YULG*, 1976).

The papers of Edith Shackleton Heald, sold at Christie's (London) on 5 July 1978, contained both letters from Yeats and manuscripts of some of his poems; most of the material was acquired by Harvard University. A very extensive collection of material from Lady Gregory's library was sold at Sotheby's (London) on 23-24 July and 17 December 1979; many of the most interesting items went to Emory University (which has also acquired the Yeats collection of Richard Ellmann). An important collection of Cuala Press publications from the holdings of Michael B. Yeats, including some with unique corrections or inscriptions, was sold individually at Sotheby's (London) on 22-23 May 1980. The published catalogs of these four sales contain numerous facsimiles and quotations and are important documents in themselves.

To the list of libraries with smaller holdings of manuscripts should be added the following: University of Delaware; Hamilton College; Historical Society of Pennsylvania; New York Public Library, Manuscript Collection (*Dictionary Catalog of the Manuscript Collection*, 1967); Pierpont Morgan Library; Pforzheimer Library; Rosenbach Foundation; and Syracuse University.

In "The Untilled Field of W. B. Yeats" (*YER*, 1978), Robert O'Driscoll and Lorna Reynolds do little more than suggest the value of studying Yeats's manuscripts.

STUDIES

In "Yeats's 'The Song of the Happy Shepherd' " (*PQ*, 1953), Marion Witt offers a transcription and discussion of a manuscript in the National Library of Ireland.

David R. Clark's series of studies of manuscripts, including facsimiles and transcriptions, can serve as models for the effective use of manuscripts for criticism and interpretation. In "After 'Silence,' the 'Supreme Theme': Eight Lines of Yeats" (in *Myth and Reality in Irish Literature*, ed. Joseph Ronsley, 1977), Clark suggests that the drafts of "After Long Silence" demonstrate that Yeats's reunion with Moina Mathers is part of the biographical background to the poem and that the "supreme theme" is not "love" but the fact that "bodily decrepitude is wisdom." In "W. B. Yeats's 'Three Things' in the Light of the Manuscripts" (*Soundings*, Stony Brook, 1977), Clark argues that the manuscripts show that the poem goes backward in time, the last stanza referring to the first encounter with the ideal lover. In "Yeats's 'From "Oedipus at Colonus" ': Transcriptions of the Manuscripts, and Two Comments" (*MBL*, 1979), he concentrates on rhythm and visual influences. In a monograph, *"That Black Day": The Manuscripts of "Crazy Jane on the Day of Judgement"* (1980), Clark's emphasis is on the manuscripts' echoes of Blake, Milton, Shakespeare, and others.

Phillip L. Marcus has published two studies based on the manuscripts of *The Death of Cuchulain*. " 'I make the truth': Vision and Revision in Yeats's *The Death of Cuchulain*" (*CLQ*, 1976) discusses the philosophical background to the play. " 'Remembered Tragedies': The Evolution of the Lyric in Yeats's *The Death of Cuchulain*" (*IUR*, 1976) shows how the nationalistic level of the final lyric was reduced during the process of composition.

An abridged edition of Curtis Bradford's *Yeats at Work*, including only the material on the poetry, was published in 1978.

EDITIONS

Curtis Bradford's edition *W. B. Yeats: The Writing of* The Player Queen was at last published in 1977, eight years after Bradford's death. From the mass of extant material, Bradford has isolated and reconstructed some thirty-two drafts. The first seventeen, written between 1907 and 1910, resulted in what Bradford describes as "a full-length play, largely in verse, which is serious in tone though it has a comic ending." After abandoning the play, Yeats returned to it in 1915 and transformed it into its present form. In addition to presenting the manuscript material with a running commentary, Bradford provides an introductory essay, a discussion of the 1919 and 1922 versions that includes much information on the unicorn symbol, and a final essay that evaluates the published criticism of *The Player Queen* and calls the drama "a triumphant success." Bradford's edition is an important contribution to Yeats studies. Unfortunately, however, some manuscript material was overlooked, and, worse, David R. Clark—who saw the work through the press—has indicated that he was denied the opportunity to read final page proof and that many of the corrections he and Russell K. Alspach had made on the galley proofs were missed. Thus the accuracy of any particular reading is always open to question. Finally, Bradford does not offer transcriptions of all the manuscripts, and in the transcriptions that are provided many canceled words and passages have been silently omitted, the result being something approaching a fair copy of Yeats's manuscript. The edition will therefore not suffice for the specialized scholar, while its bulk will deter most other readers.

William H. O'Donnell's *Literatim Transcription of the Manuscripts of William Butler Yeats's* The Speckled Bird (1976), a work clearly designed for the specialist, provides precise transcriptions of each page of the manuscripts (even including some misfiled pages that have no connection with the novel). Two appendixes—which would have been more useful if combined—cross-reference the edition with O'Donnell's The Speckled Bird *with Variant Versions*, published in 1977 despite the date of 1976 given on the title page, in the *Literatim*, and with the text of one version of the novel that O'Donnell published (*MHRev*, 1975). The edition presents all four versions of the work, named and dated by O'Donnell: "Island" (1897), "Leroy" (1897–98), "De Burgh" (1900), and "Final" (1902). Also included are Yeats's notes to the manuscripts as well as O'Donnell's textual notes, explanatory notes, and lengthy introduction. Throughout, the editing is scrupulous. For instance, O'Donnell notes that "infrared and ultraviolet photographs were taken of more than one hundred pages in a generally unsuccessful attempt to enhance cancelled words," a process he elaborates on in "Infrared and Ultraviolet Photography of Manuscripts" (*PBSA*, 1975). Of greater interest to most readers is O'Donnell's "Yeats's Fictional Fathers in *The Speckled Bird*" (*Éire*, 1980), which discusses "the radical difference between the father character in the first two and the last two versions," the early version being more nearly based on Yeats himself than on his father, the later version reversing the balance.

In "Language and Rhythm in Poetry: A Previously Unpublished Essay by W. B. Yeats" (*Shenandoah*, Summer 1975), Richard Fallis presents the text of a brief and unfinished entry from the 1921 Oxford notebook, with a minimum of editing.

In 1977 David R. Clark, Richard J. Finneran, George Mills Harper, Phillip L. Marcus, William M. Murphy, Stephen Parrish, Ann Saddlemyer, and Jon Stallworthy formed a Yeats Editorial Board to encourage, coordinate, and seek funding for editions of manuscripts. The Cornell University Press has now agreed in principle to the series, and approximately thirty to thirty-five volumes are projected. The editions will present all the manuscripts of the poems (supervised by Finneran), all the manuscripts of the plays for which sufficient material survives (supervised by Clark), and selected manuscripts of the prose works (supervised by Harper) and of the family papers (supervised by Murphy). Several editions that were in progress when the Yeats Editorial Board was formed will now appear under its auspices. The first volume in the Cornell Yeats is The Death of Cuchulain: *Manuscript Materials, Including the Author's Final Text* (ed. Phillip L. Marcus, 1982). It contains photographs and facing-page transcriptions of all extant manuscripts and typescripts. The useful introduction summarizes the process of composition and shows the value of the manuscripts for purposes of interpretation. Marcus also identifies several textual errors in the received editions.

6. Some Early Studies (to 1940)

Something of Yeats's stature and status in the early years of his career can be gleaned from his appearance in Norman Rowland Gale's satiric *All Expenses Paid* (1895). Of greater significance is the chapter on Yeats in William Archer's *Poets of the Younger Generation* (1902). Archer admires Yeats's "astonishing union of primitive imagination and feeling with cultivated and consciously artistic expression" but warns that in recent years Yeats "is becoming more and more addicted to a petrified, fossilised symbolism, a system of hieroglyphs which may have some inherent significance for their inventors, but which have now become matters of research, of speculation, of convention." Archer also touches on such topics as the parallels with Maeterlinck and the defects in Yeats's meter.

In *The Stage Irishman of the Pseudo-Celtic Drama* (1904), F. Hugh O'Donnell continues his attack on *The Countess Cathleen* and extends his criticism to *The Land of Heart's Desire* and "The Rose of Peace." James H. Cousins is more sympathetic in "William Butler Yeats: The Celtic Lyricist" (*PoetryR*, 1912), although he argues that Yeats's involvement in the theater has caused his recent work to contain "unassimilated lumps of strength which collide ungraciously with the evocations of his truer moments." In *Changing Ireland: Literary Backgrounds of the Irish Free State, 1889-1922* (1924), Norreys Jephson O'Conor describes Yeats's career in a sketch of little special interest. Yeats is briefly mentioned in Mrs. Claude Beddington's *All That I Have Met* (1929), which includes the text of a 1924 letter from him.

The chapter on Yeats in *A Cheerful Ascetic and Other Essays* (1931), by James J. Daly, S. J., attacks Yeats for his paganism and concludes that he "has succeeded in composing some graceful academic excercises; nothing more." The section on Yeats in Rebecca Pauline Brugsma's dissertation *The Beginnings of the Irish Revival* (Groningen 1933) is primarily quotation and summary. Edith Sitwell offers a sympathetic assessment in *Aspects of Modern Poetry* (1934), suggesting that some of Yeats's recent poems are "undoubtedly the greatest lyrics of the last hundred years, because of their intense fusion of spirit and matter, because of their overwhelming fire and their strange world-old wisdom, sung in the voice of one who is impatient with 'the loveless dust.' " T. R.

Barnes's "Yeats, Synge, Ibsen and Strindberg" (*Scrutiny*, 1936) is too brief to be effective. In an article admired by Yeats, "Public Speech and Private Speech in Poetry" (*YR*, 1938), Archibald MacLeish calls Yeats "the best of modern poets" because "his poetry is no escape from time and place and life and death but, on the contrary, the acceptance of these things and their embodiment." In "AE and W. B." (*VQR*, 1939), which is not a comparative study, Sean O'Faolain argues that only Yeats's late poems are effective poetry and that "if the essential Yeats has any literary affinities it is with the gregarious men of the eighteenth century." The chapter on Yeats in *Tradition and Romanticism: Studies in English Poetry from Chaucer to W. B. Yeats* (1940), by Benjamin Ifor Evans, is of little interest.

Forrest Reid's *W. B. Yeats: A Critical Study* (1915) is briefly discussed by Mary Bryan in *Forrest Reid* (1976). In "Forrest Reid on Yeats" (*Threshold*, 1977), James Simmons quotes from Reid's work at length, apparently to justify Simmons' eccentric judgment that "I have never read a better critical study." Brian Taylor also comments on the study in *The Green Avenue: The Life and Writings of Forrest Reid, 1875–1947* (1980), suggesting that "Reid perhaps reads into Yeats those elements which he saw in his own work."

7. Special Issues of Periodicals; Yeats Journals

The special Yeats issue of *Oasis* (Nov. 1951) offers only a one-page note and a selection from the poetry. The Yeats issue of *Ireland of the Welcomes* (May-June 1979) includes an essay by Liam Miller, "Yeats's West"; addressed to a tourist audience, it is accompanied by excellent photographs.

The Yeats issue of the *Colby Library Quarterly* (June 1979) was edited by Douglas N. Archibald, who contributes a brief preface. The Yeats issue of *Modern British Literature* (Spring 1979), entitled *Yeats Four Decades After: Some Scholarly and Critical Perspectives* and also issued as a monograph with that title, was edited by James Lovic Allen. In the introduction Allen offers the reductive view that "with a writer as frequently doctrinal as W. B. Yeats the intentional fallacy *must* be *intentionally* committed if interpreters are to arrive at anything like valid meanings for the poems and plays in the canon"; Allen also attempts to defend his own articles on Yeats against the criticism they have received. The essays in both these special issues are cited elsewhere in this chapter.

The special issue of *Studies in the Literary Imagination* entitled *W. B. Yeats: The Occult and Philosophical Backgrounds* (Spring 1981) was edited by Ted R. Spivey, who in his "Editor's Comment" pays particular tribute to the work of George Mills Harper. The most important essays in the volume are Harper's " 'Unbelievers in the House': Yeats's Automatic Script," which provides the most detailed account yet available of the Automatic Script (consisting, by Harper's count, of 3,627 pages), and James Olney's "Sex and the Dead: *Daimones* of Yeats and Jung," which traces the philosophical backgrounds to the theory of the daimon and shows the connections stated in Olney's title. Less useful, partly because of its brevity, is Herbert J. Levine's " 'But Now I Add Another Thought': Yeats's Daimonic Tradition," an attempt to show "what Yeats borrowed from the literary daimonic traditions known to him and to suggest the impact of his daimonic theory of creativity on the great poetry of his maturity." James Lovic Allen's "Life as Art: Yeats and the Alchemical Quest" traces the relationship between alchemy and Yeats's attempts to achieve the transformation of life into art; the attacks on several previous critics, notably Thomas R. Whitaker, are not helpful. In "Between Circle and Straight Line: A Pragmatic View of W. B. Yeats and the Occult," Weldon Thornton suggests that critical hostility toward Yeats's esoteric interests is grounded in contemporary habits of thought. Daniel Melnick's "Yeats's Image of Culture" includes some comparisons with Coleridge but is not especially original. Of negligible interest are D. S. Lenoski's "The Symbolism of the Early Yeats: Occult and Religious Backgrounds," which is little more than paraphrase and quotation, and Russell E. Murphy's "The 'Rough Beast' and Historical Necessity: A New Consideration of Yeats's 'The Second Coming,' " which is a confused and scarcely "new" argument that the "rough beast" has some positive values in the poem. In "W. B. Yeats and the 'Children of the Age': Science, Poetry, and Visions of the New Age," Spivey treats Yeats as a "postmodern" through comparisons with Whitehead and others.

In 1978 the *T. S. Eliot Review* became the biannual *Yeats Eliot Review*, Shyamal Bagchee continuing as editor. The arbitrary yoking together of the two writers seems inauspicious, and few of the essays in the four numbers published to date have been of particular significance. The contents of the several issues are cited elsewhere in this chapter.

A *Yeats Annual*, edited by Richard J. Finneran, will begin publication in 1982. The first number will contain an edition by George Mills Harper and Steve L. Adams of the "Leo Africanus" manuscript; critical essays by George Bornstein, Edward Engelberg, Ian Fletcher, Daniel A. Harris, Philip L. Marcus, and Thomas Parkinson; a reprinting of recent dissertation abstracts relating to Yeats; and numerous reviews. After the second number, to be published in the spring of 1983, Finneran will edit an annual of Yeats studies for the Cornell University Press, the first number of which will be published by the end of 1983. In addition to essays, notes, reviews, and dissertation abstracts, this volume will contain an annual classified bibliography of Yeats criticism by K. P. S. Jochum, beginning with the list for 1981.

8. Collections of Criticism

The Yeats section of *Yeats, Joyce, and Beckett: New Light on Three Modern Irish Writers* (ed. Kathleen McGrory and John Unterecker, 1976) is a disappointment. The "new light" is somewhat dim to begin with, since Unterecker's interview with Anne Yeats and Austin Clarke's "Glimpses of W. B. Yeats" are in fact reprinted from *Shenandoah* (1965). McGrory's "Scholarship Frowned into Littleness" is a survey of Yeats scholarship that, except for one work, ends in 1972 and offers little evaluation. The section of photographs includes two of Yeats and his daughter as well as eight of Yeats country by Unterecker (all in black and white). The only Yeats item of interest in this collection is Adrienne Gardner's "*Deirdre*: Yeats's Other Greek Tragedy," a commentary that concentrates on the imagery and offers some comparisons with *Antigone*.

    Yeats, Sligo and Ireland: *Essays to Mark the 21st Yeats International Summer School* (ed. A. Norman Jeffares, 1980) is an uneven gathering. Most of the selections were first presented as lectures at Sligo. For the advanced student, perhaps four essays are of value. Seamus Heaney's "Yeats as an Example?" brilliantly defends Yeats as "an example of labour, effort, perseverance" for the contemporary poet. To Heaney, what makes Yeats "finally admirable is the way his life and work are *not* separate but make a continuum, the way the courage of his vision did not confine itself to rhetorics but issued in actions." In "The 'Dwarf-Dramas' of the Early Abbey Theatre," Ann Saddlemyer shows the common characteristics of the early one-act plays by Yeats, Lady Gregory, Synge, and Hyde, with some emphasis on *The Shadow of the Glen*. Helen Vendler's "Four Elegies" is a useful discussion of Yeats's "brilliant and forcible modernisation of one of the oldest of literary forms." John S. Kelly's "Books and Numberless Dreams: Yeats's Relations with His Early Publishers" outlines the production and critical reception of *The Wanderings of Oisin and Other Poems* and *The Countess Kathleen and Various Legends and Lyrics* and the production of the 1895 *Poems*, noting Yeats's "complicated movement of response to and reaction from his critics." At the other extreme are three essays that might have been entertaining lectures but do not suffer the medium of print: John Holloway's description of Irish weather, D. E. S Maxwell's rambling commentary on images of metamorphosis in Yeats and others, and Patrick Rafroidi's eight-page study "Yeats, Nature and the Self." William M. Murphy's defense of his *Prodigal Father* (1978) against the views of Helen Vendler (*NY*, 8 Jan. 1979) is misplaced. Other than a poem by Brendan Kennelly, the remaining contributions are Lester I. Conner's "A Matter of Character: Red Hanrahan and Crazy Jane," more quotation than analysis; Denis Donoghue's "Romantic Ireland," an extended gloss on the titular term; Barbara Hardy's "The Wildness of Crazy Jane," a close reading of the relevant poems with an extended aside on Yeats's use of the word "wild"; T. R. Henn's "The Place of Shells" (rpt. from his *Last Essays*, 1976), which notes Yeats's use of Sligo in his work; A. Norman Jeffares' "Yeats and the Wrong Lever," which offers plot summaries of some works by Charles Lever and argues that Yeats's negative evaluation of him is unfair; F. S. L. Lyons' "Yeats and Victorian Ireland," which provides a context for some of the quarrels in Yeats's early years; and Augustine Martin's "Hound Voices Were They All: An Experiment in Yeats Criticism," which argues that "the best commentary on Yeat's poems is provided by his other poems" but goes outside them to interpret "Hound Voice" as "the one poem in which Yeats gives himself to the blood-dimmed stream of history and becomes personally 'fighting mad.' "

W. B. Yeats: The Critical Heritage (ed. A. Norman Jeffares, 1977) is a useful anthology of the critical response from 1884 (a letter from John Butler Yeats to Edward Dowden) to 1939 (Auden's elegy), but the editing is altogether inadequate. Although almost all 155 selections demand annotation, Jeffares has supplied notes to only 18 of them. The choice of selections is difficult to justify, as many major critics and many major volumes by Yeats are not represented. Some selections are misdated or misattributed. The fifty-eight-page introduction adequately sketches the response to Yeats and quotes from some essays not included in the edition, but it also contains misstatements, suggesting, for example, that B. L. Reid's study of the poetry, *William Butler Yeats: The Lyric of Tragedy,* demonstrates that "Yeats's drama has interested many critics."

9. Introductory Studies; Handbooks and Guides

Yeats is discussed at some length in Peter Costello's *The Heart Grown Brutal: The Irish Revolution in Literature, from Parnell to the Death of Yeats, 1891–1939* (1977) and in Richard Fallis' *The Irish Renaissance* (1977). Costello's book seldom rises above the level of plot summary and devotes excessive attention to minor writers; it also shows little sophistication in either its critical methodology or its underlying assumptions about the relation between history and literature. Fallis sticks closer to the facts and offers a solid introduction for the beginning student; the chapter on Irish history will be welcomed by non-Irish readers. Richard M. Kain's twenty-six-page entry on Yeats in *A Dictionary of Irish Literature* (ed. Robert Hogan, 1979) is somewhat discursive and contains a few uncharacteristic errors.

Richard F. Peterson's *William Butler Yeats* (1982), in Twayne's English Authors Series, is a useful introductory study. Peterson comments on most of the poems and plays as well as on *A Vision*, sometimes summarizing the critical tradition on a particular work. The volume also offers a biographical sketch and a chapter "Influences and Contributions." There are a few scattered errors, and the index is quite incomplete except for Yeats's works.

P. N. Furbank's *W. B. Yeats* (1976; with corrections, 1977) was prepared for the third-level course on twentieth-century poetry in the Open University. Except for a defective bibliography, the work provides a reliable introduction to Yeats, with emphasis on *The Wind among the Reeds* and *The Tower*. There are two new entries in the undergraduate vade mecum genre. W. T. Currie and Graham Handley's *Brodie's Notes on W. B. Yeats: Selected Poetry* (1978), in the Pan Study Aids series, is keyed to Jeffares' edition of the *Selected Poetry* (1962). *Notes on W. B. Yeats's Poetry* (1980), in the Methuen Notes series, is—to judge from the copyright notice—the work of Cyril Kemp; it treats selected poems with a biographical emphasis and also covers such topics as "Ireland," "Theosophy," and "Plato and Plotinus." There is little to choose between them.

10. General Studies

Morton Irving Seiden's "A Psychoanalytic Essay on William Butler Yeats" (*Accent,* 1946) is an early but still classic example of Freudian interpretation, in this instance of "The Cap and Bells" and especially "The Wanderings of Oisin." Seiden's approach allows only for an allegorical reading of the images and symbols. Frank Kermode's important "Poet and Dancer before Diaghilev" (*PR,* 1961) was expanded and included in *Puzzles and Epiphanies: Essays and Reviews 1958–1961* (1962). James D. Boulger's interesting discussion "Personality and Existence in Yeats" (*Thought,* 1964) argues that "Yeats asserts the value of man over the tyranny of impersonality in his later poetry by making a myth of himself and his friends."

Herbert Howarth (*WHR,* 1965) offers a balanced assessment of Yeats's achievement. A sense of balance is precisely what is missing in the chapter on Yeats in Karl Shapiro's *To Abolish Children and Other Essays* (1968). Shapiro finds that Yeats "invented or repatented the little lyric, metaphysical, symbolist gadget which is the model for the modern American poem" and that indeed Yeats is "the twentieth-century master of the gadget poem." The latest recruit to the ranks of the negative critics is Denis Donoghue, in "The Hard Case of Yeats" (*NYRB,* 26 May 1977). Having abandoned the authorized biography, Donoghue now concludes that Yeats seems peripheral to modern poetry: "what surrounds Yeats's name is not the aura of an achieved poetry, a body of work separable from its origins, but an impression of genius fulfilled chiefly in the multiplicity of its life."

B. D. Cheadle's "Yeats and Symbolism" (*ESA,* 1969) ignores almost all the relevant scholarship but provides a useful introductory commentary on the topic; discounting the influence of the French tradition, Cheadle suggests that for Yeats "truly symbolist poetry is that which deliberately attempts to achieve *profundity* through its symbols." Janet Frank Egleson's "Christ and Cuchulain: Interrelated Archetypes of Divinity and Heroism in Yeats" (*Éire,* 1969) is an interesting essay tracing the appearance of the two figures in Yeats's poetry and plays and suggesting their complex relation to each other. There are some brief comments on Yeats, particularly on "Among School Children" and "Lapis Lazuli," in Robert Langbaum's *The Modern Spirit: Essays on the Continuity of Nineteenth- and Twentieth-Century Literature* (1970). The poorly written chapter on Yeats in *Modern and Otherwise* (Delhi, 1974), by Sisirkumar Ghose, tries to demonstrate that Yeats used the mask as a means of escaping reality and criticizes his work by the standards of Indian philosophy.

In a brief section of *The Protean Self: Dramatic Action in Contemporary Fiction* (1974), Alan Kennedy asserts the importance of dramatic action in Yeats, but does not fully justify the conclusion that "Yeats's conception . . . of ritual or dramatic action and the ideal of the 'antithetical' man is of central importance to an understanding of the literature of the twentieth century." Alan Spiegel's "From Divided to Shared Love in the Art of Yeats" (*Renascence,* 1974) discusses the movement from a tripartite love situation where the lover must choose between two opposite types of women to a shared relationship where both are accepted, an insight not quite so original as is suggested. The comments on Yeats in Patricio V. Monis' "The Literary Symbol in Contemporary Poetry and Drama" (*Unitas,* 1975) are elementary; the emphasis is on "The Second Coming" and "Leda and the Swan." P. P. Sharma's "Yeats: Poet of Unified Sensibility" (*VQ,* 1974-75) offers nothing new or stimulating in a discussion of Yeats's refusal to accept simple answers and his ability to come to terms with antitheses. Also disappointing is Joseph Leondar Schneider's "Yeats's Unreconciled Opposites" (*CLQ,* 1975), which finds a "rarely noted ideological inconsistency" in that Yeats argues for the merger of opposites in most of his work but attacks marriages between different classes in *On the Boiler* and *Purgatory.*

Eleanor Wilner's "The Uncommon Eye: Vision in the Poetry of Blake, Beddoes, and Yeats," in her *Gathering the Winds: Visionary Imagination and Radical Transformation of Self and Society* (1975), tries to demonstrate that Yeats attempted "against the modern world which he too despaired of, to refind and reanimate, not only poetry and poetic drama, but the aristocratic dualism of an older Western world in a form material enough to satisfy the materialism which he shared with his age." Her scholarship is less than comprehensive: only three critics are cited, and her basic text is the *Selected Poems.* Her views of the essential difference between Blake and Yeats are close to those of Harold Bloom, who is ignored. The chapter as a whole is imprecise. Eugene Webb's *The Dark Dove: The Sacred and the Secular in Modern Literature* (1975) includes a chapter, "The One and the Many: The Ambiguous Challenge of Being in the Poetry of Yeats and Rilke," which emphasizes Rilke and, apart from stressing the importance of Nicholas of Cusa to Yeats's thought, adds little to previous accounts.

The concluding chapter of Stuart A. Ende's *Keats and the Sublime* (1976), "Yeats's Dialogues with the Voice of Enchantment," mentions Keats far less often than Shelley. Paying undue homage to the work of Harold Bloom and overlooking all other critics except George Bornstein, Ende discusses the commonplace notion of the tension between idealism and realism in Yeats; the use of Freudian terminology throughout results in a particularly muddied discussion of the mask and the daimon. "The Man and the Echo" is singled out for particular praise. The chapter on Yeats in Helen Regueiro's *The Limits of Imagination: Wordsworth, Yeats, and Stevens* (1976) offers little that has not already been said, and said with greater clarity. Ignoring all Yeats's critics except Bloom and all Yeats's prose except two sentences from *A Vision,* Regueiro asserts that "like Stevens in his later poems, Yeats affirms the capacity of poetry to sacralize profane time and to turn the gratuitous aridity of history into a landscape of imaginative redemption." Thomas Rice Henn's posthumously published *Last Essays* (1976) brings together both unpublished and published lectures and articles, including three essays cited in the 1976 review of research ("The Rhetoric of Yeats," "Towards the Values," and "Yeats and the Poetry of War"). The previously published "Yeats and the Picture Galleries" (*SoR,* 1965) appears here in slightly revised form. The collection as a whole is disappointing, since Henn often buries his erudition among rambling remarks and asides obviously intended not for posterity but for lecture audiences.

Using John Lukács' definition of "bourgeois" (in *The Passing of the Modern Age*, 1970) as a belief in "domesticity, privacy, comfort, the concept of the home and of the family," David L. Kubal argues in "Our Last Literary Gentlemen: The Bourgeois Imagination" (*BuR*, 1976) that Yeats "should not be seen as an aristocrat but rather as a defender of bourgeois moral values and spiritual standards," even though Yeats recognized that "for all its humanistic attributes the bourgeois culture lacked a metaphysical depth." Daniel S. Lenoski has written a series of articles on Yeats's aesthetics: "Aesthetic Theory and Yeats's Change in Poetic Style" (*CJIS*, 1976); "The Symbolism of Rhythm in W. B. Yeats" (*IUR*, 1977); "The Metaphysics behind Yeats's Aesthetics" (*AIS*, 1977); "The Artist as a Force for Change in W. B. Yeats" (*Albion*, 1978); "W. B. Yeats and Celtic Spiritual Power" (*CJIS*, 1979); "Yeats, Eglinton, and Aestheticism" (*Éire*, 1979); and "W. B. Yeats: God and Imagination" (*ESC*, 1980)—this last in eight pages. In all of these the previous scholarship is either ignored or quickly passed over (for instance, in a 1979 essay Lenoski suggests that Hazard Adams, in a book published in 1955, "agrees with me"). Worse, the essays are less Yeats analyzed than Yeats quoted, paraphrased, and summarized. Readers familiar with the primary material will find little of interest.

Paul A. Bove's "Cleanth Brooks and Modern Irony: A Kierkegaardian Critique" (*Boundary*, 1976) includes some interesting comments on Brooks's analyses of "Sailing to Byzantium" and *A Vision*. Bove also argues that Yeats, like "many postmodern poets," is "committed to the paradox that in and through the profane, the sacred, the creative, and the valid are to be found in the here and now." In *Literature and Western Civilization, the Modern World, III: Reactions* (ed. David Daiches and Anthony Thorlby, 1976), Daiches' "Anti-Romanticism and Reaction" offers a conventional and hostile discussion of Yeats's politics, and Angus Calder's "British Poetry and Its Audience, 1914-70" comments on Yeats's conception of his proper audience. The cassette in the Audio Learning series by C. J. Rawson and Marjorie Perloff, *Yeats and the Romantic Tradition* and *Yeats: Imagination and Symbolism* (1976), presents a somewhat rambling discussion of various topics, with long asides on Yeats's relation to Wordsworth, Coleridge, Keats, Stevens, and Williams; it is accompanied by a supplementary booklet, the work of John Sutherland and Keith Walker.

Three related essays make no great advance in our understanding of their subject. Galina Baužytě's derivative "William Butler Yeats and Symbolism" (*Literatūra*, 1976) concentrates on the plays. Denis Donoghue's "Yeats: The Question of Symbolism" (in *Myth and Reality in Irish Literature*, ed. Joseph Ronsley, 1977) discusses the conflict between symbol and history and Yeats's attempts to reconcile them, as in his use of legendary material. John Lucas' "From Naturalism to Symbolism" (*RMS*, 1977; *Decadence and the 1890s*, ed. Ian Fletcher, 1979) provided some late Victorian background on naturalism but is unoriginal in its treatment of Yeats.

A much more important contribution to Yeats studies is Robert Langbaum's *The Mysteries of Identity: A Theme in Modern Literature* (1977). Although some relevant primary and secondary material is overlooked (e.g., the lectures on personality in *Yeats and the Theatre* or Hazard Adams' *Blake and Yeats*), Langbaum effectively discusses Yeats's search for a total identity. In "Exteriority of the Self," he concentrates on the theories of the mask and the daimon, with the emphasis on *The Player Queen* and *Per Amica Silentia Lunae*. He stresses Yeats's belief in reincarnation and suggests that "without resorting to a concept of God," Yeats "restores the old supernatural confirmation of identity." "The Self as a Work of Art" analyzes the "Rosa Alchemica" stories and *A Vision*, particularly the first version. Langbaum stresses the central importance of Yeats's chapter "The Soul in Judgment" and insists that the unusual subject matter must not be allowed to obscure the role it plays in Yeats's thought or its "psychological perspicuity." In "The Self as God," Langbaum treats the importance to Yeats of Indian philosophy and comments on many of the later poems, plays, and essays. Langbaum concludes that "Yeats discovered in Indian religion the ultimate implications of all that he had been saying through a lifetime about identity" and that "Balzac showed him how he could absorb such insights while remaining European."

Suzanne Nalbantian's *The Symbol of the Soul from Hölderlin to Yeats: A Study in Metonymy* (1977) offers only some scattered and uninspired remarks on Yeats. John Montague's "Faces of Yeats" (*EI,* 1977) is a short comment on Yeats's adoption of various masks. John Bayley's "W. B. Yeats" (*Cahiers du Centre de Recherches sur les Pays du Nord et du Nord-Oeust,* 1978) is a lecture of minor interest. There are several entries on Yeats in Arland Ussher's *From A Dark Lantern: A Journal* (1978). Yeats also appears briefly in Terence Brown's "Dublin in Twentieth-Century Writing: Metaphor and Subject" (*IUR,* 1978), which notes Yeats's "assertion of the primacy of Irish rural life as a creative force in the national being." James Olney's interesting and entertaining "W. B. Yeats's Daimonic Memory" (*SR,* 1977) shows how Yeats's purposeful forgetfulness allowed him to create works in which "the essential is affirmed while the accidental is left to shift for itself among various possibilities"; Yeats "seeks to embody . . . the very essence of being, purified now of the 'accident and incoherence' of existence."

Graham Hough's "W. B. Yeats: A Study in Poetic Integration," in his *Selected Essays* (1978), is provocative, even if the basic concepts may be familiar. Hough carefully outlines the stages in Yeats's development and concludes that Yeats seeks "an organized diversity of experience: archetypes, separate and mutually irreducible, not infinite in number but each appearing in an infinity of forms, yet all to be comprehended as the substance of a single spirit." Despite some perceptive comments on individual works, Andrew Parkin's *The Dramatic Imagination of W. B. Yeats* (1978) as a whole is disappointing. The "dramatic imagination" of the title is more talked about than defined, and the attempt to show its presence in most of the plays and in a few other works is often ineffective. The study contains much plot summary and makes little effort to come to terms with the previous criticism. The intended audience also remains unclear, as it is difficult to reconcile the specialized topic with the style; for instance, Parkin suggests that if Yeats's "soul soared, his reason could not but scratch the sceptical itch" and describes MacGregor Mathers as "a magician Yeats met in London."

D. E. S. Maxwell's "Views of Yeats" (*Mosaic*, 1979) is a diffuse essay on Yeats's disinterest in the physical aspects of the landscape and his emphasis on its visionary disclosures; the discussions of Edward Thomas and of Hardy seem not so much enlightened comparisons as a means of lengthening the article. In "Yeats and Eliade: Shamanism and the Modern Poet" (*MBL*, 1979), Ted R. Spivey tries to argue that Yeats was a "shaman *manqué*," one of the proofs being "the almost unknown feat" of "writing memorable poetry after the age of seventy." Although Spivey offers some suggestive parallels, he carries the thesis much too far and ignores many aspects of both Yeats's life and work. Lionel Trilling's commentaries on "Sailing to Byzantium" and on *Purgatory* from his 1967 anthology have been reprinted in *Prefaces to the Experience of Literature* (1979). Despite its title, *Literary Landscapes of the British Isles: A Narrative Atlas* (1979), by David Daiches and John Flower, includes a chapter on the Dublin of Yeats and Joyce, with Joyce receiving the greater attention. Ashok Bhargava's *The Poetry of W. B. Yeats: Myth as Metaphor* (New Delhi, 1979) is of little value to advanced students; after some introductory remarks on Yeats's interest in myth and on *Per Amica Silentia Lunae* and *A Vision*, Bhargava comments on each of the poems from *The Wild Swans at Coole* through *Last Poems*, using a heavily biographical approach and seldom rising above the level of a reader's guide. In "Those Masterful Images" (*Crane Bag*, 1979), Richard Kearney ignores most of the relevant scholarship while presenting the unoriginal thesis that "Yeats is inspired by a visionary and sacramental imagination quite as much as by its romantic and erotic contrary." The brief comments on Yeats in Jan B. Gordon's " 'Decadent Spaces': Notes for a Phenomenology of the *Fin de Siècle*" (in *Decadence and the 1890s*, ed. Ian Fletcher, 1979) are not of great significance.

G. J. Watson's *Irish Identity and the Literary Revival* (1979) contains the interesting chapter "W. B. Yeats: From 'Unity of Culture' to 'Anglo-Irish Solitude,' " which argues that Yeats's "Anglo-Irish birth lay at the roots of all Yeats's strategies for encompassing Ireland in his poetry." Watson is particularly concerned with Yeats's attitudes toward history, suggesting that the poet's "most compelling myth of history (which clearly connects with his own history and the history of the Anglo-Irish) is that of crisis, loss, defeat and dissolution, often accompanied by monstrous eruptions of violence." Nevertheless, Yeats finds in this myth of history "an exhilarating creative freedom and a powerful resonance of statement." Unfortunately, Watson's insistence on demonstrating his thesis leads him to slight many relevant matters, especially the cyclical theories of *A Vision*; and his description of Yeats's Anglo-Irish inheritance would have been more precise had he not overlooked Donald Torchiana's *W. B. Yeats and Georgian Ireland* (1966). Less rewarding is "W. B. Yeats: Theatrical Nobility," in William H. Pritchard's *Lives of the Modern Poets* (1980). Taking Johnson's *Lives of the English Poets* as an approximate model, Pritchard offers not so much a biographical sketch as a general commentary, designed for a wide audience. He shows no particular fondness for Yeats, the heroes of his book being Eliot and Frost, and he is unduly harsh on the early poetry. He argues that Yeats "is probably the modern poet most vulnerable to affectations which are not inevitably amusing; and this weakness in style of life carries over into his poetry." Thus Yeats often practices "a display rather than an exploration of himself." One questions Pritchard's authority to suggest that Yeats's "letters also say remarkably little of interest (compared with Frost's or Pound's) about poetry" when he calls an incident found on page 109 of the Wade *Letters* a "probably apocryphal anecdote."

James Olney's *The Rhizome and the Flower: The Perennial Philosophy—Yeats and Jung* (1980) is the most fascinating and learned study of Yeats published in many years. Scrupulously researched and carefully written, Olney's work develops the parallels between Yeats and Jung; traces those parallels back to their common sources in Plato and Platonism; traces the sources of Plato and Platonism in the four great ancestors of Pythagoras, Parmenides, Heraclitus, and Empedocles; and, much more briefly, suggests that the ultimate source for all may be found in the very construct of the human brain. Olney demonstrates that "what all three sought—Yeats in poetic myth, Jung in psychological myth, and Plato in philosophic myth—was one and the same thing though under different names: Unity of Being, individuation, perfect merger with the *daimon* which will transport one to the *eidos* of his being." Further, both "as statement and as enactment," Yeats's poetry "is about life's multiplicity, behind which, before and after which, there is, for the artist-as-Demiourgos, an '*eidotic*' unity on which he fixes his gaze and his desire. Thus one characteristic movement of Yeats's poems . . . is from plurality to unity: behind many if not all of his poems is the monistic emotion and the vision of the idealist." Unfortunately, neither summary nor quotation can do justice to this study, which offers significant new insights not only on Yeats's career as a whole but also on *Per Amica Silentia Lunae, A Vision*, and many poems. *The Rhizome and the Flower* is required reading for any advanced student of Yeats.

The two chapters on Yeats in Wayne Hall's *Shadowy Heroes: Irish Literature of the 1890s* (1980) discuss the relation between some of the early works and Yeats's attitudes toward Ireland. Most of the previous scholarship on the topic is ignored, and few new insights are provided. The statement that "in 1896 Yeats moved into an apartment with Mrs. Olivia Shakespear," thus having "a shared London flat," represents an egregious misreading of a passage in *Memoirs*. V. V. Jain's *W. B. Yeats as Literary Critic* (Delhi, 1980) and Vinod Sena's *The Poet as Critic: W. B. Yeats on Poetry, Drama and Tradition* (Delhi, 1980) both use a great deal of quotation and paraphrase to present a selection of Yeats's major critical ideas, fail to come fully to terms with previous assessments, and argue for Yeats's importance as a critic. Sena even suggests that Yeats may be "the most perfect example of the poet-critic in English criticism." Sena's study is clearly the more valuable of the two—especially as Jain's is marred by numerous misprints and occasional stylistic failures—and it provides a useful introduction to the topic. Sena's "W. B. Yeats, Personality and Tradition" (*Humanities Rev.*, New Delhi, 1980) is condensed from the longer study. In "Majority: The International Yeats Summer School" (*Éire*, 1980), Peter Alderson Smith reports on the 1980 session at Sligo. Randall Jarrell's essay "The Development of Yeats's Sense of Reality" (*SoR*, 1942) is reprinted in his *Kipling, Auden and Co.: Essays and Reviews, 1935-1964* (1980).

There are some brief comments on Yeats, particularly on his battles against censorship and the divorce laws, in *Ireland: A Social and Cultural History 1922-79* (1981) by Terence Brown.

11. Studies of the Poetry

"The Poetic Development of W. B. Yeats," in D. J. Enright's *Literature for Man's Sake: Critical Essays* (1955), is a standard account of "the well-nigh miraculous nature of Yeats's development," though little sympathy toward the very late poems is evident. More provocative is Thomas Parkinson's "The World of Yeats' 'Nineteen Hundred and Nineteen,' " in *The Image of the Work: Essays in Criticism* (ed. B. H. Lehman et al., 1955), which provides a close reading of the poem combined with a statement on its essential modernity. In "William Butler Yeats" (*KM*, 1962), Patrick Kavanagh argues for the superiority of the later poems but suggests that "the bawdy of the *Last Poems* is not true to the full Yeatsian life." The chapter on Yeats in Edwin Muir's *The Estate of Poetry* (1962) surveys the poems, stressing the fact that Yeats wrote with an actual audience in mind. In *Poetry in Our Time: A Critical Survey of Poetry in the English-Speaking World, 1900-1960* (1963), Babette Deutsch offers an introductory commentary on the poems. The comments on three poems in Eavan Boland's "Precepts of Art in Yeats's Poetry" (*DM*, 1965) are of little interest.

In *English Verse: Voice and Movement from Wyatt to Yeats* (1967), T. R. Barnes gives the full texts and close readings of some of the major poems; the result is more nearly an anthology than a critical study. In " 'Principles of the Mind': Continuity in Yeats's Poetry" (*MLN*, 1968), Gayatri Chakravorty Spivak discusses the significance of the three personae in *The Wind among the Reeds* and, with less success, argues that Yeats continues to develop the three voices in his later poems. Marjorie G. Perloff's " 'Heart Mysteries': The Later Love Lyrics of W. B. Yeats" (*CL*, 1969) is a sound if unoriginal discussion of what is called the "Second Maud Gonne Cycle," "a fairly large group of lyrics written between 1919 and 1939"; Perloff concludes that Yeats "was never exclusively the poet of earth and of commitment to the body." R. W. Medlicott's survey of "Leda and the Swan: An Analysis of the Theme in Myth and Art" (*Australian and New Zealand Journal of Psychiatry*, 1970) does not emphasize Yeats but provides some useful background material. "The Modern Poet and the Public World," in Thomas R. Edwards' *Imagination and Power: A Study of Poetry on Public Themes* (1971), includes a discussion of "Easter 1916." Michael Harnett's "W. B. Yeats: Evolution of a Style" (*Irish Times*, 23 Feb. 1971) contains nothing of note. The same must be said of D. K. Lal's *W. B. Yeats: Selected Poems (A Study of Yeats's Important Poems)* (Bareilly, 1971) and S. C. Mundra's *W. B. Yeats and His Poetry (with Critical Introduction and Exhaustive Notes)* (Bareilly, 1971; 3rd ed., 1978), which both contain chapters on the life and work followed by commentary on selected poems, replete with misprints. Scarcely more useful is the chapter on Yeats in C. H. Sisson's *English Poetry 1900-1950: An Assessment* (1971), which is as inane in its evaluations as in its organization—Sisson begins with the last poems and proceeds backward through the canon. This chapter and Sisson's "Yeats and Swift" (*Agenda*, 1971-72) are reprinted in his *The Avoidance of Literature: Collected Essays* (ed. Michael Schmidt, 1978).

Charles Altieri's perceptive "From a Comic to a Tragic Sense of Language in Yeats's Mature Poetry" (*MLQ*, 1972) concentrates on "A Prayer for My Daughter" and "Coole Park and Ballylee, 1931" to demonstrate that "the comic sense Yeats had in the earlier years is no longer operable because reality does not conform to the human will." In "Yeats's 'Sailing to Byzantium' and the Limits of Modern Literary Criticism" (*RLV*, 1972), Epifanio San Juan, Jr., takes issue with some previous critics, especially Elder Olson, before presenting an overwritten reading of the poem as illustrating the triumph of art. Stuart Hirschberg's "Campbell's 'Monomyth' and the Exploration Pattern in Yeats's 'A Dialogue of Self and Soul'" (*Explor*, 1973) tries to demonstrate that the poem follows the archetypal pattern of separation, illumination, and return. More interesting is Reinhold Heller's "Edvard Munch's *Vision* and the Symbolist Swan" (*Art Quarterly*, 1973), which contains only a few remarks on "Leda and the Swan" but provides a valuable survey of the iconographic significance of the symbol. Visvanath Chatterjee's "A Reading of Yeats's Byzantine Poems" (*BDEC*, 1973-74) adds little to previous accounts. In "Crazy Jane and 'Byzantium'" (*E&S*, 1974), Nicholas Brooke discusses some parallels that are not especially enlightening.

Giacomo Cosentino's *Studies in Yeats's Later Poems* (Catania, 1974) treats "A Woman Young and Old," *Words for Music Perhaps*, and, more briefly, "Supernatural Songs." Although the book provides some scattered insights, it ignores most of the extant scholarship, and the writing is often awkward and at times overfervent ("All art is an attempt to find *God. Crazy Jane on God* is great art; large parts of the Old Testament are not"). Barbara L. Estrin's "Alternating Personae in Yeats' 'Lapis Lazuli' and 'Crazy Jane on the Mountain'" (*Criticism*, 1974) offers little more than a close reading of "Lapis Lazuli," overemphasizing the sexual level. In a more important study, Elizabeth Huberman (*ELWIU*, 1974) suggests that the structure of "Byzantium" reverses that of "Sailing to Byzantium." The chapter on Yeats in B. B. Paliwal's *The Poetic Revolution of the Nineteen Twenties* (New Delhi, 1974) contains a general discussion of the poems followed by some explications; advanced students will discover little of interest. A. G. Stock's "W. B. Yeats and the Poetry of Violence" (*JJCL*, 1974) is well written but derivative. Richard P. Wheeler's "Yeats' 'Second Coming': What Rough Beast?" (*AI*, 1974; rpt. in *The Practice of Psychoanalytic Criticism*, ed. Leonard Tennenhouse, 1976) illustrates almost all the excesses of its genre, suggesting that the poem "builds upon a deeply repressed fantasy of omnipotent, destructive rage, called into service to master an experience of intolerable, infantile helplessness." Roberta R. Armstrong's mistitled "Yeats as Nineteenth Century Poet" (*VIJ*, 1975) comments on the personae of *The Wind among the Reeds* and argues that the book has a three-part structure; unfortunately, she overlooks Spivak's article and fails to note Yeats's later rearrangement of the order of the poems. James D. Boulger's excellent "Moral and Structural Aspects in W. B. Yeats's *Supernatural Songs*" (*Renascence*, 1975) argues that "the fundamental interest of *Supernatural Songs* is that the aim of the poems is an impossible one, since the ineffable, however defined, cannot be depicted in any poetic image, Christian, Asiatic, or other. The success of the poems must rest in the originality and inventiveness of the poet in coping with this situation." Claire Hahn's essay (*Thought*, 1975), which is primarily an attack on Bloom's *Yeats*, argues that the "central theme" of *Last Poems* "is the attempt of the artist to ascend to truth through his poetry"; the article is well written if not particularly original. Rob Jackaman's analysis of "Byzantium" (*SoRA*, 1975) is similar to that of Helen Vendler (in *Yeats's* Vision *and the Later Plays*), whose position he misrepresents. In " 'The Second Coming' and Yeats's Vision of History" (in *A Festschrift for Edgar Ronald Seary*, ed. A. A. Macdonald et al., 1975), Robert O'Driscoll provides the background to the poem in Yeats's historical thought, especially as developed in *A Vision*; little is added to prior accounts. In "The Monomyth and Literary Criticism" (*CollL*, 1975), Steven R. Phillips applies Campbell's theory to "Sailing to Byzantium," the result being an interesting though partial reading of the poem. Krishna Rayan's "Yeats and the 'Little and Intense' Poem" (*EIC*, 1975) is a minor contribution, offering close readings of selected poems of eight or fewer lines, contending that "a poem with a microstructure has thus a superior quality for developing macro-meaning." Christopher Gillie's *Movements in English Literature, 1900–1940* (1975) contains some introductory remarks and a defective bibliography; "Among School Children" is given the greatest attention. "The Sacred in the Poetry of W. B. Yeats" (*Confluents*, 1975), by Mme Samson, is of no value. In "The Theme of Escape in W. B. Yeats's Early Poetry" (*JEn*, 1975), V. N. Sinha presents a standard and unresearched account of the tension between the ideal and the real worlds in some early works.

In *The Language of Modern Poetry: Yeats, Eliot, Auden* (1976), A. C. Partridge considers in detail sixteen poems, providing for each a scansion, an analysis of the rhetorical figures, and a paraphrase interpretation. There are some annoying errors in fact, some simplistic readings, and, for most readers, a bewildering array of terms from classical rhetoric (e.g., "aphaeresis," "ecphonesis," and "epizeuxis"—on a single page). His study of Yeats's versification fails to draw on the work of Beum, Dougherty, and Parkinson. The chapter on Yeats in David Perkins' *A History of Modern Poetry: From the 1890s to the High Modernist Mode* (1976) is unsatisfactory. Yeats's entire career receives but a single page more than early Eliot and three pages fewer than early Pound. After considering at some length Yeats's life—relying too uncritically on *Autobiographies*—Perkins is left with less than two pages to discuss the poems published after 1928. He argues that Yeats's distinctive qualities are the use of symbolism, the presence of a speaking voice in the poems, and the concept of antithesis and that "the persistence and depth of his Romantic belief in the possibility of human greatness . . . most essentially distinguishes Yeats from the other Modernist writers." The chapter on Yeats in *English Poetry* (ed. Alan Sinfield, 1976) is a dialogue between Richard Ellmann and Peter Wilson of interest only to beginning students. The volume also includes Laurence Lerner's "Reading Modern Poetry," which briefly comments on "Lapis Lazuli." *Essays in Modern Criticism* (ed. Raj Nath and William I. Elliot, Allahabad, 1976) contains three essays concerning Yeats. Elliot's "A Reading of Yeats's 'Lapis Lazuli' " is a close reading of moderate interest. P. S. Sastri's "The Poetics of the Lyric: An Examination of Elder Olson's Analysis of 'Sailing to Byzantium' " attempts to show the shortcomings of Olson's reading while arguing that "the poem is organized into a unity by the idea of music." Naresh Chandra's "A Critique of New Criticism," which attacks R. P. Blackmur's analysis of "The Second Coming," is the least interesting of the three essays, none of which shows much awareness of previous scholarship.

"W. B. Yeats: A Vision of Joy," in Elizabeth Jennings' *Seven Men of Vision: An Appreciation* (1976), offers little more than a paraphrase, with commentary, of selected middle and late poems, beginning with those in *The Wild Swans at Coole*. Adele M. Dalsimer's "By Memory Inspired: W. B. Yeats's 'September 1913' and the Irish Political Ballad" (*CLQ*, 1976) is a close reading with emphasis on the use of rhyme; she notes the similarities between the poem and the ballad "By Memory Inspired." In "From Parnell to O'Duffy: The Composition of Yeats's 'Parnell's Funeral' " (*CJIS*, 1976), Patrick Holland makes a convincing case for dating the composition of the second part of the poem circa August 1934. The comments on Yeats in Siegfried Mandel's "The Nightingale in the Loom of Life" (*Mosaic*, 1976) are brief and not especially perceptive, but the essay is useful for the background material. Ruth Nevo's attempt to demonstrate in "Again, Byzantium" (*Lang&S*, 1976) that "the poem is about, and also enacts, the creative process itself" is not worth the struggle with her opaque style. R. F. Fleissner's "The Second Coming of Guess Who? The 'Rough Beast' as Africa in 'The Second Coming' " (*NConL*, 1976) is either an absurd argument or a failed attempt at humor; Fleissner says that we should "associate the beast with the emergence of Third World peoples as a power to be reckoned with."

George Fraser's *Essays on Twentieth-Century Poets* (1977) reprints with some added notes "Yeats and the Ballad Style" (*Shenandoah*, Spring 1970) and the general commentary on Yeats's career from *Vision and Rhetoric* (1959). Also included are "Seven Poems by Yeats," which offers close readings of moderate interest, and "Yeats: Two Dream Poems," which provides sexual interpretations of "The Cap and Bells" and "His Dream" and comments on the stylistic changes in Yeats's poetry from 1900 to 1910. The chapter on Yeats in David Holbrook's *Lost Bearings in English Poetry* explicates "Among School Children" along familiar lines. Joseph Ronsley's "Yeats as an Autobiographical

Poet" (in *Myth and Reality in Irish Literature*, ed. Ronsley, 1977) overlooks Marion Witt's standard essay on the topic and offers nothing new. A more interesting essay in the same collection, Balachandra Rajan's "The Poetry of Confrontation: Yeats and the Dialogue Poem," concentrates on "A Dialogue of Self and Soul," "Yeats's highest achievement in a form the resources of which he himself had worked out and deepened." Among the numerous comments on Yeats in Ellen Williams' *Harriet Monroe and the Poetry Renaissance: The First Ten Years of* Poetry, *1912–1922* (1977) is a valuable listing of the changes that Ezra Pound tried to make in Yeats's poems in the December 1912 *Poetry*—although surely the change from "sides" to "eyes" in "The Mountain Tomb" is a dictated correction rather than "an alteration that Yeats apparently did not protest." There are some brief and misguided comments on Yeats in Lawrence R. Ries's *Wolf Masks: Violence in Contemporary Poetry* (1977).

Hazard Adams' "The 'Book' of Yeats's Poems" (*Cornell Rev.*, 1977) argues for the significance of the overall order of Yeats's poems, preferring the format used in the 1949 *Poems* and in the *Variorum Edition*; the essay also has some perceptive remarks on *A Vision* and Yeats's attitude toward myth. In " 'Horseman, Pass By!': Metaphor and Meaning in Yeats's Epitaph" (*CP*, 1977), James Lovic Allen provides a catalog of the possible connotations for the horseman image in "Under Ben Bulben." William C. Barnwell's interesting "The Blandness of Yeats' Rhadamanthus" (*ELN*, 1977) draws on sources in Mangan and Merriman to suggest a "positive contextual meaning" for "bland" in "News for the Delphic Oracle." Also useful is Barnwell's "The Rapist in 'Leda and the Swan' " (*SAB*, 1977), which distinguishes four different approaches to the poem. Charles J. Clancy's "Yeats's *Oisin*" (*Éire 19*, 1977) overlooks some relevant material but argues effectively that Oisin and Patrick "are not mutually exclusive" but are "linked in antagonism and in the solitude of their existence." Izolda Geniušienė's "The Rose Symbol in the Early Poetry of W. B. Yeats" (*Literatūra*, 1977) does not advance our understanding of the subject. Two well-written essays that offer close readings of selected poems with little or no reference to the critical tradition are Samuel Hynes's "All the Wild Witches: Women in Yeats's Poems" (*SR*, 1977) and Barbara Hardy's "Passion and Contemplation in Yeats's Love Poetry," in her *The Advantage of Lyric: Essays on Feeling in Poetry* (1977). Bryant E. Hoffman's "Myself Must I Remake: Yeats's *Last Poems* (1936–1939)" (*LitR*, 1977) provides unoriginal close readings of selected lyrics. The chapter " 'Sailing to Byzantium': Another Voyage, Another Reading," in Simon O. Lesser's *The Whispered Meanings: Selected Essays* (ed. Robert Sprich and Richard W. Noland, 1977), attempts to rebut Elder Olson's well-known study but presents an overpessimistic reading of the lyric's conclusion.

Michael North's "Symbolism and Obscurity in 'Meditations in Time of Civil War' " (*CritQ*, 1977) gives an explication of some interest but pays insufficient attention to previous accounts. In "Yeats's 'Lapis Lazuli' " (*N&Q*, 1977), David Parker argues that "Yeats was more or less fully aware of what the carving means [in Chinese iconography], and . . . he allowed this knowledge to play a part in the shaping of the poem." Laurence Perrine (*CP*, 1977) suggests that "love" is the "supreme theme" in "After Long Silence." Perrine's unexciting "Yeats's Response to the Experience of Rejected Love" (*MBL*, 1977) concludes that Yeats found compensation in the writing of poetry. Virginia D. Pruitt (*Expl*, 1977) calls attention to the myth of Pan and Syrinx as a possible source for the title *The Wind among the Reeds*. " 'A Mind of Winter': Yeats's Early Vision of Old Age" (*CLAJ*, 1977), by Gary Storhoff and Linda Storhoff, tries without much success to demonstrate that "The Living Beauty" and "The Cold Heaven" project "a misshapen and unresolved vision of the world," whereas "in Yeats's later poetry, he can confront his condition and accept it, and this acceptance energizes the force of his art." Eishu Sonoi's "Yeats's Tree" (*SELL*, 1977) and Masaaki Yoshino's "Yeats's Dance Image" (*SELL*, 1978) are equally derivative.

The Early Poetry of W. B. Yeats: The Poetic Quest (1978), by Thomas L. Byrd, Jr., is a rather flat study of the poems from the beginning to 1906, with emphasis on "The Wanderings of Oisin" and *The Shadowy Waters*. Byrd concentrates on the pastoral motifs and stresses the ambivalence in Yeats's attitude toward the ideal world. The different versions of *The Shadowy Waters* are discussed at length, unfortunately without reference to *Druid Craft: The Writing of* The Shadowy Waters (ed. Sidnell et al., 1971); indeed, no secondary material published after 1971 is mentioned. The close readings are more paraphrase than analysis. The two chapters on Yeats are not among the strongest in Michael Ragussis' uneven *Language and the Romantic Tradition* (1978), which sees D. H. Lawrence as the culmination of a tradition in which the artist, distrustful of the power of language, "deliberately sets out to turn a self-critical eye on his work." Ragussis concentrates on "The Song of the Happy Shepherd," "The Sad Shepherd," "Nineteen Hundred and Nineteen," and "Her Vision in the Wood." Despite numerous disparagments of anonymous "critics," some significant material is overlooked, such as Thomas Parkinson's essay on "Nineteen Hundred and Nineteen" and James Land Jones's study of Yeats and Keats.

The two chapters on Yeats in M. L. Rosenthal's *Sailing into the Unknown: Yeats, Pound, Eliot* (1978) contain numerous interesting readings but are ultimately unsatisfying. Rosenthal seems unsure of the intended audience: much of the book appears to be addressed to general readers, but a close familiarity with the poems is required to follow the arguments. Moreover, his attempt to read the poets "with a fresh eye and ear" means that almost all the scholarship is ignored. Rosenthal suggests that Yeats's essential modernism is seen in his use of the sequence poem: "Yeats remains our greatest modern architect of structures made up of lightning flashes." The chapter on Yeats in Anthony Thwaite's *Twentieth-Century English Poetry* (1978) is introductory and not free from error. More interesting are the remarks on Yeats in Howard Nemerov's *Figures of Thought: Speculations on the Meaning of Poetry and Other Essays* (1978), especially those in the chapter "Poetry and History." David Young's " 'The Living World for Text': Life and Art in *The Wild Swans at Coole*" (in *The Author in His Work: Essays on a Problem in Criticism*, ed. Louis L. Martz and Aubrey Williams, 1978) is a well-written but unoriginal discussion of Yeats's ability to use the events of his life in the poems.

"Lyric Voice and Reader Response: One View of the Transition to Modern Poetics" (*TCL*, 1978), by Ed Block, Jr., comments on three Yeats poems in a discussion of how modern poetry moves toward involving the reader in the poem, arguing that "Yeats allows semantic and stylistic indeterminancy to create open spaces for the reader's imagination." Edward Proffitt's "The Epic Lyric" (*RS*, 1978) briefly touches on Yeats as one of the modern writers who attempt to construct "a long work built on lyric principles or composed of lyric pieces welded into an integrated whole of epic significance." Lucas Carpenter's "Yeats' Crazy Jane Poems" (*CP*, 1978) gives paraphrases and commentaries for the entire series, as well as for "Crazy Jane on the Mountain"; most of his views have already been argued, and his approach to the refrains is simplistic. Norman Friedman's interesting "Permanence and Change: What Happens in Yeats's 'Dialogue of Self and Soul' " (*YER*, 1978) suggests that the "Self" in part 2 is able to resolve and integrate the positions of both "Self" and "Soul" in part 1, achieving "a transcendence, not of life, but rather of the terms of the conflict altogether." Warwick Gould's disjointed "Yeats as Aborigine" (*FDP*, 1978) notes the existence of a John Butler Yeats illustration to "The Lake Isle of Innisfree" in the *Leisure Hour* (Oct. 1896) and then discusses the relation between the poem and its major source, W. G. Wood-Martin's *History of Sligo, County and Town* (1882–92). Rob Jackaman (*ArielE*, 1978) ignores all the published criticism as he catalogs the balancing images in "Easter 1916" and those in "Nineteen Hundred and Nineteen" and then argues that the two endings are balanced against each other, "white magic" ("Easter 1916") versus "black magic" ("Nineteen Hundred and Nineteen"). Herbert J. Levine's "Yeats at the Crossroads: The Debate of Self and Anti-Self in 'Ego Dominus Tuus' " (*MLQ*, 1978) is a valuable study of the background to the poem, with particular emphasis on the "Leo Africanus" correspondence. In "Singing amid Uncertainty: Image and Idea in Yeats's 'Memory' " (*ELN*, 1978), Dwight H. Purdy discounts the biographical interpretations and substitutes an ingenious but perhaps overelaborate reading of the poem as "an exemplary philosophical lyric on two of Yeats's favorite themes, the ambiguity of idealism and the inherent contradictions in a Romantic theory of poetic remembering." Vilas Sarang's "The Byzantium Poems: Yeats at the Limits of Symbolism" (*CP*, 1978) presents the not very interesting argument that in both poems Yeats has difficulty in depicting the timeless.

Stuart Hirschberg's *At the Top of the Tower: Yeats's Poetry Explored through* A Vision (Heidelberg, 1979) summarizes the main ideas of the 1937 *A Vision*; cites some of the critical studies of the work (though Hazard Adams and Harold Bloom, among others, are ignored); and provides explications of some twenty-one middle and late poems, paying little or no attention to the previous scholarship. Indeed, since the study cites no work later than 1970, there may have been little revision in what was first a 1972 dissertation. Among the few new ideas is the forced argument that Crazy Jane represents a person of Phases 16, 17, and 18 in the order in which her poems (including "Crazy Jane on the Mountain") are placed. By and large, though, familiar poems are discussed in familiar ways. The Audio Learning cassette *Yeats: The Natural and the Supernatural* and *Yeats: Time and Death* (1979), by J. A. Berthoud and A. J. Smith, in fact consists of a close reading of "Supernatural Songs," mostly well done but somewhat weak on "Meru"; the tape is accompanied by a supplementary booklet. In some brief remarks in *The New Cratylus: Notes on the Craft of Poetry* (1979), A. D. Hope attacks the "literary dustmen" who engage in source and parallel studies, using Henn and Melchiori on "Leda and the Swan" as his prime examples. The chapter "A Fascist Poem: Yeats's 'Blood and the Moon' " in Donald Davie's *Trying to Explain* (1979) is more assertion than argument. James L. Allen's "From Traditional to Personal Myth: Yeats's Prototypes and Analogues for the Golden Bird of Byzantium" (*CJIS*, 1979), which draws on and essentially supersedes Allen's earlier essays (*DilR*, 1963; *ES*, 1967), offers a catalog, replete with extensive quotations, of the various bird symbols in Yeats, with particular reference to the Byzantium poems. Diana Arbin Ben-Merre's "The Poet Laureate and the Golden Bird: A Note on Yeats' Byzantium Poems" (*CJIS*, 1979) uses Yeats's *Bookman* letter (Nov. 1892) to demonstrate "the differing conceptions of the golden bird in the two poems," but her argument is not convincing. In "Yeats' 'Byzantium' " (*OJES*, 1979), Avadhesh K. Srivastava is content to summarize some of the standard commentaries on the poem, giving particular attention to the second stanza.

David Cowart's Freudian analysis in "Identity and Sexuality: Yeats's 'The Cap and Bells' and Its Contexts" (*YER*, 1979) adds little to previous efforts except for the suggestion that the Fool and Queen "adumbrate" the concepts of Will and Mask in *A Vision*. Sharon D. Decker's "Love's Mansion: Sexuality in Yeats's Poetry" (*MBL*, 1979) gives some emphasis to "The Three Bushes" but offers more quotation and paraphrase than analysis. Thomas H. Jackson's interesting if somewhat long-winded essay (*ELH*, 1979) discusses Yeats's and Mallarmé's differing responses to positivism and argues that William Carlos Williams is "to a remarkable extent the realizer of their goals." In "Yeats's 'When You Are Old' " (*Expl*, 1979), Erik S. Ryding suggests that the "crowd of stars" refers, by way of the Pleiades, to the group of sixteenth-century French poets named the Pléiade, thereby making Yeats (rejected by Maud Gonne) lost in "the crowd" of despondent love poets; the interpretation is unlikely. Michael J. Sidnell (*CLQ*, 1979) insists on the "allegorical basis" of the "The Wanderings of Oisin" and also argues that "Yeats's distinction between solar and lunar influences is the main feature of the symbolic structure"; the essay offers some interesting new readings (e.g., suggesting Edward Dowden as the main source for the demon of book 2), but Sidnell's statement that since "Alspach's study (in 1943) of some of the sources of the poem there has been no extended examination of any aspect of 'Oisin' " simply ignores the work then available by Daniel Albright, Charles J. Clancy, Harold Bloom, Adele M. Dalsimer, and Brenda S. Webster. In " 'Adam's Curse' and the Value of Artistic Labour" (*YER*, 1979), David Ward suggests that the conclusion of the poem is weak "because Yeats tries to use a transcendent symbol from his earlier work for which the reader—and the grammar of the poem—is simply unprepared"; but Ward does not admit that such an effect may be precisely Yeats's intention. The major argument in Joan Dayan's essay on *The Wind among the Reeds* (*CLS*, 1979) is that "the poetic experience of *The Wind* is that of the poem negating itself, its very circularity leading to a dead cipher." Why an important journal would publish an essay such as Dayan's that discusses this poem without referring to any criticism after Arthur Symons' 1899 review is a puzzling question. In "Some Observations on Myth and Legend: Irish and Canadian" (*PTRSC*, 1979), Douglas Le Pan offers an interesting if unresearched account of "Easter 1916" that shows Yeats "assisting at the birth of a modern Irish legend."

The chapter "Yeats and Oisin," in Robert Welch's *Irish Poetry from Moore to Yeats* (1980), does little beyond making the standard comparisons of Yeats with Mangan and Ferguson and providing a plot summary of "The Wanderings of Oisin." What interpretation is offered centers on the political level of book 2, suggesting that "the demon is not just England, he is also Irish recollection of English violence and misrule." "Yeatsian Myth as Seen in 'The Wanderings of Oisin' " (*Bull. of Seisen Women's Coll.*, 1980), by Eriko Takada, A.C.J., is a commentary on and paraphrase of the poem of no special significance. More interesting is N. Jeanne Argoff's "Yeats's Innovations in the Ballad Form" (*CLQ*, 1980), which concentrates on the ballads from the 1930s and suggests that Yeats's later ballads succeed in "closing the gap between the literary ballad and its popular models without giving up the sophistication and complexity achieved by the professional poet." Shyamal Bagchee (*CJIS*, 1980) tries to show that the "real significance" of "The Statues" is in "Yeats's ability to fuse together two such diverse elements as sexual desire and intense patriotism"; but he can find little of note in the third stanza, suggesting that "in the narrative structure of the poem" it "does not contribute anything significant." Harold F. Brooks (*DUJ*, 1980) presents an interesting close reading of "The Tower" but regrettably ignores many of the major prior interpretations. Virginia Pruitt's essay (*ELH*, 1980) is more properly researched but is not convincing in seeing "The Tower" as a criticism of the " 'intellectual' solution offered in 'Sailing to Byzantium,' " since such a scheme oversimplifies the opening poem in the volume. The brief comments on Yeats's early poetry in John Porter Houston's *French Symbolism and the Modernist Movement: A Study of Poetic Structures* (1980) argue that "the mood was the overriding consideration" and that the "urge to find some intellectual construct" behind the poems is misguided; the question of possible influences is not addressed. Seamus Heaney's interesting "The Makings of a Music: Reflections on Wordsworth and Yeats," in his *Preoccupations: Selected Prose, 1968-78* (1980), demonstrates that "there is a relation between the process of composition and the feel of the completed poem all through Yeats's work." The comments on Yeats in "Reading Poetry Aloud" (*ESA*, 1980), by Geoffrey Hutchings, are of no special significance. The section on Yeats in Kenneth Koch's "Inspiration and Work: How Poetry Gets to Be Written" (*CLS*, 1980) suggests that the imagery of "The Second Coming" is indebted to George Yeats's pregnancy, a possibility perhaps impossible to prove or disprove—even though Koch is not altogether accurate when he states that "Yeats wrote this poem the day before his wife gave birth to his first child." Kalu Ogbaa's poorly written "Yeats and the Irish Revolution" (*ComQ*, 1980), which discusses four poems, is of no value. In " 'The Folly of Being Comforted': Three Versions and Three Voices" (*WascanaR*, 1980), Thomas A. Pendleton misreads the poem by not perceiving that it offers more than one kind of "comfort."

Ronald Schleifer's "Principles, Proper Names, and the Personae of Yeats's *The Wind among the Reeds*" (*Éire*, 1981) contains some interesting comments on individual poems, but the writing is not always clear. Schleifer also overlooks or pays insufficient attention to the previous scholarship and commits too many errors, especially in quotations. " 'Imitate Him If You Dare': Relationships between the Epitaphs of Swift and Yeats" (*Studies*, 1981), by James Lovic Allen, is a perceptive account that also shows how Yeats draws on other epitaph conventions. Allen concludes that "Yeats's inscription is . . . a virtual exemplar of simultaneous adoption and adaptation of a . . . specific set of conventions, the conventions of writing epitaphs."

12. Studies of the Drama

GENERAL STUDIES

The chapter "Yeats, Synge, and the Irish School," in Ernest Randolph Reynolds' *Modern English Drama: A Survey of the Theatre from 1900* (1949; rev. ed., 1950), includes some brief but admiring remarks on Yeats's plays, especially *The Countess Cathleen*. Norman Newton (*ELC*, 1958) provides an interesting though partial analysis of *The Player Queen*, suggesting that "the play concerns itself with two kinds of power—revolutionary-political power and sexual power—both embodied in animal and bird symbols." Newton also comments on some of the fallacies in the conventional theories of modern poetic drama. Henry Popkin's "Yeats as Dramatist" (*TDR*, 1959) is a general appreciation of Yeats's ability to write plays that combine "seeming simplicity with extraordinary complexity." "The Plays of Yeats," in Kenneth Rexroth's *Bird in the Bush: Obvious Essays* (1959), is an admiring review of the 1953 *Collected Plays*, noting that "Yeats is certainly the greatest poet of our time" and that his best plays "achieve a purity and intensity quite unlike anything in the modern theater." "The Lyric and the Philosophic in Yeats' *Calvary*" (*MD*, 1960), by Elliott B. Gose, Jr., briefly demonstrates the relevance of *A Vision* to the play but has little of interest for advanced students. George Steiner's *The Birth of Tragedy* (1961) includes some comments, most of them negative, on Yeats's plays; Steiner asserts that even Yeats's best plays are no more than "prolegomena to a future drama." John R. Moore's "Cuchulain, Christ, and the Queen of Love: Aspects of Yeatsian Drama" (*TDR*, 1962) assesses selected plays.

Yeats is treated only briefly by J. Chiari in *Landmarks of Contemporary Drama* (1965) and by Tom F. Driver in *Romantic Quest and Modern Query: A History of the Modern Theatre* (1970), though both critics argue for a positive assessment of Yeats's contribution to the modern theater. George M. Harper's perceptive "The Reconciliation of Paganism and Christianity in Yeats' *Unicorn from the Stars*," in . . . *All These to Teach: Essays in Honor of C. A. Robertson* (ed. Robert A. Bryan et al., 1965), shows how Yeats's searach for a "satisfactory substitute" for Christianity is reflected in the play and also discusses the differences between *Unicorn* and the earlier *Where There Is Nothing*. Bobby L. Smith (*ArQ*, 1966), attempts to demonstrate that *Four Plays for Dancers* reproduces the six-play sequence of plays in the Noh; the reading of *The Only Jealousy of Emer* seems especially confused. In a chapter in *Studies in the Arts: Proceedings of the St. Peter's College Literary Society* (ed. Francis Warner, 1968), T. R. Henn offers a general survey of Yeats's work in the theater, concluding that none of the plays "can be called 'great.' " Murray Roston's *Biblical Drama in England: From the Middle Ages to the Present Day* (1968) includes readings of *Calvary* and *The Resurrection*, admiring the latter but objecting to *Calvary* because "the dual symbolism . . . serves to represent both the historical and the contemporary changes of the cycles" and thus "ultimately collapses." Oliver Snoddy's "Yeats and Irish in the Theatre" (*Éire*, 1969) simply reprints Yeats's comments on the topic from *Samhain*. Hardly more significant is Margaret Patrice Slattery's unresearched "*Deirdre*: The 'Mingling of the Contraries' in Plot and Symbolism" (*MD*, 1969). Barton R. Friedman's essay (*ArQ*, 1970) stresses such topics as the influence of Blake and Shelley on *The King's Threshold* and the function of the play's lunar imagery. Vinod Sena's "W. B. Yeats and the Storm-Beaten Threshold" (*DM*, 1970) brings together most of Yeats's comments on tragedy without much awareness of prior analyses; Sena covers much the same ground in his "Catharsis or Ecstasy: W. B. Yeats on Tragedy" (*LCrit*, 1974). Robert Coltrane's "From Legend to Literature: W. B. Yeats and the Cuchulain Cycle" (*LHR*, 1971) is an introductory study of the plays and their major sources.

There are some brief remarks on Yeats's drama, particularly the dance plays, in *Dramatic Poetry from Mediaeval to Modern Times: A Philosophic Enquiry into the Nature of Poetic Drama in England, Ireland and the United States of America* (Madras, 1972), by H. H. Anniah Gowda. In "Yeats's Symbolic Farce: *The Player Queen*" (*MD*, 1972), Michael Hinden takes issue with the readings of Ellmann, Vendler, and Wilson, arguing that "Yeats's final version of the play was not intended as a serious dramatization of his theories but rather as self-satirical treatment of ideas which earlier he had failed to render satisfactorily in abstract form." Equally interesting is Phillip L. Marcus' "Myth and Meaning in Yeats's *The Death of Cuchulain*" (*IUR*, 1972), which suggests that the Morrigu is trying to assist Cuchulain and that the play is thus concerned with the tensions between the natural and the supernatural realms. In "Treatment of Christianity in W. B. Yeats's *The Resurrection*" (*LCrit*, 1974), Sathya M. Babu gives an effective summary of and commentary on the play but does not go beyond previous studies. David L. Vanderwerken's "*Purgatory*: Yeats's Modern Tragedy" (*CLQ*, 1974) provides a competent but not especially new reading, stressing that "ironic displacement of the myth of ritual sacrifice is at the heart of the tragic act in *Purgatory*." In "The Brief and Troublesome Reign of *Cathleen ni Houlihan* (1902-1907)" (*SAB*, 1975), John A. Byars notes the presence of the Cathleen figure in Lady Gregory's *Kincora* and Synge's *Playboy*. Anthony Coleman's useful "A Calendar for the Production and Reception of *Cathleen ni Houlihan*" (*MD*, 1975) cites many of the early reviews and also refers to the promptbook in the National Library of Ireland.

"Towards Lyric Tragedy: W. B. Yeats," a disunified, unresearched chapter in David Lenson's *Achilles' Choice: Examples of Modern Tragedy* (1975), is a negligible contribution. Lenson gives considerable attention to *The Unicorn from the Stars*, the Oedipus plays, "The Gyres," and "Lapis Lazuli" and points out the importance of *A Vision* in allowing Yeats to write "tragedy whose action is the time we are living in, whose characters are all of us." Andrew Parkin's "Singular Voices: Monologue and Monodrama in the Plays of W. B. Yeats" (*CJIS*, 1975) traces Yeats's developing "mastery of dramatic structures compressed and subtle enough to give extraordinary intellectual and emotional weight to the one-act play" but fails to take into account David R. Clark's analysis of the play within a play in *The Words upon the Window-Pane* (in Clark's *W. B. Yeats and the Theatre of Desolate Reality*, 1965). *Insight IV: Analyses of Modern British and American Drama* (ed. Hermann J. Weiand, Frankfurt, 1975) includes John A. M. Rillie's explication of *Purgatory*.

John Berryman's *The Freedom of the Poet* (1976) contains a 1936 review of the *Collected Plays* (1934), making the standard charge that Yeats's plays are not dramatic: "Yeats has not written great plays or anything like great plays." Patrick A. McCarthy's "Talent and Tradition in Yeats's *On Baile's Strand*" (*Éire*, 1976) is primarily about Yeats's modification of his sources, though some perceptive comments on the symbolic value of the cloak are also included. "Neo-Modernist Drama: Yeats and Pirandello," a chapter by James McFarlane in *Modernism 1890-1930* (ed. Malcolm Bradbury and McFarlane, 1976), traces Yeats's changing dramataic styles and suggests his influence on later playwrights. Andrew Parkin's "Yeats's Orphic Voice" (*CJIS*, 1976) comments on *The Only Jealousy of Emer*, *A Full Moon in March*, and *The Resurrection* without offering significant new insights. The same might be said of Halbert A. Reeves's "Dramatic Economy of Imagery in Two of Yeats's Later Plays" (*McNR*, 1976-77), which offers solid but derivative discussions of *Purgatory* and *The Death of Cuchulain*. In "The Golden Cradle and the Beggar-Man: Problems of Yeats's Poetics" (*CRCL*, 1976)—an essay that, despite its title, is solely on the drama—Timothy J. Reiss attempts to apply Mikhail Bakhtin's distinction between "monological discourse" and "dialogical intercourse" to *The King's Threshold*, *The Unicorn from the Stars*, and *The Herne's Egg*; readers familiar with the plays will find little to surprise them other than the terminology.

Richard Taylor's *The Drama of W. B. Yeats: Irish Myth and the*

Japanese Nō (1976) contains interesting readings of some individual plays, such as *The Herne's Egg*, but as a whole is less than fully successful. Taylor constantly wavers in his judgment of exactly how crucial the Noh was to Yeats, and he proceeds through the canon regardless of the relation of any particular play to the Japanese tradition. He pays insufficient attention to the extensive research on his topic, neglecting such important studies as Thomas Parkinson's article (*CL*, 1954) and Hiro Ishibashi's *Yeats and the Noh* (1966). He also appears to have little sympathy for Yeats's plays, attacking them for their "lack of relevance to the modern predicament" and concluding that "Yeats's flaw as a dramatist lay in his failure to meet the expectations of the spectator." The lack of illustrations is unfortunate. In *The Language of Modern Drama* (1977), Gareth Lloyd Evans provides a conventional evaluation of the plays as good literature but bad drama, suggesting that Yeats's basic flaws are his themes, his habit of constant revision, and "the nature of his imagination." Barton R. Friedman's *Adventures in the Deeps of the Mind: The Cuchulain Cycle* (1977) is a disappointing study of the five-play cycle and of *Deirdre*, offering little that is new and written in a lame and digressive style. In the opening chapter Friedman tries to demonstrate that Yeats's developing dramatic aesthetic resulted in plays that "stage the mind of the artist creating his artifact," but this restrictive thesis is often lost sight of in the close readings that follow. Each play is afforded a chapter, but the analyses are interrupted by asides on such matters as the influence of Robert Bridges on *On Baile's Strand* or the parallels between John O'Leary and Cuchulain in *The Green Helmet*.

Warren Leamon's "Theatre as Dream: Yeats's Stagecraft" (*MD*, 1977) gives a rather standard account of Yeats's "absolute rejection of realism in tragedy" and refers to none of the previous scholarship. In "The Tragedy of Dogmatism: Yeats's Later Plays" (*SWR*, 1977), Leamon launches a broad attack on Yeats's plays, citing only Nathan and Wilson rather than those critics who have anticipated him. Leamon asserts that "in his plays the obsession with image confuses action and character with form and symbol. The result is neither pure poetry nor tragedy but a kind of lyric drama in which symbolism is used as a substitute for character and action." F. C. McGrath *(CJIS*, 1977) gives an unexciting close reading of *At the Hawk's Well*, suggesting that "Cuchulain's only attribute in the play is heroic personality." Liam Miller's *The Noble Drama of W. B. Yeats* (1977) is a factual account of the composition, publication, and production of each of Yeats's plays, accompanied by some splendid illustrations and extensive quotations. Particularly useful are the reproductions of all the programs for the first performances of Yeats's plays. In "The Quest for Individuality: Yeats's *Four Plays for Dancers*" (*Éire*, 1977), George M. Murphy argues for the essential unity and order of the four plays, based on Yeats's references to the Four Treasures of Ireland and on the Jungian theory of individuation; the result is more ingenious than informative. Eriko Takada's "The Quest of William Butler Yeats for Human Integrity" (*Bull. of Seisen College*, Japan, 1977) provides an introductory commentary on *On Baile's Strand*, suggesting that Cuchulain "is the most archetypal of the Yeatsian tragic heroes." The brief discussion of Yeats by Arnold P.

Hinchcliffe in *Modern Verse Drama* (1977) concentrates on *Purgatory*, "his finest verse drama."

The chapter "W. B. Yeats's *Deirdre* (1906)," in Herbert V. Fackler's *That Tragic Queen: The Deirdre Legend in Anglo-Irish Literature* (Salzburg, 1978), is of little interest, but the book as a whole is useful in providing a background for Yeats's treatment of the story. Lynn Haims's "Apocalyptic Vision in Three Late Plays by Yeats" (*SoR*, 1978) is essentially a close reading of *A Full Moon in March*, *Purgatory*, and *The Death of Cuchulain*, arguing that the "transformation of private and national selves through the medium of art is the central preoccupation of these strange and extraordinary plays"; Haims believes that the transformation succeeds in two of the plays but not in *Purgatory*. In "Ritual and Parody in *The Herne's Egg*" (*CJIS*, 1978), Sidney Poger provides much plot summary but little reference to the critical tradition on the play; he suggests that the theme of the play is that "man trivializes his rituals, making them comic or unreal, and then governs his life by them." Ronald Schuchard's cogent "W. B. Yeats and the London Theatre Societies, 1901–1904" (*RES*, 1978) is a model of scholarship, drawing extensively on unpublished materials to trace Yeats's involvement in several clubs and societies at the turn of the century. Gordon M. Wickstrom's "Legend Focusing Legend in Yeats's *Deirdre*" (*TJ*, 1978), a discussion of the differences between Yeats's play and one version of the legend in the *Book of Leinster*, is a minor contribution.

Katharine Worth's *The Irish Drama of Europe from Yeats to Beckett* (1978) stresses the influence of Yeats on the contemporary theater, particularly on the work of O'Casey and Beckett—although surely the thesis that "the Irish line running from Synge through Yeats and O'Casey to Beckett has become the main line of modern drama" is an overstatement. She sees Synge and especially Maeterlinck as the seminal forces behind Yeats's plays. Her comments on some selected plays vary in quality from perceptive analyses to sympathetic plot summaries; moreover, since Worth believes that "the plays call out, in fact, for as many interpretations as there are imaginations to respond to them," she has only a minimal interest in how the plays reflect Yeats's thinking. Nor does Worth take notice of prior responses: for instance, although she covers many of the same topics included in James W. Flannery's study (discussed on p. 126), she avoids any reference to his published work and mentions only a 1975 lecture at Sligo. And it is disturbing to find the same Eliot passage cited three times, only once correctly. Still, Worth's book offers a refreshing and interesting assessment of Yeats as "one of the great masters of the twentieth-century theatre." Her "Evolution of European 'Drama of the Interior': Maeterlinck, Wilde and Yeats" (*MuK*, 1979) summarizes one of the major theses of the longer study.

In "Yeats: A Case for Resurrection" (*CJIS*, 1979), Barry Bauska offers an appreciation of *The Resurrection* that will have little significance for readers familiar with the play. There are two chapters on Yeats in Philip Edwards' uneven *Threshold of a Nation: A Study in English and Irish Drama* (1979), which essentially incorporates his *Na-*

tionalist Theatres: Shakespeare and Yeats (1976). One chapter provides the background in both Irish tradition and Renaissance literature for the concept that the poet should have political power and offers a reading of *The King's Threshold*; the other discusses Yeats's belief in the relation between nationality and literature and compares Yeats and Shakespeare. Most of the ideas are familiar, and much relevant scholarship—even Rupin W. Desai's *Yeats's Shakespeare* (1971)—is ignored. In "Intimations of Immortality: W. B. Yeats's *At the Hawk's Well*" (*TJ*, 1979), Natalie Crohn Schmitt argues that in the play "for the first time, Yeats suggests the idea repeatedly expressed in the later plays: that the supernatural is not beyond this realm but a feeling of bursting fullness within it"; her interpretation of Cuchulain's final choice as illustrating his heroism is far more common than is suggested. In "Artist of Bones: Yeats's *Calvary* as Poem and Play" (*MSLC*, 1979), Howard D. Pearce fails to demonstrate fully that in the play "Christ as symbolic poet or dead man is engaged in the basic activity of self-completion" or that "the pull between the dramatic and the poetic forms becomes . . . the ultimate art of the play, the bodying forth of an idea." Clearer and more perceptive is W. J. McCormack's "Yeats' *Purgatory*: A Play and a Tradition" (*Crane Bag*, 1979), which notes the use of "specifically *nineteenth-century* social patterns" in the play and offers some interesting comments on the way in which "the Old Man exists in a multiple dramatic relation." Ann Peyton's "Yeats, Zen, and the Theatre of Enlightenment" (*SARev*, 1979) adds nothing to previous discussions of the topic. Only slightly more useful is Ronald Schleifer's "The Civility of Sorrow: Yeats's Daimonic Tragedy" (*PQ*, 1979), a quotation-filled essay that does little to elucidate its major topic but does make some noteworthy remarks about "That the Night Come." The claim that "commentators have not dealt with the relation between Yeats's theory of masks and his notion of tragedy" is inaccurate. Maureen Murphy's " 'What Stood in the Post Office / With Pearse and Connolly?': The Case for Robert Emmet" (*Éire*, 1979) concerns the veneration of Emmet by Pearse and does not mention Yeats.

A Needle's Eye (ed. Mary O'Malley and John Boyd, 1979) includes four essays on Yeats. Denis Donoghue's "The Politics of Yeats's Theatre" (rpt. without indication from *Threshold*, 1974) is a collection of commonplaces until the concluding and debatable assertions that "his last plays, and notably *The Herne's Egg*, are canes for punishing the bourgeoisie which had let him down" and that "he needed to 'fail' in any publicly defined way so that he could take unto himself the heroism of failure, and sing the heroic note." In "The Plays of W. B. Yeats: A Time of Re-assessment" Conor O'Malley tries to show that the plays "will eventually find acceptance in the professional theatre." Both Sam McCready's "Imperceptibly into Song" and Raymond Warren's "An Idea of Music" discuss Yeats's attempts to combine words with music in his drama, McCready offering a humorous anecdote about Yeats at the 1934 production of *The King of the Great Clock Tower* and Warren supplying samples of his music for *The Player Queen* and *Calvary*. *A Needle's Eye* also includes some black-and-white photographs of recent productions of Yeats's plays at the Lyric Players Theatre in Belfast.

Anthony Bradley's *William Butler Yeats* (1980), in the World Dramatists series, is an introductory guide to the plays, providing for each a plot summary, an indication of the date of first production, some commentary, and occasional unplaced remarks on contemporary productions (sometimes accompanied by photographs). The final chapter, "Yeats and the Irish Historical and Cultural Background," is useful for beginning students. Joseph Leondar Schneider's *Unity of Culture in Yeats's Drama* (Seoul, 1980), a somewhat disjointed study, attempts to show Yeats changing attitudes toward the possibility of attaining unity of culture in Ireland, seeing the 1907 riots over Synge's *Playboy* as a key factor in the change from optimism to pessimism. But the book sometimes loses sight of this familiar thesis in the midst of presenting close readings of *The King's Threshold, The Dreaming of the Bones, Purgatory, Deirdre, The Only Jealousy of Emer*, and *The Death of Cuchulain*. These readings refer only selectively to the extant criticism and contain a substantial amount of plot summary. Schneider is particularly distressed by *Purgatory*, "one of the least congenial of Yeats's works." In "Symbolist Drama: Villiers de l'Isle Adam, Strindberg, and Yeats" (*NYLF*, 1980), Haskell M. Block offers a brief but useful survey of the main characteristics of the genre, stressing that "the structue of the mystical drama of the turn of the century is almost always enclosed within a pattern of spiritual initiation." Although at times too allegorical and not completely satisfactory in the treatment of *Calvary*, Herbert J. Levine's "The Inner Drama of Yeats's *Four Plays for Dancers*" (*CLQ* 1980) effectively discusses the plays as "all deeply autobiographical in the way that Yeats uses their fictional settings and characters to work through problems in his own life." Bettina L. Knapp's interesting chapter "*The Only Jealousy of Emer*: Recycling the Elements," in her *Theatre and Alchemy* (1980), suggests that the play dramatizes "the alchemical operations which take his protagonists from a state of primal oneness to *separatio* and *coagulatio*" but that the process does not lead to "evolution into a higher sphere of existence, but rather to another *separatio*, another war and another rebirth." Knapp thus concludes her essentially allegorical interpretation by asserting that Emer's "sacrifice is fruitless."

J. J. Ll. Cribb (*IUR*, 1981) presents a suggestive account of the influence of Blake on *The Countess Kathleen*, arguing that the two main debts "are the character of the Countess and the action or movement of the play as a whole." He finds the ending of the play seriously flawed because "Blake points one way. The story [i.e., the source] points another," and Yeats "denies himself the possibility of writing a tragedy." Mary FitzGerald's " 'Out of a medium's mouth': The Writing of *The Words upon the Window-Pane*" (*CLQ*, 1981) demonstrates that the play was based on C. E. Lawrence's *Swift and Stella* and comments perceptively on Yeats's mastery of the dramatic form. Of no particular value are the brief discussions of three Yeats plays in John Orr's *Tragic Drama and Modern Society: Studies in the Social and Literary Theory of Drama from 1870 to the Present* (1981).

YEATS IN PRODUCTION

André Rouyer's "In Quest of W. B. Yeats: Notes on the French Production of Three Plays" (*Threshold*, 1957) describes a production at the Théâtre de Poche but laments that "Yeats is still almost unknown to-day to the French public at large." In *Benson and the Bensonians* (1960), J. C. Trewin provides some information on F. R. Benson's appearance in *Diarmuid and Grania*.

James W. Flannery's *W. B. Yeats and the Idea of a Theatre: The Early Abbey Theatre in Theory and Practice* (1976) treats the plays from the beginning to the discovery of the Noh, arguing that "Yeats's theories of drama and his own dramatic work were continually revised and reshaped in terms of his practical experience in the theatre." Flannery provides useful information about the conditions in which Yeats's plays were composed, discussing, for example, how some of the plays were written or revised to conform to the talents of the available actors. He gives good accounts of Yeats's relationships with the Fays and with Gordon Craig but undervalues the contributions of George Moore and Lady Gregory. Although the book contains much material that will be familiar to advanced students and often betrays its origins as a dissertation (Trinity Coll. Dublin 1970), it remains the fullest account available of Yeats's early dramatic career.

Karen Dorn's "Stage Production and Greek Theatre Movement: W. B. Yeats's Play *The Resurrection* and His Versions of *King Oedipus* and *Oedipus at Colonus*" (*ThR*, 1976) is an interesting and scholarly account of Yeats's interest in the movement and of the ways in which the plays discussed were written with a view to production in the Peacock (*The Resurrection*) or on the main Abbey stage (the Oedipus plays); Dorn concludes that the three works "were the culmination of Yeats's long interest in the adaptation of the Greek theatre to the modern stage." In "Two Views of Purgatory: Yeats and Beckett at the Edinburgh Festival" (*JBeS*, 1978), Richard Cave discusses a production of *Purgatory* in a Beckettian style, directed by Sé Sheridan, explaining "this was not exactly the play Yeats conceived but it was a fine realization of most of his themes and intentions; there were losses but there were powerful gains." In "His Hour Come Round at Last? W. B. Yeats, Playwright" (*Éire*, 1978), Audrey S. Eyler gives an account of the 1976 production of three Yeats plays in Dublin, directed by James W. Flannery; she does not object to, but indeed admires, the cuts made in the texts. In "A Style for Yeats's Dance-Plays: 'The More Passionate Is the Art the More Marked Is the Selection' " (*YES*, 1979), Richard Allen Cave offers an interesting account of student productions of three Yeats plays, arguing that "the explicit theatricality of Yeats's plays holds the key to their meaning" and that "to observe his every direction is to find a coherent dramatic unity in performance"; unfortunately Cave overlooks Flannery's work, but he makes some astute remarks on the use of different verse rhythms as a method of characterization, especially in *The Only Jealousy of Emer*. Gertrude Patterson's lecture "W. B. Yeats in the Theatre: The Challenge of the Poetic Play" (*YER*, 1979; *Threshold*, 1980) does not succeed as a published essay. Of more significance are Peter Alderson Smith's comments (*Éire*, 1979) on the symbolic significance of the scenery for *The Countess Cathleen*, particularly the scenery used before the 1912 revisions; Smith emphasizes the importance of the tapestry. Liam Miller (*ERA*, The Curragh, 1980) describes his design for "a seven-fold painted screen to be used as a background for certain later plays" of Yeats and provides a black-and-white illustration of it.

YEATS AND THE ABBEY

Three more volumes of *The Modern Irish Drama: A Documentary History* have been published: *Laying the Foundations, 1902–1904* (1976) and *The Abbey Theatre: The Years of Synge, 1905–1909* (1978), both by Robert Hogan and James Kilroy, and *The Rise of the Realists, 1910–1915* (1979), by Hogan, Richard Burnham, and Daniel P. Poteet. These authoritative chronicles of the period include quotations from unpublished letters to and from Yeats as well as newspaper reports of interviews and speeches. Hugh Hunt's *The Abbey: Ireland's National Theatre, 1904–1979* (1979) is far less detailed but essentially accurate and can thus be recommended for beginning students.

Harold Orel's "A Drama for the Nation," in *Irish History and Culture: Aspects of a People's Heritage* (ed. Orel, 1976), is a standard survey of the beginnings of the theater movement. In "Annie Horniman, Practical Idealist" (*CJIS*, 1977), Edward Malins stresses Horniman's importance to the movement and her disinterest in politics. Mary M. Lago's "Irish Poetic Drama in St. Louis" (*TCL*, 1977) provides details about the controversy over the production of A. E.'s *Deirdre* at the 1904 Exposition. Anthony Coleman's "AE's *Deirdre* and the Fays" (*N&Q*, 1979) gives the text of a letter from A. E. to the Fays in April 1902 and refers briefly to Yeats. In *The Dublin Drama League 1918–1941* (1979), Brenna Katz Clarke and Harold Ferrar note that Yeats's wish to include non-Irish plays in the Abbey repertoire was never fulfilled; three productions of his plays by the Dublin Drama League are also listed.

13. Studies of Other Topics

A VISION AND MYTHOLOGY

Robert Martin Adams' "Now That My Ladder's Gone: Yeats without Myth" (*Accent*, 1953) presents the best argument for the essential irrelevance of *A Vision* to Yeats's achievement. Adams also offers a brilliant close reading of "Byzantium" and a provocative summary of Yeats's career: "He was early concerned with the expression of ideas, artistic or national; then with the development of personality, natural and adventitious; and lastly with the facts of animality, *tout court*." Of less interest is the case against the importance of *A Vision* presented in Donald F. Sturtevant's "The Public and Private Minds of W. B. Yeats" (*Thoth*, 1963).

Rosemary Puglia Ritvo examines the parallels between Plotinus and

A Vision in two rather complex articles, "*A Vision* B: The Plotinian Metaphysical Basis" (*RES*, 1975) and "Plotinus's Third 'Ennead' and Yeats's *A Vision* (*N&Q*, 1976). Northrop Frye's *The Secular Scripture: A Study of the Structure of Romance* (1976) includes a few scattered and primarily unfavorable remarks on Yeats. Frye's essay "The Rising of the Moon" (from *An Honoured Guest*) is reprinted in his *Spiritus Mundi: Essays on Literature, Myth, and Society* (1976); in the preface to the collection Frye objects to the "irresponsible fatalism" of *A Vision*. In "Yeats's Esoteric Comedy" (*HudR*, 1977), Steven Helmling concentrates on the prefatory matter in the 1937 *A Vision* but ignores Hazard Adams' important study of the topic in *Blake and Yeats* (1955; rpt. 1968). Also overlooking Adams is Eugene Korkowski in "Yeats' *Vision* as Philosophic *Satura*" (*Éire*, 1977), a strained attempt to classify the book as a Menippean satire. In " 'The Whirl Becomes a Sphere': Concept and Symbol in Yeats' Poetry of Beatitude" (*C&L*, 1977), David J. Leigh, S.J., offers a conventional survey of Yeats's difficulties in presenting effective images of the divine, whether in prose or in verse. Rama Nand Rai's "A Study of W. B. Yeats's *A Vision*" (*JSL*, 1978–79) is introductory and not altogether accurate.

W. B. Stanford's *Ireland and the Classical Tradition* (1976) provides a brief but solid survey of Yeats's interest in classical mythology, particularly Greek mythology, and argues that his classical allusions "are vividly seen or felt, not just recalled."

THE OCCULT AND YEATS'S RELIGION

David Daiches' "Religion, Poetry and the 'Dilemma' of the Modern Writer," in his *Literary Essays* (1956), discusses how Yeats's "dialectical symbolic system" allowed him to come to terms with the loss of tradition. Daiches argues the same views in his "Theodicy, Poetry, and Tradition," in *Spiritual Problems in Contemporary Literature* (ed. Stanley Romaine Hopper, 1957), and makes scattered comments on Yeats's use of myth in "Myth, Metaphor, and Poetry," in *More Literary Essays* (1968). In "Religion and Literature" (*SR*, 1974), Cleanth Brooks is not completely convincing in his attempt to demonstrate that "the driving power of many of [Yeats's] poems comes from his use of religious symbols which were still vibrant in the community of which all his life he counted himself a member—symbols which therefore must still have carried some special resonance for him." "Yeats, Gnosticism, and the Sacred Void," in Harold Bloom's *Poetry and Repression: Revisionism from Blake to Stevens* (1975), gives a somewhat more sympathetic picture of Yeats's "syncretic Gnosticism" than was offered in his *Yeats*, followed by elaborate and Bloomian readings of "The Second Coming," "Byzantium," and "Cuchulain Comforted"; the previous scholarship is of course ignored, except for attacks on the unnamed and apparently synonymous "reviewers and Yeats-idolators."

Mary Catherine Flannery's disappointing *Yeats and Magic: The Earlier Works* (1978) contains many factual errors and makes little attempt to consider the details of her subject or to survey the extant criticism (she makes almost no use, for instance, of the new materials available in *Yeats and the Occult*, ed. George Mills Harper, 1975). Her attempt to conclude with a presentation of the National Library of Ireland manuscripts of "Ego Dominus Tuus" fails because of her inability to read Yeats's handwriting ("nine lines unreadable, crossed out") and her ignorance of the existence of further manuscript material in the Michael B. Yeats holdings and in the Berg Collection. Mary E. Bryson's "Metaphors for Freedom: Theosophy and the Irish Literary Revival" (*CJIS*, 1977) includes some comments on Yeats but adds little to previous assessments of his involvement in the movement. Likewise, Yeats is only briefly mentioned in *Ancient Wisdom Revived: A History of the Theosophical Movement* (1980), by Bruce F. Campbell. P. L. R. Brown's "Psychological Aspects of Some Yeatsian Concepts" (*Mosaic*, 1977) is a well-written defense of Yeats's esoteric beliefs, emphasizing their parallels in Jung. In an earlier comparative study, "Yeats and Jung: An Ideological Comparison" (*L&P*, 1963), Richard J. Wall and Roger Fitzgerald quote a 1960 letter to them from Jung, stating "as you rightly surmise, I am not acquainted with his [Yeats's] work at all. I have never read a line of his." Both of these essays are essentially superseded by Olney's *The Rhizome and the Flower* (discussed on p. 109).

IRELAND AND YEATS'S POLITICS

James D. Boulger's "Yeats and Irish Identity" (*Thought*, 1967) effectively presents the increasing Irishness of Yeats in his later career and also offers some comparisons with Eugene O'Neill. Terence de Vere White's chapter "Yeats as an Anglo-Irishman," in his *The Anglo-Irish* (1972), is of little significance. Thomas Flanagan's "Yeats, Joyce, and the Matter of Ireland" (*CritI*, 1975) compares the two writers' attitudes toward the masses and the folk tradition; it is well written but unoriginal. J. C. Beckett discusses Yeats briefly in *The Anglo-Irish Tradition* (1976). In "W. B. Yeats and the Public Life of Ireland" (*New Divinity*, 1976), F. S. L. Lyons soundly sketches Yeats's relationship with Ireland throughout his career. Harold Orel's "The Irishry of William Butler Yeats," in *Irish History and Culture: Aspects of a People's Heritage* (ed. Orel, 1976), is more introductory. There are only a few comments on Yeats in Michael Butler Yeats, "My Father and Ireland Today" (*Yeats Soc. of Japan Annual Report*, 1976).

M. C. Bradbrook's " 'A Dream within a Dream': Yeats and the Legend of Ireland" (*Mosaic*, 1977) is a hurried survey of Yeats's attitudes toward Ireland; it is of no use to advanced students. More provocative is F. S. L. Lyons' "The Parnell Theme in Literature," in *Place, Personality, and the Irish Writer* (ed. Andrew Carpenter, 1977), which concentrates on showing the differences between the facts of Parnell's life and his treatment in literature; Lyons also effectively contrasts Yeats's and Joyce's use of the Parnell materials. An essay by Robert O'Driscoll in the same collection, "Return to the Hearthstone: Ideals of the Celtic Literary Revival," consists primarily of quotations from Yeats and A. E. and avoids all previous discussions of the topic. Nor is there much of interest in John Unterecker's rambling "Countryman, Peasant and Servant in the Poetry of W. B. Yeats," in *Views of the Irish Peasantry, 1800–1916* (ed. Daniel J. Casey and Robert E. Rhodes, 1977). Seamus Deane's "Yeats, Ireland and Revolution" (*Crane Bag*, 1977), an essay based on some arguable assumptions, is unsympathetic to Yeats, finding his career "marked by incoherence and by an almost wilful mysticism." Augustine Martin provides an effective reply in "What Stalked through the Post Office? (Reply to Seamus Deane)" (*Crane Bag*, 1978).

D. E. S. Maxwell's "Yeats and the Irishry" (*CJIS*, 1975; *Threshold*, 1978) is a derivative account of Yeats's attitudes toward his audience, with particular reference to the work of the second generation of Abbey playwrights. W. J. McCormack's densely written "Yeats and a New Tradition" (*Crane Bag*, 1979) constantly invokes a host of critics and philosophers, obscuring the principal ideas and leaving only such truisms as "the element which provides continuity between Yeats's position in 1890 and in 1930 is this rejection of the primacy of the middle class." More useful is F. S. L. Lyons's *Culture and Anarchy in Ireland, 1890–1939* (1979), which gives an authoritative context for Yeats's political and cultural activities. In "Artificers of the Great Moment: An Essay on Yeats and National Literature" (*CLQ*, 1979), Phillip L. Marcus offers a good summary of the topic, with special reference to "The Grey Rock" and "The Dolls." The treatment of Yeats's relation to Ireland in Adrian Frazier's "The Ascendancy Poetry of W. B. Yeats" (*SR*, 1980) overlooks the relevant scholarship and contains little of interest. James MacKillop's " 'Beurla on it': Yeats, Joyce, and the Irish Language" (*Éire*, 1980) presents a sketchy account of Yeats's use of Gaelic, with insufficient attention to Yeats's informants, especially Lady Gregory and Douglas Hyde.

Richard M. Dorson's foreword to *Folktales of Ireland* (ed. Sean O'Sullivan, 1966) provides a good summary of Yeats's activities as a collector of folktales. Less to the point is Neil R. Grobman's "In Search of a Mythology: William Butler Yeats and Folklore" (*NYFQ*, 1974), which argues that "the great weakness in Yeats's collecting was the relative absence of ethnographic detail." Edward O'Shea's valuable "Yeats's Revisions in *Fairy and Folk Tales*" (*SFQ*, 1974), an article not altogether superseded by his *Yeats as Editor* (1975), discusses the changes Yeats made in many of the selections for his anthology. In " 'Contention is better than loneliness': The Poet as Folklorist" (*Genre*, 1979), Edward Hirsch covers much of the same ground but ignores O'Shea's essay. Mary Helen Thuente's *W. B. Yeats and Irish Folklore* (1980), a detailed and well-researched study of Yeats's work in the genre during the first fifteen years of his career, shows "how the narrative traditions of Irish folklore, in particular legends, influenced Yeats in subject, theory and style." Thuente demonstrates that Yeats's interests progressed from fairies to peasants to eighteenth-century characters to ancient heroes, and likewise from folk-belief legends to Anglo-Irish fiction to folk-hero legends to ancient mythology. She treats Yeats's editorial activities at some length but does not give sufficient consideration to O'Shea's work. The final chapter, " 'Traditional Innovations' in Literary Theory and

Style," somewhat overstates the importance of folklore in Yeats's career as a whole. Despite a few errors and some needless repetition, Thuente's book is likely to be the standard study for many years.

Roger McHugh's "Yeats and Irish Politics" (*UnivR*, 1962?; *TQ*, 1962) sketches the subject adequately, putting particular emphasis on "The People." Although F. X. Martin's "1916—Myth, Fact and Mystery" (*SH*, 1967) only touches on Yeats, it is extremely useful for a discussion not only of the rebellion itself but also of the various literary and historical interpretations of it. Mary Carden's perceptive article (*Studies*, 1969), partly a response to Conor Cruise O'Brien's essay (in *In Excited Reverie*), examines and defends Yeats's politics, stressing the influence of Vico (by way of Croce's *Philosophy of Giambattista Vico*, 1924) and of Swift. Carden argues that all three "are linked in a common hatred of abstraction and of eighteenth-century Rationalism." There are some brief remarks on Yeats in Terry Eagleton's *Criticism and Ideology: A Study in Marxist Literary Theory* (1976) and in George Watson's *Politics and Literature in Modern Britain* (1977).

Fahmy Farag's *The Opposing Virtues: Two Essays* (1978) consists of "Needless Horror or Terrible Beauty: Yeats's Ideas of Hatred, War, and Violence," treating Yeats's belief in the necessity of a cleansing violence; and "W. B. Yeats and the Politics of *A Vision*," defending the politics on the assumption that they are essentially spiritual. Both essays include much quotation and paraphrase and offer little that has not already been said. Farag is also guilty of what might be called essay cloning. It is acceptable of course that the second segment of the monograph stitches together Farag's "W. B. Yeats and the Politics of *A Vision*" (*CJIS*, 1975) and his "The Poet as the Nation's Daimon: The Cabbalistic Politics of *A Vision*" (*CJIS*, 1976), though a more scrupulous scholar might have acknowledged the prior publications. But there can be little defense of Farag's republishing his 1975 essay under the altered title "W. B. Yeats's Politics in the Thirties" (*ESC*, 1976), the only difference being the omission in the later printing of the appendix providing the text of Yeats's "Genealogical Tree of Revolution." After the publication of *The Opposing Virtues*, Farag repeated the same stratagem, reprinting the first essay under the new title of "The Staring Fury and the Blind Lush Leaf: Yeats and the Antinomial Nature of Energy" (*JEn*, 1979).

Stephen Spender's *The Thirties and After: Poetry, Politics, People 1933-1970* (1978) includes several remarks on Yeats, particularly in the chapter "Notes on Revolutionaries and Reactionaries." Spender argues that "Yeats's Fascism, not his poetry, was an excrescence. It grew rather approximately and grossly from the center of his poetic imagination which was neither approximate nor gross." In "Yeats and Revolutionary Nationalism: The Centenary of '98" (*Éire*, 1980), Peter A. Quinn traces Yeats's early political activities, with emphasis on the 1898 celebrations; he overlooks Herbert Howarth's *The Irish Writers, 1880-1940* (1958), an analysis of the messianic impulses of Yeats and Yeats's contemporaries, and adds little to previous accounts.

In *W. B. Yeats and the Emergence of the Irish Free State, 1918-1939: Living in the Explosion* (1981), Bernard G. Krimm attempts to reveal "the grounding Yeats's writing had in . . . the intense political situation in Ireland," emphasizing how Yeats tried to "reach the public about practical political concerns." Taking an essentially chronological approach, Krimm treats numerous poems, plays, and prose works. The discussion of Yeats's political life contains interesting new details but suffers from factual errors and speculations that lack firm evidence. Krimm's approach to the writings is far too allegorical, and he offers some unacceptable interpretations, such as seeing Congal in *The Herne's Egg* as a representation of de Valera. Unfortunately, the book is not indexed and has been atrociously proofread (e.g., at one point over a page of material is repeated). Grattan Freyer's *W. B. Yeats and the Anti-Democratic Tradition* (1981) offers an elementary sketch of the life and works with some special reference to Yeats's political activities. This pedestrian volume adds almost nothing to earlier accounts while committing several new errors. The level of commentary on Yeats's works seldom rises above plot summary or paraphrase. The final chapter reviews some of the previous scholarship on Yeats's politics but omits several important studies.

The best of the three books on Yeats's politics published in 1981 is Elizabeth Cullingford's *Yeats, Ireland and Fascism* (1981). Despite the title, Cullingford traces Yeats's politics throughout his career, beginning with the influence of John O'Leary. She effectively demonstrates that "the history of Yeats's involvement with Irish politics is the history of his fight to retain intellectual freedom in an environment made hostile first by the British and then by his sometime nationalist allies." Cullingford handles the question of fascism well, noting for the first time that Yeats presumably "made public his rejection of fascism" in a letter to the Second International Writers' Conference in July 1937—an event perhaps worthy of more detailed investigation. She concludes that "the nature of his convictions make it wrong to place him in any political category save that of a nationalist of the school of John O'Leary" and that Yeats's essential political belief was in "an aristocratic liberalism that combined love of individual freedom with respect for the ties of the organic social group." Since *Yeats, Ireland and Fascism* is likely to stand as the standard account of Yeats and politics for the foreseeable future, it is regrettable that Cullingford is not more comprehensive in treating the prior research: she overlooks, for instance, George Mills Harper's "Yeats's Intellectual Nationalism" (*DM*, 1965) and omits the *Senate Speeches* from her bibliography of primary works.

POETIC STYLE

James L. Allen's "Yeats's Use of the Serious Pun" (*SoQ*, 1963) gives five examples, not all convincing. In "W. B. Yeats: The Pun of a Gonne" (*MBL*, 1979), Conrad A. Balliet argues on dubious evidence (a Denver journalist's report of how Gonne stated her name should be pronounced) that Gonne rhymes with "dawn" and then proceeds to discover numerous puns on Gonne/gone; a skeptic might reply that many people still living knew Maud Gonne and pronounce her name "gun." In " 'The lion's tooth' in Yeats's 'Crazy Jane Grown Old Looks at the Dancers' " (*YER*, 1979), Matthew Little argues that the "lion's tooth" refers to "dandelion" but provides no evidence of that use of the term by contempory speakers in Ireland or elsewhere.

Harvey Gross has some brief but interesting comments on Yeats in *Sound and Form in Modern Poetry: A Study of Prosody from Thomas Hardy to Robert Lowell* (1964). Michael P. Gallagher's "Yeats, Syntax, and the Self" (*ARQ*, 1970) is a disjointed and unsatisfactory treatment of its several topics. James R. Quivey's "Yeats and the Epigram: A Study of Technique in the Four-Line Poems" (*Discourse*, 1970) discusses well the various effects Yeats can achieve in the form. Also valuable is Hugh Kenner's "Some Post-Symbolist Structures," in *Literary Theory and Structure* (ed. Frank Brady et al., 1973), which comments on Yeats's use of the "intricate long sentence." R. J. MacSween's mistitled "Yeats and His Language" (*AntigR*, 1973) argues ineffectively that Pound and Eliot are superior to Yeats, who was "betrayed by his insensitivity to rhythm and sound in verse" and whose works are filled with "tired language."

James Bailey's "Linguistic Givens and Their Metrical Realization in a Poem by Yeats" (*Lang&S,* 1975), on "The Cap and Bells," and Donald Ross's "Stylistic Contrasts in Yeats's Byzantium Poems" (*Lang&S,* 1975) are technical analyses of greater interest to linguists than to most Yeatsians. In *Aspects of Literary Stylistics: A Discussion of Dominant Structures in Verse and Prose* (1970), Anne Cluysenaar comments on the handling of tenses in "Coole Park and Ballylee, 1931" and on the revisions in "The Song of Wandering Aengus." E. L. Epstein's "Syntactic Laws and Detemporalized Expression in Modern Literature," in *Style and Text: Studies Presented to Nils Erik Enkvist* (ed. Håkan Ringbom, Stockholm, 1975), offers an interesting linguistic study of the first of the "Two Songs from a Play," especially the opening stanza; Epstein shows "how careful Yeats is with temporal verbs, and how cunningly he sets about robbing them of their temporality." Also of note is Epstein's *Language and Style* (1978), which remarks briefly on "Who Goes with Fergus?" and a few other poems. Ronald Schleifer's overwritten "Narrative in *In The Seven Woods*" (*JNT*, 1976) tries to show how "Baile and Aillinn," "The Old Age of Queen Maeve," and "Adam's Curse" illustrate Yeats's movement toward including more of the temporal world in his poetry.

In *Yeats' "Sorrow of Love" through the Years* (Lisse, 1977), Roman Jakobson and Stephen Rudy provide a detailed linguistic analysis of and contrast between the 1892 and 1925 versions of the poem, demonstrating the superiority of the later text. Both versions are interpreted by reference to *A Vision*, though the emphasis of the study is on the analysis. The monograph is reprinted in *PoT* (1980), the same issue including Jakobson's "On Poetic Intentions and Linguistic Devices in Poetry: A Discussion with Professors and Students at the University of Cologne," which includes some remarks on Yeats. Izolda Geniušienė's "W. B. Yeats's Simplification of His Poetic Tradition" (*Literatūra,* 1976) also compares the two texts of "The Sorrow of Love" but offers no new insights. In "Yeats's 'The Sorrow of Love' " (*Expl,* 1979), James E. Porter uses a comparison of the two versions to support an interesting though partial reading of the 1925 text, but he does not refer to the work of Jakobson and Rudy. Charles C. Walcutt (*Expl*, 1980) takes issue with the reading by Porter. V. N. Sinha's "Yeats's 'Remaking of Himself' in Some Early Poems" (*JEn*, 1978) is a solid if not especially original account of the revisions in four early poems, Sinha arguing that the changes are not always an improvement.

Horomu Miyauchi's "The Byzantium Poems: A Verbal Criticism" (*SELit*, 1977), while largely derivative, is a solid stylistic analysis. In "Actantial Modelling of the Love Relationship in W. B. Yeats: From 'He Wishes for the Cloths of Heaven' to 'Leda and the Swan' " (*Linguistica e letteratura*, 1977), Anthony L. Johnson argues that "each lyric operates as the other's antithesis" and, for example, that "treading" has a sexual connotation even in the earlier poem; most readers would have appreciated either a definition of "actantial model" or at least a reference to its source in A. J. Greimas' *Semantique structurale* (Paris, 1966). In "Sign, Structure and Self-Reference in W. B. Yeats's 'Sailing to Byzantium' " (*ASNSP*, 1978), Johnson presents a "signic, structural and semiotic reading" of the poem; the results are interesting but often overextended, as in the discussion of the anagrams in "men," "monuments," "magnificence," and "commend." Equally technical, if not more so, is Vladimir N. Toporov's "William Butler Yeats: 'Down by the Salley Gardens.' An Analysis of the Structure of Repetition" (*PTL*, 1978).

In "The Irishness of Yeats" (*CJIS*, 1977), Seán Lucy argues that many characteristics of Yeats's poetry are indebted to Gaelic poetry. Lucy continues this discussion in "Metre and Movement in Anglo-Irish Verse" (*IUR*, 1978), providing an analysis of "The Cold Heaven" and suggesting that possibly Yeats's greatest metrical achievement is "to bring to its highest point the interaction of the slow *amhrán* and the traditional iambic line." In "The Adjective as Symbol" (*Mosaic*, 1979), Conrad A. Balliet discusses some of the meanings of "cold," "mere," "ignorant," "blind," "foul," and "wild," showing that Yeats scholars have yet to exhaust the values of the *Concordance to the Poems*. D. G. Gillham's "Five Studies in Metaphor" (*ESA*, 1979) includes an unresearched but perceptive reading of "Long-Legged Fly," discussing Yeats's use of "symbolic metaphor." K. P. S. Jochum (*MBL*, 1978) offers a good survey of Yeats's use of the sonnet form; "Leda and the Swan" and "Meru" receive the most detailed treatment.

OTHER TOPICS

In "Yeats and the Careless Muse," in *Learners and Discerners: A Newer Criticism* (ed. Robert Scholes, 1964), John Frederick Nims suggests with both wit and insight that "Yeats was at once careful and careless, careful to seem careless; out of the tension between these opposites arise some of the finest effects of his art." Edward Craney Jacobs' "Yeats and the Artistic Epiphany" (*Discourse*, 1969) offers little beyond close readings of four poems. Richard Durkan's "The Dun Emer and the Cuala Press" (*Wesleyan Library Notes*, 1970) is a good sketch. S. B.

Minajagi's "W. B. Yeats's Poetic Ritual: 'Contraries' and Their Consummation" (*LCrit*, 1971) is chaotic. The chapter "Adam's Curse and Cussedness: Yeats's Rebellion against British English and Its Lesson to India", in Shankar Mokashi-Punekar's *The Indo-Anglian Creed and Allied Essays* (Calcutta, 1972), is a rambling essay on Yeats's language. Michael Yeats's "Words and Music" (*Yeats Soc. of Japan Annual Report*, 1973) surveys Yeats's interest in music and notes the sources for various songs. Over 350 items on Yeats are listed in Bryan N. S. Gooch and David S. Thatcher, *Musical Settings of Late Victorian and Modern British Literature: A Catalogue* (1976).

In "Yeats and the Irish Short Story" (*AntigR*, 1974), Anthony Farrow suggests the influence of Yeats on George Moore and on Joyce, but the essay is too brief to be fully convincing. Cara Ackerman's "Yeats' Revisions of the Hanrahan Stories, 1897 and 1904" (*TSLL*, 1975) shows how the changes enabled Yeats to "create and unify the three levels of his tale—the simple narrative, the nationalist political, and the occult"; unfortunately, she overlooks a rather similar analysis by Richard J. Finneran (*TSLL*, 1972). In the interesting " 'And I Myself Created Hanrahan': Yeats, Folklore, and Fiction" (*ELH*, 1981), Edward Hirsch demonstrates how the stories "maintain a fiction of community" while simultaneously undermining that concept "through the agency of their own self-consciousness." Hirsch thus concludes that "Yeats centers the poet by appearing to decenter him." In "Coming Out into the Light: W. B. Yeats's *The Celtic Twilight* (1893, 1902)" (*JFI*, 1981), Hirsch emphasizes the "hybrid nature" of the work, both a "folklore collection" and "a work of imaginative fiction." Hirsch argues that "the central animating goal of *The Celtic Twilight* was to affirm that the supernatural world exists and to demonstrate that the Irish peasantry had unique commerce with that world."

Stanley Weintraub (*CVE*, 1978) includes Yeats with Shaw and Moore in a discussion of the factual variety of autobiography, concluding that Yeats's "instincts were sound even when his facts were not." There is little of significance in two essays by David G. Wright, both of which include comparisons with Joyce: "The Elusive Self: Yeats's Autobiographical Prose" (*CJIS*, 1978) and "Behind the Lines: Strategies of Self-Portraiture in Yeats and Joyce" (*CLQ*, 1980). Daniel T. O'Hara's overwritten *Tragic Knowledge: Yeats's* Autobiography *and Hermeneutics* (1981) attempts to "show how useful [Paul] Ricoeur is for the reader of Yeats's *Autobiography*" and to "incorporate both phenomenological description and critical interpretation within an openended dialectical hermeneutic of imaginative restoration." The end result is not successful, except for readers interested in learning more about such topics as "chronic cynicism's ultimately mummifying sensibility." One turns with relief to "W. B. Yeats: Reveries over Childhood and Youth," in John Pilling's *Biography and Imagination: Studies in Self-Scrutiny* (1981), which demonstrates that "the writing of 'Reveries' is as much a struggle for self-possession and self-definition as any of the more celebrated poems." But the best recent discussion of *Autobiographies* is found in James Olney's "Some Versions of Memory/Some Versions of *Bios*: The Ontology of Autobiography," in *Autobiography*:

Essays Theoretical and Critical (ed. Olney, 1980), which suggests that Yeats provides an example of "the autobiographer as anamnesiologist": "Yeats redeems the time by simply abolishing it in favor of eternity" and presents us with "a truer truth than fact, a deeper reality than history." William L. Howarth's essay in the same collection also comments on Yeats as an example of a "poetic autobiographer."

In " 'I Seek an Image': The Method of Yeats's Criticism" (*MLQ*, 1976), Richard Fallis stresses Yeats's indebtedness to impressionism for his critical method and argues that "*transposition d'art* . . . is the basis of Yeats's critical and—on a broader scale—creative method." Michael A. Lofaro's "The Mask with No Eyes: Yeats's Vision in *Per Amica Silentia Lunae*" (*Style*, 1976) is a technical analysis of the first two paragraphs that almost completely avoids dealing with content. Bryant E. Hoffman's "All Imaginable Things: Yeats's *Per Amica Silentia Lunae*" (*IRA*, 1980) offers little more than a summary of the work and neglects Robert Langbaum's analysis in *The Mysteries of Identity* (1977). Lionel Trilling's *Speaking of Literature and Society* (ed. Diana Trilling, 1980) reprints "Yeats as Critic," a 1961 review of *Essays and Introductions*, which argues that "his essays have but one intention—to support in the way of discourse and insistence the preferences that are asserted by his poems in the way of passion." There are some brief comments on Yeats in *Night Visitors: The Rise and Fall of the English Ghost Story* (1977), by Julia Briggs.

Edward Engelberg's provocative "Space, Time, and History: Towards the Discrimination of Modernisms" (*MSLC*, 1974) contrasts the attitudes of Yeats, Eliot, and Wyndham Lewis toward space, time, and history, showing that Yeats "sees History-as-Event; reality partakes of both flux and stasis." Engelberg argues that Yeats understood "the 'humanism' in the art of Space" and "the energy and force of the visual imagination." Some other efforts to place Yeats in modernism pale in comparison with Engelberg's analysis. James Lovic Allen (*MBL*, 1977) summarizes some of the major critical definitions of the modernist movement and then offers a mechanical survey of the extent to which Yeats meets those definitions, eventually asserting that Yeats is essentially a nineteenth-century writer with the single exception of his "unquestioned membership" in the symbolist movement. Even less to the point is D. E. S. Maxwell's "Yeats and Modernism" (*CJIS*, 1977), a discursive essay that says little on the topic. In "The Left-Handedness of Modern Literature" (*TCL*, 1977), Scott Sanders does a better job of summarizing some of the main characteristics of modernism, although his comments on Yeats are unremarkable.

In "Yeats's Quarrel with Himself: The Design and Argument of *On the Boiler*" (*BRH*, 1978), Sandra F. Siegel attempts to show that "in each section of the essay, the essay as a whole, and the entire publication including the play [*Purgatory*], Yeats advances an argument and then proceeds to devalue or repudiate the view he has seemed to uphold"; her discussion of the proof materials overlooks the final page proofs in the Macmillan Archive of the British Library.

Osamu Osaka's "Yeats: *John Sherman* Reconsidered (1)" (*SELL*, 1978) summarizes much of the past criticism and argues for a favorable judgment of the work. More interesting is Mary McArdle Balk's "Yeats's *John Sherman*: An Early Attempt to Reconcile Opposites" (*YER*, 1979), although the thesis that Yeats deliberately used "symbolic tripartite combinations" to represent the Unity of Being lacking in John Sherman is forced. By far the most significant recent study of the novelette is William M. Murphy's "William Butler Yeats's *John Sherman*: An Irish Poet's Declaration of Independence" (*IUR*, 1979), which identifies the biographical sources for many of the characters and incidents; Murphy concludes that "the more one reads in the unpublished family papers and documents about the actual day-to-day life of the Yeatses, the more *John Sherman* seems to depart from fiction and to approach autobiography." In contrast, A. Norman Jeffares' "Yeats, Allingham and the Western Fiction" (*CJIS*, 1980), which concentrates on *John Sherman* and repeats much of the information from Murphy's essay, might well have remained an unpublished lecture.

14. Sources and Literary Contacts

NINETEENTH-CENTURY WRITERS (GENERAL STUDIES)

"The Last Romanticism of W. B. Yeats," in George Bornstein's *Transformations of Romanticism in Yeats, Eliot, and Stevens* (1976), demonstrates how "many of Yeats' greatest mature poems creatively develop out of romantic themes and modes." Bornstein sees Yeats's attitudes toward the romantics progressing through three stages: early enthusiasm, middle-aged rejection or avoidance, and late reconciliation. Borrowing a term from M. H. Abrams, Bornstein offers readings of eight of Yeats's "Greater Romantic Lyrics," arguing that Yeats's "greatest innovation" in the form "was to make vision into a summoning of images." Not all the readings are strikingly original, and at times they are restricted to fit the thesis; and the structure of the chapter (going from the middle to the early to the late poems) will confuse some readers. But on the whole *Transformations of Romanticism* is a valuable study that serious students should not neglect. The chapter on Yeats is reprinted with minor changes in *Romantic and Modern: Revaluations of Literary Tradition* (ed. Bornstein, 1977).

WILLIAM BLAKE

Although it is now only of historical interest, Grace Jameson's "Irish Poets of Today and Blake" (*PMLA*, 1946) might be cited as an early attempt to trace Yeats's (and A. E.'s) indebtedness to Blake. In "Yeats's Butterflies" (*CJIS*, 1976), Brian John notes sources for the imagery in Lady Wilde and Blake. Kathleen Raine's *From Blake to A Vision* (1979) is an impassioned and ascholarly attempt to demonstrate the essential similarities between Blake and Yeats and to discuss their relation to other figures of the "perennial philosophy." Raine emphasizes the importance of Yeats's interpretation of "The Mental

Traveller'' and suggests that his "instinctive sympathy" with a "diagrammatic type of thought qualified him to understand Blake better than any other editor since." The monograph includes thirty-five illustrations, though few are directly related to the text.

PERCY BYSSHE SHELLEY

In "A Source for 'A Woman Homer Sung' " (*N&Q*, 1950), A. Norman Jeffares suggests a passage in *Hellas* for "shadowed in a glass." George Bornstein's interesting "Yeats's Copy of Shelley at the Pforzheimer Library" (*BRH*, 1979) lists and comments on the annotations that Yeats made in a copy of the 1866 *Select Works*, showing that the marked pasages "pertain to the topics that most interested Yeats—the role of language and art, the frustration of love, spirits in this or the after world, figures of intense passion, and the kind of images stressed in 'The Philosophy of Shelley's Poetry.' "

OTHER NINTEENTH-CENTURY WRITERS

In "Anxiety of Influence: 'Resolution and Independence' and Yeats's 'The Fisherman' " (*YER*, 1978), Shyamal Bagchee overlooks the extant criticism of Yeats's interest in Wordsworth and makes a rather tenuous case for the influence of Wordsworth's poem. Typical of his evidence is the comment on "mighty Poets" versus "great Art": "there is striking similarity in the combination of lower case adjective with upper case noun, and in the resulting personifications." More significant and more scholarly is Patrick J. Keane's "Revolutions French and Russian: Burke, Wordsworth, and the Genesis of Yeats's 'The Second Coming' " (*BRH*, 1979), which uses the manuscripts of the poem to show how Burke's writings on the French Revolution and Wordsworth's *The Prelude* influenced Yeats's poem, though we learn little about how the detailed knowledge of the sources might affect our assessment of the finished lyric. A more naive effort is Walter Evans' "From Wordsworth's *The Prelude* to Yeats's 'The Second Coming' " (*YER*, 1979), which singles out one moment in Wordsworth's poem (bk. 10, ll. 78–93) as a major source and works through parallel passages, many of them quite debatable (Keane cites the same passage among many others from *The Prelude*).

Both Mario L. D'Avanzo (*Expl*, 1975) and William Elford Rogers (*CP*, 1975) have discovered a source for the titular image of Yeats's "Long-Legged Fly" in chapter 7 of Coleridge's *Biographia Literaria*.

David Eggenschwiler's "Nightingales and Byzantine Birds, Something Less Than Kind" (*ELN*, 1971) effectively contrasts the birds in Keats's "To a Nightingale" and "Sailing to Byzantium." R. A. Malagi's "The Artifice of Eternity: Yeats's 'Sailing to Byzantium' and Keats's 'Ode on a Grecian Urn' " (*Jour. of Karnatek Univ.*, 1975) is a brief comparison of little note. The somewhat disjointed chapter "Artist and Philistine," in Barbara Frances Fass's *La Belle Dame sans Merci and*

the Aesthetics of Romanticism (1974), provides an interesting discussion
of Keats's and Swinburne's influences on *The Wanderings of Oisin*
(*Lamia* and some other poems on bk. 1 of *Oisin*; "Hymn to Proserpine"
on bk. 3). Fass suggests that "the conflict in Yeats between his anti-
Philistinism and his anti-aestheticism can be traced in the two strains in
the nineteenth-century tradition he inherited. Like Keats, he understood
the penalties of escapism; like Swinburne, he recognized the threat to the
artist of a utilitarian culture. It is in this double dilemma that Oisin is
caught."

In " 'The Second Coming' and *Suspira de Profundis*: Some
Affinities" (*AN&Q*, 1976), Stuart Peterfreund discovers some not impossible but quite unlikely echoes of De Quincey's work in the poem.
More plausible is the suggestion by Thom Seymour, in "Yeats's 'Leda
and the Swan' " (*Expl*, 1980), that through Pater's essay "Style," Yeats
was familiar with De Quincey's distinction between "the literature of
knowledge and the literature of power."

In "Yeats and the Reinterpretation of Victorian Poetry" (*VP*,
1976), Richard Fallis quotes and comments on Yeats's views of Tennyson, Arnold, Browning, Hardy, Hopkins, Henley, Rossetti, and Morris, arguing that "throughout his quarrels with Victorianism runs the
theme that the poetry of vision is the norm against which all post-
Romantic poets should be judged." Nathan Cervo's "Hopkins, Yeats,
Eliot: The Pre-Raphaelite Heritage" (*PRR*, 1978) is more quotation than
analysis and is inexact at best. Norman Friedman (*SLitI*, 1975) discusses
Hallam's essay on Tennyson as foreshadowing many of the concepts of
modern aesthetics and comments briefly on Yeats. Gary Sloan's "Yeats,
Tennyson, and 'Innisfree' " (*VN*, 1978) overstates the influence of Ten-
nyson on both the poem and Yeats's career as a whole. M. K. Goldberg's
"Arnold and Yeats—A Note" (*CJIS*, 1977) offers some vague parallels,
such as both writers' "resistance to the afterglow of Romanticism." In
"W. B. Yeats, Matthew Arnold, and the Critical Imperative" (*VN*,
1979), Vinod Sena tries to demonstrate the importance of Arnold to
Yeats's criticism, a topic Sena mistakenly thinks "has gone unnoticed."
The possible influence of Arnold on Yeats's conception of tragic gaiety,
for instance, was suggested by Edward Engelberg (in *The Vast Design*,
1964: rev. 1974), who—unlike Sena—did not omit the attribution when
quoting Arnold's " 'All art,' says Schiller, 'is dedicated to Joy. . . .' "

James McNally (*SBHC*, 1977) employs the strange procedure of using Tuohy's *Yeats* to note some echoes of Browning in Yeats. Gerald
Monsman's "Pater and His Younger Contemporaries" (*VN*, 1975) is a
good general survey but says relatively little about Yeats. Richard Bizot
(*ELH*, 1976) argues that Yeats admired Pater to 1895, rejected him to
1915, had a tempered admiration to 1922, and an ever-greater admiration toward the end of his life; the essay provides a useful summary of
the relationship. F. C. McGrath has written three articles on Yeats and
Pater: "Heroic Aestheticism: Yeats, Pater, and the Marriage of Ireland
and England" (*IUR*, 1978), " 'Rose Alchemica': Pater Scrutinized and
Alchemized" (*YER*, 1978), and "Paterian Aesthetics in Yeats's Drama"
(*CompD*, 1979). The essays overlap, overlook the work of Monsman and
Bizot (as well as understate the work of Rupin W. Desai), and apply the

thesis of Pater's pervasive influence too restrictively. McGrath holds that Pater's essays on Shakespeare greatly influenced Yeats's development of the concept of "lyric unity" in his drama and uses the revisions in *On Baile's Strand* to demontrate that influence.

Margaret A. Lourie's "The Embodiment of Dreams: William Morris' 'Blue Closet' Group" (*VP*, 1977) is a useful addition to the Yeats-Morris criticism, suggesting the influence of Morris' early dream poetry while noting that Morris could accept "the dream at the cost of all external experience" whereas Yeats could not. Of less interest is Linda C. Dowling's " 'Rose Accurst': Yeats and Le Gallienne" (*VP*, 1978), a comparison of "Beauty Accurst" and Yeats's "Rose of the World" that shows Yeats's superiority. Michael Fixler (*PMLA*, 1959) provides a valuable discussion of the possible influence of Huysmans (especially his *À Rebours*) on the "Rosa Alchemica" stories.

In "Method in Source Study: Yeats' Golden Bird of Byzantium as a Test Case" (*TSLL*, 1975), Archibald A. Hill points out that most of the passage in Gibbon that is generally regarded as a major source for "Sailing to Byzantium" was quoted by Edmund Gosse in his *History of Eighteenth Century Literature* (1889); Hill also reasserts the importance of Marvell's "The Garden" and includes some theoretical discussion of source study. In "W. E. H. Lecky and 'The Second Coming' " (*YER*, 1978), L. M. Findlay suggests a possible source in *The Rise and Influence of Rationalism in Europe* (1865).

Herbert Howarth's "Whitman and the Irish Writers," in *Comparative Literature: Proceedings of the Second Congress of the International Comparative Literature Association* (ed. Werner P. Friedrich, 1959), suggests that Yeats "assimilated Whitman's 'heroic nudity' by writing the poetry of the human physique, by finding ecstasy in it, and by a corresponding nudity and ecstatic elementalism of style." Far less interesting is James E. Quinn's "Yeats and Whitman, 1887–1925" (*WWR*, 1974), which overlooks Howarth and merely quotes some of Yeats's comments on Whitman. Sidney Poger's "Yeats as Azad: A Possible Source in Thoreau" (*TJQ*, 1973) yet once more makes the case for the influence of Thoreau on "The Lake Isle of Innisfree"; more original but less probable is the assertion that the use of the tree in *Purgatory* is indebted to Thoreau.

Patrick Diskin's "Yeats's *Purgatory* and Werner's *Der vierundzwanzigste Febuar*" (*N&Q*, 1979) argues convincingly that a play by Zacharias Werner, as translated by James Clarence Mangan in the *Dublin University Magazine* for July 1837, is a major source for *Purgatory*. In "The Creator as Destroyer: Nietzschean Morality in Yeats's *Where There Is Nothing*" (*CLQ*, 1979), George Mills Harper provides a good survey of the use of Nietzschean concepts in the play, demonstrating, for example, that "Paul Ruttledge is modeled upon Nietzsche's character sketches of Christ and Saint Paul."

IRISH MATERIALS

In "Griffith, MacNeill and Pearse" (*Studies*, 1966), C. P. Curran suggests possible sources for "terrible beauty" in *The Writings of James Fintan Lalor* (1895) and P. H. Pearse's *From a Hermitage* (1913). Stanley M. Holberg's " 'Sailing to Byzantium': A New Source and a New Reading" (*ELN*, 1974) finds a source in "The Story of Conn-eda; Or the Golden Apples of Lough Erne," which Yeats included in his 1888 anthology of folklore; the new reading centers on a distinction between the bird as object and its song. In "A Great Ragged Black Bird" (*Hermathena*, 1974), A. Norman Jeffares argues that Yeats took his information on Lough Derg from Archdeacon St. John Seymour's *St. Patrick's Purgatory: A Medieval Pilgrimage in Ireland* (1919); what should have been a short note is expanded into an essay by excessive quotation. In "Yeats and Carleton" (*Carleton Newsletter*, 1975), Eileen Sullivan is content to reprint some of Yeats's letters that mention Carleton and to point out that many recent critics have agreed with Yeats's views. Adele M. Dalsimer's "W. B. Yeats' *The Wanderings of Oisin*: Blueprint for a Renaissance" (*Éire*, 1976) compares the first version of the poem with its major sources but adds only a few details to previous accounts. In "Yeats's Synge-Song" (*IUR*, 1976), Ole Munch-Pedersen locates the source of "I was going down the road one day" (in the 1908 version of *The Hour Glass*) in Lady Gregory and discusses the changes Yeats made. In "Padriac Pearse: The Revolutionary as Artist" (*ShawR*, 1976), Christopher Clausen cites some comments that Pearse and Yeats made about each other. Joan Towey Mitchell's rather drawn-out "Yeats, Pearse, and Cuchulain" (*Éire*, 1976) detects some echoes of Pearse's poems in "Easter 1916." In *The Damnable Question: A Study in Anglo-Irish Relations* (1976), George Dangerfield notes a reference in "Easter 1916" to a speech by Pearse: "if I die it shall be from the excess of love I bear the Gael." David R. Clark (*IrishS*, 1980) suggests that Samuel Ferguson's "Willy Gilliland" is a source for the image of the fisherman in "The Fisherman" and "The Tower."

Bruce A. Rosenberg's "Irish Folklore and 'The Song of Wandering Aengus' " (*PQ*, 1967) traces the various sources and concludes that Aengus' search is primarily "for the ineffable alchemy of poetic inspiration"; Rosenberg neglects the comments on sources in Russell K. Alspach's "Two Songs of Yeats's" (*MLN*, 1946), which also discusses "Red Hanrahan's Song about Ireland." Diane E. Bessai (*MHRev*, 1977) provides a careful survey of the sources and analogues for the figure at the end of *Cathleen ni Houlihan*, arguing that "the remarkable element in Yeats's play was that it managed to combine . . . many features of the various traditional conceptions with his own innovations, thereby giving modern Ireland what might be called her definitive personification." Less convincing is Kenneth B. Newell's "Yeats's Fergus as Sun God" (*Éire*, 1978), which admits that "no source before 1892 directly identifies Fergus as sun god" but which erects just such an interpretation by a liberal use of "may have" and "could have." Deborah Tannen gives a helpful account of Yeats's sea imagery and especially of Manannan Mac Lir in "Celtic Elements in Three Works by William Butler Yeats"

(*Folklore and Mythology Studies*, 1978), the works being *The Wanderings of Oisin*, *The Shadowy Waters*, and "Three Songs to the One Burden." Ole Munch-Pedersen (*Éire*, 1979) surveys the nineteenth-century background of Crazy Jane, beginning with a ballad by Monk Lewis and continuing through broadside ballads and chapbooks to a play by Charles A. Somerset. James Stewart's "Three That Are Watching My Time to Run" (*IUR*, 1979) traces the possible sources for the lyric in *The Unicorn from the Stars* and posits Douglas Hyde as the main author of the version used. In a few brief remarks on Yeats in *Sheridan Le Fanu and Victorian Ireland* (1980), W. J. McCormack attempts to demonstrate Yeats's "unacknowledged debt to Le Fanu's fiction."

NEOPLATONIC TRADITION

Mario M. Rossi (*Cronos*, 1947) asserts that "at every point, [Yeats's] life and his poetry touched philosophy because they touched mystery" but offers few specific examples. Robert W. Witt (*YER*, 1974) complains that most anthology editors do not indicate that the parable of the splitting of the egg in the *Symposium*, referred to in "Among School Children," was intended by Plato to be satirical. Donald T. Torchiana (*MBL*, 1979) provides a survey of Yeats's interest in Plato, drawing on some unpublished materials and listing the books by or about Plato in Yeats's library.

VISUAL SOURCES

Wayne D. McGinnis (*RS*, 1974) asserts that "the search for balance . . . characterizes both Giotto's art and Yeats's in 'The Magi' " but he does not suggest a source. More interesting is William C. Barnwell's "A Possible Italian Influence on Yeats's 'Statues' " (*PQ*, 1977), which notes a local legend about Tullio Lombardo's statue of Guidarello Guiderelli in the Academia di Belle Arti in Ravenna: young girls seeking husbands, homes, and fine children could obtain them if they kissed the lips of the statue. Yeats may well have heard of this legend on his trip to Italy with Lady Gregory. Elizabeth W. Bergmann's "Yeats's Gallery" (*CLQ*, 1979) perceptively discusses the importance of portraits to Yeats's art, indicated, for example, in his choice of illustrations for the 1908 *Collected Works*. Less stimulating is Paul Cohen's "Yeats as Portraitist" (*YER*, 1979), which is confined to the use of portraits in the poetry.

MEDIEVAL AND RENAISSANCE LITERATURE

George Bornstein's excellent "Yeats's Romantic Dante" (*CLQ*, 1979) draws on the previous scholarship and concludes with some comments on "The Second Coming," "Byzantium," and "Cuchulain Comforted." Bornstein argues that Yeats "saw Dante above all as a quest poet, with whom he shared devotion to an unattainable woman, political office in a strife-torn land, exile (voluntary in Yeats's case), acceptance of an abstruse system of belief, and a host of poetic goals, not least of which was to become a character in his own work." This essay effectively supersedes earlier studies, although David Spurr's "A Celtic Commedia: Dante in Yeats's Poetry" (*RLSt*, 1977) has a useful list of possible borrowings. The treatment of Yeats in Dominic Manganiello's "Yeats among the Moderns" (*Selecta*, 1980) is of little significance.

Roland Blenner-Hasset (*Anglia*, 1955) notes some possible sources in Chaucer for the idea of the Great Year in *A Vision* and argues that Leo Africanus draws on Scipio Africanus the Elder in *The Parliament of Fools*. W. R. Martin's "A Possible Source for Yeats's 'Sailing to Byzantium' " (*CJIS*, 1977) suggests Bembo's eulogy of the soul's spiritual love in Castiglione's *The Book of the Courtier*.

In "Shakespeare's *Hamlet* and Yeats's 'Under Ben Bulben' " (*LCrit*, 1972), S. R. Swaminathan argues unconvincingly that Hamlet is the speaker of the poem and also sees his presence in several other late poems. More plausible is Laurence Perrine's tracing of echoes from *The Tempest* in "Yeats and Shakespeare: 'The Old Stone Cross' " (*MBL*, 1978). In " 'There Struts Hamlet': Yeats and the Hamlet Mask" (*HSt*, 1979) R. W. Desai only slightly extends the conclusions in his *Yeats's Shakespeare*.

The chapter "Yeats, Donne and the Metaphysicals," in Joseph E. Duncan's *The Revival of Metaphysical Poetry: The History of a Style, 1800 to the Present* (1959), concerns mainly the parallels with Donne and Herbert rather than the question of direct borrowings. Elise Leach's "Yeats's 'A Friend's Illness' and Herbert's 'Vertue' " (*N&Q*, 1961) suggests that Yeats found the image of the soul surviving the burning of the world in Herbert's poem. Ronald E. McFarland (*FDP*, 1976) argues that "Sailing to Byzantium," especially the third stanza, is indebted to Herbert's "Love (II)." Leonard Unger's "Yeats and Milton" (*SAQ*, 1962) is largely speculative and at times farfetched; he emphasizes the influence of *Areopagitica* in several ways and sees it as a source for "The Second Coming."

JAPANESE TRADITION

The section "Some English Imitations," in Peter Arnott's *The Theatres of Japan* (1969), includes a discussion of Yeats, arguing that his "adaptations remain one of the happiest instances of the transposition of styles." Myung Whah Kim's "Dance and Rhythm: Their Meaning in Yeats and Noh" (*MD*, 1972), which ignores all previous work on the subject except Kermode's, is of little interest. In a brief note (*NConL*, 1976), Stuart Hirschberg finds some parallels between the Japanese Noh *Nishikigi* and the "Crazy Jane" sequence, particularly in that each builds toward a climactic dance and employs a chorus (i.e., the refrains in the poems). Shotaro Oshima's remarks on Yeats's relation to the Noh, in "Between Shapes and Shadows" (in *Myth and Reality in Irish Literature*, ed. Joseph Ronsley, 1977), have little significance.

Naito Shiro (*EB*, 1972) concentrates on "The Statues," locating a source for "Buddha's emptiness" in Diasetz Suzuki's *Essays in Zen Buddhism, First Series* (1938). Gerald Doherty (*Young East,* 1979) suggests that "Demon and Beast" and "Lapis Lazuli" show a "remarkable closeness in insight and structure to the Zen Buddhist experience of satori."

INDIAN THOUGHT

A. Davenport (*RES,* 1952) notes some echoes of the Upanishads in Yeats, especially in the Byzantium poems. Mary M. Lago (*IndL,* 1963; *Mahfil,* 1966) provides a solid if at times simplistic sketch of the relationship between Yeats and Tagore, suggesting that "despite their apparent similarities, the basic difference . . . lay in their concepts of time." Pranabendu Dasgupta (*JJCL,* 1964) offers an interesting comparison of Yeats's and Tagore's stage techniques and dramatic theories as well as of a few plays; he does not suggest direct indebtedness on either side. The chronology of "Yeats and India," in *W. B. Yeats and India Centenary 1865-1965: A Seminar and Festival at Jadavpur University 25 to 27 December 1965* (1965), is more detailed and accessible in Naresh Guha's *W. B. Yeats: An Indian Approach* (Calcutta, 1968). In a provocative but at times confusing note, "The Vedantic Logic of Yeats' 'Crazy Jane' " (*Renascence,* 1966), Anselm Atkins argues that Jane uses both a "logic of convergence" and a "logic of mutual exclusion" and that her "way of thinking is most readily comprehensible from the point of view of Eastern or Vedantic logic." In "Bhartrihari, Yeats and Tagore: The History of a Poem" (*VQ,* 1972-73), S. R. Swaminathan finds a source for "What Then?" in Bhartrihari's *Satakatrayam.* In an important note, "The Source of Yeats's 'What Magic Drum?' " (*PLL,* 1973), Dennis E. Smith and F. A. C. Wilson draw on the Swami's *The Holy Mountain* to demonstrate that Yeats's poem has only two participants, "a devotee who might be Ribh and the apparition of a saint or 'divine master,' and that the poem is a description of a vision analogous to that in *The Holy Mountain*"; thus the poem is "the evocation of vision in which the spiritual and the atavistic merge." Mokashi Punekar's brief "An Introduction to Shri Purohit Swami and the Avadhoota Geeta" (*LCrit,* 1974) notes that the Swami used "a good many Yeatsian turns of phrase in his translation," which was unpublished in his and Yeats's lifetime. Subhas Sarkar's discussion of Yeats and the Swami (*BDEC,* 1975-1976) adds only a few biographical details on the Swami to earlier accounts.

William A. Gordon's "Eastern Religions and the Later Yeats" (*DR,* 1975-76), though well done, does not go beyond the previous scholarship or pay sufficient attention to *how* Yeats uses Indian materials. Santosh Pall (*Studies,* 1976) stresses the influence of Indian thought on Yeats's conception of the dancer. B. M. Singh's "Yeats and *Gitanjali*" (*RUSEng,* 1976) is of little significance. More interesting is the attempt by Vilas Sarang (*N&Q,* 1978) to show that "The Four Ages of Man" presents "an ironic account of the four asramas" of Hindu tradition. Although almost all the extant criticism is ignored, Brian Keeble's " 'Myself Must I Remake': W. B. Yeats and Unity of Being" (*SMLit,*

1980) offers a good introduction to the influence of Indian thought on Yeats, arguing that "Yeats' final assault on Unity of Being can be said to begin with his friendship with Shree Purohit Swami." Keeble also provides an interesting commentary on "Supernatural Songs."

FRENCH LITERATURE

In "Yeats's Debt to Ronsard on a *Carpe Diem* Theme" (*Comparative Lit. Studies*, Cardiff, 1946), William F. Mackey provides the text of the Ronsard poem that is the basis for "When You Are Old" (apparently unaware that C. L. Wrenn has preceded him in 1919 in an essay in *DUJ*) and argues that "though the material debt to Ronsard is great in pattern, theme and subject matter, it is negligible in taste, emotion and spirit." Ian W. Alexander's "Valéry and Yeats: The Rehabilitation of Time" (*Scottish Lit*, 1947) is a good comparative study. Carl Benson, in his valuable essay "Yeats and Balzac's *Louis Lambert*" (*MP*, 1952), suggests the importance of Balzac to Yeats and sees a progression in Yeats's interests from Blake to Shelley to Balzac. Lloyd Parks's "The Influence of Villiers de l'Isle Adam on W. B. Yeats" (*NCFS*, 1978) summarizes the major parallels but does not altogether demonstrate that "Yeats found in the writing of the French master a confirmation of his own nascent philosophy at perhaps the most crucial point of his development." In "Flaubert: *Trois Contes* and the Figure of the Double Cone" (*PMLA*, 1980), John R. O'Connor shows that "the double cone is simply not in the text of 'La Spirale' in the fully realized way that Yeats said it was [in *A Vision*]" but that Flaubert indeed used the symbol as "a geometrical matrix or motive form underlying the *Trois Contes*." James McNally (*HS*, 1981) notes an "interesting resemblance" in "images and theme" between "Sailing to Byzantium" and Anatole France's *Penguin Island* (trans. 1909), but it is unclear whether a source is being suggested or a parallel being discovered.

OTHER SOURCES

In "Yeats's 'Cat and the Moon' " (*N&Q*, 1950), Grover Smith cites Plutarch's *Isis and Osiris* as a source for the changing pupils of the cat's eyes. In "The Honey-Bees of W. B. Yeats' 'The Stare's Nest at [sic] My Window': Echoes of Orpheus" (*CJIS*, 1979), Lee M. Whitehead finds a reference to the story of Aristaeus in Vergil's *Fourth Georgic* but strangely neglects to refer to the biblical version of the myth in "Vacillation." Stuart Hirschberg (*NConL*, 1976) suggests the influence of Masefield's "A Creed" on "Under Ben Bulben," because of similar ideas and parallels in diction. Reinhard F. Spiess (*RLV*, 1976) makes an interesting but tenuous case for the influence of Wittgenstein on "The Circus Animals' Desertion" and "A Bronze Head." In "Possible Sources for Yeats's 'The Statues' " (*CJIS*, 1977), W. R. Martin suggests Wyndham Lewis' *Time and Western Man* (1927) and Edith Hamilton's *The Greek Way* (1930).

SOME LITERARY CONTACTS

Norman H. MacKenzie's "Hopkins, Yeats and Dublin in the Eighties," in *Myth and Reality in Irish Literature* (ed. Joseph Ronsley, 1977), provides little new information on Yeats's contacts with Hopkins. Marion Witt (*N&Q*, 1960) points out some echoes in Yeats of Symons' poems and translations. The fullest study of the relationship is the chapter "Arthur Symons, Symbolist," in John M. Munro's *Arthur Symons* (1969). There are few references to Yeats in *The Memoirs of Arthur Symons: Life and Art in the 1890s* (ed. Karl Beckson, 1977). Christopher S. Nassaar's "Vision of Evil: The Influence of Wilde's *Salome* on *Heart of Darkness* and *A Full Moon in March*" (*VN*, 1978) is not fully researched and becomes absurd when it suggests that the "Swineherd is surely meant to suggest the decadent artist, and especially the Oscar Wilde of *Salome*."

Mark Mortimer (*Studies*, 1977) argues that Yeats's famous advice to Synge, to go to the Aran Islands, was probably never given or was at best one of several factors influencing Synge's decision. Sean McMahon's "Art and Life Blended: Douglas Hyde and the Literary Revival" (*Éire*, 1979) includes some brief and unoriginal remarks on Yeats's relationship with Hyde. Also of only passing interest is the sketch of Yeats's contacts with George Moore in Donald M. Michie's "A Man of Genius and a Man of Talent" (*TSLL*, 1964).

In *The Poetry of Ezra Pound: The Pre-Imagist Stage* (Bern, 1960), N. Christoph De Nagy traces Yeats's influence on Pound's early career; the appendix lists twenty-five poems "reminiscent of the poetry of the 'Nineties and, in particular, of the young W. B. Yeats." There are also some brief remarks on Yeats in De Nagy's *Ezra Pound's Poetics and Literary Tradition: The Critical Tradition* (Bern, 1966). Peter Faulkner's "Yeats, Ireland and Ezra Pound" (*Threshold*, 1963?) ignores all previous studies while discounting the influence of Pound on Yeats. Thomas H. Jackson's *The Early Poetry of Ezra Pound* (1968) stresses the influence on Pound of Yeats's doctrine of the "Moods" and also notes Pound's adoption of some of Yeats's stylistic devices, such as "his characteristic manipulation of run-on lines so as to produce simultaneously a feeling of enjambment and of pause." A valuable study by George J. Bornstein and Hugh H. Witemeyer (*CL*, 1967) shows Yeats's early acceptance of Pound's view of Villon as a realist and Yeats's later conception of Villon as a visionary. Witemeyer's *The Poetry of Ezra Pound: Forms and Renewal, 1908-1920* (1969) also comments on Yeats's influence on Pound, arguing that Pound saw Yeats as a "living apostle" who symbolized "the craft of 'poetry as pure art.' " There are some scattered remarks on Yeats and Pound in Ronald Bush's *The Genesis of Ezra Pound's* Cantos (1976) and also in Bornstein's *The Postromantic Consciousness of Ezra Pound* (1977). William Pratt's interesting "Ezra Pound and the Image," in *Ezra Pound: The London Years, 1908-1920* (ed. Philip Grover, 1978), touches on Yeats, as does Donald Davie's chapter "Ezra Pound and the English," in *Trying to Explain* (1979).

Luigi Schenoni's "Some Comments upon Joyce's Meeting with Yeats" (*WN*, 1977) is of passing interest at best. In "James Joyce and the Theory of Magic" (*JJQ*, 1978), Craig Carver discusses Joyce's interest in the idea of a "great memory" and sees Yeats's writings on the subject as an influence. Anita Gandolfo (*JJQ*, 1978) demonstrates that Joyce used the 1893 Ellis-Yeats edition of Blake and adopted some of Yeats's views of Blake. Bonnie Kime Scott's underresearched "Joyce and the Dublin Theosophists: 'Vegetable Verse' and Story" (*Éire*, 1978) discusses Joyce's indebtedness to Yeats's early work, particularly the occult fiction. Robert Adams Day's interesting "How Stephen Wrote His Vampire Poem" (*JJQ*, 1980) suggests Yeats's essay on Blake and his introduction to W. T. Horton's *A Book of Images* as sources for Stephen's poem in *Ulysses*. In " 'He Lumped the Emancipates Together': More Analogues for Joyce's Mr. Duffy" (*JJQ*, 1980), Joseph C. Voekler offers "The Tables of the Law" as a major source for "A Painful Case," arguing that "Joyce's story may well have been a necessary act of exorcism."

Helen Gardner's *The Composition of* Four Quartets (1978) demonstrates that for the figure of the ghost in "Little Gidding" Eliot "began with Yeats in mind and worked towards a greater generality"; she also cites a 1942 letter from Eliot to John Hayward in which Eliot indicates that the figure "will no doubt be identified by some readers with Yeats though I do not mean anything so precise as that." The authors of two earlier studies quote from Eliot's letters to them about the identity of the figure: Maurice Johnson, in "The Ghost of Swift in *Four Quartets*" (*MLN*, 1949), and Kristian Smidt, in "T. S. Eliot and W. B. Yeats" (*RLV*, 1965).

Harold H. Watt's "The Tragic Hero in Eliot and Yeats" (*CentR*, 1969) considers only the drama. Gina White's poorly done "Modes of Being in Yeats and Eliot" (*Modern Occasions*, 1971) has some absurd errors and misquotations. Ted R. Spivey offers some elementary comparisons in "The Apocalyptic Symbolism of W. B. Yeats and T. S. Eliot" (*Costerus*, 1972). In "Eliot on Yeats: 'East Coker, II' " (*YER*, 1976), Christopher Brown suggests that part of the section is an attack on Yeats's style. There is little of interest in Keith W. Schlegel's "Yeats' 'The Magi' and Eliot's 'The Journey of the Magi' " (*Cithara*, 1976) or in Shun'ichi Takayanagi's "Yeats and T. S. Eliot: Ageing and Apocalypse" (*ELLS*, 1976). In "Yeats and Eliot on 'Traditional Culture': A Few Long Thoughts" (*Spirit*, 1977), David Rogers provides a string of quotations and little else. Likewise, Joanne Seltzer's "The Kings of the Cats: Eliot and Yeats" (*PRR*, 1977) is little more than a summary of Eliot's 1940 lecture on Yeats. More interesting is Phillip L. Marcus' " 'I declare my faith': Eliot's 'Gerontion' and Yeats's 'The Tower' " (*PLL*, 1978), which suggests that Yeats's poem is probably a response to Eliot's but that in any case there are fruitful parallels between them. Though Subhas Sarkar's *Eliot and Yeats: A Study* (Calcutta, 1978) is listed here because of its title, it is not a comparative study; the four essays on Yeats are badly written and of no significance.

In "Shaw, Yeats, Nietzsche, and the Religion of Art" (*Komos*, Melbourne, 1967), Margery M. Morgan provides an interesting comparison of *Major Barbara* and *The Resurrection*, indicating their common debt to Nietzsche and suggesting, more tenuously, the influence of

Shaw's play on Yeats's. In "The Rejection of Shaw's Irish Play: *John Bull's Other Island*" (*Éire*, 1975), Norma Jenckes discusses the rejection but also provides a capsule history of the Irish dramatic movement. Harold Ferrar's "The Caterpillar and the Gracehoper: Bernard Shaw's *John Bull's Other Island*" (*Éire*, 1980), an appreciation of the play, includes yet another discussion of its rejection by the Abbey. There are also some comments on the episode in Terence de Vere White's "An Irishman Abroad," in *The Genius of Shaw: A Symposium* (ed. Michael Holroyd, 1979).

Paul Geneson's "The Yeats-O'Casey Relationship: A Study in Loyal Opposition" (*SORev*, 1975) is an elementary sketch. Ronald G. Rollins' predictable and unexciting "O'Casey, Yeats, and Behan: A Prismatic View of the 1916 Easter Rebellion" (*SORev*, 1976) discusses "Easter 1916." The essay "O'Casey's Letters: Litir O Cathasaigh" (*SORev*, 1978) simply reprints Yeats's 20 April 1928 letter on *The Silver Tassie* and O'Casey's response. Richard F. Peterson's "Polishing Up *The Silver Tassie* Controversy: Some Lady Gregory and W. B. Yeats Letters to Lennox Robinson" (*SORev*, 1978) summarizes the correspondence, without quoting from it, and adds little to previous accounts. In "Yeats and O'Casey: Exemplary Dramatists" (*Threshold*, 1979), Seamus Deane argues that Yeats is "more stimulating" because his "experiments indicate to us now that the search for a new form is also a search for a new mode of feeling." Walter C. Daniel's "Public vs. Private Commitment in Two Plays of W. B. Yeats and Sean O'Casey" (*CLAJ*, 1979) contrasts the "public commitment" of Yeats, as seen in *Cathleen ni Houlihan*, with the "private commitment" of O'Casey, as seen in *The Plough and the Stars*. Katharine Worth (*IUR*, 1980) makes no reference to previous accounts while attempting to show that Yeats replaced Synge as a major influence on O'Casey beginning with *The Silver Tassie*. More useful is Mary FitzGerald's "Sean O'Casey and Lady Gregory: The Record of a Friendship," in *Sean O'Casey: Centenary Essays* (ed. David Krause and Robert G. Lowery, 1980), which provides full details on *The Silver Tassie* incident and shows "the vehemence of O'Casey's reaction." Although somewhat biased in favor of O'Casey, Krause's essay in the same collection, "The Druidic Affinities of O'Casey and Yeats," is a good summary of the relationship, noting the affinities between "these two angry and visionary Irish titans."

Éamon Grennan's "Careless Father: Yeats and His Juniors" (*Éire*, 1979) offers an introductory survey of Yeats's attitudes toward his younger contemporaries. Richard F. Peterson's "The Crane and the Swan: Lennox Robinson and William Butler Yeats" (*JIL*, 1980) draws on some unpublished correspondence to trace the relationship.

Marilyn Gaddis' "The Purgatory Metaphor of Yeats and Beckett" (*LonM*, 1967) is an adequate comparative study that discounts the idea of Yeats's influence. Thomas Kilroy's "Two Playwrights: Yeats and Beckett," in *Myth and Reality in Irish Literature* (ed. Joseph Ronsley, 1977), includes some interesting comments on three of Yeats's plays but makes few comparisons with Beckett. Ronald G. Rollins' "Old Men and Memories: Yeats and Beckett" (*Éire*, 1978) avoids the published criticism while comparing *Purgatory* with *Krapp's Last Tape* in a discussion that offers little beyond plot summaries. John P. Harrington's " 'That Red Branch Bum was the Camel's Back': Beckett's Use of Yeats in *Murphy*" (*Éire*, 1980) is not altogether convincing in arguing that the novel shows the difference between Yeats's and Beckett's views of astrology and the concept of opposition and that Becket is deliberately criticizing Yeats.

Jon Stallworthy's "W. B. Yeats and Wilfred Owen" (*CQ*, 1969) neglects Joseph Cohen's earlier study (*JEGP*, 1959) but provides a good survey of the relationship, noting Yeats's influence on Owen. Sasi Bhusan Das overlooks both essays in the drawn-out study "W. B. Yeats's Charges against Wilfred Owen" (*Modern Rev.*, Calcutta, 1976). David C. Nimmo (*ES*, 1975) discusses Yeats's omission of a line from W. J. Turner's "The Seven Days of the Sun" in *The Oxford Book of Modern Verse* (1936). Lucy S. McDiarmuid's "Poetry's Landscape in Auden's Elegy for Yeats" (*MLQ*, 1977) offers a good analysis of the structure of Auden's poem. In an interesting essay "Auden and W. B. Yeats: From Singing-Master to Ogre" (*Commonweal*, 13 May 1977), Edward T. Callan traces the shift in Auden's opinion of Yeats from admiration to dislike. There are some brief comments on Auden's relationship with Yeats in Samuel Hynes's *The Auden Generation: Literature and Politics in England in the 1930s* (1977). In "Auden, Yeats, and the Word 'Silly': A Study in Semantic Change" (*South Atlantic Rev.*, 1981), Edith Whitehurst Williams effectively traces the historical changes in the meaning of "silly" and demonstrates how the presence of the word in Auden's elegy mirrors his ambivalent attitudes toward Yeats and his work.

In "Yeats, Noyes and Day Lewis" (*N&Q*, 1950), George Brandon Saul notes some echoes and parallels; in a reply (*N&Q*, 1950), Noyes states that the borrowings were deliberate. In " 'From the Master's Lips': W. B. Yeats as C. S. Lewis Saw Him" (*CSLBull*, 1974), Joe R. Christopher gives an interesting account of Lewis' early reading and admiration of Yeats, his two visits to Yeats in Oxford in 1921, and his ambivalent hostility toward Yeats's occult interests, reflected in Lewis' 1926 narrative poem *Dymer*. Patrick J. Keane's *A Wild Civility: Interactions in the Poetry and Thought of Robert Graves* (1980) is a sound study of the parallels between Graves and Yeats, the hostility of Graves (and Laura Riding) toward Yeats, and the numerous borrowings from Yeats by Graves. Keane demonstrates that "both have created mythographic systems to provide a wider and more coherent framework for their poems; both are attracted to cyclicism; both submit themselves to a barbaric Muse, a femme fatale with lunar affiliations. Above all, both locate their central and obsessive theme in the human sexual relation of man and woman." Timothy Materer's "Lewis and the Patriarchs: Augustus John, W. B. Yeats, T. Sturge Moore," in *Wyndham Lewis: A Revaluation: New Essays* (ed. Jeffrey Meyers, 1980), offers a brief discussion of Yeats and Lewis, arguing that Lewis saw Yeats as a father figure and that they "meet on the common ground of Bishop Berkeley's philosophy."

15. Influence and Comparative Studies

INFLUENCE STUDIES

In "The Poetry of Padraic Fallon" (*Studies*, 1975), Maurice Harmon explains that "the influence of Yeats manifests itself in Fallon's work in two ways: in . . . the conscious recognition and adaptation of a mode of rhetoric and of organization; and in the determination . . . to find a personal world and a distinctive voice." In "The Literary Myths of the Revival: A Case for Their Abandonment," in *Myth and Reality in Irish Literature* (ed. Joseph Ronsley, 1977), Seamus Deane attempts to argue against the influence of Yeats on contemporary Irish literature, finding Yeats's view of history particularly objectionable; he points to the greater significance of Joyce and of Kavanagh, "the great de-mythologizer." Brendan Kennelly also shows a preference for Yeats in an interview, "On Language and Invention" (*LitR*, 1979), saying of Yeats that "the thing to do is to write your way through him and to emerge with your own voice." In a review essay on the Irish number of *LitR*, "Re-membering: Irish Poetry after Yeats" (*Éire*, 1980), Kevin P. Reilly stresses the extent to which the younger poets prefer Kavanagh to Yeats and regard the latter as "a funny old uncle who could jump higher than the moon." In the introduction to *Irish Poetry after Yeats: Seven Poets* (ed. Maurice Harmon, 1979), Harmon argues that "Yeats's legacy is a primary factor in the development of all Irish poets" and briefly considers that legacy under the categories of "his sense of the Irish past, its history, folklore, myth and legend; the symbol-making impulse of his imagination; the emphasis on personality; his belief in personal utterance." The poets discussed are Clarke, Kavanagh, Devlin, Murphy, Kinsella, Montague, and Heaney. Some readers may be interested in Yeats's appearance as a character in part 3 of *The Non-Stop Connolly Show: A Dramatic Cycle of Continuous Struggle in Six Parts* (1977–78), by Margaretta D'Arcy and John Arden.

John Press's *Rule and Energy: Trends in British Poetry since the Second World War* (1963) includes some brief comments on Yeats's influence on English poets. In "W. B. Yeats, Thomas Hardy and Philip Larkin" (*AJES*, 1978), Press suggests that Yeats's influence on Larkin's poetry was more lasting than Larkin has admitted.

In *The Echoing Wood of Theodore Roethke* (1976), Jenijoy La Belle comments on Roethke's interest in and indebtedness to Yeats, with particular attention to "Four for Sir John Davies." William Heyen's "The Yeats Influence: Roethke's Formal Lyrics of the Fifties" (*John Berryman Studies*, 1977), apparently written in 1966–67 and unrevised since, is a more mechanical account of the relationship, arguing that "the primary lesson [Roethke] learns from Yeats is that . . . a poet comes to lean on the examples of admired ghosts, but that ultimately his poems must declare themselves a part of his own self." In some remarks in *Cry of the Human: Essays on Contemporary American Poetry* (1975), Ralph J. Mills, Jr., notes the influence of "the decidedly personal character of Yeats' voice, growing bolder and more idiosyncratic as his career lengthened." Marjorie Perloff (*Centrum*, 1976) uses Yeats an an example of the older school of "symbolism" as against the newer school of "antisymbolism" (Pound, Williams, Roethke, Ashberry, et al.) and suggests that contemporary poets regard Yeats as "a great but remote figure." At least one who apparently did not was Sylvia Plath. Gary Lane's "Influence and Originality in Plath's Poems," in *Sylvia Plath: New Views on the Poetry* (ed. Lane, 1979), argues that "the influence of Yeats on Plath, extending more broadly than the poetic fatherhoods of Thomas, Roethke, or Stevens, is such as to legitimize him [as] grand- or god-father." Likewise, Barnett Guttenberg's "Plath's Cosmology and the House of Yeats," in the same collection, uses a plethora of quotation to try to demonstrate that "Plath builds a complete system, with a Yeatsian antithetical vision and consistent clusters of Yeatsian imagery. In addition, she seems to offer a series of rejoinders on various points of disagreement."

In "Brennan and Yeats: An Historical Survey" (*Southerly*, 1977), Mary A. Merewether carefully uses archival materials to trace the influence of Yeats's early work, especially *The Wind among the Reeds*, on the Australian poet Christopher Brennan. A similar effective discussion of influence is provided by John C. Wilcox in "Enticing Yeats to Spain: Zenobia and Juan Ramón Jiménez" (*YER*, 1978), which suggests that "Jiménez had been inspired by a Yeats who, though haunted by tradition, had never permitted the *Soul* to obliterate the *Self*; by a poet who had never entirely yielded his life-in-time to the *Absolutes* of the Symbolist aesthetic." An even fuller discussion of this influence is found in the chapter on Yeats in Howard T. Young's *The Line in the Margin: Juan Ramón Jiménez and His Readings in Blake, Shelley, and Yeats* (1980), which demonstrates the "extreme attraction" that Jiménez felt for Yeats. In "W. B. Yeats: Image of a Poet in Germany" (*SHR*, 1968), Susanne Schaup laments that "Yeats is sadly neglected compared with other English poets" and finds the main topics of interest to Germans to be "Yeats the symbolist and Yeats the dramatist." In "Chinese Views of Anglo-Irish Writers and Their Works in the 1920's," in *Modern Chinese Literature and Its Social Context* (ed. Göran Malmqvist, Stockholm, 1977), Irene Eber notes that, "although many an essay was written about Yeats, the Nobel Prize winner, relatively few of his works were translated," amounting to a few poems, *The Hour Glass*, and some of the stories from *The Celtic Twilight*.

COMPARATIVE STUDIES

L. R. Lind's brief "Leda and the Swan: Yeats and Rilke" (*ChiR*, 1953) argues the superiority of Rilke's "Leda" because "in his economy he allows no bifurcation of attention." Jane Davidson Reid's "Leda, Twice Assaulted" (*JAAC*, 1953) is a solid comparative study that does not attempt to choose between the poems. A good survey of the basic parallels and affinities between the two writers is offered by Patricia Merivale in " 'Ultima Thule': Ghosts and Borderlines in Yeats and

Rilke" (*CL*, 1978), which suggests that "the more complex, mature work of both poets—'Byzantium,' the *Duino Elegies*—are subtle visionary meditations on the contiguity of life and death."

In the interesting essay "Fin de Siècle, Fin du Globe: Yeats and Hardy in the Nineties" (*BuR*, 1977), Edward Alexander contrasts Hardy's pessimism with Yeats's apocalyptic tendencies, showing that "Hardy was not a fin de siècle writer in the same sense that Yeats was, because he could find no consolation for present evil in the prospect that the century's end would bring cataclysm and a new revelation." Theodore Weiss's "The Many-Sidedness of Modern Literature" (*TLS*, 1 Feb. 1980), a review of Rosenthal's *Sailing into the Unknown*, comments at some length on—and rightly objects to—the current tendency to elevate Hardy at the expense of Yeats and other modern poets. A good instance of such a trend is "Leda and the Dumbledore" (*SR*, 1980), by James Hepburn, which compares "Leda and the Swan" with Hardy's "An August Midnight," the expressed aim being to elevate Hardy's stature and lower Yeats's. Hepburn concludes that "it is tempting to say that 'An August Midnight' makes 'Leda and the Swan' seem like a cheap bauble, but that would be to exaggerate." Indeed.

Robert W. Hill's "A Phenomenological Approach to Hopkins and Yeats" (*HQ*, 1978) is an unexciting attempt to show that "Hopkins' vision is more consistently phenomenological than Yeats's" but that "Hopkins' excellence of vision is less than Yeats's excellence of technique"; Hill criticizes Yeats for failing to develop "a completely satisfactory relationship with the things of earth." Leonard Conversi's "Mann, Yeats and the Truth of Art" (*YR*, 1967) contains more rhetoric than enlightenment. There is also little of interest in the comparative survey "Chesterton and W. B. Yeats: Vision, System and Rhetoric" (*CRev*, 1976), by David L. Derus. Thomas Mallon's "All Souls' Nights: Yeats, Sassoon and the Dead" (*IrishS*, 1980) suggests that "the most important common ground" between the two writers is "their sense of the influence of the dead, especially those departed whom they knew in life."

The appendix on Faulkner and Yeats in Cleanth Brooks's *William Faulkner: Toward Yoknapatawpha and Beyond* (1978) notes some interesting similarities and argues that "a fruitful comparison of Yeats and Faulkner must proceed from a recognition of the general parallels between the provincial cultures that nourished the genius of both men." In "Look at the Sea" (*RUSEng*, 1977), B. M. Singh compares "A Dialogue of Self and Soul" with Frost's "Neither Out Far nor in Deep."

In "Lyric as Performance: Lorca and Yeats" (*CL*, 1977), Murray Baumgarten notes that both poets show "a common concern for magic as the vehicle by means of which the poet becomes a communal spokesman, like the link between magic and lyric" and compares "An Irish Airman Foresees His Death" with "Canción de jinete." In "Mount Abiegnos and the Masks: Occult Imagery in Yeats and Pessoa" (*LBR*, 1968), Sol Biderman discusses the occult interests of Yeats and the Portuguese poet Fernando Pessoa, concluding that "what links Pessoa most directly to Yeats is the idea of the Mask." Rubén García's "The Unexpected Affinities: W. B. Yeats and Fernando Pessoa" (*JAPS*, 1976) covers much the same ground but makes no reference to Biderman's essay.

In "Reaching Back to Glory: Comparative Sketches in the 'Dreams' of W. B. Yeats and W. E. B. DuBois" (*Crisis*, 1976), W. Maurice Shipley argues that both men "succeeded in getting their people to grasp the nobility of their heritage and realize a new feeling of racial pride." The chapter "Yeats and His Enchanted Stone," in Lois Hughson's *Thresholds of Reality: George Santayana and Modernist Poetics* (1977), offers a standard account of Yeats's development and some scattered parallels with Santayana. Alan D. Perlis (*WSJour*, 1978) compares "Byzantium" with Stevens' "To an Old Philosopher in Rome," suggesting that "the significant departure from Romanticism is that in both poems artifact replaces nature."

The chapter on the novel *The Red and the Green* in Donna Gerstenberger's *Iris Murdoch* (1975) includes numerous comparisons with "Easter 1916," mainly to Yeats's advantage. Margaret Scanlan's "Fiction and the Fictions of History in Iris Murdoch's *The Red and the Green*" (*ClioI*, 1980) notes some allusions to Yeats and Joyce and argues that they "define some limitations of the visions of revolutionaries and artists" as well as "suggest resemblances, points of collusion, between the two groups: a tendency to simplify reality, a willingness to glamorize violent death." Wallace G. Kay's " 'As Recollection or the Drug Decide': Images and Imaginings in 'Among School Children' and *Blowup*" (*SoQ*, 1974) makes a minor contribution, arguing that "what the Yeats poem, the Cortazar story, and the Antonioni film suggest is that complete life cannot deny any of its parts." In "Exorcisms" (*Theater*, 1978), Oscar Giner makes an interesting comparison between *Purgatory* and *The Fanlights*, a play by the contemporary Puerto Rican writer René Marqués, showing how they are "exemplars of a critical national situation."

J. M. SYNGE

Weldon Thornton

1. Editions and Correspondence

The four-volume Oxford *Collected Works* (1962–68) remains the standard edition of Synge, but caveats continue to surface about Alan Price's selective and eclectic editing of the prose works (vol. 2). For example, Andrew Carpenter, in "Synge and Women" (*EI*, 1979), warns us that "the text of Synge's autobiography provided in the Oxford Synge is not satisfactory as it is conflated from at least five separate manuscript sources." It appears increasingly likely that we shall need a clearer and fuller edition of the miscellaneous essays and prose works that exist in several drafts in the notebooks.

The only textually noteworthy edition published in the last five years is Malcolm Kelsall's New Mermaid edition of *The Playboy of the Western World* (1975). In his note on the text, Kelsall expresses his respect for and debt to Ann Saddlemyer's work in volume 4 of the *Collected Works* but points out that his edition differs from Saddlemyer's text because of his "less flexible procedure." For Kelsall, "the authority of the final typescript has been preferred when it differs from the galley proof, and revisions in proof are preferred to the typescript." In addition to textual notes, Kelsall's edition contains substantial annotations, often clarifying passages in *Playboy* by quoting from Synge's other works.

In Wicklow West Kerry and Connemara (1980) reprints Synge's essays about these places, along with essays by George Gmelch and by Ann Saddlemyer, more than fifty photographs by Gmelch, and indexes of places and subjects. Gmelch's essay sets the geographical and demographic context for the Synge essays and praises Synge for his evocation of the mood of a locale, for his unusual attention to the landless people of his day, and for the accuracy of his accounts of the customs and stories of the people among whom he lived. Saddlemyer's piece, summarized on p. 180, discusses Synge's essays as literature and as literary source.

Andrew Carpenter (*Hermathena*, 1976) edits drafts of two passages of about four hundred and three hundred words from the notebook Synge used over the winter of 1897-98 (MS. 4382). Neither has any literary merit, but both cast some light on Synge's attitude toward women and sensuality and exemplify his desire for "epiphanic" experiences.

Another addition to Synge's canon is an unpublished essay discovered by Ann Saddlemyer, written by Synge in April or May 1906 and titled "The Dramatic Movement in Ireland" (*MD*, 1981). Apparently intended for publication in the *Manchester Guardian* soon after the Irish National Theatre Society's midlands tour in April 1906, this two-thousand-word essay summarizes the aims and progress of the dramatic movement from its inception to 1906, offering evaluations of several of the early dramatic productions. Most interesting is Synge's praising Hyde's play *The Twisting of the Rope* as "in some ways the most important of all those produced by The Irish Literary Theatre, as it alone has had an influence on the plays that have been written since."

No new Synge correspondence has been published since 1975. Ann Saddlemyer's long-awaited edition of correspondence between Yeats, Lady Gregory, and Synge—*Theatre Business: The Correspondence of the First Abbey Directors*—is scheduled for early 1982.

Saddlemyer is also editing a projected two-volume edition of Synge's *Collected Letters* for Oxford University Press; the first volume should appear in 1982. (Saddlemyer is interested in learning of yet undiscovered letters.)

2. Bibliography

There is still no full-length primary bibliography for Synge; the best sources remain those cited in the earlier edition of this work.

One book-length secondary bibliography has been published: Edward A. Kopper's *John Millington Synge: A Reference Guide* (1979), an annotated bibliography of criticism and commentary about Synge. In aim and scope it falls between the listing of materials offered by Levitt (1974) and by Mikhail (1975), and the summarizing of essays and books in *Anglo-Irish Literature: A Review of Research* (1976). Kopper lists nine hundred to a thousand items (fewer than half the number in Levitt or Mikhail), each of which is briefly characterized or annotated. The entries are arranged chronologically, alphabetized within each year, and complete through 1976, with some items from 1977. A thirteen-page introduction offers an intelligent but cursory review of Synge criticism; the index lists authors, titles, and some topics.

Richard M. Kain's review essay, "The Image of Synge: New Light and Deeper Shadows" (*SR*, 1976), discusses eight volumes on Synge appearing between 1971 and 1975 and reflects on the image of Synge that they present—reserved, contemplative, melancholy, intense, enigmatic. Synge is one of five Anglo-Irish dramatists included in Robert D. Boyer's

Realism in European Theatre and Drama, 1850-1920: A Bibliography (1979). Boyer's brief section on Synge is of little use; it is marked by a puzzling pattern of inclusion and some errors, and it lists nothing on Synge published after 1975.

3. Biography and Studies of Synge's Personality

No major biographical work on Synge has appeared in the last five years. Ann Saddlemyer has written brief, astute biographical sketches for *Great Writers of the English Language: Dramatists* (ed. James Vinson, 1979) and for *The Dictionary of Irish Literature* (ed. Robert Hogan, 1979); there have been one book-length collection of reminiscences and several essays interpreting aspects of Synge's personality.

E. H. Mikhail, in the preface to his slim *J. M. Synge: Interviews and Recollections* (1977), expresses the hope that "the present collection of conversations and recollections will throw further light on this shy-mannered man," but the items Mikhail includes are mostly old familiar ones. In contrast to his informative companion collection on Yeats, much of this volume simply reprints the well-known and readily available opinions of Yeats, Lady Gregory, Moore, Colum, and W. G. Fay. Only eight of the thirty-two items—and these are among the briefest in the book—are from newspapers or magazines. The annotations are uneven; for example, Mikhail identifies A. E. as George Russell and summarizes the plot of *Playboy*, but he neglects to clarify Synge's putative kinship to Lafcadio Hearn or to identify several contemporary writers referred to. Some of his annotations are simply inappropriate. The index is unreliable: some of the information in the annotations is indexed and some not, and some indexed items are hidden away where they are unlikely to be found. In short, this volume has little to justify itself beyond the convenience of having this material gathered between two covers.

François Boulaire (*CCET*, 1977) briefly discusses several of Synge's ancestors, providing only slightly more detail about them than is given in the genealogical chart in M. Bourgeois' *John Millington Synge and the Irish Theatre* (1913). Boulaire focuses on similarities between Synge and two of his clerical ancestors named Edward Synge (the first, archbishop of Tuam, died in 1714; the second, his son and the bishop of Elphin, died in 1762). According to Boulaire, these two Edwards showed an impressive degree of religious tolerance and some scepticism about political institutions—both traits found later in the playwright.

Jeanne Flood's "Synge's Ecstatic Dance and the Myth of the Undying Father" (*AI*, 1976) offers a Freudian analysis of Synge's psychology as it is reflected in the "Autobiography," "Under Ether," and the first chapter of *The Aran Islands*. Flood's purpose, like that of so many other critics of Synge, is to explain why the Aran Islands experiences were so important a turning point for Synge; her explanation is the most complicated that has been offered. She begins by discussing the absence of Synge's father (who died when Synge was less than one

year old) and Synge's early experiences that Flood claims resulted in fear
of the devouring mother and "an equation of uterine entrapment and
hell." Synge's refusal to marry reflects his wish to protect himself from
the fate of his father. Other elements of this complex, Flood says, were
contributed by Synge's reading of Darwin, Frazer, and Alfred Nutt.
Frazer and Nutt "offered Synge a myth in which the death of the father
is the fatal necessity that lies behind all life and all history." Turning to
"Under Ether," Flood argues that the operating room, "site of past
dismemberings, is the devouring womb of the fantasy" and that "by
presenting the operating table as a wooden scaffold, Synge makes his
operation into the crucifixion of the divine son." Flood also sees this idea
reflected in the first chapter of *The Aran Islands*, arguing that Synge
achieves the death of the symbolic father and rebirth as the miraculous
son through his identification with Old Mourteen and with Pat Dirane
and through the ecstatic dance dramatized in his famous dream. In
Flood's words, "By the transformation of Pat Dirane into himself
symbolically achieved in the dream dance, Synge denied the finality of
the pre-historic death of the father. The threat against himself posed by
the incorporative mother ceased to paralyze him because he became able
to accept the dissolution of ego-boundaries as a recurrent experience
leading to the perpetual transformation of the now eternal self," and this
"made it possible for him to submit himself to the feared and desired loss
of ego boundaries involved in creative work." Flood's convoluted thesis
does contain some germs of truth; Synge's psychological inclinations
doubtless operate on several levels and involve difficulties with his
mother, with sexuality, and with his concern for the integrity of his ego.
But Flood weakens whatever sympathy we may have for her argument by
selecting only those elements of Synge's works conducive to her thesis,
by elevating conjecture into evidence, and by reading passages in
narrowly sexual terms. Interesting and suggestive as Flood's essay is, it
fails by overstating what might have been a revealing analysis of certain
aspects of Synge's mind.

   Sean McMahon's " 'Leave Troubling the Lord God': A Note on
Synge and Religion" (*Éire*, 1976) revives the question of Synge's
anticlericalism and insensitivity to religion, claiming that the outrage of
the early audiences was misdirected but not baseless. The essay both
insinuates Synge's insensitivity and defends Synge against similar charges
brought by Daniel Corkery, in *Synge and Anglo-Irish Literature* (1931).
McMahon apparently would like to condemn Synge as a Protestant
agnostic incapable of appreciating the nuances of Irish Roman
Catholicism, but he seems to fear that such a stance is fifty years out of
date. He contents himself with pointing to Synge's suppression and
distortion of detail in *The Aran Islands* and with making the ominous
but unclarified charge that "the portrayals that were damned as un-Irish
for all the wrong reasons were more dangerously un-Irish than the most
extreme agitators realized." McMahon ends with a weak paean to artistic
freedom that further obscures the point he retreats from making.

   Ann Saddlemyer's "Synge and the Doors of Perception" (in *Place,
Personality and the Irish Writer*, ed. Andrew Carpenter, 1977) draws
skillfully on Synge's aesthetic and religious statements, published and

unpublished, to explore his philosophic and spiritual values. Beginning with a look at passages in Synge's prose describing moments of "heightened awareness," Saddlemyer stresses Synge's inclination to see nature and the individual personality as complementary. Then, describing Synge as having a mystic's regard for nature's mysteries and for the wholeness and the potential intensity of human experience, she explains that for Synge "the work of a great artist will be *unique*, carrying with it the shock of joy given by 'a thing never done before and never to be done again'; it will be *profound*, because it 'finds the inner and essential mood of the things it treats . . .'; and being rich, many-sided, and universal, it will be *sane*." Saddlemyer goes on to discuss how this religious-aesthetic belief is reflected in Synge's handling of locale, dialogue, and love and death.

Robin Skelton's "The Politics of J. M. Synge" (*MR*, 1977) is built on inferences from Synge's essays and plays rather than on any new evidence. Beginning predictably with Yeats's claim that Synge was unfitted to think a political thought, Skelton concludes that this was untrue but that Synge was no party man. Drawing on analogies between certain statements of Synge's and some of William Morris', and on material from Synge's essays and from *Well of the Saints* and *Playboy*, Skelton claims that "Synge's detestation of modern capitalist society was as strong as his distrust of religious dogma" and says that in his plays Synge "presented themes whose political implications were, in fact, much more fundamental than perhaps he himself realized." *Well of the Saints* "can be regarded as politically loaded," and the rise and fall of Christy in *Playboy* evoked disturbing memories of Parnell in the minds of Irish politicians. Skelton sees Synge as concerned about the welfare of the Irish people and as moved to work "for the cause of Irish freedom, by endeavoring to free it from the prison of its own self-delusions."

Patrick Hederman's "The Playboy versus the Western World" (*Crane Bag*, 1977) is a pastiche of spirited adjurations and superficial observations purporting to deal with "Synge's political role as artist." Hederman accepts the simplifications that Synge was incapable of a political thought, that he was totally estranged from the Irish nationalists' aspirations, and that on Aran he found reality. The vagueness of Hederman's presentation obscures whatever point he is making.

Mark Mortimer (*Studies*, 1977) challenges the received idea that Synge went to the Aran Islands as a direct result of Yeats's urging. Mortimer argues that Synge's decision was more complex and influenced by "a family connection, a knowledge of Irish, an interest in Brittany and a yearning to discover in his own country a primitive, unspoiled civilization."

Synge is one of several persons touched on by Terence de Vere White in "Richard Irvine Best and His Irish Literary Contemporaries" (*IUR*, 1977). White briefly mentions the acquaintance of Best and Synge in Paris and Best's visit to Synge during his last days in the hospital, but he tells us nothing new about their relationship.

Andrew Carpenter (*EI*, 1979) discusses Synge's attitude toward women and traces its development in his life and his works. Carpenter's thesis is that Synge's women "developed from the cardboard Celliniari of the *Etude Morbide* . . . through the earthy extravagance of the brash Pegeen . . . to the stately dignity of Deirdre" and that "in many respects the progression of Synge's plays parallels the progression of his life." But while Carpenter's analysis of the effects of Synge's social and religious background makes a good start on the study of this potentially rich topic, Carpenter falters when presenting the stages of Synge's development. He pinpoints several crucial junctures in Synge's life—his going to Italy and meeting Hope Rea in 1896, his going to the Aran Islands, his meeting Molly Allgood, and his experiencing the death of his mother—but he is vague about their significance.

G. J. Watson's *Irish Identity and the Literary Revival: Synge, Yeats, Joyce, and O'Casey* (1979) explores these four writers' struggles with "the nature or meaning of Irish identity, and the resultant effects on the content and form of their art." Synge is seen as "paradigmatic of the situation and problems of the Ascendancy writer in Ireland, torn between the desire to identify and merge with a community and the desire to assert the distinguishing and defining values of the individual self." Watson emphasizes Synge's social and religious background and shows how it blends with his personality to produce his distinctive attitudes. In Synge's disdain of the middle class and his elegaic treatment of the peasantry and its lack of emotional inhibition, Watson sees an inextricable intertwining of "romantic primitivism and Ascendancy attitudes" in "what might be called an Irish version of pastoral." The characteristics of Synge's language noted by Watson are a uniformity among all the characters, verb forms suggesting stasis, and an elaborate syntax, all expressing Synge's wish for continuity and community. Watson comments on Synge's fascination with primitive energy and finds Synge's penchant for violence not simply in the events he depicts but in the fabric of his language. *Playboy* is seen as a celebration of the demonic, and the audience's hostility to it as a response to the play's implicit support for violent revolution against England when most Irishmen were content with constitutional measures. Finally, the complexity of Synge's denouements, his "consistent thwarting or complication of the straightforward comic pattern" expresses simultaneously the pull toward community and toward individuality.

4. General Books and Essays

Nicholas Grene, in the preface to his *Synge: A Study of the Plays* (1975), claims that the book is "the first full study to concentrate exclusively on the plays" and that it offers "the detailed criticism, analysis and evaluation" required for the work of a writer of Synge's stature. Grene also points to the possibility of looking closely at Synge's six plays "without needing to explain who he was and where he lived when, what else he wrote and in which order." The chapters that follow do not adhere to the New Critical method that the preface suggests will be adopted, but they do resemble the preface in their unevenness. Valid and perceptive criticism alternates with sheer summary of the plays, and analyses of the sources and progress of Synge's language alternate with grammatical classifications. Grene also has a penchant for arguing himself into a corner. In his first, mainly biographical chapter, for example, Grene contends that Synge was "an observer among the peasants . . . unable to understand" or "communicate with them" because he retained "much of the arrogance, the unconscious assumption of superiority of the upper class." Then, to account for Synge's acknowledged ability to represent the peasant mentality, Grene contradictorily speaks of his being "gifted with a unique feeling for what he saw among the Irish peasants."

In his discussion of Synge's Aran experiences, Grene emphasizes the shaping of language and Synge's account of the islands as selective, partial, and inaccurate—a reflection of Synge's wish to believe that the people were primitive and had a rapport with nature that he deeply envied.

Grene's discussion of *Riders to the Sea* (involving a lengthy summary of the plot) makes the dubious assumption that this play was completed before Synge turned to *Shadow of the Glen*, stresses the realistic props Synge insisted on, and worries over the false problem of how a play with so much "surface realism" manages to win a sophisticated audience over to the supernatural. He sees the play as a tragedy, though not quite a classical one, and he describes Maurya's state at the end of the play as a "Christian resignation . . . much more impressive . . . because it has been seen to overcome the pagan feeling of bitter resentment."

Grene devotes a full chapter to the development of Synge's dialect, stressing that its poetry is a product of selection and shaping, not a quality inherent in the language Synge drew on. The linguistic forms and constructions Synge preferred and consistently used are described. Grene also points out that Synge's characters differ in their attitudes toward language, some regarding it as poetic and liberating and others seeing it as blather.

In an overview of the Wicklow essays, Grene categorizes their subjects as sheep farmers, people of the villages and valleys, and tramps and tinkers, and twits Synge for blurring the distinction between the last two. Grene summarizes *Shadow of the Glen* to illustrate his claim that the play's unity arises from a harmony involving balance and contrast, growing out of Synge's subtle exploitation of the audience's expectations. Synge's technique here is "to make us constantly re-group his characters, and to revise the criteria by which they had been grouped before."

Grene proposes to do justice to the neglected merits of *Tinker's Wedding*, but finally sees it as at best a failure from which we may learn something. His discussion of its background is overliteral, and he says the play fails because "the story on which it was based was not suitable for Synge's purposes."

Grene's intelligent but problematic discussion of *Well of the Saints* defers too much to Synge's schematic analysis of the play but does focus clearly on the theme of truth and illusion, comparing the play to other writers' plays on the same theme. Grene suggests that the fullness of *Well* enables Synge to take a "serio-comic view of the world which is deeply committed and yet austerely detached." But Grene does not make clear how any richness in the drama can answer the basic confrontation between dream and reality the play dramatizes through Martin and Mary's witting choice of blindness and their elaboration of dreams they know to be baseless.

In his discussion of *Playboy*, Grene rejects mythic or literary parallels and the view that Christy is best seen as an artist, proposing instead to "establish the simple theatrical forms on which it is based, and then to look at the way Synge develops them towards something more complex." He concludes that "the central effect of the play depends upon the relation between . . . extravagant comedy and a more realistic form of drama." In an overview of what Grene terms Synge's four "unhappy comedies"—*Shadow of the Glen, Tinker's Wedding, Well of the Saints*, and *Playboy*—he acknowledges that both Synge and O'Casey write "tragicomedy" but stresses that, unlike O'Casey, "Synge never writes tragicomedy . . . where the comedy threatens to pull apart from the serious drama which surrounds it." Grene then observes that Beckett, Ionesco, and Pinter all made breaches of theatrical convention far more sensational than Synge's.

Grene sees *Deirdre of the Sorrows* as a failure because the writing of that play "took Synge outside the landscape he knew" and because the story of Deirdre "was not ultimately real to him as a whole, and it was not susceptible to transformation into the terms of his reality."

K. S. Misra's *The Plays of J. M. Synge: A Critical Study* (New Delhi, 1977) has a general introductory chapter, a chapter on each of the six plays, and a brief conclusion. The introduction discusses the general aims of the Irish dramatic movement, stressing its blend of nationalistic and aesthetic elements. Praising Synge's comprehensive depiction of the Irish folk-ethos, Misra points out that the dramas are serious but not didactic, that Synge cultivated in his plays a broad-based "humor" to counter morbidity and sophistication, and that he challenged the artificial language of contemporary plays by drawing on the idiom of the people.

Riders to the Sea Misra praises as realistic but not naturalistic, finding that Synge's genius transforms naturalistic detail into something universal. He is not, however, satisfied with Maurya's characterization, saying that "the genuine tragic emotion of pity seems to be diluted to sentimentalism because of Maurya's passivity." He admires the economy of the plot, though "the action of the play is thin and the plot is uneventful," and finds the language appropriate and the creation of atmosphere masterly. Misra sees the central theme of *Shadow of the Glen* as women's loneliness, their helplessness and dependence on men, and male indifference to their sufferings. He believes that Nora's emancipation promises to be fruitful, in view of the sympathetic nature of the Tramp. The play is not uniformly satisfying, however; "it has a thin plot in which little happens" and "there is not much in the way of characterization."

Finding *The Tinker's Wedding* a masterly blending of the comic and the serious, Misra praises its humor and its "seriousness devoid of any didacticism." About *Well of the Saints* Misra says that "illusion and reality are once again juxtaposed, leaving the individual free to make his choice of either." How these two categories interact in the play is not made fully clear, but the Douls' rejection of the return to sight at the play's end is seen as positive, "the reconstruction of their life." Misra acknowledges that this play, like some others of Synge's, is not easily analyzable through set, conventional dramatic forms but finds in the play's fusion of the tragic and comic moods a rare artistry transcending conventional categorizations.

Misra sums up the theme of *Playboy* as " 'self-discovery' —Christy's 'discovery' of himself and the Mayoites' 'discovery' of themselves specifically represented by Pegeen." By the end of the play, Christy's self-discovery is complete, but Pegeen's realizations lead her toward tragedy, while "the Mayoites remain tied to their constricting environment." The inescapable conclusion is that "people who can thrive on myth and make-believe can hardly survive in the world of reality. The two worlds are incompatible and compromise between them is impossible." *Deirdre* exemplifies Synge's maturity as an artist in his handling of the legendary source, his mastery over ironies, and his sense of exaltation in high tragedy. Though the element of fate is large in the play, by its end Deirdre has become transfigured and "expresses the realized 'eternity' of her love." "The themes of fatalism and old age and death are concluded on a note of 'joy' and 'triumph.' "

Misra's book draws on a limited number of secondary sources and offers nothing distinctive in its view of Synge or his plays. It consists of a great deal of summary of the plays and relatively little interpretation. The effect is marred by typographical errors and misnomers (e.g., Edwin Martyn; P. P. Powe, for Howe).

Three essays have appeared in *Studies on Synge* (ed. Dapo Adelugba, Ibadan, 1977). René Frechet's "The Theme of Speech in the Plays of J. M. Synge" (pub. in French in *EA*, 1968) introduces and briefly discusses each of the six plays, concluding that for Synge "it is by means of words, of speech, that a life can realize itself, and discover joy." In A. W. Thomson's essay, the brief assessments of the plays are collections of critical observations rather than full-scale interpretations. *Shadow* is praised as going beyond farce by virtue of its subtle handling of tensions within and among the characters and its evocation of a "queerness" surrounding all experience. *Tinker's Wedding* explores the incompatability of the two "estates" of the tinkers and the priest and gains richness from the character of Mary, whose ripe age signifies a power greater than that of priest or tinkers. *Well of the Saints* is judged Synge's least successful play—its language pallid, its themes too explicit. *Riders* offers not a tragic formula but the intensification of the tragic, best seen in Maurya's vision of the mingled worlds of the living and the dead. *Deirdre*, while tragedy in a high or accustomed sense, is not great tragedy, though its language is beautiful. Most expressive of Synge is *Playboy*—a magnificent comedy built around violent separation and no less violent conjunction. Tadgh F. O'Sullivan's "Synge and the Ireland of His Day" is a brief résumé of Synge's life and career drawn from published sources. Of some value for its intended general audience, it holds nothing for those knowledgeable about Synge.

Maurice Harmon's "Cobwebs before the Wind: Aspects of the Peasantry in Irish Literature from 1800 to 1916" (in *Views of the Irish Peasantry, 1800-1916*, ed. Daniel J. Casey and Robert E. Rhodes, 1977) deals briefly with Synge but gives him a distinctive place among the writers discussed. For Harmon, "Synge stands apart, in that he broke through the barriers of the Ascendancy world and penetrated deeply into the native, Catholic, and rural world," and he "had the capacity to portray more deeply and with greater clarity the essential psychological and social problems of the time."

T. R. Henn's "John Millington Synge: A Reconsideration" (in Henn's *Last Essays*, 1976; first pub. in *Hermathena*, 1971) is an overview that passes quickly over the prose and poetry, turning in more detail to the plays. Henn describes them as "one tragedy, two near-tragedies, and two 'critical' comedies," leaving us to infer which are which and which one has been passed by in this schema. He touches on Synge's language, calling its quality variable, its diction uneven. He concludes by focusing on the "ambivalence of Synge's outlook, which [is] the force behind his irony and his anti-clericalism, his understanding and compassion and intense apprehension of place."

W. A. Armstrong's "Synge's Communities and Dissenters" (in *Drama and Society*, ed. James Redmond, 1979) deals with isolation in Synge's life and works. Armstrong's thesis is that each play involves "a central character whose intuitions lead him to move away from a community less perceptive than he is" and that "the adversity, the alienation, and the danger" that he may face as a result "are justified because of the intensification, the inner development, and the enriched vision achieved." Each of the plays is discussed briefly in terms of this claim.

Seamus Deane's "Synge's Western Worlds" (in *A Needle's Eye*, ed. Mary O'Malley and John Boyd, 1979), while written with great facility, touches too many topics too briefly to leave any clear impression. Deane deals mostly with Synge's attitude toward Ireland and with the status of language in his plays. According to Deane, Synge believed that Ireland had great cultural potential, and he aimed to help it find its way to a vigorous new identity. Synge's plays persistently involve "inner longing . . . confronted by a hostile or closed world," and characters must either overcome that hostile world or recognize that nothing can be done. Deane finds the plays oddly ahistorical, maintaining that "the only historical detail in Synge is the language." Deane's suggestions are impressive in their variety, but his meanings are often disappointingly hard to pin down.

Weldon Thornton's *J. M. Synge and the Western Mind* (1979) challenges prevailing opinions by arguing that Synge was deeply concerned about the integrity of his political and religious beliefs. Partly because of the Aran Islands experience, Synge came to see that implicit ideas—an unacknowledged intellectual frame of reference—exert great power in people's lives. This realization, which was crucial to Synge's intellectual and aesthetic development, forms a progressively developed theme throughout his dramatic canon.

Thornton explores Synge's social and familial background, showing how the religious dogmatism of his family bred into Synge a deep concern about integrity of belief and an obligation to search for the "truth."

Thornton suggests that on the Aran Islands of the 1890s Synge could have found a world view that was archaic and pre-Western, one characterized not only by a different set of beliefs (especially about nature and the supernatural) but by a different attitude toward the importance of beliefs generally. Thornton then discusses Synge's reactions to life on the islands, as reflected in *The Aran Islands*, arguing that the main value of the experience was in making Synge "aware of the cultural variability of deeply implicit attitudes and beliefs."

Turning to the plays, Thornton examines each one from the perspective of the influence exerted by received assumptions. According to Thornton, this theme is behind Synge's penchant for evoking and then undercutting his audience's stereotypical religious or political attitudes, thus throwing the audience into that "cognitive dissonance" that occurs whenever our implicit frames of reference are challenged. In *The Shadow of the Glen*, Synge intentionally evokes and then undercuts the traditional story of the January-May marriage, and the frustration and anger the early audiences felt stemmed more from the shattering of that stereotype than from the more local causes usually adduced. In *Riders to the Sea*, Synge's concern with this theme manifests itself more directly in his evocation of the distinctive world view he had experienced on the Aran Islands. Whether Synge simply wanted to re-present what he had felt on the islands or to evoke another form of cognitive dissonance from an audience to whom this milieu would be foreign, the effect has been to send critics scurrying for traditional Western frames of reference to assimilate the events and mood of the play. Accordingly, most of the critical comment on the play is devoted to the false issue of whether the play succeeds as Aristotelian tragedy—a concern that again illustrates Synge's point about the power of received forms of judgment. *The Tinker's Wedding* testifies to this power both through its themes and through the challenge it offered to the contemporary audience. The Abbey refused to stage it for fear of the responses likely to be provoked by the impious handling of the priest. The play shows two world views poised against each other—that of the tinkers versus that of the "establishment"—and the difficulty of moving between the two is shown by Sarah's initial attraction to the institution of marriage and her rejection of it on closer inspection.

Thornton sees in the longest plays, *Well of the Saints* and *Playboy*, Synge's fullest exploration of the philosophical issues implicit in the relation among experience, ideas, and "truth." Thornton agrees with those critics who have regarded as pessimistic and even nihilistic the Douls's final choice of a blindness that permits them to construct whatever dreams they wish, but he argues that these dark implications do not represent Synge's final judgment on these issues. For Thornton, *Playboy* complements *Well of the Saints* in its more subtle and affirmative exploration of the same philosophical issues. In *Well of the Saints*, idea and "reality" are presented in static opposition, and the play's ending shows the Douls opting for a dream so contrary to reality that it must be seen as a lie. In *Playboy*, on the other hand, the relation of idea and reality is more subtle; the "reality" of Christy's personality is transformed during the play, largely through the medium of language, so that the idea or the dream (or what Christy calls "the power of a lie") has in fact modified reality. And this, Thornton claims, represents Synge's more subtle and mature response to the dilemma of idea versus reality.

In *Deirdre*, Thornton sees Synge moving beyond this dilemma and even turning his awareness of the power of implicit ideas to advantage. When he came to write his Deirdre play, Synge realized that previous writers had been limited by received nineteenth-century attitudes toward the Irish saga material. He set himself the challenge of consciously setting aside that frame of reference and developing his own, so that he could see the characters of the story not as icons but as persons with complex needs and motives. The result is a version of the Deirdre story that is psychologically far more astute and rewarding than any other.

Joan Templeton, in "Synge's Redeemed Ireland: Woman as Rebel" (*Caliban*, 1980), claims that Synge's major theme is the demand for freedom achieved through "the assertion of individual self over the norms of a restrictive society" and sees this theme embodied primarily in the dilemmas of the women in his plays. In this context she discusses Nora Burke, Maurya, Mary Casey, Pegeen Mike (deemed an exception, since she is a conformist at heart), and Deirdre. But Templeton constricts an otherwise perceptive speculation about why Synge so persistently uses "trapped females" as protagonists by proposing the narrowly political thesis that "their conflict dramatizes what Synge and his contemporaries view as Ireland's own" and by saying that "They are models for Ireland's redemptive future."

In " 'There's Talking for a Cute Woman!': Synge's Heroines" (*Éire*, 1980), F. A. E. Whelan and Keith N. Hull discuss all six plays from the point of view that "Synge's principal women think and behave in a basic pattern that acts as a unifying theme in his plays: all suffer from . . . dissatisfaction with their lives, seek escape, and in the process become the movers and shakers of dramatic action." Whelan and Hull's application of this idea, however, is too general and too uneven to tell us anything new. Their thesis draws them into seeing Mary Doul as "ultimately in control of the Douls' life and happiness," and they must acknowledge that the nature of Maurya's tragedy "apparently reverses the theme of woman initiating the main action of the play."

5. Synge and the Literary Movement

Micheál Ó hAodha's chapter on Synge in his *Theatre in Ireland* (1974) says nothing new about Synge's works or about his relation to other Abbey playwrights. Ó hAodha deals briefly (and inaccurately) with Synge's biography and touches on each of the plays but offers no new interpretations. The chapter consists mainly of bland observations and long, predictable quotations from Synge's works.

James W. Flannery's "W. B. Yeats and the Abbey Theatre Company" (*ETJ*, 1975) says little about Synge; it does show Synge's opposition to taking continental municipal theaters as a model (i.e., his preference that the Abbey continue to do "native work"), and Flannery characterizes Synge's and Lady Gregory's opposition to Yeats's ambitions for the theater as arising from "intransigence, theatrical ignorance and downright selfishness."

Harold Orel's "Drama for the Nation" (in *Irish History and Culture*, ed. Orel, 1976) briefly assesses Synge's contribution to the theater movement. He points out that Synge more than any of the others was able to write both plays dealing with peasant life and plays dealing with romantic and heroic life such as one finds in folktales, and he emphasizes that because Synge could not be made to serve political ends, he played a decisive role in making the victory of the Abbey "a victory for an apolitical, imaginative, and innovative play, for Literature."

Richard Fallis, in *The Irish Renaissance* (1977), discusses Synge in the context of the rise of the Abbey. Emphasizing the controversy that constantly surrounded Synge, Fallis praises his accomplishments as a dramatist: *Shadow of the Glen* offers a "powerful evocation of the glens of Wicklow and its subtle symbolism"; *Riders* is "the great short tragedy in our language"; *Playboy* is Synge's masterpiece, and "no play of the Irish renaissance has a richer, more various language"; *Deirdre* is "a play which misses greatness only because its author did not live to give it the final revisions," and "there is no greater speech in Irish drama" than Deirdre's final keen over Naisi. Fallis concludes that Synge "was surely the greatest playwright Ireland has produced."

Robert Hogan and James Kilroy's *The Abbey Theatre: The Years of Synge, 1905–1909* (1978) necessarily touches continually on Synge's role in the movement. Documentary rather than evaluative, this volume presents scores of excerpts from contemporary newspapers and journals as well as from letters, diaries, and unpublished manuscripts. Almost all the material relating to Synge is available in print elsewhere, but here it becomes more coherent as gathered around the story of the Abbey Theatre.

The Revels History of Drama in English, Volume VII: 1880 to the Present Day (1978), by Hugh Hunt, Kenneth Richards, and John Russell Taylor, gives a mere two paragraphs to Synge, proclaiming the high quality of his "peasant drama" and saying that his "vital quality is the constant link he keeps with reality, even in his wildest flights of invention."

Hugh Hunt's *The Abbey: Ireland's National Theatre, 1904–1979* (1979) contains no extended discussion of Synge or of his plays. The five pages Hunt devotes to describing the uproar caused by *Playboy* tell us nothing new.

Katharine Worth, in *The Irish Drama from Yeats to Beckett* (1978), plays down Synge's realism and dwells on the European influences on him, especially that of Maeterlinck. Among the similarities she traces between these two are their musicality and their concern with visualization, with monotony and stillness, and with the "fluidity of their characters." Worth focuses on *The Well of the Saints*, the play that "pushes the hardest towards incongruity and absurdity, forcing us into uneasy relation with its dreamers and non-dreamers alike." Synge first piles up the odds against the Douls but then "puts his weight behind the rightness of the final choice . . . by showing how with the return of physical blindness, a kind of inner light is restored." Synge's characteristic mode is "a knife-edge balance of the comic and the somber," which "becomes a way of confronting without despair the really bad jokes of life; physical afflictions, ugliness, old age, death." Worth considers that, in spite of certain nineteenth-century traits in his style and technique, Synge is "one of the most modern of the moderns" by virtue of his "sardonic humor and by his subtle handling of the self-conscious theatricality that seems so natural to his characters." Worth also says that Synge's career "remarkably anticipates" Beckett's and that Synge (and Maeterlinck) influenced the drama of Yeats.

In "Pious and Impious Peasants: Popular Religion in the Comedies of Lady Gregory and John M. Synge" (*CLQ*, 1978), William M. Clements proposes that at the turn of the century there were two operative Irish stereotypes: the stage Irishman inherited from the nineteenth century and the peasant fostered by Celtic nationalists. According to Clements, the characters of Lady Gregory and Synge conformed to neither, mainly because of their impiety.

In his "The Fall of the Stage Irishman" (*Genre*, 1979) Declan Kiberd deals briefly with Synge and *Playboy*. While *Playboy* is "an attack on the lyric gush, pugnacity and violence popularly associated with the Stage Irishman," it "is also, though covertly, an assault on the anti-stage Irishman of Wilde and Yeats" (i.e., a sensitive figure cultivating "the mask of the elegant anti-self").

6. Sources, Influences, Languages, and Translations

SOURCES

Mark Mortimer's "Synge and France" (*France-Ireland: Literary Relations*, ed. Patrick Rafroidi et al., Paris, 1974) attempts to elucidate Synge's debt to France. Mortimer says that this question has been clouded by the intentional underestimation of this debt by early commentators—by George Moore because he wished to be the sole Irishman able to speak about France and by Stephen MacKenna because he wanted to defend Synge against the slanders of French influence. Mortimer reminds us of the great influence of Pierre Loti's *Pêcheur d'Island* on Synge and of the debt of *The Well of the Saints* to de la Vigne's farce *L'Aveugle et le boiteux*. He observes that Villon and Ronsard left a lasting mark on Synge but that the influence of Racine and Molière is more difficult to plot. In short, this brief overview says nothing new.

Gérard Leblanc's "J. M. Synge in Paris," in the same collection of essays, recapitulates in some detail Synge's stays in Paris, discussing his political sentiments, acquaintances, schooling, and reading. Leblanc's interest in the influences of Paris and of French literature on Synge focuses not so much on the effects of individual works as on what Synge gleaned from all this that helped him find his own aesthetic and learn how to express himself effectively. For Leblanc, Synge's artistic theory and expression turn largely on successful "collaboration" between the artist and his environment, something Synge found only after his French experiences. Thus, while Leblanc does not see Synge's stays in Paris as an "unnecessary stage," he does feel that no French writer of his time represented to Synge what he was looking for, and only in Ireland and in the drama could Synge "conciliate his principles and his practice and . . . express in a specific medium the significant bond between man and the world in which he lives, loves, acts and dies."

Jean C. Noël's "J. M. Synge and Some French Writers" (*CCEI*, 1977) focuses on Synge's articles—on Huysmans and Loti and one on Anatole France—that are only partially reprinted in *Collected Works*, vol. 2. Noël deplores the disdain in which these articles have been held, praising Synge's perspicacity and independence of judgment and saying that these articles speak well for Synge's achievement as a critic of French literature.

INFLUENCES

In *A Comparison of Plays by John Millington Synge and Frederico García Lorca: The Poets and Time* (Madrid, 1978), Jean J. Smoot carries out the first full-scale comparison of these writers. The introduction notes that affinities between these two have been suggested but never thoroughly studied. The first chapter, purportedly about the two writers' "aesthetics," is more an exploration of their basic attitudes toward life than a coherent discussion of their theory of art; Smoot also misleads us by declaring that "Synge read Greek, Latin, Hebrew, French, German, Irish, and Italian" and that "Synge could read Greek tragedy in the original," citing no documentation for these claims. Smoot then compares *Riders to the Sea* and *Bodas da sangre*, *In the Shadow of the Glen* and *Yerma*, *Playboy* and *La casa de Bernarda Alba*, and *Deirdre* and *Doña Rosita la soltera*. The last comparison shows that both writers see time as death, as bringing a fading of beauty, a loss of vitality, a lessening of emotional ties, thereby making life itself tragic. But both writers measure time not by years but by intensity, and "the poet is the one who destroys time, who makes our brief space on this earth meaningful and worthwhile."

In "Synge and Comedy" (*YeatsS*, 1972), Alec Reid begins his comparison of Synge and Beckett by generalizing about the Anglo-Irish sensibility produced in those who are "English to the Irish, Irish to the English"—a sensibility often "finding its expression through the tragicomic." Reid acknowledges that Synge and Beckett seem to give diametrically opposite responses to the questions of what is to be done and how we are to go on. Synge, "recognizing the inevitability of the dark still defies it by seeking exultation," while Beckett, "turning from such emotional response, drives his intellect to the creation of a world where there is nothing left to lose." But looking more closely, we frequently find the tragic beneath the comic surface in Synge and "an equally surprising humor in Beckett." Reid concludes that "the tragic overtones in Synge and the laughter in Beckett are precisely what we would expect from men seeing life in the double terms of the tragi-comic vision."

James Knowlson's "Beckett and John Millington Synge" (*Frescoes of the Skull: The Later Prose and Drama of Samuel Beckett*, 1980; *Gam-*

bit, 1976) notes that Beckett acknowledged the influence of Synge in a letter to Knowlson. Knowlson judges the most fundamental thematic parallel to be "the sense of a profound rift between God and man and between the ideal and the actual." But "Beckett may owe his greatest debt" to Synge in another, more aesthetic direction—namely, that in Synge's plays "many basically poetic (and musical) devices are exploited dramatically to arrive at a text characterized by density, ambiguity, resonance, and multiplicity of levels, both intellectually and emotionally."

Katharine Worth's "O'Casey, Synge and Yeats" (*IUR*, 1980) discusses the influence of Synge and of Yeats on the theme of dreaming in O'Casey's plays. Claiming that Synge's influence is most discernible in the plays down through *The Plough and the Stars* and Yeats's in the plays from *The Silver Tassie* on, Worth looks specifically at certain similarities between *Playboy* and *The Shadow of a Gunman*. She then uses these similarities to highlight differences in the handling of the dream in each play—in Synge "the action can be seen indeed as a maturing process in which dream is brought into a fruitful relation with reality," whereas there is no happy ending for Davoren when the fantasy of his being a gunman collapses.

LANGUAGES

Declan Kiberd has published an array of material dealing with Synge's knowledge of the Irish language and his use of native language sources. Several of Kiberd's essays (*Maynooth Rev.*, May 1978, Dec. 1978, and May 1979; *RES*, 1979; *Hermathena*, 1979) are replicated in his *Synge and the Irish Language* (1979) and need not be separately summarized. Kiberd's book is the only full-scale discussion by someone competent to judge of Synge's knowledge of the Irish language and his indebtedness to Irish-language sources. Kiberd is best on scholarly or linguistic issues. He concludes that Synge's spoken Irish was quite good, his written Irish only moderately good, and his academic Irish very good, showing a knowledge of the history of the language and literature in all its phases. These conclusions are grounded in a careful study of Synge's translations and the Irish originals. Less convincing is Kiberd's discussion of the influence of Irish literature on Synge's works. His presentation of *Vita Vecchia* as "Synge's attempt to recreate a romance of the Gaelic mode in modern English" fails because the spirit of *Vita Vecchia* is alien to that of Gaelic romance, despite the technical similarities. More valid is Kiberd's view of *Playboy* as "heroic parody" built around parallels (mostly ironic) with the Cuchulain stories, but he takes no note of these suggestions having been made by M. J. Sidnell in 1965 and Diane E. Bessai in 1968. Kiberd is more specific and convincing in discussing the influence of Irish folk songs—and especially Douglas Hyde's several volumes—on Synge's poetry and plays. But here again the critical judgment is flaccid when Kiberd describes Martin Doul as "a latter-day Avicenna, whose love for Molly's beauty increases his virtue." In his discussion of Synge and folklore, Kiberd is better at establishing Synge's distinctively comparatist approach to the topic than in showing how Synge's study of folklore bears on his plays. In his discussion of how Synge, Yeats, and A. E. treated the Deirdre legend, Kiberd attributes the fundamental differences among the works to Synge's reliance on the Irish originals, ignoring the more basic temperamental differences among these three writers. Kiberd's conclusions about Synge's Anglo-Irish dialect are the same as those of Alan Bliss (1972) and others but are based on a fuller examination of unpublished materials. Kiberd concludes that Synge's literary Anglo-Irish "represents not the talk of the folk, but a colorful intensification of the peculiarly Irish elements of their idiom." Kiberd demonstrates Synge's sympathy with much of what the Gaelic League was striving for (except, of course, the restoration of Irish as the language of the country) and his efforts within the Abbey Theatre to "maintain the national character of its productions." Kiberd's unearthing of the laudatory view of Synge espoused in *An Claidheamh Soluis* in April of 1910 gives us a better appreciation of the sympathies between Synge and the Gaelic advocates of his day.

Kiberd's "Writers in Quarantine? The Case for Irish Studies" (*Crane Bag*, 1979) decries the continuing practice of separating Irish from Anglo-Irish studies and regards Synge as the "first and most spectacular victim" of this division, but he says that "it was Synge's particular achievement to ignore this foolish devision and to take both literatures out of quarantine." Kiberd's "The Frenzy of Christianity: Synge and Buile Shuibhne" (*Éire*, 1919) calls attention to similarities of situation, motif, and theme between the Irish story *The Frenzy of Sweeny* and Synge's *Playboy* (and, briefly, *Well of the Saints*). These parallels include the frenzy and resultant poetic capacities of Sweeny and Christy, the predicted deaths of Sweeny at spear point and of Christy by hanging, and the motif of "threefold death" in both works. Kiberd's case is built entirely on internal evidence, though it seems likely Synge did know the Sweeny story. His scanty discussion of the meanings of these parallels for *Playboy* is less than satisfying.

Uwe Stork's monograph *Der Sprachliche Rhythmus in den Bühnenstücken John Millington Synges* (Salzburg, 1980) discusses the nature and function of the speech rhythms in Synge's plays. The first third of the monograph surveys the literature on rhythm and uses the categories of structural linguistics (i.e., stress, juncture, pitch) to give a precise account of prose rhythms. After establishing the rhythmic features that occur in Synge's works, Stork cites Synge's comments about the rhythmical and musical aspects of language, comments of the plays' characters, and the evolution of certain passages in the plays to argue that Synge consciously strove to achieve these rhythmic effects. Stork then surveys the developments of Synge's prose rhythms progressively through the plays. In *Riders to the Sea* and *The Shadow of the Glen*, sentences are lengthy and have unobtrusive but persistent rhythms. In *Tinker's Wedding* and *Well of the Saints*, the language is less satisfying, less dramatically appropriate, and less individualized, the rhythmic and musical effects being sought too much for their own sake. The language of *Playboy* is more satisfying, with some of Synge's rhythmic effects reaching their greatest intensity. Examination of successive drafts of the play shows the sentences becoming tighter, less florid, with better marked rhythms and more dramatic appropriateness. Finally, in *Deirdre*, Stork finds that the language is slower paced, less intense, and less obtrusive than *Playboy*—all in keeping with its slower movement.

TRANSLATIONS

Irene Eber (in *Modern Chinese Literature and Its Social Context*, ed. Göran Malmqvist, Stockholm, 1977) explains that Chinese critics of the late 1920s considered the Irish an oppressed people and generally accorded their literature a warm reception. Interest in Synge was strong enough that all six of his plays were translated; Eber cites a 1926 volume publishing the translations but says she has not seen it.

Per Denez' brief note "The Breton Translations of Synge's Plays" (*CCEI*, 1977) cites translations into Breton of *Riders* and *Shadow* by Youenn Drezen and of *Riders* and *Playboy* by Remi Derrien.

Carlo Bigazzi, in "*Riders to the Sea*: Problemi di Traduzione" (*EM*, 1977-78), compares the Italian translations by James Joyce and by Carlo Linati. He generally prefers Joyce's translation, describing it as more accurate and precise and as being in a more generic (if sometimes archaic) Italian than Linati's, which approximates the Tuscan dialect. Comparing their translations of certain Irish terms (e.g., *hooker, curragh*), Bigazzi favors Joyce's choices over those of Linati. He faults both translators for avoiding some distinctively Irish terms (e.g., *kelp, poteen, Samhain, hags*), but Bigazzi's criticisms and suggestions are often literalistic. (Thanks to Anna Battigelli for translating this essay.)

7. Studies of Drama

THE SHADOW OF THE GLEN

Dapo Adelugba's essay on *The Shadow of the Glen* and *The Tinker's Wedding* (*Studies on Synge*, ed. Adelugba, Ibadan, 1977) approaches these plays through the terms "shadow" and "wedding," but his use of the words is too loose and metaphoric to have any clarifying power. This brief, impressionistic essay grew out of Adelugba's experiences as director of student productions of these plays at Ibadan University. S. O. Yabuku's "A Student's Production Diary," in the same collection of essays, describes rehearsals and performances of these productions. It casts some light on the problems of an amateur production by non-English speakers but no light on either of the plays.

Robin Wilkinson's "structuralist" comparison of *Shadow* and *Deirdre* (*CCEI*, 1979) uses a set of complexly related polarities. For Wilkinson, both plays are structured around two principal axes, the first arising from a contrast between "interior" values (those of house or cottage) and "exterior" values (those of the natural world), the second from a contrast between virile and feminine values (not equatable with male and female characters). Complicating this is the association of death with aspects of both ends of these polarities (e.g., with immobility in the interior and with dissolution or madness in the exterior). Wilkinson points out that in both plays the central pair of characters chooses the risks of exterior life over the stasis of interior life.

Thomas Morrissey's "The Good Shepherd and the Anti-Christ in Synge's *The Shadow of the Glen* " (*IRA*, 1980) goes to great lengths to find Christ parallels and parodies among the characters of the play. Dan is "a comical but potentially vicious anti-Christ who exemplifies the concept of death-in-life," whereas Darcy, identified with the Good Shepherd, exemplifies life-in-death. Undeterred by the paucity of evidence for such analogues, Morrissey can excuse the imprecisions in his schema by calling Dan "a distorted type of Christ" or by saying that "Synge's deification of Patch Darcy is tongue-in-cheek." Morrissey satisfies his belief that "biblical allusion is a major vehicle in the play for [Synge's] heretical ideas on religion and politics" by concluding that "by pitting a humorous type of Christ against a farcical anti-Christ, Synge strikes at the heart of bourgeois Christianity in Ireland."

RIDERS TO THE SEA

In "Structural Dynamics in *Riders to the Sea*" (*CLQ*, 1975), William J. Free disagrees with those who see *Riders* as presenting only death and resignation, arguing that *"Riders* also presents a dramatic image of striving against the inevitability of fate . . . in two senses: in the active intentions of the younger characters [specifically Cathleen and Bartley] and in the physical contrast on stage between their expression of those intentions and Maurya's more passive reaction to the forces threatening to overwhelm her."

John A. M. Rillie's discussion of *Riders to the Sea* (in *Insight IV: Analyses of Modern British and American Drama*, ed. Hermann J. Weiand, Frankfurt, 1976) argues that the play's tragedy "is not consummated in the death of a hero, but in the agony of coming to realize life as tragedy, and that it must be lived." He points out that Maurya is prostrate with grief at the play's opening but at the end, "through grieving, she is erect, presiding over the service for her dead." Against those who argue that the play is pathetic or that the true protagonist and victor is nature, Rillie claims that such views arise from reading rather than seeing the play, for "what we see and hear is that, in spite of all that sea and wind can do, humanity does live there," and "it is overwhelmingly as an affirmation of life . . . that Maurya's acceptance of death speaks to us."

Almire Martin (*CCEI*, 1977) develops a convoluted and murky thesis about the process Maurya goes through in the play. Rejecting as inadequate earlier views of Maurya as simply tragic or pagan or Christian, Martin proposes the darker and more complicated view that Maurya is "the priestess in a human sacrifice, [and] she is also the one that suffers most." Faced with the loss of her last son, Maurya attempts to come between Bartley and his fate by refusing him her blessing, but in doing so, she descends into a bitter self-knowledge: "convinced as she is of the absoluteness of the sea's demands . . . Maurya reaches the half-conscious knowledge that there exists but one way to keep her son to herself, which is to destroy him herself.''

Paul F. Bötheroyd's ''J. M. Synge's *The Aran Islands, Riders to the Sea* and Territoriality: The Beginnings of a Cultural Analysis'' (*Studies on Synge*, ed. Dapo Adelugba, Ibadan, 1977) attempts to approach *Riders* through the categories of ''cultural analysis.'' But Bötheroyd's use of ''cognitive maps'' and ''territoriality'' at best provides an alternative vocabulary for discussing the play, and it sometimes involves belaboring the obvious. The main ''boundaries'' Bötheroyd finds in the world of the play are the threshold of the cottage and ''a line drawn through the spring well some distance from the cottage,'' though further boundaries are marked by the seashore, by Galway/Connemara, and by ''the north.'' Around each of these, Bötheroyd explains, the meanings of the play gather.

THE WELL OF THE SAINTS

Anthony Roche (*Genre*, 1979) focuses on the sources of *The Well of the Saints* in Irish myth and folklore. Claiming that the various literary sources suggested by others ''remain hypothetical,'' Roche turns instead to the story of the miraculous well that Synge recounts in *The Aran Islands*; to the traditional Irish *immran*, or sea voyage; and to the story of Ossian and Patrick as more relevant sources. Drawing most on this last, Roche claims that the world of blindness Martin and Mary persist in preferring has parallels to Ossian's Other World, in that both are ''avowedly illusionistic.''

THE PLAYBOY OF THE WESTERN WORLD

Malcolm Kelsall's ''The Playboy before the Riots'' (*ThR*, 1975) attempts to determine the mode of presentation of the first performances of *Playboy* to see whether there may have been some justification for the response of the Abbey audience. Kelsall points out that, while recent productions and interpretations of *Playboy* have emphasized the comic and fantastic elements of the play, the aim of the company that first performed it was realism and verisimilitude. To support this contention Kelsall draws on contemporary accounts of the play and statements of intention by members of that acting company, as well as on Synge's statements in defense of the play. According to Kelsall, ''darker realism won the day,'' and the audience was presented with an interpretation playing up the griminess of the protagonist and apparently dealing seriously with attempted father murder and with the claim that the people of Mayo would warmly receive such a figure. Naive as such a view may seem to us now, Kelsall reminds us that the Dublin audience had to judge what was given them, and he suggests that if ''this reconstruction of the Fay/Synge interpretation is correct, the riots were natural, even, dare one suggest, healthy.''

Kelsall argues, in the introduction to his edition of *Playboy* (1975), that the play was both the finest embodiment and a subversion of the goals of the dramatic movement. It does in general fulfill the desire for realism and for poetic beauty that were the ideals of the Abbey, but on its realistic foundation it rears an extravaganza that rises to fantastic absurdity, leading the audience to "mutually irreconcilable reactions." Kelsall points out that the "difficulty of Synge's work is not in discovering hidden meanings . . . but in determining its tone and the validity of its style," and in this context he examines the actions and language of the play, concluding that "Synge was not intending to be taken seriously."

John A. Byars (*SAB*, 1975) approaches *Playboy* in the context of Yeats's *Cathleen Ni Houlihan* and Lady Gregory's *Kincora* as "a new version of a familiar myth." According to Byars, "Pegeen does perform the same function as Cathleen Ni Houlihan in that she creates a hero, even if this requires, as it does with Lady Gregory's Gormleith, betrayal to complete the task."

Paul M. Levitt (*CLQ*, 1975) briefly proposes that *Playboy* would more appropriately be divided into two acts. Claiming that Synge used the three-act format "because turn-of-the-century theatrical conventions made it impractical if not impossible to present a two-act play for production," Levitt proposes to divide the play at the first entrance of old Mahon, thus reinforcing the play's thematic unity and focusing the two major themes—the growth of the man and the growth of the poet.

Paul F. Bötheroyd's "Clichés and Barriers between Cultures" (in *Modern Britain,* ed. Frank Jolles, Düsseldorf and München, 1976) briefly uses *Playboy* to illustrate the tactics and problems of *Landeskunde* and lists several books that would be helpful in establishing a cultural context for reading the play.

John A. M. Rillie's discussion of *Playboy* (in *Insight IV: Analyses of Modern British and American Drama,* ed. Hermann J. Weiand, Frankfurt, 1976) consists mostly of a detailed précis of the play, but an interpretation does emerge. For Rillie, the play operates in a gap "between the understanding and the imagination," and by the end of the play Christy "has lived his fiction into truth." Thus Synge shows us that "life touched by the imagination can be transfigured." But Rillie also presumes that the point, which the people of the village do not see, is that "value lies not in any fact, true or false, but in the dream and in following the dream," so he is forced to conclude that the strongly optimistic strain in the play is shadowed by darker ambiguities, since "poetry is indifferent apparently to truth or falsehood."

Michel Bariou (*CCEI*, 1977) anatomizes the progress of the love between Christy and Pegeen, defending at every point Synge's psychological astuteness. But while Bariou views the play through the lens of comedy and argues puzzlingly that Pegeen, being the comic type of the cantankerous old woman, is "incapable of changing," he sees the dissolution of the love at the play's end not as signaling a triumph of self-sufficiency on Christy's part but as involving tragic misunderstanding and loss for both of them. The dark ending, then, reflects both Synge's "basic pessimism about human nature" and his belief in "the irreconcilable clash between the world of reality and the world of the imagination."

In *"The Playboy of the Western World* as Antidrama" (*MD*, 1977), Bruce Bigley pursues with new subtlety the old idea that the effect of *Playboy* on its audiences owes something to Synge's intentional rejection of generic conventions. Leaning heavily on a dubious distinction between Christy the protagonist and Christy the narrator, Bigley claims that Christy himself learns a great deal from his experiences and further that he "teaches" the audience something about the nature of reality. For Bigley, "True reality in this play exists only beyond the back wall of the stage, and we can perceive it only indirectly, through the storytellers, the fabulists, mainly Christy, but also the others." What disturbs the audience about this play is not the theme of parricide but the lesson "that the reality we live in is not necessarily so well-founded as we believed." And finally the play is "truly anti-drama, a form which undercuts its own conventions and refuses to resolve the problems it raises."

C. L. Innes' "Naked Truth, Fine Clothes and Fine Phrases in Synge's *Playboy of the Western World*" (in *Myth and Reality in Irish Literature*, ed. Joseph Ronsley, 1977) uses clothing images and the relations among the play's characters to explore how the play provides the reality and the joy Synge calls for in his preface and to discuss the play's implications about "the power of the poetic word to transform." For Innes, "the struggle between Christy and his father . . . suggests Synge's opposition of naturalism with the imaginative transcendence of reality" ("Mahon represents the reality half of Synge's dichotomy"), while Pegeen suggests an unredeemable equation of the poetic with the exotic. Accordingly, Christy is fed, clothed, and even transformed by Pegeen and the villagers, but "he fails to transform Pegeen." Thus, though "the play does deal with the power of the poetic word to transform, it also deals in its tragicomic ending with the failure of poetry."

Gérard Leblanc, in "The Three Deaths of the Father in *The Playboy of the Western World*" (*CCEI*, 1977), argues that while *Playboy* evokes the traditional story of the overthrow of the old order by a youthful savior, it neutralizes it by relegating that overthrow to a safely distanced realm of story and by having the father survive. Christy's attempt to regain through actual murder the position he loses when his story collapses is doomed to failure because "one cannot re-enter a story by choosing reality as the field of one's action." But when this attempt at real murder expels the villagers (and the audience) from the conventions of the romantic mode, Christy "refuses the logic of reality and chooses the infinite freedom of the story," once more becomes a "narrator," and verbally murders his father: "Are you coming to be killed a third time or what ails you now?" This according to Leblanc is "the only effective murder in the play," for "the murder is really achieved when turned into a metaphor," and the relation of Christy and his father at the end of this play "vouches for the ultimate triumph of the story over the real."

Deirdre McKeown-Laigle's "The Liberation of Christy Mahon" (*CCEI*, 1977), while broaching several perspectives on the play's characters, approaches them mainly through Celtic myth. She draws several parallels between the career of Christy and that of Cuchulain (taking no note of the earlier essays by Sidnell and Bessai), and she replaces Augustine Martin's Dionysian-Apollonian dichotomy with a Christian-Druid one.

Mark Mortimer (*CCEI*, 1977) points to several facets of *Playboy* that exemplify Synge's outstanding stagecraft: the skillful use of stage directions, of exits and entrances, of contrasts physical and situational, of absent characters (especially Father Reilly), of indirect presentation of certain important incidents, and of Widow Quin as a "key-figure." Aware of the many revisions the play went through, Mortimer sees the final version as "the fruit of long reflection and immense care, an unalterable work of art."

Elizabeth Hale Winkler, in *The Clown in Modern Anglo-Irish Drama* (Frankfurt, 1977), discusses Christy and more briefly Shawn Keogh as clowns. While her general observation about the play—that it intrigues and attracts us by maintaining a fine line between realism and fantasy—is not new, her subtle handling of the clown figure generally and of Christy in particular gives us a new perspective and new appreciation of Synge's achievement in this play. Winkler concludes that "primarily it is the clown Christy who helps to lift the play out of the particular Irish setting into the universal."

In "The *Playboy* of the *Western World*" (*Éire*, 1978), Arthur H. Nethercot, after reviewing dictionary definitions and the opinions of earlier Synge scholars, attempts on the basis of internal evidence to pinpoint the meaning of the phrase "Playboy of the Western World." But in spite of his scrutiny of the relevant passages in the play, Nethercot's conclusion is less than satisfying, for it expresses not a gathering up of the meanings of the phrase within the play but his own inferences from the whole of the play. For him, this Playboy is "a play actor who . . . has become in reality what at first . . . he only pretended to be," but Christy's championship is limited since it grows out of competition with the males only of "the small, retarded western county of Mayo."

Robert B. Heilman's brief discussion of *Playboy* in *The Ways of the World: Comedy and Society* (1978) presents the play as a subtle reenactment of society's perennially ambivalent response to the energetic young intruder. While this thesis is not new, Heilman's larger interpretive frame of reference and his finely tuned sense of the social and psychological currents within the play give his discussion great scope and clarifying power, so that we come away with a renewed sense of how rich a play this is and how much human experience it manages to encompass.

Warren Akin IV (*SAB*, 1980) says that in *Playboy*, "Synge masterfully forms, through radical revision, a plot compounded of fairy tale and reality with which to tell one aspect of the oedipal struggle." But though Akin attends to Synge's drafts, to fairy-tale analogues, and to oedipal elements in the play, his essay summarizes too much and does not provide a full-scale oedipal interpretation.

René Agostini's essay (*CVE*, 1979) purports to trace Christy's evolution from an imaginary to a real identity, but on this much written-about aspect of the play, Agostini offers nothing new. Poorly written and poorly typeset, the essay cites not one earlier critical comment on the play.

James C. Pierce (*Éire*, 1981) sees the Widow Quin as "the only realist in this Mayo community . . . the only reliable commentator on *The Playboy* world" and "the touchstone for Synge's satiric but not unsympathetic assessment of Mayo society." Pierce argues, rather too intricately, that the Widow's proposal to Christy is the "high point of *The Playboy* in terms of thematic development" (though not of plot) and that the sense of potential tragedy we glean from Christy's rejection of her proposal forms "Synge's most elusive structural irony" and alters our assessment of Christy. Pierce also dwells on purported personality likenesses of Pegeen and the Widow, claiming that "the greatest difference between them, perhaps the only difference of real significance, is age" but that the greater experience of the Widow enables her to understand the significance of her tragedy, whereas Pegeen cannot understand her own. Pierce claims that the play is inevitably, intentionally ironic, because, while Christy lives up to the ideals of the Western world and is thus heroic, the play's broader perspective shows these ideals to be empty fantasies and not worth living up to.

DEIRDRE OF THE SORROWS

Ronald L. Baker's brief discussion of the Deirdre legend in the plays of A. E., Yeats, and Synge (*Indiana English Journal,* 1975) judges A. E.'s the weakest and Synge's the best rendition of the legend, mainly because of Synge's more realistic language and his refusal to soften the traditional story.

Ellen S. Spangler (*Éire*, 1977) argues that, in spite of earlier critics' misgivings, *Deirdre* can be seen as drama and as tragedy and that certain apparent inconsistencies in Deirdre's character can be resolved if the play is understood as feminine tragedy. For Spangler, "feminine tragedy involves not struggle and then the horror of sudden discovery, as does masculine tragedy, but the horror of a perpetual knowledge, whose presence means that the self can never be entirely deluded into active struggle." Spangler's claim for *Deirdre* as feminine tragedy is grounded in the presence in the play of many archetypically feminine elements and in the distinctive character of Deirdre, who is portrayed as both human and divine, a duality that explains her apparent inconsistency in act 3.

Herbert V. Fackler's chapter on Synge's play, in *That Tragic Queen: The Deirdre Legend in Anglo-Irish Literature* (Salzburg, 1978), substantially repeats his 1969 *Modern Drama* essay.

8. Poetry, The Aran Islands, and the Essays

Synge's poetry has received scant attention in the past five years. David Perkins' *A History of Modern Poetry from the 1890s to the High Modernist Mode* (1976) devotes only a few paragraphs to Synge, stressing his achievement of "a powerful coarsening of image, diction, and rhythm." Perkins takes Synge's statements in the preface to the 1908 edition of his *Poems* to reflect the influence of Yeats, rather than vice versa as some earlier critics have suggested.

Jane McClellan's brief "J. M. Synge: Poet of Irreverence" (*Forum*, Houston, 1977) approaches Synge's poetry as an expression of his world view. Noting his wish to bridge realism and fancy in his poetry, she discusses the influence of fin de siècle French writers and of Gaelic tradition. She finds in Synge's poetry a persistent irreverence, "deeply grounded in an essentially religious attitude toward life." Acknowledging that "Synge's own vision was firmly fixed on earth," she suggests that his writings are also permeated by a mysticism much like that of the cabala, which she feels it is possible Synge read. Reemphasizing the link between his world view and his verse, McClellan says that "For Synge, religion lay in things as they are, and poetry was a way of saying these things honestly and sincerely."

In Rigby Graham's summary of writings about the Aran Islands (*ABC*, 1975), Synge figures more prominently through reproductions—of some of his photographs, of Jack B. Yeats's illustrations, of book title pages—than he does in the text. Graham's brief discussion of Synge contains several errors.

In "Synge in Aran" (*IUR*, 1975), Malcolm Kelsall claims that Synge's aestheticism and morbidity prevented his seeing the "Homeric" (a term Kelsall uses several times) quality of life on the Aran Islands. Contrasting Synge's account with Pat Mullen's *Man of Aran* and Tomás Ó Crohan's *The Islandman*, Kelsall shows that Synge's is colored by decadent aesthetic attitudes. He argues that Synge lacks the ability to see the culture from the inside and often, "like the pre-Raphaelites, misses the spirit for the decorative exterior." Synge's account has a "Lotiesque morbidity," and his "subjective gloom is at times, clearly literary in its origins." Stressing that *The Aran Islands* presents a "subjective vision," Kelsall says, "Probably [Synge] was unaware that he was composing a work of fiction." But Kelsall's emphasis on Synge's inability to get inside the culture attacks a straw man, for no critic, nor even Synge himself, has claimed that Synge was able to become one of the island people. And Kelsall exaggerates Synge's aestheticism, not realizing that this was one of several approaches Synge tried out and that he gleaned far more from the Aran Islands than he did from Paris.

Wolfgang Sänger's *John Millington Synge: The Aran Islands, Material und Mythos* (Frankfurt, 1976) offers the fullest discussion to date of *The Aran Islands*. Sänger's interest in the book turns mainly on ways in which Synge made aesthetic use of the materials he found on the islands. Disagreeing with those earlier critics who described the work as a mere sourcebook for the materials of the plays, he believes with Robin Skelton that the book ought to be considered as an aesthetic construct in its own right. Sänger briefly discusses the received ideas about why Synge went to the Aran Islands (antiquarian interest, philological studies, a romantic fascination with primitive modes of life and thought), only to find them insufficient to explain many qualities of the resulting artistic creation. Sänger argues that the "narrator" of the work is not John Mill-ington Synge, reporter of facts and events, but a persona characterized by a persistently subjective and "romantic" stance toward the raw material. After examining some of the stages and stylistic devices by which this subjective shaping of the material is carried out, Sänger looks at several "myths" through which the material is given form. The most important of these myths is the Quest, especially as it is seen in such traditional Irish stories of the search for a primitive world as the voyage of Bran and the voyage of Maeldun. For Synge, Sänger claims, the life of Inishmaan became paradigmatic of the life of the golden age of antiqui-ty. Sänger quotes extensively from Rousseau to show that Synge's ac-count of life on these islands depicts qualities of life traditionally associated with the golden age, halfway between the impulsive life of the savage and the decadence of modern civilization. In his last chapter Sänger discusses the place of *The Aran Islands* in Synge's canon and in his view of life. He develops more specifically Donna Gerstenberger's suggestion that Synge and William Morris are kindred spirits and ex-amines the relationship between *The Aran Islands* and such works as *News from Nowhere* and *The Earthly Paradise*. Sänger contrasts the romantic subjectivism of *The Aran Islands* with Synge's later, more dispassionate essays and articles and with the intellectual maturity of his plays, concluding that this early prose work constitutes one phase in the writer's overall development.

Paul F. Bötheroyd's " 'Athenry That Was, Galway That Is, Aran That Will Be': Recent Works on Aran" (*EI*, 1980) is a review of several works about the Aran Islands. Nearly half of it deals with Sänger's book, which Bötheroyd finds disappointing. Most of the other Aran literature Bötheroyd mentions has no direct bearing on Synge.

Mary C. King's "Synge and *The Aran Islands*: A Linguistic Apprenticeship" (*IrishS*, 1980) treats the four sections of *The Aran Islands* as reflective of a steady progression in Synge's knowledge of Irish in four successive trips to the islands. But her contribution to the topic of Synge's knowledge of Irish is overshadowed by D. Kiberd's *Synge and the Irish Language* (1979).

William Daniels' "AE and Synge in the Congested Districts" (*Éire*, 1976) presents a running comparison of the reactions of A. E. in 1898 and Synge in 1905 to their travels in the west of Ireland. While the routes they traveled were often closely parallel, Daniels' presentation of their comments leaves the reader wondering what point is being made. The most specific inference Daniels draws is that "Synge tended to be pessimistic about what had been done or could be done in the Congested Districts. . . . AE tended to write more optimistically. . . . Yet, although optimistic, AE saw the West as realistically as did Synge."

William Daniels (*Éire*, 1980) deals with the seven Wicklow essays in volume 4 of the 1910 *Works* and with "An Autumn Night in the Woods" as "Synge's introduction to [these] seven essays." Daniels' stated pur-pose is to "demonstrate the unity" of the essays and to show that in each "Synge patterns times of day, weather conditions, places, landscapes, and people and their stories to develop his major theme of decay." But while Daniels catalogs the situations and settings of these essays, frequently refers to "patterns," and speaks promisingly of "one last demonstration of Synge's conception of this group of seven essays as a whole," he does not follow through on his stated aim. These essays predictably have much in common, having been written by one man about one locale. But the claim for unity must involve more than that, implying as it does coherence and progression, and it remains unproved.

Ann Saddlemyer's "The Essays as Literature and Literary Source" (in *In Wicklow West Kerry and Connemara*, ed. G. Gmelch, 1980), while acknowledging that Synge's essays are a storehouse of imagery, expression, and character for the plays, deals mainly with similarities of perspective, of attitude, of tonality, of an underlying consistency of vision and mood, in the essays and plays. She judges these essays to be "excellent examples of what would now be called 'essay journalism' " and praises them for their balanced, considered presentation of their subjects, their skillful use of isolated incident, and their striking detail.

Declan Kiberd's "Synge's *Prós* and Verse in *Vita Vecchia*" (*Éire*, 1980) discusses this early work as an example of Synge's deliberately setting his work within the Gaelic tradition. Stressing Synge's knowledge of the Irish language and literature, Kiberd points out that the basic form of the *Vita Vecchia* as well as certain of its flaws stem directly from Gaelic models, especially the "Three Sorrows" tales and *Buile Shuibhne*. Among traits traceable to these models are the alternation of verse and prose, the attribution of the verse directly to the narrator, the use of the prose as recapitulatory, experimentation among verse forms, alliteration, and, on the negative side, the increasing redundancy of the prose narrative as the story progresses.

JAMES JOYCE

Thomas F. Staley

From the prospect of the centennial year of Joyce's birth, 1982, we can take a long view of Joyce criticism and observe several important trends, the most important being the broadening of its outlook or theoretical approach. Recent criticism, say in the past decade, has become more sensitive to the contemporary literary context and to the intellectual and historical context in which Joyce wrote. There are both good and bad examples of this development. Although the most important work published in Joyce studies during the past five years has been in textual studies, lexicons, and reference works, recent criticism has begun to reflect the central currents and conflicts in the theoretical study of literature. If those dozen or so years after the Second World War deserve to be called the "age of criticism," certainly this past decade is equally deserving of the title "the age of theory." These developments, in spite of the constant reference to texts, have not generally drawn readers to particular or individual texts in the way that the New Criticism did, but the influence of these theoretical activities has been felt in recent Joyce criticism.

1. Bibliography

During the latter half of the seventies Joyce criticism has continued unabated and has achieved significant development in the area of manuscript reproductions, textual studies, and bibliography. The format of this supplement is slightly altered from the 1976 chapter to accommodate more precisely the nature of the work discussed.

The second edition of Robert H. Deming's *A Bibliography of James Joyce Studies* (1977) incorporates the listings from the first edition that covered the years to 1961, and new entries bring the coverage up to 1973. Deming has added about 770 items from the pre-1961 period that were not included in his first edition. This new edition has 5,885 entries and three new sections: "Reviews of Joyce's Works," "Dissertations," and "Musical Settings, Theatrical Productions, Films, Radio Broadcasts, and Recordings." Deming has eliminated nearly all the annotations provided for entries in the first edition, noting that "the sacrifice of this information should be compensated for by the greater completeness of this edition." One cannot help agreeing with him.

Two tests of a good bibliography are completeness and, in a bibliography this large, skill in classification. Omissions in Deming's work include books of European criticism that deal in passing with Joyce and introductions to editions, such as James S. Atherton's introduction and notes to the Heinemann edition of *A Portrait* (1964). Some of Deming's classifications are, of course, arbitrary, and the material is so broad and diffuse that one can find surprises in the listing of some articles under certain categories. But after using the bibliography for some time, I find Deming's classification and arrangement of material to be generally clear and helpful. The work is accurate, and the general principles of inclusion and classification are sound. For bibliographical coverage of the years 1974–1975, the *PMLA* annual bibliographies need to be supplemented by Alan Cohn's annual checklists in *JJQ*. For the years 1976 and following, however, Cohn's lists attempt to be current and comprehensive and are published in each issue of *JJQ*.

2. Manuscript Holdings and Catalogs

Two major Joyce collections have been purchased by American libraries. The University of Tulsa has acquired the Harriet Shaw Weaver Collection from the National Book League, supplementing the university's already strong Joyce holdings. This collection consists of more than two hundred volumes and includes works by and about Joyce as well as books presented by Joyce to Weaver. A catalog is in preparation. Joyce's Trieste library has only recently (1980) been acquired by the Humanities Research Center of the University of Texas. An appendix in Richard Ellmann's *The Consciousness of Joyce* (1977) lists "about 600 items which comprise all or nearly all the library that Joyce left behind in Trieste." Ellmann's list includes about a hundred books that are not in the surviving collection, although a few books in the collection do not appear on Ellmann's list. Some of the books contain marginal notes by Joyce, and dots appear in the margins of some texts. In examining these marks, I was unable to ascertain their significance; some scholars contend they have elaborate meaning. We need to wait for proof, however.

The Lockwood Memorial Library, State University of New York, Buffalo, has issued a descriptive catalog marking a six-month exhibition of their rich holdings. Entitled *James Joyce Exhibition: A Catalogue* (1978), it was prepared by Thomas E. Connolly with the assistance of K. C. Gay. Although the catalog includes only a representative portion of the Buffalo holdings, its chronological arrangement gives it solidity, ranging from the early epiphanies to the page proofs of *Finnegans Wake* bound in a dust jacket that Faber and Faber sent to Joyce for his birthday in 1939. In 1975 the University of Pittsburgh published a catalog of the exhibition that displayed the notable private collection of Alice and David Holliday. Steven Lund and Alan Cohn survey the Southern Illinois University Joyce holdings in *ICarbS* (1975).

3. Editions, Concordances, and Textual Studies

The major publishing event in Joyce studies is the completion of the publication of *The James Joyce Archive*. An introduction to this indispensable archive of Joyce's manuscripts is given in Michael Groden's *James Joyce's Manuscripts: An Index* (1980), a comprehensive index to the sixty-three-volume archive as well as the most complete checklist of all extant manuscripts, typescripts, and proofs. Groden also includes an index to the various library collections that hold Joyce manuscript material. The *Archive* itself, printed on acid-free paper, publishes in fascimile all extant and available notes, drafts, manuscripts, typescripts, and proofs—Joyce's entire "workshop." Letters are not included. Each *Archive* volume contains a preface by one of the editors, and collectively the *Archive* reproduces some twenty-five thousand pages of original documents from all of the known Joyce collections. Groden is general editor of the project, and associate editors are Hans Walter Gabler, David Hayman, A. Walton Litz, and Danis Rose. The *Archive* brings together in one place the widely and erratically dispersed prepublication materials, but as the editor cautions in his "General Introduction": "It must be recognized . . . that these volumes are only reproductions, and a scholar would be irresponsible to rely exclusively on them." One minor disappointment is that each volume is not numbered on the spine or elsewhere. A massive and unique enterprise, the *Archive* makes available to scholars a body of material that will in the coming years have a profound effect on Joyce studies.

Much space was devoted in the 1976 essay to the complex problem of Joyce's texts, and in the past few years the subject has generated important new projects and published works. Hans Walter Gabler, with the help of computer technology, is currently preparing a critical edition of *Ulysses* that promises to be definitive. The work will consist of "an authoritative reading text, and the critical apparatus is divided between a synopsis of the episodes [each of the eighteen], textual genesis (the synoptic text) and appended apparatus." This quotation is from the preface of *Prototype of a Critical Edition in Progress* (München, 1979), a trial edition of the eighth episode of *Ulysses*, "Lestrygonians." It is intended only for the use of the Joyce scholars who might aid or comment on the procedures and is not for sale. A thorough discussion of the textual problems of *Ulysses* and a comment on Gabler's work appear in an essay by Hugh Kenner, "The Computerized *Ulysses*" (*Harper's*, 1980). Another essay on the subject by Michael Groden appears in *Scholarly Publishing* (1980). The edition will evidently offer interesting and innovative ways of presenting a corrected text that will at the same time be easily readable, along with the necessary apparatus. The specimen edition offers assurance that we shall soon have a definitive one that will approximate what Joyce intended.

An elaborate and expensive undertaking has been the publication in 1975 of the facsimile of the manuscript titled *"James Joyce's Ulysses,"* now reposited at the Rosenbach Foundation of Philadelphia. The work consists of three boxed volumes, two of which are the faces of the manuscript and the third a reduced face of the first edition, "marked to show the differences between it, the serial installments as published in *The Little Review*, and the manuscript." Clive Driver provided a preface and annotations, and a number of textual scholars have challenged his claims. A flurry of letters appeared in *TLS*, and Hans Gabler noted that "by reason of the markedly divergent genetic and transmissional status of its several parts, it [the Rosenbach ms] does not have either the bibliographical or the textual integrity on which to base the claim that it be the manuscript of *Ulysses*." Gabler asserts that "there is not, and never was such a thing." The value of this manuscript lies not in its being *the* manuscript of *Ulysses* but in its being a link in the stemma. Its authority in certain episodes is questionable and complex, however, and it should be used with caution.

Michael Groden's Ulysses *in Progress* (1977) is an excellent and detailed account of how the novel came to be. Groden traces with impeccable care the process of composition and examines how Joyce wrote the book in three major stages rather than two. As Groden notes in his introduction, "one major aspect of *Ulysses* that has remained obscure is its complicated and bizarre prepublication history." The manuscript history of the work remains "bizarre," but thanks to Groden's study it is no longer obscure. In some instances Groden had to work with as many as thirteen different stages of development. His study, with its intelligent if not definitively established speculation, is a clear and insightful examination of an incredibly complex process.

Phillip Herring's important textual studies continue with the publication of *Joyce's Notes and Early Drafts for* Ulysses: *Selections from the Buffalo Collection* (1977). Herring's edition provides a reliable transcription of notebooks VIII.A.5 and V.A.2 and of the early manuscripts of "Cyclops" and "Circe," so that scholars now have printed access to all the extant notes for *Ulysses*. Herring's rendering of the text is scrupulous, his introductions are illuminating, and his editorial apparatus is sound and consistent.

Gabler, Herring, and Groden have made truly significant contributions to Joyce scholarship. Their work has at last shown us the shape and proportions of the genetic process of *Ulysses*, and their diligence and precision are inspiring.

Another contribution to textual scholarship is *James Joyce's The Index Manuscript* Finnegans Wake *Holograph Workbook VI.B.46* (Colchester, 1978), transcribed, annotated, and introduced by Danis Rose. Joyce compiled this workbook (now at Buffalo) in 1938 as the "Work in Progress" was nearing its conclusion. Rose elucidates the complexity of this text and the way in which its parts were used and incorporated into *Finnegans Wake*, demonstrating how this notebook and others act as textual witness to the first stage in the genetic process. More important, the evidence gathered by Rose enables him to draw several hypotheses related not only to the composition but to the basic structure of *Finnegans Wake*.

The most sophisticated and extensive concordance ever done in Joyce studies is Wilhelm Füger's *Concordance to James Joyce's* Dubliners (New York, 1980). Füger's work includes a comprehensive concordance organized in the form of the key word within a context of 120 characters, keyed to the Viking Compass edition with conversion tables to the Penguin and Cape editions. A "reverse index" lists words according to the alphabetical order that results from reading them backward, a principle of arrangement used in traditional rhyming dictionaries. Such an arrangement is helpful in analyzing the microstructure of the text's vocabulary. A third part of this massive volume is a frequency list that comprises five columns per entry and gives additional data. For example, the word "like" appears 131 times, holds the sixtieth rank of frequency, and has a relative frequency of 0.1939%. The user of this concordance will find even further refinements. Füger's concordance is an excellent example of how the computer can be brought into the service of literary studies. Once the text of *Ulysses* is established, one can hope that Füger will do the concordance.

Two textual works on *Exiles* have been published by Garland. John MacNicholas' *James Joyce's* Exiles: *A Textual Companion* (1979) appraises the sources, text, and extant manuscripts of the play. Mac-Nicholas set out "to provide the reader with comprehensive information concerning the genesis, composition, and final authorial intent," and he achieves his aim. Besides establishing a critical text of *Exiles*, Mac-Nicholas devotes two chapters to the historical background of the play's genesis and its chronology of composition and publication. Of special interest is MacNicholas' revelations about Bertha, who was initially conceived as meek but was changed to an enormously strong character in the final manuscript. This thorough and intelligent study is the most important and comprehensive work to appear on *Exiles*.. Ruth Bauerle's *A Word List to James Joyce's* Exiles (1981) is based on the Penguin text, the one most widely available, and includes an index of Joyce's important notes to the play. Bauerle incorporates departures from the Penguin text established in the MacNicholas study and indicates alternative frequency counts where omissions or additions noted by MacNicholas affect the count of a word.

A number of new and additional translations of Joyce's work have been published, including Italian and German editions of his letters. Of considerable interest is *Scritti Italiani* (Milan, 1979), a collection of Joyce's writings in Italian brought together by Gianfranco Corsini and Giorgio Melchiori. Included are Joyce's essays in *Il Piccolo della Sera* and his lectures at the University of Trieste as well as the essay examination papers that were recently discovered by Louis Berrone; these will be discussed below. This volume also includes the "Anna Livia Plurabelle" passages from *Finnegans Wake*, which Joyce translated in collaboration with Nino Frank. These are fragments, but they are published for the first time in their unaltered versions. They had been slightly changed by

Ettore Settanni without Joyce's supervision when they first appeared in the *Prospettive* number of 1940. While all the contributions to this volume have been well edited, Jacqueline Risset's work on the holograph of the fragments is especially impressive. She maintains that the fragments are a further rewriting of the original texts and not merely translations. As Rosa Maria Bosinelli has noted, Risset's rigorous examination of these passages reveals Joyce's mastery of Italian (*JJQ*, 1980). The entire book testifies to Joyce's total immersion in the Italian language and culture.

As part of an examination that Joyce sat for at the University of Padua in April of 1912 to be certified as an English teacher, Joyce wrote two essays, "The Universal Literary Influence of the Renaissance" and "The Centenary of Charles Dickens," the first in Italian and the second in English. These essays were discovered by Louis Berrone and published in *James Joyce in Padua* (1977). The book contains photographs of each essay, printed transcriptions, a translation of the one in Italian, and long "afterwords" on both essays. Berrone's interesting discovery fills in another piece in our picture of Joyce's long Italian sojourn. It should be noted that Joyce passed his examination in English by fifty points above his next rival but failed to get an official teaching job anyway.

Joyce's translation of Gerhart Hauptmann's *Before Sunrise*, which scholars have long known about, has now been published by the Huntington Library, the holders of the manuscript, under the title, *Joyce and Hauptmann:* Before Sunrise, *James Joyce's Translation* (1978). The introduction and notes are by Jill Perkins (the daughter of the owner of the manuscript, from whose estate Huntington acquired it). Joyce translated the play during his student days at University College in an attempt to provide a modern continental play for the Irish Literary Theatre. Perkins describes the manuscript and its provenance, Joyce's familiarity with and interest in European drama from 1900 to 1906, and the difficulties and inaccuracies of the translation itself.

A new and expanded edition of *The Critical Writings* (1959) under the joint editorship of Richard Ellmann and Ellsworth Mason is also planned.

4. Journals and Special Issues

James Joyce Quarterly and *A Wake Newslitter*, the latter after a brief hiatus, continue to be the major periodical forums for Joyce studies. These are supplemented by the *James Joyce Foundation Newsletter*, which publishes news and announcements and lists many current publications; Morris Beja and Fritz Senn have taken over the editorship from the founding editor, Bernard Benstock. The *Newsletter* is the official publication of the James Joyce Foundation, which is governed by an international board of Joyce scholars and sponsors biennial Joyce symposia.

A new publication, the *James Joyce Broadsheet*, was begun in 1979 and is published from the James Joyce Centre, University College, London. Edited by Alison Armstrong, Peter Bekker, and Richard Brown, a typical issue publishes one article, current book reviews and critical surveys, news of Joycean events, especially activities of the various European Joyce societies, and a notes-and-queries section. The first three issues are extremely promising. The second (May 1980), for example, features a review essay by Colin MacCabe, "Joyce and Chomsky: The Body and Language." The layout of the issues thus far is good and the writing lively and informed. Properly, the paper covers the European scene very well, and it is a welcome addition to Joyce publications.

A two-volume edition, one volume in French and one in English, *Joyce and Paris 1902 . . . . . . 1920–1940 . . . . . . 1975* (Paris, 1979), edited by Jacques Aubert and Maria Jolas, brings together selected papers from the Fifth International James Joyce Symposium held in Paris, 16–20 June 1975, though many of the items are merely summaries of the papers delivered. The two volumes form an interesting contrast in approach as well as in subject matter. The French volume, presenting the talks and remarks of Jacques Lacan, Michel Butor, Philippe Sollers, Nathalie Sarraute, and other French authors and critics, seems remote from the more traditional American concerns in the English volume. But that was 1975. By 1979, at the Zurich Symposium, the critical approaches and theoretical concerns of the American and European participants had much more in common. This new balance reflects the shifting concerns in Joyce criticism mentioned earlier. This is not to say that Joyce studies have been taken over by the structuralist, poststructuralist, and deconstructionist camps; but Joyce criticism in the latter half of the seventies—especially the work of a number of younger American critics—has obviously come under the influence of the theoretical developments in Europe, mainly in France, during the past fifteen years. Umberto Eco, Hélène Cixous, Philippe Sollers, and others, however, have done work on Joyce that predates these more recent developments.

The Fall 1978–Winter 1979 issue of *JJQ* (special *Structuralist/Reader Response Issue*) provides further evidence of these developments of Joyce criticism. Articles such as Jean Ricardou's "Time of the Narration, Time of the Fiction," Jennifer Levin's survey of Joyce criticism in *Tel Quel,* Robert Scholes's "Semiotic Approaches to a Fictional Text," and Herbert Schneidau's "One Eye and Two Levels: On Joyce's 'Cyclops,' " indicate shifting theoretical and critical concerns. The Spring 1981 issue of *JJQ* offers a special section in response to Seymour Chatman's work on narrative structure, such as his article "New Ways of Analyzing Narrative Structure, with an Example from Joyce's *Dubliners*" (*Lang&S,* 1969). Essays by Jonathan Culler and James Sosnoski on Joyce are also included.

While these trends are important, they do not dominate Joyce studies, for most of the criticism continues to stem from more traditional scholarship and criticism. Psychoanalytic criticism, for example, is featured in a special issue of *JJQ* guest-edited by Mark Schechner (1976). The articles in this issue and in a later supplement (1977) represent refutations, revisions of former positions (see Darcy O'Brien's "A Critique of Psychoanalytic Criticism''), and energetic new formulations. Schechner's selected checklist of psychoanalytic studies on Joyce is a useful starting point for further study on the subject.

A special two-number Joyce issue of *Modern British Literature* (1980) contains nine essays by such critics as Fritz Senn, Bernard Benstock, Thomas F. Staley, and Zack Bowen. It also includes Joseph Kestner, "Joyce, Wagner and Bizet: *Exiles, Tannhauser,* and *Carmen*"; Michael Groden, "James Joyce and the Classical, Romantic, and Modern Tempers"; and Brook Thomas, "Reading, Writing, and Joyce's Dublin." This issue is also published as the second volume in the *Modern British Literature* Monograph Series, under the title *James Joyce: New Glances* (1980), edited by Edward A. Kopper, Jr., the founding editor of *MBL*.

Phoebus (1980), a journal published by the Department of English of Chung-Ang University of Seoul, Korea, brought out a special Joyce number in English under the editorship of Chong-Keon Kim. It includes essays by John P. Daly, S.J., Thomas F. Staley, and three Korean scholars, and an appendix offering a "Korean Version of *Pomes Pennyeach,*" by Chung-Ho Chung. Korean interest in Joyce continues to be lively.

Poétique devoted a special issue to *Finnegans Wake* in 1976, edited by Hélène Cixous, and *The Crane Bag* (1978) has a large section on Joyce with essays by Vivian Mercier and Bernard Benstock, among others.

5. Biography

Further biographical study of Joyce is limited. Ellmann's biography remains the cornerstone. Stan Gébler Davies' *James Joyce: A Portrait of the Artist* (1975) is insignificant; except for some mean-spirited comments on the man and some humorous commentary on the Dublin literary scene, the book follows either Ellmann or his sources. When Davies veers away from Ellmann, as he does only occasionally, he makes errors.

An excellent collection of recollections of Joyce by European friends and acquaintances is brought together, edited, and in some instances translated by Willard Potts in his *Portraits of the Artist in Exile* (1979). Represented are Silvio Benco, Francini Bruni, August Suter, Nino Frank, and others. Seven of the reminiscences appear for the first time in English and, as might be expected, vary in length and value. This is a well-edited collection with informative headnotes, substantial identifications in the footnotes, and accurate translations from the various European languages. Several of these recollections appeared earlier in a special *Joyce Reminiscences Issue* of *JJQ* (1977), coedited by Potts. That issue also contained further material on and by Ole Vinding, a Norwegian acquaintance of Joyce's.

6. Criticism

Because of space limitations the emphasis in this section as in the 1976 essay is on books rather than on essays. Over five hundred essays of widely varying importance have been written during the period covered here and only the particularly pertinent ones are included. As noted earlier, virtually complete annual bibliographies appear in *JJQ* and the *MLA International Bibliography*.

GENERAL STUDIES

The most important general and comprehensive study of Joyce's work published in recent years is C. H. Peake's *James Joyce: The Citizen and the Artist* (1977). One could say that Peake's study looks backward rather than forward, that it assimilates rather than innovates, but such a view would be superficial; the book offers far more than its unpromising title suggests. Peake's commentaries on *Dubliners* and *A Portrait* are sound and frequently richly suggestive, but his work on *Ulysses* is especially praiseworthy. His sections on the "Nestor," "Proteus," "Aeolus," and "Cyclops" episodes are of particular value for their close and revealing analysis of the text. Peake's emphasis on political themes is illuminating in his treatment of "Aeolus" and "Cyclops" and especially informative and original regarding the function of the interpolations in "Cyclops." A careful reader, Peake knows the previous scholarship well and does not bore us with half a hundred details that are already known. For example, his treatment of the "Aeolus" episode emphasizes not the rhetorical forms but the three specimens of oratory—those of Dan Dawson, Seymour Bushe, and John F. Taylor—thereby altering the reading stressed in previous criticism. In Peake's view it is these three speeches, "epideictic, forensic, and deliberative," and not the rhetorical forms stressed by Stuart Gilbert, that underlie the rhetorical basis of the episode. As Peake points out, all the forms that Gilbert stresses in "Aeolus" can be found almost as frequently in the other chapters. Peake's illuminating discussion of Stephen's "parable of the plums" examines its nature and function, explains why it is called a "Pisgah Sight of Palestine," and stresses the parable's relation to the themes of the episode and the novel as a whole, especially regarding Stephen's problems and ambition. Peake's book is filled with insights and carefully developed arguments that alter and expand our understanding of many passages and even of substantial themes in *Ulysses*. His study is rare in that it is both a fine introduction for the general reader and a valuable work for the specialist.

Dominic Manganiello's *Joyce's Politics* (1980) is much more directly concerned with Joyce's political thinking as it is reflected in the life and works. A thorough and interesting study, it brings much new material to light, especially the political aspects of Joyce's work that were informed by continental sources and events. Manganiello blunts some of the easy assumptions in Joyce criticism that Joyce cared little for politics or political theory unless it was Irish. Manganiello is well informed in political thought and convincing in his analyses of Joyce's eclectic assimilation and in his demonstration of political ideas in Joyce's work.

Two books by Hugh Kenner have come out: *Joyce's Voices* (1978) and *Ulysses* (1980); the latter is treated later. Many regard Kenner's work as the most important current criticism on Joyce. The concerns presented in his first book, *Dublin's Joyce* (1956), have lain at the center of Joyce studies, and most serious Joyce scholarship on *Ulysses* has had to come to terms with Kenner's work. *Joyce's Voices* (1978), a study of a little over one hundred pages, comes out of Kenner's four T. S. Eliot Memorial Lectures delivered at the University of Kent. The first chapter is inspired in part by the setting of Kenner's lecture and the subject the lecture series memorializes. Drawing on Eliot's essay *"Ulysses,* Order and Myth,'' Kenner focuses on objectivity and its effect on Joyce's language. In Joyce's work the fictional event is inseparable from its linguistic manifestation. Kenner uses the early story "Grace" as an example of how Joyce worked with the resources of language. The second chapter coins a phrase that has already become a standard term in Joyce criticism: "The Uncle Charles Principle." As Kenner puts it, "This is a small instance of a general truth about Joyce's method, that his fictions tend not to have a detached narrator though they seem to have. . . . One reason the quiet little stories in *Dubliners* continue to fascinate is that . . . the illusion of dispassionate portrayal seems attended by an iridescence difficult to account for until we notice one person's sense of things inconspicuously giving place to another's.'' This principle, though a developed one, has some relation to what Ellmann once called "the blurred margin technique.'' The two remaining chapters also focus on Joyce's use of language and the varying voices that give energy and dimension to his texts. The growing general interest in narrative theory in contemporary criticism is only one reason for the central position of Kenner's work on Joyce. More important are the originality of Kenner's insights, the thoroughness of his arguments, and his mastery of the entire modern period.

Two books on Joyce's Irish background are John Garvin's eccentric *James Joyce's Disunited Kingdom* (1976) and Bernard Benstock's thorough and reliable *James Joyce: The Undiscover'd Country* (1977). Garvin contends that *Ulysses* and *Finnegans Wake* are based on Irish history, folklore, and legend and are deeply rooted in Irish culture generally, a probability that has certainly not escaped earlier critics. From this position, however, Garvin makes many curious and sundry observations, some arcane and interesting, others unformulated, random, and remote. Though unsystematic and frequently bizarre in its interpretations, the book is not without value. Garvin knows a great deal about Dublin, especially nineteenth-century bureaucracy, and can capture the milieu of Joyce's youth. Benstock's study is very different. He is a thorough and knowledgeable guide through the complex political and social history that forms so much of the background of Joyce's work. Joyce used Ireland in nearly every way a writer can use a native country, and his love-hate relation is deeply and, in a way, hopelessly complex. While convincingly arguing that Joyce ultimately rejected Ireland and made his commitment to the larger European literary tradition, Benstock treats the full complex of Irish cultural and political thought bearing on Joyce's work.

Leo Knuth's *The Wink of the Word* (Amsterdam, 1976) is a study of ingenuity and perception dealing with Joyce's phatic communication. The opening chapters present a close argument for linking Joyce the man and artist to his work; Knuth concentrates on the formation of Joyce's thought and argues against the restrictive and narrow model set up for reading Joyce by S. L. Goldberg in *The Classical Temper* (1961). Knuth's later chapters trace Joyce's movement from realist to multivalent writer, offering rigorous analyses of passages and sections, such as the treatment of "Wandering Rocks." The book is difficult to summarize, and several of Knuth's larger contentions elude me; but his commentary on motifs, words, and even letter arrangements is engrossing, and his analysis of Shem's riddle in *Finnegans Wake* is highly original.

Another European study is Carla Marengo Vaglio's *Invitio alla lettura di Joyce* (Milan, 1977), which is the best introductory study of Joyce to appear in Italy. It provides a full chronology of Joyce's life and work, discussions of all the works, and a good bibliography. Of less interest is Dolf Sörensen's *James Joyce's Aesthetic Theory* (Amsterdam, 1977); Jacques Aubert's important book on the subject, *Introduction à l'esthétique de James Joyce* (Paris, 1973), is not even mentioned in the bibliography, and the observation that Joyce drew on Vico and Bruno is commonplace. Manto Aravantinou's *Ta Hellenikā ou Tzaīems Tzōys* (*The Greek of James Joyce*, Athens, 1977) not only accounts for Joyce's use of Greek but also notes Joyce's Greek friends and his interest in modern Greek generally. This work, meant for Greek readers, is remote from Joyce studies and not carefully documented (see M. Byron Raizis' review, *JJQ*, 1979).

Barbara Reich Gluck's *Beckett and Joyce: Friendship and Fiction* (1979) traces the complex relationship between Joyce and Beckett and the influence of Joyce on Beckett. Kenner, Hayman, and Melvin Friedman have all written well on this subject, and Gluck has herself discovered some interesting parallels between the two men. Her informative treatment of Beckett's trilogy demonstrates that Beckett uses themes of circularity, recurrence, and time in much the same way as Joyce does. Deirdre Bair's biography, whatever its limitations, has given us considerable information about Beckett's close contact with Joyce between 1928 and 1932, but Gluck slights and even ignores some of Bair's revelations. There is a great deal in Gluck's book, but many aspects of the complicated Joyce-Beckett relationship, both literary and human, are still to be unraveled.

Breon Mitchell's distinguished Oxford dissertation on Joyce's influence on the German novel, mentioned in the 1976 essay, has been published as *James Joyce and the German Novel, 1922-1933* (1976). Mitchell's volume is a careful and judicious comparative study that deals with an important period of development in the German novel.

Matthew Hodgart's *James Joyce: A Student's Guide* (1978), though an ample introduction, is idiosyncratic, occasionally inaccurate, and often arch. Kenneth Grose has also written an introductory study, *James Joyce* (1975), in the Evans Brothers Literature in Perspective series, and

Peter Costello has written a brief biographical introduction, *James Joyce* (1980), in Gill and Macmillan's Irish Lives series. There are four essays on Joyce in *Yeats, Joyce and Beckett* (1976), edited by Kathleen McGrory and John Unterecker, dedicated to William York Tindall. The volume includes a selection of Tindall's fine photographs of the Joyce landscape. The essays by Raymond J. Porter on Joyce's Irishness and by Margaret Solomon and Nathan Halper are all strong. Bernard Benstock's essay is a thorough, informative, and often witty discussion of "the James Joyce industry." There is also a valuable interview with Joyce's close friend from Zurich, Carola Giedion-Welker.

The interesting work of Robert M. Adams continues with his latest study, *After Joyce: Studies in Fiction after* Ulysses (1977). Among many other observations, Adams suggest that the novel still attracts intense study because the "questions we ask about it have been changed by our experience of other art-forms, other novelists" and the "very shape and tempo of life as we experience it have changed, underlining some new patterns in the arabesque and erasing others." Adams curiously omits consideration of *Finnegans Wake* in his study, perhaps because he is convinced *Ulysses* had little influence on Joyce's last work.

Richard Ellmann's *The Consciousness of Joyce* (1977), which is in part an outgrowth of his earlier *Ulysses on the Liffey*, tries "to measure Joyce's response to his principal sources" and, as I noted earlier, includes a listing of Joyce's Trieste library in 1920. Almost none of the books in this collection are annotated; there are a few markings, but they are not sufficient to suggest any direct response from Joyce to the works that made up his working library during his years in Trieste. Ellmann, obviously at home with *Ulysses*, ponders how Joyce may have interwoven and responded to many of these works, ending the book with a chapter on Joyce and politics. Ellmann's study includes little that is conclusive and lacks the force that marked his earlier work.

An extremely valuable reference work is Shari Benstock and Bernard Benstock's *Who's He When He's at Home: A James Joyce Directory* (1980). A work of careful scholarship and great industry, the *Directory* lists and discusses over 3,000 personages who appear in Joyce's work—mythical, fictional, legendary, historical, and anonymous. All Joyce's work is covered except *Finnegans Wake,* which is served by Adaline Glasheen's *Third Census of* Finnegans Wake (see p. 200). Presented in a clear format with carefully prepared introductions, Benstocks' work has many uses. So far I have not detected any omissions, even to the "singing cake of soap" in "Circe." The introduction, also of great value, discusses the use of names and particular problems associated with each work and with each episode in *Ulysses*. Also provided are appendixes entitled "The Joycean Method of Cataloguing" and "Molly's Masculine Pronouns."

Psychoanalytic interest in Joyce continues with the publication of Sheldon Brivic's thorough *Joyce between Freud and Jung* (1980). Brivic investigates all Joyce's work from the psychoanalytic point of view and attempts to trace Joyce's mental process through his works. The contributions to psychoanalytic theory by such thinkers as Klein, Lacan, and Winnicott are recognized by Brivic, perhaps even exploited. Brivic's study is expansive and flexible, his methodology eclectic. He examines *A Portrait* from a Freudian perspective, goes on to connect the unconscious determinants of Joyce's personality to Joyce's sense of meaning and value (Brivic would say "system"), and concludes with an examination of Joyce's mythology. Brivic's prose is frequently dense and a bit unrelieved, but the work as a whole is solid, insightful, and well-informed.

Joyce's texts are as self-conscious as any found in modern literature; the reader is constantly being made aware of the language used, whatever else the text may be about. Colin MacCabe's energetic and original *James Joyce and the Revolution of the Word* (1978) comes out of the context of structuralism, Freud, Marx, and Lacan and gives new attention to Joyce's use of language and to how we read him. MacCabe's thesis has implications and extensions, especially political ones, that seem to push Joyce into political corners, but MacCabe's fresh examination of Joyce's work and the questions it raises about the relation between reader and text are critically important.

The enormous interest in narrative theory in recent years has brought a number of theoreticians to Joyce's text. Such critics as Wolfgang Iser in *The Implied Reader* (1974) and Dorrit Cohn in *Transparent Minds* (1978) have both dealt with *Ulysses* at length. Iser devotes two chapters of his book to *Ulysses*. His concentration is reader-oriented, his orientation is phenomenological, and his work seems to fall theoretically between Stanley Fish and Norman Holland. Adopting neither Holland's "transactive" relationship nor Fish's theory of interpretative strategies or "affective stylistics," Iser sees an interaction between reader and text. While Holland assumes an at least partially stable text, for Iser the text is primarily indeterminate. This indeterminacy is reflected in his view that *Ulysses*, "Instead of providing an illusory coherence of the reality it presents . . . , offers only a potential presentation, the working out of which has to be done actively by the reader." Dorrit Cohn analyzes the confessional scene in *A Portrait* and illustrates various narrative methods in *Ulysses*, concentrating on Molly's monologue. Cohn is concerned with such methods as *style indirect libre*, or *erlebte Rede*. This device, the presentation of characters' thoughts in the third person and the past tense, is usually used for present external actions and scenes in narrative. Cohn takes issue with Erwin Steinberg's *The Stream of Consciousness and Beyond in* Ulysses (1973) and other studies. She is especially critical of Steinberg's view that Bloom's and Stephen's monologues are like prespeech speeches made of preverbal words, noting that Steinberg's "non-verbal conception of the stream of consciousness . . . blinds him to Joyce's primary purpose in choosing the quoted-monologue technique over the other available techniques for depicting the inner life, namely to record his characters' verbal responses to their experiences." Cohn is concerned primarily with a theoretical framework; although her observations on *Ulysses* are challenging, one is uncertain how specifically helpful they are with Joyce's text. One could take issue with Cohn's theoretical models, but to do so would require extensive argument (see John Paul Riquelme's review essay, *CLS*, 1980, for one such argument).

Joyce's relation to Catholicism has been a persistent and important question in Joyce scholarship, if not a major one. Robert Boyle's *James Joyce's Pauline Vision* (1978) is the best work on this subject to date. Although many have seen Joyce's relationship with the Catholic church as a great struggle for freedom from the oppressive Catholicism of his childhood and adolescence and have regarded his work as a vindictive chronicle of his attempts to escape, this view is reductive and absurd, for it reduces Joyce's art to the level of personal animus and ignores the depth and richness of his texts. Such an interpretation has in the past also equated Stephen Dedalus' pronouncements with those of Joyce, failing to account for the transformation of experience into language, to say nothing of the extratextual evidence that separates Joyce from his creations. It is equally absurd to construct an elaborate apologetic view that Joyce never really escaped the church's hold on him and longed to be at least spiritually reconciled. Joyce's mind and personality were such that no orthodoxy, no single world view, could contain him. He saw truth in fragments of everything from Boehme, Vico, and the occult to Aristotle, Aquinas, and Dante. Boyle has attempted to deal with Joyce's affinities with the various aspects of Catholicism by exploring its imaginative rather than its rational impact on Joyce. Boyle tells us in his foreword that he has grown increasingly suspicious of "rational certitude," and this suspicion sets the foundation for his book. Those readers who have not read Boyle's earlier work on Hopkins and Joyce might well wonder what they are in for at this point, but they need not be uneasy, because few critics penetrate a text as deeply, skillfully, and relentlessly as Boyle does.

The texts of Shakespeare, St. Paul, and Hopkins form important correlations for Boyle's study. Boyle offers a brilliant analysis of Joyce's images to reveal the intricately interladen texture and development of Joyce's themes. The Trinitarian theme, for example, which assumes so much importance in *Ulysses*, is revealed by Boyle to be a vigorous and well-thought-out aspect of Joyce's aesthetic theory. Boyle's treatment of *Finnegans Wake* in the light of the Pauline vision is also illuminating. Difficult to summarize because of the way ideas are developed, this work is an insightful and fascinating exegesis even for those to whom much of what Boyle says may seem remote.

Interest in Joyce within the context of the Irish revival is sustained by G. J. Watson in *Irish Identity and the Literary Revival* (1979) and by Wayne E. Hall in *Shadowy Heroes: Irish Literature of the 1890s* (1980). In discussing Joyce, Watson is careful from the outset not to draw the easy contrast between the Ascendancy ethos of Yeats and Synge and Joyce's discontent and desires to escape his native country. Joyce's art, as Watson points out, is far too complex for such contrast, especially in the attitude it reveals toward Ireland. Joyce is chronologically beyond Hall's study, but in his conclusion Hall correctly notes that Stephen in *A Portrait* "maintains much of the conventional aestheticism of the 1890s," with his "preferences for vision over experience, heroic failure over practical success, art over life." Hall goes on to note, however, "that Joyce's work completes the transformation of the 1890s hero into the humbled and suffering common man." Hall's fine study offers an engaging and thorough background study for students of Joyce.

Leo Daly's *James Joyce and the Mullingar Connection* (1975) is a handsome illustrated volume published by Dolmen in which Daly argues for the importance of Mullingar in Joyce's work.

It is rare to find scholars with a deep professional interest in both D. H. Lawrence and Joyce, in spite of these writers' dominant positions in modern literature. Robert Kiely's *Beyond Egotism: The Fiction of James Joyce, Virginia Woolf, and D. H. Lawrence* (1980) is the first study to treat their literary relationship in any detailed and extended way. Kiely concentrates on the convergence of several themes but particularly on the role of the ego in the relationship between author and reader, between character and author, and among the characters in a given work. It is from this perspective that Kiely explores the writers' similarities. Although his angle seems confining at times, it yields some interesting common ground on which to view the three novelists.

EARLY FICTION

Fewer extended studies have been devoted to Joyce's early fiction during the past five years than during any comparable five-year period for the last fifteen years. Even the flow of articles has abated.

Thomas F. Staley and Bernard Benstock have followed their *Approaches to* Ulysses (1970) with *Approaches to Joyce's* Portrait: *Ten Essays* (1976). The book includes Staley's essay on *Portrait* scholarship, Hans Walter Gabler's history of the text, Breon Mitchell's essay on *Portrait*'s relation to the tradition of the bildungsroman, James Naremore's quasi-Marxist approach, Chester Anderson's uncompromising Freudian reading, Hugh Kenner's well-known and updated "The Cubist *Portrait*," Benstock's essay on the symbolic structure, and Darcy O'Brien's "In Ireland after *A Portrait*." The volume provides a multiplicity of approaches to the novel, and many of the essays give prominence to the best previous scholarship on the various perspectives. The first issue of *Irish Renaissance Annual* (1980), edited by Zack Bowen, contains Maurice Beebe's extensive essay "The *Portrait* as Portrait: Joyce and Impressionism," a thorough historical and analytical study that carefully compares Joyce's techniques to those of the impressionists.

Remo Ceserani's *Argilla* (Naples, 1975) provides the English text of "Clay," an Italian translation, a chronological bibliography, and a long discussion of the story with an extensive review of the criticism. It is an introductory volume but fairly comprehensive. An extended study of the *Dubliners* stories is Marilyn French's long "Missing Pieces in Joyce's *Dubliners*" (*TCL*, 1978). For French the focus of *Dubliners* is less on character than on an ethos, a Dublin way of thinking dominated by two sets of ideals, popular Catholicism and propriety. The two major devices French sees Joyce using in all the stories to convey the Dublin mode of thinking are "masking language" and "gaps." Masking language is euphemistic and cliché-ridden; gaps are ellipses in logic, language, or information. French demonstrates how these modes of thinking. and devices operate throughout the individual stories.

John Russell's *Style in Modern British Fiction* (1978) devotes a chapter to *Dubliners*. Although Russell reveals a rather limited notion of rhetoric, restricting his considerations to the "expressive experience," he finds several revealing stylistic patterns in the stories through his analysis of Joyce's use of the colon, semicolon (formal compounding), cadence, and the like. Charles Rossman's interesting "Stephen Dedalus and the Spiritual-Heroic Refrigerating Apparatus: Art and Life in Joyce's *Portrait*" (in *Forms of British Fiction*, ed. Alan Warren Friedman, 1975) is a fully developed discussion of the relation between Stephen's aesthetic theory and the manner in which the aesthetics express Stephen's character and experience. Rossman contends that just as Stephen's discourse on Shakespeare in *Ulysses* reveals more about Stephen that it does about *Hamlet*, so too does the aesthetic theory reveal more about Stephen's character than has previously been recognized. An argument similar to Rossman's but less amply developed appears in Harold Kaplan's *The Passive Voice* (1966). Others, of course, have also written on this subject, but Rossman's discussion is the most lucid and detailed.

It has been noted previously that the enormous contemporary interest in literary theory has been reflected in recent Joyce criticism, and the *Dubliners* stories have been used as examples of various approaches on several occasions. Seymour Chatman's previously cited essay, p. 187, offers an extended narrative analysis of "Eveline" in a test of Roland Barthes's and Tzvetan Todorov's methods of analysis of narrative. Robert Scholes's "Semiotic Approaches to a Fictional Text: Joyce's 'Eveline' " (*JJQ*, 1979) is as much a small-model demonstration of the critical resources in the theories and methods of Todorov, Genette, and Barthes as it is a reading of the story. Staley's "A Beginning: Signification, Story and Discourse in Joyce's 'The Sisters' " (*Genre*, 1979) is also as much a demonstration of the possibility in the methods of those three theorists, along with glances at Maria Corti and Edward Said, as it is an analysis of the beginning of "The Sisters." An example of how divergent criticism of *Dubliners* remains can be seen by comparing Staley's essay with Jackson I. Cope's "Joyce's Waste Land" (*Genre*, 1979). Cope argues that *Dubliners* is primarily a nineteenth-century text, and Staley argues just as strongly for its modernist affinities. Both of these essays are reprinted in *The Genres of the Irish Literary Revival* (1980), edited by Ronald Schleifer.

In *Modes of Modern Writing* (1977), David Lodge discusses Joyce's early work as a transition between Roman Jakobson's metaphoric and metonymic poles, between the realistic and modernist texts. Lodge's work is especially interesting in its application of a linguistic model to Joyce's texts since most such studies of Joyce's work in the past have been devoted to *Finnegans Wake*. Also of interest is Fred Miller Robinson's *The Comedy of Language* (1980), which argues that comedies of language are the essential texts in the study of modern comedy. His theory of comedy, which is especially revealing when applied to modern works such as *Ulysses*, is based on the contradiction between the descriptive capacity of language and the nature of reality as metaphysical flux.

Robinson says that *Ulysses* is strengthened by this contradiction and calls the book, along with other modern works, a comedy of language. His chapter on *Ulysses* both supports his theory and reveals how Joyce worked in this mode.

ULYSSES

Hugh Kenner's latest book, *Ulysses* (1980), is published in the Unwin Critical Library, a series "addressed to serious students and teachers of literature, and to knowledgable non-academic readers" and intended "to provide a scholarly introduction and a stimulus to critical thought and discussion." Kenner's volume succeeds admirably in these purposes, and in spite of the limited format suggested by the series, it is also an extension of the sustained engagement Kenner has had with Joyce's work for more than twenty-five years. This study brings the broad range of Kenner's ideas from *Dublin's Joyce, The Counterfeiters, The Pound Era,* and *Joyce's Voices* into perspective. Just as Kenner illuminates Joyce's texts by applying to them the principle of parallax, an organizing principle in *Ulysses,* and the second look, so does he in his *Ulysses* frequently give us a renewed and fresh look at some of his earlier observations and judgments—a critical parallax. Ever since his discussion of "double writing" in *Dublin's Joyce,* Kenner has been concerned with Joyce's rhetoric—its repetitions, its locutions, its interwoven system of referents. "Virtually every scene in *Ulysses* is narrated at least twice," Kenner notes in his *Ulysses*. Narrative idiom that need not be the narrator's, the "Uncle Charles Principle" of *Joyce's Voices,* is also prominent in this study; Kenner's discussion of the mimetic gives way to the vast playfulness of styles, the text itself. Kenner also reexamines the Homeric parallel and its function—primarily ironic in the earlier chapters and "coercive" in the last eight. Technique binds the episodes; Kenner calls the complex narrative voices "the aesthetics of delay," further revelations that refocus the reader's previous thoughts. This aesthetics of delay engages the reader as active participant. Such a technique "restores a governing rhythm of the book, whereby impression in the first half is modified by knowledge in the second, though only after resolute rereading has extracted the knowledge from a stylistic that tends to render it inconspicuous." Kenner's is not a complete and systematic study that covers each episode; rather it is another look at those aspects of *Ulysses* that continue to engage him and that he judges the central concerns of the text. This is a work by a major critic that modifies, reasserts, refocuses, and renews his reading and interpretation of a text, and the results are important and enduring.

As Kenner's study affirms, the thematic and structural ties between *Ulysses* and Homer have, since Stuart Gilbert's early study, been the frequent subject of critical investigation. Michael Seidel's *Epic Geography: James Joyce's* Ulysses (1976) argues cunningly that Joyce recreates the epic geography of the *Odyssey* in *Ulysses* and does so according to the Homeric action as cartographed by Victor Bérard in *Les Phéniciens et L'Odyssée.* Bérard's influence has long been acknowledged, but it has never been so comprehensibly accounted for, nor have its implications been so thoroughly discussed. Some of the elaborate charting and epic movement and placement seem inflated, even remote to the action, but Seidel's study is especially interesting for its discussion of mythology, philosophy, and epic poetry generally, in the light of Bérardian parallels. Bérard's discoveries lead Seidel to conclusions that account for major patterns within *Ulysses*. For example, we are given a Homeric reason for Bloom's drifting too far east at the beginning of "Lotus-Eaters." *Epic Geography* is an intriguing source study.

James H. Maddox, Jr.'s, *Joyce's* Ulysses *and the Assault upon Character* (1978) emerges out of the critical environment of S. L. Goldberg's *The Classical Temper* (1961), with its emphasis on character and moral enactment. Maddox, whose study of character develops Goldberg's treatment of Joyce's aesthetic theories, proposes that Joyce's characterization is predicated on the coexistence of opposites and, furthermore, that his stylistic variations are the corollary of Stephen's axiom: "Proteus thought the world can be known only through refracted signatures." Goldberg can see no redeeming features in the stylistic narrative and extravagance of the last part of *Ulysses,* but Maddox can, through these "refracted signatures" and Joyce's profound faith in the individual. Proceeding from these propositions, Maddox's *Ulysses* becomes an integrated work, though not a schematized one. Maddox is a careful reader, and his book reflects a struggle for openness and precision.

Stanley Sultan's brief Ulysses, The Waste Land, *and Modernism* (1977) does not dwell on what has now become a critical commonplace, the influence of *Ulysses* on *The Waste Land,* but looks at the two works together and sees them as the richest expression of modernism.

Three later and more specialized studies of *Ulysses* are Elliott B. Gose, Jr.'s, *The Transformation Process in Joyce's* Ulysses (1980), Craig Wallace Barrow's *Montage in James Joyce's* Ulysses (Madrid, 1980; distributed in the United States by Studio Humanitos), and Constantin-George Sandulescu's *The Joycean Monologue: A Study of* Ulysses (1979). All three studies are uneven, but they may have some interest for the specialist. Gose emphasizes Bergson's influence and contends that Bergson's ideas helped Joyce develop his own about life as a process of transformation, along with other ideas. This thesis is not convincing. Sandulescu's study is needlessly rigid and at the same time discursive; it attempts to set Joyce's monologues and character development against the modern literary tradition. But Sandulescu's treatment of Dorothy Richardson, for example, is quite inadequate for the conclusions he draws, and his contentions regarding Joyce's influence on Svevo do not seem valid. Barrow's work is slightly better informed.

It has been generally agreed, although perhaps less firmly held of late, that Anglo-American literary criticism insists on a less speculative, more practical orientation than does its European counterpart. For example, in spite of Georges Poulet and others phenomenological criticism has never taken a firm hold on the American scene. Thus when an American critic such as Suzette Henke proposes in her *Joyce's Moraculous Sindbook* (1978) to examine *Ulysses* from a phenomenological and existential orientation one expects something both unusual and original. The results, however, are disappointing in the extreme. The work is not an informed example of phenomenology and its method, and Henke's effusive prose is a mishmash of pretension, cliché, and fantasy. Waxing about the ending of *Ulysses,* she writes: "By inflating the content of our own experience, by exalting joy and compensation for pain, we become artists of the imagination. . . ." To the uninitiated such readings—and they occur throughout the book—must make the phenomenological method seem like an exercise in free association, substituting euphoria for rigor. Some critics see such a study as damaging; I am more sanguine—surely its faults and pretentions are self-evident, even to students. There is danger, however, not in its extravagantly banal commentary on Joyce, but in its potential for making student readers despair of ever coming to terms with important European intellectual currents.

Roy K. Gottfried's *The Art of Joyce's Syntax in* Ulysses (1980) takes us far away from such loose and impressionistic criticism; his is a thorough and informative study of the diverse sentence patterns in *Ulysses* and the stylistic variations that Joyce's syntactical arrangements create. Gottfried's work is especially valuable for the close attention it gives Joyce's use of various sentence patterns to form the different styles from episode to episode and the way in which these styles reflect the tension in the novel between freedom and order. Roger Moss's "Difficult Language: The Justification of Joyce's Syntax in *Ulysses*" (in *The Modern English Novel: The Reader, the Writer, and the Work,* 1976) offers further discussion on this subject.

Four books published in Europe that deal with *Ulysses* are Hartmut Mietzner's *Immanenz und Transzendenz in Joyces* A Portrait . . . *und* Ulysses (Frankfurt, 1978); a collection of essays edited by Therese Fisher-Seidel, *James Joyces* Ulysses (Frankfurt, 1977); Paul P. J. van Caspel's *Bloomers on the Liffey* (Groningen, 1980); and Eckard Lobsien's *Der Alltag der* Ulysses (Stuttgart, 1978), a sound phenomenologically oriented study that perhaps argues too strenuously with positivistic-oriented criticism. Fischer-Seidel's collection contains contributions by Fritz Senn, Hans Gabler, Arno Esch, Franz K. Stanzel, and Viktor Link, as well as an excellent bibliography of *Ulysses* studies. Paul van Caspel's curious and enjoyable study examines a number of introductions and guidebooks for errors and finds an incredible number of misquotations and factual errors in all of them. Translations are in an equally bad state, as this interesting study reveals. The error-filled Random House text of *Ulysses* seems reliable by comparison.

Many who teach *Ulysses* frequently have over the years drawn up modest chronologies of the lives of Leopold and Molly Bloom; these can now be replaced by John Henry Raleigh's *The Chronicle of Leopold and Molly Bloom* (1977), which also includes lists of Bloom's addresses and jobs and more than a half-dozen maps and diagrams of such things as the floor plan of 7 Eccles Street. Raleigh subtitles his work Ulysses *as Narrative,* because its year-by-year chronicle highlights, "as no other method could, the immense and detailed naturalistic base upon which *Ulysses* is constructed." Raleigh's task was not easy, because the naturalistic base itself has as many conflicting facts as one finds in the life it reflects. Leopold and Molly often disagree on what he or she did when. Raleigh, rather than speculate on who is right in the absence of further evidence, presents the conflicting facts. There are even more difficult problems in *Ulysses* that Raleigh must encounter, not the least of which is what constitutes evidence. Are we to accept anything that appears in "Circe," for example? While the Benstocks in their *Directory* accept as reality "absolutely nothing" in "Circe" that is not corroborated in a succeeding chapter, Raleigh is less restrictive. Or how do we distinguish between the many actual events of 16 June 1904 recorded in *Ulysses* and, for example, Bloom's attendance at Paddy Dignam's funeral? Raleigh's chronology does not make a distinction between fictional and historical reality, but it is virtually complete. Raleigh puts the facts of the Blooms' life in order and, in so doing, gives the reader yet another, if partial, view of the controlled universe Joyce created in *Ulysses*. Hart and Knuth's *A Topographical Guide to James Joyce's* Ulysses has come out in a second edition with corrections (1976) and will remain a valuable tool for the specialist and student as well.

FINNEGANS WAKE

Adaline Glasheen's *Third Census of* Finnegans Wake (1977) initiates what has been an active and productive period in *Wake* scholarship. The *Third Census* greatly amplifies the list of personal names and the other litter of the "divine and human comedy," and although the author modestly claims that even this *Third Census* is an interim report, it is of enormous value to the student of the *Wake*. Glasheen's revised synopsis is more detailed than previous ones, and her chart "Who Is Who When Everybody Is Somebody Else" is extremely helpful in putting the almost hopelessly variegated connections in some kind of order. To use her own words in a different context, Glasheen is the archaeologist and augur who reads the signs of the *Wake* as well as anyone.

Louis Mink's *A* Finnegans Wake *Gazetteer* (1978), Brendan O Hehir and John Dillon's *A Classical Lexicon for* Finnegans Wake (1977), and Roland McHugh's *Annotations to* Finnegans Wake (1980) provide strong evidence of the sustained scholarly work that the text evokes. O'Hehir and Dillon's volume gives a glossary of the Greek and Latin in all of Joyce's work as well as in *Finnegans Wake,* and the appendixes provide a more detailed explanation of Joyce's use of classical language. Mink's study belongs beside James Atherton's *The Books at the Wake* (1960; rpt. 1974) and Glasheen's work. Mink gives 2,800 topographical identifications from the *Wake,* "topographical" referring not only to geographical allusions but also to words and phrases that have literary, biographical, and historical overtones. The latter category is especially valuable for the Dublin references. We learn, too, that many places are not places as we had assumed but things that might have been named after places. The book is divided into two parts, a "Linear Guide" and an "Alphabetical Gazetteer." The second part is arranged according to the "plain-text" rubric in part 1, and it includes a complete inventory of the same identifications numerically listed by page. Part 2 also includes four well-detailed maps. Mink prefaces this work of impeccable scholarship with a number of short introductions that discuss the patterns of topographical allusion in the *Wake.* Mink's book is indispensable to the serious study of *Finnegans Wake.* McHugh's study, as he readily notes in his preface, is the outgrowth of many years of exegetical study by Hart, Knuth, Senn, and many others; it "attempts to cope with the formidable secondary task of identifying the components of the text, by applying the cream of all available exegesis in as condensed and accessible a form as possible." The form of McHugh's volume is a masterstroke, providing as it does a single numbered page for every numbered page of the *Wake,* with annotations appearing on the lines corresponding to those of the text of the *Wake.* The value of this volume will be tested after extensive use by knowledgeable readers.

Critical studies of the *Wake* continue to appear with frequency. Margot Norris' *The Decentered Universe of* Finnegans Wake: *A Structuralist Analysis* (1976) is one of the first books on the *Wake* to make extensive use of the structuralist method; Norris is also indebted to psychoanalytic approaches to literature. For Norris the dislocated dream meanings produce a decentered universe in the *Wake.* The method in this study is more revealing than the author's interpretation. Roland McHugh's *The Sigla of* Finnegans Wake (1976) is primarily exegetical, but his "sigla" approach substitutes ciphers for established terminology. Both Norris' and McHugh's works reflect a current critical context. Clive Hart in his 1962 study of the *Wake,* for example, speaks of assembled structures and motifs, but Norris admits to no such patterning; she sees Hart's work as too rigid and confining. Michael H. Begnal and Grace Eckley's *Narrator and Character in* Finnegans Wake (1975) is more traditional in approach. Begnal analyzes the ironies of the *Wake* in his study of narration and point of view, which is actually a careful isolation of the separate speakers in the *Wake* to determine who is speaking. He contends that once the reader isolates the various characters and determines points of view the book is not quite so complicated as previous critics have made out. Eckley analyzes the "Anna Livia Plurabelle" chapter and sees it at the center of the book. Of little note is Reighard Motz's *Time As Joyce Tells It* (1977), a bizarre book that comments on, among other diversions, what Motz concludes are "time" passages in the *Wake.*

Originally an issue of *TriQuarterly, In the Wake of the* Wake (1978), edited by David Hayman and Elliott Anderson, contains essays responding to the *Wake* and pieces written in the spirit of the *Wake.* It would be simplistic and therefore rash to categorize the contributors to this volume, but all of them reflect either a postmodern orientation, as in the contributions by Samuel Beckett, John Cage, Raymond Federman, and William Gass, or fairly recent European theoretical concerns, as in the contributions by Philippe Sollers, Michael Finney, and Hélène Cixous. The editors' introduction sets an excellent context both for the *Wake* and for the contributions that follow. Finney's essay provides interesting commentary and context for "Work in Progress" as it appeared in Eugene Jolas' *transition,* especially in the light of Jolas' manifesto "Revolution of the Word" and other pronouncements that were running concurrently in *transition* with "Work in Progress." As Finney points out, Joyce surely only tolerated these views because Jolas was the editor and was publishing parts of the *Wake* in each issue. A thorough history of *transition,* which includes a great deal on Joyce's relation with the magazine and the Jolases, is Dougald McMillan's tran-sition: *The History of a Literary Era, 1927–1938* (1975). Though sometimes a bit awkward and confusing in its organization, it gives important information. Both Finney and McMillan provide the historical and intellectual context that is far too often lacking in studies of the *Wake.*

John Cage's curious *Writing through* Finnegans Wake (1978, a special supplement to vol. 15 of *JJQ*) grew out of his piece for Elliott Anderson, in *TriQuarterly.* Cage rewrites the *Wake* in "mesostics," always spelling "James Joyce" vertically. Using a fine line structure, he attempts to show the relation of Joyce's text to Joyce's name. Jacob Drachler's *Id-Graphs and Ego-Graphs* (1979) is a suite of forty-four black-and-white mixed-media graphics described as "a confabulation with *FW.*"

Alchemy and Finnegans Wake (1980), by Barbara DiBernard, is a detailed study of alchemy and its various uses in the *Wake.* That Joyce was interested in the subject fairly early in his literary career has been discussed before by critics as early as Stuart Gilbert. Eliphas Lévi's theories of magic were known to Joyce and to Stuart Gilbert, and magic, spirtualism, mysticism, and Freemasonry were also of interest to Joyce. DiBernard sees Joyce using alchemy as a metaphor for change and the artistic process, especially the idea of transmutation. This is a clear and well-developed study of a difficult and elusive subject.

FOUR REVIVAL FIGURES

Lady Gregory, A. E. (George W. Russell),

Oliver St. John Gogarty, and James Stephens

James F. Carens

During the past five years there have been major publications on Lady Gregory, A. E., Oliver St. John Gogarty, and James Stephens. Though Lady Gregory has not yet become the subject of a definitive "life," her works have been attended to by publishers, editors, scholars, and critics, as have been the works of A. E., whose definitive biography we now have. The works of James Stephens and Oliver Gogarty have not appeared in the critical editions they deserve; and, in recent years, neither individual works nor aspects of the works of these two writers have been treated frequently enough in brief periodical essays that can stimulate new understanding. Yet the works of Stephens and Gogarty have been given full-scale critical analyses, and Gogarty has also been the subject of a new biography. It is to be hoped that recent publications will encourage further critical study of all four figures, especially in periodical essays devoted to particular issues and critical perspectives, and that the texts, letters, and biographies we continue to need may be expedited as well.

All four writers figure to some degree and sometimes prominently in recent general studies. Herbert A. Kenny's *Literary Dublin* (1974), a cultural history, gives a popular account of the personal role of each in the literary revival and thus will be of limited use in advanced scholarly research. Peter Costello's *The Heart Grown Brutal: The Irish Revolution in Literature from Parnell to the Death of Yeats, 1891–1939* (1977) alludes to Lady Gregory and A. E. frequently, to Stephens scarcely at all, not even to his account of the Easter Rising or to the nationalist impulse in his later work, and to Gogarty extensively but with no understanding of his political attitudes. Costello does not provide a reliable guide to the political dimensions of the writers' works or to their nationalist roles. In contrast, Richard Fallis' *The Irish Renaissance* (1977), even if one might dispute this or that observation on one or another of the four writers, has the quality of solid literary history.

Among more specialized works, the four published volumes in the documentary history *The Modern Irish Drama* are a useful source of information concerning the dramatic and literary activities and opinions of the four writers. Lady Gregory figures extensively in the four volumes, *The Irish Literary Theatre, 1899–1901* (1975), *Laying the Foundations, 1902–04* (1976), *The Abbey Theatre: The Years of Synge, 1905–09* (1978), all by Robert Hogan and James Kilroy; and *The Rise of the Realists, 1910–15* (1979), by Hogan, Richard Burnham, and Daniel P. Poteet. Information of various degrees of usefulness about A. E. may also be found in these volumes; Gogarty appears fleetingly in all but the first volume and Stephens only in the fourth. Hugh Hunt's *The Abbey: Ireland's National Theatre, 1904–1979* (1979) is worth consulting, too, for Lady Gregory's and A. E.'s roles in the development of the theater.

Of a different nature entirely, *The Letters of Sean O'Casey* (vol. 2, ed. David Krause, 1980) is a storehouse of subjective opinion and colorful and prejudiced comment about all four writers.

1. Lady Gregory

MANUSCRIPTS AND LETTERS

An important acquisition of Lady Gregory manuscripts, typescripts, proofs, and first editions has been made by the Robert W. Woodruff Library for Advanced Studies at Emory University. The major portion of the acquisition was the property of Lady Gregory's grandson; it had been a part of her personal library not included in the Gregory archives acquired by the Berg Collection of the New York Public Library. The Emory acquisition includes a number of letters from Yeats to Lady Gregory. Among the Gregory items are page proofs with autograph revisions of nine of her published works, including *Cuchulain of Muirthemne* and *Gods and Fighting Men*; and among the manuscripts are an autograph diary, kept in the early years of her marriage, that describes life in London, at Coole, on the Continent, and in Egypt. There is also an autograph of "An Emigrant's Notebook," an autobiographical essay composed about 1884 that offers insights both into Lady Gregory's life and into her later development as a dramatist. If not as extensive as the Gregory materials at the Berg, the Emory collection is very choice.

As badly as an edition of Lady Gregory's collected letters is needed, it would be unrealistic to expect one in the very near future. Important Gregory correspondence may, on the other hand, at least be anticipated. Ann Saddlemyer has completed a collection of the letters of Yeats, Synge, and Lady Gregory, *Theatre Business*—the publication of which, though delayed, is anticipated in 1982—and Daniel Murphy has completed a selection from the correspondence of Lady Gregory and Yeats. As I indicated in my 1976 chapter, Murphy also projects an edition of the correspondence of Lady Gregory and John Quinn and has completed extensive work on the project.

EDITIONS AND BIBLIOGRAPHY

Among the eight remaining announced volumes in the Coole Edition of Lady Gregory's writings, only the first of the two volumes of Lady Gregory's journals has been published. *Lady Gregory's Journals: Books One to Twenty-Nine, 10 October 1916–24 February 1925* (1978) has been edited with a foreword by Daniel Murphy. In a note on the text, Murphy explains that it is based not on the surviving holograph but on Lady Gregory's typescript, which omits some minor details and identifications found in the former and thus "represents all that Lady Gregory wanted to preserve" of her journals. There are puzzles and inconsistencies in the endnotes and index to the volume. To cite random instances: Theodore Roosevelt, unidentified in the text, is mistaken for his young cousin, Franklin Delano, in the index; no page references to Lady Gregory's comments on Proust are found in the index, but endnote references to these passages are provided. In general, the endnotes are helpful—though, in this volume, they would be more so as footnotes in the text. The *Journals* themselves, while dominated by Lady Gregory's efforts to secure for Ireland her nephew Hugh Lane's collection of impressionist paintings (retained by the National Gallery, London, which refused to honor an unwitnessed codicil to Lane's will), are rich in their revelation of her character, intellect, and literary career, as in their revelation of her theatrical, social, and political associations. Lady Gregory had her minor vanities, enjoying and recording any praise that came her way, but even in the casual gossip she confides to her journals, she is never petty. Whether startling us by revealing that she picked up an idea for the opening of *Aristotle's Bellows* from Proust's *Swann's Way* or recording the horrors perpetrated by the Black and Tans in the area around Coole, she has a sharp sense of the particular. Her conversations and encounters with Yeats, Shaw, O'Casey, and others, as well as her opinions of them, are firmly defined; and she gives us not only information about her experience but brave and humane insights into the English and Irish literary and political worlds of the period. In particular, A. E., James Stephens (who broke with her, as she records, in a fit of petulance characteristic of Dublin literary society but later became reconciled), and Gogarty make frequent appearances in this volume. The second volume of the *Journals* has not yet appeared, but *Mr. Gregory's Letter-Box*, the twentieth volume of the edition, appeared in 1981, with a brief foreword by Jon Stallworthy. Mary M. FitzGerald is currently editing the shorter writings, which will include incidental poems, stories, portraits, folk legends, translations, and reviews, in addition to political, travel, and agricultural writings, and should display this author's considerable virtuosity.

According to Colin Smythe, publisher of the Coole Edition, a number of the first thirteen volumes were delayed in publication so that actual publication dates did not necessarily coincide with publication dates given on the title pages (cited in my 1976 chapter); Smythe hopes to correct these matters in reprints and paperback editions, thereby causing some bibliographical confusion against which students should be forewarned. The final volume in the Coole Edition, a bibliography of Lady Gregory's writings, is to be (to revise my earlier description of it) the work of Smythe and FitzGerald. Individual volumes of the Coole Edition—*Our Irish Theatre, Poets and Dreamers*, and the *Journals* (vol. 1)—have appeared in the United States (1973, 1974, 1978) under the imprint of an American publisher.

Colin Smythe has reprinted *Gods and Fighting Men* with corrections (1976) and Elizabeth Coxhead's 1962 edition of the *Selected Plays* (1975). The 1901 *Ideals in Ireland*, a document in the history of the Irish renaissance, edited by Lady Gregory, has appeared in another reprint (1978).

E. H. Mikhail's *Lady Gregory: An Annotated Bibliography of Criticism* was published in 1982.

BIOGRAPHY

In a brief preface to *Lady Gregory: Interviews and Recollections* (1977), E. H. Mikhail laments that we have nothing approaching a definitive biography of Augusta Gregory and hopes the collection of interviews and reminiscences he has edited "will provide a warm, anecdotal view of an important literary figure." Mikhail's selection contains classic passages on Lady Gregory from autobiographical works by Moore, Yeats, and O'Casey, recollections by others, such as John Quinn, Wilfrid Scawen Blunt, and Walter Starkie, and a variety of newspaper reports and interviews. It is a useful compilation, particularly in its selections from the less accessible news stories, interviews, and memoirs. Biographical in its approach and impressive in its command of the subject is Ann Saddlemyer's "Augusta Gregory, Irish Nationalist: 'After all, what is wanted but a hag and a voice?' " (in *Myth and Reality in Irish Literature*, ed. Joseph Ronsley, 1977). Saddlemyer traces Lady Gregory's nationalsim from its origin in her childhood, examining its impact on her role in the theatrical movement, her Republican leanings, "her keen admiration for the image-makers of her nation," and her independence, in old age, from the political views of Yeats. Granting that "the arrogance which characterized some of Yeats's most famous utterances . . . belonged to Lady Gregory's also," Saddlemyer argues that "that very arrogance fed her nationalism as surely as did her love of country."

Mary Lou Stevenson's "Lady Gregory and Yeats: Symbiotic Creativity" (*JRUL*, 1978) is another essentially biographical essay; Stevenson treats Lady Gregory's patronage of Yeats and her friendship and collaboration with him. She argues that practically and socially Lady Gregory was "superior" to Yeats but that emotionally and creatively she was his "inferior"; she further argues that Lady Gregory was the better playwright; that "Yeats' plays, though beautiful, are boring"; and that the relationship "was of immense benefit to both" but was not "in itself, a thing of beauty." Stevenson concludes that "In their thirty-five years of friendship, there was much enthusiasm, much intellectual interest, many shared hopes and fears, but little intimacy and little love." Commendably free of psychoanalytic cant but simplistic in its approach to the collaboration and in its critical judgments, Stevenson's essay highlights the pressing need for a comprehensive, sophisticated, and searching study of Lady Gregory that will treat both the life and the works with fresh, sensitive, and firm perceptions. The information needed for that definitive life has at last begun to emerge. For instance, Elizabeth Longford's *A Pilgrimage of Passion: The Life of Wilfrid Scawen Blunt* (1979) not only gives an account of the lifelong Gregory-Blunt friendship but also reveals, on the evidence of Blunt's "secret memoirs," the Gregory-Blunt love affair, which occurred during her marriage to Sir William and occasioned her twelve-poem sequence "A Woman's Sonnets."

LITERARY HISTORY AND CRITICISM

A number of recent essays dealing in whole or in part with Lady Gregory provide something akin to footnotes or addenda to our present understanding of her work. Sean McMahon's *"Casadh an tSugáin*: The First Irish Play" (*Éire*, 1977) describes how Lady Gregory provided the scenario that permitted Douglas Hyde to escape the "debilitating" symbolism of his source in Yeats's story "The Twisting of the Rope" and thus helped to deflect Irish drama toward realism. In "Pious and Impious Peasants: Popular Religion in the Comedies of Lady Gregory and J. M. Synge" (*CLQ*, 1978), William M. Clements concludes that Lady Gregory rejected both the stereotypical stage Irishman and the nationalist stereotype of the industrious, courageous, and pious peasant, depicting in her folk characters rather the reality she discerned. It was her realism, he argues, that resulted in nationalist attacks on her works. Richard F. Peterson's "Polishing Up *The Silver Tassie* Controversy: Some Lady Gregory and W. B. Yeats Letters to Lennox Robinson" (*SORev*, 1978) draws on unpublished letters to confirm the widely held assumption that, in decisions affecting the Abbey Theatre, Lady Gregory deferred to Yeats.

Among essays in literary criticism, "Lady Gregory: Shaw's 'Charwoman' or Cinderella?" by Clement T. Goode (*McNR*, 1977–78), is, despite its title, a study of the character development of the sergeant in *The Rising of the Moon*. In an impressive essay (*CJIS*, 1977), Joseph Ronsley takes issue with both Elizabeth Coxhead (author of a Gregory biography) and Ann Saddlemyer (editor of the *Collected Plays*), who had earlier seen *Grania* as an essentially personal and private work lacking the tragic dimension. In a rigorous examination of the play's tone, action, characterization, and thematic implications, Ronsley demonstrates that Lady Gregory at her best can stand up under—and reward—a searching analysis; he also argues persuasively for describing the play as a tragedy, as Grania's tragedy, "because she has really lost her humanity with her love in playing out her tragic role."

Edward A. Kopper's *Lady Isabella Persse Gregory* (1976), in Twayne's English Authors Series, gives a useful, brief account of the life and work; Kopper treats Lady Gregory's early years and growing interest in the literary revival, her major prose renderings of the heroic cycles, and the contributions she made to the emergence and growth of the Irish theater; he then offers analyses and summaries of the short plays, comedies, folk history plays, and "tragic comedies," concluding with an account of the closing years of Lady Gregory's life, darkened as these were by political violence in Ireland and by the Lane controversy. Often using earlier critical studies by Ann Saddlemyer and Hazard Adams as a point of reference, Kopper provides a generally sane and cogent introduction, though as Saddlemeyer has pointed out in a review (*MD*, 1978), there are inaccuracies of detail. In setting out "to demonstrate the worth of Lady Gregory, the much neglected but highly talented creative artist and person who has been overshadowed by Yeats," he does not entirely avoid the tendency, manifest at its most extreme in Elizabeth Coxhead's biography, to depict Yeats as something of a villain. If we are to have, in time, either a definitive life or full-scale critical studies of the work commensurate with the character and accomplishment of Lady Gregory, moral sympathy and critical sophisication must liberate her defenders from such smothering attitudes.

2. A. E. (George W. Russell)

LETTERS

Letters to W. B. Yeats (ed. Richard J. Finneran, George Mills Harper, and William M. Murphy, 1977) contains a series of letters from A. E. to Yeats that reveals something of the complexity of their association from 1896, when Yeats could be addressed as "Dear Willie," to the time of A. E.'s death. A. E.'s letter of 14 June 1935, a dying man's tribute to genius and his own apologia, at once dignified and pathetic, is essential to an understanding of A. E. and the friendship. *Some Unpublished Letters from AE to James Stephens* (ed. Richard J. Finneran and Mary M. FitzGerald, 1980; title page misdated 1979) includes thirty-two letters, ranging from 1913 to 1934. The next section contains further information about A. E.'s letters.

EDITIONS

A collected edition of the writings of George W. Russell is being published by Colin Smythe, who, along with Henry Summerfield, serves as general editor. As now planned, the edition will include selections from A. E.'s contributions to the *Irish Homestead* and the *Irish Statesman*, the poems, and the letters, as well as volumes devoted to the mystical writings, the political works, and the writings on art and literature. A volume on A. E.'s paintings and a revised edition of Alan Denson's bibliography will complete the edition. At present, only Henry Summerfield's two-volume *Selections from the Contributions to* The Irish Homestead (1978) is available; scrupulously chosen, edited, and annotated, the work includes Summerfield's introduction and also reprints Diarmuid Russell's memoir of his father. Aimed at an Irish farm audience and intended to advance principles of Sir Horace Plunkett's Irish Agricultural Organisation Society, the *Irish Homestead* was so extraordinary a farm publication under the editorship of A. E. (1905–23) that these two volumes of A. E.'s contributions remain absorbing reading even today. In addition to advancing the cooperative movement and dealing with all aspects of husbandry, A. E. addressed himself to such subjects as Irish national and political concerns, the European situation, the condition of women, and the problems of modern democracy and capitalism. A. E. also contributed literary reviews of Irish writers, including George Moore, Douglas Hyde, Katharine Tynan, James Stephens, Lady Gregory, and Oliver Gogarty, whose work he wished to bring to the attention of his readers. Though he had certain editorial quirks— such as his campaign against the drinking of tea and alcoholic beverages—A. E. surely created the most literate and humane of all agricultural journals. The selections from the *Homestead* are an invaluable resource for those interested in the intellectual and cultural history of modern Ireland. Of the volumes that are to follow in the collected edition of the writings, a volume of selections from A. E.'s contributions to the *Irish Statesman* (1923–30), also chosen and edited by Summerfield, has been completed in manuscript, and *The Descent of the Gods: The Mystical Writings*, edited by Raghavan and Nandini Iyer, is near production. A. E.'s spiritual autobiography, *The Candle of Vision*, always of interest to Theosophists, was reprinted again in 1974.

Biography

Henry Summerfield's *That Myriad-Minded Man: A Biography of G. W. Russell, "A. E."* (1975) offers a definitive life of A. E. A traditional treatment of the life and the works, solidly grounded in all the available sources, both published and unpublished, Summerfield's work manages to show how A. E.'s early visionary experiences and his lifelong commitment to theosophy (a system effectively outlined by Summerfield) sustained both his artistic endeavors as poet and painter and his practical efforts as agricultural organizer, journalist, and editor. Summerfield is not influenced by psychoanalytic technique or psychological assumptions, though he uses Jung's mystical experiences to validate and interpret those of A. E. Clearly sympathetic to his subject, Summerfield nevertheless avoids reverence, and if he discerns certain strengths in A. E.'s creative works, he is fully cognizant of his subject's limitations, particularly as a poet. His summary of A. E.'s achievements is not exaggerated: "a career of service to Ireland and her farmers, the blueprint of the cooperative parish . . . , the fostering of generations of Irish writers and of an Irish theatre, a handful of fine poems, a moving record of mystical experiences, the vigorous and flexible prose of his periodical writing, and the creation of a personality of rare perfection. . . . " If he has not quite got to the heart of A. E.'s love-hate relationship with Yeats, Summerfield is admirably evenhanded and restrained in his treatment of the subject. (It should be reported that Peter Kuch has completed a study of the Yeats–A. E. friendship.) Reviewing *That Myriad-Minded Man*, William Daniels (*IUR*, 1976) complains that Summerfield mentions but does not really go into the subject of A. E.'s relationship with Susan Mitchell, but Daniels does not indicate how Summerfield could have come to more explicit conclusions.

The rare perfection of A. E.'s personality is T. R. Henn's subject in "The Sainthood of A. E." (*Last Essays*, 1976); originally delivered as a lecture at the Yeats Summer School (Sligo, 1964), this essay is a genial discussion of the life of A. E., marked by bits of donnish name-dropping. Given Summerfield's work, it is useful now only as an introduction.

A. E.'s painting is almost inaccessible at present; Henry Summerfield's biography reproduces several of the paintings, including passages from symbolist murals—in short, just enough to tantalize. It is to be hoped that Colin Smythe will succeed in producing a volume of reproductions. Though A. E. was so notoriously careless with the medium of oils that many of his works have deteriorated, he does have a place in the history of symbolist painting. His Theosophic paintings illuminate the works of such continental artists as Kupka and Kandinsky, as Marian Burleigh has argued (Diss. New York Univ. 1978).

LITERARY HISTORY AND CRITICISM

A number of recent essays in literary history have approached A. E. comparatively. Robert O'Driscoll's "Return to the Hearthstone: Ideals in the Celtic Literary Revival" (*Place, Personality and the Irish Writer*, ed. Andrew Carpenter, 1977) attributes to A. E. as well as to Yeats the "imaginative leap" that led to the "artistic articulation of the ideals of the Celtic Revival." His essay puts the case for A. E.'s major contribution to the revival all the more strongly by developing a running parallel between the ideas of Yeats and those of A. E. without being defensive. O'Driscoll finds that both Yeats and A. E., rejecting English materialism and imperialism, turned to folklore and heroic myth to give expression to the qualities of Irish national experience that most distinguished their land from England. Furthermore, "The language that Yeats and AE use to advocate cultural and political separation from Britain was as uncompromising and as calculated to stir the soul of the nation as the language of Patrick Pearse, James Connolly, and their revolutionary associates." "George Russell," a chapter in Wayne E. Hall's *Shadowy Heroes: Irish Literature of the 1890s* (1980) gives a less sanguine view. Hall, whose subject is the heroic ideal among revival figures of the period, makes a familiar case against A. E.'s first two volumes of poetry and develops the ironic view that Russell's greatest national contribution was, through the cooperative movement, to the materialism he disdained. Working on a much more particularized topic, William Daniels (*Éire*, 1976) compares the responses of A. E. and Synge to the congested districts of western Ireland, explaining that Synge and A. E. made complementary journeys and that each then gave a realistic picture of actual social conditions, though A. E. tended to be more optimistic about the possibility of change. Ronald L. Baker's "The Deirdre Legend in Three Irish Plays" (*Indiana English Jour.*, 1975) finds A. E.'s *Deirdre* weak by comparison with the Yeats and Synge plays based on the Deirdre legend, too remote in language and conception from its legendary source. Herbert V. Fackler's valuable introduction to the De Paul's Irish Drama Series edition of *Deirdre* (1970) has been reprinted in his inclusive study *That Tragic Queen: The Deirdre Legend in Anglo-Irish Literature* (Salzburg, 1978). (In my 1976 review, I should have attributed the fine textual work of the De Paul *Deirdre* to William J. Feeney.)

A number of diverse aspects of A. E.'s career have been examined in other recent essays. In "AE's Use of Blake in *The Irish Homestead*" (*JIL*, 1976), Jack W. Weaver reveals that, despite an extensive familiarity with Blake's poetry, A. E. made editorial use only of *The Marriage of Heaven and Hell*, because, Weaver concludes, A. E. found its aphoristic lines useful to suggest the necessary reconciliation of opposites. Elsewhere (*ELT*, 1976) Weaver argues that A. E. developed a satirical portrait of Moore in *Avatars*, after a long silence on the subject of Moore that resulted from a quarrel the two had had over Susan Mitchell's satiric book on Moore. Weaver points out that the *Avatars* portrait criticizes "Moore's realism, his obsession with physical love, and his use of Ireland as subject matter" and continues the criticism of Moore and of *Hail and Farewell* that A. E. consistently and publicly made in the *Homestead* and the *Statesman* when the two were on better terms. Lis Christensen's "George Moore's Portrait of AE in *Hail and Farewell*" (*IUR*, 1974), primarily a close analysis of Moore's technique, convincingly demonstrates that Moore treats A. E. with much the same mocking irony he uses for the other characters in his picture of the revival. Two hitherto unpublished letters from A. E. to Quiller-Couch found in F. G. Atkinson's article (*EA*, 1976), while not in themselves particularly interesting, demonstrate that, at a time when English reviewers were hostile to Yeats and other Irish poets, Quiller-Couch and his unacknowledged coeditor, York Powell, supported them. Quiller-Couch generously included Yeats, A. E., and other Irish poets in *The Oxford Book of English Verse* (1900) and later in *The Oxford Book of Victorian Verse* (1912), though by that time the tide had begun to turn in favor of Yeats and A. E.

A. C. Bose's *Three Mystic Poets* (1945), a discussion of A. E., Yeats, and Tagore, was most recently reprinted in 1978; Bose treats A. E. as representing that stage of mystic experience marked by inner illumination which expresses itself in eloquence and grandeur. To Bose, whose perspective differs radically from that of recent critics, A. E. seems a "great poet, and one of the greatest of modern mystic poets." More modest in the claims he makes for A. E.'s poetry is William Daniels, who, in " 'Glory and Shadow': AE's Supernatural Imagery" (*Éire*,

1978), writes of A. E.'s early work. Drawing attention to experiences described by Violet North, A. E.'s wife, and by such different poets as Synge and Austin Clarke, Daniels suggests ways in which imagination responds to the actual lighting of the Irish landscape and demonstrates that A. E.'s symbolism emerges from contact with Irish light itself. Writing of one of A. E.'s prose fables in "*The Interpreters*: AE's Symposium and Roman à Clef" (*Éire*, 1976), Patricia McFate aptly describes the work as a "synthesis of philosophical discourse, political discussion, and A. E.'s memories of his literary friendships"; McFate argues that all the major characters are not only aspects of A. E. or of the human soul but also Yeats, Moore, Stephens, and others among A. E.'s associates. A convincing case for the value of A. E.'s literary criticism is made by Henry Summerfield in "AE as a Literary Critic" (*Myth and Reality in Irish Literature*, ed. Joseph Ronsley, 1977), a comprehensive treatment both of A. E.'s aesthetic and of his practical criticism of traditional English and modern English, Irish, and American literature.

Robert Bernard Davis' *George William Russell ("AE")* (1977), in the Twayne series, is a concise and informed introduction to all the major aspects of A. E.'s career except the painting. Davis treats the poetry not by dealing with the individual volumes but by examining characteristic types of poems he finds in the *Collected Poems* (1935) and in one other volume, *The House of Titans and Other Poems* (1934). While Davis sees a new strength in the poems A. E wrote during and after World War I, he finds the unusual "The Dark Lady" to be A. E.'s most accomplished poem because it "shows clearly that he had the ability to write other than in the mystical vein and that he is at his best when he is least didactic." Emphasizing A. E.'s political and economic writings, Davis manages to show the vitality of A. E.'s best prose and the power of his commentary on the modern Irish nation.

3. Oliver St. John Gogarty

MANUSCRIPTS AND LETTERS

An interesting group of letters and occasional manuscripts from Gogarty to novelist Norah Hoult, located in 1978 and 1979, has been added to the Gogarty Collection at Bucknell University. There are more than a hundred of these Gogarty-Hoult items, dating mostly from the 1930s and reflecting the atmosphere within a particular set of Dublin friends and associates; they also provide some evidence of Gogarty's Yeats watching. Three letters from Gogarty to Yeats, 1929–30, indicative of the discourse between the two, appear in *Letters to Yeats* (ed. Richard J. Finneran, George Mills Harper, and William M. Murphy, 1977).

Editions and Bibliography

Only a recent reprint of the American edition of *As I Was Going down Sackville Street* (1980) has been added to the scant list of Gogarty reprints. But for a particularly rich bibliography, J. B. Lyons' recent biography, described next, should be consulted.

Biography

Oliver St. John Gogarty: The Man of Many Talents (1980) is the work of J. B. Lyons, Dublin neurologist and author; his biography complements Ulick O'Connor's earlier one (1964), provides additional information and new anecdotes, and focuses more on chronology and detail than its impressionistic predecessor did. Lyons' book is at its best in its first dozen chapters and in those sections dealing with Gogarty's family, education, and medical and social careers in Dublin. (Lyons' own experience and sympathy particularly qualify him to interpret Gogarty's training and practice in medicine.) This biography draws extensively on Gogarty's letters and quotes not only his bawdy verse (which can almost always be defended) but also the occasional verses and missives that Gogarty did not regard as publishable; indeed, these casual, rough, and unfinished or rejected verses are perhaps given too much emphasis, at the expense of the more significant works. While Lyons says that his checklist of Gogarty's publications and of secondary works is not complete, it is the most extensive available. Lyons' succinct account of Gogarty's medical career (in his *Brief Lives of Irish Doctors*, 1978) should be noted.

Literary History and Criticism

Jack W. Weaver's "Moore's Sainted Name for Gogarty in *Hail and Farewell* " (*ELT*, 1971), overlooked in my 1976 chapter, offers the plausible suggestion that George Moore, who refers directly to Gogarty in *Salve*, calls him Conan as a private joke when he appears in *Vale*, mockingly attaching the familiar name of an Irish saint to an anything but saintly figure. Two pieces by J. B. Lyons, "Oliver St. John Gogarty: The Early Phase" (*Jour. of the Irish Coll. of Physicians and Surgeons*, 1975) and "Oliver St. John Gogarty: The Productive Years" (*Studies*, 1977), were later incorporated in his biography of Gogarty. James F. Carens' *Surpassing Wit: Oliver St. John Gogarty, His Poetry and His Prose* (1979) attempts to distinguish Gogarty from Joyce's Buck Mulligan and also from the personal legend Gogarty himself helped to create; it offers a critical analysis of his development as a poet and an account of the mutually stimulating association with Yeats. *Surpassing Wit* also examines Gogarty's accomplishment as a creator, in his best "autobiographical" works, of highly distinctive prose fictions. It is the first full critical treatment of the entire Gogarty canon.

4. James Stephens

LETTERS

Richard J. Finneran's "Some Unpublished Letters from James Stephens to James Sullivan Starkey and Thomas MacDonagh" (*CJIS*, 1978) includes a series of eight letters and notes written between 1908 and 1912 and two notes dating from 1923 and 1936; the earlier group is of some interest, both personal and literary, since little correspondence survives from that period.

EDITIONS AND BIBLIOGRAPHY

Though both critical and popular editions of Stephens' works are still needed, the number of Stephens reprints has increased. Reprints of *Etched in Moonlight* and *Here Are Ladies*, his collections of short stories, were issued in 1977, as was a reprint of his *Deirdre*. The Poolbeg Press, Dublin, now promises a paperback selection from the two short story collections for 1982. Selected and introduced by Augustine Martin, this publication may prove a useful popular edition. Reprints of *Irish Fairy Tales* and *Mary, Mary* (the American title of *The Charwoman's Daughter*) appeared in 1978. A new edition of *The Insurrection in Dublin* (1979) contains a useful introduction and afterword by John A. Murphy.

I. A. Williams' early, outdated, and brief descriptive bibliography of Stephens has been reprinted twice (*John Collings Squire and James Stephens*, 1973, 1978), and Birgit Bramsbäck's more important *James Stephens: A Literary and Bibliographical Study* has been reprinted three times (1973, 1975, 1977). Dean H. Keller's "*On Prose and Verse* by James Stephens" (*BC*, 1975) describes a "trial copy" of a book Stephens published in 1928, a bibliographical rarity recently acquired by the Kent State University Libraries.

LITERARY HISTORY AND CRITICISM

Alan M. Cohn's "James Joyce and James Stephens: The Coincidence of the Second of February" (*ICarbS*, 1975) adds little that is new on the subject of Stephens' actual birth date or the shared birthday with Joyce, but it does include hitherto unpublished holograph notes to "Sarasvati" and to "Minuette" that provide information about the poems in question and about Stephens' friendship with Joyce. A more important Stephens friendship, that with W. B. Yeats, is Richard J. Finneran's concern in *The Olympian and the Leprechaun: W. B. Yeats and James Stephens* (1978). Finneran gives a carefully detailed account of the impact of the two writers on each other and of the evolution of their attitudes toward each other; the study offers valuable insights into both writers. Appended are important writings by Yeats and Stephens on each other and a descriptive bibliography of Stephens volumes in Yeats's library and Yeats volumes in Stephens' library. Birgit Bramsbäck's "The

'Dublinscape' of James Stephens'' (*MSpr*, 1977) shows how, through ample realistic and evocative detail, Dublin pervades Stephens' poetry and prose and creates a range of moods. Bramsbäck's essay is an effective introduction to Stephens and to the variety of his work.

Augustine Martin's *James Stephens: A Critical Study* (1977) and Patricia McFate's *The Writings of James Stephens* (1979) are the first substantial, extended critical studies of Stephens' work; each of these books is bound to influence subsequent critical thinking, and each deserves attention. Although Martin and McFate may differ in emphasis and in particular judgments, they both prefer Stephens' early poems and his redactions from Irish originals to his later poetry, regard his fiction as more important than his poetry, admire his later legendary works, and insist that Stephens was a serious artist, not to be seen merely as another talented product of the revival. (I should note that Sylvia McLaurin's dissertation, Louisiana State University 1979, argues that Stephens' prose interpretations of Irish legendary materials were superior to the attempts of Yeats, Synge, and others to capture the essential mood of the originals.) McFate's critical approach to Stephens is biographical, historical, textual; Martin's more formalistic and mythic. McFate is strong on the development of the works from earlier stages and in her knowledge of existing manuscripts; she is effective in treating Stephens' sources in Irish legend, Blake, and Theosophy and in showing how he modified and synthesized to achieve particular artistic ends. Her book is comprehensive, too, covering even the early minor prose works. Martin is strong in particularized analysis of structure, tone, and technique; especially compelling are his distinction between the visionary Blakean element in Stephens and the mystic, or Theosophic, element and his assessment of the unfortunate effects of the latter on the poetry. McFate emphasizes the Irishness of Stephens and the relation of the works to the realities of modern Irish experience and to the ideals of the revival, though she also argues that everything Stephens produced, from patriotic essay to lyric, was a variation on the theme of love. Martin, emphasizing the experimental quality of Stephens' techniques and the mythic qualities of his imagination, rebuts the tendency of some critics to regard Stephens as an Irish provincial and to fail to see that Stephens' "life was a persistent, arduous and frequently brilliant experiment with experience and form." Yet Martin also recognizes that Stephens' departure from Dublin marked the end of his creative period and that his influence was strong on subsequent Irish novelists, such as Joyce, Eimar O'Duffy, Flann O'Brien, Austin Clarke, and Benedict Kiely. Both McFate's book and Martin's are essential to any subsequent study of Stephens.

SEAN O'CASEY

David Krause

1. Bibliographies

Ronald Ayling and Michael J. Durkan's *Sean O'Casey: A Bibliography* (1978) is a complete and invaluable record of all O'Casey's work: his plays, books, essays, contributions to books and periodicals, manuscripts, typescripts and proof pages, first stage productions and major revivals, translations and adaptations of his works, recordings, radio and television broadcasts and films, and motion pictures. Many entries in this model of bibliographical scholarship contain richly detailed notes that describe, clarify, or comment on the background of the material.

E. H. Mikhail's *A Research Guide to Modern Irish Dramatists* (1978) lists all the major bibliographical reference works on O'Casey. Mikhail also performs an important service with his continuing "Sean O'Casey: An Annual Bibliography" in the fall issue of *SORev,* every year since 1975. The 1980 issue lists sixty-nine newspaper and magazine articles dealing with the controversy that arose over the banning of *Within the Gates* in Boston in 1935. This is a significant catalog of previously unused material relating to a historical episode of literary censorship. Everyone is deeply indebted to Mikhail for his fine detective work. If there is one problem with his lists, it is the placement side by side of important and unimportant, provocative and superficial, references without any indication of their content or quality.

For a useful record of O'Casey scholarship in progress, see the *Handlist of Work in Progress* (1970–   ) produced by the Royal Irish Academy, Dublin, Committee for the Study of Anglo-Irish Language and Literature. Maurice Harmon's *Select Bibliography for the Study of Anglo-Irish Literature and Its Backgrounds* (1977) is too selective and woefully inadequate for O'Casey studies. It lists only four bibliographical references and omits any mention of the obviously important *Sean O'Casey Review*. A significant contribution to the study of O'Casey's work, Robert G. Lowery's *Sean O'Casey Review*, begun in 1974, is a rich mine of bibliographical and critical material about O'Casey's life and work. Beginning in 1982, Lowery will also edit a regular *O'Casey Annual* in book form, and the *Review* will continue to appear in a slightly shortened format. By providing an international forum for O'Casey scholarship and criticism, organizing O'Casey conferences, and encouraging new research, Lowery has emerged as an outstanding champion of O'Casey. He is an accomplished historian as well as editor, and his book reviews in the *Review* reflect his gritty and eloquent impatience with writers who have inadequate historical and critical perspectives.

2. Editions, Letters, and Manuscripts

The Harvest Festival: A Play in Three Acts was published in 1979 with a foreword by Eileen O'Casey and an introduction by John O'Riordan. This is O'Casey's earliest extant play, probably written in 1919 and rejected by the Abbey Threatre in 1920 (for the Abbey's critique and rejection, see the *Letters*, vol. 1). The original manuscript is in the Berg Collection of the New York Public Library. O'Casey's refusal to publish this work during his lifetime indicates that he considered it an uneven and unfinished example of his apprenticeship as a dramatist, and it should be studied and judged in this light. In many ways it anticipates *Red Roses for Me*.

Pan Books published *Three Plays: Juno and the Paycock, The Shadow of a Gunman, The Plough and the Stars* (1980), a reprint of the paperback edition (1957).

The paperback edition of *Autobiographies* (2 vols., 1963), long out of print, was at last reprinted by Pan Books in 1980. This inexpensive and important edition is available only in Great Britain and Ireland, and it is to be hoped that a publisher will soon bring it out in the United States. Macmillan of London has reprinted a new hardcover edition of *Autobiographies* (2 vols., 1981), with an index by J. C. Trewin. It is a handsome and long-overdue edition, but the index is a superficial effort that barely scratches the surface of the multitudinous O'Casey references. A comprehensive index remains to be published.

Volume 2 of *The Letters of Sean O'Casey* (ed. David Krause, 1980) covers 1942–54. A third and final volume, covering 1955–64, is in preparation. The unpublished letters from Gabriel Fallon (1898–1980) to O'Casey, written over a twenty-year period, are in the University of Texas Library at Austin.

For a descriptive catalog and useful editorial comment on manuscript material in the Berg Collection of the New York Public Library, see Ronald Ayling's "Detailed Catalogue of Sean O'Casey's Papers at the Time of His Death" (*SORev*, 1975–76).

3. Biographical, Critical, and Historical Studies

In *Eileen* (1976), a lively sequel to *Sean* (1971), Eileen O'Casey provides another behind-the-scenes look at her life with Sean. We see more of his daily habits and thoughts as a writer and family man, his determination to go on writing new plays even though few were performed, and above all his compassionate and courageous influence on Eileen's life. Unlike some widows of famous men, she offers many profound insights into her husband's character.

Dublin is still full of people who say they knew people who knew O'Casey. In " 'Always Complainin': The Politics of Young Sean" (*IUR,* 1980), Roger McHugh reports that a friend of a friend said he had worked as a laborer with O'Casey on the Great Northern Railway and recalled only one thing about him: "Sean O'Casey? Ah, yes, I remember him all right: a long, thin fella with a drop on the end of his nose, always complainin'. Always complainin'!" This general description might have identified nine-tenths of the adult male working-class population of Dublin early in the twentieth century, including the friend of the friend. What we may have here is a quick portrait of the archetypal Dubliner, who eventually became a vivid character in O'Casey's plays. McHugh goes much further with this portrait and associates O'Casey's "complainin' " with the role of the Socratic gadfly whose sharp stings help to keep the city awake and aware of danger. He traces the young Sean's shift from Irish nationalism to international socialism, basing his evidence on O'Casey's early writing in the *Irish Worker* and *Irish Freedom* during the 1912–14 period and on his first book, *The Story of the Irish Citizen Army* (1919). At a time when some contemporary Irish critics and journalists are dismissing O'Casey's autobiography as a distorted work of self-inflating fiction, it is interesting to observe McHugh's comments on the subject:

> the autobiographies themselves seem to me to resemble George Moore's in that they are partly factual, partly fictional, but give such a vivid impression of life that one often prefers them to historical accounts, and discounts their egocentric hindsights. They also cast a good deal of light on the various influences and loyalties of O'Casey himself; his mixed religious background, his father's evangelical strain; his mother's loyalty to the English crown and her pride in Irish ancestry, his Protestant teachers and the Catholic companions of his boyhood, a true background for the vital conflicts of his plays.

McHugh is perceptive and fair here, but some sceptical and cynical Irishmen who reject the autobiographies as bad or deceitful writing should consider the possibility that, as their distinguished countryman Oscar Wilde firmly believed, art can often be more vital and more authentic than life.

Unlike McHugh, C. Desmond Greaves, in *Sean O'Casey: Politics and Art* (1979), is seldom perceptive or fair. Greaves tells us more about the politics of Greaves than he does about the art of O'Casey, and along the way he makes some wild and unlikely speculations about the life of O'Casey. As a doctrinaire republican-socialist committed to the cause of an Irish revolution, Greaves measures everything in O'Casey's life and art by the uncompromising principles of the 1916 Easter Rising, die-hard principles that O'Casey questioned and mocked in his plays. Not surprisingly O'Casey the man and dramatist fails the Greaves political test. Like the intractable Peadar O'Donnell (see Michael McInerney's *Peadar O'Donnell, Irish Social Rebel,* 1974), Greaves is distressed that there are no characters in the Dublin trilogy who might have led a revolt to liberate Ireland from British tyranny. It never occurred to either of these men that it might not be the primary function of art to change the political destiny of the nation and that no Irish artist, beginning at the top with Yeats and Joyce, could have passed that litmus test. Determined to find a reason for the political weaknesses in O'Casey's art, Greaves offers the simplistic psychoanalytical speculation that O'Casey's failure must have been related to his traumatic guilt over not having fought for Ireland in 1916.

Since there have never been any signs of such a traumatic guilt complex throughout the eighty-four years of O'Casey's life, or anywhere in his voluminous writing, this charge can only be seen as a reprehensible attempt to call him a coward or, worse, a renegade. But socialists like Greaves, above all, should remember that O'Casey was "out" in 1913 during Jim Larkin's general strike for the cause of labor, considered by O'Casey to be more crucial for the fate of the working people of his country than the 1916 cause of nationalism, a middle-class rising that he accurately predicted would eventually undermine the future of the labor movement in Ireland. Perhaps it would be pointless to ask Greaves, a Connolly republican-socialist, to be tolerant of O'Casey's position as a Larkin labor-socialist. Greaves dismisses Larkin as "the agitator" and brands him as a mere "ultra-leftist." Leveling the charge at O'Casey as well as at Larkin, Greaves says, "Ultra-leftism is a phenomenon of untrained emotions and common in those whose socialism is insufficiently educated to be scientific." Only a flint-hearted scientific materialist could pass muster here. Another of Greaves's favorite terms of abuse is "artistic elitism," the taint of which he finds in just about all of O'Casey's plays, except *The Star Turns Red,* the one political work that for Greaves "celebrates O'Casey's conversion to communism." According to the Greaves gospel—and he often sounds like a priggish Covey spouting his Jenersky—any writer who dares to place art above politics is an "artistic elitist." As the most obvious example of this cardinal sin, Greaves quotes a passage from a letter O'Casey wrote to Lady Gregory in 1928: "And one thing is certain—that so long as God or Nature leaves us one atom of strength, we must continue to use that atom of strength to fight on for that which is above & before all governments & parties—Art & Literature which are the mantle & mirror of the Holy Ghost, and the Sword of the Spirit" *(Letters I).*

Now some of us may feel that this was one of O'Casey's most powerful and poetic statements of his artistic faith, but for Greaves it is only an "elitist's" self-damning confession of political and emotional failure because "Art had become his substitute religion." On page after page of his book Greaves argues that scientific socialism is the only genuine religion for a writer. He raises political objections about every play, even *The Star Turns Red,* in which he feels that the profusion of symbols and language get in the way of the militant theme. Greaves bristles over O'Casey's deviation from the orthodox path of socialist-realism and accuses O'Casey of imitating Synge with excessive "decoration" in the dialogue of his early plays and of succumbing to "Tollerization" with the expressionistic techniques of the later plays.

As a drama critic Greaves has serious limitations. He seldom rises above simplistic plot summaries and moralistic messages and fails to cope with the comic genius of O'Casey and Synge, perhaps because Synge was the most apolitical of playwrights. He is amazed that *The Playboy,* " this slight comedy of rebellious youth should arouse strong emotions" since it is for Greaves "completely non-moral and lacks a reference point." By this he means, of course, a *political* reference point. As for the innovative symbolic and fantastic theatrical techniques in O'Casey's later plays, Greaves never recovers from the shock that, in the works beginning with *The Tassie,* O'Casey jumped "holus-bolus into Expressionism."

Greaves is similarly misleading when he jumps into what he calls the nonscientific account of O'Casey's life in the autobiography. Whenever there is some doubt about O'Casey's family background, Greaves draws conclusions based on wild guesses or on outright misrepresentation. Using the so-called evidence of Martin Margulies and Anthony Butler, he decides that O'Casey's father Michael must have been a man of means with considerable standing in the Unionist or Anglo-Irish community of Dublin. He presumes, without any more evidence than O'Casey's comment in the autobiography that his father knew Latin, that "Michael Casey may have been a 'spoiled priest' who turned Protestant and married a Protestant girl." Yet it is known that Michael, the son of a mixed marriage, was raised as a Protestant by his uncompromising Church of Ireland mother after his Catholic father died.

Greaves uses dubious methods of research to expose the "inaccuracies"in the autobiography. Two characteristic examples will suffice. When O'Casey writes that his father's funeral took place "on a very cold day," Greaves does not examine the context of the passage to see why an ailing six-year-old boy was chilled and frightened by his first encounter with death in the family. Instead Greaves consults old meteorological records and concludes that "the day was by no means cold." When O'Casey writes that he placed sprigs of musk, fuchsia, and geranium on his mother's coffin as symbols of the gold, frankincense, and myrrh she never had in her lifetime, Greaves ignores the elegaic and symbolic context and on the basis of data in the horticultural records declares that "these plants do not usually flower in November." Greaves is apparently concerned with verifiable statistics, not the validity of metaphoric or symbolic insight in an autobiographical work of art.

Finally, something must also be said about the faulty reasoning in Greaves's book. O'Casey often chose to ignore or was not certain about specific dates of past events, but Greaves makes far too much of this minor and understandable frailty. Finding that O'Casey, twenty years after his mother died, was off by a year in remembering the date of her death, Greaves writes: "To be uncertain with dates is to be unsure of the succession of events. To be unsure of the succession of events is the most certain way to lose their significance. And if their objective significance is lost, a subjective one can take its place." Perhaps a writer who can draw serious conclusions from such choplogic is likely to lose the objective significance of his own subject.

Martin Margulies has contributed to some of the misinterpretations and distortions of Greaves and Butler, the leaders of the anti-O'Casey movement. In "Sean O'Casey Revisited" (*Univ. of Bridgeport Quart.*, 1980), Margulies presents what might have been an addition to or a reassessment of his monograph *The Early Life of Sean O'Casey* (1970). But the article turns out to offer nothing new, nothing to indicate that Margulies had revisited O'Casey or Dublin. It is misleading, inaccurate, and full of unsupported generalizations; in some instances it contradicts information previously presented in the monograph.

For someone with a self-advertised legal training, Margulies is extremely careless with documents and facts, too often accepting as "evidence" the testimony of people who knew people who disliked O'Casey's antiheroic plays, distrusted his Larkinite politics, or found his forthright views discomfiting. Misrepresentations and distortions in the Margulies version of O'Casey's early life are assessed in the 1983 edition of the *O'Casey Annual*.

Anthony Butler, the Dublin yellow journalist, has savaged O'Casey for many years. Long reluctant to dignify Butler's accusation that O'Casey was a liar, a thief, and a coward, David Krause finally wrote a detailed refutation, "The Maiming of Sean O'Casey" (*Dublin Evening Herald,* 26 Nov. 1976). The article and Butler's response to it are reprinted in *SORev* (1977).

Frank Robbins' *Under the Starry Plough: Recollections of the Irish Citizen Army* (1977) is a personal memoir of the author's experiences during the 1916–21 period of Irish history, from the Easter Rising to the civil war. Robbins, taking a nationalistic pro-Connolly point of view, is vigorously anti-Larkin and anti-labor and hence also anti-O'Casey. He celebrates at length the nationalistic movement that O'Casey mocked in his plays, mentioning O'Casey by name mainly to belittle his work in the Citizen Army. The book offers many insights into the middle-class attitudes of the idealistic nationalists.

It is evident that many Irish nationalists have never forgiven O'Casey for taking an ironic view of the blood sacrifice of the Easter Rising in *The Plough and the Stars*. Even a highly respected old warrior like the republican Peadar O'Donnell, himself a talented writer as well as a militant nationalist and socialist, has called the play "nauseating." His significant reaction is recorded in Michael McInerney's *Peadar O'Donnell, Irish Social Rebel* (1974):

> O'Donnell has some of that bitter vision which many Republicans have towards Sean O'Casey. He says that he knew O'Casey as a cranky man rather than a revolutionary. He lived through a period of history when "resistance was the theme of the

people in Dublin from 1913 onwards particularly, yet O'Casey's characters showed none of this. He was a great dramatist and will be remembered long after I am forgotten as a literateur. A great dramatist he was, and his plays are very good theatrically, yet his plays do not excite or stimulate me. His *Plough and the Stars* I find nauseating. There is no character in that play from whom any revolutionary action could proceed.

"The O'Casey plays of that period gave the opportunity to the good, fat Dublin middle-class to have a laugh at Dublin's workers. The women in his plays were as patient as donkeys, they accepted their lot without revolt. Yet he was a writer, a dramatist of great ability. But compare Juno with Gorki's 'Mother' with all her sense of injustice and revolt."

O'Donnell's grudging admiration for O'Casey's theatrical genius cannot hide the fact that political rebels have difficulty understanding artistic rebels. How can anyone describe the dominant women in the Dublin trilogy as patient donkeys? How can anyone ignore the courage of Juno Boyle in defending her family, the wisdom of her ironic speech about sacrificial principles? For an extension of O'Donnell's views, held by a much younger man, a politically biased Irish academic and poet of exceptional talent, see Seamus Deane's "Irish Politics and O'Casey's Theatre" (*Threshold,* 1973; rpt. in *Sean O'Casey,* ed. Thomas Kilroy, 1975). For a response to O'Donnell's and Deane's political approach to art, see David Krause's "Some Truths and Jokes about the Easter Rising" *(SORev,* 1976).

The demand that art should be subservient to politics comes up again in Carl Reeve and Ann Barton Reeve's *James Connolly and the United States: The Road to the* 1916 *Irish Rebellion* (1978). The Reeves are careful and dedicated scholars, but they reject O'Casey's belief that the patriotic nationalism of 1916 undermined the labor movement in Ireland; they support O'Donnell's argument that the Easter Rising was the most sacred event in Irish history and that any writer who does not glorify it is an enemy of the Irish people. The Reeves try bravely to be fair to O'Casey, yet they end up by damning him: "There can scarcely be divided opinion on O'Casey's superb writing talent. . . . Yet . . . his fancy, his biting irony, his brilliant comedy were, in 'The Plough and the Stars,' directed against the Irish working class, depicting the workers as caricatures and their revolt as laughable." If O'Casey had sanctified the Rising and idealized his slum characters, he probably would have written an undistinguished political tract, instead of a powerful tragicomedy directed against war and bloodshed, not against the Irish people, who in the play are presented with a depth of compassion and without the taint of caricature. Why are the defenders of Irish nationalism so priggish, so dour in their dedication to their holy cause, so suspicious of artistic complexity in the techniques of "biting irony" and "brilliant comedy"? The solemn Reeves are in no mood for comedy, even the rich Dickensian comedy of O'Casey, which laughs with as well as at the sharply drawn characters. At one point the Reeves enlist the help of Michael Gold in their reluctant denigration of *The Plough.* In a review of the film version of the play (*Daily Worker*, 15 Feb. 1937), which is described as a bad film because it was based on a bad play, Gold argued that O'Casey was not a revolutionary but "a muddled liberal" who "did not understand the great place of Easter Week in history, and hence he could not portray it dramatically." The Reeves quote with approval Gold's conclusion about the play: "What a program of futility, cowardice and impatience. But it is the same program O'Casey had for Ireland. His play was really an artistic statement of this shabby, un-Irish creed."

Paradoxically both communists, like Gold, and anticommunists have problems accepting O'Casey's self-styled communism, a personal creed perhaps more characteristic of the man than of his works of art. In the first issue of his *Sean O'Casey Review* (1974), Robert G. Lowery, the founder-editor, in "O'Casey, Critics, and Communism," protests that "There is as yet no comprehensive analysis of Sean O'Casey's politics, though whole chapters of books and columns of print have been devoted to proving that he was not the Communist he thought he was. There are certain fallacies in the analysis presented so far and many questions O'Casey himself raised have gone unanswered." This article exposes many inadequate and inaccurate accounts of O'Casey's communism. Lowery's review of Greaves's *Sean O'Casey: Politics and Art* (*SORev*, 1980) says that the title is right but the work wrongheaded, that Greaves fails to come to grips with his complex subject because his book is mostly "a rebuttal and contradiction of nearly everything O'Casey said politically and otherwise about himself." Lowery concludes that "the O'Casey chapter on politics and art has still to be written." Perhaps Lowery himself will eventually write that chapter. He has made his first effort in that direction in his "Sean O'Casey: Art and Politics" (*Sean O'Casey Centenary Essays*, ed. David Krause and Robert G. Lowery, 1980).

Little has been written about what might be called O'Casey's Protestant politics, and in an important if sometimes imprecise essay (*IUR*, 1980), Alan Simpson makes some valuable and hitherto unknown revelations about the northside area of Dublin City known as the East Wall, where O'Casey lived with his mother and brothers from 1889 to 1920. Simpson (1921–1980), a theatrical director of outstanding talent and a courageous man of rare insight who will be sorely missed, describes the East Wall as a largely Protestant enclave of lower-middle-class and working-class families traditionally and emotionally linked to Britain, living in a drab and unattractive area surrounded by docks, railway lines, and sooty bridges, isolated from the rest of the predominantly Catholic northside of the city. The Caseys moved into this Protestant ghetto shortly after the death of the father. At first, they lived in a modest section of the neighborhood, but subsequently, as their economic situation worsened, they moved to a two-room flat in a section much lower in the social scale and more insular. "The retrograde move," Simpson observes, "must have been extremely traumatic for O'Casey," since everyone in the neighborhood would have witnessed the family's decline.

This crumbling neighborhood of working-class Protestantism, not the Georgian slum tenements of the Catholic poor outside the Pale, was the main influence on O'Casey's life, Simpson claims. Simpson's thesis thus far is sound and illuminating, and, most important, it opens new ground for investigation. He believes that the Dublin scenes in *Red Roses for Me* and *The Silver Tassie* are set in the East Wall, and he might have included the recently published early play, *The Harvest Festival*, probably O'Casey's most Protestant, most East Wall work, the prototype for *Red Roses*. We should remember, however, that the first three major plays—*Gunman, Juno,* and *Plough*—which presented life in the Georgian slum tenements, not the decaying East Wall, might then be called his most Catholic plays, with the intrusion of some Protestants like Bessie Burgess. Like William Carleton in the nineteenth century, O'Casey was one of the few modern Irish writers who had a profound understanding of lower-class Protestants and Catholics. To take such a broad view, he would have had to know the disintegrating conditions of life in Catholic Dublin beyond the East Wall. We should remember that in 1920 O'Casey had shared a single-room flat with Michael Mullen, the Aran Islander, in one of the Georgian tenements in Mountjoy Square.

When Simpson moves away from the plays, however, and tries to make the East Wall area the only dominating and crucial influence in O'Casey's life, his thesis tends to become too rigid and deterministic. He argues that the young O'Casey was trapped "within the narrow confines of East Wall" and concludes that "the aggressive side of O'Casey's character owes as much to the geographical location in which he spent more of the first half of his life as it does to his family circumstances and inherited traits." There may be no way to prove or disprove such a palpable half-truth, but it must be recognized that Simpson has thrown a powerful light over a hitherto dark area of O'Casey's life. Nevertheless, it would be a mistake to assume that the young O'Casey was a frustrated prisoner of East Wall, for he was well launched on his escape from that narrow enclave by his mid-twenties.

Although O'Casey comically scolded Protestants and Catholics in his plays and autobiography, ordinary Dubliners of both faiths were usually attracted to his work. Micheál Ó hAodha's "O'Casey and After," in his *Theatre in Ireland* (1974), points out that it was only the special-interest groups like the rabid Nationalists and Catholics who consistently denounced O'Casey, adding: "It is worth recalling that the ordinary public and the theatre-goers in Dublin were on O'Casey's side from the beginning. They flooded to his plays whenever they were given an opportunity to do so." When he turns to the dramatist's life and the autobiography, however, Ó hAodha separates himself from the ordinary Dubliners who admired O'Casey; instead, he shares the view of Butler and Margulies that O'Casey "fabricated" the early years of hardship and exaggerated his self-education: "Nor is it a fact that he grew up in relative ignorance and was largely self-educated. In later years he certainly suffered poverty through illness and unemployment but it is difficult to understand how, with his background and above-average opportunities, he was unable to get a better job that that of a labourer." Ó hAodha does not say what he means by implying there was something impressive in O'Casey's "background." Does he mean the untruth that O'Casey's father was a Protestant of high "standing" in Dublin? And what does he mean by alluding to those "above-average opportunities," which simply did not exist for an undernourished and half-blind young man who was not qualified for any work other than manual labor. It is not without cause that Dublin has earned the reputation of being the city of brotherly malice.

For some enlightenment about O'Casey's early life, particularly his voracious method of self-education, we must turn to John Jordan, an astute scholar and one of the few reliable Irish critics of O'Casey. In his valuable "The Passionate Autodidact: The Importance of *Litera Scripta* for O'Casey" (*IUR*, 1980), Jordan looks at the books and authors mentioned in the autobiography and the plays to investigate "O'Casey's laborious self-education and the effect it had on his life and dramatic canon." It is an outstanding piece of critical research. Besides many known and little-known literary references in O'Casey's work, Jordan identifies a number of hitherto overlooked passages, like the allusion to Robert Stawell Ball's *Story of the Heavens* in *Juno* and allusions to *The Winter's Tale* in *Red Roses* and to Canon Sheehan's *Under the Cedars and the Stars* in *The Bishop's Bonfire*; and there are dozens of identified quotations and allusions that open up some of the rich subtext in O'Casey's work. Jordan rightly maintains that O'Casey's complex learning and writing technique grew out of the monumental pride and sometimes reverse snobbery of the courageous autodidact as self-conscious underdog. It was a rigorous method of broad reading and intensely personal writing that could only have been self-motivated and self-taught.

O'Casey's books were his defense against an alienating world, and his own written words, which were often inspired by those books, became the weapons of his self-preservation and creative energy. In some ways he modeled himself in his middle years after the fiery Jim Larkin, another highly literate and "passionate autodidact," who published some of O'Casey's early writings in his labor newspaper, the *Irish Worker*. Robert G. Lowery is editing a book of Larkin's writings in his newspaper. This important and long overdue work also includes some articles by James Connolly, O'Casey, and many lesser-known but significant writers who contributed to the *Irish Worker*.

Ronald Ayling's "Sean O'Casey and Jim Larkin after 1923" (*SORev*, 1977) prints part of a letter O'Casey wrote to Ayling in 1960; its full text will appear in the *Letters* (vol. 3). The letter contains interesting information about O'Casey's later contact with Larkin and with some Dublin labor people who had attacked Larkin and O'Casey. It also gives a sharp account of what was probably Larkin's last visit with the dramatist, during which it became apparent to O'Casey that the one-time Prometheus of the Irish working people had in his declining years become too cautious and compromising in his friendly relationship with the Catholic hierarchy in Dublin.

There are signs of critical failure and omission in some recent studies of modern Irish literature that lend silent approval to the belief that everything O'Casey wrote after he left Ireland in 1926, including the autobiography, was unimportant. For example, G. J. Watson, in *Irish Identity and the Literary Revival* (1979), relates the theme of "Irish identity" to the works of Synge, Yeats, Joyce, and O'Casey. His treatment of

O'Casey, however, is limited to the Dublin trilogy on the assumption, apparently, that the dramatist lost his "Irish identity" when he left Ireland. Robert G. Lowery's review of this book (*IUR*, 1980) astutely exposes Watson's critical failure.

Peter Costello, in *The Heart Grown Brutal: The Irish Revolution in Literature, from Parnell to the Death of Yeats, 1891–1939* (1977), concentrates on works that deal with the revolutionary period and therefore discusses only the Dublin trilogy. His comments on these plays, however, are so erratic and so distorted by the introduction of psychological identity games that his critical judgments become questionable. In his treatment of *The Shadow of a Gunman*, for example, Costello trots out the well-worn but erroneous contention that Davoren represents O'Casey; he also identifies O'Casey with the Covey in *The Plough*.

Richard Fallis' more reliable *The Irish Renaissance* (1977) presents a reasonable introduction to the major figures of modern Irish literature. Nevertheless, his point of view is conventional and safe to such an extent that he seems to be intimidated by such eccentric masterpieces as *Finnegans Wake* and O'Casey's autobiography. He tries hard to be fair to O'Casey, but sometimes his approach to the "flawed genius" leads him into stock catalogs of strengths and weaknesses in which he appears to be temporizing. He moves freely beyond the trilogy and praises some of the later plays, like *Red Roses* and *Cock*, yet he is uneasy about O'Casey's innovative experiments with dramatic technique and is unable to respond to the unorthodox form and linguistic freedom in the autobiography.

In *The Irish Drama of Europe from Yeats to Beckett* (1978), Katharine Worth, usually an alert and learned drama critic, creates difficulties for herself because she is so determined to do justice to the European origins of Yeats's dance plays and to connect O'Casey's comic fantasies to Yeats. By making the static drama of Maeterlinck one of the main sources of Yeats's symbolic theater, Worth struggles unsuccessfully to associate O'Casey with that esoteric tradition. Ignoring all the early plays, ignoring the substantial evidence that the O'Casey of the later plays was inspired by the many-sided Gaelic muse of low comedy and high fantasy as well as by the uninhibited theater of music-hall farce, Worth presses on with her unconvincing arguments that "O'Casey adapts the Yeatsian total theatre techniques" in *Red Roses*, that the mysterious Figure in the final flood scene in *Purple Dust* "provides a Yeatsian moment," that the stylized dance scenes in *Oak Leaves and Lavender* are "Yeatsian territory," and that *Cock-a-Doodle Dandy* "shows most clearly the impact made by Yeats's dance plays on [O'Casey's] imagination." In an interview with Christopher Murray (*IUR*, 1980), Tomás MacAnna, who produced many of O'Casey's later plays at the Abbey Theatre, makes pertinent remarks on Worth's book. For an extension of Worth's argument, see her "O'Casey, Synge and Yeats" (*IUR*, 1980), which tries unsuccessfully to prove that the dance and dream sequences in *Within the Gates* indicate that O'Casey was "moving . . . close to Yeats's methods."

A number of book-length studies of O'Casey's work have appeared during the past five years. A useful introduction to the range of characters in O'Casey's work, Bernard Benstock's *Paycocks and Others:*

Sean O'Casey's World (1976) classifies the various characters in all the plays according to type and traits, an arduous if often transparent labor of love that the intelligent and well-informed author handles effectively. Since such a study stresses character isolated from dramatic structure, it can provide only a limited view of O'Casey's dramatic genius. For some of the characters, Benstock tries to identify the real-life models. For example, he suggests that Lionel Robartes in *Behind the Green Curtains* is based on Yeats; but the model was actually Lennox Robinson, with the matching initials, since the funeral scenes in the play are based on incidents involving burial services for Robinson.

Ronald Ayling's *Continuity and Innovation in Sean O'Casey's Drama* (Salzburg, 1976), a monograph composed of four previously published articles, is a more impressive work than its pedantic title and limited printing in Austria suggest. One piece, "Expressionism, Epic Theatre, and O'Casey's Further Experiments," presents a careful assessment of the relation between O'Casey's work and innovative techniques in the plays of Strindberg, Toller, O'Neill, and Brecht. In a more formidable article, originally entitled "To Bring Harmony: Recurrent Patterns in O'Casey's Drama" (*Éire*, 1975), Ayling applies a comment O'Casey made about Strindberg to O'Casey himself: "Harmony there was none, and Strindberg used all his energy, all his imaginative thought to bring harmony out of disorder and selfishness." This article illustrates why Ayling is one of the outstanding critics of O'Casey's work.

A variation of Ayling's concept of "harmony out of disorder" appears in B. L. Smith's *O'Casey's Satiric Vision* (1978). Smith stresses the cathartic aspect of O'Casey's satire by showing how the targets of the dramatist's comic wrath must be unmasked in a broad display of fun and games to expose potential evil and restore harmony. Smith places O'Casey in the main tradition of satire: "Like Jonson, Swift, and Twain before him, O'Casey recognized that society's authorities . . . enforce the boundaries that can become repressive or destructive, reject questions that threaten those boundaries, and question those who persist in questioning the unquestionable." Smith rightly distinguishes, however, between the pessimistic vision of the traditional satirist, and O'Casey's affirmative vision, which develops gradually through all his work and reaches full maturity in the symbolic fantasy of his later comedies. O'Casey's "healing satire," Smith argues, is both critical and fun-provoking. Some of Smith's comments about the plays may be predictable or repetitive, and sometimes there is too much plot summary, but on the whole his approach to the satire in O'Casey's work is highly intelligent.

Some recent critical studies are disappointing because they are inept or because they cover familiar ground. John P. Frayne's inadequate and unenlightening *Sean O'Casey* (1976), in the Columbia Essays on Modern Writers series, is a cranky "yes, but" essay in which the author parrots many of the usual canards about O'Casey, such as that he was only successful in his first three "naturalistic" plays and that his work declined thereafter because he left Ireland. Since Frayne mainly limits himself to thumbnail plot summaries of all the plays, he cannot present a fair or penetrating assessment of O'Casey's work and of his significance as a writer. Frayne makes some rewarding comments on *The Plough* because he takes the time to understand the complexity of O'Casey's tragicomic ironies in relation to the Easter Rising.

Two recent books—Doris da Rin's *Sean O'Casey* (1976), in the World Dramatists series, and James R. Scrimgeour's *Sean O'Casey* (1978), in the Twayne series—represent conscientious yet undistinguished efforts. They are both more descriptive than critical, more cautious than courageous in their approach to the complexities of O'Casey's art. Perhaps these introductory surveys will be of some interest to the uninitiated, for whom they are apparently intended. Da Rin's enthusiasm for her material may provoke some readers to go further into O'Casey's work, and Scrimgeour's lively prose style makes his book a readable if not too original document.

Katie Brittain Adams Davis' *Federico García Lorca and Sean O'Casey: Powerful Voices in the Wilderness* (Salzburg, 1978) reads like an inept dissertation. Davis seldom moves beyond simplistic plot summaries; seldom knows what to do with the terms "realism" and "symbolism" with which she belabors both dramatists; seldom realizes that Lorca may have close affinities to Synge, closer than to O'Casey; often misunderstands the historical background of O'Casey's life and plays; often misspells the names of characters and critics; often relies on some secondary sources to such an extent that her own point of view is hidden or nonexistent; and often makes the reader wonder why this book was written.

Ronald Gene Rollins' *Sean O'Casey's Drama: Verisimilitude and Vision* (1979) reproduces some interesting letters O'Casey wrote to Rollins, but they alone are not capable of lifting this little book above its own pretentiousness, which sometimes threatens to place the author on a par with O'Casey as the two men engage in profound and trivial dramatic discourse. Although Rollins can be a fairly bright and enthusiastic critic, he tries to wring too much significance out of the rather obvious dualism of his concepts of verisimilitude (realism) and vision (poetry). The importance of this book lies mainly in O'Casey's expression of his artistic intentions in the letters.

Hugh Hunt's *Sean O'Casey* (1980) is a short introduction to the life and work of the dramatist in the new Gill's Irish Lives series. A borrowing of well-worn or dubious material from many unacknowledged and some unreliable sources, it is a trivial effort without any discernible purpose. On O'Casey's life, Hunt merely repeats the misrepresentations of Butler, Margulies, and Greaves; and on O'Casey's plays he seems satisfied to present behind-the-scenes gossip at the Abbey Theatre and endless cuttings from newspaper reviews. The text is marred by many errors, some of which might be cited here: O'Casey's father was always a tenant, never a "householder"; the date of the Irish premiere of *The Silver Tassie* was 1935, not 1936; the off-Broadway production of *Purple Dust* in 1956 ran not for four months but for just over one year, the longest run ever for an O'Casey play; Horace Reynolds taught at Harvard, not Yale; and some of the titles of O'Casey's works are misspelled or mispunctuated.

The most recent book on O'Casey's plays, Jack Mitchell's *The*

Essential O'Casey (1980), is a Marxist interpretation that, predictably, treats O'Casey narrowly as a political writer. Unpredictably, two of the twelve plays Mitchell considers essential—*Behind the Green Curtains* and *Figuro in the Night*—are minor works; and he ignores the essential late comedy *The Drums of Father Ned*, perhaps because it is on the whole a nonpolitical work. Like Greaves, Mitchell considers "artistic elitism" the cardinal sin, and when he suspects that O'Casey has placed art before politics, Mitchell objects and warns that this "approaches the elitist views of a Yeats"! Ironically, Mitchell does not realize that such censure is actually high praise. Nevertheless, when he allows himself to depart temporarily from his strident political dogma and Marxist slogans, Mitchell can sometimes be an enlightened critic of drama, as he indicates in his analysis of the panoramic structure of *Plough* and in his treatment of the unconventional comic techniques in *Purple Dust* and *Cock*. His comparison of the dramatic methods of O'Casey and Brecht contains many theatrical insights.

In John Orr's *Tragic Drama and Modern Society* (1981), the chapter on O'Casey considers only the first three plays, Orr arguing that O'Casey's career really ended after *Plough* because O'Casey could no longer write tragedy. Orr's rigidly sociopolitical approach makes it difficult for him to accept that many of O'Casey's plays, not only the Dublin trilogy, are tragic *and* comic, or tragicomic in an intentionally ironic counterpoint between the two dramatic modes. Orr's difficulty is particularly evident in his charge that *Juno* fails as a tragedy because the comic "Captain" Boyle upstages the tragic Juno. He insists that the play should have ended with Juno's tragic lament for her dead son. "This is the climactic moment of the play," Orr claims, "and the ensuing scene where Boyle and Joxer enter drunk and incapable, thick-skinned and oblivious, ends up as bathos." Result: "The comic and tragic elements in the play thus fall apart." No time for comedy in O'Casey?

O'Casey's position as a significant modern writer continues to be slighted: most of his books remain out of print. Commenting on what she calls the typical "critical blindness" toward *The Silver Tassie*, Barbara Brothers (in a review of B. L. Smith's *O'Casey's Satiric Vision, SORev*, 1980) calls attention to some unfortunate sins of omission: "neither Bernard Bergonzi in *Heroes' Twilight* nor Paul Fussell in *The Great War and Modern Memory*, two recent important studies of literature of World War I, mention the play though they give space to R. C. Sherriff's *Journey's End*, which both dismiss as 'a glib though theatrical contrivance.' " And John O'Riordan (*SORev*, 1980) points out another regrettable omission: "In *The Spectator* (1-12-'79), some angularities appeared by way of comment on the centenary of the birth of Patrick Pearse in relation to the Easter Rising from the pen of Richard West. In an article, 'The Myth of 1916,' he expatiates on the need to refute Pearse's extreme republican ideals, giving overwhelming commendation to Conor Cruise O'Brien and others for having the temerity, with the situation in the north, to 'debunk' Pearse's ideas, never once, of course, mentioning O'Casey or *The Plough and the Stars*."

O'Casey's centenary celebration in 1980, however, produced a revival of interest in the dramatist's work and a considerable amount of critical and scholarly activity. In Ireland, Micheál Ó hAodha edited a program of talks on Radio Éireann under the auspices of the Thomas Davis lecture series. The talks, which were presented throughout the spring of 1980, have been published as *The O'Casey Enigma* (ed. Micheál Ó hAodha, 1980). The volume contains Tomás MacAnna, "O'Casey's Toy Theatre"; Denis Johnston, "Sean O'Casey in the Twenties"; Cyril Cusack, "O'Casey and the Actor"; James Plunkett, "O'Casey and the Trade Unions"; C. Desmond Greaves, "Sean O'Casey and Socialism"; Hans-Georg Simmgen, "O'Casey Stage Productions in the German Democratic Republic"; Robert Hogan, "O'Casey: The Pose in the Prose"; and Micheál Ó hAodha, "The Enigma of Sean O'Casey."

A collection of papers was read at the O'Casey Centenary Conference, organized by Robert G. Lowery, at Hofstra University on 27–28 March 1980. Maik Hamburger, drama adviser of the Deutsches Theater in East Berlin and a translator of O'Casey's plays into German, in "Music and Song in O'Casey's Plays," draws some effective analogies between O'Casey and Brecht in their use of song and comedy as alienating devices. At the conclusion of *Mother Courage*, Hamburger feels, Brecht cannot avoid the element of pathos as the defeated heroine bravely drags her wagon offstage without any ironic or alienating accompaniment. By contrast, he points out, O'Casey is much more successfully Brechtian in the conclusion of *Juno*, where the tragic pathos of the defeated but brave heroine is broken and the audience comically alienated from that intense feeling by the arrival of the two dissolute clowns, Boyle and Joxer, with their tragicomic bravado and farcical chaos. William Maroldo, in "O'Casey's Tributes to Joyce in the First Irish Book," continues his important work of identifying and analyzing O'Casey's debt to Joyce, revealing the texture and form of the autobiographies. Mary FitzGerald and Carol Kleiman, in separate papers on *The Silver Tassie*, study the background of the rejection of the play and O'Casey's innovative technique, respectively, using some new material in the New York Public Library's Berg Collection. Bernard Benstock, in "Chronology and Narratology in O'Casey's Beginnings," analyzes the structure and symbolic nuances in the long opening sentence of the first volume of the autobiography. Violet O'Valle, in "Melville, O'Casey, and *Cock-a-Doodle Dandy*," draws some striking and hitherto unexplored analogies between O'Casey's symbolic play and Melville's allegorical tale, significantly titled "Cock-a-Doodle Doo." Martin Margulies, in "The Early Life of Sean O'Casey," revisits the material in his ten-year-old book. David Krause, in "The Continuing Self-Portrait," examines the image of the man and writer that emerges in the newly published volume 2 of the *Letters*.

David Krause and Robert G. Lowery have edited a special commemorative volume, *Sean O'Casey Centenary Essays* (1980). Ronald Ayling's article tends to minimize the influence the Abbey Theatre directors had on O'Casey's early career. He feels that in a practical sense O'Casey received more help and encouragement from Lennox Robinson than is realized, that Lady Gregory's exaggerated influence was more emotional than literary, and that in the final accounting "O'Casey soon outgrew the playwriting possibilities of the Abbey directorate." Bernard

Benstock concentrates on biographical and literary parallels between O'Casey and Joyce, stressing passages in the autobiography that maintain O'Casey's unique style while reflecting many verbal and rhythmic Joycean games. Mary FitzGerald uses the unpublished sections of Lady Gregory's journal in the Berg Collection to reveal some new insights into the literary friendship of O'Casey and Lady Gregory, two seemingly contrary yet specially compatible people, and she traces the unfortunate timing of events that led up to the Abbey's rejection of *The Tassie*. This paper strongly modifies Ayling's view of Lady Gregory's influence on O'Casey. David Krause analyzes the inevitable conflict that arose between O'Casey and Yeats and examines the pattern of their gradual reconciliation, with an assessment of their theories of art and the creative affinities that ironically linked such dissimilar writers. Robert G. Lowery makes an ambitious attempt to study the dramatist as a Marxist artist whose works are compatible with the aesthetic theories of Marx and Lenin. William Maroldo illustrates that the young O'Casey was emotionally closer to the Roman Catholicism of his comrades than he was to the Protestantism of the Church of Ireland, in which faith he was brought up. Concentrating on the last three chapters of *Pictures in the Hallway*, Maroldo reveals a rich texture of religious symbolism with allusions to a Dantean hell in Dublin and some Miltonic echoes of pandemonium. Alan Simpson presents an "unholy trinity" composed of Synge, O'Casey, and Behan, and as a theater director he is at his best when discussing the stage performance of their plays. He is most convincing in his comments on Behan, less so on Synge and O'Casey; he is least interesting when he imitates Greaves and talks about O'Casey's "guilt complex" over not having been "out" in 1916. Stanley Weintraub illustrates the Shavian affinities in O'Casey's plays, going beyond the obvious connections between *Purple Dust* and *John Bull's Other Island* to suggest that *Juno* is O'Casey's version of *Heartbreak House* and that *The Plough* has ironic associations with *Major Barbara*.

The indefatigable Lowery has also edited a collection of essays on the autobiography, *Sean O'Casey's Autobiographies: Reflections upon the Mirror* (1981). Ronald Ayling uses O'Casey's holograph exercise books, now in the Berg Collection, to trace the origin and evolution of the autobiography and to justify the strategic shift from the first-person to a third-person narration. Bernard Benstock treats the autobiography as a mock epic, studies many of the comic catalogs of names and places, and defends and explicates O'Casey's use of puns and wordplay, with effective connections to Joyce. Deirdre Henchy surveys conditions in Dublin during the first thirty years of O'Casey's life. David Krause defends the use of fictional techniques in a life story and analyzes some passages to show how verbal and visual imagery are fused in O'Casey's creative imagination. Robert G. Lowery concentrates on the years 1900 to 1912, when O'Casey rejected his early nationalist sympathies and, under the influence of John Ruskin, Bernard Shaw, and Jim Larkin, began to develop his life-long commitment to socialism. William Maroldo continues his valuable explication of the autobiography by looking at some key passages in the first four volumes, the "Irish Books," and identifying allusions to the work of Homer, Vergil, Dante,

Milton, Keats, Darwin, and Verdi. E. H. Mikhail uses passages from the autobiography and the *Letters* to illustrate the emotional and literary terms of the O'Casey-Shaw affinities. Carmela Moya reveals the method O'Casey used to connect his personal history with the history of Ireland, and she points out how the ordinary daily events of his childhood assume an epic and universal significance. Moya also stresses the function of Celtic myth and legend as a way of broadening the historical and political implications of O'Casey's life story. Micheál Ó Maolain's essay, originally written in Irish and published in *Feasta* (Beltaine, 1955), now translated into English by Maureen Murphy, presents a first-hand view of the young O'Casey by his Aran Island friend, with whom he shared a room in a Mountjoy Square tenement during the Black-and-Tan war in 1920. Ó Maolain was probably one of many models for Seumas Shields in *The Gunman*. Raymond J. Porter examines the writings of O'Casey and Pearse to discover the two men's attitudes toward literature and nationalism during the years that led to the Easter Rising.

The centenary saw several revivals of O'Casey's plays throughout the world, but perhaps no production had a greater impact than the Royal Shakespeare Company's staging of *Juno and the Paycock* at the Aldwych Theatre on 9 September 1980. Seldom had the London critics reviewed an O'Casey play with such universal and eloquent praise. The rave notices were reprinted in the *Irish Times* (10 Sept. 1980).

There has been a steady interest in O'Casey's work in the German theater. Regina Heidenreich-Krawschak, in "Critical Reception of Sean O'Casey in Berlin since 1953" (*SORev,* 1978), comments on the critical responses to twenty-four productions of O'Casey's plays performed in German translation in West and East Berlin from 1953 to 1977. The most successful presentation in East Berlin was the Berliner Ensemble's 1966 staging of *Purple Dust*, a popular work that has since remained in the company's regular repertory. The most successful play in West Berlin, surprisingly, was Wilfried Minks's production of *The Bishop's Bonfire* in 1972 at the Schlosspark-Theater. Mixed or controversial receptions have greeted performances of *Gunman, Juno, Tassie, Red Roses,* and *Cock* in both Berlins, though a production using a new translation of *Juno* by M. Hamburger and A. Dresen was well received in East Berlin in 1972. The one-act plays have also been favorably received. Heidenreich-Krawschak makes the following significant distinction between the productions in the two Berlins: "Whereas, in East Berlin, Brecht and Gorki very often stand as godfathers to O'Casey's plays, productions in West Berlin suffer from the influence of Hauptman." The point about these O'Casey godfathers in Germany is that the emphasis of his work is probably shifted into two directions that distort his dramatic art. The Hauptman influence in West Berlin is excessively naturalistic and leads to a sociological bias; the Brecht and Gorki influence in East Berlin is excessively ideological and leads to a political bias.

This emphasis on the political aspects of O'Casey's art is also evident in *Gulliver 7* (1980), a bilingual West German literary magazine that honored the centenary by devoting a special issue to articles on O'Casey's work. Thomas Metscher claims that "the national literature of modern Ireland cannot be divorced from the political and ideological context of the Irish struggle for independence." As a Marxist critic, Metscher approaches O'Casey's plays in the context of the "class struggle," which is not precisely what the bourgeois Easter Rising was all about. Manfred Pauli comments on the notable productions of the plays in East Germany. Rüdiger Hillgärtner sets out to refute C. Desmond Greaves's charges in *Sean O'Casey: Politics and Art* that O'Casey had "misrepresented" and "corrected" his life story in the autobiography. In his refutation, however, Hillgärtner unknowingly adopts some of the Greaves misrepresentations. For example, Hillgärtner mistakenly assumes that O'Casey's father had owned and lost the house on Upper Dorset Street in which he was a tenant; he mistakenly assumes that O'Casey had, like his father, worked as a clerk; he mistakenly assumes O'Casey suffered from a "guilt complex" because of 1916 and practically paraphrases Greaves when he writes: "Then there is the Easter Rising, in which he took no part, that O'Casey could understand neither in 1916 nor later on in its complicated national and international context." In the same issue of *Gulliver 7*, Jack Lindsay, who shares the Marxist sympathies of Greaves, writes a review of the Greaves book in which he praises the author's interpretation of O'Casey's politics but questions his evaluation of the plays. Jack Mitchell's article, if one makes reasonable allowances for his sometimes rigidly Marxist bias, quarrels with three German critics who dismissed O'Casey's five one-act plays: they are "totally at variance with the rest of his dramatic work" (Kurt Wittig, 1937); "O'Casey never took much trouble with the form of the one-acter" (Klaus Völker, 1968); "It is hardly necessary to point out that O'Casey's farces were written without any serious intent" (Heinz Kosok, 1972). Mitchell counters with some illuminating comments on *A Pound on Demand*, for example, in which he reveals the comic humanity of O'Casey's two early Beckett-like tramps, Sammy and Jerry. To refute Kosok's charge that O'Casey had no "serious intent" in his one-act plays, however, Mitchell replaces the comic seriousness with a political seriousness that distorts O'Casey's dramatic aim. The whole subject of the "serious" function of the comedy in all O'Casey's plays, to say nothing of the structure of the comedy, demands further critical investigation. David Krause has begun some of this work in *The Profane Book of Irish Comedy* (1982).

The special issue of *Gulliver 7* should provoke some challenging arguments about O'Casey's intentions and achievements. Readers interested in further investigating German criticism on O'Casey's work should see Kurt Wittig, *Sean O'Casey als Dramatiker: Ein Beitrag zum Nachkriegsdrama Irlands* (Leipzig, 1937); Kaspar Spinner, *Die alte Dame sagt: Nein! Drei irische Dramatiker: Lennox Robinson, Sean O'Casey, Denis Johnston* (Berne, 1961); Thomas Metscher, *Sean O'Caseys dramatischer Stil* (Braunschweig, 1967); Heinz Kosok, *Sean O'Casey: Das dramatische Werk* (Berlin, 1972); Werner Besier, *Der junge Sean O'Casey: Eine Studie zum Verhältnis von Kunst und Gesellschaft* (Berne, 1974); Manfred Pauli, *Sean O'Casey: Drama, Poesie, Wirklichkeit* (Berlin, 1977); Burchard Winkler, *Wirkungstrategische Verwendung popularliterarischer Elemente in Sean O'Caseys dramatischem Werk unter besonderer Berücksichtigung des Melodramas*

(Göppingen, 1977); Peter Stapelberg, *Sean O'Casey und das deutsch-sprachige Theater (1948-1974)* (Frankfurt, 1979); Jochen Achilles, *Drama als problematische Form: Der Wandel zu nichtrealistischer Gestaltungsweise im Werk Sean O'Caseys* (Frankfurt, 1979).

Interest in O'Casey's work has grown rapidly in France in recent years, partly because of the efforts of Patrick Rafroidi, Raymonde Popot, and William Parker, who have edited a series of volumes on Irish literature at the Université de Lille. In their *France-Ireland: Literary Relations* (Paris, 1974), E. J. Dumay reports that while French critics and audiences have been aware of O'Casey's plays since the 1926-27 winter season, when *Juno* was performed in Paris in English, the "formidable public recognition of O'Casey's prestige as a dramatist" in France began in 1961 "with Jean Vilar's magnificent production of *Red Roses for Me* at the Théâtre National Populaire." From that time up to the early 1970s, at least thirteen different O'Casey plays have been staged in Paris or the provinces. He stands "second only to Brecht," Dumay says, "with whom he has sometimes been wrongly compared." This view should be contrasted with the tendency in East Berlin to equate O'Casey with Brecht. In France the only major work by O'Casey that remains unknown and unpublished in a French translation is the autobiography. For the translation and criticism of O'Casey's work in other languages, see the Ayling-Durkan *Sean O'Casey: A Bibliography* (1978), Mikhail's *A Bibliography of Modern Irish Drama, 1899-1970* (1972), and his subsequent annual bibliographies in the *Sean O'Casey Review*.

Rafroidi, Popot, and Parker also edited *Aspects of the Irish Theatre* (Paris, 1972), in which a number of articles deal with O'Casey's work. Rafroidi presents a brief and generalized discussion of theater and nationalism in Ireland. He draws some vague comparisons between several plays by O'Casey and Denis Johnston—*The Plough and the Stars* and *The Scythe and the Sunset*, *Juno and the Paycock* and *The Moon in the Yellow River*—that deal ironically with the Easter Rising and the civil war period. Since Rafroidi provides no evidence from the plays and no critical analysis, one must question his impressionistic and unsubstantiated conclusion: "Johnston's is a more intellectual attitude, a lighter and yet deadlier irony which touches on the absurdity of any struggle and perhaps any action whatsoever."

Also in *Aspects of the Irish Theatre*, Jeanne Lezon traces the connections between the historical events and the dramatic action in *The Plough* to establish the working-class attitude toward the Easter Rising. Lezon's main point is that O'Casey was trying to write not an objective history of the Rising but rather a tenement dweller's view of the event. She illustrates Pearse's view of the tenement dwellers to show how he failed to understand their desperate economic and social needs; and she reminds us that when the looting broke out during the Rising, as we see it in act 3 of *The Plough*, Pearse had issued a manifesto in which he cruelly condemned the looters as "the hangers-on of the British Army." Finally, Lezon emphasizes what too many patriotic defenders of the Rising miss—the ironic legacy of 1916 for the Irish working class: "It is certain that, in O'Casey's opinion, the social results of the Rising and subsequent 'troubles' did not amount to much more than the advent of 'the terrible beauty of the tall-hat,' that of a bourgeois class which took little heed of the plight of the poor."

The two other articles in *Aspects of the Irish Theatre* are disappointing. Bernard Mathelin's obvious, generalized presentation—a series of plot summaries of O'Casey plays that deal with war—lacks a critical point of view. Bernard Leroy's "Two Committed Playwrights: Wesker and O'Casey" is more ambitious, but it inflates Wesker's achievements and deflates O'Casey's. Leroy refers to some superficial similarities of theme and characterization in their plays and in their working-class and socialist sympathies; nevertheless, he fails to account for the comic energy and intensity of language, the sharp irony and symbolic vision, and the innovative transfigurations of reality that set O'Casey apart from the naturalistic limitations of Wesker.

In O'Casey's native country the *Irish University Review* published a special 1980 issue in honor of the centenary, *Sean O'Casey: Roots and Branches*. Included in this issue is an important dialogue between Christopher Murray, who edited the issue, and Tomás MacAnna, the most successful director of O'Casey's later plays. On the basis of his experience directing the Abbey productions of *Red Roses for Me* (1967), *Purple Dust* (1975), *Cock-a-Doodle Dandy* (1977), and *The Star Turns Red* (1978), MacAnna believes that theatrically O'Casey's comedy and farce are more vital than his "message"—indeed, the comedy *is* the message, "a rich vein of O'Casey gold." MacAnna considers that O'Casey's concept of "total theatre," a completely different drama from Yeats's "secret theatre," is based on his daring and even hilariously outrageous use of comedy and fantasy, the multiple elements of farce, satire, allegory, poetry, and music-hall antics. MacAnna is convinced that his comic-epic staging of *Purple Dust* captured these qualities most effectively. Recognizing that *Cock-a-Doodle Dandy* is in many ways a darker comedy than *Purple Dust*, MacAnna nevertheless insists it would be a mistake to produce it "in a deadly serious manner." Since he believes O'Casey was writing about a repressed Ireland of the 1940s that was no longer valid for present-day Ireland, MacAnna felt he had to maintain the historical gap by minimizing the priest's apparent tyranny and by concentrating on the positive aspects of the Cock's wild tricks and comic joy. Possibly this accommodation to past and present history was MacAnna's concession to an Irish audience with hypersensitive religious beliefs. Apparently MacAnna felt he was confronted by a similar challenge in his production of *The Star Turns Red*, where he softened the proletarian "message" and heightened the theatrical spectacle with considerable success. As a practical and imaginative man of the theater, MacAnna seems to be saying that all O'Casey's later plays, despite their serious and satiric themes, are music-hall-inspired comic fantasies that must not be produced as "thesis" drama.

In the same special issue as the MacAnna interview, Micheál Ó hAodha gives an account of his relationship with O'Casey during the years when Radio Éireann dramatized some of the plays for Irish audiences. He also mentions a number of informal talks O'Casey recorded in 1955 to accompany a festival of O'Casey plays, and it is to be hoped that they will one day be published. Ó hAodha lists all the productions of

O'Casey's works presented on Radio Telefis Éireann radio from 1943 to 1979 and on RTE television from 1962 to 1977, with the names of the producers (directors) and casts. (Comments on the remaining pieces in the O'Casey issue of *IUR* appear elsewhere in this essay.)

Another Irish critic, this time from Northern Ireland, to respond to O'Casey's work is Conor O'Malley (*SORev*, 1980), who reviews the Lyric Theatre's productions of O'Casey's plays. Unlike the Abbey Theatre in Dublin, O'Malley points out, the Lyric in Belfast "was not contained by a narrow-minded, unsophisticated public which demanded a nationalistic rather than an artistic perspective." He also argues that since the Lyric's approach to a "poetic" theater was not limited to the presentation of verse drama, it could produce the plays of O'Casey as well as of Yeats, the company's two major dramatists, with contrasting yet parallel concepts of poetic vision.

In "A Symposium: The Staging of Sean O'Casey's Plays" (*SORev*, 1979), Robert G. Lowery presents the responses of theater artists, critics, and observers from many countries who were invited to comment on their experiences producing the plays: Heinz Moog, the Austrian actor who played "Captain" Boyle in *Juno*; Alan Simpson, the Irish director of Beckett and Behan plays; Sylvia O'Brien, the Irish actress who played in a number of O'Casey's works and was the mother in the successful New York production of Hugh Leonard's *Da*; Vincent Dowling, the Abbey Theatre actor-director now working in America; Ingeborg Pietzsche, the drama critic for *Theater der Zeit* in East Berlin; Philip Burton, the American director who staged *Cock* in New York; and Emile Jean Dumay, the advisor to a number of French productions of O'Casey's plays. Many important insights emerge, but perhaps Burton's directorial approach to *Cock*, especially his comment on how the actors should interpret their roles, should be singled out. Like MacAnna, Burton insists the play must be performed as "a pondeorus moral tract" but rather in O'Casey's intended "vividly comic light" with "a Dickensian profusion of wonderful characters, who seem larger than life because they are bursting at the seams with it." The key to that Dickensian touch, according to Burton, lies in the paradoxical way O'Casey mixes positive and negative traits in his comic characters.

4. General Criticism

Thomas Kilroy's introduction to the collection of essays he edited, *Sean O'Casey* (1975), has posed critical problems about O'Casey's achievements and shortcomings in the theater that still have to be resolved. He raises the issue of O'Casey's stylized language, pointing out examples of the "artificial" and excessively "literary" dialogue in *The Silver Tassie* and *Red Roses for Me*. The defense that O'Casey's dialogue is always "artificial" in that it is not meant to be "realistic" conversation does not entirely come to terms with Kilroy's objections, especially the one about "literary" or purple prose. Kilroy also questions O'Casey's use of "pervasive symbolism" because he feels the symbols "do not ex-

tend the meaning of the scene in any complex way." On this point, however, on the deep and extended symbolic values that reverberate in a play
like *The Tassie*, for example, Kilroy and those who share his view might
begin by reading Jacqueline Doyle's penetrating article on the complex
religious symbolism in the play. Her original seminar paper, referred to
in the 1976 review of research, has now been published (*MD*, 1978).

In many instances Kilroy recognizes O'Casey's power and courage
as a dramatic artist. Nevertheless, he makes two comparisons—between
O'Casey and Dickens and between O'Casey and O'Neill—calculated to
denigrate O'Casey. Kilroy sees any comparison of O'Casey and Dickens
as "superficial" in that it "takes no account of the differences between
the two modes of fictional narrative, one proper to the novel and the
other to drama." But the comparison is more relevant than Kilroy
realizes, as we can see if we look at the fictional and dramatic techniques
O'Casey developed in his autobiography, especially the first two volumes
where his rendering of the tragicomic and epic experiences of alienated
childhood contains remarkable parallels to the frustrated world of the
child in Dickens. And while we wait for some alert critic to pick up these
and many other parallels in the plays, we can look at Christopher Murray's "A Dickens Parallel" (*SORev*, 1980), which explores striking
similarities between "Captain" Boyle and Captain Cuttle in *Dombey
and Son*, two richly drawn clowns, who resort to curiously similar mock-
heroic posturing and pompously inflated comic language. O'Casey's link
to Dickens is important and calls for further investigation.

When he moves on to O'Casey and O'Neill, the pedantic Kilroy
damns them both for experimenting with new dramatic forms and for
abandoning naturalistic drama. He finds

> . . . a more profitable comparison to be made between O'Casey
> and O'Neill. Both had early successes and later neglect, and this
> was related to the efforts of both playwrights to impose form that
> would be acceptable in the modern theatre on material that was
> traditional and retrospective. Their careers in the theatre came to
> an end when human identity was being redefined in drama in terms
> that excluded . . . the idea of consecutiveness implied by
> tradition. . . . The virtues of both playwrights are histrionic, not
> literary. Both dramatized the pressures of modernity upon the units
> of traditional domesticity, upon the young imprisoned within hide-
> bound systems of an older generation or of older gods; but despite
> their rage and passion, each is, at heart, too traditional to proceed
> beyond the crisis of the family or to do more than memorably catch
> the point of transition. Both seek, too, to renew the experience of
> classical or Shakespearean tragedy in a modern setting. Both re-
> spond, at times overenthusiastically, to contemporary experi-
> mentation, as if the devices exist simply as an available property
> and not as (what they are) evidence of a radical change in our view
> of man and his moral place in the world. Despite the expressionism,
> the symbolism, the stylization, neither is at all times at ease with the
> stage-figure of nonnaturalistic drama, divested of a social reality.

Yet the wide range of their plays indicates that both dramatists show their creative strength of renewal because they can be, in different works and even in the same works, traditional and innovative, classical and modern, realistic and expressionistic, histrionic and literary. In many of their plays O'Neill and O'Casey move beyond "the crisis of the family." And O'Casey and O'Neill may also be closer to the "redefined" and dissociated drama of Beckett than Kilroy realizes—O'Casey in most of his one-act plays and in his tragicomedies and comic fantasies whenever his paycocks and tramps enact their farcial duets of "chassis"; O'Neill in most of his one-act sea plays and certainly in *Iceman*, where his down-and-outs seem to anticipate Gogo and Didi. Then Kilroy ignores the occasions when O'Neill and O'Casey are not trying to do the same thing at all, when, for example, O'Neill consciously tries to recapture the form of classical tragedy and O'Casey deliberately avoids that genre to pursue the newer form of tragicomedy. Perhaps Kilroy has set up some straw men that must be demolished before we can see O'Neill or O'Casey in the round and on their own individual terms, with their valid strengths and weaknesses in the theater.

For a start toward that demolition process we might turn to John Arden's fascinating "Ecco Hobo Sapiens: O'Casey's Theatre" (in *Sean O'Casey*, ed. Kilroy), which clears the ground by connecting some traditional and modern structures of historical drama in O'Casey's plays. Rejecting the commonly held belief that O'Casey, beginning with *The Silver Tassie*, was directly influenced by the nonrealistic techniques of German expressionism, Arden insists that "there is a much older and more immediate source of [O'Casey's techniques] in the old British theatrical tradition," which is "a combination of medieval morality-play, Shakespeare, Bunyan, and Victorian popular melodrama." Arden thus sees O'Casey's loosely structured modern chronicle plays, his political and comic-ironic motifs, as outgrowths of morality plays like Lindsay's *Three Estates*, Shakespeare's history plays, and Boucicault's melodramatic extravaganzas. But the main surprise and hitherto ignored element in Arden's article is his stress on Bunyan's *Pilgrim's Progress* as an indirect yet potent influence on O'Casey. One would like to see Arden's new and plausible argument developed much further, with more concrete evidence of the structural and thematic links between Bunyan and O'Casey and between Bunyan and Ireland. The argument may even be made with stronger evidence in the early volumes of the autobiography, where there could be a quest-motif for the allegorical Casside as Christian. There is reason to wonder if those religious and historical structures and resonances were functioning ironically and satirically in Arden's own work, particularly in a savagely antiwar play like *Serjeant Musgrave's Dance*, a work that the older O'Casey greatly admired. Arden also recognizes the Gaelic influences on O'Casey's work. He points to the young O'Casey's keen interest in the Gaelic revival movement and suggests that his plays "also reflect the prevailing divine machinery of the pre-Christian Gaelic legends." Some work has already been done on the influence of the Celtic and Christian motifs in the Ossianic dialogues on O'Casey's tragicomic writing, and it is also likely that the tradition of the Gaelic genre of the *aisling*, or dream vision, influenced the visionary structures of some later plays. Finally, since Arden himself is, as O'Casey was, a nondoctrinaire Marxist as well as an innovative and eclectic playwright, he argues that O'Casey's symbolic and socialist theater "would not fit into any recognizable Marxist-bureaucratic pigeon-hole." This declaration of O'Casey's political independence is no doubt intended to disturb some Marxist critics. On another controversial issue, Arden considers O'Casey's paradoxical support of the discredited Stalin an inseparable part of his loyalty to the original principles of the Russian Revolution and its great idealism.

As if to prove that O'Casey's instinct for dramatic rituals of joy is more important than his political beliefs, Emile Jean Dumay (*SORev*, 1975) calls attention to the dramatized rituals of celebration around which much of the action in O'Casey's plays is organized. This enlightened and creative piece establishes an effective overview of O'Casey's festive vision, arguing that "If there is one theme that is resorted to or illustrated with unflinching steadiness in Sean O'Casey's plays, it is that of merry-making and celebration as a pervasive sign of free and creative life." Dumay provides copious and convincing evidence from just about all the plays to support his claim, and he extends his approach by identifying "counter-festivals" that appear in some of the early, middle, and later plays "like ridiculous, disturbing or monstrous reversals, a hollow mould of the world, a negative picture big with death, sadness or nonsense." Dumay cites as an example the "excessive rhetoric in the second act [of *The Plough and the Stars*], the call to blood in Pearse's speech and the flag dragged into the pub by men wearing silly uniforms." Dumay then mentions some of the "counterfeit festivals," such as "the last ball of the middle classes in *The Star Turns Red* " and "the march-procession-masquerade of the Dublin intelligentsia together with the Children of Mary, bishops, and some mistaken workers, decked with brightly-coloured sashes and rosettes—a fair lot of demonstrators in *Behind the Green Curtains*"; these activities are in contrast to the celebrations and transfigurations in *The Tassie* and *Red Roses*; the apocalyptic rituals in *Purple Dust* and *Cock*; and the Celtic Tostal in *The Drums of Father Ned*, "a gay, untrammelled festival, full of hope and creative power."

Naomi Pasachoff (*Éire*, 1977), whose attempt to deal with O'Casey's "festive" elements is not so enlightened as Dumay's, concentrates on O'Casey's "most exuberant works"—*Within the Gates, Purple Dust*, and *Cock-a-Doodle Dandy*—because they best illustrate "his affirmation of life." This conventional approach to some unconventional plays contains few surprises, except perhaps for some potentially interesting analogues to Blake's cosmology that Pasachoff finds in *Purple Dust* and *Cock*. Much remains to be done with the sources and techniques of the apocalyptic motifs in all the later comedies.

Carol Kleiman's "*The Silver Tassie* and Others: A Revaluation in the Light of the Absurd" (*SORev*, 1978) provides some answers to the problems raised by Thomas Kilroy's charge that O'Casey's theater is too traditional in spite of its experimental adventures. Kleiman offers copious examples of innovative techniques, mainly from *The Tassie* and *Red Roses*, to show that O'Casey could be as antitraditional and ironically symbolic in his stagecraft as any of the modern avant-garde playwrights. Nevertheless, a difficulty in terminology emerges when she tries to prove that O'Casey was an "Absurdist" and "Artaudian" before these terms became popular, and she acknowledges that O'Casey himself, in the last essay he wrote, "The Bald Primaqueera," adamantly rejected the ideas and techniques of the theater of the absurd. Disagreeing with an author's conception of his own work is certainly permissible, and it can even lead to new insights. Such is not the case here, however, when Kleiman tells us, for instance, that the final scene in *Juno* indicates that O'Casey "understood instinctively the Artaudian concept of a 'theatre of cruelty' "; that Bessie's cry of "Choke th' chicken" in *The Plough* is an "absurd image"; that the name "Sister Peter Alcantara" repeated five times in *The Tassie* "is the kind of repetition that frequently occurs in the dialogue of Absurd plays"; that the "structural image" of the "man in the wheelchair" in *The Tassie* reveals "O'Casey's relation to the Theatre of the Absurd"; and that the "severed head of Dunn-Bo" in *Red Roses* suggests the "severed" heads of Nagg and Nell in *Endgame*. Trying to force O'Casey into the fashionable theater of absurdity or cruelty by wrenching episodes out of their ironic, satiric, or symbolic contexts, where they are vivid reflections of particular themes, illuminates neither the episodes nor the plays. On the other hand, there are some significant links between the farcical and alienated tramps of O'Casey and Beckett, as the younger Beckett himself unwittingly anticipated in his 1934 review of O'Casey's *Windfalls,* but Kleiman is too busy cataloging dubious "absurdities" to develop this connection. Perhaps she has been too strongly influenced by Robert P. Murphy's "Sean O'Casey and 'The Bald Primaqueera' " (*JJQ,* 1970), a debt she acknowledges. She even quotes with approval Murphy's unconvincing attempt to make O'Casey an absurdist by insisting on a similarity of symbolism in *Cock* and *Rhinoceros*: "Is the rooster really so different from Ionesco's rhinoceroses (that the playwright stipulates are to have a certain kind of savage beauty) except that the one is a symbol of the expansion and liberation of man's humanity while the others represent a loss of humanity?" Yes, totally different, not only in the obvious contrast between the figure and function of a rooster and a rhino, but also in that overriding "except," which cannot in any way unite the symbol of liberation and life with the symbol of loss and death. For all her overstatements, Kleiman indicates that she does understand some of the qualities that separate O'Casey from the theater of absurdity and cruelty, and from expressionism as well: "What distinguishes O'Casey's vision from that of either the Expressionists or the Absurdists is this unerring ability to harmonize discords, to integrate successfully both thematically and in terms of stagecraft, all the wildly disintegrating elements of the world in which we live." Kleiman's *Sean O'Casey's Bridge of Vision* is scheduled for publication in 1982.

David Brunet (*SORev,* 1979) illustrates how Boucicault's use of visual spectacle and melodrama directly influenced O'Casey, who adapted these external techniques to make them "contribute to ironic and metaphoric resonances" in his plays rather than allow them to become part of a gratuitous theatrical spectacle. Comparing the effects of these techniques in Boucicault's *The Poor of New York,* Racine's *Phèdre,* and O'Casey's *Gunman, Plough, Tassie,* and *Red Roses,* Brunet concludes that O'Casey's "method of representing spectacular action" is different from the others' and that his plays "resemble melodrama in making the sensational action both visible and audible; but he focusses simultaneously upon the response (or non-response) of the characters to the event."

Herbert Goldstone (*SORev,* 1974) disagrees with critics who say that O'Casey moved suddenly into German expressionism in act 2 of *The Tassie,* for he insists that the whole play is constructed with nonrealistic elements. This point of view is not original, and Goldstone's approach to it is too general. Goldstone also makes several obvious comparisons between *The Harvest Festival* and *Red Roses,* saying nothing concrete or useful. His generalizations about O'Casey's politics are confusing, and his implication that the early *Harvest Festival* is a fervent communist play is neither supported nor illustrated.

Little has been written about O'Casey's short stories, and Susan Allison McCormack's "The Moral Impulse in Sean O'Casey's Fiction" (*SORev,* 1978) adds nothing to our understanding of them. McCormack approaches the stories in such a mechanical and rigidly utilitarian way that they are all reduced to trite sociopolitical sermons: "His fiction," we are told, "exhibits the Marxist-Leninist belief that art must serve a social function, which is to bring about the inevitable transformation of society and man." No one reading the McCormack article would realize that some of the stories are allegorical or visionary, some of them reveal the frustration and alienation of working-class people, some of them strike the lyrical and tragic mood of Joycean paralysis that characterizes *Dubliners*; and, contrary to what McCormack says, none of the stories are programmed for a communist transformation or indeed for any didactic purpose.

Christopher Gillie, in *Movements in English Literature, 1900–1940* (1975), offers some limited but damning comments on what he calls the failure of O'Casey's language in tragic scenes. Surprisingly, he singles out Juno Boyle's powerful lament for her dead son as a prime example of this failure, comparing it unfavorably with Maurya's poetic lament for her drowned men in Synge's *Riders to the Sea*: "The difference is between emotion half baffled by language and emotion elucidated by language." If anyone is baffled here it must be the reader of this vague and unjustified comparison.

In "Sean O'Casey," *Dictionary of Irish Literature* (ed. Robert Hogan, 1979), Hogan concentrates on what seem to be equal measures of strength and weakness in an attempt to say something definitive about everything O'Casey wrote. The result is a questionable and somewhat glib balancing act that keeps breaking down. O'Casey emerges as an awkward and constantly flawed genius who, even in his best works, was never in full control of his craft. Even in the general account of O'Casey's reputation today and the present state of O'Casey scholarship, Hogan invokes his too facile plus-and-minus prognosis calling the current strong interest in O'Casey "probably an overreaction to the years in which he was neglected."

Elizabeth Hale Winkler's "The Clown and Satire: Sean O'Casey," in her *The Clown in Modern Anglo-Irish Drama* (1977), presents a somewhat simplistic approach to the comic characters in the plays. The clowns in O'Casey's work, Winkler believes, possess negative traits that must be satirized for the good of society. This fairly conventional and predictable view leaves out much of O'Casey's comedy. Although Winkler does not seem to realize it, she is often concerned not so much with clowns as with the play's comic villains, or *alazons*, the rigid characters O'Casey laughs at because they are guilty of what Bergson called automatism. Sometimes she is tempted to venture into the world of the genuine clowns that we laugh with as well as at, like Seumas Shields and Fluther Good, who in spite of their folly also represent what she rightly calls "common sense or folk wisdom"; but she quickly adds that "this function is not the most important in O'Casey." What is most important to Winkler, then, is "the clown as a butt, as object of mockery, due to his socially negative characteristics." This means that in *Purple Dust,* for example, she ignores the wise and eccentric peasant clowns and identifies the satirized or negative Stoke and Poges as the typical O'Casey clowns, although they are clearly the comic villains of the piece; and in *Red Roses* she does the same thing with the fanatical Foster and Dowzard, two minor *alazons,* again ignoring the more significant and flexible clowns led by Brennan. Furthermore, since the vividly comic women in O'Casey's plays are not treated as negative butts, Winkler ignores them too, although they present a variety of rich clowns. The reader must be on guard to look beyond Winkler to the many clownish characters O'Casey treats with his characteristically sly double view, satirically *and* sympathetically. In "The Clown in O'Casey's Drama" (*IUR,* 1980), Winkler again overemphasizes the negative or satiric aspects of clowning. The real clowns elude her.

In "O'Casey, Influence and Impact" (*IUR,* 1980) Robert Hogan justifies his opening warning that "the premises of this article are somewhat dubious." He refers to some superficial "resemblances" between O'Casey's first three plays and some third-rate Dublin slum plays by other writers and concludes that the "question of significant influence is just beside the point," a judgment that seems obvious from the start. O'Casey's "most literary influences seem to me his most pernicious," Hogan says, and for this unhappy association he singles out "the incongruous pair of George Jean Nathan and James Joyce." Describing *The Flying Wasp* as "a most Nathanish book," he does not distinguish between possible Nathan echoes, which are not identified, and O'Casey's own authentic critical voice, which is not illustrated. Hogan's two quick paragraphs on O'Casey-Joyce parallels are inadequate as well as unconvincing. Instead of providing concrete examples and a critical point of view, he simply damns both writers for playing with puns.

Philip Edwards' *Threshold of a Nation: A Study of English and Irish Drama* (1979) is a frustrating book, and Edwards provides the stick with which we must beat him for his misplaced labor. He tells us in his preface, "The balance between the English section (six essays, some of them very long) and the Irish section (three) looks like English arrogance." It does. The material on English drama runs to 170 pages, the Irish to 53 pages, and Edwards says, "I hope that as a result my treatment of the corpus of twentieth-century Irish drama does not seem in its brevity altogether too tangential." It does. Of the three short chapters on the "corpus" of Irish drama, one is on Yeats without any treatment of his plays; one is on George Moore, who didn't write many plays; and the final chapter, all of twelve pages, makes cursory remarks that praise several plays by O'Casey, Johnston, and Behan. So much for Irish drama. Readers interested in the subject can ignore this book.

5. Criticism of Specific Works

THE HARVEST FESTIVAL

Ronald Ayling *(IUR,* 1980) presents a definitive assessment of *The Harvest Festival,* the 1979 edition of which was briefly discussed on page 217. The action of the play deals with the struggle for improved conditions for the working people, in a religious as well as a political context. O'Casey was to return to this subject in many subsequent plays, and Ayling finds significant affinities not only to *Red Roses* but also to *Gunman, Juno, Within the Gates,* and *The Star Turns Red.* The play's powerful indictment of the Anglo-Irish Ascendancy and its servile parishioners shows that the early O'Casey could be as harsh a judge of the hypocritical and unchristian practices of Irish Protestantism as he later was of Irish Catholicism. Ayling points out that O'Casey often oversimplifies his theme by using ideological speeches or by exaggerating the traits of his heroes and villains. Ayling also believes that the language of the play is often artificial and editorialized. In spite of these flaws, Ayling says, the play also exhibits significant signs, in some crude yet effective episodes, of what was to become O'Casey's characteristic use of comedy and compassion in a tragic situation. We see these brief but brilliant flashes in the treatment of Tom Nimmo, an earthy Catholic laborer whose frailties and ironic attitudes suggest Seumas Shields in *Gunman,* and in the martyred hero's mother, Mrs. Rocliffe, a complex woman whose humanizing contradictions prefigure Juno Boyle.

In his introduction to the new edition of *The Harvest Festival,* John O'Riordan sees definite traces of the tram conductor, O'Casey's comic friend in the autobiography, in Tom Nimmo "with his humorous catchphrases and asides, such as, 'Protestants is curious animals.' " O'Riordan points out a number of links to *Red Roses;* he feels that Williamson, the churchwarden, has overtones of Grigson in *Gunman;* and he says that the conflicts that take place between the rector and his select vestry "parallel those described by O'Casey in the pages of his autobiography *Pictures in the Hallway,* in the chapter 'The Sword of Light.' " It is likely that many more parallels will be discovered in future studies.

JUNO AND THE PAYCOCK

Errol Durbach, in "Peacocks and Mothers: Theme and Dramatic Metaphor in O'Casey's *Juno and the Paycock*" (*MD*, 1972), rejects the common notion that the dramatist is a realist in *Juno* and claims that O'Casey's so-called realism resembles that of Dickens and Ben Jonson: "It emphasises something non-human within the recognisably 'true' depiction of character, so that what we observe in action is a human being moving slowly out of the realm of the real into the surreal." Durbach offers a convincing argument, but unfortunately he does not develop any specific connections to Jonson and Dickens; instead he supports his case with some "surreal" parallels in the plays of O'Casey and Chekhov. The subject calls for deeper investigation.

James Coakley and Marvin Felheim (*CompD*, 1970–71) find Plautine models for all the characters in *Juno*, not only the obvious braggart and parasite-slave of Boyle and Joxer, and identify traditions in the work of Plautus and Terence for most of the comic scenes. Coakley and Felheim conclude that the "most important relationship between *Juno* and Roman Comedy lies in similarity of characterization." This observation suggests that the whole tradition of comedy, particularly the way the comic models develop and change and yet remain more or less constant from Plautus to Shakespeare to Jonson to Dickens to O'Casey, must be studied more intensely.

Mary Papke (*SORev*, 1977) starts off with a sound attempt to show how in *Juno* O'Casey was dramatizing the anguish of Jim Larkin's desperate workers in Dublin, but along the way she resorts to an abstract and inflated critical jargon that obscures her ideas. Her analysis is "socio-formalist in methodology"; O'Casey uses his characters "as parabolic vehicles or symbols for larger socio-political groups"; the play is "a parable for the regression of working-class consciousness in Ireland"; and her critical "methodology" is "neither pure sociology nor pure formalism but both." Whatever it is supposed to be, in its application here it is ill-digested and impure Papke that calls more attention to itself that it does to O'Casey's play.

John Russell Taylor, in *Hitch: The Life and Times of Alfred Hitchcock* (1978), presents some curious and interesting information about the 1930 film version of *Juno*. Taylor tells us that Hitchcock "tends to dismiss [the film] *Juno and the Paycock* as just a photograph of the stage play." In an attempt to expand the limitations of the stage play, Taylor goes on, Hitchcock "persuaded O'Casey to write a new opening scene in the pub leading up to an energetically staged riot and shooting. The rest of the film follows the play so exactly that it has, Hitch says, nothing to do with cinema." Although there are considerable doubts about how "exactly" Hitchcock presented O'Casey's stage play—Hitchcock and his wife, Alma, wrote the screenplay—Taylor concludes, "Despite Hitch's anxieties about making the text cinematic, the film turned out very successfully, and was praised by the critics of the time to such an extent that it seriously embarrassed him. James Agate, famously difficult to please, wrote in the *Tatler*, '*Juno and the Paycock* . . . is a magnificent British picture.' "

No doubt that comment was one reason O'Casey was more seriously embarrassed than Hitchcock. Although he never saw the film, which was burned in the streets of Limerick when it was released (see the *Letters,* vol. 1), O'Casey knew he had not written a "British" play; and he had protested unsuccessfully when Hitchcock decided to cast the British actor Edward Chapman as "Captain" Boyle instead of O'Casey's natural choice, Barry Fitzgerald. Over the years, as information about the film reached O'Casey from various sources, he became completely disenchanted with its British sentimentalization and its cheapening of his original text. He not only rejected any responsibility for the film but wanted to have it destroyed.

On the matter of Hitchcock's "exact" reproduction of the play in the film, in 1955 two Americans, Charles Rosenberg and Martin Kesselman, after seeing a revival of the film, wrote to O'Casey objecting to what they called the characterization of the tailor as "a whimsically vicious anti-semitic caricature." Apparently what Hitchcock had done, without consulting O'Casey, was to change the original character of the tailor, "Needle" Nugent, into a "Mr. Kelly" and cast a Jewish actor, Fred Schwarz, to play the role with a heavy stage-Jewish accent. The change gave the whole scene an antisemitic taint that had no place in the play or film. O'Casey was so shocked to learn about this cheap trick that, in his letter of reply on 23 March 1955 (which will appear in the *Letters,* vol. 3), he wrote a blistering attack against antisemitism and the "bugger" who had corrupted his play and the film. It is time now that someone with a background in cinema and drama made a critical study of Hitchcock's version of *Juno* and also of John Ford's 1937 film version of *The Plough* to understand why both productions failed to do justice to O'Casey's work.

THE PLOUGH AND THE STARS

Gabriel Fallon's "The First Production of *The Plough and the Stars*" (*SORev,* 1976) provides a valuable firsthand account of the backstage tensions at the Abbey Theatre in 1926 that distorted the play and prevented the audience on the opening night and throughout the rest of the run from seeing *The Plough* exactly as O'Casey had written it. Although much of this information is known, Fallon gives an objective and graphic report of the situation. As the director of the production, Lennox Robinson, perhaps with malicious or jealous intent, went about miscasting and undermining some of the roles; some of the actors in the company were openly antagonistic to O'Casey as a "playwright of the slums" and refused to say lines that they felt were "indecent" or "immoral"; Michael Dolan, the actor and the manager of the Abbey, deviously tried to prevent the production of the play; to appease the Irish government's representative on the Abbey board, Yeats and Lady Gregory decided that Rosie Redmond's slightly bawdy song had to be cut out of the second act; and Yeats himself, the guiding genius of the theater, fanned the flames of political controversy behind the scenes. In view of all this subversion, which contributed to the riots that broke out in the theater against O'Casey and his play, Fallon concludes, "If Yeats wanted to provoke the Republicans at O'Casey's expense he had certainly succeeded. If Michael Dolan wanted to have the play rejected, he had a double victory, for he had the author rejected into the bargain. If Robinson was indeed jealous of O'Casey's reputation he too had reason to congratulate himself."

Ronald Ayling (*SORev*, 1976) comes to terms with a number of controversial issues about *The Plough*, two of which—O'Casey as realist and O'Casey as pacifist—are effectively resolved. About O'Casey's so-called realism, Ayling says that in *The Plough* the "loose narrative structure of the chronicle-play afforded greater opportunities for non-realistic techniques"; and he observes that even the language of this play reflects a sharp departure from realism. Ayling is also enlightening about O'Casey as a pacifist, an issue that has led some critics, like Gabriel Fallon, to detect what they call a confused state of mind in the playwright's seemingly contradictory pacificism and militancy in different plays. Ayling provides two incisive answers that should be noted here, one regarding O'Casey's position as an artist, the other regarding his view as a socialist:

> [Fallon] poses the question of how any dramatist could write of war from a pacifist view-point in the Abbey plays and in *The Tassie* and then endorse violent military action in *The Star Turns Red* and *Oak Leaves and Lavender*. . . . The same question could be asked in relation to, say, Shakespeare's writings, too: how could the man who wrote the poignant scene between The Father Who Has Killed His Son and The Son Who Has Killed His Father in *Henry VI* also write the battle speeches of *Henry V* ? and how can one account for the vastly different attitudes to war shown in, say, *Henry V* and *Troilus and Cressida*? The dilemma is one which confronts any artist, particularly a socialist one, who thinks and feels deeply about the subject. . . . Socialists have traditionally stood for resistance to economic and imperialist exploitation and, where it is necessary, support armed rebellion to change the structure of society. But . . . a strongly-felt pacifist tradition has remained embedded in the movement, and this is hardly surprising considering that warfare has always imposed greater hardship and suffering on the working people than upon any other section of the population.

In a less successful but well-meaning attempt to present O'Casey as an artist and socialist (*SORev*, 1976), Jack Lindsay sets out to offer a new and complex socialist interpretation of *The Plough*. His high intentions are so impressionistic, however, that he does not get beyond his more modest attempt to reply to a doctrinaire Marxist attack by Francis Mulhern, a critic in the *New Left Magazine*, who in 1975 wrote that the play was a political betrayal, a naturalist and "humanist critique of all forms of political violence." Like Greaves's "artistic elitism," Mulhern's antiviolent "humanism" is apparently another code term for bourgeois decadence. Lindsay mounts a formidable reply to Mulhern, insisting that the play is symbolic, not naturalistic, and that O'Casey's humanism, deeply rooted in socialism and the labor movement, cannot be called a bourgeois betrayal. Lindsay also points out that O'Casey would have been falsifying history if he had pretended, for the sake of the Easter Rising, that political nationalism and economic socialism were united in 1916, when they were in fact only driven further apart in Ireland. It is clear from modern history, as well as from *The Plough*, that the Rising as a revolution did nothing for the working people or for socialism in Ireland.

Robert G. Lowery, who edited the special issue of his *Sean O'Casey Review* for spring 1976 in honor of the fiftieth anniversary of *The Plough*, discusses the historical background of the play in his article in that issue. Lowery points out that up to 1916 O'Casey was "a radical and militant agitator and organizer" who was "in the mainstream of Irish nationalist, then socialist, activity." By examining O'Casey's early writing in the *Irish Worker* and other labor journals, his active role in Larkin's 1913 general strike, and the views he expressed in *The Story of the Irish Citizen Army*, Lowery illustrates why O'Casey felt he had to shift his loyalties from nationalism to socialism, why his dedication to the immediate cause of labor made him break with the middle-class nationalism that led to the Easter Rising. It was therefore the undermining of Larkin and of labor's economic struggle by the nationalist volunteers headed by Pearse and Connolly that prompted O'Casey to take an ironic and critical view of the Rising in *The Plough*. "It is clear," Lowery says, "that he had a decided socialist preference, but it is also clear that he was neither a reformist Labourite in the mold of the world socialist community of that time, nor was he a wild-eyed romantic committed to revolutionary martyrdom." Lowery does not believe that O'Casey could have written a political play in support of the Rising "unless he engaged in fantasy or divorced himself totally from his role in his early years."

Raymond J. Porter (*SORev*, 1976) does well to remind us that, although O'Casey in *The Plough* had mocked Pearse's fanatical call for blood sacrifice for the national liberation of Ireland, the ironic playwright admired and respected the 1916 martyr as a creative educator and courageous fighter. Porter's carefully documented article draws on the writings of both men to illustrate that the many areas of agreement between them, mostly in matters of cultural nationalism, should be balanced against their opposing political attitudes toward the Easter Rising.

Ellen Baile, O.P., in "Bessie Burgess: Cathleen Ni Houlihan of the Tenements" (*SORev*, 1976), indicates how O'Casey used his women characters, mainly Bessie Burgess, "to demythologize the Easter Rising" and to mock the efforts of Irishmen to celebrate "the exhilaration of war." Contrasting the mythic "Kathaleen Ny-Houlihan" of James Mangan's sentimental poem with the rough and courageous Bessie, Baile decides that O'Casey's tenement woman is the genuine Cathleen Ni Houlihan: "Through such a woman, O'Casey fleshes out his artfully designed profanation of Cathleen the queen in the belief that Ireland can be liberated by demythologizing her spurious gods and by confronting the rich continuity of the race that lies beneath the torment of the ni Houlihan of the Troubles.''

Bernard Benstock (*SORev*, 1977) presents the interesting view that *The Plough* is not only O'Casey's best work but "a paradigm of O'Casey's art. It summarizes the materials of his earlier efforts and lays the groundwork for his later plays." Though Benstock has no problem illustrating how *Gunman* and *Juno* are prefigured in *Plough*, he becomes vaguely metaphoric about just how the various innovative techniques and themes of the later plays all grow out of *The Plough*. "From this neck of the hourglass," that is, *The Plough*, he tells us, "almost a score of later plays evolve." This is what he tells us, but he doesn't show us how that ingenious hourglass image works for so many diverse themes and structures. Perhaps he will develop the substance of his metaphor in some future work.

Ronald Rollins' "O'Casey and Johnston: Different Reactions to the 1916 Easter Rising" (*SORev*, 1977) compares *The Plough and the Stars* with *The Scythe and the Sunset* (Johnston is parodying O'Casey's title) and states that, despite "great differences" between the works, "the attitudes of the two playwrights regarding motivation and conduct of men in conditions of crisis are virtually identical." Rollins grants that the women in the two plays are strikingly dissimilar, since O'Casey's women all mock the notion of glorious death for Ireland while Johnston's women, especially his Emer, the rabid patriot with the hot machine gun, defend the sacrficial bloodshed. Nevertheless, Rollins tends to minimize the differences, telling us that both plays are "anti-heroic works," despite the openly heroic and romantically patriotic mood and thrust of Johnston's play and Johnston's attempt, in his introduction to *The Scythe*, to separate his play from O'Casey's.

For the record, Ronald Ayling and Michael J. Durkan (*SORev*, 1976) note that O'Casey considered the "Woman from Rathmines" episode in act 3 redundant and asked the Abbey Theatre to eliminate it from their productions. In further support of this view, O'Casey wrote in *The Green Crow* that the Woman from Rathmines "had neither rhyme nor reason for being there; a character that was in every way a false introduction."

THE SILVER TASSIE

Richard F. Peterson (*SORev*, 1978) presents some important new evidence on the Abbey's rejection of *The Silver Tassie*. As Peterson points out, in letters to Gabriel Fallon and Bernard Shaw (in *Letters*, vol. 2) O'Casey said he suspected that the Abbey directors might have been determined, even in a conspiratorial way, to reject his new play before he had submitted it. From the evidence in unpublished letters Yeats and Lady Gregory wrote to Lennox Robinson, Peterson concludes that although O'Casey's suspicions about a conspiracy were unfounded, he might have been a victim of Yeats's arrogance: "This arrogance that O'Casey apparently sensed and came to resent was part of a belief held by Yeats and Lady Gregory and Robinson that the Abbey was as much a state of mind as it was a physical reality. . . . [Yeats] clearly identifies himself, Robinson, and Lady Gregory with an aristocratic level of intelligence, imagination, and taste far superior to that of the common herd represented by the audience, many of the players, and some of the would-be dramatists submitting plays for production." Peterson cites passages in the letters suggesting that O'Casey was considered one of the common herd who did not represent the true Abbey spirit; that Yeats believed Robinson's *Ever the Twain* was the greatest Abbey success and far superior to *Juno and the Paycock*; and that two years after Yeats had rejected the most original and experimental play by the Abbey's leading dramatist, he was lamenting, Peterson tells us, "the lack of originality and experimentation in the plays submitted to the Abbey." In the letters Lady Gregory wrote to Robinson, Peterson finds evidence that "only Yeats had the power to decide the fate of a play entirely on his own" and that Lady Gregory as well as Robinson accepted Yeats "as the supreme judge" and therefore gave consent to his arrogant and unjust rejection of O'Casey's play. All this unpublished evidence in the letters, Peterson concludes, adds up to a hard judgment of the Abbey directors in their unfair treatment of O'Casey: "O'Casey's bold new step in the direction of expressionism challenged Yeats's self-assurance that only he possessed the bold vision to transform the Abbey into a truly experimental theatre. Ironically, an aristocratic posture and an intellectual arrogance, bred by Yeats and supported by Robinson and Lady Gregory, did more than any narrow political or religious force to damage the spirit and enterprise of the Abbey." There has seldom been just cause for such a strong indictment of the Abbey directors or such a strong defense of O'Casey.

In *A Hundred Different Lives* (1979), Raymond Massey's autobiography, the distinguished actor and director devotes a chapter to his experiences directing the world premiere of *The Silver Tassie* in London in 1929. Scholarly and literary people, who sometimes underestimate or misunderstand the vital contribution of the theatrical profession, should be enlightened by Massey's backstage account of the collaborative shaping of a significant play that was far ahead of its time. Massey says he was aware that the so-called realistic acts—the first, third, and fourth, in contrast to the savagely expressionistic second act—were in fact "anything but realistic," since they combined "poetry, symbolism, and riotously funny Irish comedy" in a series of thematic interrelationships that were not immediately apparent. It was a daring and powerful play, he writes, a new kind of drama that was "not for tidy minds." Massey had to nurse the unpredictable Augustus John through the designing of the symbolic set for the crucial second act; he persuaded a reluctant Charles Laughton, who played Harry Heegan, to waltz in a wheelchair in the fourth act; and when the play opened to favorable notices but had to close after twenty-six performances, he shared the view of the producer, C. B. Cochran: "It's the proudest failure I ever had!"

Heinz Kosok (*SORev*, 1978) points out that of about thirty alterations O'Casey made in the text of *The Tassie*—the differences between the first printed edition (1928) and the final "Stage Version"

(1949)—half of them are to be found in the stage directions. This indicates that O'Casey probably based most of the changes on what he had learned about the use of the stage space from seeing Massey's production, which was put on after the play had been published. Kosok assesses all the changes and finds that the most important one, occurring at the end of the play, is an additional speech for Susie Monican, in which she says that she and her friends are not to blame for what happened to the to war victims, Heegan and Foran, and can do nothing to help them. With this speech, Kosok claims, "O'Casey makes it quite clear that it would be too easy a solution to hope for a general change by altering a few individuals' behaviour. Only by eliminating war altogether will it be possible to prevent other people from suffering as Harry does." This is probably an accurate explanation of O'Casey's purpose in adding the speech. The war, not Susie, is the real enemy. Kosok adds, however, that the new speech raises a different problem by making Susie's seemingly contradictory and complex character even more difficult to interpret and perform: "Susie has here become a mouthpiece of the author's opinions, which—considering her earlier 'conversion' from religious fanaticism to sexual liberation—makes her part even more difficult to play."

Susie Monican therefore remains a crux in the play, a character who must undergo a sudden transition at several points in the action but most significantly in the final scene. In "Notes on the French Premiere of *The Silver Tassie*" (*SORev*, 1978) Emile Jean Dumay discusses Guy Restore's 1967 production of the play in France, and he remembers particularly "the successful way Susie was played, mixing fits of piety and fanaticism with the extreme liveliness of a hot temper to the amazement of the audience who had indeed no idea that such extremes could be reconciled in Irish characters." Perhaps, then, the successful interpretation of Susie depends on the ability of the actress, Irish or otherwise, to achieve that amazing reconciliation of extreme emotions.

Marguerite Harkness (*SORev*, 1978) disagrees with critics who find elements of hope in *The Tassie*, which she considers O'Casey's darkest play. She is persuasive in her rejection of Walter Starkie's notion that the courage shown by the suffering in the three earlier Dublin plays can help explain and resolve the continuing war theme in *The Tassie*, of Saros Cowasjee's statement that Susie and Maxwell at the end of the play represent O'Casey's affirmation of life, and of Jack Lindsay's conviction that the play is a political work with the necessary upbeat element of a socialist's indictment of religion and war. Harkness argues instead that *The Tassie* is an unrelieved "wasteland" play that demythologizes O'Casey's earlier characterization of heroic women as symbols of hope and therefore offers "no light in the darkness." Convincing as Harkness is, one cannot help wondering, without trying to reach for illusory hope, if there is not an implicit flash of light in the darkness of O'Casey's towering rage, the creative light of his passionate outcry against the destruction and dehumanization of war.

Elizabeth Freundlich (*SORev*, 1978) discusses the political tensions that led to two controversial productions of *The Tassie* in German translation, one in Zurich in 1952 directed by Berthold Viertel, the other in West Berlin in 1953 directed by Fritz Kortner. The play was translated as *Der Preispokal* by Elizabeth Freundlich and Gunther Anders. (See also O'Casey's 1953 letter to Freundlich about the right-wing German protests against the Kortner production, *Letters*, vol. 2.) The article calls attention to Viertel's interesting comparison between the work of O'Casey and Karl Kraus, the powerful Austrian satirical writer. Freundlich quotes these comments by Viertel:

> When the second act [of *The Tassie*] begins, the backwall of the room seems to open and the audience is magically transported into a fantastic war-landscape which millions of contemporaries had seen and in which millions had died, while others had seen it only in their nightmares. Strange creatures, no longer human ones, begin to talk, to sing, to murmur prayers which transform themselves into street-ballads; complaints turn into curses against the torturers of the millions. Where else had I heard something of that kind? Where had I even directed something of that kind? Of course I speak of the gigantic drama "The last days of mankind" by Karl Kraus, which like O'Casey's second act was a mixture of sarcastic and apocalyptic vision, of prose and poetry, of prayer and operetta. Such similarity of playwrights, otherwise utterly different, cannot be mere coincidence.

Simon Williams (*SORev*, 1978) shows how the distortion and dehumanization in the symbolic second act of *The Tassie* are mirrored in diverse ways in the other three acts, serving to unify the "theme and conflicting styles" throughout the work. His analysis is sound as far as it goes, but he does not place enough emphasis on the predominant religious imagery and symbolism that provide perhaps one of the main unifying structures linking all the acts and giving the play its ritualistic enactment of a faltering Christianity with a victimized or crucified hero who ironically suffers for all of us without redemption.

THE STAR TURNS RED

Heinz Kosok's "Unity Theatre and *The Star Turns Red*" (*SORev*, 1980) provides the historical background and purpose of Unity Theatre as an amateur club-theater dedicated to "mirroring the life of ordinary people and contributing to the reform of society." O'Casey doubtless shared this double dedication when he chose Unity for the world premiere of *The Star Turns Red* in 1940. This is probably the only O'Casey play, says Kosok, whose appeal could have confined it to a particular theater. Kosok also mentions that when Unity produced the play again in 1946, a controversy arose between O'Casey and the management of Unity. Although Kosok says that "little is known" about the dispute, an explanation of its causes can be found in O'Casey's letter to William Rust, 23 September 1946 (in *Letters*, vol. 2). According to O'Casey, Unity had erred on two counts: it had mounted a poor production of his play, and its officers had failed to send him his very reasonable royalty payment.

The most successful production of the seldom performed *The Star Turns Red* was probably Tomás MacAnna's original and provocative staging of its Irish premiere at the Abbey Theatre in 1978. Discussing that production in "The Old Man Said 'Truflais!' " (*SORev*, 1978), MacAnna says he interpreted O'Casey's proletarian parable as something of an operatic miracle play, what he calls "a mixture of Toller and Wagner, but not altogether free from the realistic images of *Plough* and *Juno*." He stressed the play's vivid and turbulent theatrical images and symbols: "the great star above," "the Saffron Devil and Red Saviour in final conflict," and the characters who "have no names: they are symbols—the Old Man, the Old Woman, the Purple Priest, Red Jim, the Lord Mayor." At the same time, MacAnna calls the play "splendidly classical, truly Aristotelian, a play of conflict: Power against Poverty; militant Church and State against militant Proletariat." While one wonders whether this collision of abstract symbols is "truly Aristotelian," MacAnna goes further and claims that O'Casey has in this play created a profound mystical experience: "the Miracle of the Star turning Red—surely one of the most stunning moments in modern theatre—heralding a new nativity. Toller would never have imagined it; Gorki might; O'Casey did." MacAnna also imagined it, and his production and article seem to reach for the visionary spirit of the later O'Casey. MacAnna's inspired work calls for a reassessment of the play. For a list of the largely favorable reviews of the production in the Dublin newspapers, see E. H. Mikhail's "Annual Bibliography" (*SORev*, 1980).

Robert G. Lowery's glowing review of MacAnna's production (*SORev*, 1978) claims that critics who have consistently faulted the play as a "political tract" fail to realize that on the stage it can be a work of rare theatrical power and beauty. The play not only "deals bluntly with Fascism and Communism," Lowery says, but it also "expresses the love and joy of life that is so prevalent in all his plays . . . in the beautifully lyrical language of the Old Testament (as Shaw said) and of the Elizabethans. The play also exhibits O'Casey's masterful use of sound, music and color, devices found in most of his plays."

COCK-A-DOODLE DANDY

Christopher Murray (*SORev*, 1977) explicates two comic and thematic allusions in *Cock-a-Doodle Dandy* that illustrate how effectively some of O'Casey's satiric stratagems work in the play. Refuting the notion of some critics that O'Casey's literary allusions are merely a form of sub-Joycean pedantry, Christopher Murray reveals that when the lonely and defeated Michael Marthraun in *Cock* counts his rosary beads, he is echoing a rosary-accompanied prayer by the lonely Owen, a character in T. C. Murray's *Autumn Fire* who has similarly been abandoned by a young wife. O'Casey is enjoying a comic jest at the expense of the tragic melodrama in Murray's play, which O'Casey saw at the Abbey in 1924. His allusion is particularly appropriate considering that Murray in his Dublin newspaper reviews denigrated O'Casey's works. Furthermore, Christopher Murray provides copious and convincing evidence of O'Casey's attitude toward Irish cultural puritanism and sexual repression as they are represented in T. C. Murray's play. Christopher Murray suggests that the satirical exorcism of Marthraun's "demon-possessed" house in *Cock* is probably aimed at the sensational exorcism scene in Frank Carney's *The Righteous Are Bold*. Evidence subsequently disclosed in the O'Casey *Letters* (vol. 2) strongly supports Christopher Murray's claim that O'Casey was reacting directly against the exploitation of religious hysteria and superstition in Carney's play, which had been a popular and (O'Casey believed) a cheap success at the Abbey in 1946 shortly before he wrote *Cock*. Christopher Murray also pinpoints the chain of events that associates Michael Dolan, the Abbey manager and actor who played the main role in the original production of *Autumn Fire* and who was one of O'Casey's early opponents at the theater, with the game of comic allusions in T. C. Murray and O'Casey. Christopher Murray's article is a first-rate piece of literary detective work.

THE AUTOBIOGRAPHY

Roy Pascal's *Design and Truth in Autobiography* (1960) is primarily concerned with the creative energy that makes an autobiography not just a historical record or a social document but a work of art. Commenting on the remarkable exhilaration with which O'Casey was able to write about personal hardship, Pascal says, "Few autobiographies can tell of a harder and more desperate childhood and youth, yet one can think of few that are less depressing. What is characteristic is at all times the fierce energy of O'Casey's response and the exhilaration of the fight." Pascal also feels that writing the autobiography in the third person enabled O'Casey to cast the imaginative insight of the mature man on his younger struggling self and thus enrich as well as relive all past experiences. Concentrating on the first four volumes, which Pascal says are free from the circuitous arguments that clog the last two, he makes an impressive case for their creative power. It remains to be seen to what extent future criticism will treat the last two volumes as O'Casey's retrospective attempt to close out his life by condemning his enemies and celebrating his ideals. Are there possibly some unifying principles that bind the last two volumes to the first four?

William J. Maroldo, in "A Darwinian Garden of Eden: A Major Emphasis in Sean O'Casey's Autobiographies" (*SORev*, 1979), once again provides a learned and lively explication of symbolic passages in the autobiography. Discussing the "Green Fire on the Hearth" chapter in *Drums under the Windows*, he shows us how O'Casey enlists the sporting fun of allusions to Shaw and Darwin and Frazer in creating the comic fantasy of Sean's strange adventures in Eden with the timid Adam and the bold Eve and the clever Serpent with the thick Irish brogue, adventures that occurred in spite of some misconceptions in Genesis and miscalculations by "Jeecaysee" (G. K. Chesterton). We are presented with such an illuminating commentary on the elaborate theological jokes, puns, portmanteau words, and literary allusions that no one will hereafter be able to read O'Casey's anthropologically satiric version of creation in that chapter without acknowledging a profound debt to the nimble Maroldo. One can only hope that he will continue to act as our Vergilian guide to the comic and symbolic realms of hell, purgatory, and paradise in the autobiography.

James Scrimgeour (*SORev*, 1977) applies Lady Gregory's early comment about O'Casey's first plays—"Your strong point is characterization"—to the treatment of some minor yet memorable people in the autobiography to prove that O'Casey "had the ability to make us feel that the lives of apparently unimportant little people were important after all." Scrimgeour concentrates mainly on O'Casey's descriptive powers, his ability to create "finely chiselled" portraits of uncommonly common people who somehow manage to survive courageously in the Dublin slums. Studied in detail are four such characters: Mild Millie, the Tram Conductor, Mr. Moore, and the old Jewish glazier.

For two diametrically opposed views of the autobiography, see Lawrence J. Dessner's "Art and Anger in the Autobiographies of Sean O'Casey" (*Éire*, 1975) and Heinrich Böll's "The Curses of Poetry" (1969) in his *Missing Persons and Other Essays* (1977). Dessner concedes that the first two volumes of the autobiography contain some "highly artistic" writing, but he insists that the final four volumes "disintegrate into a congeries of memoir, argumentation, and angry polemic." In a somewhat pedantic, neoclassical manner, Dessner scolds O'Casey for not adhering to a formal structure of "organizing principles" and an overall control of the "shaping context" to contain the sprawling account of his life story, which, Dessner feels, "is presented without art or intention, and lacks the form which would have wrought catharsis out of pain." Heinrich Böll, on the other hand, believes that O'Casey's eloquent anger is an integral part of his life and art, both of which were "disputatious and disputed till his last breath"—and "to be disputed," Böll says, "is the only possible status for an author." More concerned about the content than the form of the autobiography, Böll feels that it is full of justified Old Testament wrath, "biblical dimensions and biblical greatness. This fierce torrent of beatifications and curses is the Protestant counterpart to Joyce's *Ulysses*, not yet properly recognized as such and yet the necessary complement, not one iota less 'blasphemous.' " Where Dessner was shocked at O'Casey's "despicable treatment" of George Orwell (no mention of Orwell's prior and shabby treatment of O'Casey), Böll cheerfully reports that "not even those sacred cows Chesterton, Belloc, Knox and Orwell are spared." Böll recognizes that O'Casey was, and had to be to survive, "stubborn, radical, uncompromising, unreasonable." These traits are viewed by Böll as virtues: "I have the impression that O'Casey was one of the most undiplomatic writers who ever lived—and that, to me, is just as flattering as his 'disputedness.' "

MODERN DRAMA

Robert Hogan

The last five years have seen some increase in books about the modern Irish drama. Much of the critical writing still concerns Yeats, Synge, O'Casey, and Beckett, but general studies of the drama have appeared, as well as volumes on particular aspects of individual dramatists. Most notable, however, is the marked increase in the publication of new plays. Broad reference books or critical studies of well-known writers are generally safe ventures, even in the harassed publishing situation of today. Plays, however, even in the best of times, have always been economically perilous to publish; and so it is startling, though of course salutary, that several publishers are taking a chance with them.

But although new plays by new writers are coming out with some frequency, the able dramatists of an older generation remain nearly as neglected as they were five years ago, their works neither being brought back into print nor being accorded much critical attention. Nor has the need for an adequate anthology been met—a disappointment both for teachers and for students.

Instead, there have been a plethora of elementary encyclopedias, introductory studies, bibliographies of criticism, and checklists of checklists. Neither the neglected dramatists of the past nor the recently published dramatists of the present have been comprehensively or sensitively treated. Most endeavor has been directed to refighting old battles on familiar battlegrounds, and some of the battles seem now to be fought with cardboard swords.

An ambitious project, however, is in the offing, which may go far to answer some of these problems. The project, from the publisher Colin Smythe and under the general editorship of Ann Saddlemeyer and Joseph Ronsley, is a series of collections, edited by various hands, of the major works of most of the notable dramatists from the first days of the theater movement to nearly the present. This worthy project should definitely establish a basic canon.

1. Bibliography

As in 1976 there is still no adequate formal bibliography of the dramatic movement from its beginnings to the present, although we have in the interim seen some inadequate additions. The skimpy general dramatic bibliography in *The Dictionary of Irish Literature* (1979) appears the effusion of a tired or weakened brain, and the bibliography attached to the article on the Abbey Theatre is no more than basic. The volume's bibliographies of individual dramatists, however, are on the whole probably the best available.

E. H. Mikhail, the most active of contemporary bibliographers in the field, describes his *A Research Guide to Modern Irish Dramatists* (1979) as "a bibliography of bibliographies of one hundred and two Irish dramatists who wrote from the beginning of the Irish Dramatic Movement in 1899 to the present time." I counted only eighty-nine dramatists and found little information that was not in the previous edition of this volume. If Mikhail's book were combined with his two previous checklists on the Irish drama, the result would still be inadequate. But should he ever harness his diligence to sound bibliographic principles and curb his tendency to hasten into print, he might well produce the one indispensable volume.

Kimball King's *Ten Modern Irish Playwrights: A Comprehensive Annotated Bibliography* (1979) does not attain even Mikhail's standards. King's choice of playwrights is so curious that the value of his book and the extent of his knowledge are highly suspect. The book is far from comprehensive even in the listing of its ten writers. The annotations are terse and errors are abundant. More a checklist than a bibliography, the volume is probably the most elementary and untrustworthy on the market.

2. Anthologies and Series

No general anthologies of the drama have appeared, although some short dramatic works have been included in general literary anthologies, like those of Freyer and of Fallon and Golden (see p. 9).

William J. Feeney, however, has edited a particular anthology of works produced by Edward Martyn's Irish Theatre. This collection appeared first in *George Spelvin's Theatre Book* (nominally 1979, but published in 1980) and then as a separate book, *Edward Martyn's Irish Theatre* (vol. 2 of *Lost Plays of the Irish Renaissance*). The work includes Feeney's knowledgeable introduction followed by Martyn's *Romulus and Remus,* Thomas MacDonagh's *Pagans,* H. B. O'Hanlon's *To-morrow,* and Eimar O'Duffy's *The Phoenix on the Roof* and *The Walls of Athens.* Feeney was unable to secure permission to reprint works by John MacDonagh, a major director and minor author whose plays remain for the most part unpublished.

Richard Burnham's anthology, *The Cork Dramatic Society,* is due to appear as volume 3 of *Lost Plays of the Irish Renaissance* in 1983 and is to include obscure or previously unpublished works by Daniel Corkery, Lennox Robinson, T. C. Murray, J. Bernard MacCarthy, and Terence MacSwiney.

One of the two paperback series listed in the previous volume, the Irish Drama Series of De Paul University, edited by William J. Feeney, has ceased publication through lack of funds. The other, the Irish Play Series of Proscenium Press, has continued with the following volumes: Liam Mac Uistin's *Post Mortem* (1977), David Hayes's *Sorry! No Hard Feelings?* (1978), John B. Keane's *The Good Thing* (1978), James Douglas' *The Savages* (1978), Maurice Davin-Power's *Shadows in the Sun* (1980), Hugh Carr's *Encounter in the Wilderness* (1980), Kevin Grattan's *Go Away, Billy Wind!* (1980), G. P. Gallivan's *Watershed* (1981), and Michael J. Molloy's *Petticoat Loose* (1982). In the press at this writing is a volume of four short plays by Douglas, Hayes, Judge, and Mac Uistin. All these plays, save Keane's, appeared also in the Society of Irish Playwrights series in Ireland. Among other Proscenium plays of Irish interest were two in the Lost Play series—Dorothy Robbie's *Ribbon with Gold* (1977) and George Fitzmaurice and John Guinan's *The Wonderful Wedding* (1978); three in the Adaptations series—P. J. O'Connor's *The Scarperer* (1978) after Brendan Behan, Robert Hogan's *An Unsocial Socialist* (1978) after Bernard Shaw, and Eugene McCabe's television adaptation of his story *Cancer* (1980); one in the Contemporary Drama series—Michael Judge's *Saturday Night Women* (1977); one in the Short Play series—Sidney Bernard Smith's *Sherca* (1979); and three in the New Abbey Theatre series—P. J. O'Connor's *Tarry Flynn* (1977) after Patrick Kavanagh, Jack White's *The Last Eleven* (1978), and Frank O'Connor and Hugh Hunt's *The Invincibles* (1980).

Several other publishers have begun issuing Irish plays, the handsomest volumes being those of Peter Fallon's Gallery Press, which has brought out Eugene McCabe's *Pull Down a Horseman/Gale Day* (1979) and several of Thomas Murphy's plays: *On the Outside/On the Inside* (1976), *Famine* (1977), and *A Crucial Week in the Life of a Grocer's Assistant* (1978), which is a revision of the play published earlier as *The Fooleen*. In conjunction with Proscenium, Gallery has published McCabe's *King of the Castle* (1978), Heno Magee's *Hatchet* (1978), Thomas Kilroy's *Talbot's Box* (1979), and reissued Brian Friel's *The Enemy Within* (1979). It has also published Brendan Behan's *Poems and a Play in Irish* (1981).

Poolbeg Press, a new Irish house that has been successful with its paperback novels and collections of short stories, began with one play, Murphy's *The Sanctuary Lamp* (1976), and then decided quite justly that the market for plays was much poorer than that for fiction.

The Writer's Co-operative, which began publishing fiction under the imprint of Co-op Books, has lately published several volumes of plays, including James Plunkett's *The Risen People* (1978), G. P. Gallivan's *Dev* (1978), Jim Sheridan's *Mobile Homes* (1978), Peter Sheridan's *The Liberty Suit* (1978) and *Emigrants* (1979), Bernard Farrell's *I Do Not Like Thee, Doctor Fell* (1979), J. Graham Reid's *The Death of Humpty Dumpty* (1979), and two volumes of short plays. The first of these, *Collection One* (1979), contained Paschal Finnan's *The Swine and the Potwalloper* and Desmond Hogan's *A Short Walk to the Sea*. The second, *Collection Two* (1979), contained Sean McCarthy's *Rise and Shine* and John Lynch's *Poor Ol' Joe*. The Co-op's latest publications are of recent Abbey and Peacock plays: Neil Donnelly's *Upstarts* (1980), Martin Boylan's *Thompsons* (1981), and William Trevor's *Scenes from an Album* (1981).

And finally the new Irish feminist press, Arlen House, has brought out three television plays under its Turoe Press imprint: Maeve Binchy's *Deeply Regretted By* (1979), Eugene McCabe's *Roma* (1979), and Alun Owen's *Passing Through* (1979).

These plays are certainly uneven in merit: there are no masterpieces, but several have strong theatrical or literary qualities, and a few are shockingly banal, puerile, and poorly edited. Nevertheless, when the amount of published original work begins to outweigh the amount of secondary criticism, we must greet the phenomenon as a symptom of health.

3. History, Criticism, and Memoirs

The third, fourth, and fifth volumes of the documentary history *The Modern Irish Drama* have appeared. Like the first two volumes, the third volume—*The Abbey Theatre: The Years of Synge, 1905-1909* (1978), by Robert Hogan and James Kilroy—quotes extensively from contemporary documents and lists the full casts of nearly any play with some pretension to merit. The fourth volume—*The Rise of the Realists, 1910-1915* (1979), written by Hogan, Richard Burnham, and Daniel P. Poteet—indicates by its greater length the increasing dramatic activity of those years. Perhaps the weakest addition to the series is the fifth volume—*The Art of the Amateur, 1916-1920* (1982), by Hogan and Burnham—in which the voluminous dramatic activity in Ireland may have defeated even these diligent grubbers. A sixth volume, *The Years of O'Casey, 1921-1926,* will continue the story to the *Plough* riots and O'Casey's departure from Ireland and will probably appear in 1983. By that time the history will have swelled to about 2,500 pages of minutiae and may possibly stand as a prime example of academic bloat.

Hugh Hunt's *The Abbey, Ireland's National Theatre, 1904-1978* (1979) is something of a semiofficial publication since the author was asked by the directors of the theater "to write an up-to-date history" and was given exclusive access to the theater's records. The chief virtue of the book is that it provides the fullest account in print of the theater's last fifty years as well as a generally accurate list of productions through 1978. Errors are few, and the events of the early, much discussed years are adequately summarized. The book's chief disappointment is its dryness and academic flavor. Those years that Hunt knew personally and that have been rarely discussed by insiders are treated with a reticent factuality and an impersonality that give little insight into what it was like to be there. (Indeed, the author even refers to himself in the third person.) These are minor faults, however, and the book will doubtless for several years be the standard historical reference to the Abbey's recent history.

The country's three major literary theaters each issued commemorative publications. *The Abbey Theatre, Dublin, 1966–1976* (1977), compiled by Deirdre McQuillan, celebrated the theater's first ten years in its new building. The booklet contains a list of the plays performed during the period, but only by year, not by month and day. The bulk of the text is a short year-by-year commentary written by Tomás MacAnna and accompanied by many handsome production photos. There are also short biographies of the company.

In 1978, the Gate Theatre celebrated the fiftieth anniversary of its founding, and although Micheál Mac Liammóir did not live to see that celebration, the event produced two volumes of warm tribute to him and his partner, Hilton Edwards. Peter Luke's *Enter Certain Players: Edwards-Mac Liammóir and the Gate, 1928–1978* (1978) contains essays by Michael Scott, Brian Friel, Terence de Vere White, Mary Manning, Denis Johnston, Lady Longford, and other associates and admirers. Manning's account of Mac Liammóir's death is particularly touching, and there are important discussions of Mac Liammóir by Edwards, Emlyn Williams, and especially Richard Pine. Patricia Turner contributes a list of Gate productions but gives only the month and year. The volume contains many characteristic costume and set designs by Mac Liammóir but not nearly as many production photos as did the original "Gate Book." Richard Pine's *All for Hecuba* (1978), a souvenir catalog of the Gate Jubilee Exhibition in October and November 1978 at the Municipal Gallery, is indispensable for a study of the Gate Theatre. It lists not only first productions, as does Turner, but also revivals and many—though hardly all—exact dates of those productions. Pine's summary of the Gate and his notes on particular productions are quite the best things in print on this topic.

A Needle's Eye (1979), edited by Mary O'Malley and John Boyd, was published by the Lyric Players Theatre to mark the tenth anniversary of the new playhouse in Ridgeway Street, Belfast. This uneven but necessary volume presents the fullest account of the theater available. It is profusely illustrated by production photos; it contains a useful essay by John W. Boyle on the theater's early years from 1951 to 1968; and it lists productions in the new house from 1969 to 1979. Most valuable among the remaining material are a thoughtful essay by Raymond Warren on music in Yeats's plays and a short account of *Threshold,* the theater's literary magazine, by John Montague. The other matter includes verses by various notable Irish poets, a self-interview by Patrick Galvin, and the texts of several of the theater's annual lectures. These pieces, by Denis Donoghue, Thomas Kinsella, Roger McHugh, and others, are oriented toward an academic view of literature rather than toward theater.

Irish Theatre (1979), by Christopher Fitz-Simon, might be described as a coffee-table pamphlet. In some two thousand words it summarizes the entire history of theater in Ireland. It contains a few errors, but its pictures are handsome.

The Dublin Drama League, 1918–1941 (1979), by Brenna Katz Clarke and Harold Ferrar, is composed of a short and uninformed academic essay and a muddled and inaccurate listing of casts. There has probably been no more garbled pamphlet about the Irish drama since Brinsley MacNamara's list of Abbey plays, and everything in it should be treated with great skepticism.

At least four particular studies might be noted. Elizabeth Hale Winkler's *The Clown in Modern Anglo-Irish Drama* (1977) carries its burden of learning very heavily indeed; and, although it contains much interesting matter about the clown figure in Western drama, the discovery of that figure in Boucicault, Shaw, Lady Gregory, Synge, O'Casey, and Beckett is a rather arbitrary exercise, sometimes farfetched and rarely illuminating. Herbert V. Fackler's *That Tragic Queen: The Deirdre Legend in Anglo-Irish Literature* (1978) discusses most of the recent dramatic and nondramatic versions of the story. The survey makes no particular point but has the merit of justly discussing some neglected and often worthy work. Katharine Worth's *The Irish Drama of Europe from Yeats to Beckett* (1978) is not the comprehensive survey the title suggests but basically a discussion of Yeats's plays, the influences on them, and their influence on a handful of other dramatists. Most interesting is a needed discussion of the influence of Maeterlinck on Yeats. The less sound portions of the book seem caused by the apparently unrealized contradictions between academic criticism and theories arising from Worth's involvement in a few experimental productions. The first view asserts that Yeats is a marvelous, perhaps *the* marvelous, twentieth-century playwright, and the second view is that he is marvelous because he can be staged in any fashion a director's fertile imagination suggests. But despite such problems, or perhaps even because of them, the book is more forceful and lively than many of its kind.

David Krause's *The Profane Book of Irish Comedy* (1982) promotes the thesis that the best Irish plays are highly critical of Ireland and discusses some of the work of Beckett, Behan, Boucicault, Boyle, Carroll, Fitzmaurice, Lady Gregory, Johnston, O'Casey, Robinson, Shaw, Shiels, Synge, and Yeats. The general soundness of the thesis and of the many particular judgments is obscured by a weight of critical symbolism and a perfervid style. The volume throws little light on the plays as works for the theater but is quite useful in considering them solely as literature.

A critical summary of recent Irish plays may be found in Christopher Murray's "Irish Drama in Transition, 1966–1978" (*EI*, 1979).

Theatre Business (1982) is a collection of early letters between Yeats, Synge, and Lady Gregory about the running of the Abbey Theatre. It is an indispensable volume, and the editing by Ann Saddlemeyer is distinguished by her usual authority and meticulousness.

One noteworthy volume of memoirs has appeared: Val Mulkerns' edition of Ria Mooney's *Players and Painted Stage,* which was printed in two numbers of *George Spelvin's Theatre Book* (1978). Ria Mooney was associated for many years with the Abbey as actress and director; she also worked at the Gate, at the Gaiety, and with Eva Le Gallienne in New York in the late 1920s. Her memoirs have been trimmed of some understandable spleen about her late days in the Abbey, but many of her accounts—for instance, her creation of the role of Rosie Redmond—are both illuminating and delightful.

Kevin Rockett's *Film and Ireland: A Chronicle* (1980), a pamphlet issued for the London Festival of the Irish Arts, lists the major films shot in Ireland or by the Irish. It is a useful, slightly annotated interim report that will serve until Liam O'Leary's book on the Irish cinema makes its appearance. Seamus de Burca has assembled an informal history of the Queen's Theatre, which is to appear in 1982.

The Irish Theatre Archive, formed in 1981 to collect theatrical memorabilia, publishes a short occasional magazine called *Prompts*. Its second number (1981) contained a pleasant general essay by Cyril Cusack, entitled "The Irish Actor."

A new quarterly, *Theatre Ireland*, is to begin publication in Ulster in September 1982. A book of essays, *Since O'Casey*, by Hogan, is to appear early in 1983.

4. Individual Authors: Texts and Criticism

Edward Martyn (1859–1923). An excellent account of Martyn's Irish Theatre in Hardwicke Street forms the introduction to William J. Feeney's *Lost Plays of the Irish Renaissance* (vol. 2, 1980), which also reprints Martyn's satiric play *Romulus and Remus*. Wayne Hall's "Edward Martyn: Politics and Drama of Ice" (*Éire*, 1980) is a pleasant, short evaluation.

Gerald MacNamara (1866–1958). A collection of most of MacNamara's plays, including the unpublished *The Mist that Does Be on the Bog*, is being edited by Kathleen Danaher Parks and Robert Hogan and should appear in 1983.

Countess Markievicz (1868–1927). The Countess is hardly noted for her contribution to the theater, although she did act, and not always execrably, the leading parts with her husband's Independent Dramatic Company. She also wrote one short, dreadful, patriotic play entitled *The Invincible Mother*, which has been disinterred and printed (*JIL*, 1977). The same issue of the journal contains Dorothy Robbie's full-length play *Ribbon with Gold*, an adulatory, thinly disguised account of the Countess as an Irish patriot.

T. C. Murray (1873–1959). See T. Gerald Fitzgibbon's "The Elements of Conflict in the Plays of T. C. Murray" (*Studies*, 1975).

James Cousins (1873–1956). William A. Dumbleton's *James Cousins* (1980) is a short, appreciative critical biography that is adequately full and fair but justly makes no extravagant claims.

George Fitzmaurice (1877–1963). Works of this once neglected Kerry author continue to be discovered, although none has added to his reputation. New publications are the short story "Chasing a Ghoul" (*JIL*, 1977) and a three-act play written in collaboration with John Guinan and entitled *The Wonderful Wedding* (*JIL*, 1978). The play was published separately in the same year by Proscenium. Carol Gelderman's *George Fitzmaurice* (1979) repeats the biographical facts gleaned from Howard K. Slaughter's original investigations, analyzes the notable characteristics of the works, and attempts some evaluation. The approach is bookish and the judgments occasionally dubious—none more so than the relegation of *The Ointment Blue* to "The Lesser Plays"—but the author does deal in ideas rather than in plot summary. Matthew N. Coughlin makes greater claims about the early play *The Toothache* than probably most people would admit, but his article "Farce Transcended" should certainly be read (*Éire*, 1975).

Thomas MacDonagh (1878-1916). *Pagans* appeared in *George Spelvin's Theatre Book* (1979) with several other plays performed at Martyn's Irish Theatre, and the collection of these plays, edited by Feeney and noted on p. 256, appeared separately also. Johann Norstedt's *Thomas MacDonagh: A Critical Biography* (1980) recounts the significant details of MacDonagh's life, gives a sound evaluation of his literary work, and makes as plausible an interpretation of his character as has appeared in print.

Patrick Pearse (1879-1916). The biography by Ruth Dudley Edwards, *Patrick Pearse: The Triumph of Failure* (1977), supersedes earlier accounts and contains considerable information about Pearse's connection with the drama.

Joseph Campbell (1879-1944). A complete issue of the *Journal of Irish Literature* (1979), edited by Assumpta Saunders, marked Campbell's centenary. The issue included the editor's detailed notes toward a Campbell biography, a recension of two short radio talks on Campbell by Austin Clarke, an anthology of poems, Campbell's previously unpublished *Northern Autobiography*, and a reprinting of his Abbey play, *Judgment*.

St. John Ervine (1883-1971). A lengthy selection of Ervine's drama criticism from the *New York World* in 1928-29, edited by Peter Drewniany and A. Freund, appeared in two numbers of *George Spelvin's Theatre Book* (1981).

Lennox Robinson (1886-1958). A short Robinson number of the *Journal of Irish Literature* (1980), edited by Lloyd Worley and Gary Phillips, included two short stories, the first publication of the pseudonymous comedy *The Red Sock,* Worley's account of its production by the New Players, and an essay about Robinson's relations with Yeats by Richard F. Peterson.

J. Bernard MacCarthy (1889-1979). This prolific writer of plays and stories was a County Cork postman. His more notable plays are *Crusaders* (1918) and *The Long Road to Garranbraher* (1928). A partial bibliography of his works appears in *The Dictionary of Irish Literature* (1979), and Richard Burnham is reprinting MacCarthy's short tragedy *Wrecked* in the forthcoming *Lost Plays of the Irish Renaissance* (vol. 3).

Eimar O'Duffy (1893-1935). The O'Duffy number of the *Journal of Irish Literature* (1978) includes some early poems and reviews and reprints the play *Bricriu's Feast* and the novel *Printer's Errors.* Two more of O'Duffy's plays, *The Phoenix on the Roof* and *The Walls of Athens (*1914), were reprinted in Feeney's *Lost Plays of the Irish Renaissance* (vol.2).

Austin Clarke (1896-1974). Two posthumous plays appeared, *The Third Kiss* (1976) and *Liberty Lane, a Ballad Play of Dublin* (1978).

Micheál Mac Liammóir 1899-1978). Mac Liammóir died in the

fiftieth year of the Gate Theatre, which he and Hilton Edwards founded. His principal late publication was a short autobiographical novel, *Enter a Goldfish* (1977). Conrad Balliett has an interview with Mac Liammóir on Maud Gonne (*JIL*, 1977). See also Luke's *Enter Certain Players* (1978) and Pine's *All for Hecuba* (1978), noted on p. 259.

Paul Vincent Carroll (1900–68). Marion Sitzmann's *Indomitable Irishry* (1975) is a short study, completed in 1965, of Carroll's plays. The book is less interesting for its critical comments than for its taped interviews with Carroll. A neglected area of the playwright's career was discussed in John D. Conway's "Paul Vincent Carroll and the Theatre in Scotland" (*Éire*, 1977).

Christine, Countess Longford (1900–80). Several fragments of autobiography appeared in the *Irish Times* in 1981.

Denis Johnston (1901–). The Dolmen Press did not, as was noted in the previous volume, reissue *A Bride for the Unicorn,* but that play is included in a three-volume collected edition, *The Dramatic Works of Denis Johnston,* being published by Colin Smythe. Volume 1 (1977) contains five plays, volume 2 (1979) contains four older plays with some revisions, a previously unpublished opera libretto, and a patriotic pageant. The third volume, yet unpublished, is to contain seven previously unpublished radio plays. Gene A. Barnett's *Denis Johnston* (1978) is a short, sound analysis of all Johnston's important work, save *The Brazen Horn.* That curious enigmatic volume appeared under the Dolmen imprint in 1976; an earlier version had been privately printed (1968). Joseph Ronsley edited a collection of critical essays in *Denis Johnston: A Retrospective* (1981) and also contributed to it an excellent checklist of Johnston's writings. The essays range from personal reminiscence to academic criticism and from the important to the trivial and turgid. However, all the major works and many of the important facets of Johnston's varied life are covered by colleagues and critics, such as Edwards and Mac Liammóir, Curtis Canfield, Thomas Kilroy, John Boyd, and Vivian Mercier.

Frank O'Connor (1903–66). *The Invincibles,* written with Hugh Hunt, was first published in the New Abbey Theatre series (1980).

Andrew Ganly (c. 1905–). Two of Ganly's one-act plays have appeared: "The Dear Queen" (*JIL*, 1976) and its sequel "The Dance in Nineteen Hundred and Ten" (*JIL*, 1977).

Samuel Beckett (1906–). *Ends and Odds,* a collection of short pieces, appeared in 1976. The most notable addition to Beckett scholarship has been Deirdre Bair's long biography, *Samuel Beckett* (1978). This book was much attacked, although not entirely justly. As the first substantial biography, it offers a wealth of information as well as some plausible interpretation of Beckett's personality and works. Recent literary criticism of note includes *Shape Changer: A Symposium,* edited by Katharine Worth (1975), *Beckett/Beckett,* by Vivian Mercier (1977), and *Just Play: Beckett's Theatre,* by Ruby Cohn (1980),

Donagh MacDonagh (1912–68). *Lady Spider,* a verse play about the Deirdre story, appeared (*JIL*, 1980) with a critical introduction by Gordon M. Wickstrom.

John Boyd (1912–), who was unlisted in the previous volume, is literary advisor to the Lyric Theatre in Belfast, which has produced several of his plays. His published work includes *The Flats* (1974) and *Collected Plays* in two volumes (1982).

Michael J. Molloy (1917–   ). Molloy's essay "The Making of Folk Plays" appeared in *Literature and Folk Culture: Ireland and Folk Culture* (1977), edited by A. Feder and B. Schrank. His recent Abbey play, *Petticoat Loose,* was published by the Society of Irish Playwrights and by Proscenium in 1982.

Conor Cruise O'Brien (1917–   ). O'Brien's *Herod: Reflections on Political Violence* (1978) contains a number of essays on political matters but also three short plays: "King Herod Explains," "Salome and the Wild Man, or the Quiet Galilean," and "King Herod Advises." P. R. O'Connor Lysaght's monograph *End of a Liberal: The Politics of Conor Cruise O'Brien* (1976) is a quite critical discussion of O'Brien as a political man rather than as a creative writer. See also Denis Sampson's "Passion and Suspicion: An Approach to the Writings of Conor Cruise O'Brien" (*CJIS,* 1976).

David Hayes (1919–   ). This Dublin-born playwright has published *Sorry! No Hard Feelings?* (1978), and his one-act "Legend" is to appear in *Four Irish Plays* in late 1982.

G. P. Gallivan (1920–   ). *Dev* appeared in 1978, and *Watershed* in 1981.

James Plunkett (1920–   ). *The Risen People* appeared in 1978.

Michael Judge (1921–   ). Works by this Dublin teacher have appeared at the Abbey and other Dublin theaters since the 1960s. His *Saturday Night Women* was published in 1978, and his one-act "The Chairs" is to be included in the above-noted *Four Irish Plays.*

Brendan Behan (1923–64). All the plays in English were published in *The Complete Plays of Brendan Behan* (1978). Peter Fallon edited a collection of fugitive material, *After the Wake* (1981), for the O'Brien Press; and his own Gallery Press published *Poems and a Play in Irish* (1981), the play being the early work whose English title would be *The Landlady.* Frank McMahon's adaptation of *Borstal Boy* appeared in 1975, and P. J. O'Connor's adaptation of *The Scarperer* in 1978. Two racy memoirs of Behan and other Dublin figures of the 1950s were John Ryan's *Remembering How We Stood* (1975) and Anthony Cronin's *Dead as Doornails* (1976). In a class by itself is Peter Arthurs' *With Brendan Behan* (1981), which illustrates in great detail the disarray, the drinking, and the alleged sexual peccadilloes of Behan's last years. A notable addition to Behan criticism was Colbert Kearney's academic but sympathetic *The Writings of Brendan Behan* (1977). E. H. Mikhail's *Brendan Behan: An Annotated Bibliography of Criticism* (1980) is the fullest in print and cites many useful and some obscure items. The annotations are terse descriptions rather than evaluations, however; and neophyte students may find themselves wading through much elementary, repetitive, and trivial material. Rather than offer such an uncritical assemblage, the compiler might have used some of his space to list Behan's own fugitive writings, not all of which were caught by Fallon's *After the Wake.*

Thomas Coffey (1925–   ). *Anyone Could Rob a Bank,* the popular 1959 farce, was published by James Duffy in 1974 but escaped citation in the previous volume.

Hugh Leonard (1926–   ). In 1978 Leonard's *Da* appeared on Broadway, won several awards, and settled down for a long run and a subsequent American tour. Somewhat reivised, the play was republished in 1979 by Atheneum. In the last five years, Leonard also published *A Life* (1980) and *Three Plays* (1981), which included *Da, A Life,* and *Time Was.* His nondramatic publications included *Home before Night* (1979), a superb autobiographical novel about boyhood, and *Leonard's Last Book* (1978) and *A Peculiar People* (1980), two collections of humorous pieces gleaned from his prolific Irish journalism. Keith Cushman's "Stand-Up Poker in Hugh Leonard's *The Poker Session*" (*JIL*, 1979) persuasively analyzes the play's main faults.

J. P. Donleavy (1926–   ). Kurt Jacobson published "An Interview with J. P. Donleavy" (*JIL*, 1979).

Criostoir O'Flynn (1927–   ). This Limerick-born playwright and short story writer published *A Man Called Pearse* (1980).

Patrick Galvin (c. 1927–   ). This Cork-born poet and playwright has been attached in recent years to the Lyric Theatre in Belfast. A 1976 issue of the theater's magazine, *Threshold*, entitled *Three Plays*, included Galvin's *The Last Burning, Nightfall to Belfast,* and *We Do It for Love.* Niall Kelly's published interview with Galvin is apparently somewhat inaccurate (*Irish Times,* 24 July 1976).

John B. Keane (1928–   ). Keane's recent publications have been mainly fiction and collections of essays. His *Death Be Not Proud and Other Stories* was published in 1976, his *Dan Pheaidí Aindí* in 1978, and his *Stories from a Kerry Fireside* in 1980. New plays have continued to be produced, however, and *The Good Thing* was published in 1978. John M. Feehan's *Fifty Years Young: A Tribute to John B. Keane* (1979) is a pleasant collection of criticism, apppreciation, poetry, and reminiscence by ten of the playwright's associates, friends, and well-wishers. James N. Healy, who has created many of Keane's best character roles, writes well on "The Birth of *Sive*"; Phylis Ryan, who has produced many of his plays, writes on his women characters; Christy Brown produces a characteristic tribute; Hogan writes, considering the circumstances, perhaps too grudgingly about Keane's art and craft; but Tony Butler probably veers too far in the opposite direction in "Authentic Genius."

William Trevor (1928–   ). This much admired novelist and short-story writer turns to television drama more as a craft than as an art. His published plays include two not cited in the previous review of research, *Going Home* (1972) and *A Night with Mrs. da Tonka* (1972), and his unfortunate Abbey play, *Scenes from an Album* (1981).

Conor Farrington (1928–   ). Primarily a verse dramatist, he is a member of the Radio Éireann Repertory Company. His published plays include the one act "The Ghostly Garden" (in *Prizewinning Plays of 1964,* 1965) and *Aaron Thy Brother* (1975). See also his essay "Playwrights and the Stationary Carrot" (*Theatre Arts,* 1962).

Brian Friel (1929–   ). He has published *Living Quarters* (1978);

Volunteers (1979); a new edition of *The Enemy Within,* with notes by him and Thomas Kilroy (1979); *Aristocrats* (1980); *Faith Healer* (1980); *Translations* (1981); and his Chekovian adaptation, *The Three Sisters.*

James Douglas (1929–   ). He has published *The Savages* (1979), and his one-act "Catalogue" is to appear in *Four Irish Plays.* A collaborative effort under the pseudonym "Robert James" appears in three issues of the *Journal of Irish Literature* (1981). Collectively called *The Writers' Trilogy,* this work includes the plays *There Are Joys, What Is the Stars?* and *Cast a Cold Eye.*

Eugene McCabe (1930–   ). A dairy farmer for ten years before the success of his stories, short novels, and plays allowed him to turn to full-time writing, McCabe includes among his published plays *The King of the Castle* (1978), *Pull Down a Horseman/Gale Day* (1979), and the television plays *Roma* (1979) and *Cancer* (1980). See also Frank Byrne's interview, "Eugene McCabe's Finished with the North!" (*Sunday Independent,* 31 October 1976).

Desmond Forristal (1930–   ). The plays of this Dublin-born priest have been among the recent successes of the Gate. He has published *Black Man's Country* (1975) and *The True Story of the Horrid Popish Plot* (1976).

Edna O'Brien (1930–   ). One of the best-known Irish novelists, O'Brien has also occasionally written for the theater or for films. Her published plays include *A Cheap Bunch of Nice Flowers* in *Plays of the Year* (vol. 26, ed. J. C. Trewin, 1963), "Wedding Dress: A Play for Television" (*Mademoiselle,* Nov. 1963), *Zee & Co.* (1971), *A Pagan Place* (1973), and *Virginia* (1981). Grace Eckley has written a short critical study (1974).

John Arden (1930–   ). This English playwright has lived for a few years in the west of Ireland with his wife, Margaretta D'Arcy, with whom in recent years he has usually collaborated. The Ardens have occasionally written plays on Irish themes, including the published *The Ballygombeen Bequest* (*Scripts,* Sept. 1972) and *The Non-Stop Connolly Show.* The lengthy *Connolly Show* was given an all-night reading at Liberty Hall and was published in six parts (1977–80).

Liam Mac Uistin (c. 1930–   ). This Dubliner has written plays in Irish and English that have been produced at the Abbey, the Peacock, and the Damer. His *Post Mortem* has been published and his one-act "The Glory and the Dream" is to appear in *Four Irish Plays.*

John Wilson Haire (1932–   ). He has been resident dramatist at the Royal Court in London and has had plays produced at the Lyric in Belfast and at the Abbey. He has published *Bloom of the Diamond Stone* (1973), *Within Two Shadows* (1974), *Echoes from a Concrete Canyon* (1975), and *Lost Worlds* (1978).

James McKenna (1933–   ). His early play *The Scatterin'* has been published (1977).

Thomas Murphy (1935–   ). His published works include *The Sanctuary Lamp* (1976), *On the Outside/On the Inside* (1976), *Famine* (1977), and *A Crucial Week in the Life of a Grocer's Assistant* (1978), a revision of *The Fooleen.*

Lee Gallaher (c. 1935–   ). This Bray-born writer has had work produced at the Lantern and the Project. His *Two Plays* (1974) contains the one-act plays "Kiss Me, Mr. Bogart" and "All the Candles in Your Head."

Thomas Kilroy (1936–). His *Talbot's Box* has been published (1979), as has his Chekovian adaptation, *The Seagull*.

Sidney Bernard Smith (1936–). His *Sherca* has been published (1979).

Heno Magee (1939–). Born into a Dublin working-class background, he has had several forceful plays produced at the Peacock. His only published play is *Hatchet* (1978).

Stewart Parker (1941–). This Belfast-born poet and playwright wrote *Spokesong,* which was favorably received in London in 1976. His radio play "The Ice-Berg" appeared in the *Honest Ulsterman* (Winter 1975). He has also published *Catchpenny Twist* (1980) and *Nightshade* (1980).

Ron Hutchinson (1947–). Born in Lisburn, Northern Ireland, and raised in Belfast, he received the George Devine Award for his first play, *Says I, Says He* (1980), and he has been playwright in residence at the Royal Shakespeare Company.

Jim Sheridan (1949–). This Dublin-born playwright and director has been mainly associated with the Project Arts Centre, which produced his *Mobile Homes* (1978).

Peter Sheridan (1952–). A brother of Jim Sheridan, he also worked at the project, where his *The Liberty Suit* (1978) and his *Emigrants* (1979) were produced.

MODERN FICTION

Diane Tolomeo

Anglo-Irish fiction can finally be spoken of as an identifiable entity in the twentieth century. It is no longer limited to writers concerned mainly with reviving a Gaelic heritage or awakening a patriotic fervor in their country, for this century has given rise to a group of Irish writers whose diversity is more pronounced than any apparent similarities or national ties. It is now more than ever possible, and sometimes desirable, to speak of Irish writers in a regional sense—the Ulster writers, the Listowel school, the Dublin writers, or the Irish writers "in exile," usually in England or the United States.

Few critics have attempted to deal with the development of Irish fiction. Most critical interpretations confine themselves to the work of a single literary figure, though the past decade has shown an increasing interest in more general surveys and attempts at broader evaluations. Such studies are often cursory, attending only to a handful of writers, especially during the lifetime of the writers. Other writers, such as Patrick Kavanagh, St. John Ervine, Padraic Colum, and Brian Friel, are known less for their prose fiction than for their poems, plays, or nonfiction. Nevertheless, such writers are included in the present survey (along with more obvious candidates for discussion) for their contributions to Irish fiction. Two writers have been excluded from the survey on the grounds that, though they are Irish by birth, their lives and writings reflect more accurately their experiences of another culture. The Dublin-born Iris Murdoch was educated at Somerville College, Oxford, and her novels belong to the tradition of English fiction. Donna Gerstenberger's monograph on her is included in the Bucknell Irish Writers series mainly because one novel, *The Red and the Green* (1965), deals with the unrest in Ireland and the troubles of Anglo-Irish families after the Easter Rising. Joyce Cary has also been excluded, although the argument against his being considered an Irish writer is slightly more tenuous. His work for the British government in East Africa and India colors many of his novels, which generally do not give evidence of particularly "Irish" concerns. Two articles and one book that place him more squarely in the Anglo-Irish tradition should, however, be noted: Lionel Stevenson's "Joyce Cary and the Anglo-Irish Tradition" (*MFS,* 1963); a more recent study by Barbara Fisher that discusses James Joyce and Joyce Cary, with the emphasis on Cary (*CJIS,* 1978); and John Wilson Foster's *Forces and Themes in Ulster Fiction* (1974).

Arguing in the other direction, I include Brian Moore, even though he emigrated to Canada and then to the United States, because his concerns remain chiefly connected to the Irish temperament and culture.

Confining this survey to those writers who have published in this century inevitably leads to some overlap with nineteenth-century fiction, such as some writings of Lord Dunsany, Standish O'Grady, Shan Bullock, Padraic Colum, and Daniel Corkery. These writers are included because of the amount of writing they produced in this century and because of their status as major figures not only in literature but also in Irish history and culture.

1. Bibliographies and General Studies

A full bibliography of twentieth-century writers of fiction cannot of course be compiled before the close of the century. Most material at present is concerned chiefly with individual writers, and where such bibliographies or checklists exist they are given in section 3. Other more general sources that are not exclusively or even mainly Irish include the Contemporary Authors series (published by Gale Research) and its companions, Contemporary Authors, permanent series, and Contemporary Literary Criticism (published under various editorships from 1973 to 1979). Also useful for brief references are Ruth Temple's *Twentieth Century British Literature: A Reference Guide* (1968) and Fred B. Millett's *Contemporary British Literature: A Critical Survey and 232 Author Bibliographies* (3rd rev., 1969). Alan R. Eager's *A Guide to Irish Bibliographical Material* (2nd ed., 1980) lists various bibliographies, although most of them deal with the early part of this century and before.

Some early bibliographical sources are Stephen J. Brown's *Ireland in Fiction* (1915) and Richard Best's *Bibliography of Irish Philology and of Printed Irish Literature* (1913) and his *Bibliography of Irish Philology and Manuscript Literature: Publications, 1913-1941* (1942; rpt. 1969). More recent is Patrick Rafroidi's *Irlande et Romantisme* (Paris, 1972). Brian Cleeve's *Dictionary of Irish Writers* (1966) is full of errors but until recently was the main source for brief biographies of minor as well as major figures. It has been supplanted by the more reliable and informative *Dictionary of Irish Literature* (1979), edited by Robert Hogan. This volume, which contains biography, criticism, and both primary and secondary bibliography, is the obvious starting point for students of Irish literature. For writers of the past twenty years, some of the best sources of both biographical and bibliographical information are periodicals and special issues of journals. Maurice Harmon's *Select Bibliography for the*

Study of Anglo-Irish Literature and Its Backgrounds: An Irish Studies Handbook (1977) is a companion to his earlier *Modern Irish Literature, 1800–1967* (1967), a guide listing novels, poetry, plays, and criticism. The more recent work provides general references to libraries, books, and periodicals; a section on Ireland and its historical and cultural backgrounds; a section on Anglo-Irish literary history and reference materials; and a useful listing of bibliographies of individual authors. The bibliographies are the most important part of Harmon's work, although it omits many secondary sources and includes some unreliable information.

Also recent is *A Bibliography of Modern Irish and Anglo-Irish Literature* (1976), by Frank Kernowski, C. W. Spinks, and Laird Loomis. In a more general context, Stephen Gwynn's *Irish Literature and Drama* (1936), while dealing primarily with prerevolutionary writing, contains a final chapter on literary developments after the revolution and briefly introduces what were then the "new" writers: Liam O'Flaherty, Sean O'Faolain, Peadar O'Donnell, Frank O'Connor, Lord Dunsany, Brinsley MacNamara, Elizabeth Bowen, and Francis Stuart. Peter Costello's *The Heart Grown Brutal: The Irish Revolution in Literature, from Parnell to the Death of Yeats, 1891–1939* (1977) discusses the same period from a more updated perspective. The book's third and final section on reaction to the revival and revolution, as well as the chapter called "The New Novel: Romantic Realism," comments briefly on literature since *Ulysses* (1922). Estella Ruth Taylor's *The Modern Irish Writers: Cross Currents of Criticism* (1954) has some useful comments on Colum, Dunsany, Ervine, Martyn, O'Connor, Strong, Tynan, and others. The festschrift for William York Tindall, *Modern Irish Literature* (1972), edited by Raymond J. Porter and James D. Brophy, contains essays on three modern fiction writers: Frank O'Connor, Brian Moore, and Flann O'Brien. Susan Cahill and Thomas Cahill's *A Literary Guide to Ireland* (1973), more a travelogue than a literary guide, attempts to combine a survey of literature with a depiction of writers in their geographical contexts, but the emphasis is on the geography and Ulster is entirely omitted.

Until recently, the best single introduction to Irish fiction in this century has been Benedict Kiely's *Modern Irish Fiction* (1950), which surveys over sixty writers as well as representative types in Irish fiction. Richard Fallis' *The Irish Renaissance* (1977), intended, according to its preface, to "sketch men, women, and events" in Ireland from 1880 to 1940, provides an introductory survey of Irish books and plays most useful for the beginning student. Three chapters on Irish fiction survey the major figures before 1940 (Joyce, Stephens, Beckett, Brian O'Nolan [Flann O'Brien], O'Connor, O'Flaherty, and O'Faolain), and a summary chapter on literature since 1940 deals, again very generally, with Mary Lavin, Michael McLaverty, Benedict Kiely, and a few others.

Herbert A. Kenny's *Literary Dublin* (1974) attempts to deal with the Dublin influence and atmosphere in Irish writing and oratory over the past three centuries. Many of the newer writers are introduced briefly in the final chapter. The book is, however, full of errors and likely to mislead a beginning student of the literature.

Vivian Mercier's indispensable *The Irish Comic Tradition* (1962) deals with fiction as well as with poetry and drama. Joseph Ronsley has edited *Myth and Reality in Irish Literature* (1977), a collection of essays, mostly on earlier figures, that includes an essay on Flann O'Brien and an interesting survey by Kate O'Brien, "Imaginative Prose by the Irish, 1820-1970." Andrew Carpenter's *Place, Personality and the Irish Writer* (1977) contains eight essays by different scholars. The first seven deal with aspects of the revival and some individual figures (Parnell, Synge, Joyce, Devlin), but the last, by Carpenter, "Double Vision in Anglo-Irish Literature," attempts to locate those traits that distinguish the Irish writer from writers of other cultures. Another general look at writers since Joyce (Beckett, Flann O'Brien, McGahern, Aidan Higgins, Banville, and Stuart) is Richard Kearney's "A Crisis of Imagination: An Analysis of a Counter-Tradition in the Irish Novel" (*Crane Bag*, 1979). And the recent work by F. S. L. Lyons, *Culture and Anarchy in Ireland, 1890-1939* (1979), while not predominantly literary in its perspective, has comments and anecdotes on literary figures throughout, especially in its chapter on Ulster.

Easily the most thorough and useful recent examination of Irish fiction is the collection of essays edited by Patrick Rafroidi and Maurice Harmon, *The Irish Novel in Our Time* (Villeneuve-d'Ascq, 1976). It includes twenty essays on the Irish novel from 1950 to 1975 in historical, social, and literary contexts and separate essays on twelve contemporary novelists. The first section on traditions and conventions contains Patrick Rafroidi's "A Question of Inheritance: The Anglo-Irish Tradition," Sean Ó Tuama's "The Other Tradition: Some Highlights of Modern Fiction in Irish," and Maurice Harmon's "Generations Apart: 1925-1975." The section "Forces and Themes in Modern Irish Fiction" contains more general essays: Kathleen O'Flaherty's "Catholicism and the Novel: A Comparative View," John Wilson Foster's "The Geography of Irish Fiction," Noël Debecr's "The Irish Novel Looks Backward," and Richard Deutsch's " 'Within Two Shadows': The Troubles in Northern Ireland." The essays on individual authors are listed in their appropriate places in section 3. Also of value is the book's section of selected primary and secondary bibliographies of individual authors.

A companion volume, *The Irish Short Story* (1979), edited by Patrick Rafroidi and Terence Brown, accomplishes an equivalent survey of writers who are best known for their shorter fiction. The initial chapters deal with the Anglo-Irish short story tradition and include a survey by Maurice Harmon of short stories written in the decade 1968-78 and appearing in the *Irish Press*. Sixteen chapters are devoted to individual writers from Carleton to McGahern. An earlier and briefer look at the short story is Vivian Mercier's "The Irish Short Story and Oral Tradition," in *The Celtic Cross: Studies in Irish Culture and Literature* (1964), edited by Roy B. Browne, William J. Roscelli, and Richard Loftus. Mercier sees the short story as the gifted genre of Irish writing and surveys it from the nineteenth century to more recent times, giving special emphasis to George Moore and Frank O'Connor. A more recent survey by Maureen Murphy, "The Short Story in Irish," appeared in *Mosaic* (1979).

Two Decades of Irish Writing: A Critical Survey (1975), edited by Douglas Dunn, deals mainly with poetry but also includes Lorna Sage's essay on Flann O'Brien, Tom Paulin's "A Necessary Provincialism: Brian Moore, Maurice Leitch, Florence Mary McDowell," and Roger Garfitt's "Constants in Contemporary Irish Fiction," which shows how Stuart, McGahern, and Aidan Higgins each present a different image of Ireland and also mentions some other contemporary writers.

Several articles dealing with more recent writings have appeared in various journals. Seán McMahon (*Éire,* 1966) briefly examines some of the categories of representative Irish types set forth by Benedict Kiely (*Modern Irish Fiction,* 1950) and discusses some recent southern writers, notably Edna O'Brien, John McGahern, and John Broderick. A subsequent article by McMahon (*Éire,* 1974) looks at writers then just beginning their publishing and cursorily surveys some of the work of Thomas Kilroy, Jennifer Johnston, Kevin Casey, Julia O'Faolain, and Tom MacIntyre, and the northern writers Maurice Leitch, Vincent Lawrence, and his brother John Banville. Also listed are a number of new writers who as yet had not published in hardback (among whom are Evelyn Haran, Kate Cruise O'Brien, Eithne Strong, Maeve Kelly, and Desmond Hogan). An earlier study by McMahon (*Éire,* 1968) provides a good general review of the importance of the priest in the life and literature of Ireland. Maurice Harmon (*Éire,* 1973) looks at the new generation of writers in the fifties, chiefly the poets, but he also discusses Higgins' novel *Langrishe, Go Down* and Thomas Kilroy's *The Big Chapel.* An earlier, more general study by Harmon is "The Era of Inhibitions: Irish Literature 1920-60" (*EUQ,* 1966).

Among the more specific studies on writers of the North, the most thorough is John Wilson Foster's *Forces and Themes in Ulster Fiction* (1974), which contains critical studies of the major northern novelists, including McLaverty, Kiely, Reid, Friel, Brian Moore, Leitch, Janet McNeill, and Bullock. Briefer and more superficial discussions of Ulster writers include John Boyd's "Ulster Prose," in *The Arts in Ulster* (ed. Sam Hanna Bell, Nesca A. Robb, and John Hewitt, 1951), which surveys the period from the late nineteenth to the early twentieth centuries, ending with writers who were just beginning to be known then but who have since become more established (such as McLaverty and Buchanan). Another shorter essay is Seán McMahon's "The Black North" (*Éire,* 1966), which focuses primarily on Moore, Kiely, and McLaverty. John Cronin's "Ulster's Alarming Novels" (*Éire,* 1969) regards both Catholic (McLaverty, Moore) and Protestant (Reid, Leitch) writers as mournful and bitter. Also by Cronin is a brief forward-looking study, concerned mainly with writers since 1950, that appeared in *Causeway: The Arts in Ulster* (ed. Michael Longley, 1971).

Finally, three journals have devoted special issues to the general subject of Irish literature. In 1976 *Sewanee Review* published an issue, *The Literature of Modern Ireland,* that includes a short story by James Plunkett, poetry, a brief essay by Edna O'Brien (later included in her *Mother Ireland*), and articles on Frank O'Connor and Elizabeth Bowen. A special issue of *Mosaic, The Irish Tradition in Literature,* edited by

Daniel S. Lenoski, appeared in 1979. It contains thirteen articles on individual figures (Yeats, Bowen, Lavin, Kavanagh, Beckett, Le Fanu, and Joyce) as well as on the more general topics of music and language. Also in 1979, *Genre* published a special issue, *The Genres of the Irish Literary Revival,* edited by Ronald Schleifer (rpt. 1980). Among its articles is Terence Brown's "After the Revival: The Problem of Adequacy and Genre," which considers Kavanagh and O'Flaherty at length.

2. Anthologies

Apart from anthologies of short stories by a single author, numerous collections of prose seek to capture a particular period or aspect of Irish writing. A comprehensive collection assembled by Seán McMahon, *The Best from the* Bell: *Great Irish Writing* (1978), excerpts forty-one articles, poems, and items of fiction from the Irish literary magazine that ran from 1940 to 1954 (excepting a two-year gap from 1948 to 1950). Following each item is a brief but useful biographical note on the contributor.

Stories of earlier writers of this century are collected in George A. Birmingham's *Irish Short Stories* (1932), which contains twenty-five stories by authors such as Lynn Doyle, Bullock, Lord Dunsany, and Birmingham. Diarmuid Russell's *The Portable Irish Reader* (1946, reissued in 1956) contains nonfiction, plays, and poetry as well as short stories by O'Flaherty, Lavin, Bowen, and others. A more comprehensive anthology is Vivian Mercier and David H. Greene's *1000 Years of Irish Prose* (1952), which ranges from translations from the Gaelic to more recent selections by O'Connor, Flann O'Brien, and others. David H. Greene's *An Anthology of Irish Literature* (1954; reissued in 1971) covers a similar chronological span and includes some short stories by twentieth-century writers.

Devin A. Garrity has collected thirty-two stories in *Irish Stories and Tales* (1955; Pocket Library, 1957) and has also assembled *44 Irish Short Stories* (1955; rpt. as *Irish Stories and Tales,* 1961). Frank O'Connor has a short but useful introduction to twenty stories by fifteen authors in *Modern Irish Short Stories* (1957). Valentin Iremonger's *Irish Short Stories* (1960) anthologizes fifteen stories by writers ranging from George Moore to John Montague. Edited by John Montague and Thomas Kinsella, *The Dolmen Miscellany of Irish Writing* (1962) contains prose and poetry, including stories by Brian Moore, John Jordan, and James Plunkett, and excerpts from the then unpublished novels of Higgins *(Langrishe, Go Down)* and McGahern *(The Barracks).*

Two volumes of *Winter's Tales from Ireland* (1970, 1972), respectively edited by Augustine Martin and Kevin Casey, contain twenty-six stories, many by newer writers who had not yet published a hardback collection of their own. David Marcus has edited a series of anthologies of Irish short stories: *Modern Irish Short Stories* (1965; reissued in 1972); *New Irish Writing 1* (1970); *Modern Irish Stories* (1972); *Tears of the*

Shamrock (1972), which contains short stories on Ireland's struggle for nationhood; *Best Irish Short Stories* (1976), almost half of which had not previously been published; *Best Irish Short Stories 2* (1977); and *Best Irish Short Stories 3* (1978).

An essay by Francis Stuart introduces *Paddy No More* (1977), a collection of eighteen stories by ten modern authors. Edna O'Brien has assembled *Some Irish Loving: A Selection* (1979), which contains letters, poems, and fictional excerpts ranging from letters from Kitty O'Shea to passages from Joyce, Shaw, Kiely, McGahern, and others. Twenty-six short stories, by writers ranging chronologically from George Moore to John McGahern, appeared recently in *Modern Irish Short Stories* (1981), edited by Ben Forkner, with a preface by Anthony Burgess. It is a comprehensive collection, well chosen for its diversity and high quality.

One of the best sources for recent short stories remains the *Journal of Irish Literature.* Since its beginning in 1972 it has published works by (among others) Desmond Hogan, Fred Johnston, Mary Rose Callaghan, Juanita Casey, and Vic Wortley. And of course there is the *Irish Press,* which has carried a weekly literary feature since April 1968.

3. Individual Authors: Texts and Criticism

The information in this section is by no means exhaustive. The bibliographical references, where given, provide more complete information about individual authors' published writings. The secondary studies are only a selection from what is frequently a much lengthier bibliography. The articles included here represent different points of view and reflect a period of several years. The listing is given chronologically according to date of birth to indicate the development of the literature over the period.

Standish James O'Grady (1846-1928) did most of his writing in the nineteenth century, and a good deal of it was nonfiction, but his influence on this century is pervasive enough that he must at least be mentioned in any survey of modern fiction in Ireland. Frequently called the father of the Irish literary revival, he contributed to the literature novels and tales based on early Irish mythology and Irish history in the Elizabethan age. Although he was called to the Irish bar, he preferred writing and helped to awaken Ireland to its past through an interest in its history and legend. Some of his works are *The Bog of Stars and Other Stories* (1893), *Red Hugh's Captivity* (1889), *Finn and His Companions* (1892; reissued for young people in 1970 as *Fionn and His Companions),* *The Masque of Finn* (1907), and a three-volume novelization of portions of the Cuchulain cycle: *The Coming of Cuculain* (1894), *In the Gates of the North* (1901), and *The Triumph and Passing of Cuculain* (1920). An early study of O'Grady's writing is the memoir by his son, Hugh Art O'Grady, *Standish James O'Grady: The Man and the Writer* (1929). A recent evaluation is Phillip L. Marcus' *Standish O'Grady* (1971). There has been little periodical criticism on O'Grady as a fiction writer. *A Bibliography of Books Written by Standish O'Grady* (1930) was compiled by P. S. O'Hegarty, who also contributed to "Bibliographies of

Irish Authors, no. 2: Standish O'Grady" (*DM,* 1930). John R. McKenna has published "The Standish O'Grady Collection at Colby College: A Checklist" (*CLQ,* 1958).

Bram Stoker (1847-1912) (Abraham Stoker) was an unpaid drama critic and a private secretary to Henry Irving. Of his twelve novels, the only one remembered today is *Dracula* (1897).

Edward Martyn (1859-1923), a playwright, wrote his first work, the novel *Morgante the Lesser* (1890), under the pseudonym Sirius. Most criticism deals with his dramatic works, but a more general approach may be found in Dennis Gwynn's *Edward Martyn and the Irish Revival* (1930) and more recently in Wayne Hall's "Edward Martyn (1859-1923): Politics and Drama of Ice" (*Éire,* 1980).

Katharine Tynan (1861-1931), known chiefly as a poet, also wrote over a hundred titles of fiction. While their merit is often questioned, their number is impressive. Marilyn Gaddis Rose has written *Katharine Tynan* (1974) for the Irish Writers series.

Henry de Vere Stacpoole (1863-1951) practiced medicine briefly as a ship's doctor and also took a great interest in sea birds. These subjects led him to write about fifty novels, mainly romantic and tropical. His most famous, *The Blue Lagoon* (1908), is a childhood fantasy that has twice been made into a motion picture.

Shan F. Bullock (1865-1935)—in English, John William Bullock —was the son of a northern Protestant bailiff, magistrate, and farmer, and he himself entered the civil service in London. A prolific writer, he produced over twenty volumes of short stories and novels as well as several works of nonfiction. His best-known novel, *The Loughsiders* (1921), deals with peasant life. Other fictional works include *Irish Pastorals* (1901), *The Squireen* (1903), *The Red Leaguers* (1904), *Dan the Dollar* (1906), *Master John* (1910), *Hetty: The Story of an Ulster Family* (1911), and *Gleanings* (1926). He is discussed in Foster's *Forces and Themes in Ulster Fiction* and in Kiely's *Modern Irish Fiction.*

Violet Russell (1868-1932), the wife of A. E., wrote *Heroes of the Dawn* (1913) and short stories based on the legendary Finn cycle.

Louie Bennett (1870-1956), a journalist interested in social justice, is being rediscovered because of her early concern with women's rights. Her novels include *Prisoner of His Word* (1908).

Robert Erskine Childers (1870-1922) was a clerk in the House of Commons for fifteen years and an Irish republican executed by the Free State government. He is also known for his thriller, *The Riddle of the Sands* (1910), which foresaw the coming of World War I. There is a bibliography of him by P. S. O'Hegarty (*DM,* 1948), and there are two studies of his life, Burke Willinson's *The Zeal of the Convert* (1974) and Andrew Boyle's *The Riddle of Erskine Childers* (1977).

Jack B. Yeats (1871-1957) is primarily known as a painter, but he also wrote several works of fiction, including *Sligo* (1930), *The Amaranthers* (1936), *The Charmed Life* (1938; rpt. 1974), and *The Careless Flower* (1947). Hilary Pyle's *Jack B. Yeats: A Biography* (1970) contains a bibliography, and *Jack B. Yeats: A Centenary Gathering* (1971), edited by Roger McHugh, contains a chronology and a bibliography by Martha Caldwell.

Lynn C. Doyle (1873-1961) was the punning pseudonym ("linseed oil") used by Leslie Alexander Montgomery, an Ulster banker and writer known mainly for his humor⌐us short stories, many of which he broadcast on the BBC in Belfast. Most are set in his imaginary locale of Ballygullion. Titles of his collected stories include *Ballygullion* (1908), *Lobster Salad* (1922), *Dear Ducks* (1925), *Me and Mr. Murphy* (1930), *Rosabelle* (1933), *The Shake of the Bag* (1939), *A Bowl of Broth* (1945), *Green Oranges* (1947), *Back to Ballygullion* (1953), and *New Stories* (1957). He is dealt with briefly in Foster's *Forces and Themes in Ulster Fiction*.

Annie M. P. Smithson (1873-1948) was a nurse and midwife who became an ardent republican in the civil war. She began writing late, but her romantic and patriotic novels are still to some extent popular, such as *Her Irish Heritage* (1917), *For God and Ireland* (1931), and *The Marriage of Nurse Harding* (1935).

Conal O'Riordan (1874-1948), a managing director of the Abbey, wrote seventeen volumes of fiction, many of which were historical. He created the character of David Quinn in his series of novels *Soldier Born,* (1927), *Soldier of Waterloo* (1928), *Soldier's Wife* (1935), *Soldier's End* (1938). Before World War I he wrote under the pseudonym Norreys Connell.

Forrest Reid (1875-1947) was an Ulster writer who produced over twenty volumes, consisting of novels, autobiography, short stories, and critical works. His many popular novels include *The Bracknels* (1911, rev. as *Denis Bracknel*, 1947), *Following Darkness* (1912; rev. as *Peter Waring*, 1937), *Brian Westby* (1934), and a trilogy written in reverse order: *Young Tom* (1944), *The Retreat* (1936), and *Uncle Stephen* (1931). His short stories are collected as *The Garden God* (1905), which was dedicated to Henry James (who did not like it); *A Garden by the Sea* (1918); and *Demophon* (1927). Reid is the subject of an early study by Russell Burlingham (1953) and of a more recent one by Mary Bryan (1976). He is also discussed in Foster's *Forces and Themes in Ulster Fiction* and in Brian Taylor's *The Green Avenue: The Life and Writings of Forrest Reid, 1875-1947* (1980).

Daniel Corkery (1878-1964), who helped revive interest in eighteenth-century Gaelic poetry and the Irish cultural heritage, had such famous pupils as Frank O'Connor and Sean O'Faolain. Often called the greatest single influence on Irish prose today, he wrote, besides verse plays, one novel, *The Threshold of Quiet* (1917), and several volumes of short stories: *A Munster Twilight* (1916), *The Hounds of Banba* (1920), *The Stormy Hills* (1929), *Earth out of Earth* (1939), and *The Wager and Other Stories* (1950). He has also written critical works on the Irish language, history, and Synge. George Brandon Saul's *Daniel Corkery* appeared in the Irish Writers series (1973), and Seán Lucy's chapter on his short stories is in *The Irish Short Story*. There is an article on him by O'Faolain in *DM* (1936).

Lord Dunsany (1878-1957), Edward John Moreton Drax Plunkett, the eighteenth Baron Dunsany, is known as a writer of poems and plays, but he also wrote a staggering amount of prose—about three dozen volumes of novels, short stories, and critical writings, including his three-volume autobiography (beautifully penned with a goose quill). His works often show a dreamworld quality, except for the tall tales of his popular character Jorkens. His fictional titles include *The Sword of Welleran* (1908), *The Last Book of Wonder* (1916), *The King of Elfland's Daughter* (1924), *The Blessings of Pan* (1927), *The Curse of the Wise Woman* (1933), *Guerrilla* (1944), *The Strange Journeys of Colonel Polders* (1950), *The Travel Tales of Mr. Joseph Jorkens* (1931), *Jorkens Remembers Africa* (1934), and *Jorkens Has a Large Whiskey* (1940).

The earliest book on Dunsany is Edward H. Bierstadt's *Dunsany the Dramatist* (1917). A study of his later years is Hazel Littlefield Smith's *Lord Dunsany, King of Dreams: A Personal Portrait* (1959), and a fuller biography is Mark Amory's *Lord Dunsany: A Biography* (1972). A study of Dunsany as poet may be found in R. F. Rattray's *Poets in the Flesh: Tagore, Yeats, Dunsany, Stephens, Drinkwater* (1961). Briefer assessments are Montrose J. Moses' "Lord Dunsany's Peculiar Genius" (*Bellman*, 1917), Norreys Jephson O'Conor's essay on Dunsany in *Changing Ireland* (1924), Oliver St. John Gogarty's "Lord Dunsany" (*Atlantic Monthly*, March 1955), R. Sencourt's "Memoirs of Lord Dunsany" (*ContempR*, 1958), and G. B. Saul's "Strange Gods in Far Places: The Short Stories of Lord Dunsany" (*ArQ*, 1963). H. M. Black has compiled "A Check-List of First Editions of Works of Lord Dunsany" (*Trinity College Dublin Annual Bulletin*, 1957).

Seumas O'Kelly (c. 1878–1918) was a journalist, editor, and deputy for Arthur Griffith. A friend of revolutionary leaders, he died of a heart attack following a raid of his offices by British soldiers. His best-known work is the long short story *The Weaver's Grave*, published posthumously. Other short story volumes are *By the Stream of Kilmeen* (1906), *The Leprechaun of Kilmeen* (1908), *Hillsiders* (1909), *The Golden Barque* (1912), and *Waysiders* (1917). He wrote two novels, *The Lady of Deerpark* (1917) and *Wet Clay*, unrevised at his death and published posthumously (1923). Seumas O'Sullivan's *Seumas O'Kelly: Essays and Recollections* (1944) is an early view of his life and work. George Brandon Saul's *Seumas O'Kelly* (1971) is a full-length version of Saul's earlier essay (*Éire*, 1967). One of the best studies is Anne Clune's essay in *The Irish Short Story*. His novels are discussed briefly by Kiely in *Modern Irish Fiction*. P. S. O'Hegarty published two early bibliographies of O'Kelly, *A Bibliography of Books by Seumas O'Kelly* (1924) and "Seumas O'Kelly" (*DM*, 1934).

Maurice Walsh (1879–1964), an employee of the Customs and Excise Service, wrote short stories and novels of a romantic Scotland and west of Ireland and is probably remembered best for his character Thomasheen James, a gardener. In 1939 he coauthored an article with Sean O'Faolain for the *Saturday Evening Post* in favor of Ireland's neutrality in World War II. Some of his works are *Thomasheen James, Man of No Work* (1941), *Sons of the Swordmaker* (1938), *Castle Gillian* (1948), *Danger under the Moon* (1956), and *The Smart Fellow* (1964). There is a Walsh checklist by Joanne L. Henderson (*JIL*, 1972).

Padraic Colum (1881–1972) wrote mainly poems and plays, but in the realm of fiction he also produced children's books and tales and both edited and introduced anthologies of other Irish writers, among them A. E., Lord Dunsany, Samuel Ferguson, and James Stephens. His novels and tales include *The King of Ireland's Son* (1916), *The Boy Who Knew What the Birds Said* (1918), *Castle Conquer* (1923), *The Fountain of Youth* (1927), *Three Men* (1930), *The Frenzied Prince* (1943), *The Flying Swans* (1957), and *Images of Departure* (1969). Zack Bowen has written a full-length study (1970) and together with Gordon Henderson has edited a special issue on Colum (*JIL*, 1973). Checklists of Colum's writings by Alan Denson appeared in two issues of *Dublin Magazine* (1967).

St. John Greer Ervine (1883-1971) is known mainly for his plays, but he wrote a considerable amount of prose as well. Born in the North, he emigrated to London in 1900. In addition to biographies of Wilde, Shaw, and others, he produced seven novels: *Mrs. Martin's Man* (1914), *Alice and a Family: A Story of South London* (1915), *Changing Winds* (1917), *The Foolish Lovers* (1920), *The Wayward Man* (1927), *Sophia* (1941), and *The Christies* (1949). A recent article on Ervine by John Boyd appeared in *Threshold* (1974). He is also discussed by Foster in *Forces and Themes in Ulster Fiction*. Paula Howard has compiled a primary bibliography (*IBl*, 1971).

Joseph O'Neill (1886-1953) served as permanent secretary in the Irish Department of Education. He was elected to the Irish Academy of Letters for his novel *Wind from the North* (1934). Also popular was his *Land under England* (1935), a novel about the world under Hadrian's wall.

J. H. Pollock (1887-1964) wrote a volume of short stories, *Irish Ironies* (1930), and five novels: *The Valley of the Wild Swans* (1932), *Peter and Paul* (1933), *The Moth and the Star* (1937), *Mount Kestrel* (1945), and *The Last Nightingale* (1952).

Maurice Collis (1889-1973), a close friend of Jack Yeats, wrote twenty-nine books. His most popular novel is *She Was a Queen*. He also wrote as an art critic.

Geraldine Dorothy Cummins (1890-1969) turned from writing plays to writing novels of peasant life as well as short stories. She is also known for her writings on psychic research, mostly on esoteric aspects of early Christianity and extrasensory perception. Her novels include *The Land They Loved* (1919) and *Fires of Beltane* (1936), and her short stories are collected as *Variety Show* (1959).

Brinsley MacNamara (1890-1963) was the pseudonym of John Weldon, who was a writer of plays and prose fiction and also an actor, then a director of the Abbey for a short while. His first novel was the controversial *The Valley of the Squinting Windows* (1918), which raised a furor because of similarities between its characters and the people of his own town, Delvin. A crowd of Delvin citizens gathered for a ritual burning of it when it first appeared. It was followed by the less upsetting story of a disillusioned patriot, *The Clanking of Chains* (1920), and then by others including *The Irishman* (1920), written under the pseudonym of Oliver Blyth; *The Smiling Faces and Other Stories* (1929); a fantasy, *The Various Lives of Marcus Igoe* (1929); *Return to Ebontheever* (1930), reissued in 1942 as *Othello's Daughter*; and a novella, *The Whole Story of the X. Y. Z.* (1951). The controversial first novel has been looked at afresh by Seán McMahon (*Éire*, 1968). There is a brief discussion of *The Clanking of Chains* in Kiely's *Modern Irish Fiction*. Michael McDonnell has compiled "Brinsley MacNamara: A Checklist" (*JIL*, 1975).

Patrick MacGill (1891–1963) was a northern writer of poems, one play, and nineteen novels. His best-known novels are the semiautobiographical *Children of the Dead-End* (1914), *The Rat-Pit* (1915), and *Moleskin Joe* (1923). Foster deals with him in *Forces and Themes in Ulster Fiction*.

Peadar O'Donnell (1893–) was a schoolteacher until 1918 and then an organizer for the Irish Transport and General Workers Union. He began writing while in jail, having been sentenced to execution by the Free State after his capture in the battle of Four Courts, but he managed to escape. He left the IRA in 1934 and founded the Irish Republican Congress. He is better known for his politics than for his writings, which are often influenced by his political experiences. From 1940 on, he was business manager for the *Bell*. O'Donnell's first novel, *Storm* (1925), deals with the Anglo-Irish war. One of his best-known novels, *Islanders* (1927), was written in southern France after his release from jail, where he had been sentenced for his Land Annuities agitation; it was published in the United States as *The Way It Was with Them* (1928). *Adrigoole* (1929) deals with peasant life, while *The Knife* (1930), published in the United States as *There Will Be Fighting* (1931) and considered one of his best writings, concerns the 1916 Rising. *The Gates Flew Open* (1930) is the story of his imprisonment after the fall of Four Courts. Later novels by O'Donnell are *On the Edge of the Stream* (1934); *The Big Windows* (1954); *There Will Be Another Day* (1963), an autobiographical account of the IRA; and *Proud Island* (1976). Two books on O'Donnell are Grattan Freyer's *Peadar O'Donnell* (1973) and Michael McInerney's *Peadar O'Donnell, Irish Social Rebel* (1974). Freyer has also written a good essay on the writings of O'Donnell (*Éire*, 1976). Paul A. Doyle has compiled "Peadar O'Donnell: A Checklist" (*BB*, 1971).

Eimar O'Duffy (1893–1935) has only recently been rediscovered in literary circles. He trained as a dentist, although he never practiced. He was opposed to the 1916 Rising and spent some time in England after World War I and then in Paris as a journalist. His writing is extremely diverse, including novels, satirical essays, poetry, plays, detective stories, and textbooks on economics. His first novel, *The Wasted Island* (1919), is an autobiographical account of the revolution. *The Lion and the Fox* (1922) is also a historical novel, and *Printer's Errors* (1922) describes pre-1916 Dublin. His fantastic trilogy, set in the twenty-first century, consists of *King Goshawk and the Birds* (1926), *The Spacious Adventures of the Man in the Street* (1928), and *Asses in Clover* (1933). *The Secret Enemy* (1932), *The Bird Cage* (1932), and *Heart of a Girl* (1935) are all mystery novels. Robert Hogan's *Eimar O'Duffy* (1972) is an excellent appraisal of O'Duffy's work, which is also discussed very favorably in Kiely's *Modern Irish Fiction*. Most early periodical criticism took the form of book reviews or obituary notices, except for Vivian Mercier's essay "The Satires of Eimar O'Duffy" (*Bell*, 1946). More recent is Gary Caret's "The 'Irish Lie': Mystic Art and Politics in Eimar

O'Duffy's *The Wasted Island"* (*Éire*, 1976). The *Journal of Irish Literature's* special O'Duffy issue (1978) contains four poems and four reviews by O'Duffy (all from the *Irish Review*), a play, fiction, and a primary bibliography that supplements the earlier work of Alf Mac-Lochlainn, "Eimar O'Duffy: A Bibliographical Biography" (*IB*, 1959–60).

Kenneth Sheils Reddin (1895–1967), who served as a justice of the district court from 1922 to 1959, was active in Sinn Fein, the Gaelic League, and the 1916 Rising. He wrote two plays for the Abbey, children's books (under the pseudonym Kenneth Sarr), and several novels, including *Somewhere to the Sea* (1936), about the revolution, and *Another Shore* (1945), published in the United States as *Young Man with a Dream* (1946).

Austin Clarke (1896–1974), while chiefly known for his lyric and dramatic poetry, also wrote the novels *The Bright Temptation* (1932), which was banned until 1954 in Ireland; *The Singing Men at Cashel* (1936); and *The Sun Dances at Easter* (1952). His works include the autobiographical *Twice Round the Black Church: Early Memories of Ireland and England* (1960) and several other works of nonfiction. A full-length study of his work is Susan Halpern's *Austin Clarke: His Life and Works* (1974). John Montague compiled *A Tribute to Austin Clarke on His Seventieth Birthday, 9 May 1966* (1966), and Maurice Harmon edited a special Austin Clarke issue of the *Irish University Review* (1974), which includes a bibliography of Clarke by Gerard Lyne.

Liam O'Flaherty (1896–   ) is best known for his stories, though he has also written sixteen novels as well as plays, criticism, and historical studies. His most famous novel, *The Informer* (1925), is based on the revolution. *Skerrett* (1932) and *Famine* (1937), two novels of Irish peasant life, have also received acclaim. Short story collections include *Spring Sowing* (1924), *Red Barbara* (1928), *The Mountain Tavern* (1929), *The Wild Swan* (1932), *Two Lovely Beasts* (1948), *The Wounded Cormorant* (1973), and *The Pedlar's Revenge* (1976). There have been a number of recent books on O'Flaherty and his work. Anthony Canedo's *Liam O'Flaherty: Introduction and Analysis* (1965) was one of the first manifestations of an O'Flaherty revival. It was followed by John Nicholas Zneimer's *The Literary Vision of Liam O'Flaherty* (1970), which interprets O'Flaherty from a less "Irish," more existential point of view. Zneimer's emphasis on the theme of religious quest is refreshing, albeit somewhat limiting. Paul A. Doyle's *Liam O'Flaherty* (1971) is a useful introduction with a good bibliography. James H. O'Brien's monograph on O'Flaherty, in the Irish Writers series (1973), concentrates on the novels, which are divided into those concerned with the "peasant" life, with the war, and with the era after the revolution. Only one chapter is devoted to the short stories and one other to the autobiographical writings.

Two specialized studies of the novels and the short stories are Angeline A. Kelly's *Liam O'Flaherty the Storyteller* (1976) and Patrick F. Sheeran's *The Novels of Liam O'Flaherty: A Study in Romantic Realism* (1976). Kelly gives an account of the stories' themes, narrative structure, and style and then turns to a study of death, life, nature, and violence in the works. Her study may be too superficial for all but beginning readers of O'Flaherty. Sheeran's assessment of the novels provides a survey of the "critical heritage" of O'Flaherty. Sheeran also discusses O'Flaherty's early life in the Aran Islands. His is the more scholarly and readable of the two studies. Several of the novels are also discussed, briefly, in Kiely's *Modern Irish Fiction*.

One of the earliest articles on O'Flaherty is Sean O'Faolain's "Don Quixote O'Flaherty" (*London Mercury*, 1937). It was reprinted with some revisions in the *Bell* (1941). O'Faolain also contributed an essay on O'Flaherty to *Writers of Today 2*, edited by Denys Val Baker (1948). Another early study is Benedict Kiely's "Liam O'Flaherty: A Story of Discontent" (*Month*, 1949). Later studies include George Brandon Saul's "A Wild Sowing: The Short Stories of Liam O'Flaherty" (*REL*, 1963), Michael H. Murray's "Liam O'Flaherty and the Speaking Voice" (*SSF*, 1968), Helene O'Connor's "Liam O'Flaherty: Literary Ecologist" (*Éire*, 1972), Maureen O'Rourke Murphy's "The Double Vision of Liam O'Flaherty" (*Éire*, 1973), and Angeline A. Hampton's "Liam O'Flaherty's Short Stories: Visual and Aural Effects" (*ES*, 1974). Brendan Kennelly contributed an insightful chapter on O'Flaherty to *The Irish Short Story*. The most complete bibliography is Paul A. Doyle's *Liam O'Flaherty: An Annotated Bibliography* (1972). It expands his earlier "A Liam O'Flaherty Checklist" (*TCL*, 1967) and Angeline A. Hampton's "Liam O'Flaherty: Additions to the Checklist" (*Éire*, 1971).

Kate O'Brien (1897–1974), a journalist who had an interest in Spanish literature, wrote novels as well as plays, diaries, and journals. Her best-known novel, *That Lady* (1946; pub. in the United States as *For One Sweet Grape*), is a historical novel about Philip II; because of the book's treatment of the monarch O'Brien was refused entry to Spain until the Irish ambassador intervened on her behalf. Her other novels include *Without My Cloak* (1931), *Mary Lavelle* (1936), *Pray for the Wanderer* (1938), *The Land of Spices* (1941), *The Flower of May* (1953), *As Music and Splendour* (1958), and *Presentation Parlour* (1963). An early article by John Jordan on *The Flower of May* appeared in the *Bell* (1954). A more recent appraisal by the same author is "Kate O'Brien: A Passionate Talent" (*Hibernia*, 1974).

Elizabeth Bowen (1899–1973) (Dorothea Cole) published over forty volumes of novels, short stories, children's books, essays, and editions of other writers. Some of her best-known works are *The Death of the Heart* (1938), *The Heat of the Day* (1949), *Eva Trout: or, Changing Scenes* (1968), *The Cat Jumps and Other Stories* (1934), and *Bowen's Court* (1942). Bowen's characters tend to be upper-middle-class, and while her early work is often close to being a social comedy of manners, her later writings, which are more concerned with human relations, at times border on tragedy. Sean O'Faolain sees her characters as like those of fable or as allegorical versions of "primitive urges" (*The Vanishing Hero*, 1956).

Jocelyn Brooke's *Elizabeth Bowen* (a British Council pamphlet, 1952) was too early to see Bowen in the larger context of English fiction, and Brooke does not regard *The Heat of the Day* as one of Bowen's most successful works. William Webster Heath's *Elizabeth Bowen: An*

Introduction to Her Novels (1961) bears some marks of its origin as a thesis as it surveys Bowen's place in the evolution of the English novel. Heath sees Bowen as a realistic novelist who deals with moral and aesthetic as well as literary concerns but who is limited by her insistence on the necessity of art as the means of learning to live with a kind of predetermined fate. A more cursory sketch is Allan E. Austin's *Elizabeth Bowen* (1971), which is designed for the general reader and, unlike Heath's book, focuses primarily on Bowen's style and thematic concerns. Edwin J. Kenney, Jr.'s *Elizabeth Bowen* (1975) consists of three short untitled sections; the lack of an index limits the book's usefulness. In an insightful if brief survey of Bowen's fiction, Kenney describes her recurring theses of lost innocence and the energy inherent in one's identity. Harriet Blodgett's *Patterns of Reality: Elizabeth Bowen's Novels* (1975) and Victoria Glendinning's *Elizabeth Bowen: Portrait of a Writer* (1977) are two recent studies of Bowen. Blodgett refutes the view of Bowen as a social realist and sees her instead as a psychological realist relying on Christian symbolism and the use of the imagination to bridge the gap between the human will and the divine will. Glendinning gives us a readable and sensitive biography that includes reminiscences by Bowen's friends and a perceptive portrayal of Bowen's conflict between her private and public lives. Robert Coles's *Irony in the Mind's Life: Essays on Novels by James Agee, Elizabeth Bowen, and George Eliot* (1974) deals primarily with Bowen's *The Death of the Heart*. Her work until 1949 is discussed by Kiely in *Modern Irish Fiction*.

Periodicals and journals have published numerous studies of Bowen's works. Early evaluations include Edward Sackville-West's "Ladies Whose Bright Pens . . . ," which also discusses the work of Ivy Compton-Burnett, in *Inclinations* (1949); David Daiches' "The Novels of Elizabeth Bowen" (*EJ*, 1949); Bruce Harkness' "The Fiction of Elizabeth Bowen" (*EJ*, 1955); and Barbara Seward's "Elizabeth Bowen's World of Impoverished Love" (*CE*, 1956). Among the most useful articles appearing in the past two decades are Geoffrey Wagner's "Elizabeth Bowen and the Artificial Novel" (*EIC*, 1963); M. Corona Sharp's "The House as Setting and Symbol in Three Novels by Elizabeth Bowen" (*XUS*, 1963); George Brandon Saul's "The Short Stories of Elizabeth Bowen" (*ArQ*, 1965); Richard Henry Rupp's "The Post-War Fiction of Elizabeth Bowen" (*XUS*, 1965); George Greene's "Elizabeth Bowen: Imagination as Therapy" (*Perspective*, 1965); Edward Mitchell's "Themes in Elizabeth Bowen's Short Stories" (*Critique*, 1966); two articles on the relation between Bowen's fiction and the Big House, Benedict Kiely's "The Great Gazebo" (*Éire*, 1967) and Gary T. Davenport's "Elizabeth Bowen and the Big House" (*SHR*, 1974); Paul A. Parish's "The Loss of Eden: Four Novels of Elizabeth Bowen" (*Critique*, 1973); Walter Sullivan's "A Sense of Place: Elizabeth Bowen and the Landscape of the Heart" (*SR*, 1976); and Barbara Brothers' "Pattern and Void: Bowen's Irish Landscapes and *The Heat of the Day*" (*Mosaic*, 1979).

Blodgett's book, listed above, has a good bibliography. There are also two separate bibliographical studies: J'Nan Sellery's "Elizabeth Bowen: A Check List" (*BNYPL*, 1970) and a primary and secondary bibliography in volume 1 of Robert J. Stanton's *A Bibliography of Modern British Novelists* (1978).

Paul Vincent Carroll (1900–68) is known mainly as a playwright, but he also wrote a number of short stories. A checklist of these as they appeared in *Ireland's Own* from 1920 to 1930 has been compiled by Diane Roman and Mary Hamilton (*JIL*, 1972).

Michael Farrell (1900–62) turned from medicine to writing in the thirties to produce a semiautobiographical and epic-sized novel, unedited when he died but later published as *Thy Tears Might Cease* (1963).

John O'Donoghue (1900–64) was in the Garda Siochana before emigrating to England. His autobiographical novel, *In a Quiet Land* (1957), is his best-known work. It was followed by *In a Strange Land* (1958) and *In Kerry Long Ago* (1960).

Sean O'Faolain (1900–)—in English, John Whelan—is well known for his fiction, biographies, travel books, and numerous works of literary criticism. He came to the United States to study at Harvard in 1926 and stayed to lecture at Boston College before returning to Ireland and beginning his writing. He was editor of the *Bell* from 1940 to 1946, and as a man of letters he encouraged many younger writers. In 1946 he converted to Roman Catholicism after his trips to Italy. His novels—*A Nest of Simple Folk* (1933), a family history; *Bird Alone* (1936); and *Come Back to Erin* (1940)—are generally less well known than his many volumes of stories. These include his first, *Midsummer Night's Madness* (1932), the translations from the Irish in *The Silver Branch* (1938), *Teresa* (1947), *The Man Who Invented Sin* (1948), *I Remember! I Remember!* (1961), *The Heat of the Sun* (1966), *Foreign Affairs* (1976), and *Selected Stories* (1978).

The earliest book on O'Faolain is Maurice Harmon's *Sean O'Faolain* (1966). Paul A. Doyle's *Sean O'Faolain* (1968), like his earlier "Sean O'Faolain and the *Bell* " (*Éire*, 1966), examines both the fiction and the editorial work on the *Bell*. Most recent is Joseph Storey Rippier's *The Short Stories of Sean O'Faolain: A Study in Descriptive Techniques* (1976), which, however, examines only eight stories. R. H. Hopkins discusses a single story in "The Pastoral Mode of Sean O'Faolain's 'The Silence of the Valley' " (*SSF*, 1964). More general studies are Katherine Hanley, C.S.J., "The Short Stories of Sean O'Faolain: Theory and Practice" (*Éire*, 1971); L. V. Harrod, "The Ruined Temples of Sean O'Faolain" (*Éire*, 1974); Gary T. Davenport, "Sean O'Faolain's Troubles: Revolution and Provincialism in Modern Ireland" (*SAQ*, 1976); and Denis Sampson, " 'Admiring the Scenery': Sean O'Faolain's Fable of the Artist" (*CJIS*, 1977). Guy Le Moigne has written an excellent survey, "Sean O'Faolain's Short-Stories and Tales," in *The Irish Short Story*. O'Faolain is also discussed throughout Kiely's *Modern Irish Fiction*.

The best recent work on O'Faolain is a special issue of the *Irish University Review* (1976), edited by Maurice Harmon, which contains ten essays on O'Faolain: Hubert Butler's "The *Bell*: An Anglo-Irish View," Joseph Duffy's "A Broken World: The Finest Short Stories of Sean O'Faolain," Dermot Foley's "Monotonously Rings the Little Bell," Hilary Jenkins' "Newman's Way and O'Faolain's Way," F. S. L.

Lyons' "Sean O'Faolain as Biographer," Robie Macauley's "Sean O'Faolain, Ireland's Youngest Writer," Donal McCartney's "Sean O'Faolain: A Nationalist Right Enough," Vivian Mercier's "The Professionalism of Sean O'Faolain," Julian Moynahan's "God Smiles, the Priest Beams, and the Novelist Groans," and Sean O'Faolain's own "A Portrait of the Artist as an Old Man."

Christine, Countess Longford (1900–   ) (Christine Patti Trew) is known for her plays, but she has also written the novels *Making Conversation* (1931), *Country Places* (1932), *Printed Cotton* (1935), and *Sea Change* (1940).

Norah Hoult (1901–   ) wrote more than two dozen popular novels and short stories. Her first book, a collection of short stories called *Poor Women* (1928), was a popular success and was followed by such novels as *The Last Days of Miss Jenkinson* (1962), *A Poet's Pilgrimage* (1965), and *Only Fools and Horses Work* (1969).

Francis Stuart (1902–   ) was born in Australia but moved to Ireland the same year. He was initially made famous by his first marriage, to Iseult Gonne in 1920, but his writings soon established him as a major literary figure. He has written more than twenty volumes of novels and short stories as well as plays, poems, and essays on such diverse figures as Jacob Boehme, de Valera, Yeats, and Kavanagh. Among his many works are *Women and God* (1931), *Pigeon Irish* (1932), *The Angel of Pity* (1935), *Julie* (1938), *The Pillar of Cloud* (1948), *Good Friday's Daughter* (1952), *Victors and Vanquished* (1958), *Memorial* (1973), and *A Hole in the Head* (1977). One of his best works is *Black List, Section H* (1971), an autobiographical novel.

Critical evaluations of Stuart's work have become increasingly popular, though his importance was already recognized in Kiely's *Modern Irish Fiction* (1950). In 1972 William J. McCormack edited *A Festschrift for Francis Stuart on His Seventieth Birthday*, which contains a bibliography, and J. H. Natterstad's *Francis Stuart* (1974) is a good study in the Irish Writers series. An early article of interest is David H. Greene's "The Return of Francis Stuart" (*Envoy*, 1951). Among recent articles, H. J. O'Brien's "St. Catherine of Siena in Ireland" (*Éire*, 1971) discusses, despite its misleading title, Stuart's *Pigeon Irish*. Of some interest too is O'Brien's "Francis Stuart's Cathleen Ni Houlihan" (*DM*, 1971). Other articles are J. H. Natterstad's "The Artist as Rebel: Some Reflections on Francis Stuart" (*ICarbS*, 1973) and his "Francis Stuart: At the Edge of Recognition" (*Éire*, 1974); Roger Garfitt's "The Novels of Francis Stuart" (*LonM*, 1976) and his "Constants in Contemporary Irish Fiction" (in *Two Decades of Irish Writings*); William C. Barnwell's "Looking to the Future: The Universality of Francis Stuart" (*Éire*, 1977); and Ronan Sheehan's interview, which includes John Banville as well, in "Novelists on the Novel" (*Crane Bag*, 1979).

A special Stuart issue of the *Journal of Irish Literature* (1976) includes an interview conducted by J. H. Natterstad as well as his "Francis Stuart: A Voice from the Ghetto." There are five letters from Iseult Gonne Stuart to Francis Stuart and a portfolio of writings by Stuart: poems, a short story, and a novel in progress, "A Hundred Wild Decembers." The checklist by Natterstad updates William J. McCormack's in *Long Room* (1971). Stuart is the only writer to receive two chapters in *The Irish Novel in Our Time*: Pierre Joannon's "Francis Stuart or the Spy of Truth" and William J. McCormack's "Francis Stuart: The Recent Fiction."

Vivian Connell (1903–), though she wrote some plays, is mainly known for novels, which include *The Chinese Room* (1943), *The Golden Sleep* (1948), *A Man of Parts* (1950), *Hounds of Cloneen* (1951), *September in Quinze* (1952), *Peacock Is a Gentleman* (1953), and *Corinna Lang, Goodbye* (1954).

Frank O'Connor (1903–66) was the pseudonym of Michael O'Donovan, one of Ireland's most popular and best-known short story writers. He was born in the Cork slums, joined the Gaelic League, and fought with the republicans in the civil war until he was imprisoned. He was employed as a clerk in the Great Southern Railway office and then as a librarian in Cork. As a director of the Abbey from 1935 to 1939, O'Connor worked closely with Yeats. He lectured in the United States and frequently contributed to the *New Yorker*. He returned to Ireland in 1962. Besides short stories, O'Connor has written novels, poems, travel books, literary criticism, and a two-volume autobiography. He was also the poetry editor for the *Bell*.

The short stories in *Guests of the Nation* (1931) depict the conflict between England and Ireland. They were followed by a novel, *The Saint and Mary Kate* (1932), a character study adapted for the stage by Mary Manning in 1970. Other story collections include *Bones of Contention* (1935), *Crab Apple Jelly* (1944), *The Common Chord* (1947), *Traveller's Samples: Stories and Tales* (1951), *Domestic Relations* (1957), *My Oedipus Complex* (1963), and *Collection Two* (1964). Reissued collections have continued to be published posthumously, often with new titles.

One of the most interesting books on O'Connor is a diverse collection of studies compiled by Maurice Sheehy, *Michael/Frank: Studies on Frank O'Connor* (1969). Its eighteen contributors include Richard Ellmann, Brendan Kennelly, Honor Tracy, Wallace Stegner, and Dermot Foley. The essays portray views of O'Connor in the academic world, as a librarian, poet, short-story writer, and Platonist. They avoid the humdrum, formally critical approach of so many similar collections of essays on literary figures. The book also contains an extensive primary bibliography.

James H. Matthews' *Frank O'Connor* (1976), in the Irish Writers series, is necessarily brief, in keeping with the format of that series, but brevity is almost an insult to a writer as prolific as O'Connor. Matthews limits himself to the fiction, and the study is so short that it is at best a superficial introduction, though useful to a beginning student. Matthews is currently working on a full-length biography of O'Connor, and part of this study appears as a rather long essay entitled "Women, War and Words: Frank O'Connor's First Confessions" (*Irish Renaissance Annual I*, 1980). It is a thorough and interesting account of O'Connor's "fumbling" for his own style in his first two books.

Maurice Wohlgelernter's *Frank O'Connor: An Introduction* (1977) deals not only with O'Connor's work but also with his character and thought in relation to his contemporaries and to historical events during his lifetime. Wohlgelernter discusses O'Connor's treatment of the Irish clergyman and Irish life but attempts no analysis of the stories themselves. A more interpretative, but less interesting, work is William M. Tomory's *Frank O'Connor* (1980), a thorough introductory study that covers a little of everything in a highly readable way. Roger Chatalic's "Frank O'Connor and the Desolation of Reality," in *The Irish Short Story*, is a biographical overview that addresses itself to some of the individual stories.

A special O'Connor issue of the *Journal of Irish Literature* (1975) contains an article by James H. Matthews, "Frank O'Connor: Improvising an Irish Writer," and poems, two stories, letters, talks, speeches, and a play by O'Connor himself. Other periodical criticism since his death includes Roger McHugh's "Frank O'Connor and the Irish Theatre" (*Éire*, 1969); Gary Davenport's "Frank O'Connor and the Comedy of Revolution" (*Éire*, 1973); Paul F. Casey's "Studying out of the Self-Educator: Frank O'Connor and German Literature" (*Éire*, 1976), which analyzes O'Connor's admiration for Goethe and for German culture; James H. Matthews' "Magical Improvisation: Frank O'Connor's Revolution" (*Éire*, 1975); James H. Matthews' "Frank O'Connor's Stories" and B. L. Reid's "The Teller's Own Tale: The Memoirs of Frank O'Connor," both in a special Irish literature issue of the *Sewanee Review* (1976); and Daniel J. Casey's "The Seanachie's Voice in Three Stories by Frank O'Connor" (*AIS*, 1977), which discusses "Peasants," "In the Train," and "The Majesty of the Law" in terms of the storyteller or "tradition bearer," the seanachie. Of interest also is Patrick Kavanagh's "Coloured Balloons: A Study of Frank O'Connor" (*JIL*, 1977), with a reply by Sean O'Faolain and a rejoinder by Kavanagh in the same issue, all reprinted by Hogan from the December 1947 issue of the *Bell*. Richard J. Thompson's "A Kingdom of Commoners: The Moral Art of Frank O'Connor" (*Éire*, 1978) argues that O'Connor's best work is his first four volumes and that he is trying to recapture a lost order and decency in our world. Because the essay attempts too much in too brief a space, it becomes cursory in dealing with specific stories. More interesting but also somewhat limited is Anthony T. McCrann's "Frank O'Connor and the Silence" (*Irish Renaissance Annual I*, 1980), which sees O'Connor as waging a lifelong battle against the silence of repression and censorship. While McCrann's readings are sensitive, they sometimes overemphasize the concept of noise in O'Connor's stories.

John Desmond Sheridan (1903–   ) writes humorous essays and popular novels, including *Paradise Alley* (1945), *The Magnificent MacDarney* (1949), and *God Made Little Apples* (1962).

George Buchanan (1904–   ) is an Ulster novelist whose best-known work is *Rose Forbes* (1950). A special issue on Buchanan put out by the *Honest Ulsterman* (no. 59, 1977) contains an article on his fiction by Val Warner.

Patrick Boyle (1905–   ) has written the short stories in *At Night All Cats Are Grey* (1966) and *All Looks Yellow to the Jaundiced Eye* (1969), which were published together in two volumes in paperback as *The Betrayers and Other Stories* (1969). His novel *Like Any Other Man*

(1966), based loosely on the story of Samson and Delilah, won him election to the Irish Academy of Letters. More recently he has written *A View from Calvary* (1976). He is discussed briefly in *Forces and Themes in Ulster Fiction* and in Henri-Dominique Paratte's chapter, "Patrick Boyle's Tragic Humanity," in *The Irish Short Story*.

Bryan Walter Guinness (1905-   ), the second Baron Moyne and a member of the well-known family of brewers, is also a patron of the arts who has himself written prose, poetry, and plays. His novels include *Singing out of Tune* (1933), *Lady Crushwell's Companion* (1938), *A Fugue of Cinderellas* (1956), and *The Giant's Eye* (1964). His short stories have been collected as *The Girl with the Flower* (1966).

Patrick Kavanagh (1905-67), while known chiefly as a poet, has also written two novels generally regarded as classics: *The Green Fool* (1938) and *Tarry Flynn* (1948, reissued in 1965), which was adapted for the stage in 1966 by P. J. O'Connor. Alan Warner's *Clay Is the Word* (1973) and Darcy O'Brien's *Patrick Kavanagh* (1975) form a useful introduction to his work. Larry Morrow's interview "Meet Mr. Kavanagh" and John Nemo's "Notes toward a Critical Biography" appear in a special Kavanagh issue of the *Journal of Irish Literature* (ed. John Nemo, 1977). Nemo's *Patrick Kavanagh* (1979) discusses the fiction, as does a brief passage in Kiely's *Modern Irish Fiction*. There are two bibliographies: John Nemo's "A Bibliography of Writing by and about Patrick Kavanagh," (*IUR*, 1973) and the bibliography in Peter Kavanagh's *Garden of the Golden Apples* (1973).

Nigel Fitzgerald (1906-   ), one-time president of the Irish Actors' Equity Association, is known mainly for his thrillers, which include *Midsummer Malice* (1953), *The House Is Falling* (1955), *Imagine a Man* (1956), *The Candles Are All Out* (1960), and *The Day of the Adder* (1963; rpt. in 1965 as *Echo Answers Murder*).

(Patrick) Rearden Connor (1907-   ) was a landscape gardener before becoming a writer of boys' books (under the pseudonym Peter Malin), short stories, and novels. His first novel, *Shake Hands with the Devil* (1933), was followed by *Salute to Aphrodite* (1935), *Time to Kill* (1936), *I Am Death* (1936), *Men Must Live* (1937), *The Sword of Love* (1938), *To Kill Is My Vocation* (1939), *River, Sing Me a Song* (1939), *The Devil among the Tailors* (1947), *My Love to the Gallows* (1949), *Hunger of the Heart* (1950), *The Singing Stone* (1951), and *The House of Cain* (1952).

Michael McLaverty (1907-   ), a northern writer, is a regional writer in the most positive sense of the term. One of the best-known Irish writers outside of Ireland, he writes mainly about ordinary people and has a gift for detail. His novels are *Call My Brother Back* (1939), *Lost Fields* (1941), *In This Thy Day* (1945), *The Three Brothers* (1948), *Truth in the Night* (1952), *School for Hope* (1954), *The Choice* (1958), and *The Brightening Day* (1965). A recent anthology, *Collected Short Stories* (1978), has an introduction by Seamus Heaney. Earlier collections are *The White Mare and Other Stories* (1943), *The Game Cock and Other Stories* (1948), and *The Road to the Shore* (1976). Two extremely good essays on his work, both by John Wilson Foster, are "McLaverty's People" (*Éire*, 1971) and "Private Worlds: The Stories of Michael McLaverty," in *The Irish Short Story.* Foster also discusses McLaverty in *Forces and Themes in Ulster Fiction.*

Janet McNeill (1907–   ) is an Ulster writer of novels, children's books, and plays for the stage and radio. Her novels include *A Child in the House* (1955), *The Other Side of the Wall* (1957), *As Strangers Here* (1960), *The Early Harvest* (1962), *The Maiden Dinosaur* (1964, pub. in the United States in 1966 as *The Belfast Friends*), *Talk to Me* (1965), and *The Small Widow* (1967), which is set not in Belfast but in an English suburb. Foster discusses her briefly in *Forces and Themes in Ulster Fiction* and at greater length in "Zoo Stories: The Novels of Janet McNeill" (*Éire,* 1974).

James Norris Goddard Davidson (1908–   ), a filmmaker and scriptwriter, has also written the novels *Galore Park* (1934) and *The Soft Impeachment* (1936).

Mervyn Wall (1908–   ) worked for Radio Éireann before becoming secretary of the Irish Arts Council. He has written plays, short stories, and the novels *The Unfortunate Fursey* (1946), *The Return of Fursey* (1948), *Leaves for the Burning* (1952), *No Trophies Raise* (1956), and *Heritage* (serialized in three consecutive issues of *JIL,* 1978–79). Robert Hogan has written the volume on his work for the Irish Writers series (1972).

Sam Hanna Bell (1909–   ) has worked for Northern Island radio and written a number of BBC documentaries and short stories, collected as *Summer Loanen and Other Stories* (1943). His novels are *December Bride* (1951), *The Hollow Ball* (1961), and *A Man Flourishing* (1973).

Bryan MacMahon (1909–   ) is a Listowel writer, teacher, man of letters, and frequent director of workshops on fiction writing. His volumes of short stories are *The Lion Tamer and Other Stories* (1948), *The Red Petticoat and Other Stories* (1955), and *The End of the World and Other Stories* (1976), which contains stories from the previous two collections plus others written for periodicals and BBC broadcasts. His earliest novel is *Children of the Rainbow* (1952). A subsequent novel, *The Honey Spike* (1967), was later made into a play. MacMahon has also written children's books, among them *Jack O'Moora and the King of Ireland's Son* (1950), *Brendan of Ireland* (1965), and *Patsy-O and His Wonderful Pets* (1970). An interview with MacMahon conducted by Gordon Henderson has appeared (*JIL,* 1974), and Patrick Rafroidi's "From Listowel with Love: John B. Keane and Bryan MacMahon" is in *The Irish Short Story.* A partial bibliography may be found in Joanne L. Henderson's "Checklist of Four Kerry Writers: George Fitzmaurice, Maurice Walsh, Bryan MacMahon, John B. Keane" (*JIL,* 1972).

Francis MacManus (1909–65), the author of thirteen novels, has also written short stories, essays, biographies, poetry, and some works in Irish. He was a schoolteacher and then a director in Irish radio. His novels about Ireland are generally regarded as patriotic but not blind to the faults of his homeland. His first novels formed a trilogy of eighteenth-century Ireland: *Stand and Give Challenge* (1934), *Candle for the Proud* (1936), and *Men Withering* (1939). They were followed by *This House Was Mine* (1937); *The Fire in the Dust* (1942), considered by some to be his best work on the themes of family, religion, and country;

Flow on Lovely River (1941); *Watergate* (1942); *The Greatest of These* (1943); *Statue for a Square* (1945); and *American Son* (1959). An early essay on MacManus is Benedict Kiely's "Praise God for Ireland" (*IM*, 1948), and a more recent one is Seán McMahon's "Francis MacManus's Novels of Modern Ireland" (*Éire*, 1970). A "Study Guide" for *Men Withering* has been compiled by Tom Halpin (1973).

Sheila Pim (1909–   ) wrote mainly detective stories with a botanical slant, such as *Common or Garden Crime* (1945), *The Flowering Shamrock* (1949), *The Sheltered Garden* (1964), and *The Wood and the Trees* (1966).

Anthony C. West (1910–   ) is an Ulster writer of short stories, collected in *River's End* (1960), and novels: *The Native Moment* (1963), *The Ferret Fancier* (1963), and *As Towns with Fire* (1968). He is discussed in Foster's *Forces and Themes in Ulster Fiction*.

Flann O'Brien (1911–66), born Brian O'Nolan, wrote under many pseudonyms, including Myles na Gopaleen (sometimes spelled na gCopaleen) as a columnist for the *Irish Times*, Brother Barnabas, George Knowall, and John James Doe. He wrote verse in Old Irish while a student at University College, where he edited the magazine *Blather*. After working in the civil service and local government until 1953, O'Brien spent over twenty years writing newspaper columns; a selection of these were published as *Cruiskeen Lawn* (1943). His most famous work, *At Swim-Two-Birds* (1939), has been regarded as a comedy and a fantasy in the Joycean tradition. His other works have also aroused much interest, and he has become something of a cult figure. *The Third Policeman*, written in 1940, was published posthumously in 1967. *The Hard Life: An Exegesis of Squalor* (1961) was dedicated to Graham Greene. It was followed by *The Dalkey Archive* (1964), *Stories and Plays* (1973), and *The Poor Mouth (An Béal Bocht): A Bad Story about the Hard Life* (1973), which had been written in Irish in 1941.

Most critical studies focus either on O'Brien's first novel or on his many-sided personality. Only one was written before his death: Thomas Hogan's early essay in the *Bell*, "Myles na gCopaleen" (1946). Anne Clissman's *Flann O'Brien: A Critical Introduction to His Writings* (1975) is the first and, to date, the only full-length study of O'Brien's work and is intended for both the general reader and the serious student. It discusses the several sides of Brian-Flann-Myles and examines him chronologically—as novelist, journalist, and playwright. A very different book on O'Brien is Timothy O'Keeffe's collection, *Myles: Portraits of Brian O'Nolan* (1973), which contains five essays, a poem by John Montague, and a good primary and secondary bibliography. The essays are Kevin Nolan's "The First Furlongs," in which O'Brien's younger brother sees him in the context of their family; Niall Sheridan's "Brian, Flann and Myles," which discusses the source of Brinsley in *At Swim-Two-Birds;* John Garvin's "Sweetscented Manuscripts" and Jack White's "Myles, Flann and Brian," which consider O'Nolan as civil servant and as columnist, respectively; and J. C. C. Mays's "Brian O'Nolan: Literalist of the Imagination." Four other books contain excellent essays on O'Brien's writings: Stephen Knight's "The Novels of Flann O'Brien," in *Cunning Exiles; Studies of Modern Prose Writers* (ed. D. Anderson and S. Knight, 1974); Lorna Sage's "Flann O'Brien," in *Two Decades of Irish Writing;* Danielle Jacquin's "Never Apply Your Front Brake First, or Flann O'Brien and the Theme of the Fall," in *The Irish Novel in Our Time;* and Denis Johnston's "Myles na Gopaleen," in *Myth and Reality in Irish Literature.*

A special Flann O'Brien issue of the *Journal of Irish Literature* (1974) includes Seamus Kelly's "Brian O'Nolan; Scholar, Satirist, and Wit," David Powell's "Who Was Myles, and What Was He?" and Myles Orvell's "Entirely Fictitious: The Fiction of Flann O'Brien," as well as plays, stories, and letters by O'Brien and a checklist by David Powell. John Wain's " 'To Write for My Own Race': The Fiction of Flann O'Brien" (*Encounter,* 1967) provides an interesting account of the evolution of *At Swim-Two-Birds,* a summary of the novel, and a discussion of Joyce's influence on it. It is reprinted in Wain's *A House for the Truth: Critical Essays* (1972). Bernard Benstock discusses the Brian Flann-Myles trinity in "The Three Faces of Brian Nolan" (*Éire,* 1968) and examines O'Brien's second novel in "Flann O'Brien in Hell: *The Third Policeman*" (*BuR,* 1969). L. L. Lee takes an American approach in his interesting "The Dublin Cowboys of Flann O'Brien" (*Western American Lit.,* 1969), while Del Ivan Janik more traditionally compares O'Brien with Joyce in "Flann O'Brien: The Novelist as Critic" (*Éire,* 1969). Another conventional look at O'Brien's first novel is Ruth apRoberts' "*At Swim-Two-Birds* and the Novel as Self-Evident Sham" (*Éire,* 1971), while Joycean affinities occur again in J. C. C. Mays's essay (*JJQ,* 1974). Jerome Klinkowitz briefly attempts a reappraisal of *At Swim-Two-Brids* (*New Republic,* 1975). Myles Orvell and David Powell examine O'Brien's many roles in "Myles na Gopaleen: Mystic, Horse-Doctor, Hackney, Journalist and Ideological Catalyst" (*Éire,* 1975). Individual works are discussed in J. M. Silverthorne's "Time, Literature, and Failure: Flann O'Brien's *At Swim-Two-Birds* and *The Third Policeman*" (*Éire,* 1976); Mary Power's "Flann O'Brien and Classical Satire: An Exegesis of *The Hard Life*" (*Éire,* 1979); and Ninian Mellamphy's "Aestho-autogamy and the Anarchy of Imagination: Flann O'Brien's Theory of Fiction in *At Swim-Two-Birds*" (*CJIS,* 1978). The term "aestho-autogamy," which is found in the novel itself, means to create characters in such a vivid way that they come to life. Rüdiger Imhof makes an original and lengthy comparison of O'Brien with Sterne in "Two Meta-Novelists: Sternesque Elements in Novels by Flann O'Brien" (*AIS,* 1979). Two noteworthy checklists of O'Brien have been published: David Powell's "An Annotated Bibliography of Myles na Gopaleen's 'Cruiskeen Lawn' Commentaries on James Joyce" (*JJQ,* 1971) and his more comprehensive "A Checklist of Brian O'Nolan" (*JIL,* 1974).

Stephen Gilbert (1912–   ) dedicated his first novel, *The Landslide* (1943), to Forrest Reid. His later *The Burnaby Experiments* (1952) borrows much from Reid. Other novels are *Bombadier* (1944), *Monkeyface* (1948), and *Ratman's Notebooks* (1968). Gilbert is discussed by Foster in *Forces and Themes in Ulster Fiction* and by Boyd in *The Arts in Ulster.*

Shaun Herron (1912–   ) wrote *The Whore-Mother* (1973), a novel that was well received initially but is now considered by some to be a tasteless fantasy or a "politico-sexual thriller." Other novels of his are *Miro* (1968), *The Miro Papers* (1972), *Through the Dark and Hairy Wood* (1972), and *The Bird in Last Year's Nest* (1974).

Mary Lavin (1912–), whose works have been characterized as being concerned mainly with "the nature of love," has written several novels—*The House in Clewe Street* (1945), *Mary O'Grady* (1950), and *A Likely Story* (1957)—but is mainly known as a writer of short stories. Her first collection, *Tales from Bective Bridge* (1942, with a foreword by Lord Dunsany in the 1943 edition; rpt. 1978), remains her best known, but many subsequent collections are considered at least of equal merit: *The Becker Wives and Other Stories* (1946), *At Sallygap* (1947), *Patriot Son and Other Stories* (1956), *The Great Wave and Other Stories* (1961), and *The Shrine and Other Stories* (1977). Two books on Lavin's work are Zack Bowen's *Mary Lavin* (1975) and Richard F. Peterson's *Mary Lavin* (1978). Peterson also discusses Lavin in "The Circle of Truth: The Stories of Katherine Mansfield and Mary Lavin" (*MFS*, 1978). The early stories are discussed by Robert W. Caswell in "Irish Political Reality and Mary Lavin's *Tales from Bective Bridge*" (*Éire*, 1968). A more general study is Thomas J. Murray's "Mary Lavin's World: Lovers and Strangers" (*Éire*, 1972). Janet Egleson Dunleavy has contributed three useful approaches to Lavin's work in "Men in Mary Lavin's Fiction" (*CJIS*, 1976), "The Making of Mary Lavin's 'A Memory' " (*Éire*, 1977), and "The Fiction of Mary Lavin: Universal Sensibility in a Particular Milieu" (*IUR*, 1977). A special issue of *Irish University Review* on Mary Lavin (1979) contains an interview with her, a short story of hers, three articles on her work, and a bibliography by Heinz Kosok. The special Irish number of *Mosaic* contains Catherine A. Murphy's "The Ironic Vision of Mary Lavin" (1979), and *The Irish Short Story* has a chapter on her work by Seamus Deane. Paul A. Doyle's "Mary Lavin: A Checklist" (*PBSA*, 1969) is now outdated.

Terence de Vere White (1912–) is a critic, biographer, and man of letters. His novels include *An Affair with the Moon* (1959), *Prenez Garde* (1961), *Lucifer Falling* (1966), *The Distance and the Dark* (1973), and *The Radish Memoirs* (1974).

Honor Tracy (1913–) has written over a dozen novels, including *The Straight and Narrow Path* (1956), *Settled in Chambers* (1967), *In a Year of Grace* (1975), and *The Man from Next Door* (1977).

Patrick Joseph Purcell (1914–), a sports journalist, has also written novels, including *Hanrahan's Daughter* (1942), *A Keeper of Swans* (1944), *The Quiet Man* (1945), and *Fiddler's Green* (1949).

Anne Crone (1915–) wrote several popular novels: *Bridie Steen* (1948), *This Pleasant Lea* (1951), and *My Heart and I* (1955).

Ernest Gebler (1915–), the former husband of Edna O'Brien, has written several novels; the best known is *Plymouth Adventure* (1950).

Walter Macken (1915–67) began his literary career as an actor and dramatist, joining the Abbey during the 1940s. He is perhaps best known, however, for his novels, especially the historical trilogy of the seventeenth century: *Seek the Fair Land* (1959), *The Silent People* (1962), and *The Scorching Wind* (1964). He also wrote three volumes of short stories and more than half a dozen other novels.

John Ross (1917–   ), before turning to script writing and television journalism, wrote thrillers and spy stories: *The Moccasin Men* (1939), *The Tall Man* (1940), and *Federal Agent* (1941).

Benedict Kiely (1919–   ), a literary critic and one-time literary editor of the *Irish Press,* is also a writer of fiction. His work includes eight novels and four volumes of short stories, as well as individual stories mostly written for the *New Yorker.* His first three novels are set in the town of Omagh—*Land without Stars* (1946), *In a Harbour Green* (1949), and *Call for a Miracle* (1950). These were followed by *Honey Seems Bitter* (1952), published in the United States as *The Evil Men Do;* a folktale novel, *The Cards of the Gambler* (1953); *There Was an Ancient House* (1955), which is based on his experiences in a Jesuit seminary; *The Captain with the Whiskers* (1960); and *Dogs Enjoy the Morning* (1968). His short stories appear in *A Journey to the Seven Streams* (1963); *A Ball of Malt and Madame Butterfly* (1973); *Proxopera* (1977), a long short story; and *A Cow in the House and Nine Other Stories* (1978), set in Ulster. Two books on Kiely's work have already appeared, both parts of series: one by Grace Eckley (1972) for Twayne, the other by Daniel J. Casey (1974) for the Irish Writers series. John Wilson Foster discusses Kiely in his *Forces and Themes in Ulster Fiction* as well as in "Dog among the Moles: The Fictional World of Benedict Kiely" (*DM,* 1970–71). An earlier survey is Grace Eckley's "The Fiction of Benedict Kiely" (*Éire,* 1968). There is also a chapter on Kiely by Kevin Sullivan in *The Irish Novel in Our Time.*

Eamon Francis (c. 1920?–   ) resigned his military career in 1966 and began writing novels and short stories: *Ballydoolin Privates* (1969) and *The Sunburst and the Dove* (1969).

Paul Smith (c. 1920–   ) has worked at many odd jobs. His first novel, *Esther's Altar* (1959), shocked the Dublin censors. It was followed by *The Countrywoman* (1962), *The Stubborn Season* (1962), and *Stravaganza* (1963).

Eilis Dillon (1920–   ) has written over forty children's books as well as novels and plays. Her titles include *Lost Island* (1952), *The San Sebastian* (1953), *The House on the Shore* (1955), *Plover Hill* (1957), *The Singing Cave* (1959), *The Fort of Gold* (1961), *Bold John Henebry* (1965), *Across the Bitter Sea* (1973), and *Blood Relations* (1978).

James Plunkett (1920–   ) is the pseudonym of James Plunkett Kelly, who has worked as a producer for Telefís Éireann and written radio plays. His story collections—*The Eagles and the Trumpets* (1954); *The Trusting and the Maimed* (1955), which includes the first title; and *Collected Short Stories* (1977)—are far less well known than his two novels, *Strumpet City* (1969) and *Farewell Companions* (1977). His stories are surveyed briefly by Thomas MacIntyre (*Studies,* 1958). His first novel is discussed in Godeleine Carpentier's "Dublin and the Drama of Larkinism: James Plunkett's *Strumpet City*" (in *The Irish Novel in Our Time*) and James M. Cahalan's "The Making of *Strumpet City:* James Plunkett's Historical Vision" (*Éire,* 1978), which also touches on some aspects of Plunkett's radio plays.

Jack White (1920–   ) is a journalist who has written novels about the Dublin middle class: *One for the Road* (1956), *The Hard Man* (1958), *The Devil You Know* (1962), and *The Last Eleven* (1979).

Brian Cleeve (1921–   ), a journalist and script writer, has written radio and television plays and a volume of short stories, *The Horse Thieves of Ballysaggert* (1966). He is well known for his spy thrillers and novels, such as *Birth of a Dark Soul* (1953, pub. in the United States as *The Night Winds* in 1954), *Death of a Painted Lady* (1962), *Death of a Wicked Servant* (1963), *Vote X for Treason* (1964), *The Judas Goat* (1966), *Exit from Prague* (1970, pub. in the United States as *Escape from Prague* in 1973), and *A Question of Innocence* (1974).

Brian Moore (1921–   ) was born in Belfast, emigrated to Canada, and now resides in the United States. His writings have been immensely popular. At various times each country has "claimed" him as one of its own writers, but most of his works remain basically Irish both in concern and in outlook. *The Executioners* (1951) and *Wreath for a Redhead* (1951) are little known, and his first success was the still popular *Judith Hearne* (1955; retitled in 1964 *The Lonely Passion of Judith Hearne*). It was followed by *Intent to Kill* (1956) and *Murder in Majorca* (1957), both written under the pseudonym Michael Bryan and not generally known as works of Moore. There followed a chain of successful novels: *The Feast of Lupercal* (1957), *The Luck of Ginger Coffey* (1960), *An Answer from Limbo* (1962), *The Emperor of Ice Cream* (1965), *I Am Mary Dunne* (1968), *Fergus* (1970), *The Revolution Script* (1971), *Catholics* (1972), *The Great Victorian Collection* (1975), *The Doctor's Wife* (1976), and *The Mangan Inheritance* (1979).

Critical work on Moore has been abundant, most of it in periodicals. Two exceptions are Hallvard Dahlie's *Brian Moore* (1969), part of the Studies in Canadian Literature series, and Jeanne Flood's somewhat Freudian *Brian Moore* (1974), in which she argues, not entirely convincingly, that the protagonists of Moore's novels are engaged in combat with their fathers, or superegos, or God, or all these at once. Other articles cited here are meant to represent a cross-section of criticism over the past two decades; the list is by no means complete. Jack Ludwig regards Moore as an adopted Canadian writer in "A Mirror of Moore" (*CanL*, 1961) and "Brian Moore: Ireland's Loss, Canada's Novelist" (*Critique*, 1962). Also Canadian is Naim Kattim's study (*CanL*, 1963). Philip French discusses Moore's novels (*LonM*, 1966), and Marion B. Smith, in "Existential Morality?" (*CanL*, 1966), raises philosophical speculations on Moore's writing. Moore is placed in an Irish context by John Wilson Foster's "Crisis and Ritual in Brian Moore's Belfast Novels" (*Éire*, 1968), which discusses *Judith Hearne* and *The Feast of Lupercal*. Another approach is Frank L. Kersonowski's "Exit the Anti-Hero" (*Critique*, 1967), which argues that the contemporary tendencies of withdrawal and lack of belief are the basic elements in Moore's characters, who are entirely different from the antiheros of the 1920s.

"An Interview in London with Brian Moore," conducted by Richard B. Sale, appeared in *SNNTS* (1969). John Cronin includes Moore in his essay "Ulster's Alarming Novels" (*Éire*, 1969). Foster's

"Passage through Limbo: Brian Moore's North American Novels" (*Critique*, 1970) was later worked into his *Forces and Themes in Ulster Fiction*. Other studies of the novels include Michael Paul Gallagher's general survey (*Studies*, 1971), Murray Prosky's more specific "The Crisis of Identity in the Novels of Brian Moore" (*Éire*, 1971), and DeWitt Henry's overview (*Ploughshares*, 1974). Bruce Cook takes a biographical approach in "Brian Moore: Private Person" (*Commonweal*, 1974), and Raymond J. Porter studies Moore's provoking novella in "Miracle, Mystery, and Faith in Brian Moore's *Catholics*" (*Éire*, 1975). Kerry McSweeney (*CritQ*, 1976) provides another overview of Moore's development. Brian Moore himself writes on his ambiguous position in "The Writer as Exile" (*CJIS*, 1976). John A. Scanlan surveys the ten years between the writing of *Ginger Coffey* and *Fergus* (*Éire*, 1977). Two approaches to Moore's religious position are David Staines' "Observance without Belief" (*CanL*, 1977) and J. H. Dorenkamp's "Finishing the Day: Nature and Grace in Two Novels by Brian Moore" (*Éire*, 1978), which discusses *Mary Dunne* and *Catholics*. Dorenkamp's essay is the more useful of the two, placing Moore's writing in the context of the conflict between Catholic belief and secular art. Tom Paulin's chapter in *Two Decades of Irish Writing* discusses Moore (along with Leitch and McDowell), and Patrick Rafroidi writes on Moore in *The Irish Novel in Our Time*. "A Brian Moore Bibliography," by Richard Studing, appears in *Éire* (1975), and there is also a primary and secondary bibliography in volume 1 of Robert J. Stanton's *A Bibliography of Modern British Novelists* (1978). Both are more comprehensive than the earlier checklist by Hallvard Dahlie (*Critique*, 1966).

Tony Gray (1922–), a columnist and script writer, has also written several novels: *Starting from Tomorrow* (1965), *The Real Professionals* (1966), *Gone the Time* (1967), and *The Last Laugh* (1972).

Michael Campbell (1924–), a member of the Irish bar and a journalist in London, has written several novels: *Peter Perry* (1956), *Oh, Mary, This London* (1959), *Across the Water* (1961), and *The Princess in England* (1964).

Juanita Casey (1925–) has written two novels, *The Horse of Selene* (1971) and *The Circus* (1974), and some poems but is mainly known for her short stories. Some have been collected in *Hath the Rain a Father?* (1966); others appear in anthologies and periodicals. A special Casey issue of the *Journal of Irish Literature* (1972) included an interview with her by Gordon Henderson.

J(ames) P(atrick) Donleavy (1925–), an American living in Ireland, writes what have been called picaresque novels with alliterative titles, such as *Meet My Maker, the Mad Molecule* (1964), *The Saddest Summer of Samuel S.* (1966), *The Beastly Beatitudes of Balthazar B.* (1968), and *The Destinies of Darcy Dancer, Gentleman* (1977). His most popular novel, *The Ginger Man* (1955), was also a play that was censored in Dublin. He is interviewed on the occurrence by Richard Harris in *Flight from the Celtic Twilight* (ed. Des Hickey and Gus Smith, 1973). Another interview was conducted by Kurt Jacobson (*JIL*, 1979). Gerald Weales' essay comparing the fiction of Donleavy and James Purdy appears in *Contemporary American Fiction* (ed. Harry T. Moore, 1964).

Dean Cohen discusses the allegorical origins of *The Ginger Man* in the children's tale of the gingerbread man (*Critique*, 1970). A lengthy appraisal of Donleavy's humor is offered in Thomas LeClair's "Death and Black Humor" (*Critique*, 1975).

John Broderick (1927–) writes mainly of life in an Irish provincial town in his novels: *The Pilgrimage* (1961); *The Fugitives* (1962); *Don Juaneen* (1963); *The Waking of Willie Ryan* (1965), which Seán McMahon called "the book of the year"; and *An Apology for Roses* (1973). Two major essays on his work are Seán McMahon's "Town and Country" (*Éire*, 1971) and Michael Paul Gallagher's chapter in *The Irish Novel in Our Time*.

Aidan Higgins (1927–), who has worked as an engineer in England, South Africa, and Spain, writes fiction that is often concerned with aspects of death as grotesque or tragic-comic. Best known for his novel *Langrishe, Go Down* (1966, reissued 1978), he has also written six short stories in *Felo de Se* (1960), published in the United States as *Killachter Meadow*, and later as *Asylum and Other Stories* (1978). *Balcony of Europe* (1972) deals with the postwar period, and some of its characters reappeared in *Scenes from a Receding Past* (1977), a novel about his Irish childhood in Sligo and his adult life in London. His work is discussed briefly in Roger Garfitt's chapter in *Two Decades of Irish Writing* and more extensively in Morris Beja's "Felons of Our Selves: The Fiction of Aidan Higgins" (*IUR*, 1973) and Robin Skelton's "Aidan Higgins and the Total Book" (*Mosaic*, 1977).

John B. Keane (1928–), a Listowel writer who has written mainly plays, has recently turned his pen to short stories as well. He writes chiefly of peasant life and its accompanying poverty. At one time a worker in the Scottish potato fields, he later became a reporter and then an editor of ancient manuscripts. The titles of most of his works begin with the word "Letters"; it is followed by *of a Successful T. D.* (1967), *of a Love-Hungry Farmer* (1974), *of a Matchmaker* (1975), *of a Civic Guard* (1976), *of a Country Postman* (1977), and *of an Irish Minister of State* (1978). He has also written *Strong Tea* (1963), *The Gentle Art of Matchmaking* (1973), and *Is the Holy Ghost Really a Kerryman?* (1976). Patrick Rafroidi provides a chapter on Keane and Bryan MacMahon in *The Irish Short Story*, and Joanne L. Henderson has published "Checklist of Four Kerry Writers: George Fitzmaurice, Maurice Walsh, Bryan MacMahon, John B. Keane" (*JIL*, 1972).

Richard Power (1928–70) (Risteard De Paor) contributed to periodicals in both Irish and English. Most of his writing was in Gaelic, but some short stories and poems were written in English. He wrote two novels, *The Land of Youth* (1964) and *The Hungry Grass* (1969). Terence Brown has an essay on his work in *The Irish Novel in Our Time*.

William Trevor (1928–) is the pseudonym of Trevor Cox, who began his career as a sculptor before entering advertising and then becoming a writer. His popular novels and short stories exist in many translations. They include *A Standard of Behaviour* (1958), *The Old Boys* (1964), *The Love Department* (1966), *Mrs. Eckdorf in O'Neill's Hotel* (1969), and *Elizabeth Alone* (1973). There is an essay on him by Mark Mortimer (*EI*, 1975).

Brian Friel (1929–   ) is best known for his plays, the most popular of which is *Philadelphia, Here I Come!* He has also written numerous short stories for the *New Yorker, Argosy*, and the *Saturday Evening Post*. His two story collections, *The Saucer of Larks* (1962) and *The Gold in the Sea* (1966), were also published in one volume titled *The Saucer of Larks* (1969). Most criticism is on Friel as a playwright, though D.E.S. Maxwell's *Brian Friel* (1973), Milton Levin's "Brian Friel: An Introduction" (*Éire*, 1972), and Foster's *Forces and Themes in Ulster Fiction* are useful for studying the stories as well. Other recent discussions of the stories are Edmund J. Miner's "Homecoming: The Theme of Disillusionment in Brian Friel's Short Stories" (*KanQ*, 1977) and Seamus Deane's introduction to Friel's *Selected Stories* (1979).

John Montague (1929–   ), the popular contemporary poet, must be mentioned here for his short stories, especially his collection *Death of a Chieftain and Other Stories* (1964). Frank Kersnowski's *John Montague* (1975) has been issued in the Irish Writers series. The short stories are discussed by Foster in *Forces and Themes in Ulster Fiction*.

Jennifer Johnston (1930–   ), daughter of playwright Denis Johnston, has written novellas about the Great War and the decline of the Big House gentry and about relationships between youth and old age: *The Captains and the Kings* (1972), *The Gates* (1973), *How Many Miles to Babylon?* (1974), and *Shadows on Our Skin* (1977). Seán McMahon discusses her novels briefly in "Anglo-Irish Attitudes" (*Éire*, 1975).

Maeve Kelly (1930–   ), one of the recent generation of Irish writers, has published a collection of short stories, *A Life of Her Own* (1976).

Maurice Leitch (1930–   ), an Ulster novelist who writes of the bitterness of the North, is often praised for his ability to establish a "sense of place" in his descriptions of County Antrim. His novels are *The Liberty Lad* (1965), *Poor Lazarus* (1969), and *Stamping Ground* (1975). His work is discussed in Foster's *Forces and Themes in Ulster Fiction* and in Tom Paulin's "A Necessary Provincialism: Brian Moore, Maurice Leitch, Florence Mary McDowell," in Dunn's *Two Decades of Irish Writing*. Seán McMahon's "May the Lord in His Mercy" (*Éire*, 1969) discusses Catholics and Protestants in Northern Ireland in terms of Leitch's novels.

Bernard Share (1930–   ) has written the novels *Inish* (1966) and *Merciful Hour* (1970).

Christy Brown (1932–   ) was raised in a Dublin slum and, because of his paralysis, does his writing by typing with one toe. He has published three volumes of poems and several novels: the autobiographical *My Left Foot* (1954), *Down All the Days* (1970), *A Shadow on Summer* (1974), and *Wild Grow the Lilies* (1976). An essay on his work by Françoise Borel, " 'I Am without a Name': The Fiction of Christy Brown." is in *The Irish Novel in Our Time*.

Edna O'Brien (1932–   ) has written television and film scripts but is best known for her many novels and short stories, some of which have appeared in the *New Yorker*. Her novel *The Lonely Girl* (1962) was made into a film, *The Girl with Green Eyes* (1964). Among her other works of fiction are *Girls in Their Married Bliss* (1964), *August Is a Wicked Month*

(1965), *Casualties of Peace* (1966), *The Love Object* (1968), *A Pagan Place* (1970, later dramatized), *Zee & Company* (1971), *Night* (1972), *A Scandalous Woman* (1974), *Johnny I Hardly Knew You* (1977), and *Mrs. Reinhardt and Other Stories* (1978). She has recently assembled an anthology, *Some Irish Loving* (1979), which includes a few excerpts from her own work but mainly contains passages from other writers. Grace Eckley's *Edna O'Brien* (1974) is in the Irish Writers series. An early survey is Seán McMahon's "A Sex by Themselves: An Interim Report on the Novels of Edna O'Brien" (*Éire*, 1967). Most recent are Raymonde Popot's "Edna O'Brien's Paradise Lost," in *The Irish Novel in Our Time*, and Lotus Snow's " 'That Trenchant Childhood Route'? Quest in Edna O'Brien's Novels" (*Éire*, 1979).

Julia O'Faolain (1932–   ), the daughter of Sean O'Faolain, lives in the United States and writes satires on the wealthy, showing a strong sense of social and moral concern. Her first novel, *Godded and Codded* (1970), was preceded by the short stories in *We Might See Sights!* (1968). She wrote a historical study of feminism, *Not in God's Image* (1973), and her stories in *Man in the Cellar* (1974) raise feminist questions. She also wrote *Women in the Wall* (1975).

Tom MacIntyre (1933–   ) has written a novel, *The Charollais* (1969), and a volume of short stories, *Dance the Dance* (1970). A useful essay on his writing is Peter Denman's "Form and Fiction in the Stories of Tom MacIntyre" (*EI*, 1975).

Lee Dunne (1934–   ) has written the novels *Goodbye to the Hill* (1965), *A Bed in the Sticks* (1968), *Does Your Mother* (1970), *Paddy Maguire Is Dead* (1972), *Midnight Cabbie* (1974), *The Cabbie Who Came In from the Cold* (1975), *The Cabfather* (1975), and *Maggie's Story* (1975).

J(ames) G(ordon) Farrell (1935–   ) was born in Liverpool but spent much of his childhood in Ireland, about which he has written *Troubles* (1970). His *A Man from Elsewhere* (1963) is a thriller, while the *The Lung* (1965) and *A Girl in the Head* (1967) are comic works. *The Siege of Krishnapur* (1973) sets Western values against East Indian civilization.

John McGahern (1935–   ) was a schoolteacher in Clontarf until 1964, when he left to take up a MacAuley Fellowship and write *The Dark* (1965), which has been called a rural version of Joyce's *Portrait of the Artist*. His first novel, *The Barracks* (1963), won him the A. E. Memorial Award as well as the MacAuley Fellowship. Subsequent works are collections of short stories, *Nightlines* (1970) and *Getting Through* (1978), and two novels, *The Leavetaking* (1974) and *The Pornographer* (1979). He is a regular contributor to the *New Yorker*. McGahern's dismissal from his teaching position is discussed by Owen Sheehy-Skeffington (*Censorship*, 1966) and by Bruce Cook in "Irish Censorship: The Case of John McGahern" (*CathW*, 1967). A general discussion of the major characters in the novels is offered by F. C. Molloy (*Critique*, 1977). Other studies have appeared as chapters in critical collections: Roger Garfitt's "Constants in Contemporary Irish Fiction," in Dunn's *Two Decades of Irish Writing*; Henri-D. Paratte's "Conflicts in a Changing World: John McGahern," in *The Irish Novel in Our Time*, probably the most thorough assessment to date; and Terence Brown's "John McGahern's 'Nightlines': Tone, Technique and Symbolism," in *The Irish Short Story*.

Thomas Kilroy (1936–   ) has written several plays and critical writings as well as short stories and one novel. *The Big Chapel* (1971), a historical novel set in the 1870s, is discussed by Brian Cosgrove in "Ego contra Mundum," in *The Irish Novel in Our Time*. Kilroy is also evaluated by Maurice Harmon in "By Memory Inspired: Themes and Forces in Recent Irish Writing" (*Éire*, 1973).

Gillman Noonan (1937–   ) published his first collection of short stories, *A Sexual Relationship*, in 1976.

Jack Wilson (1937–   ) is an Ulster writer whose works include *The Wild Summer* (1963), *The Tomorrow Country* (1967), and *Dark Eden* (1969), a diary of an Ulster plantation in 1616–18. He is discussed briefly in *Forces and Themes in Ulster Fiction*.

Kevin Casey (1940–   ) has written *The Sinner's Bell* (1968), a novel concerned with the problem of social opportunity; *A Sense of Survival* (1974), generally regarded as less successful; and *Dream of Revenge* (1977).

John Banville (1946–   ) has written four novels: *Long Lankin* (1970); *Nightspawn* (1971); *Birchwood* (1973), sometimes referred to as an Irish Gothic novel; and *Dr. Copernicus* (1976). He is interviewed, with Francis Stuart, by Ronan Sheehan in "Novelists on the Novel" (*Crane Bag*, 1979). Seamus Deane's " 'Be Assured I Am Inventing': The Fiction of John Banville" appears in *The Irish Novel in Our Time*.

Maura Treacy (1946–   ) has written a volume of short stories, *Sixpence in Her Shoe* (1977).

Lucile Redmond (1949–   ) won the Hennessy Literary Award for her short story "The Shaking Trees" (1975; rpt. in *Paddy No More*, 1977).

Desmond Hogan (1951–   ), one of Ireland's newest young writers, has published a collection of short stories, *Charing Cross Road Revisited* (1974), and a novel, *The Ikon Maker* (1976).

Neil Jordan (1951–   ) has written a highly regarded collection of short stories, *Nights in Tunisia and Other Stories* (1976).

MODERN POETRY

Mary M. FitzGerald

Although most scholars acknowledge W. B. Yeats as Ireland's greatest poet and have awarded him the lion's share of literary analysis, they have not altogether ignored the lesser-known figures in modern Irish poetry. This chapter considers works about poets who were contemporaries or successors of Yeats, with the exception of those whose poetry is covered elsewhere in this volume.

The literary criticism that addresses the work of these poets has largely followed the course of history. In the opening years of this century, critical emphasis centered on national identity: the definition and articulation of a distinctively Irish voice. As Yeats took on the status of an establishment figure, younger poets struggled to escape his influence and to chart their own directions, searching for new themes and new modes of expression. By mid-century, Patrick Kavanagh had turned "regionalism" into an honored term. The Irish voice had given way to the Ulster voice, the rural voice, the Dublin voice. More recently, the renewal of violence in the North of Ireland has urged poetic energies into new directions again.

Within the overall pattern of history, smaller cycles of literary criticism have developed. As each new phase has begun, scholarly commentators have defined it, isolated its characteristics, charted its development. As it has become more fully established, analysis of specific features or of individuals has taken the place of definition; and after it has melted into a new phase, retrospective overviews have become more prevalent. Accordingly, much of the criticism cited in this chapter is of historical value; only a few major works stand out from the whole. These major works, whether definitive biographies or definitive analyses of their times, are highlighted in the text, but the historical perspective predominates. Critical works are given, where possible, in chronological order. When some future scholar writes the history of Irish literary criticism, such a slant may not be needed, but for the present it helps to follow the shaping of ideas.

Several of the poets examined in this chapter are equally well known as dramatists or as writers of novels and short stories. Their work in other genres will be found in the appropriate chapters of this book.

1. Bibliographies, Dictionaries, and Directories

At present, there are no comprehensive bibliographies for Anglo-Irish literature in general or for Anglo-Irish poetry in particular. Attempts to fill this gap have met with varying degrees of success. Bibliographies of primary and secondary materials relating to poetry generally occur as portions of larger bibliographies or as checklists in studies of individual poets, but these are necessarily incomplete. It is best to measure any one of them against others for possible omissions and to supplement each with further research.

Among the early general bibliographies in the field, one of the best is Stephen J. Brown's *A Guide to Books on Ireland* (1912), which contains sections on poetry, biography, and literary criticism. Brown's book is nearly exhaustive through 1912, and his succinct annotations are helpful. Richard Irvine Best's *Bibliography of Irish Philology and Printed Irish Literature* (1913) and his *Bibliography of Irish Philology and Manuscript Literature: Publications, 1913-1941* (1942; rpt. 1969) are indispensable, as are Alan R. Eager's *A Guide to Irish Bibliographical Materials* (1964; rev. 1980) and Richard J. Hayes's *Manuscript Sources for the History of Irish Civilisation* (1965; supplemented 1979). In addition, most of the standard bibliographical guides to English writers contain listings on Irish poets, and the National Library of Ireland's new subject catalog, still in progress, will include listings under the heading of Irish poetry.

Periodical bibliographies have recently shown increasing numbers of entries for modern Irish poetry, usually under the individual poets' names. Those published by the Modern Language Association, the Humanities Research Association, the International Association for the Study of Anglo-Irish Literature (in *IUR*), the American Committee for Irish Studies (in its *Newsletter*), *Twentieth Century*, *Études Irlandaises*, and *The Year's Work in English Studies* are standard sources. Other periodical bibliographies that are especially useful for their listings of recent or forthcoming publications are *Bibliotheca Celtica*, which annually prints listings of Anglo-Irish literature; the Royal Irish Academy *Handlist of Work in Progress*, which has appeared annually since 1973; and *Books Ireland*, a monthly publication that lists and reviews new books. The new *Irish Literary Supplement* (1982), appearing semiannually, is already indispensable. *Hibernia*, the *Irish Times*, and the *Irish Press* regularly note the appearance of new creative work, though they are less exhaustive then *Books Ireland* in their coverage and somewhat less reliable for information about new critical work. Indexes for *Hibernia* and the *Irish Times* will presently become available and will greatly facilitate access to the various fugitive pieces about contemporary Irish poetry that have appeared in their pages.

Among dictionaries and directories, the best for bibliographical items are *Contemporary Writers of the English Language* (ed. James Vinson et al.; rev. 1980), which has a volume on contemporary poets, and Robert Hogan's *Dictionary of Irish Writers* (1979). Both supply very good primary bibliographies (books only) for their entries; Hogan's work offers more extensive coverage of the field and some selected secondary bibliography as well.

Maurice Harmon's *Modern Irish Literature, 1800–1967: A Reader's Guide* (1967) has now been superseded by his *Select Bibliography for the Study of Anglo-Irish Literature* (1977). Written primarily for students, Harmon's work names the major literary and historical sources in the field and offers checklists for individual writers. Its annotation is more descriptive than evaluative, and it does not claim to be comprehensive; but it is helpful nonetheless, especially for those commencing study in the field or researching one of its major figures. On the other hand, *A Bibliography of Irish and Anglo-Irish Literature* (ed. Frank Kersnowski, C. W. Spinks, and Laird Loomis, 1976) claims to be comprehensive but is not. Worse, its many misprints and errors render it highly unreliable, as does its substitution of dates of recent editions for dates of first editions. Students should be warned of its shortcomings, and users would do well to check its citations against the sources. Irish literature could use a more extensive compilation like the *New Cambridge Bibliography of English Literature*. Several items of more limited bibliographical scope are Marian Keaney's *Westmeath Authors* (1969), Helen Maher's *Galway Authors* (1976), Marion Sader's *Comprehensive Index to English Language Little Magazines, 1890–1970* (1970), an index to the first fifty volumes of *Studies* (1966), and Rudi Holzapfel's indexes of contributors to the *Dublin Magazine* (1966) and to the *Bell* (1970).

All previous dictionaries and directories of Irish writers, including D. J. O'Donoghue's *The Poets of Ireland* (1912) and Brian Cleeve's three-volume *Dictionary of Irish Writers* (1969–76), have recently been superseded by Robert Hogan's *Dictionary of Irish Writers* (1979). A cornucopia of biographical, bibliographical, and critical information, Hogan's book is a dictionary in the Johnsonian sense, strongly flavored by the opinions of its contributors. Hogan's entries, roughly half the total, are often not only astute but also astringent. The tone is sometimes so provocative that readers and even writers may well be outraged, but one can be grateful for the sheer energy of the prose and the enormous scope of the enterprise, as well as for an excellent introductory essay, which is especially salutary for the American readers to whom it seems addressed. Unfortunately, not all the writers covered are well served by the commentary, but most are, and the biographical and bibliographical information is invariably full and valuable.

Other dictionaries are also useful. *Contemporary Poets of the English Language*, in the Contemporary Writers collection, includes perceptive, evaluative essays on poets by their colleagues. Martin Seymour-Smith's *Who's Who in Twentieth Century Literature* (1976) contains entries on the better-known Irish poets. Seymour-Smith compares writers to their European contemporaries. Henry Boylan's *A Dictionary of Irish Biography* (1978) considers poets who are no longer living. His entries follow *DNB* style. *Who's Who, What's What and Where in Ireland* (1973) provides much useful background information, as does *The Encyclopedia of Ireland* (1968). Users of the *New Columbia Encyclopedia* will want to check Kevin Sullivan's helpful list of corrections to the fourth edition (*Éire*, 1980). More reference works are in progress: the American Committee for Irish Studies is compiling a dictionary of Irish biography, which will consist of long essays about each subject; and a multivolume, multinational, multigenre *Dictionary of Literary Biography*, currently in progress under various editors in the United States, will include the more renowned Irish writers among its entries.

2. General Studies

Among background histories of the twentieth century in Ireland, a most helpful recent volume for literary scholars is Richard Fallis' *The Irish Renaissance* (1977), which covers literature and history from the early renaissance to the present day. Fallis concentrates on the broad span of history, explaining thematic concerns in the literature as he progresses. Although those with a sure grasp of Irish history will not need this book, it makes an excellent starting place for newcomers to the field. There are some minor flaws, but on the whole it is sure and sound. On the other hand, Herbert A. Kenny's *Literary Dublin: A History* (1974) is riddled with factual errors and is no more than a casual history for armchair readers.

The *Course of Irish Verse in England* (1947), by Robert Farren (Riobeard Ó Farachain), remains useful. Frank O'Connor's *A Short History of Irish Literature: A Backward Look* (1967) is required reading. Though highly idiosyncratic and occasionally simply wrong, it carries a certain personal truth, and of course O'Connor's opinions on Irish literature are significant in themselves. Patrick C. Power's two books, *A Literary History of Ireland* (1969) and *The Story of Anglo-Irish Poetry: 1800–1922* (1967), are both balanced and informative. A. Norman Jeffares provides a brief introduction to Irish writing in Bruce King's *Literatures of the World in English* (1974). Augustine Martin's *Anglo-Irish Literature* (1980) in the Irish government's Aspects of Ireland series is the most concise, informative monograph on the subject.

Histories of Ireland that provide useful background include F. X. Martin and T. W. Moody's *The Course of Irish History* (1967), Giovanni Costigan's *A History of Modern Ireland* (1969), J. C. Beckett's *A Short History of Ireland* (1952; 4th ed., 1971), F. S. L. Lyons' *Ireland since the Famine* (1969) and *Culture and Anarchy in Ireland, 1830–1939* (1979), and the projected nine-volume *A New History of Ireland*, edited by T. W. Moody, F. X. Martin, and F. J. Byrne. *The Gill History of Ireland*, edited by James Lydon and Margaret MacCurtain, is a useful series currently in print; especially helpful is the volume by Joseph Lee, *The Modernisation of Irish Society, 1848–1918* (1973), which places the literary revival in its economic and social background. Oliver Mac-Donagh's *Ireland* (1968; rev. 1978) is a good short history. The standard history of the early part of the literary movement in this century is Ernest

A. Boyd's *Ireland's Literary Renaissance* (1916; rev. 1922; rpt. 1968). Terence Brown's *Ireland: A Social and Cultural History 1922-79* (1981) is the best study of the period to date.

The present wealth of Ulster writers has occasioned a renewed emphasis on the literary and cultural distinctiveness of that province. The definitive study of modern Ulster poetry and the best introduction to the subject is Terence Brown's *Northern Voices: Poets from Ulster* (1975), although some of it is dated by the continuing development of younger writers and the emergence of new ones. An earlier survey of Ulster writers by Daphne Fulwood and Oliver Edwards in *Rann* (1953) has some historical significance. One of the first items to separate Ulster's literary achievement from that of the main stream of nationalist Irish writing was an anonymous essay, "Ulster's Share in the Revival," in a special Northern Ireland supplement to the London *Times* (Dec. 1922). In 1942 the *Bell* published an Ulster issue, and in 1945 John Hewitt provided an excellent historical analysis of the roots of Ulster writing in *Lagan*, pointing out that the province was not really experiencing a renaissance but rather was having its ongoing literary tradition highlighted by a contemporary fashion for regionalism. Hewitt's seminal essay also emphasized that poets need to be "rooted" and therefore find it difficult to address audiences in modern industrial societies. He urged—prophetically—the formation of a writers' group at Queen's University and counseled his fellow poets to follow Robert Frost's advice and "forthwith [find] salvation in surrender" to the land of their birth. Many of Hewitt's points are echoed in subsequent articles by other Ulster writers. Also in 1945, Oliver Edwards discussed Yeats and Ulster in the *Northman*. In 1948 John Hewitt's "Overture for Ulster Realism" appeared in *Poetry Ireland*, and in the following year *Poetry Quarterly* carried an article by Howard Sergeant on regionalism in contemporary Ulster poetry. An Ulster issue of *Poetry Ireland* (1950) included another important Hewitt essay. The next major item to appear was *The Arts in Ulster: A Symposium* (1951), edited by Sam Hanna Bell, Nesca A. Robb, and John Hewitt. It claimed to be "the first book to be concerned specifically with the arts in Ulster" and contained a good historical summary of poetry in the region by J. N. Browne. In 1950-51 the *Bell* published a series, "Fears and Convictions of Ulster Protestants," which dealt with some underlying tensions, if not specifically with poetry. Following this, the *Bell* carried an article by George Buchanan on being an Ulsterman ("Letter from the North," 1952) and an article by John Hewitt on being an Ulster writer ("Some Notes on Writing in Ulster," 1952). In 1953 *Rann* published articles by Howard Sergeant on regionalism, by John Hewitt on the history of Ulster literature, and by Daphne Fulwood and Oliver Edwards on the literary heritage of the province.

After a relatively quiet period, Roy McFadden evaluated contemporary Ulster writers in *Threshold* (1966) and Padraic Fiacc announced the arrival of a new generation of poets in *Hibernia* (Nov. 1967, Feb. 1969). With the appearance in print of such new and obviously authentic poetic voices as those of Seamus Heaney, Derek Mahon, and Michael Longley, as well as the ballad poetry of James Simmons, Ulster writing was spotlighted again. In the late sixties the political strife in Belfast and Derry increased the interest focused on the North and on northern writers. In November 1969 Longley's "Strife and the Ulster Poet" appeared in *Hibernia*, and in August 1970 Eavan Boland's important symposium, "The Northern Writer's Crisis of Conscience," was published in successive issues of the *Irish Times*. The symposium included nearly all the major young Ulster writers and gave their views on how the violence had affected them. Also in 1970, Derek Mahon supplied a more simply literary history of his contemporaries in *Twentieth Century Studies*. In 1971 a survey of the current artistic situation appeared in *Causeway: The Arts in Ulster*, edited by Michael Longley. Longley's essay on poetry in this volume distinguished briefly among the voices and styles represented by northern writers. From time to time in the succeeding months, *Hibernia* turned its attention, largely in reviews, to the poetry coming from the North. In 1973 D. E. S. Maxwell, drawing heavily on Eavan Boland's *Irish Times* symposium, provided a thoughtful essay on the problem of violence for Ulster writers (*Éire*). Further speculations on the subject have come from Britta Olinder (*MSpr*, 1977), in an article occasioned by reading Padraic Fiacc's anthology, *The Wearing of the Black* (1974), and in another *Irish Times* series initiated by Eavan Boland's "The Weasel's Tooth" (7 June 1974). James Liddy's two articles in *Éire* (1979), one each on the Catholic and Protestant writers of Ulster, are brief and somewhat inconclusive. Mention should also be made of two recent, handsomely illustrated volumes of background material, John Hewitt's *Art in Ulster I* (1978) and Mike Catto's *Art in Ulster II* (1978). Roger Garfitt's *TLS* review article (15 Feb. 1980) evaluates new poetry by northern writers, and a recent *Threshold* (1982), edited by Seamus Deane, brings the literary and cultural coverage up to date.

The history of modern Irish poetry is of course much more than the history of Ulster poetry. Robert Farren, in his introduction to *The Course of Irish Verse* (1975), discusss the larger picture, as does David Perkins—very briefly—in *A History of Modern Poetry from the 1890's to the High Modernist Mode* (1976). Seán Lucy collects thirteen fine essays by poets and scholars in *Irish Poets in English* (1973). Frank Kersnowski's *The Outsiders: Poets of Contemporary Ireland* (1975) groups the writers according to the periodicals in which they regularly appeared, a pioneering approach that provides a helpful and unique perspective on contemporary poetry. Although flawed by misquotation and errors of fact, the book is still useful as an introduction. Thomas Cahill and Susan Cahill's *A Literary Guide to Ireland* (1973; rpt. 1980), which groups Irish writers according to geography, is a guide to literary landmarks, not to the literature itself. It is somewhat in the spirit of such earlier studies as David O'Donoghue's *The Geographical Distribution of Irish Ability* (1906) and John Freeman's *Literature and Locality: The Literary Topography of Britain and Ireland* (1963). The *Oxford Literary Guide to the British Isles*, compiled by Dorothy Eagle and Hilary Carnell (1977), includes Irish literary landmarks.

Perhaps the earliest history of the Irish literary movements of the twentieth century is W. P. Ryan's *The Irish Literary Revival* (1894). Although it predates the century by six years, its discussion of the early days and founding figures of the Irish Literary Society in London and in Dublin is particularly valuable. Information about literature at the turn of the century was added by Maurice Harmon in "Aspects of the Peasantry in Anglo-Irish Literature from 1800 to 1916" (*SH*, 1975) and by Richard Burnham in an article on the publishing firm of Whaley and Company (*JIL*, 1977). The best overall study is Phillip L. Marcus' *Yeats and the Beginning of the Irish Renaissance* (1970); although it focuses on Yeats, it deals extensively with other major figures. A shortened version of this study appears as a chapter in Brian de Breffny's *The Irish World: The History and Cultural Achievement of the Irish People* (1977), a bountifully illustrated volume that offers more substance in its essays than its pictorial format might suggest. Also of note are John Wilson Foster's "The Western Island in the Irish Renaissance" (*Studies*, 1977) and "The Topographical Tradition in Anglo-Irish Poetry" (*IUR*, 1974). Austin Clarke's "Anglo-Irish Poetry," published in *Literature in Celtic Countries* (1971), is required reading, both as a landmark analysis and as a literary artifact. Seán Lucy's "Meter and Movement in Anglo-Irish Verse" (*IUR*, 1978) is an indispensable study of modern Irish prosody.

Many early studies are too close to their subject to be more than historically valuable. Among these are Oliver Elton's essay on living Irish literature in *Modern Studies* (1907), which gives only passing reference to Yeats's contemporaries; Lionel Johnson's *Post Liminium* (1911), edited by Thomas Whittemore, which considers poetry and patriotism; Darrell Figgis' *Studies and Appreciations* (1912), which deals only with Yeats and Synge; Authur Clery's *Dublin Essays* (1919), which treats prose and theater but not poetry; and John W. Cunliffe's *English Literature during the Last Half Century* (1919; rev. 1923), which has only one chapter on Irish literature. But Ernest Boyd's *Ireland's Literary Renaissance* (1916; rev. 1922; rpt. 1968) is a detailed and valuable history, and some contemporary memoirs supply anecdotal literary information. Among the more illuminating are Simone Téry's *L'Ile des bardes* (1925), A. Rivoallen's *Littérature irlandaise contemporaine* (1939), David Morton's *The Renaissance of Irish Poetry 1880-1930* (1929), Lily MacManus' *White Light and Flame: Memoirs of the Irish Literary Revival and the Anglo-Irish War* (1929), Oliver St. John Gogarty's *As I Was Going down Sackville Street* (1937) and *It Isn't This Time of Year at All* (1954), "An Englishman's" *Dublin: Explorations and Reflections* (1917), Willard Connely's *Adventures in Biography* (1956), and C. P. Curran's "The Side Walks of Dublin" (*Studies*, 1962).

Also recently, scholars have gone over the early literary history to good effect. Augustine Martin has written persuasively on Pearse, Connolly, and MacDonagh (*Studies*, 1959). One of the very best histories, now out of print, is Herbert Howarth's *The Irish Writers, 1880-1940: Literature under Parnell's Star* (1958), which deals mainly with revival figures. John S. Kelly gives the historical background for the revival in much the same vein (*AIS*, 1976). Estella Ruth Taylor's full-length study, *The Modern Irish Writers: Crosscurrents of Criticism* (1954), is more general than Howarth's, as is Lloyd Morris' *The Celtic Dawn: A Survey of the Renascence in Ireland, 1889-1916* (rpt. 1970). William I. Thompson's *The Imagination of an Insurrection: Dublin Easter 1916* (1961) is an exceptionally fine study of the literature and history of the period, and Richard J. Loftus' *Nationalism in Modern Anglo-Irish Poetry* (1964) provides excellent analyses of the writers in their historical context from Yeats through Austin Clarke. Peter Costello's more recent *The Heart Grown Brutal* (1977) and Malcolm Brown's *The Politics of Irish Literature from Thomas Davis to W. B. Yeats* (1972) subsume the literature under considerations of the cultural context.

Most studies that do not attempt an overview of Irish literary movements but rather concentrate on immediately contemporary events have now only historical significance. An early example is Geraldine E. Hodgson's "Some Irish Poetry," which appeared initially in *Contemporary Review* (1910) and was reprinted in *Living Age* in the same year. William Boyle discussed the various Irish character types encountered in Anglo-Irish writing in *Studies* (1912), and the St. Patrick's Day issue of the 1913 London *Times* contained the article "Modern Irish Poets: Irish Literature and English Influences." Of special historical importance is a 1913 *Studies* article by Padraic Pearse on various aspects of Irish poetry. The *London Quarterly Review* (1914) printed Saidee Kirtlan's "Irish Poets and Poetry," which primarily concerned Yeats and the nineteenth century but also discussed Nora Hopper and Althea Gyles. Mary Sturgeon's *Studies of Contemporary Poets* (1916) included commentary on Irish work, and Katharine Tynan (*Studies*, 1917) considered recent Irish poetry in general. Another important historical document is Thomas MacDonagh's *Literature in Ireland: Studies Irish and Anglo-Irish* (1916), which isolated the two traditions of Irishness and Anglo-Irishness in contemporary literature and pointed to the merits of the primarily Celtic aspects of modern Irish art. Apparently in answer to this volume, George A. Birmingham (Canon Hannay) published *An Irishman Looks at His World* (1919), decrying Celticism as an escape from present reality and suggesting innovation instead: "we cannot again become artists like the ancient Irish by copying the things they did." Stephen Gwynn's *Irish Books and Irish People* (1919) is more anecdotal and less critical than its predecessors. Padraic Colum discussed Irish poetry briefly in the *Bookman* (New York, 1921). Norreys Jephson O'Conor's collection of essays, *Changing Ireland: Literary Backgrounds of the Irish Free State, 1899–1922* (1924), is important both for the buoyant optimism of its title, which implies the emergence of a new Irish literature for a new Irish state, and for the essays themselves. O'Conor writes about almost every poet of his time, and although the essays are mostly introductory and filled with quotation, they nonetheless provide valuable historical data and show some literary insight. Also important for historical reasons is Hugh Alexander Law's introductory study, *Anglo-Irish Literature* (1926), for which A. E. provided a foreword. In 1929 David Morton produced *The Renaissance in Irish Poetry*, and the *Irish Statesman* carried two articles by Stephen J. Brown on Irish and on Anglo-Irish literature (23 and 30 Nov.).

The best overall views of the thirties are Samuel Hynes's essay in *Modern Irish Literature* (ed. Raymond J. Porter and James D. Brophy, 1972) and his full-length study *The Auden Generation: Literature and Politics in England in the 1930s* (1977). Of the earlier studies of the thirties, some of the best are a series of essays by Roy McFadden and Geoffrey Taylor in the *Bell* (1943). McFadden and Taylor's "Poetry in Ireland" attempts to clarify the position of the poet in the recent past and in the coming decade. They trace the changing values that they have perceived in the preceding three years and provide a rallying cry for the forties. Another important survey of the period is Robert Greacen's "Contemporary Irish Writings," in *Life and Letters* (1949), which takes stock of the twenty-five-year consolidation of Irish modernism; Greacen notes the disproportionately large number of contemporary Ulster writers and briefly discusses individual contributions to the development of a modern Irish poetry. He sees enough vitality to ensure future literary growth, but he remarks on the absence of leadership since Yeats's death. Midway through the thirties, other writers took stock of the literary scene. Among these the most notable are Austin Clarke, Samuel Beckett, and Anthony Cronin, whose essays in this vein are reprinted in the *Lace Curtain* (1971). Sean O'Faolain's "Irish Poetry since the War" in the *London Mercury* (1935) and Norreys Jephson O'Conor's "The Trend of Anglo-Irish Literature" in the *Bookman* (1934) are also worth study. Francis Shaw (*Studies*, 1934) discusses the relation between Anglo-Irish poetry and the early Celtic twilight, and Stephen Gwynn covers more history in his *Irish Literature and Drama in the English Language: A Short History* (1936). Another useful, more specialized item for the study of the thirties is Anthony Cronin's "Decade of Decision: Literary Journals of the 1930's" (*Hibernia,* 25 June 1971). D. E. S. Maxwell's essay (*JML,* 1975) on the poets and politics of the thirties has largely been superseded by Samuel Hyncs's book.

A possible keynote address for the forties is John V. Kelleher's "Irish Literature Today" (*Atlantic Monthly,* 1945; rpt. in the *Bell,* 1945). More specifically addressed to the situation of poetry in the forties is Anthony Cronin's series of essays "Aspects of Poetry Today" (*Bell,* 1945-46). Cronin sees the influence of the Anglo-Irish and Celtic schools of poetry waning in the face of world war and personal danger, and he notices a growing elegiac tone in contemporary poetry commensurate with the increasing preoccupation with the fate of individuals and of mankind in general. Also in the *Bell* (1947), an article by Austin Clarke and a continuing series of essays by Geoffrey Taylor comment on the state of Irish poetry in the forties. In the introduction to *The Course of Irish Verse* (1948), Robert Farren surveys the poetry of the decade and considers its essentially Irish quality.

The emergence of new writers in the fifties called for another backward look, and several critics provided one, among them Lorna Reynolds (*Studies,* 1951), David Marcus (*Meanjin Papers,* 1952), Sean O'Faolain (*Bell,* 1953), and Austin Clarke in *Poetry in Modern Ireland,* a full-length study (1951). In 1951 the *Bell* held an important symposium under the title "The Young Writer." Participants included John Montague, Valentin Iremonger, John Ryan, James Plunkett, and Mary Beckett. The tone was almost unrelievedly negative, leading to a conclusion that Ireland might well be left without a contemporary literature because of animosities between young writers and the establishment. Francis MacManus answered the arguments rather bitterly in the same pages. The gloomy prognosis proved faulty, however, and some five years later Vivian Mercier was discussing Anglo-Irish literary history in a brief essay in *Studies* (1956) and John Montague was providing a brief, annotated catalog of the major names in the field (*Poetry*, 1957). Since then, the fifties have merited two memoirs and several critical studies, quite apart from those that concern particular figures. Anthony Cronin's *Dead as Doornails* (1976) and John Ryan's *Remembering How We Stood* (1975) are complementary reminiscences that cover the same ground from slightly different perspectives. Both books are esentially sentimental views of literary and pub life in the Dublin of the fifties. Anthony Cronin's *The Life of Riley* (1969) is a fictionalized account of the same period. Maurice Harmon's introduction to *Irish Poetry after Yeats* (1977) provides a more scholarly consideration of the time, as do other, more general studies of Irish poetry published in the sixties and seventies.

The sixties brought a new set of poets to prominence. The first defining note of the new decade was exhortative: John Hewitt's Yeats-echoing " 'Irish Poets, Learn Your Trade' " (*Threshold*, 1959). Denis Ireland's "Fog in the Irish Sea: Some Afterthoughts on Anglo-Irish Literature" (*Threshold*, 1961–62) gave a pessimistic reading of the contemporary situation, as did Denis Donoghue, in cataloging the literature on sale in Dublin (*Studies*, 1961). Sean O'Faolain surveyed fifty years of Irish writing and offered a lengthy analysis of the problems faced by contemporary Irish writers, who, he says, must see themselves as outcasts, abandon writing about Ireland, and go in search of larger themes (*Studies*, 1962). Augustine Martin's answer (*Studies*, 1965) suggested that perhaps the time of the artist-as-pariah had passed and that what was needed now was a more affirmative attitude and a rejection of "inherited dissent." In 1966 Douglas Sealy's two-part article in the *Irish Times* (24–25 Jan.) gave a brief survey of the major contemporary writers and urged publishers to exercise discrimination in choosing materials for publication. Benedict Kiely discussed the landed aristocracy's impact on Irish writing (*Éire*, 1967). Alice Curtayne's *The Irish Story: A Survey of Irish History and Culture* (1967) moved away from particulars to a more general approach; her final chapter deals with contemporary writers. Three prominent studies that appeared in mid-decade enhanced the reputation of Irish writing and provided sound critical evaluations of their subjects: Richard Loftus' landmark, *Nationalism in Modern Irish Poetry* (1964), the best study of its subject to date; *The Celtic Cross* (1964), a collection of essays edited by William J. Roscelli et al.; and M. L. Rosenthal's *The New Poets: American and British Poetry since World War II* (1967), which devotes a significant portion of its text to contemporary Irish poets of the fifties and sixties. In the same period, *Hibernia* articles commented more freely and more frequently on emerging poets, and although the essays are too brief to allow for sufficient reflection, there are illuminating pieces on contemporary trends and on individual writers, especially in articles by Eavan Boland, Rivers Carew, Maurice Harmon, and Aidan Higgins. Other writings included Brendan Kennelly's "The Rebirth of Irish Poetry" (*Hibernia*, 29 Aug. 1969) and two brief retrospective examinations of the decade: Leland Bardwell's "Poetry in the Sixties," in her commemorative *Dublin Arts Festival* publication (1970), and Macdara Woods's "Ten Years of Irish Poetry" (*Hibernia*, 17 Apr. 1970).

At the start of the seventies Eavan Boland discussed the future of Irish poetry in an article in the *Irish Times* (5 Feb. 1970), and Thomas Kinsella's Thomas Davis lecture over Radio Telefís Éireann provided a keynote address for the problems of the coming decade. The lecture, "The Divided Mind," was printed in Seán Lucy's collection of essays, *Irish Poets in English* (1973), which among other important items for students of contemporary Irish poetry, includes Robert Farren's essay on the Gaelic voice in Anglo-Irish poetry and studies by various poets and critics of the preceding generations of Irish writers. In 1971 (Jan. - Mar.) the *Irish Times* ran a series of retrospective essays on the major figures of the early part of the century; these articles are as important for the light they shed on the opinions of those who wrote them—including Michael Hartnett, Benedict Kiely, Padraic Fallon, John Broderick, Michael Longley, and Eavan Boland—as they are for the assessments of the major figures. John Montague briefly surveyed the current scene in the 1972 St. Patrick's Day number of *TLS*, under the unfortunate title "Order in Donnybrook Fair." Patrick Diskin considered the Gaelic background in Anglo-Irish poetry once more (*Topic*, 1972); Richard Kain suggested that Irish literary periodicals are "an untilled field" for research (*Éire*, 1972); John Unterecker interviewed Liam Miller about the poets and publications associated with the Dolmen Press in *Modern Irish Literature* (1972); the catalog of the Project Arts Centre's 1972 "Irish Poetry Now" exhibit included John Jordan's useful summary of Irish poetry since Yeats; and *Les Lettres Nouvelles* produced a special issue (1973), edited by Serge Faucheron, which introduced contemporary Irish poets to a French audience and included valuable interviews (in French) with Seamus Heaney, Derek Mahon, Michael Longley, Michael Hartnett, and John Montague, as well as translations of their poems. Maurice Harmon discussed a change in tone from the old nationalism to a new cosmopolitanism in such writers as Thomas Kinsella, John Montague, and Richard Murphy (*Éire*, 1973). There followed John Wilson Foster's article on topography in Irish poetry (*IUR*, 1974), Dillon Johnston's summary of poetry in the early seventies (*Shenandoah*, 1974), and Sean McMahon's essay on new Irish writers (*Éire*, 1974). The most important item of criticism to emerge in the seventies was *Two Decades of Irish Writing: A Critical Survey* (1975), edited by Douglas Dunn: this collection of excellent essays, many of them reprinted from journals, examined contemporary Irish literature from different angles. Essays about individual poets are cited below in the appropriate discussions; noteworthy here are Michael Smith's and Seamus Deane's essays about contemporary poetry in general and D. E. S. Maxwell's brief survey of northern poetry. Of less importance for Irish studies is G. S. Fraser's *The Modern Writer and His World* (1975), which places Irish writers in a general discussion of contemporary writing. In 1976 *SR* produced a special issue dedicated to Irish writing, with relevant essays by Denis Donoghue and George Brandon Saul, and a pertinent review essay by Seamus Deane. In a collection of essays edited by Joseph Ronsley, *Myth and Reality in Irish Literature* (1977), Deane argued for a departure from the traditional literary myths of the revival, especially Yeats's views of the implicit superiority of Anglo-Irish writing. A special number of *MSpr* (1977), introduced by Johannes Hedberg, examined Irish writers. Maurice Harmon discussed a cross-section of contemporary Irish poets (*EI*, 1977), and reviewed Irish literary nationalism since 1922 (*KM*, 1978). Eamon Grennan (*Éire*, 1978) considered the state of contemporary publishing and, while celebrating the strength of the small presses, called for more discriminating standards. Desiree Hirst (*AWR*, 1978) also considered the general poetic scene.

Recently, more specialized studies have begun to appear. Terence Brown examines the Dublin influence in "Dublin in Twentieth-Century Writing: Metaphor and Subject" (*IUR*, 1978), and C. L. Innis compares the rhetoric of Irish literature to the rhetoric of black American literature (*MR*, 1975; *ALT*, 1978). Sean Golden's general survey "Traditional Irish Music in Contemporary Irish Literature" (*Mosaic*, 1979) offers readings that are occasionally reductive, as when Golden calls Seamus Heaney's "Requiem for the Croppies" a "recent treatment of the Croppy Boy theme." The capstone of general criticism in the 1970s is Adrian Frazier's brief, well-written "Irish Poetry after Yeats" in the special number of the *Literary Review* dedicated to the subject (1979). Frazier surveys and analyzes the major writers and major trends succinctly and memorably. Also in the late seventies the *Honest Ulsterman* provided a forum for vigorous literary and political debate: much lively literary criticism appeared under the pseudonym "Jude the Obscure." A new Irish journal, the *Crane Bag*, has proved a platform for further debate on social and literary issues. In late 1979 one issue was given over to a multidimensional examination of the state of Irish letters at the end of the decade, by such critics as Edna Longley and Robert Tracy. Included in the same issue is Sean Golden's "Post-traditional English Literatures" and Timothy Kearney's "Ulster Poetry: A Post-modernist Perspective." Aidan Mathews has perhaps sounded the keynote for the 1980s in his "Modern Irish Poetry: A Question of Covenants" (*Crane Bag*, 1979), while Seán Lucy looked back over the poetry of the decade (*IUR*, 1979). Two other important special issues appeared in 1979, a *Ploughshares* number edited by Seamus Heaney and composed primarily of recent poetry and fiction, and the *Literary Review* number edited by Adrian Frazier. John Montague provides a history of *Threshold* in *A Needle's Eye* (1979), and in the same publication Thomas Kinsella's Lyric Theatre lecture reveals that he is working on the new *Oxford Book of Irish Verse*, calls for the inclusion of Anglo-Irish and Irish literature in "a single embrace," and provides a stringent and astute analysis of the present state of Irish letters.

The 1980s have begun with a retrospective glance from Kevin Reilly (*Éire*, 1980), who examines Irish poetry from 1940 to the present, and an extremely valuable special number of *Threshold* (1982), edited by Seamus Deane, on the subject of nationalism and literature. In addition to representative contributions from poets and other writers, it contains five important essays by Deane, Vincent Buckley, Timothy Kearney, Niall Crowley, and Hugh Maxton, which study the subject from genuinely helpful perspectives. The issue is bound to provoke further discussion, if not controversy. It bodes well for future criticism.

3. Anthologies

Anthologies of Irish poetry offer material enough for at least one good study, as yet unwritten. Yeats's *A Book of Irish Verse* (1894; rev. 1900) effectively began the century and was soon joined by the more comprehensive *A Treasury of Irish Poetry in the English Tongue* (1900), edited by Stopford Brooke and T. W. Rolleston. A. E. introduced the work of younger writers in his *New Songs* (1904), and two multivolume, multigenre collections appeared: Charles Read's *The Cabinet of Irish Literature* (1904), in four exquisitely crafted volumes, and Justin McCarthy's *Irish Literature* (1904), in ten volumes. Eleanor Hull's *A Textbook of Irish Literature* appeared in two volumes (1906, 1908). John Cooke's *The Dublin Book of Irish Verse, 1798-1909* (1909) included modern writers and supplied helpful notes to the poems. *Poems of the Irish Revolutionary Brotherhood* appeared in 1916. The next major collection was Lennox Robinson's *A Golden Treasury of Irish Verse* (1925), which held precedence in the field for many years thereafter. Mention should also be made of Alfred Perceval Graves's *The Book of Irish Poetry* (1914); Yeats's *Oxford Book of Modern Verse* (1936), which included more Irish poets than earlier editions of that work; and Geoffrey Taylor's *Irish Poets of the Nineteenth Century* (1951), some of whose subjects continued writing poetry well into the twentieth century.

In the forties and fifties, the emergence of new writers called for the production of new anthologies, and Roy McFadden and Robert Greacen compiled a Northern Ireland collection called *Ulster Voices* (1943). Geoffrey Taylor collected poetry from the *Bell* for *Irish Poems of Today* (1944); Donagh MacDonagh edited a sample of contemporary Irish poetry from the North and South, *Poems from Ireland* (1944); and Robert Greacen edited an Ulster collection, *Northern Harvest* (1944). Diarmuid Russell's *The Portable Irish Reader* (1946) supplied a generous helping of poetry as well as fiction; it was followed by Kathleen Hoagland's *1,000 Years of Irish Poetry* (1947) and Padraic Colum's *An Anthology of Irish Verse* (1948). Next came two books on contemporary writers: Devin A. Garrity's *New Irish Poets: Representative Selections from the Work of 37 Contemporaries* (1949) and Valentin Iremonger and Robert Greacen's *Contemporary Irish Poetry* (1949). David H. Greene edited *An Anthology of Irish Literature* (1954) in the Modern Library series. Donagh MacDonagh and Lennox Robinson joined forces to produce *The Oxford Book of Irish Verse* (1958) for the Clarendon Press, a sure sign that Irish poetry as such had "arrived."

After Padraic Colum's *The Poet's Circuits* (1960; rpt. 1982), other vigorous new voices began the sixties, with the appearance of *Three Irish Poets: John Montague, Thomas Kinsella, Richard Murphy* (1961), followed by John Montague's *The Dolmen Miscellany of Irish Writing* (1962)—called *The Dolmen Anthology of Irish Writing* in its American form (1962). Robin Skelton included the same writers and others in *Six Irish Poets* (1962), as did Devin A. Garrity in *The Mentor Book of Irish Poetry* (1965) and Donald Carroll in *New Poets of Ireland* (1963). Going back to earlier times, George Brandon Saul edited *The Age of Yeats: The Golden Age of Irish Literature* (1963), a rather arbitrary selection of works chosen apparently for their range as much as for their intrinsic worth; it contains little poetry. The sixties also saw theme collections of Irish literature, with Desmond Ryan's *The 1916 Poets: Pearse, MacDonagh, Plunkett* (1963) and Seán Lucy's *Love Poems of the Irish* (1967).

The enormous burst of creative vitality that was released in Ireland as the sixties merged into the seventies provided a bounty of anthologies. Brendan Kennelly's *The Penguin Book of Irish Verse* (1970) aimed for a broad historical sweep rather than for an in-depth coverage of individuals. The work of previously uncollected poets appeared in Seán Lucy's *Five Irish Poets* (1970) and David Marcus' *New Irish Writing* (1970). Marcus' volume, which includes fiction as well as poetry, was the first in a series of such books that he edited, using material culled from his Saturday pages in the *Irish Press*. Robin Skelton featured "Five Irish Poets" (*MH Rev*, 1971). In recent years *New Irish Writing* (1976) has appeared at various intervals and has tended to include more fiction than verse. In 1972 Derek Mahon edited *The Sphere Book of Modern Irish Poetry*, William Cole produced *Poems from Ireland*, and Seamus Heaney began editing *Soundings*, billed as an annual anthology of new Irish writing. A second issue appeared under Heaney's editorship in 1973, and a third and final one under the editorship of James Simmons in 1975. In Simmons' own anthology, *Ten Irish Poets* (1974), most of the writers are from Ulster. Padraic Fiacc's *The Wearing of the Black: An Anthology of Contemporary Ulster Poets* (1974) was composed of works on the theme of northern violence and arranged, said Fiacc, in symphonic form. His book is as much an important historical document as an anthology of verse. For altogether different reasons, Desmond Egan's *Choice: An Anthology of Irish Poetry Selected by the Poets Themselves with a Comment on Their Choice* (1973) is also an important volume: it contains valuable information from the poets about the composition of some of their poems. Irish poets appear in *The Oxford Book of Twentieth Century Verse* (1973), *A Patrick Kavanagh Anthology* (1973), *Living Poets* (1974), *The Faber Book of Twentieth Century Verse* (1975), *New Poems* (1975), *The Oxford Book of Contemporary Verse, 1945–1980* (1980), and *Pomes for Joyce* (1982). John Montague provides a helpfully inclusive introduction to his *The Faber Book of Irish Verse* (1974), published in the United States as *The Book of Irish Verse: An Anthology of Irish Poetry from the Sixth Century to the Present* (1977). Montague selects judiciously for both breadth of range and depth of individual coverage, and his book is still one of the best available. David Marcus' more narrowly focused *Irish Poets, 1924–1974* (1975) deals only with poets born after 1924, thereby giving a fuller perspective on the recent scene. *The Wolfhound Book of Irish Poems for Young People* (1975) includes major contemporary poets. *Poetry Now*, intended as a periodical anthology, also began appearing in 1975. Sean McMahon collected poetry, fiction, and essays from the *Bell* into a volume, *The Best from the* Bell (1978), but there was much more of "the best" that he did not have room to include. Grattan Freyer published *A Prose and Verse Anthology of Modern Irish Writing* (1978), with a useful but brief introduction by Conor Cruise O'Brien. Maurice Harmon edited *Irish Poetry after Yeats: Seven Poets* (1979); the poets are well chosen and amply represented, and Harmon's lengthy introduction is especially valuable for beginning students. Peter Fallon and Dennis O'Driscoll observed an anniversary with *The First Ten Years: Dublin Arts Festival Poetry* (1979), and Jim Fitzgerald commemorated the Irish visit of John Paul II, "a poet who is also Pope," with *Celebration: A Salute to a Visiting Artist* (1979), a gathering of poetry from a stellar array of contemporary writers. Frank Ormsby edited a fine anthology, *Poets from the North of Ireland* (1979), and provided an excellent introduction.

The new decade is beginning well with an Irish issue of *Ploughshares* (1980), edited by Seamus Heaney, and four estimable anthologies: Frank Ormsby's *Poets from the North of Ireland* (1979), Peter Fallon and Sean Golden's *Soft Day: A Miscellany of Contemporary Irish Writing* (1980), Anthony Bradley's *Contemporary Irish Poetry* (1980), and Andrew Carpenter's *The Writers: A Sense of Ireland* (1980). Fallon and Golden include fiction; Bradley does not, but his volume is twice the size of theirs, contains a useful introduction, and supplies both pictures and brief biographical sketches at the head of each poet's entry. Carpenter's anthology conveys an impression of the wealth of contemporary Irish writing by offering not only all new work from the full range of living Irish writers (with a few exceptions, duly noted in the preface) but also fine portrait photographs of each.

4. Studies of Individual Poets

The better-known poets among Yeats's contemporaries are discussed in other parts of this volume. Poets of lesser reputation, however, have not been neglected. Phillip L. Marcus' *Yeats and the Beginning of the Irish Renaissance* (1970) is the best overall study of these minor figures of Yeats's day and, together with Robert Hogan's *Dictionary of Irish Writers* (1979), provides the fullest critical treatment of many of the individual poets. Virtually all the poets mentioned in this chapter are accorded some critical treatment by Hogan's or Marcus' book in addition to the other works cited here, and most are discussed in works listed under General Studies in this chapter.

Although John Todhunter (1839–1916) merited a bibliography at the time of his death (*Irish Book Lover*, 1916) and a posthumous *Selected Poems* (1929), he has not been the subject of any individual study since 1953, when Yeats's essay on his poetry was reprinted in *W. B. Yeats: Letters to Katharine Tynan*. T. W. Rolleston (1857–1920), whose *Sea Spray, Verses and Translations* (1909) was followed by further translations from the Irish, has been the subject of two studies, one by Norreys Jephson O'Conor in his *Changing Ireland* (1924) and the other by C. H. Rolleston in *Portrait of an Irishman* (1939), neither of which treats his poems at length. O'Conor also briefly discusses Dora Sigerson Shorter (1866–1918) in his book, finding her poetry typical of the Celtic revival; she receives more extended consideration in the *Bookman* (London, 1905) as a "New Young Irelander," along with Yeats and A. E., and in William Archer's *Poets of the Younger Generation* (1902), a reasoned appraisal of her merits and faults. A memorial to her, by one

"Benmore," entitled *Remembered, a Daughter of Erin, Dora Sigerson Shorter, Died 6th January 1918, Gifted and Patriotic,* appeared in the year of her death. Her many volumes of verse have not been collected.

Katharine Tynan (1861–1931) figures in Yeats's *Autobiographies* (1955) and in several biographical and critical studies of Yeats. William Archer praised her thoughtfully in *Poets of the Younger Generation* (1902), as did A. E. in the preface to her *Collected Poems* (1930) and, more effusively, Michael Walsh (*IM*, 1930). Other analyses include reviews of her career by C. E. Maguire in the *Bookman* (New York, 1931), and by Russell K. Alspach (*Ireland-America Rev.,* 1940). The standard studies of her life and work are Anne Connerton Fallon's book in the Twayne series (1978) and Marilyn Gaddis Rose's study in the Irish Writers series (1973). Roger McHugh's *W. B. Yeats: Letters to Katharine Tynan* (1953) and David DeLaura's "Such Good Friends: Four Letters of Gerard Manley Hopkins to Katharine Tynan" (*Studies,* 1964) supplement her autobiographical works, *Twenty-Five Years* (1913), *The Middle Years* (1916), *The Years of the Shadow* (1919), and *The Wandering Years* (1922).

The poetic importance of Douglas Hyde (1860–1949) derives chiefly from his translations of Irish verse. P. S. O'Hegarty published a bibliography of his works in 1939. It has been updated by Dominic Daly, in *The Young Douglas Hyde* (1974); by Gareth Dunleavy, in his Irish Writers series study (1974); and by Tomás de Bhaldraithe—in Irish—in *Galvia* (1957). Of the many smaller studies of Hyde, the most relevant to his poetry is Robert Welch's "Douglas Hyde and His Translations of Gaelic Verse" (*Studies,* 1975). Lester Conner's "The Importance of Douglas Hyde," in *Modern Irish Literature* (1972), gives short consideration to the poems, and Monk Gibbon's preface to Hyde's *Poems from the Irish* (1963) is too effusive and too brief to be trustworthy. No collected poems exists.

Less prominent in the revival were such figures as James Cousins (1873–1956), whose major publishing occurred after he emigrated to India. J. N. Browne discusses him in *The Arts in Ulster* (1951), and John Hewitt offered a centenary commemoration in the *Irish Press* (21 July 1973), but Alan Denson's *James H. Cousins and Margaret E. Cousins: A Bibliographical Survey,* privately printed in 1967, provides the major bibliography and evaluation of his work. Despite its obvious advocacy of Cousins' "cause" and several authorial interruptions, it is a work of scrupulous scholarship. Cousins wrote his autobiography with his wife, *We Two Together* (1950); his poems remain uncollected. Frederick Herbert Trench (1865–1923) received notice in *Poets of the Younger Generation* (1902) for his long poem, *Deirdre Wedded* (1901), but his work has gone largely unnoticed since, except for its influence on the young Austin Clarke and for Herbert Fackler's "Herbert Trench's *Deirdre Wedded* (1901): Neglect Merited" (*Éire,* 1978) and a fuller treatment in Fackler's *The Deirdre Legend in Anglo-Irish Literature* (1976). G. F. Savage-Armstrong (1845–1906) has been virtually ignored by everyone except Marcus and Hogan, but Richard Rowley (1877–1947) has benefited from the general revival of interest in Ulster writers. Articles about his poetry appear in *The Arts in Ulster* (ed. Sam Hanna

Bell et al., 1951) and in the *Honest Ulsterman* (1976), and Terence Brown considers him briefly in his *Northern Voices* (1975). A selection of his work, edited by Victor Price, appears in *Apollo in Mourne: Poems, Plays and Stories* (1978), with a brief bibliography. Seumas O'Sullivan (James Sullivan Starkey, 1879-1958) has been the subject of several bibliographies; the latest one, by Alan Denson, appears in Liam Miller's celebratory *Retrospect: The Work of Seumas O'Sullivan and Estella F. Solomons* (1973), which also contains brief notes by Padraic Colum. Lorna Reynolds' discussion of his work appeared earlier (*UnivR,* 1955). The poetry of Daniel Corkery (1878-1953) is considered at some length in *Irish Writing* (1953); that of Ethna Carberry (1866-1902) is remembered by Alice Furlong in a slight article (*IM,* 1918). Alice Milligan (1866-1953) is the subject of Thomas MacDonagh's "The Best Living Irish Poet" (*IrishR,* 1914); Amanda M'Kittrick Ros (1860-1939) is discussed in *O Rare Amanda!* by Jack Loudan (1957); Susan Mitchell (1866-1926) is well served by Richard M. Kain's 1972 book in the Irish Writers series; and John Moore, a "Donaghadee poet," is introduced in the first volume of *Irish Booklore.* Nora Hopper (1871-1906) is treated at length in *The Arts in Ulster* (1951) and in Phillip L. Marcus' *Yeats and the Beginning of the Irish Renaissance* (1970).

Four Irish poets died in the turbulent years of 1916 and 1917 before they reached full poetic voice. Three of them, Joseph Mary Plunkett (1887-1916), Thomas MacDonagh (1878-1916), and Padraic Pearse (1879-1916), are considered in William Irwin Thompson's *The Imagination of an Insurrection: Dublin, Easter 1916* (1961), in Richard J. Loftus' *Nationalism in Modern Anglo-Irish Poetry* (1964), and in Malcolm Brown's *The Politics of Irish Literature from Thomas Davis to W. B. Yeats* (1972). Articles about Plunkett appeared in *University Review* in 1954, and Padraic Gregory wrote on his poetry in *IM* (1918). Thomas MacDonagh's *Literature in Ireland: Studies Irish and Anglo-Irish* (1916) is important for its analysis of the fundamental differences between English and Irish literature as they appeared during the revival, and Padraic Colum's introduction to the volume is also of interest. The text of an address by MacDonagh's sister has been published (*UnivR,* 1956), and two full-length studies exist: E. W. Parks and A. W. Parks's *Thomas MacDonagh: The Man, the Patriot, the Writer* (1967), and Johann Norstedt's *Thomas MacDonagh: A Critical Biography* (1980), which supersedes the Parks study. Norstedt discusses the historical impact of MacDonagh's writing and uses family papers. Both Plunkett and MacDonagh are discussed from a historical perspective by Donagh Mac-Donagh in F. X. Martin's *Leaders and Men of the Easter Rising: Dublin 1916* (1967). Brendan Kennelly's essay on Plunkett appeared in the *Dublin Magazine* in 1966, as did Eavan Boland's on Padraic Pearse. Pearse is the subject of two articles by David Thornley in *Studies* (1976, 1979) and several by Raymond J. Porter, most of which are subsumed into his Twayne study, *P. H. Pearse* (1973). Other works on Pearse include an early bibliography by P. S. O'Hegarty (*DM,* 1931); two descriptions of St. Enda's College by Desmond Ryan (*Threshold,* 1957; *UnivR,* 1955); C. P. Curran's combined study of Griffith, MacNeill, and Pearse (*Studies,* 1966), in which he claims that Yeats partially derived the refrain for "Easter 1916" from Pearse's words; Christopher Clausen's examination of Pearse as a revolutionary and artist (*ShawR,* 1976); and Ruth Dudley Edwards' full-length biography, *Patrick Pearse: The Triumph of Failure* (1966), which deals only briefly with the poetry. Séamas Ó Buachalla has edited his letters and writings (1979-80). The fourth poet to die in this decade of strife, Francis Ledwidge (1887-1917), perished in World War I. His *Complete Poems* (1919) was published shortly after his death by his friend and mentor, Lord Dunsany, but a fuller version, including many previously unpublished items, appeared in 1974 under the editorship of Alice Curtayne, who is also his biographer (1972). A memorial address by her (*Éire,* 1980) is of only historical significance. Seamus Heaney considers Ledwidge's literary importance in an essay in his *Preoccupations* (1980).

Yeats's contemporaries included several younger poets who were his friends or acquaintances. Among them were Monk Gibbon (1896-) and John Lyle Donaghy (1902-47). Patricia Dingwall notes the resemblance of Gibbon's work to that of Pierre Bonnard, the French painter, and otherwise comments on his independence from contemporary literary movements (*Bell,* 1948). In the *Capuchin Annual* (1973), James Coulter considers Donaghy, whose poems Yeats published at the Cuala Press, finding him "one of the two major Irish poets in the English language in my own lifetime" (the other is Austin Clarke); and in *The Arts in Ulster* (1951), R. N. Browne praises Donaghy's lyric poetry for its "sterness without *hauteur*" but notes an "undercurrent of pessimism" that reveals itself in "stoical defiance of . . . time."

Nearly every history of the Abbey Theatre discusses Padraic Colum (1881-1972), and he has been well covered by literary scholarship. Alan Denson has provided a checklist of his works (*DM,* 1967), and Zack Bowen has written the definitive study of his life and work (1970). In addition, the reminiscences of his wife, Mary Colum, contain much valuable biographical information about him (1928), as do the many recollections published after his death by various friends (*Capuchin Annual,* 1973; *CLC,* 1973; *IBl,* 1972; *JIL,* 1973; *DM,* 1974). The Padraic Colum number of the *Journal of Irish Literature* (1973) contains an interview, several reminiscences, an article on his plays, and some previously uncollected poetry, prose, and drama. Also of interest are Douglas Campbell's examination of Colum's "celebration of littleness" (*Éire,* 1974), Hugh Shields's discussion of "She Moved through the Fair" (*IUR,* 1975), Carolyn Walsh's article in the *Irish Times* (19 July 1977), and L. A. G. Strong's memories of Colum in *Personal Remarks* (1953). A recent evaluation is Richard J. Loftus' chapter on his work in *Nationalism in Modern Anglo-Irish Poetry* (1973). J. F. Cassidy's "The Poetry of Padraic Colum" (*IM,* 1921) is overwritten and excessively romantic in its view of the Gael. In 1971 Alan Denson noted on Colum's ninetieth birthday (*Irish Times,* 8 Dec.) that no collected poems has yet appeared; that situation still prevails. His papers have been purchased by the State University of New York, Binghamton; Zack Bowen has supplied an annotated catalog and bibliography of the collection.

Colum wrote a brief reminiscence of one of his contemporaries, Joseph Campbell (1879-1944), which appeared in *Rann* (1945), and although Campbell has yet to receive the honor of a full-length study, he has had good essays written about his work. P. S. O'Hegarty supplied a bibliography during Campbell's lifetime (*DM,* 1940), and after his death J. N. Browne paid tribute to his "shining simplicity" (*Lagan,* 1945), as did Seumas O'Sullivan in a note in *The Rose and Bottle and Other Essays* (1946). Browne treated Campbell more analytically in *The Arts in Ulster,* (1951), calling him "the most accomplished of the poets associated with the Ulster literary movement prior to 1914" and praising his fastidious economy of language and his classical restraint of feeling. More recent considerations of his work have agreed with that assessment. David R. Clark provides a close reading and analysis of "The Dancer" (*Éire,* 1969), finding its strength in its fusion of dancer as individual and dancer as type. The most extensive Campbell commemorative to date appears in honor of his centenary (*JIL,* 1979); the same special issue includes a thorough chronology of his life by Assumpta Saunders.

Another poet of the period, F. R. Higgins (1896–1941), was Yeats's close friend in his final years. M. J. MacManus prepared a bibliography of Higgins' work through 1937 (*DM,* 1937), and Frank O'Connor, Yeats's other good friend among the younger poets, lamented Higgins' early death, describing him as "a Keats disguised as a Falstaff" and a "[b]ridge between the obstinate anti-romanticism of our time and the lofty and fantastic imagination of pre-revolutionary poetry" (*Bell,* 1941). Geoffrey Taylor noted Higgins' originality and found in him "an Irish analogue to English pastoral poets" (*Bell,* 1946); Taylor also remarked that Irish poets who do not gain the ear of England or America remain essentially unrecognized, citing this as the prime reason for the failure of Higgins and others to achieve a renown commensurate with their poetic skills. This flattering appraisal of Higgins has not prevailed; Padraic Fallon's reassessment of the poet in the *Irish Times* (30 Mar. 1971) finds in his poetry both good and bad, greatness and decline. Thomas Dillon Redshaw (*Hibernia,* 1971) says much the same, and Richard Burnham (*Éire,* 1978) notes that Higgins owed much of his literary reputation to Seumas O'Sullivan, who published the bulk of Higgins' poems in the *Dublin Magazine.* Richard Loftus, in *Nationalism in Modern Anglo-Irish Poetry* (1973), considers Higgins a prime example of a poet influenced by nationalism. Fellow poets Austin Clarke and W. R. Rodgers supply reminiscences of Higgins (*DM,* 1967), as do Rodgers' BBC broadcasts, collected in *Irish Literary Portraits* (1973).

Although the poetry and prose of Frank O'Connor (Michael O'Donovan, 1903–66) are equally important, his prose has received more critical attention, no doubt because there is so much more of it. As a poet, however, he is significant not only for the beauty and precision of his translations of Irish poetry but also for his influence on and collaboration with W. B. Yeats (and vice versa). Three full-length studies of O'Connor are James H. Matthews' *Frank O'Connor* (1976), in the Irish Writers series, which does not discuss the poetry; Maurice Wohlgelertner's *Frank O'Connor: An Introduction* (1977), which concentrates primarily on the life; and *Michael/Frank* (1969), edited by Maurice Sheehy, a collection of essays and bibliography that is still the most important single item of O'Connor criticism to date. It includes essays on his poetry by Brendan Kennelly and David Greene and informative reminiscences from a range of friends, scholars, and critics. In another important early essay on O'Connor's poetry, Geoffrey Taylor (*Bell*, 1945) favorably compares his translations with those of Mangan and Stephens. More sharp-tongued is Patrick Kavanagh's appraisal (*Bell*, 1947), which implicitly denigrates the significance of O'Connor's poetry and stories. Douglas Sealy's study of O'Connor's Irish translations (*DM*, 1963) is especially helpful for its comparisons of specific passages to the originals; Sealy demonstrates the superiority of O'Connor's renderings to those by other translators and finds his work to be the best available. O'Connor's poetry is also discussed in various books on Yeats, but a definitive commentary on the poems has yet to be written, and the poems themselves have yet to be collected. The autobiographical information found in his *An Only Child* (1961) and *My Father's Son* (1968) is supplemented by interviews such as those in the *Bell* (1951), *The Paris Review Interviews* (1958), and *Monitor: An Anthology* (ed. H. W. Weldon, 1962), as well as by reminiscences, the best of which are collected in Sheehy's *Michael/Frank*. Alan Anderson has compiled a bibliography of O'Connor's published books (1979), but Sheehy's should also be consulted for its listing of many fugitive pieces. The Frank O'Connor issue of the *Journal of Irish Literature* (1975) contains letters, broadcasts, speeches, and journalism, in addition to an unpublished play and several poems, some of which are reprinted from other published sources.

Two Ulster contemporaries of O'Connor, W. R. Rodgers (1909–69) and John Hewitt (1907–   ), have earned substantial critical commentary. Rodgers, whose *Collected Poems* was issued posthumously (1971), as were his BBC interviews with writers, *Irish Literary Portraits* (1973), is the subject of one of the better volumes in the Irish Writers series, Darcy O'Brien's brief but highly informative *W. R. Rodgers* (1970), which is the major study of Rodgers' work. Earlier treatments include a 1941 article in the *Bell* by Geoffrey Taylor and a 1950 one by H. A. L. Craig, who found Rodgers to be "one of the most original of modern poets," though difficult and elliptical. R. N. Browne noted Rodgers' similarities to Hopkins in *The Arts in Ulster* (1951). In more recent studies, Terence Brown has examined his style briefly in *Hibernia* (1969) and at greater length in *Northern Voices* (1975). Less significantly, Frank Ormsby quotes the poems and summarizes the career in the *Honest Ulsterman* (1970). Michael Longley points briefly to Rodgers' distinctive achievement in *Causeway: The Arts in Ulster* (1971). Robert Greacen's comparison of Rodgers and Hewitt (*Rann*, 1969) has been superseded by Terence Brown's exemplary essay in *Two Decades of Irish Writing* (ed. Douglas Dunn, 1975), which describes Rodgers' poetic style as "plenitude without passion."

John Hewitt, who did not collect his poems until 1968, continues to add to his work. Geoffrey Taylor's 1941 article in the *Bell* considered his work along with Rodgers', noting similarities between the two poets and to Edward Thomas and Robert Frost; Taylor concluded that Hewitt's verse is inferior for its "flatness unrelieved by a single memorable line," an overly negative view. R. N. Browne, on the other hand, praised

Hewitt in *The Arts in Ulster* (1951) for a simplicity like "wheaten bread." Recent scholarship has been more analytical and less impressionistic, notably John Montague's essay (*Poetry Ireland*, 1964), Douglas Sealy's (*DM*, 1969), and Seamus Heaney's (*Threshold*, 1969; rpt. in *Preoccupations*, 1980). All three treat Hewitt primarily as historically significant for Ulster writers who have followed him, a verdict Michael Longley corroborates in his brief remarks on the poet in *Causeway: The Arts in Ulster* (1971). An important article on Hewitt's poetry appeared in 1972 in *Aquarius* under a title often borrowed since—"The Planter and the Gael." In it, Hewitt (the planter) is compared with John Montague (the Gael), and each is seen as representative of the different types of Ulstermen. John Wilson Foster's "The Landscape of the Planter and the Gael in the Poetry of John Hewitt and John Montague" (*CJIS*, 1975) adopts this terminology, used by the poets themselves on a poetry-reading tour in the early 1970s. For Hewitt, as well as for Rodgers and other Ulster writers, Terence Brown's criticism is definitive. In *Two Decades of Irish Writing* (1975), Brown cites Hewitt's "syntax of careful logic which is never allowed to become the intellectual equivalent of emotional or verbal imbalance," and at greater length in *Northern Voices* (1975) he judiciously evaluates Hewitt's achievement in the Ulster literary tradition. Britta Olinder perceptively examines Hewitt's view of his own poetry in *Papers from the First Nordic Conference for English Studies* (Oslo, 1981). Alan Warner has edited *The Selected John Hewitt* (1981).

Francis MacManus' "The Exasperating Padraic Fallon" (*Bell*, 1951) is a good introduction to the life and work of Fallon (1905–74). The cause of MacManus' exasperation, Fallon's preference for fugitive forms of publication, was not alleviated until 1974, when his *Poems* was printed posthumously; the long absence of a collection accounts for the scarcity of Fallon criticism before 1974. Since then, only a few articles have appeared, among them Eavan Boland's brief assessment of the poet's work (*Hibernia*, 19 Jan. 1973) and John Broderick's similar article (*Hibernia*, 25 Oct. 1974), which have been superseded by Maurice Harmon's lengthy commentary on the *Poems* (*Studies*, 1975). Harmon finds Fallon's work primarily a reaction against Yeats, a view shared by Donald Davie in *Two Decades of Irish Writing* (1975).

Largely thanks to the reprinting of Samuel Beckett's favorable review of Thomas MacGreevy's *Poems* (*Lace Curtain*, 1970–71), MacGreevy (1893–1967) has been rediscovered, most notably by Brian Coffey (*Hibernia*, 1971), Anthony Cronin (*Lace Curtain*, 1978), Stan Smith (*Lace Curtain*, 1978), and Thomas Dillon Redshaw (afterword to rpt. of MacGreevy's *Collected Poems*, 1971). Of these four evaluations, Cronin's and Redshaw's are the more helpful, since they are the more detailed.

Brian Coffey's poetry has not been extensively examined in print; apart from reviews of individual volumes and of his *Selected Poems* (1971), Coffey (1901–   ) has been studied primarily in broadly historical books and essays. Even the special Coffey issue of the *Irish University Review* (1975) is *by* him rather than *about* him except for James Mays's introduction. One notable essay has appeared, however: Stan Smith's evaluation of the "systolic/diastolic" progression in the poems, in *Two Decades of Irish Writing* (1975). Parkman Howe's interview with Coffey appeared in *Éire* (1978).

Coffey's energies have done much to promote the reputation of his friend Denis Devlin (1908–59). Coffey edited Devlin's complete poems for a special issue of *University Review* (1963; pub. separately in 1964) and prepared the *Denis Devlin Special Issue* for Advent Books in 1976, which contains articles on Devlin's work by Mervyn Wall, Lorna Reynolds, James Mays, Robert Welch, and Stan Smith, as well as by Coffey. Coffey's early articles (*UnivR*, 1961, 1965) initiated the main critical discussion of Devlin's work. M. L. Rosenthal, in *The New Poets* (1967), considers him briefly in context with the other poets of the forties. Niall Montgomery (*Lace Curtain*, 1971) contributes little beyond praise for Devlin's "humanity." More significant are Frank Kersnowski's article (*SR*, 1973) and Mary Salmon's close analysis of Devlin's *Lough Derg* (*Studies*, 1973). Coffey's essay in *Place, Personality and the Irish Writer* (ed. Andrew Carpenter, 1977) consists mostly of quotation and reminiscence, and Maurice Harmon discusses Devlin briefly in his introduction to *Irish Poetry after Yeats* (1977). Two articles by Roger Little and by Stan Smith examine him at greater length (*IUR*, 1978), and William G. Downey provides useful background and a good reading of *Lough Derg* (*Éire*, 1979).

Poets of this period whose work is less widely known have received correspondingly less critical analysis. The poetry of Patrick MacDonogh has been recently reintroduced to literary study by Caroline MacDonogh (*CCEI*, 1977), but there has not as yet been any extended treatment. The same is true for Ewart Milne (1908–   ), John Irvine (1903–64), Robert Farren (1909–   ), and other contemporaries of Devlin and Coffey. Farren's participation in the Dublin Verse-Speaking Society with Austin Clarke earns him one article, by Tina H. Mahony (*IUR*, 1974). George Buchanan (1904–   ) has been the subject of two brief items, one by James Simmons in the *Honest Ulsterman* (1978) and the other by Frank Ormsby in the introduction to *Poets from the North of Ireland* (1979).

For the generation that succeeded Yeats, scholars have concentrated their energies on the three major poets of the time: Austin Clarke (1896–1974), Patrick Kavanagh (1904–1967), and Louis MacNeice (1907–63). Clarke's many volumes of poetry were collected in 1974. Bibliographies of his work have been compiled by Gerald Lyne (*IUR*, 1974); Thomas Dillon Redshaw (*Éire*, 1974); and G. Craig Tapping, in *Austin Clarke: A Study of His Writings* (1980). Perhaps the earliest serious literary criticism of Clarke is Patrick J. Gibbons' *"The Vengeance of Fionn*: An Appreciation" (*IM*, 1918), but Clarke's poems did not receive widespread critical analysis, other than reviews, until comparatively recently, because of the poet's penchant for publication by private presses, occasional journals, and the like. He was given only passing notice in "Some Poets and Others" (*Bookman*, London, 1929) and in Gerald Griffin's *The Wild Geese: Pen Portraits of Famous Irish Exiles* (1938). B. Belitt's 1937 article in *Poetry* (Chicago) placed Clarke in the Gaelic mode, but it was not until M. J. Craig's essay in the *Bell* (1942) that Clarke's poetic achievement came under full critical scrutiny. This important article found him "an intellectual poet" and quoted him on the subject of his method of composition. Vivian Mercier discussed his verse plays in two essays (*DM,* 1944; *Life and Letters,* 1947), and John Montague mentioned him briefly in *Poetry* (Chicago, 1957). Criticism from the sixties expanded from these beginnings. Douglas Sealy surveyed the work somewhat too cautiously, obviously aware that Clarke would read his words, but found that the poetry "deserves to be ranked with the best that any Irishman has written" and noted its intensity and irony (*DM,* 1963). John Jordan praised Clarke (*Poetry Ireland,* 1964), and William John Roscelli and Richard Loftus' *The Celtic Cross: Studies in Irish Culture and Literature* (1964) included three major articles on Clarke, by Roscelli, George Brandon Saul, and Maurice Harmon. Augustine Martin provided a perceptive study of Clarke's metrical and thematic development (*Studies,* 1965). In 1966 John Montague's *A Tribute to Austin Clarke on His Seventieth Birthday* collected contributions from a fairly broad range of contemporaries and indicated Clarke's stature in Irish letters. M. L. Rosenthal's multinational study, *The New Poets* (1967), included Clarke, and John Jordan considered him briefly in *Hibernia* (1967). Kevin Sullivan examined him at greater length in "Literature in Modern Ireland," in Owen Dudley Edwards' *Conor Cruise O'Brien Introduces Ireland* (1969), where he calls Clarke "after Yeats, the most complete poet of twentieth century Ireland."

Criticism of Clarke in the 1970s begins with the first full-length study of his work, John Jordan's volume in the Irish Writers series (1970), followed by Richard Weber's "Austin Clarke: The Arch-Poet of Dublin" (*MR,* 1970) and Kathleen McGrory's brief chapter in Porter and Brophy's *Modern Irish Literature* (1972). Eavan Boland provides a portrait of Clarke in old age (*Hibernia,* 1973), and Carol Gelderman, in an article on George Fitzmaurice, corrects some misapprehensions about Clarke and Yeats (*Éire,* 1973). Robert Welch locates Clarke in the Gaelic poetic tradition in a special Clarke number of the *Irish University Review* (1974). The volume also contains articles on the religious lyrics by Vivian Mercier, on the epics by Brendan Kennelly, and on the later poems by Austin Dodsworth, as well as an analysis of the poet in transition by Robert F. Garratt, a survey of the work as a whole by Thomas Kinsella, and biographical notes by Maurice Harmon. In a less weighty reflection on Clarke's literary reputation, John Jordan sees Clarke as one of the "behated brethren" (*Hibernia,* 1974). A student's guide, *Patrick Kavanagh and Austin Clarke,* by D. J. Murphy (1979), emphasizes the Gaelic tradition in Clarke's poetry and gives a chronology of his life. Susan Halpern's pioneering *Austin Clarke: His Life and Works* (1974) has largely been superseded by G. Craig Tapping's excellent *Austin Clarke: A Study of His Writings* (1980). *Two Decades of Irish Writing* (1975) reprinted Donald Davie's essay on Clarke and Fallon, in which Davie discusses Clarke's alleged lack of sufficient mythopoeia. Michael Wood (*Parnassus,* 1975) considers Clarke along with D. J. Enright and Philip Larkin. Thomas Kinsella edited a selection of Clarke's poetry (1976), and Robert F. Garratt examines Clarke's debt to Swift for his satiric vein (*Éire,* 1976). In Joseph Ronsley's *Myth and Reality in Irish Literature* (1976), J. C. C. Mays describes Beckett's apparent parody of

Clarke as Austin Ticklepenny in *Murphy*, thereby providing an important biographical footnote; and Daniel J. Murphy discusses both satirical and religious poems somewhat briefly in *Hermathena* (1976). Robert F. Garratt evaluates Clarke's debt to Jonathan Swift (*Éire*, 1976), and Maurice Harmon's introduction to *Irish Poetry after Yeats* (1977) places him in the modern Irish tradition. Roger Little compares Devlin and Saint-John Perse (*IUR*, 1978). Adrian Frazier (*Éire*, 1979) considers the poetry of Clarke's last years, and Stan Smith (*IUR*, 1978) provides one of the better general essays on his poetry as a whole. William G. Downey recalls Devlin in a recent article (*Éire*, 1979), but the major sources of information about Clarke's life remain his autobiographical *Twice Round the Black Church* (1962) and *A Penny in the Clouds* (1968). Tina H. Mahony discusses Clarke's association with Robert Farren in forming the Dublin Verse-Speaking Society (*IUR*, 1974). Gregory A. Schirmer's study of Clarke's early narrative poetry (*Éire*, 1981) covers some of the same ground as Tapping's book.

Patrick Kavanagh's rejection of Yeats's influence and his strong thematic insistence on his home ground and on everyday reality have made him the most important figure in Irish poetry among the generation after Yeats, especially to the younger poets whom his example liberated from the shadow of the master. Consequently much scholarly attention has been directed at his work, most of its treating his historical rather than his literary significance. Kavanagh's *Collected Poems* appeared in 1964, and two bibliographies, one by John Nemo (*IUR*, 1973) and the other by Kavanagh's brother Peter, in his *Garden of the Golden Apples* (1973), demonstrate the extent not only of his poetic publication but also of his prose fiction and criticism. Nemo's bibliography is especially detailed in its coverage of secondary materials, but it does not discriminate between lengthy literary analysis of the poetry and passing reference to the man—a minor complaint to make about a very thorough work but one that might well be corrected in future bibliographies. In a 1950 article in *Envoy*, surveying Irish poetry from 1930 to 1950, Paul Gerard noted that Kavanagh's uniqueness contributed to his greatness and distinguished him from those of his contemporaries who had not yet emerged from Yeats's shadow. Articles of some biographical significance appeared in 1951: Hubert Butler's essay in the *Bell*, giving the reasons for the failure of Kavanagh's *Envoy*, and Phelim Brady's report in *Empire News*, providing a profile of the poet. A more infamous profile, a parody of Kavanagh that appeared in 1952 in the *Leinster Leader*, occasioned several articles of biographical significance, both in response to the profile itself and by virtue of the libel suit against the *Leader* that Kavanagh initiated and lost. (For details, see the major Kavanagh studies, cited below.) James Plunkett (*Bell*, 1952) had earlier found the defining characteristics of Kavanagh's poetry to be his "compression and unerring selection" and his "ability to make the smallest action clamorous with emotional conflict." Richard Weber briefly considered *A Soul for Sale* as the book on which Kavanagh's reputation depended (*Icarus*, 1954), but Anthony Cronin, surveying the work in more detail, preferred to locate Kavanagh's achievement in his insistence on ordinary rather than symbolic themes (*Nimbus*, 1956). Donald Macalernon provided a short descriptive essay on Kavanagh in *Focus* (1960), and John Hewitt produced a longer, more critical study in *Threshold* (1961). Hewitt saw Kavanagh's voice as having lost impetus and energy after *A Soul for Sale* and faulted *Come Dance with Kitty Strobling* for its unimaginative use of assonance and its mixed metaphors. Of some interest are subsequent articles by Paul Potts (*LonM*, 1963) and John Jordan (*Poetry Ireland*, 1964), two positive views by J. M. Newton (*Delta*, 1965) and John Ryan (*DM*, 1965), and one negative view by Donald Torchiana (*TriQ*, 1965). Douglas Sealy produced a thorough survey and analysis of the *Collected Poems (DM,* 1965), balancing the good against the bad. M. L. Rosenthal dealt briefly with Kavanagh's poems in *The New Poets* (1976), placing him in context with the other poets of the forties.

Immediately after Kavanagh's death on 30 November 1967, predictably generous essays began to appear, especially in newspapers. Those by Proinsias MacAonghusa in the *Sunday Independent*, Augustine Martin in the *Independent*, John Montague in the *Irish Times*, and Paul Potts in *The Evening Herald* (rpt. from the London *Times*) are representative. More thoughtful retrospective analyses of Kavanagh's achievement appeared in 1968, along with major studies of his work. Paul Pott's essay (*TC,* 1968) is primarily the uncritical praise of a friend; Maryanna Childs's piece (*CathW*, 1968) is similar in tone. John Montague's item in the *Guardian* (1968) reminisces about Kavanagh and describes the commemoration of the Canal Bank seat in his honor. Other tributes included those by Raymond Rosenfield (*Irish Times,* 1968), David Wright (*LonM,* 1968), Michael Hartnett (*Irish Times*, 1968), and a collection of writers' memorials that appeared in *Hibernia* (Jan. 1968). Michael Longley, Derek Mahon, and John Ryan supplied tactful but fruitful literary analysis (*DM,* 1968), noticing in Kavanagh's work those aspects that affect their own. Grattan Freyer's article (*Éire,* 1968) introduced Kavanagh to American readers but has been superseded by later studies. Alan Warner's early articles about Kavanagh (*DM,* 1968; *Threshold,* 1969; *English,* 1969) have been absorbed into his later book (see below). Kevin Sullivan considers Kavanagh's poems briefly in Owen Dudley Edwards' *Conor Cruise O'Brien Introduces Ireland* (1969), noting that Kavanagh is original "in the sense that his work seems so spontaneous as not to have been shaped or inspired by literary influences of any kind." Thomas McLaughlin (*Honest Ulsterman*, 1969) comments on Kavanagh's distinction between "provincial" (debilitating regionalism) and "parochial" (enabling regionalism) and applies the principle to Kavanagh's work. In an article replete with quotation, Brendan Kennelly discusses Kavanagh's comic vision (*AR*, 1970). Leland Bardwell, in the Dublin Arts Festival pamphlet (1970), speaks briefly about Kavanagh, as do Timothy O'Keeffe (*Two Rivers,* 1970) and C. H. Sisson in *English Poetry, 1900-1950: An Assessment* (1971). Bernard Share offers another consideration of *A Soul for Sale* in *Hibernia* (1972), and Rachel Doherty supplies a pleasant memoir of her friendship with Kavanagh in the *Irish Press* (27 Jan. 1973).

The first major Kavanagh study was Alan Warner's *Clay Is the Word: Patrick Kavanagh, 1904-1967* (1973). Broad in scope, introductory in intention, and based in part on recollections of Kavanagh's friends and relatives, it remains necessary reading for any Kavanagh student. All subsequent criticism of the poet is indebted to it, and even more recent studies have not entirely superseded it; it is still the liveliest of the full-length studies of Kavanagh. A festschrift of poems, *A Patrick Kavanagh Anthology,* edited by Eugene Robert Platt, and various articles on Kavanagh's poetry appeared in 1973 as well: John Boland's brief celebration in *Hibernia,* Desmond Swan's discussion of autobiographical elements in *The Great Hunger (Era 2),* and Brendan Kennelly's chapter in Seán Lucy's *Irish Poets in English.* Subsequently John Nemo surveyed Kavanagh's literary criticism (*Studies,* 1974), and D. J. Murphy produced a simple, straightforward student guide to Kavanagh's work in *Patrick Kavanagh and Austin Clarke* (1979). Seamus Heaney gave a plain-speaking, somewhat negative analysis of Kavanagh's poetry in the *New Review* (1975; rpt. in *Two Decades of Irish Writing,* 1975, and in *Preoccupations,* 1980); it is as important for what it implies about Kavanagh's impact on Heaney's poetry as for what it says about Kavanagh. In another article in *Two Decades of Irish Writing,* Michael Allen weighs the balance of provincialism and metropolitanism in Kavanagh's work and gauges its effect on Heaney and Montague. Darcy O'Brien's monograph on Kavanagh in the Irish Writers series (1975) is almost too brief—seventy-two pages—to be of use; it is a critical survey of the work that leans somewhat on Warner's *Clay Is the Word* but gives more coverage to Kavanagh's libel action than Warner does. It has been largely superseded by Nemo's 1979 study (see below). Francis Stuart makes a brief statement in *Hibernia* (1975), in which he describes Kavanagh as an "earthy visionary"; John Nemo surveys Kavanagh's journalism (*JIL,* 1975); and Daniel J. Casey offers a long article on Kavanagh's "calculations and miscalculations" (*CLQ,* 1975). Maurice Harmon's *Irish Poetry after Yeats* (1977) evaluates Kavanagh's poetry briefly in its introduction to a selection from his work, and the special Kavanagh issue of the *Journal of Irish Literature* (1977) contains some uncollected poems, a stage adaptation of *Tarry Flynn,* and notes toward John Nemo's forthcoming critical biography (in fact, the introduction). It also reprints Larry Morrow's interview with Kavanagh from the *Bell.* "Jude the Obscure's" commentary in the *Honest Ulsterman* (1978) ranges across the long poems and the autobiographies in a rambling, eclectic way, and Peter Kavanagh's *Patrick Kavanagh Country* (1978) offers a guide to Kavanagh's Monaghan, together with some biographical information and several fugitive items from Kavanagh's work. Richard F. Fleck considers the poet's work only briefly (*Paintbrush,* 1979), but Terence Brown's essay in the special number of *Genre* (1979; rpt. as *The Genres of the Irish Literary Revival,* ed. Ronald Schliefer, 1980) describes the difficulty that Kavanagh and other young writers after Yeats had in locating for themselves a unique thematic territory. Brown concentrates his attention on Kavanagh and O'Faolain as representative artists and finds that they both moved toward a concept of an "Irish Ireland" very different from that of Yeats. John Nemo's full-length *Patrick Kavanagh,* in the Twayne series (1979), provides the most thorough examination of the poet's career thus far, together with a chronology of important events and an updated bibliography. The volume does not entirely supersede Warner's *Clay Is the Word,* but it should prove the standard point of departure for all future studies of Kavanagh. Two articles of note also appeared in *Mosaic* (1979): Weldon Thornton's somewhat negative reappraisal of *The Great Hunger* and John Wilson Foster's penetrating reevalution of Kavanagh's work as a whole, in which Foster finds, as others have, that Kavanagh's literary reputation is important chiefly for its effect on the poets who followed him. Kavanagh's autobiographies, *The Green Fool* (1938) and *Tarry Flynn* (1948), although fictional accounts of his life, contain much pertinent information, which should be supplemented by his essays in *Envoy* and in *Kavanagh's Weekly,* his short-lived newspaper, recently issued in a facsimile volume (1981), together with interviews, such as that in the *Bell* (1948), and autobiographical-critical articles by Kavanagh (*Bell,* 1948; *Studies,* 1959). Both John Ryan, in *Remembering How We Stood* (1976), and Anthony Cronin, in *Dead as Doornails* (1976), have collected flavorful reminiscences of Kavanagh and his contemporaries in Dublin. Ryan and Cronin cover the same ground and in fact occasionally use the same stories. The background thus provided is both amusing and depressing by turns, but the occasional contradictions in the two volumes warn against an overreliance on the information they contain. Peter Kavanagh's recent biography, *Patrick Kavanagh: Sacred Keeper* (1980), has the advantages and disadvantages of a brother's eye view.

Louis MacNeice, the Ulsterman in this trio of famous contemporaries, is only partly an Irish poet, since his literary concerns tie him as closely to W. H. Auden and to Stephen Spender as they do to Ireland. He first received extended critical attention as one of the poets of the thirties, and as a result he is still thought of as a British writer. But, as Terence Brown has shown, his native place and his characteristic skepticism mark him as Irish as well. One of the earliest studies of his work occurs in a chapter of James Southworth's *Sowing the Spring* (1940); Southworth notes MacNeice's unusual imagery, prosody, and themes, which he attributes to MacNeice's Irish origins. Valentin Iremonger, in "A First Study" (*Bell,* 1947), noted MacNeice's attention to commonsense detail as well as his urban imagery and inherent skepticism. R. N. Browne, in *The Arts in Ulster* (1951), praised MacNeice's technical brilliance and identified a "darting intelligence" that conveys a sense of impending doom and present diasaster. G. S. Fraser described MacNeice's "evasive honesty" in *Vision and Rhetoric* (1959). All these themes have become part of the standard view of MacNeice's poetry. After his death, major evaluations began. John Press's *Louis MacNeice* (1965) provided a good overview. Douglas Sealy's long appraisal of MacNeice's career (*DM,* 1964) is balanced and lucid, and his summation is masterful: he cites MacNeice's "extraordinary talent" but suggests that he was not ultimately a great poet, because he "kept the balance too carefully between the witty surface and the serious undertones of his poems," because he "has not shown us ourselves transfigured as a great poet can," and, finally, because he possessed an "admirable aloofness" that "hindered him from reaching the heights." Terence Brown briefly refines these early views (*Hibernia,* 1970), calling MacNeice a "stoical exile" and finding that his refusal to commit himself to any single philosophy gives him a poetry of "wit, sophistication, and brilliance" and "the skeptic's sense of tragedy and loss, a sense that makes life's simple gifts things precious, poignant and fragile." Brown sees this as a sign of MacNeice's greatness and expands this view in two longer pieces (*Studies,* 1970), both of which are subsumed into his full-length study of the poet (1975). Elton Edward Smith's *Louis MacNeice* (1970) has been superseded by later studies. Michael Longley refers briefly to MacNeice's place in the historical context in *Causeway: The Arts in Ulster* (1971).

William T. McKinnon's landmark volume, *Apollo's Blended Dream: A Study of the Poetry of Louis MacNeice* (1971), was a major study of the poet's full career; it emphasized the philosophical underpinnings of his work and provided a bibliography. Two years later, McKinnon added a further item, an article on MacNeice's *Pale Panther (EIC,* 1973), and Christopher Armitage and Neil Clark provided *A Bibliography of the Works of Louis MacNeice* (1973). Samuel Hynes included MacNeice in a discussion about Yeats's influence on the poets of the thirties (*Modern Irish Literature,* 1972). D. B. Moore, in *The Poetry of Louis MacNeice* (1972), and Ian Hamilton, in *A Poetry Chronicle* (1973), added further to the expanding scholarship on his poems. Terence Brown supplied an article about MacNeice and Walter Pater (*Hermathena,* 1973) and joined forces with Alec Reid to produce a valuable collection of essays, *Time Was Away* (1974), on the poetry, plays, and life of the writer. The volume's most significant essays on the poetry—by Brown, Derek Mahon, and Robin Skelton—concern MacNeice's relation with his father, with Ireland and England, and with Celtic verse models. Other important articles include those by W. B. Stanford and by E. L. Stahl on MacNeice's Greek and German translations, and there are also many and various reminiscences by family members and other contemporaries. D. E. S. Maxwell's article (*MSLC,* 1974), ostensibly about MacNeice's relationship to the political poetry of the thirties, is in fact an amalgam of several different ideas and is mostly about MacNeice's dual vision and his attitude toward Yeats. The major study of MacNeice is Terence Brown's *Louis MacNeice: Skeptical Vision* (1975). Brown proposes that "the central determining factor in MacNeice's poetry and thought . . . was a tense awareness of fundamental questions, rooted in philosophical scepticism"; but unlike McKinnon, with whom he takes issue, Brown pays close attention to the manifestation of the skepticism in the technical and thematic structures of the poems. The third chapter of the book holds Brown's main argument: that the poetry manifests a positive skepticism that can be seen both to cherish life and to perceive death as that which gives life its significance. The final chapters attend closely to the syntax and other technical aspects of the poetry. Brown's work is clearly the definitive study of the life and the poetry. It has not proved to be the final word on the subject, however, and other items continue to appear, among them a lengthy and useful study of the pattern in MacNeice's poems, by A. J. Minnis (*YES,* 1975), as well as shorter references to MacNeice in articles that consider groups of poets and in reminiscences, such as Dan Davin's "In a Green Grave" (*Encounter,* 1972) and *Closing Times* (1975). Also of use are

Tom Paulin's article (*RMS,* 1976) on *Letters from Iceland,* Eric Homberger's final chapter in *The Art of the Real* (1977), Cherry Wilhelm's "Four Poems from *Inscapes*" (*CRUX,* 1978), Margot Heinemann's chapter on three left-wing poets in *Culture and Crisis in Britain in the Thirties* (1979), and Barbara Coulton's *Louis MacNeice in the BBC* (1980).

Of the generation of poets who came into prominence in the 1950s, the three major figures are Thomas Kinsella (1928-), John Montague (1929-), and Richard Murphy (1927-). Since they continue to write and develop, definitive analysis would be premature. There have been, however, some significant and useful studies. Edna Longley's excellent essay on Kinsella's poetic technique (*DM,* 1966) concentrates on his stylistic development and his characteristic repetition and shifts of mode. Kinsella has since moved beyond this stage, but the essay is the first important study of his work. M. L. Rosenthal included him in *The New Poets* (1967), where he examines his poetry as typical of postwar themes, and Maurice Harmon treats his work briefly in *Hibernia* (1969). Thomas Dillon Redshaw's seminal and informative "The Wormwood Revisions" (*Éire,* 1971) notes variants and traces the developoment of the poems. Redshaw also provides a gloss to *Butcher's Dozen (Éire,* 1972), Kinsella's poem about Bloody Sunday in Derry, when British troops opened fire on marching demonstrators. The poem provoked an interesting response in a fugitive pamphlet entitled *Kinsella's Oversight: A Reply to the Butcher's Dozen, a Poem on Bloody Sunday by Thomas Kinsella* (available in the National Library of Ireland). In an essay on Montague in *Modern Irish Literature* (1972), James D. Brophy spends some time on Kinsella's work. The major study of Kinsella's work up to 1973 is Maurice Harmon's *The Poetry of Thomas Kinsella* (1974), which traces themes and techniques in the early writings. Now outdated by Kinsella's recent work, it nonetheless remains a good introduction to the poet. Calvin Bedient included Kinsella in his *Eight Contemporary Poets* (1974); the others are Tomlinson, Davie, R. S. Thomas, Ted Hughes, Larkin, Graham, and Stevie Smith.

Bedient's important essay places Kinsella in the contemporary milieu and compares his poetry favorably to that of the others. Vernon Young (*Parnassus,* 1975) examines Kinsella as one of four modern poets who sing in "raptures of distress." Here again, Kinsella is the only Irish poet considered. Edna Longley's perceptive article on Kinsella, Murphy, Montague, and Simmons, in *Two Decades of Irish Writing* (1975), is the best recent study of his work and required reading for anyone wishing to understand Kinsella in his Irish literary context. Maurice Harmon's introduction to *Irish Poetry after Yeats* (1977) performs a similar function. Hugh Kenner analyzes Kinsella's poetic diction in an essay that was intended as an introduction to the American edition of his *Selected Poems, 1956-1968* (1973) but that was published in *Genre* (1979; rpt. as *The Genres of the Irish Literary Revival,* 1980); Kenner's essay is predictably excellent, though his anecdotal details of its earlier rejection by Kinsella's American publisher seem misplaced. Two articles by Peggy Broder (*CJIS,* 1979; *Éire,* 1979) propose a thematic dichotomy in Kinsella's later poetry, which she characterizes as masculine (orderly) and feminine (chaotic); she finds that Kinsella, in recognizing and balancing these opposing forces, continues to grow in poetic integrity and in linguistic strength. A Kinsella interview appears in John Haffenden's *Viewpoints* (1981). Michael G. Freyer's checklist of Kinsella's books (*DM*, 1966) has been superseded by Hensley C. Woodbridge's bibliography (*Éire*, 1967), but an updated bibliography would be welcome, as would a new evaluation of the poetry as a whole.

Richard Murphy's poetry first garnered protracted critical attention after the publication of his 1960 elegy, *The Woman of the House,* which occasioned a running debate on modern metrics in the *London Magazine, TLS,* and *Threshold.* M. L. Rosenthal included him in *The New Poets* (1967), and he is discussed in introductions to the various anthologies appearing in the late sixties and early seventies. James D. Brophy mentions him briefly in his article on John Montague in *Modern Irish Literature* (1972), but he calls Murphy the most Irish of the trio that includes Kinsella, because "his poetry has the least interpretive comment and thus seems to stand as most autonomously Irish." In a St. Patrick's Day number of *TLS* (1973), Montague briefly discusses Murphy's work, among others; and Murphy's additions to Yeats's *King Oedipus* for the Abbey production of that play are the subject of two brief articles by Rebecca Schull (*Irish Times,* 17 May 1973; *The Arts in Ireland,* 1973). Two essays in Seán Lucy's *Irish Poets in English* (1973), by Maurice Harmon and by Bryan MacMahon, discuss Murphy among other poets of his generation, as Harmon also does in *Éire* (1973). Edna Longley's article in *Two Decades of Irish Writing* (1975) comments perceptively on Murphy's relation to Anglo-Irish and Irish Ireland and compares his poems to those of Montague, Kinsella, and Simmons. Elgy Gillespie's "Richard Murphy upon Omey" (*Irish Times,* 21 Nov. 1975) gives sources of some poems. The major collection of scholarly articles about Murphy's work to date is contained in the 1977 special issue of the *Irish University Review,* reprinted with an extra essay by Maurice Harmon as *Richard Murphy: Poet of Two Traditions* (ed. Harmon, 1978). The volume contains a background essay on the history of the battle of Aughrim, the subject of Murphy's major epic poem, by J. G. Simms; archaeological notes on the "High Island" of his poems, by Michael Herity; ornithological notes on the storm petrels of the later poetry, by Anthony Whilde; a glossary on the major works, by Jonathan Williams; a briefly annotated bibliography of primary and secondary materials, by Mary FitzGerald; and critical essays by Maurice Harmon and Seamus Heaney on the literary merits of the poems. This useful compendium of information about the poetry is a good guide for students. Dennis O'Driscoll briefly introduces Murphy's poems (*PAus,* 1979), and Mark Kilroy (*Éire,* 1980) uses Murphy's Connemara locale as a significant ground for explicating the poems, providing a good rehearsal of the importance of place in Murphy's work. The American edition of *High Island* (1976) incorporates Murphy's earlier volumes and is therefore a collected poems; his *Selected Poems* (1979) should provoke a new evaluation of his achievement. An early autobiographical-critical essay, "The Pleasure Ground" (*Listener,* 1963; rpt. in *Writers on Themselves,* 1964), can be supplemented with several good interviews with Murphy, most notably those in the *Irish Times* (21 Nov. 1975), the *Irish Press* (2 Nov. 1971, 7 June 1973) and the *London Magazine* (1980; rpt. in *Viewpoints: Poets in Conversation with John Haffenden,* 1981).

In "Living under Ben Bulben" (*KM,* 1966), John Montague offers the opinion that Yeats's "direct influence on Irish poetry has been disastrous," a remark that had been foreshadowed by others he had made in a symposium, published under the heading "The Young Writers" (*Bell,* 1951) and amplified in his commentary on his own epic poem, *The Rough Field,* in the *Spectator* (26 Apr. 1963). Montague also touched on the subject of Yeats's influence in his Thomas Davis lecture in 1971, which appeared in Seán Lucy's *Irish Poets in English* (1972). Montague's sense of land and of language is adumbrated in an article in the Northern Ireland supplement to the *Irish Times* of 10 July 1970 and in "The Planter and the Gael" (*Aquarius,* 1972), a discussion with John Hewitt. The first important critical articles on his poetry appeared in *Studies* (1964): an introductory note, by Seán Lucy, which provides a good brief guide to stages of progress in *The Rough Field,* and Thomas Dillon Redshaw's longer article, which examines the poem in detail. Sidney B. Poger compares the poem to Hart Crane's *The Bridge* (*Éire,* 1981). M. L. Rosenthal's *The New Poets* (1967) includes him among the writers of the forties and fifties, as does Michael Longley in *Causeway: The Arts in Ulster* (1971). Geoffrey Squire's note "Public Poetry" (*Irish Times,* 30 Mar. 1971) is of only passing interest. James D. Brophy, in *Modern Irish Literature* (1972), places Montague midway between two poles represented by Murphy and Kinsella; Brophy notes a "central theme of imaginative imitation" and a technique of memory that he calls "recovering the scene," but he has no ear for the traditional Irish assonant patterns in Montague's poetry and misses these completely. Seán Lucy, again, is more illuminating (*IUR,* 1973), as is Thomas Dillon Redshaw (*Éire,* 1974). John Wilson Foster, in "The Landscape of the Planter and the Gael in the Poetry of John Hewitt and John Montague" (*CJIS,* 1975), makes a useful comparison of themes and techniques in the work of both poets. Terence Brown discusses Montague against the history of Ulster poetry (*Northern Voices,* 1975) in one of the better extended studies of his work, and Frank Kersnowski concentrates on Montague's life and work in his volume in the Irish Writers series (1975). Two essays in *Two Decades of Irish Literature* (1975) consider his poetry in detail: Edna Longley studies him among his contemporaries and examines his technique, and Michael Allen discusses his poetry in an article on Patrick Kavanagh. Honor O'Connor examines the early poetry (*EI,* 1977), and both Donald Hall (*Parnassus,* 1977) and Maurice Harmon (in *Irish Poetry after Yeats,* 1977) give him a moderately extended treatment in comparing him with his contemporaries. James Liddy (*Éire,* 1978) argues unpersuasively that Montague's "craftsmanship" keeps him from being as good a poet as Padraic Fiacc; more convincing is Benedict Kiely's assessment and analysis (*HC,* 1978). Adrian Frazier's excellent interview with Montague (*LitR,* 1979) deserves serious attention. Thomas Dillon Redshaw discusses Montague's "The Northern Gate" (*CJIS,* 1979). In an earlier article (*Éire,* 1976), he described Montague's work and produced a bibliography of selected criticism, as did

Kersnowski in his full-length study; however, neither bibliography is complete. Montague has recently issued a selection of his poetry (1981), but, as with *A Slow Dance* (1975), he continues to revise and reprint individual pieces. Since the apppearance of *The Great Cloak* (1978), it seems clear that his work is due for a study that considers his development to the present.

A less well known contributor to John Ryan's symposium "The Young Writers" (*Bell*, 1951) was Valentin Iremonger (1918-), one of those who began publishing in the fifties, along with Montague, Murphy, and Kinsella, but whose work has not yet occasioned extended literary criticism. Since some, like Seán Lucy (1931-), have only recently collected their poetry into a volume (Lucy's appeared in 1979), and others, like Robert Greacen (1920-), have not yet done so, much of the commentary on their work can be found only in reviews. Ulster writers have fared better than others because they have tended to be discussed in studies of Ulster literature as a whole. Thus Roy McFadden (1921-) is discussed by Michael Longley in *Causeway: The Arts in Ulster* (1971) and by Terence Brown in *Northern Voices* (1975). Similarly, Robert Greacen is discussed in the same publications. Of the southern Irish writers, Anthony Cronin (1926-) is represented by his own excellent criticism in the *Bell* (esp. 1954) and by an interview in *Icarus* (1976); his memoir, *Dead as Doornails* (1976), vividly recreates literary Dublin in the fifties. A good article on Patrick Galvin (1927-)—a lengthy interview—appears in the *Irish Times* (24 July 1976), and Eavan Boland writes judiciously of Donagh MacDonagh (1912-68) in *Hibernia* (11 Sept. 1970). But for Rupert Strong (1911-) and Eithne Strong (1923-), as for others, reviews and newspaper items remain the chief source of information.

In the late sixties and early seventies a particularly strong group of poets emerged, most of them coming from the North. One of them, James Simmons (1933-), is discussed by Michael Longley in *Causeway* (1971) and by Terence Brown in *Northern Voices* (1975), as well as in articles by Michael Allen (*Éire*, 1975), who argues for the influence of Longley on Simmons, and by Edna Longley (*Two Decades of Irish Writing*, 1975), who compares him with Murphy, Montague, and Kinsella, his contemporaries in years if not in time of publication. Simmons himself supplies a useful introduction to his work in a brief interview in *Phoenix* (1968) and discusses his role in the *Honest Ulsterman*, which he founded. His poem satirizing the departure from Ulster of other Irish poets (*Irish Times*, 7 June 1974) occasioned a running controversy in the press. He has lately received more serious attention from critics and was interviewed by Adrian Frazier (*LitR*, 1979). Padraic Fiacc (1924-), another poet of this generation, has had careful critiques by Terence Brown in *Northern Voices* (1975) and in Brown's introduction to his edition of *The Selected Padraic Fiacc* (1979). Fiacc's chief apologist is James Liddy, who argues that Fiacc is "perhaps the most considerable poet emerging from the Ulster disturbances" because he is "more involved than Yeats" in the political turmoil of his time and because he presents "an urgent working class articulation conceptualized as a genital wound" (*Éire*, 1978; and *Varieties of Ireland, Varieties of Irish-*

America, ed. Blanche M. Touhill, 1976). Liddy's characteristic method is to compare Fiacc with Baudelaire, Yeats, or Whitman and to claim—rather than to demonstrate—Fiacc's equal status. Brown's more modest claims for the poet are more convincingly presented. He argues that Fiacc's virtues lie in his "intense realization of states of consciousness" and his "ambitious experimentalism." The poetry of Brendan Kennelly (1936–   ) is the subject of an interview in the *Literary Review* (1979), and several of his poems have been interpreted in music by composers Jane Strong O'Leary and Seoirse Bodley for performance over Radio Telefis Éireann and at the Project Arts Theatre in Dublin. The major study of his work is Erwin Otto's *Das lyrische Werk Brendan Kennelly* (1976); Otto's careful analysis of Kennelly's public voice (*EI*, 1976) is also significant. The absence of a collection of his poems accounts in part for the scarcity of extended critical commentary.

Of the poets appearing in Ulster in the sixties, the most important are Seamus Heaney (1939–   ), Michael Longley (1939–   ), and Derek Mahon (1941–   ). Heaney's work has attracted an appropriately large amount of critical analysis; Mahon and Longley deserve more attention than they have so far received. All three poets, however, have recently issued volumes of selected poems, which should lead to more analytical commentary on their work as a whole. One of the earliest items concerning Seamus Heaney is a brief interview and sketch of the poet by Padraic Fiacc (*Hibernia*, May 1968). It was followed by Longley's brief consideration of the poems in *Causeway* (1971) and by Montague's short notice in the 1972 St. Patrick's Day number of *TLS*. The first protracted study of Heaney's work was Benedict Kiely's (*HC*, 1970), which was followed by George A. Brinton's note on the second volume of poems (*ConP*, 1973), Seán Lucy's discussion of three Ulster poets (*IUR*, 1973), and Jon Silkin's brief analysis of Heaney's language in *New Blackfriars* (1973). Clive James devoted a chapter of *The Metropolitan Critic* (1974) to dissecting Heaney's work. John Wilson Foster's article (*CritQ*, 1974) judiciously evaluates Heaney's achievement to that point, as does a very fine piece by Thomas Dillon Redshaw (*Éire*, 1974). Terence Brown concentrates on what he sees as subliminal violence in Heaney's central self (*Northern Voices*, 1975) and gives a less enthusiastic evaluation of the poetic voice than most critics; but in an article on W. R. Rodgers and John Hewitt in *Two Decades of Irish Writing*, Brown cites Heaney's "The Tollund Man" as an example of what Hewitt's "professed 'regionalism' *could* do but doesn't." Heaney's poem, he says, "has broken through to universal areas of psychic and cultural truth." In the same volume, Michael Allen, Seamus Deane, and Edna Longley mention Heaney in the course of discussing other poets or broader themes; it is a measure of Heaney's growing reputation that his fellow poets write about his work and that critics cite his poetry in articles about other writers. For example, Michael Allen (*Éire*, 1975) writes of Michael Longley but discusses Heaney's influence on Longley's development. Julian Gitzen (*StHum*, 1975) compares Heaney's style to imagism; the article is based only on Heaney's first two books and is primarily a summary, but it is significant as an early American response to his poems. Robert Buttel's full-length study in the Irish Writers series (1975) is now out of date, but it is a helpful introduction to Heaney's first three volumes of poetry, and it has some historical significance as the first full-length study of the poet. Buttel argues that Heaney "is worth serious study" for the way in which his "language coalesces into living texture and movement" and that he is "a special instance of a poet who has transcended the limitations of the provincial by being inordinately true to the material of his locality." Heaney's fourth volume, *North* (1975), moves beyond his local territory; two background pieces are helpful to an understanding of the book, even though they do not treat the poetry as such: P. V. Glöb's *The Bog People* (1963), from which Heaney takes the material of several of the poems; and G. F. Dalton's "The Tradition of Blood Sacrifice to the Goddess Eire" (*Studies*, 1974). As Heaney's poetry has become better known, reviewers have tended to make the appearance of a new volume the occasion for a retrospective analysis of his previous work. One of the better of these is Richard Murphy's review of *North* (*NYRB*, 1976). Bernard Sharratt's article in *New Blackfriars* (1976) takes a dim view of Heaney's sexual themes and imagery. Monie Begley's references to Heaney in *Rambles in Erin* (1977) have more biographical then literary interest. Donald Hall discusses Heaney at some length in an article about Irish poets (*Parnassus*, 1977). John Wilson Foster's analysis of the sources and themes of Heaney's "A Lough Neagh Sequence" is required reading (*Éire*, 1977), as are the references to Heaney in Seamus Deane's article in *Myth and Reality in Irish Literature* (ed. Joseph Ronsley, 1977). Arthur E. McGuinness' 1978 examination in *Éire* of tradition and ritual in the poems becomes reductive on occasion, as when McGuinness seeks overt evidence of a Catholic theology in the poems and finds none, but he makes a useful comparison of collected versions of poems with their earlier counterparts and cites an uncollected poem, "A Flourish for the Prince of Denmark." Few will see the logic in his assertion that Heaney's slight, graceful "St Francis and the Birds" is "very like Yeats's *Byzantium*" or the validity of his reducing some of Heaney's more complex poems to a single meaning. Similarly, few will agree with James Liddy, who argues that Heaney is only potentially a good poet who does not yet measure up to Padraic Fiacc's level of excellence (*Éire*, 1978). Rita Zontonbier's examination of the matter of Ireland in Heaney's poetry is more helpful (*DOR*, 1979). Arthur E. McGuinness' valuable article on revisions in the poems (*IUR*, 1979) supplies drafts of several poems and traces their evolution in manuscript; his study of Heaney's "Act of Union" is especially rewarding. David Lloyd considers the "two voices" found in *North* (*ArielE*, 1979), and Maurice Harmon places him in the contemporary Irish tradition in *Irish Poetry after Yeats* (1977). Anthony Bailey has provided several readable recountings of visits with Heaney, one in *Quest* (1978) and another in the *New Yorker* (1979; rpt. in his *Acts of Union: Reports on Ireland, 1973–79*, 1980). The bibliography in Buttel's study needs to be expanded and amended in the light of Heaney's *Selected Poems* (1980), his collected prose (*Preoccupations*, 1980), and his continuing development.

P. R. King's *Nine Contemporary Poets* (1979) contains a chapter on Heaney, and Gregory A. Schirmer (*Éire*, 1980) answers A. Alvarez' objection (*NYRB*, 1979) that Heaney is not a major poet by outlining his themes and analyzing his handling of language and symbol. Jay Parini also concludes that Heaney is a major poet in a very fine article in the *Southern Review* (1980). Roberta Berke's consideration of his work in *Bounds out of Bounds* (1981) is too brief to be of more than passing interest, but Timothy Kearney's article on Heaney's manner of engaging the Ulster troubles is both perceptive and enlightening (*Threshold*, 1982). Vincent Buckley's more general approach (*Threshold*, 1982) finds him avoiding nationalism, along with other Irish poets past and present, and reads some of Heaney's poems too simply.

Seamus Heaney has been interviewed very frequently in the last few years, and those interested in his biography and his personal statements about his art should consult not only his *Preoccupations* (1980) but also interviews with Caroline Walsh (*Irish Times* , 6 Dec. 1975), with Eavan Boland (*Irish Times*, 12–14 August 1970), in the *Book of the Month Club News* (1976), with Seamus Deane in the *Crane Bag* (1977), with Randall James in *Ploughshares* (1979), with Robert Druce (*DQR*, 1979), with John Haffenden in the *London Magazine* (1979; rpt. in Haffenden's *Viewpoints*, 1981) and in the excellent Danish *Sköleradioen* volume, *Seamus Heaney* (1977), which provides one of the best introductions to his work.

Eavan Boland interviewed Derek Mahon on the Northern Ireland writer's situation (*Irish Times*, 12 Aug. 1970), and Harriet Cook interviewed him on the state of Irish letters and on his use of urban imagery (*Irish Times*, 17 Jan. 1973). Before then, Hayden Murphy (*Hibernia*, 1969) and Michael Longley (*Causeway*, 1971) had short pieces on his work. In 1975, his poetry, like Heaney's, was considered in studies of other writers or of the movement in general: Michael Allen, writing of Michael Longley (*Éire*); Seamus Deane, discussing nationalism in Irish poetry in *Two Decades of Irish Writing*; and Terence Brown, in *Northern Voices*. Of these three analyses, Brown's is by far the most detailed and the most important; he accurately attests to Mahon's clarity, profundity, and wit. Brian Donnelly has replied to the publication of Mahon's *Poems, 1962–78* with a good review article (*Ploughshares*, 1980), as did Blake Morrison (*TLS*, 1980); others will presumably follow.

Similarly, Michael Longley's poems seem to be studied primarily in works that treat the Ulster writers as a group. Except for a first-person description of how he began to write (*Phoenix*, 1969) and for Michael Allen's article (*Éire*, 1975), which traces his technical development and notes parallels with Mahon's work and influences from Heaney's, Longley has been cited mainly as one of the movement's new voices. Eavan Boland interviews him in the *Irish Times* (12 Aug. 1970), and Anthony Thwaite, in the introduction to his *Penguin Modern Poets* (1970), claims that Longley's is "the most promising voice in the province," and Terence Brown praises him in *Northern Voices* (1975). His new volume of *Collected Poems* (1980) should likewise induce further scholarly appraisal of his considerable achievement.

Michael Hartnett's *Selected Poems* (1977) produced some reviews of his total work, as did his much celebrated announcement, in *A Farewell to English* (1975), that henceforth he would write only in Irish. Most critical attention, however, has focused on Hartnett's transition to Irish and not upon the merits of the poetry in English. He is interviewed by Eavan Boland in the *Irish Times* (5 Feb. 1970).

A great many other poets are beginning their careers or are midway through them, without yet having attracted much notice beyond reviews. To see the total contemporary picture, one should know about their work. Some of them deserve far greater critical attention than they have received, and many would repay study. Robert Hogan's *Dictionary of Irish Literature* lists those among them who had published a volume of poems by 1979; beyond that, one will need to check reviews in Irish publications.

Although much good work has already been done on modern Irish poetry, more remains to be done. Thomas Kinsella's diagnosis that "We lack proper criticism in Ireland to a crucial degree, and such of it as there is has been odd in certain ways" (*A Needle's Eye*, 1979) is uncomfortably correct, not only for Irish criticism but for American and European criticism of Irish writing as well. Comparatively few of the critical works cited in this chapter address their subject at the level of scholarly analysis. The lack of in-depth criticism may be understandable, since most of the work is introductory, but it also points a direction for future Irish literary studies.

Perhaps the primary need is for updated bibliographies. Present critical works need revision in the light of recent evaluations. Definitive studies are lacking for some poets who clearly deserve them. Reassessments are needed for others, especially for those poets who are in mid-career. And new poets continue to appear, more than a few of them showing substantial promise. In short, a great many opportunities remain for productive research in modern Irish poetry.

INDEX